GREAT BOOK *of* TATTOO *Designs*

Revised Edition

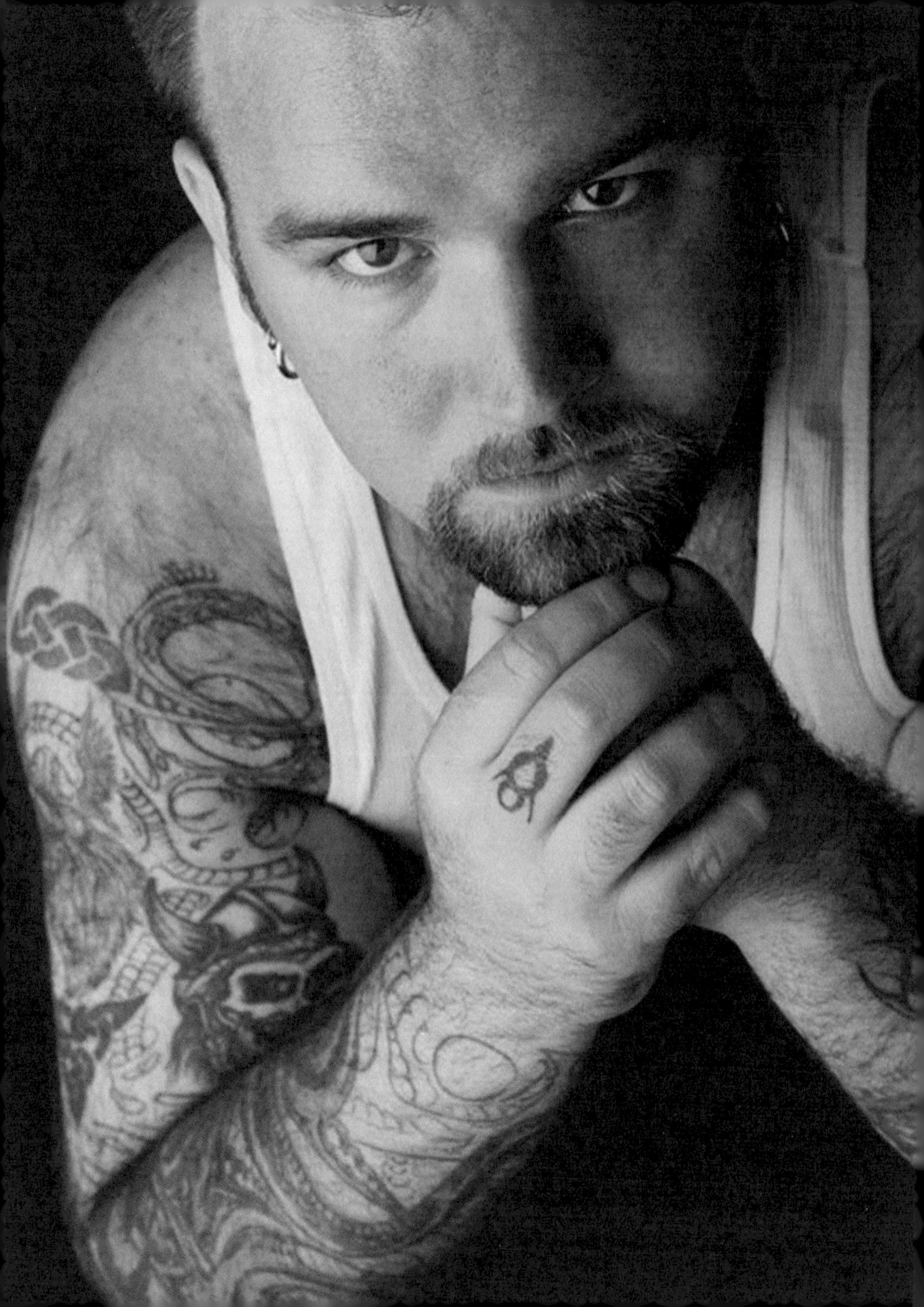

GREAT BOOK *of* TATTOO *Designs*

Revised Edition

Lora S. Irish

FOX CHAPEL
PUBLISHING

Great Book of Tattoo Designs, Revised Edition (ISBN 978-1-56523-813-8, 2013) is a revised edition of *Great Book of Tattoo Designs* (ISBN 978-1-56523-332-4, 2007), both published by Fox Chapel Publishing Company, Inc. Revisions include new patterns.

ISBN 978-1-56523-813-8

Printed in China
Eighth printing

Contents

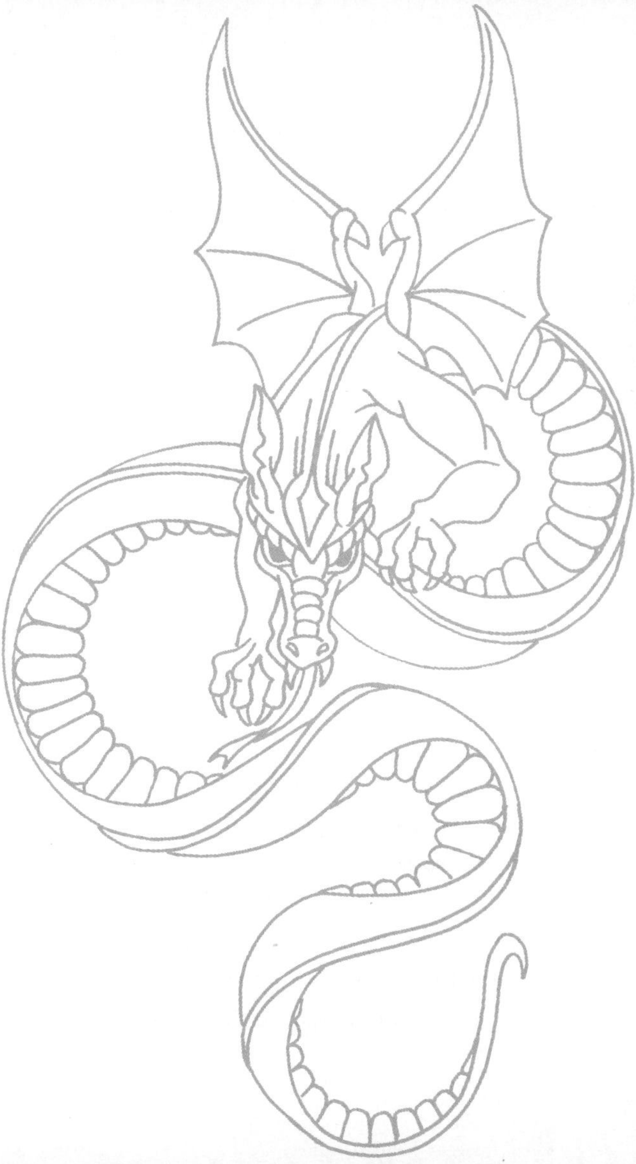

Introduction

The first edition of this book was a surprise seller. Lora S. Irish is a noted graphic designer and a successful design book author in her own right. Her work was entirely new to the field of tattoo art, and the fresh new portfolio found an eager audience among tattoo artists around the world. The book is even available in Russian and Japanese editions.

We've added 36 new patterns to this revised edition to replace designs that no longer fit today's styles and interests. In particular, you'll find wonderful new steampunk, Mayan, Native American and tribal designs inside this edition.

Working with the author, I've always been impressed by how she throws herself into each and every design. It's not enough for her to just draw a few handsome dragons. For example, if you've read her *Great Book of Dragon Patterns*, you'll see that she delves deep into the history and mythology of both Eastern and Western dragons, creates color and anatomical studies, and does much, much more.

Part of what makes this book so popular is the balance of art and craftsmanship contained in each design. The subjects are drawn with the eye of an artist, but are also carefully crafted so they can be turned into functional art. Too much detail in the design and it would become a blob on the skin. Too little detail and the design would lack impact.

Body art carries a powerful message about an individual: It is an expression of individual creativity, a way to tell the world who you are and what you believe, a visual language with specific cultural meanings and social values.

Your choice of tattoo design is a powerful statement for the rest of your life. Whatever your age, sex, social status, or reason for getting tattooed, you'll want to select high quality art for this permanent display.

Inside this volume, you'll find more than 500 beautifully drawn line and shaded tattoo designs worthy of being a permanent personal statement on human canvas. Use them in their original format or mix and match elements to create something more personal. Envision the possibilities!

Sincerely,
Alan Giagnocavo, Publisher

P.S. Since choosing a tattoo is such a permanent and personal decision, I'd love to hear which design you choose (with or without a picture of the actual tattoo). Please write or email Attn: Tattoo Art. As a thank you, everyone who writes in will be sent a few new tattoo designs that didn't make it into this edition.

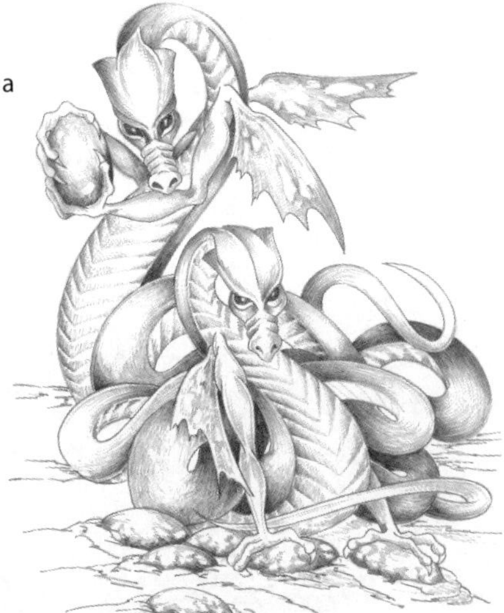

Fox Chapel Publishing
903 Square Street
Mount Joy, PA 17552
publisher@foxchapelpublishing.com

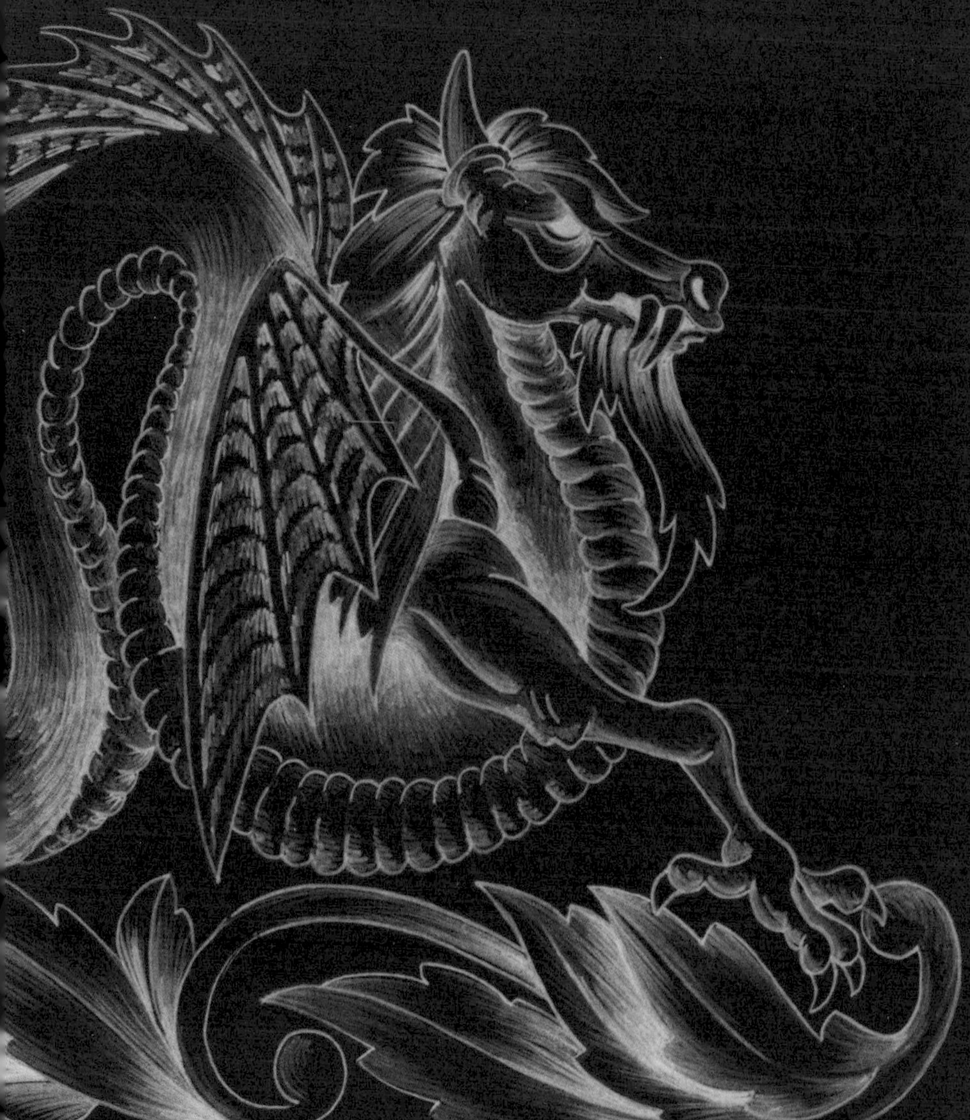

Fantasy

Fantasy figures are found in countless cultures from Celtic to tribal to Asian. For those wishing to make a commanding individual statement, the fire-breathing dragon can represent good (hope, purity, women as creators, protection against hostile spiritual forces) and evil (Satan, rage, raw power, jealousy, maleficence). Other fantasy figures are more whimsical. Fairies can symbolize the nurturing and maternal nature of women or the power of the human spirit. Green men, creatures whose faces are surrounded by or made from leaves, personify nature and are symbols of rebirth.

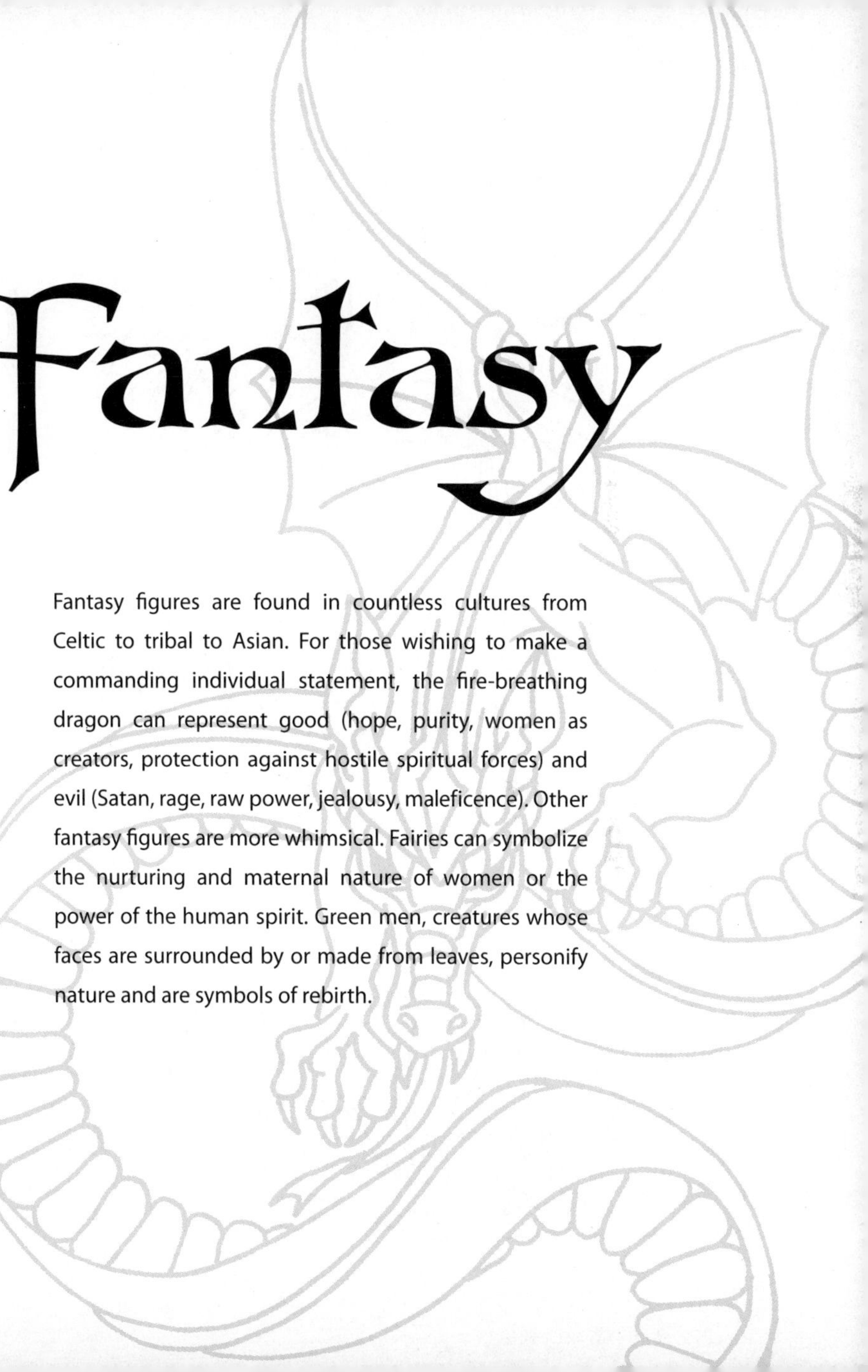

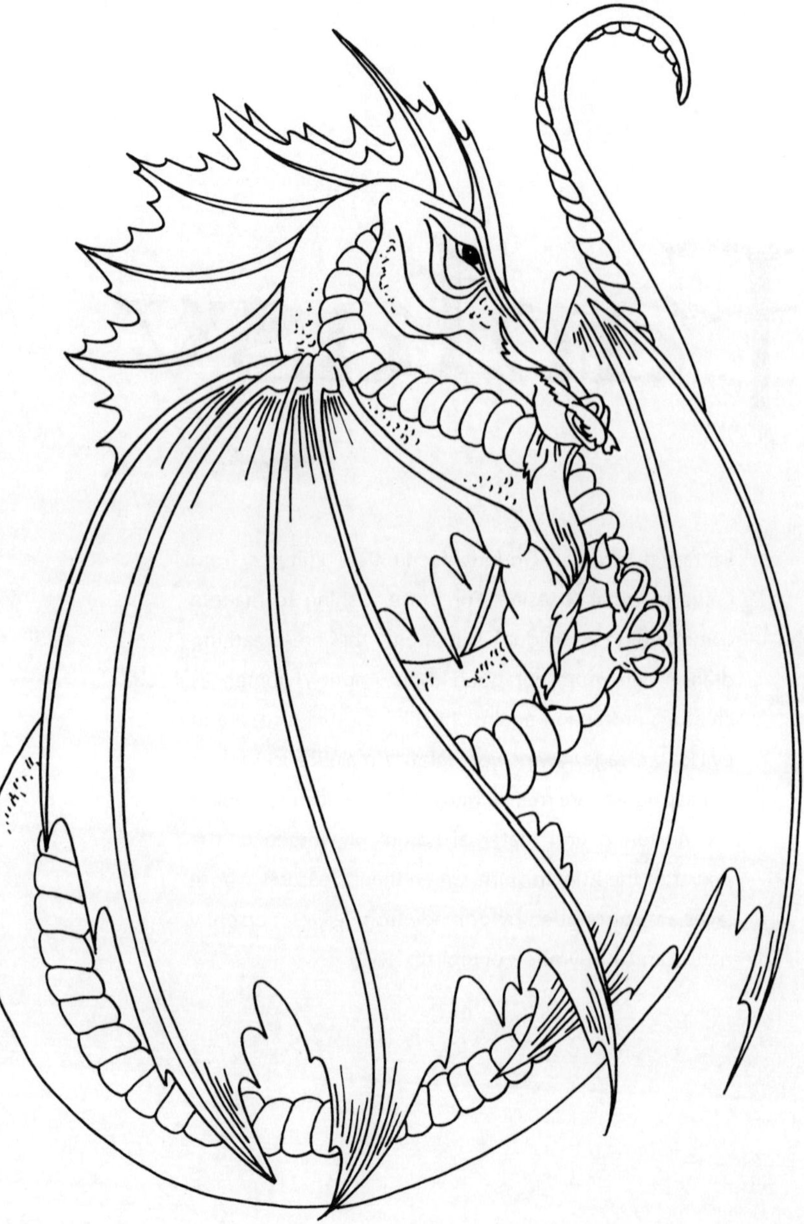

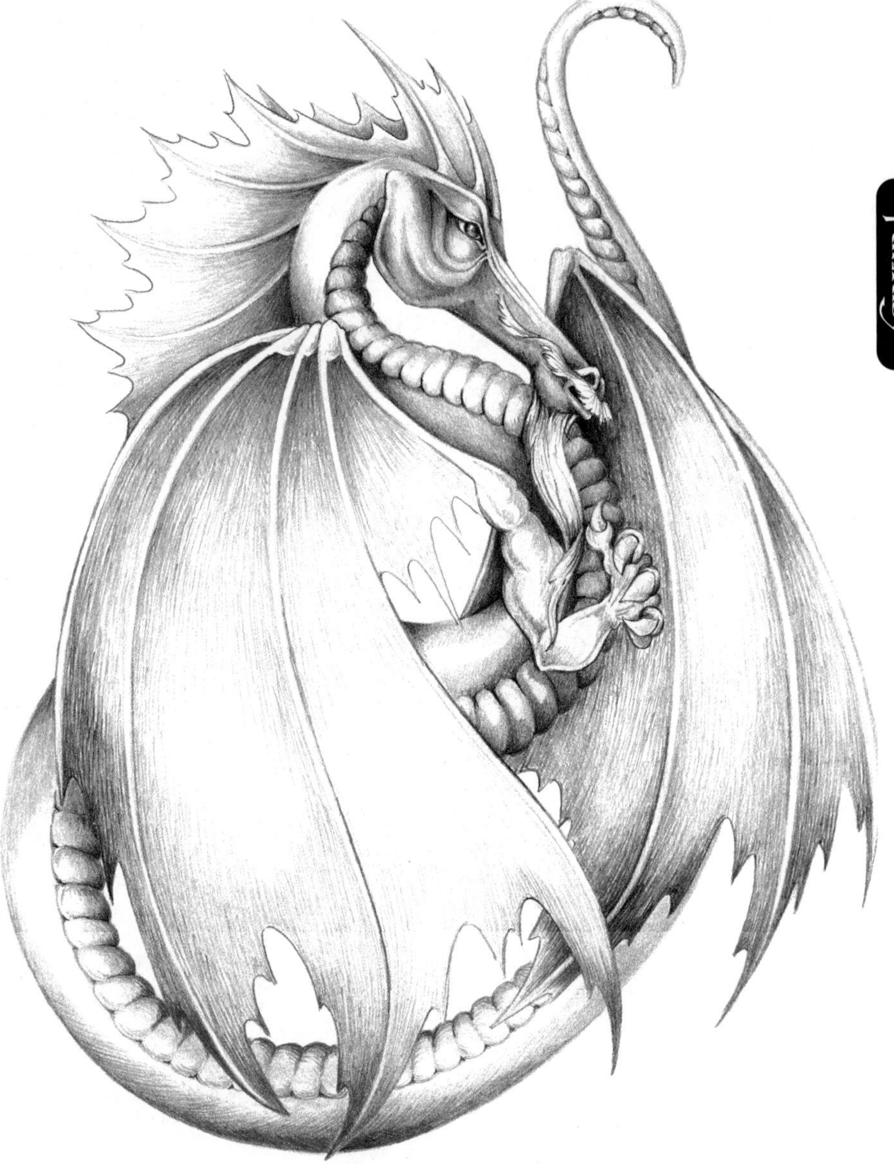

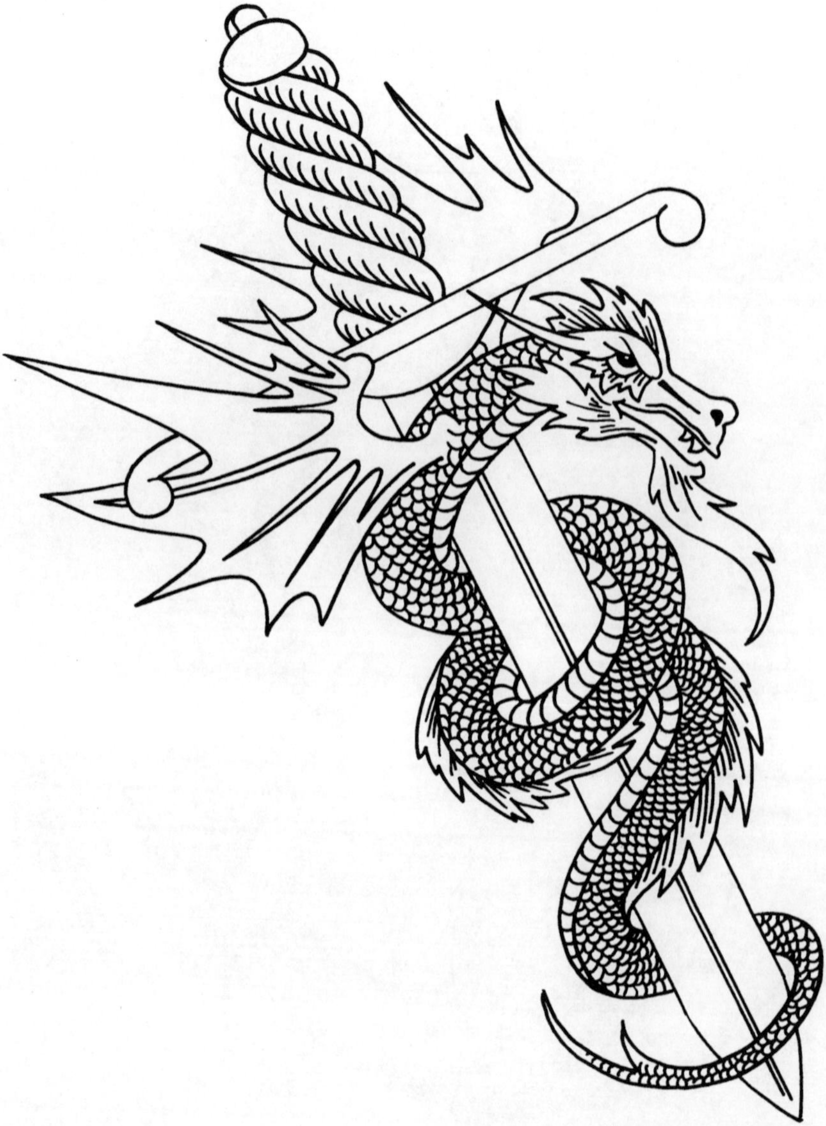

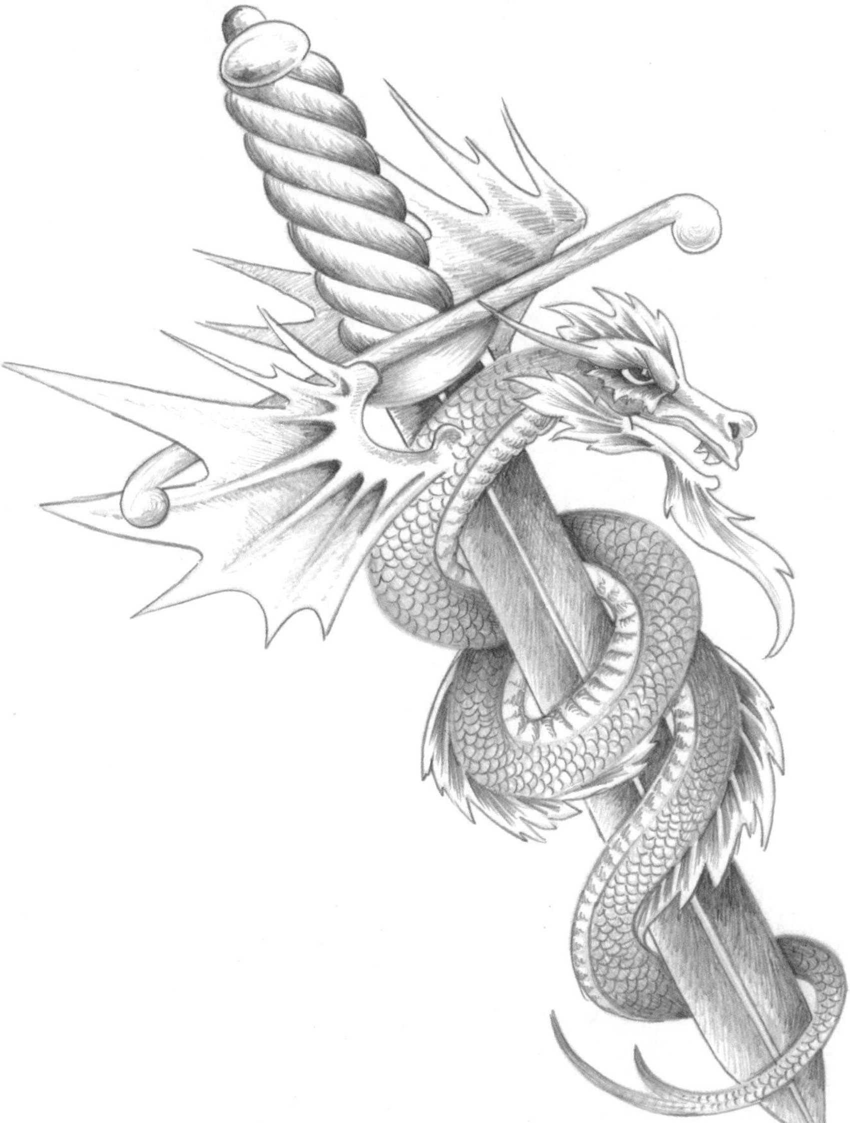

Fantasy

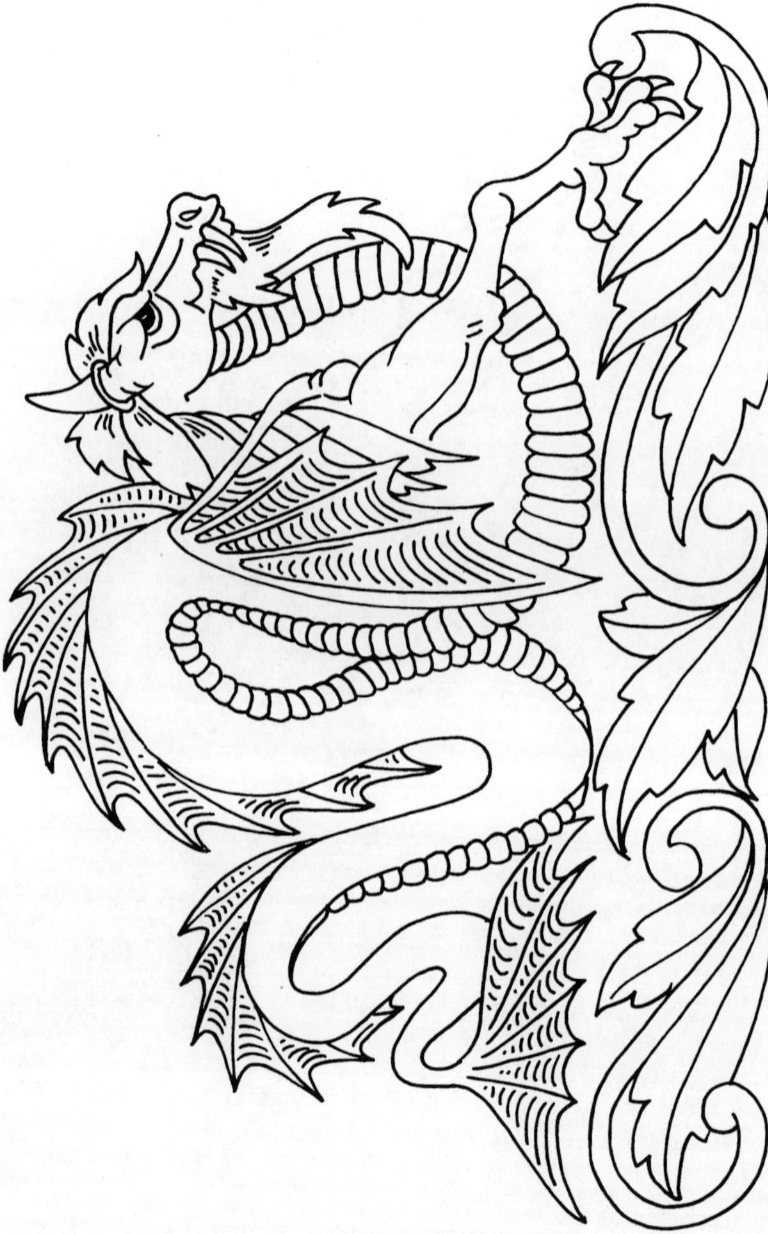

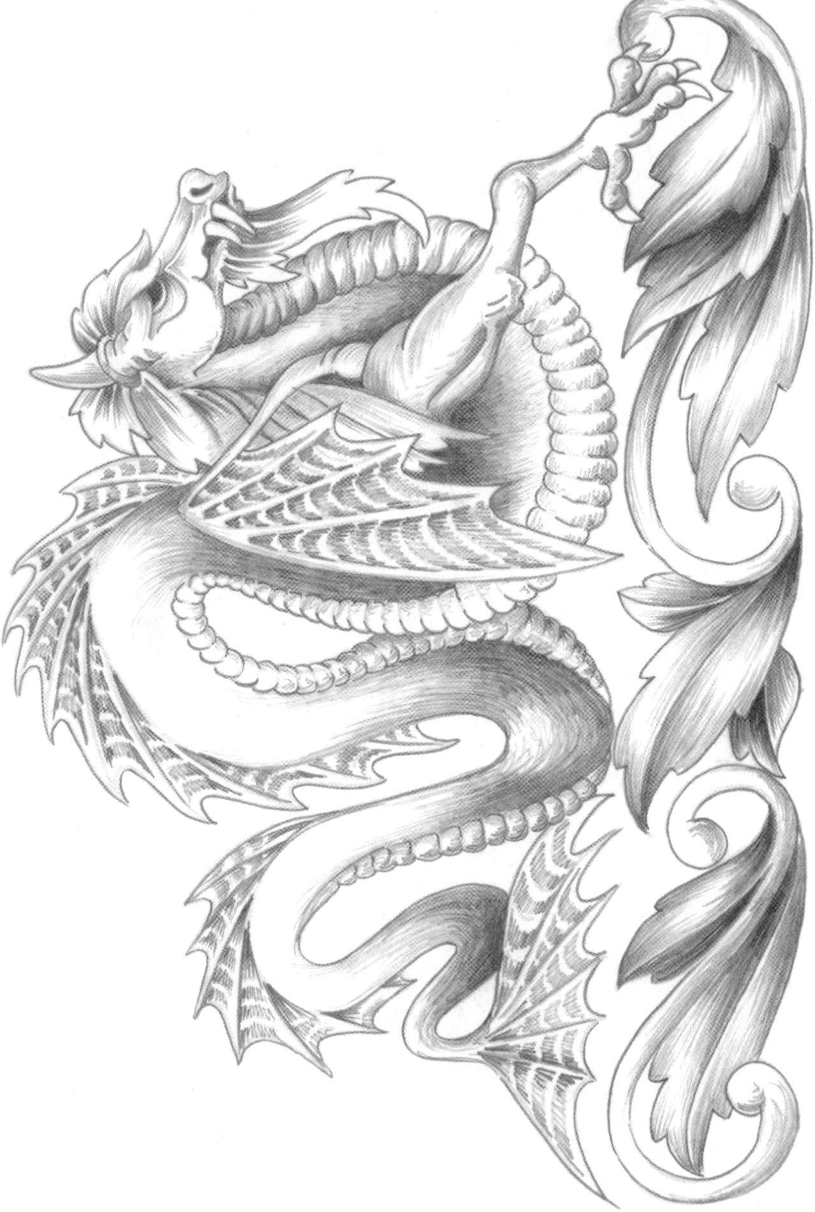

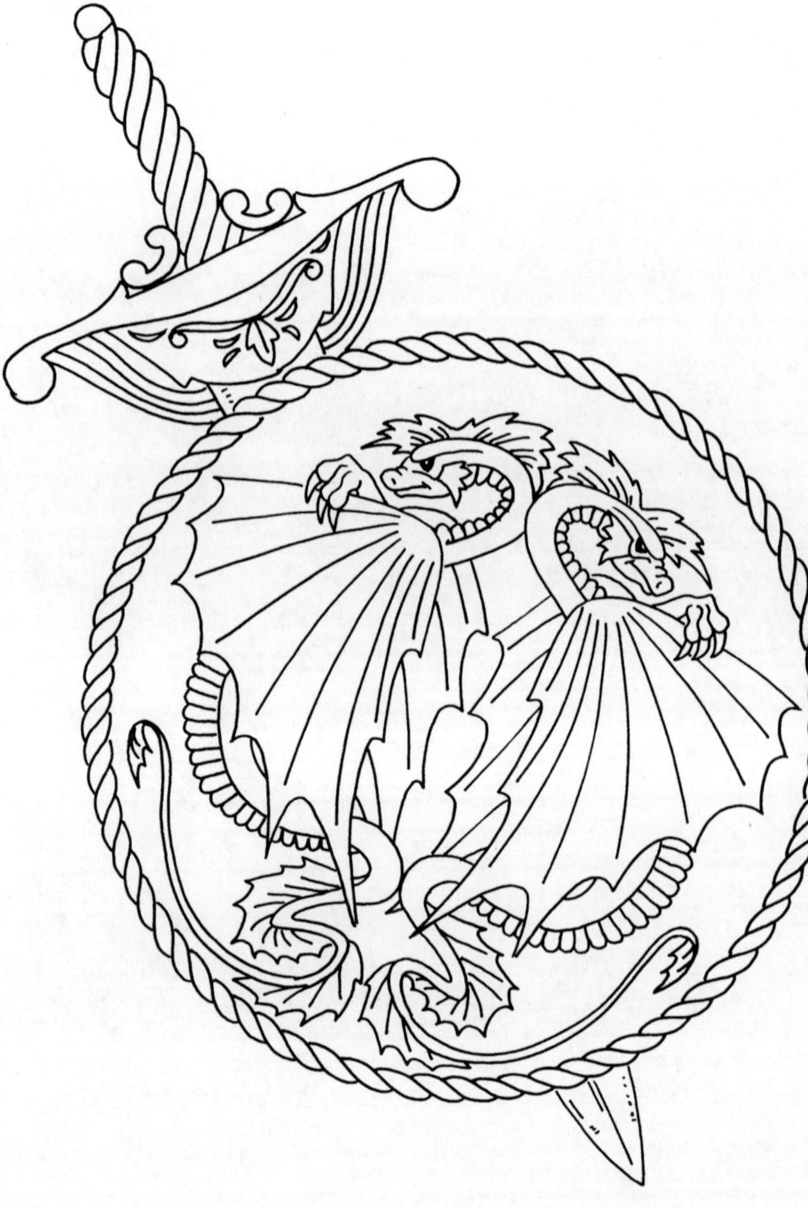

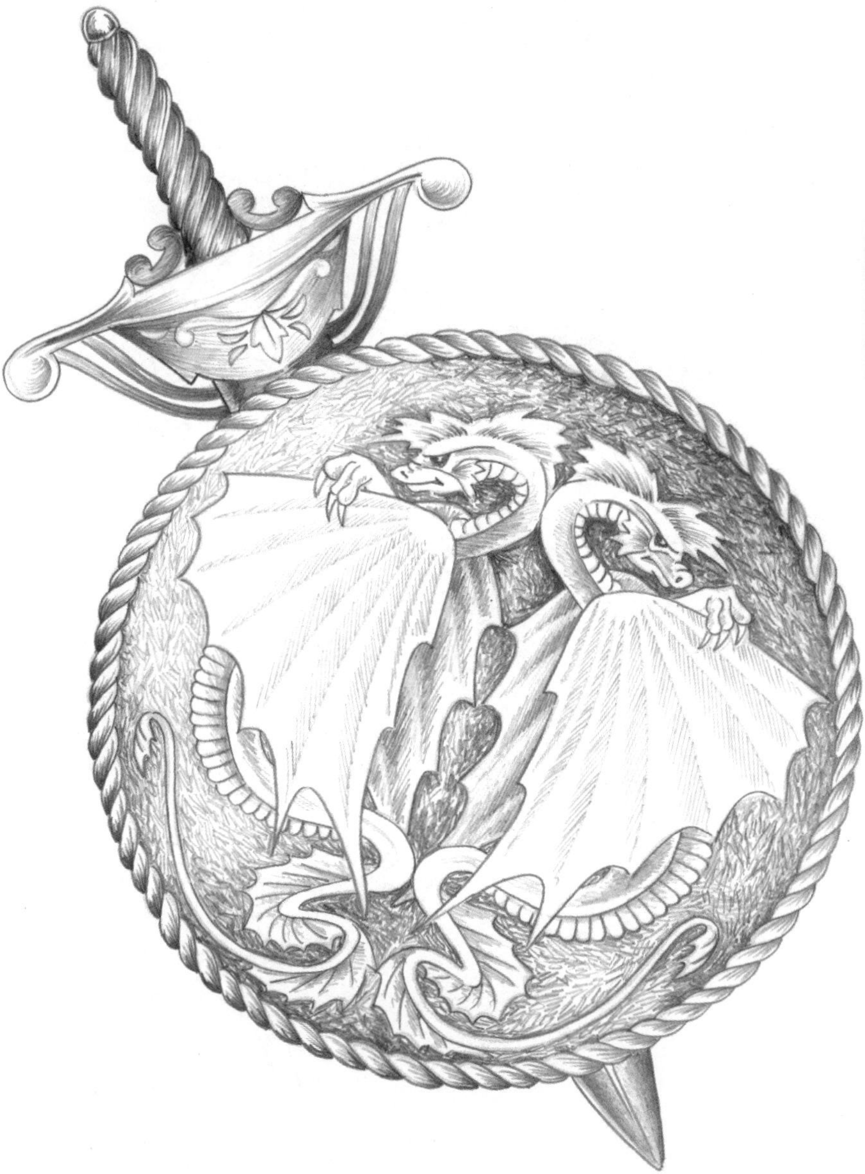

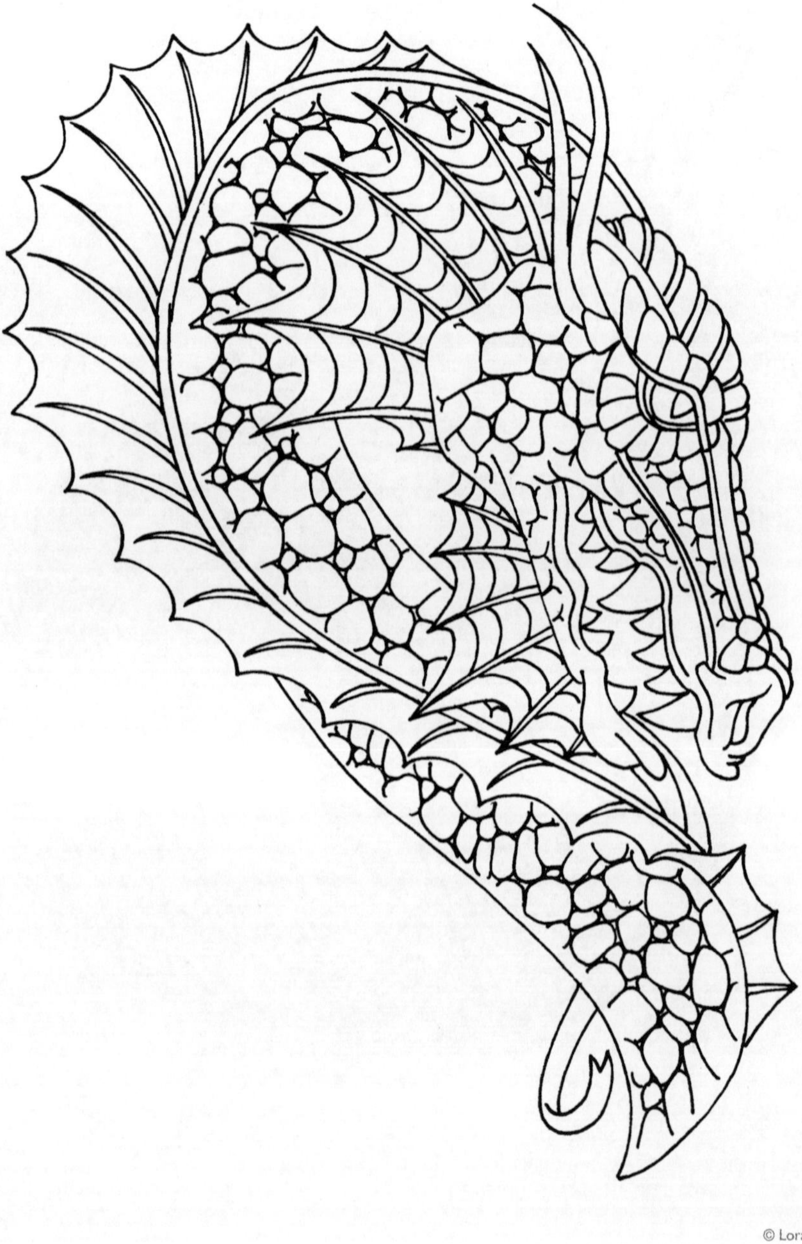

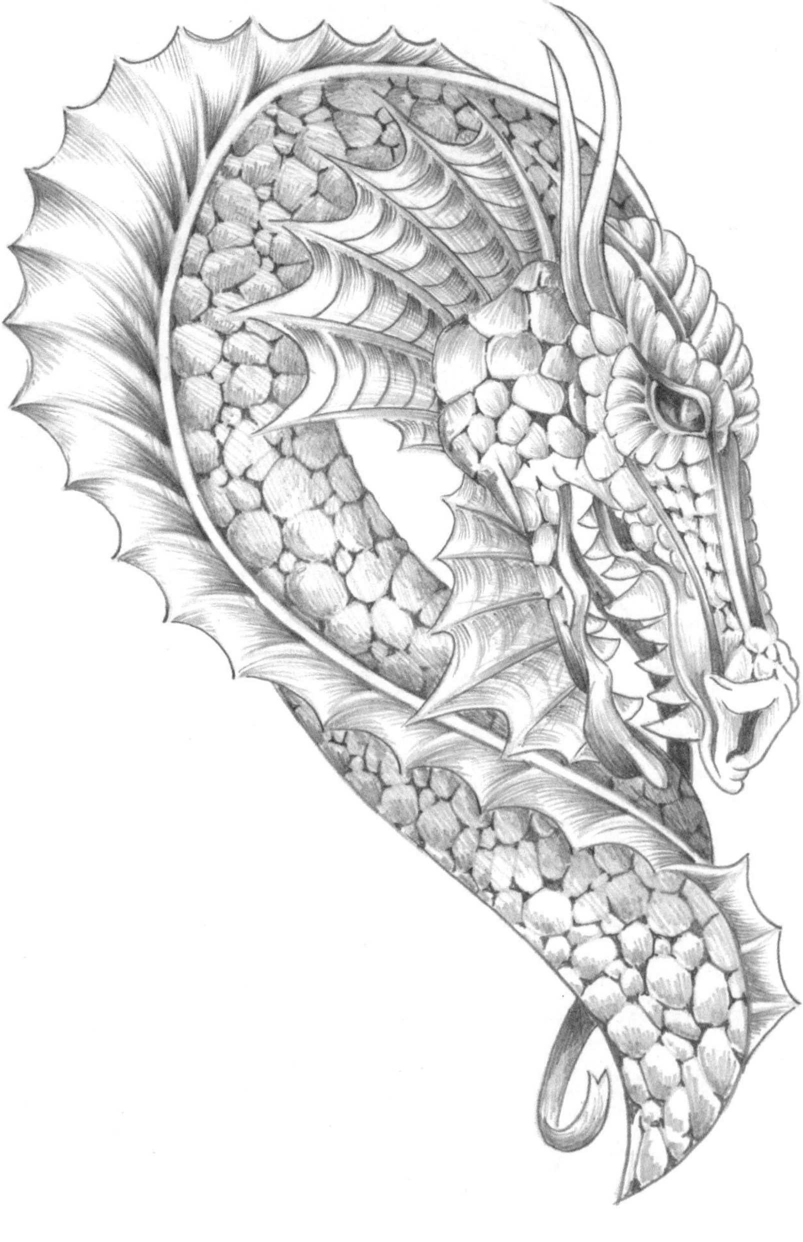

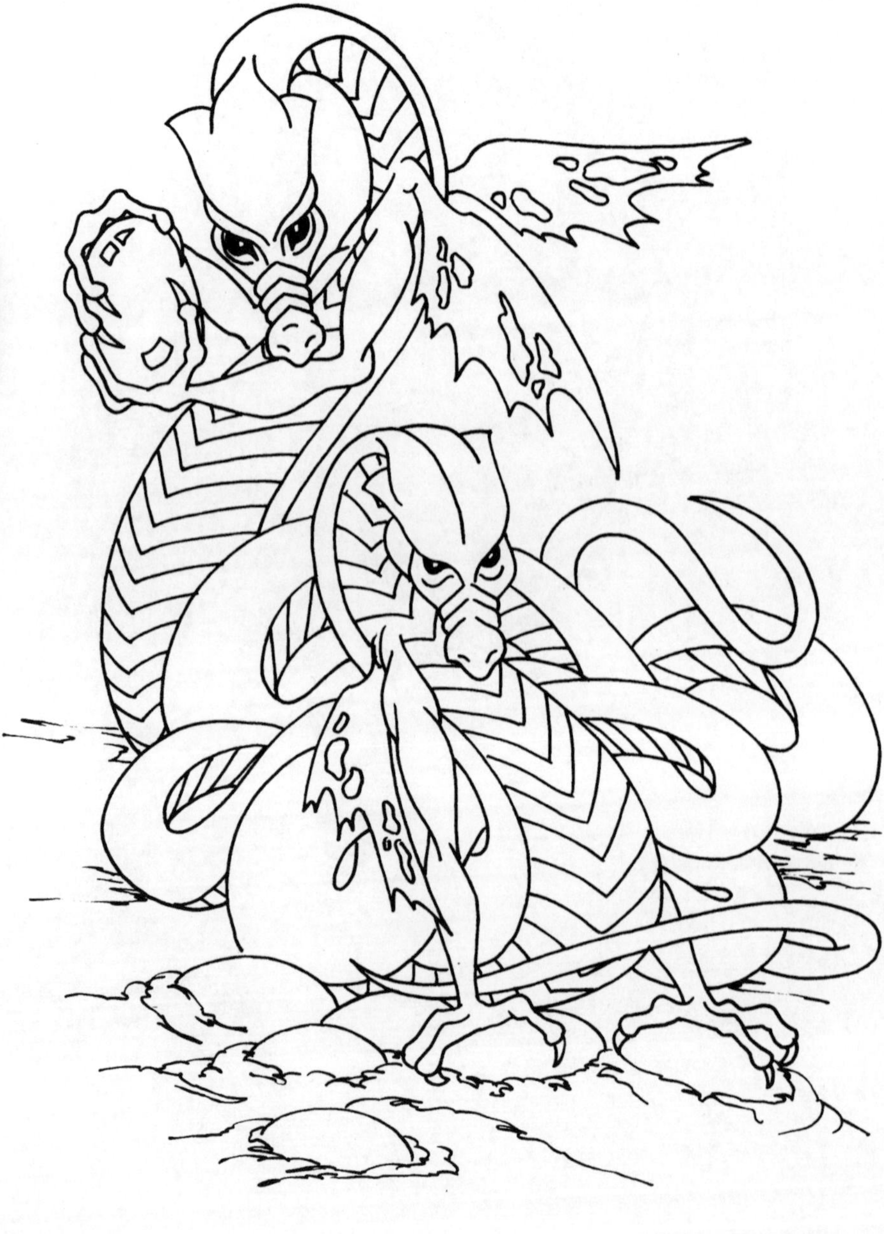

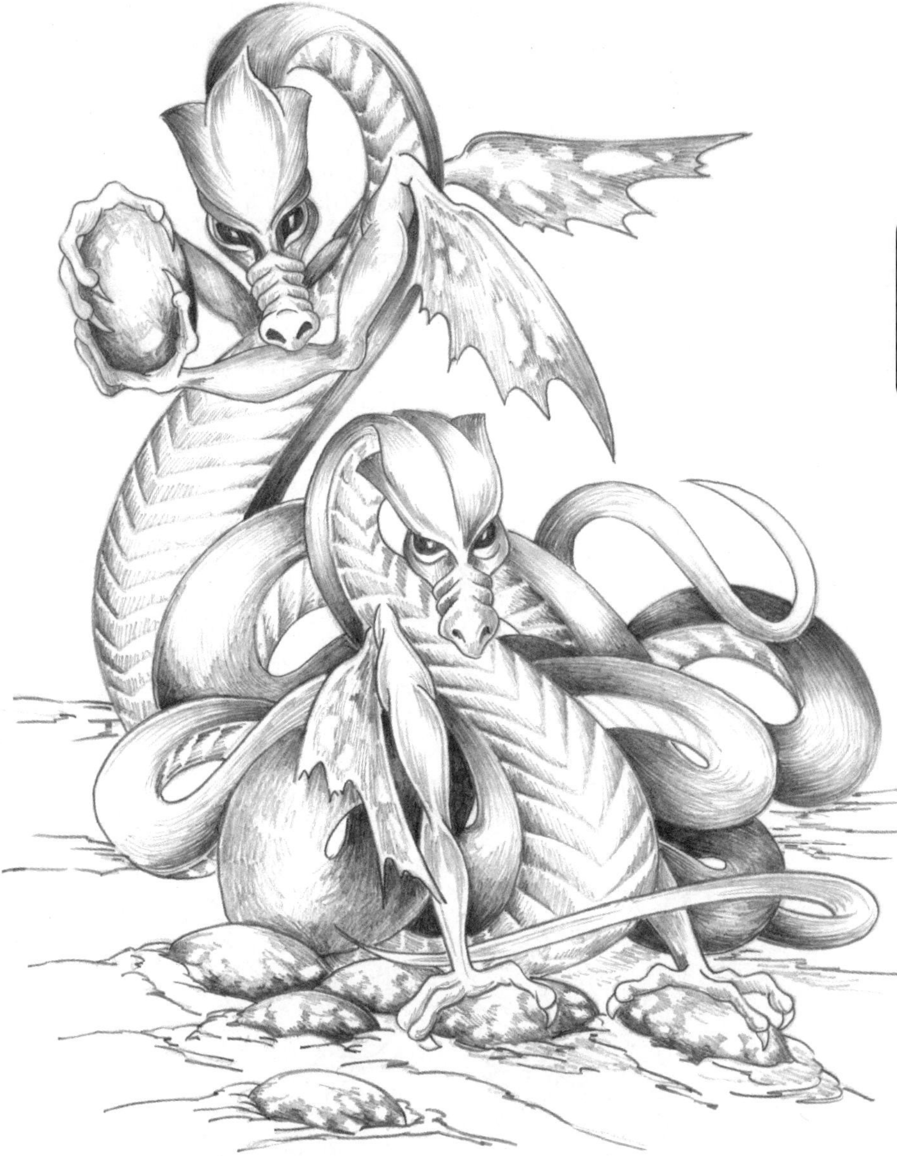

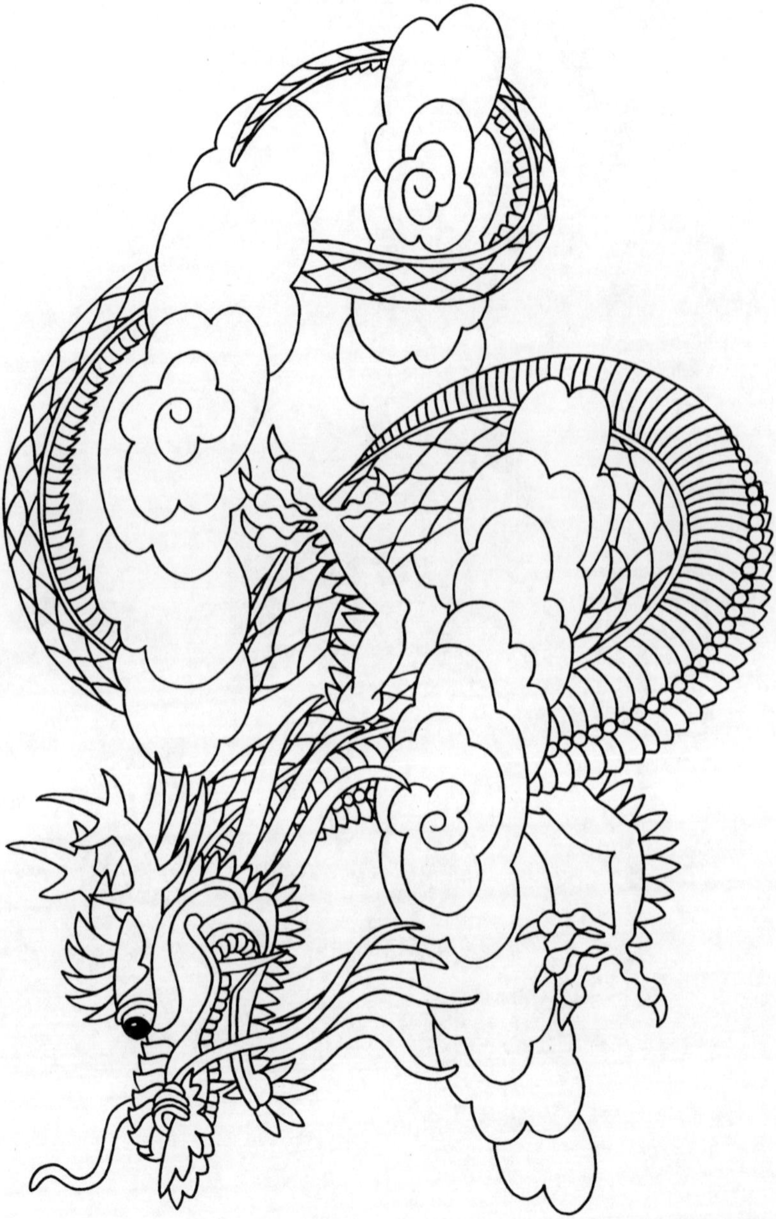

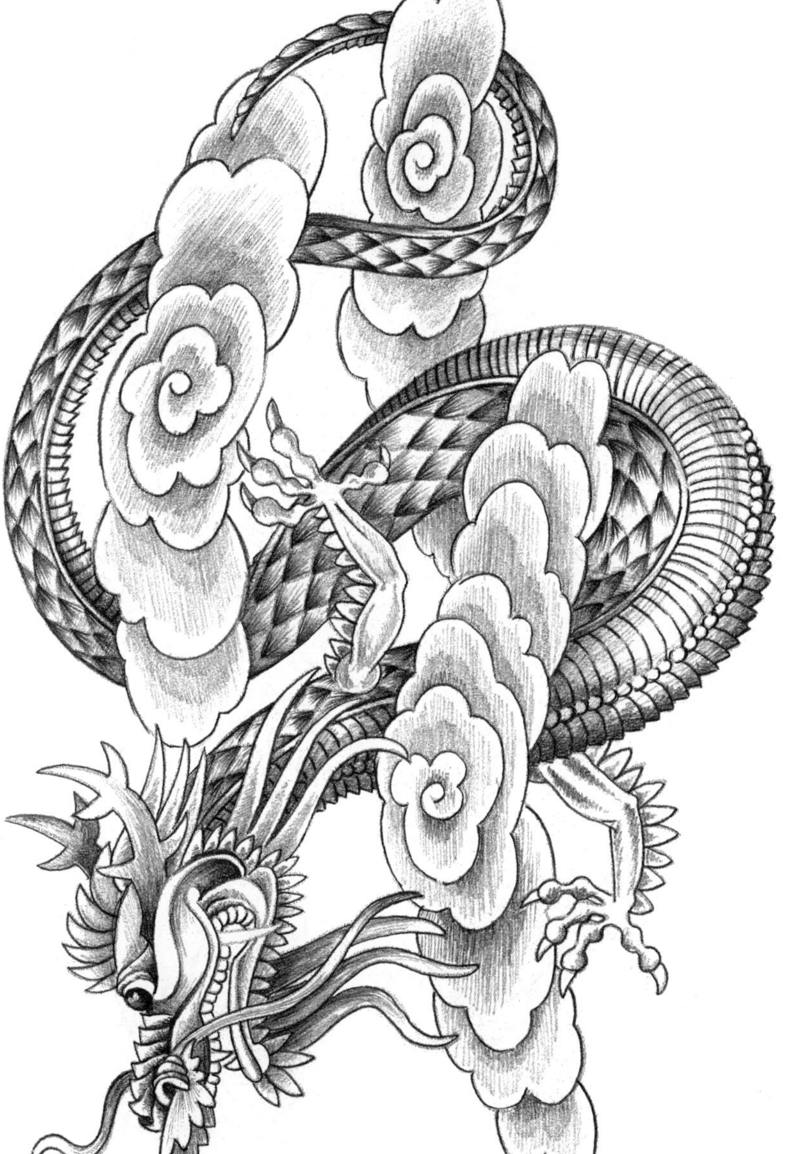

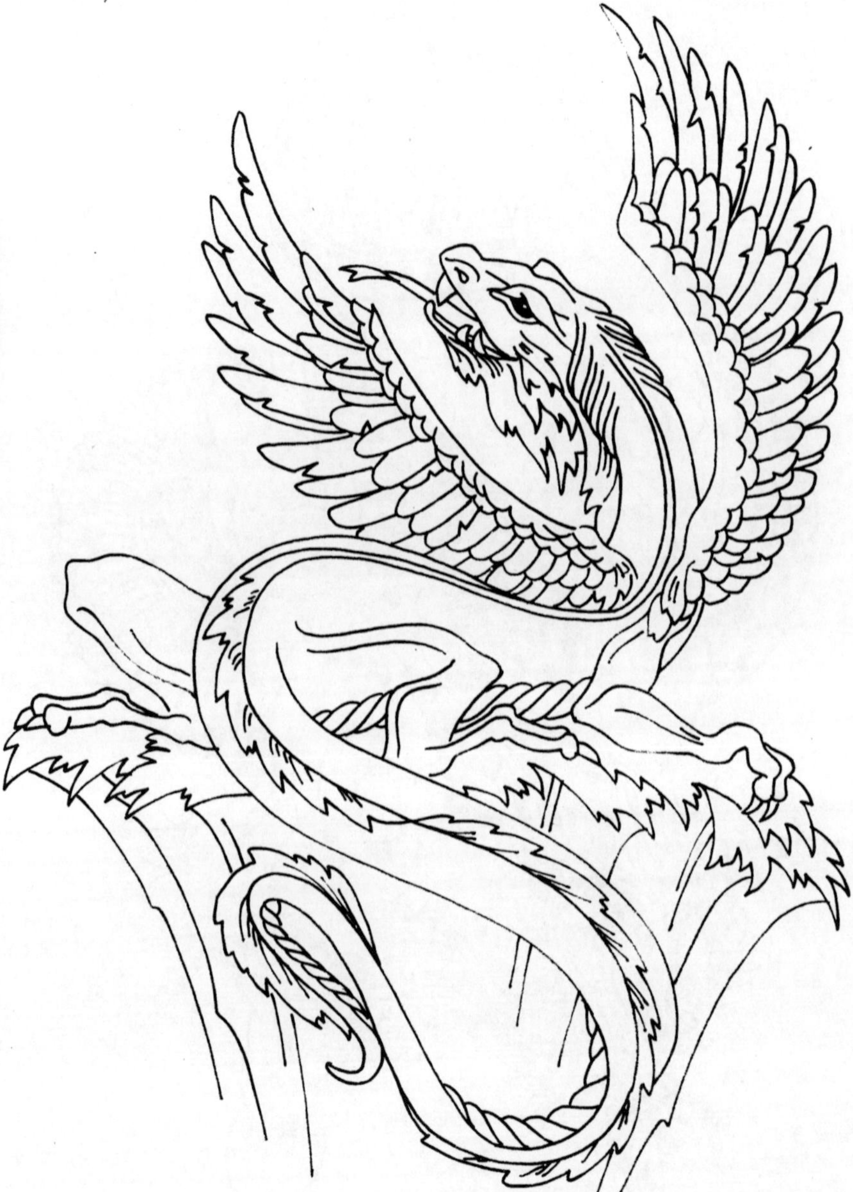

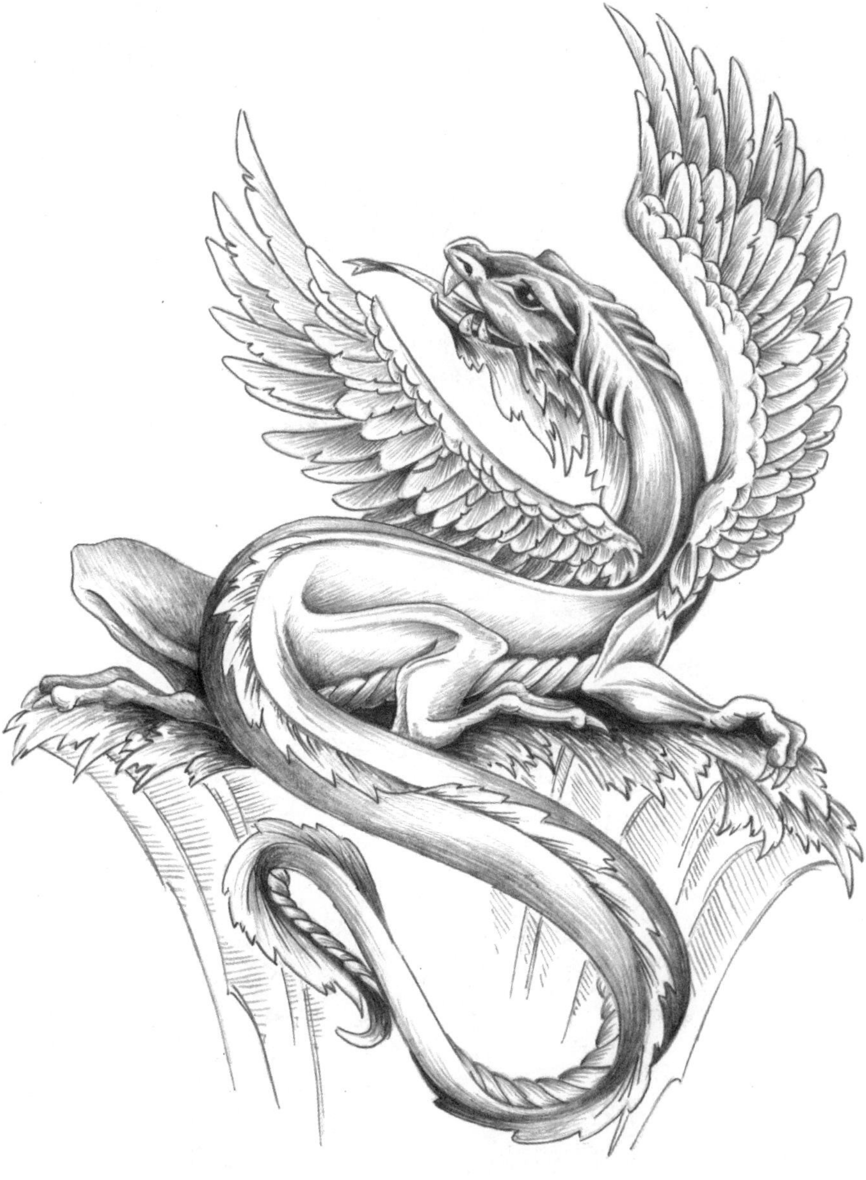

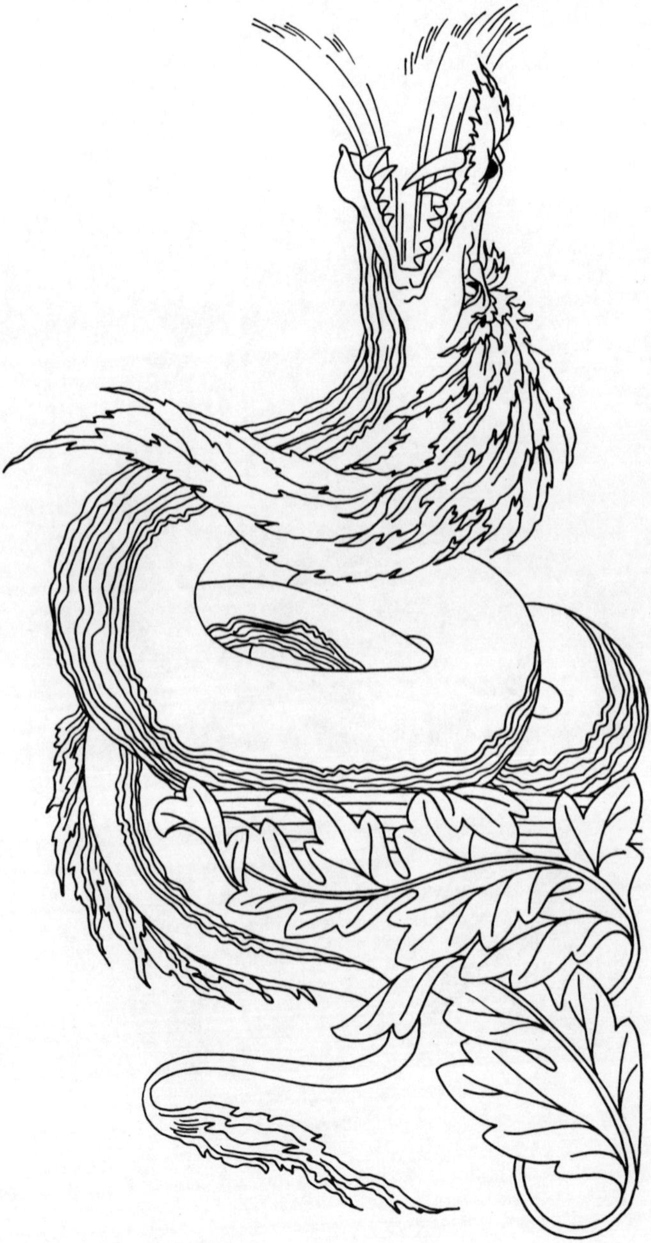

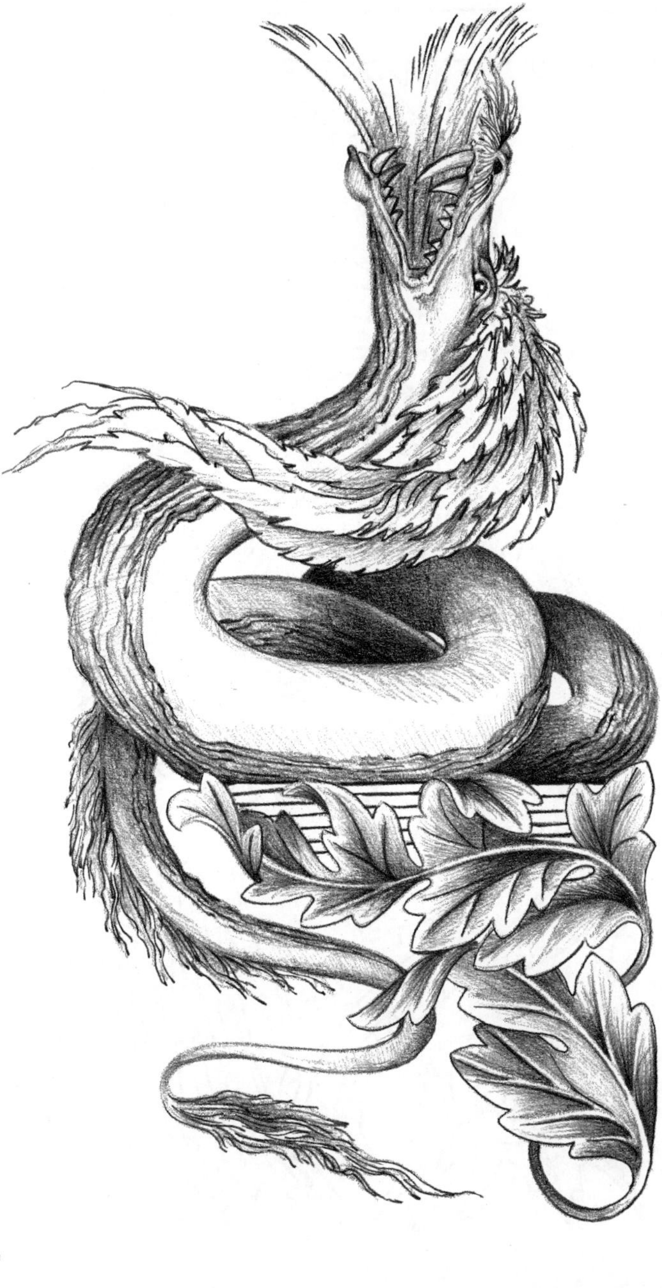

Fantasy

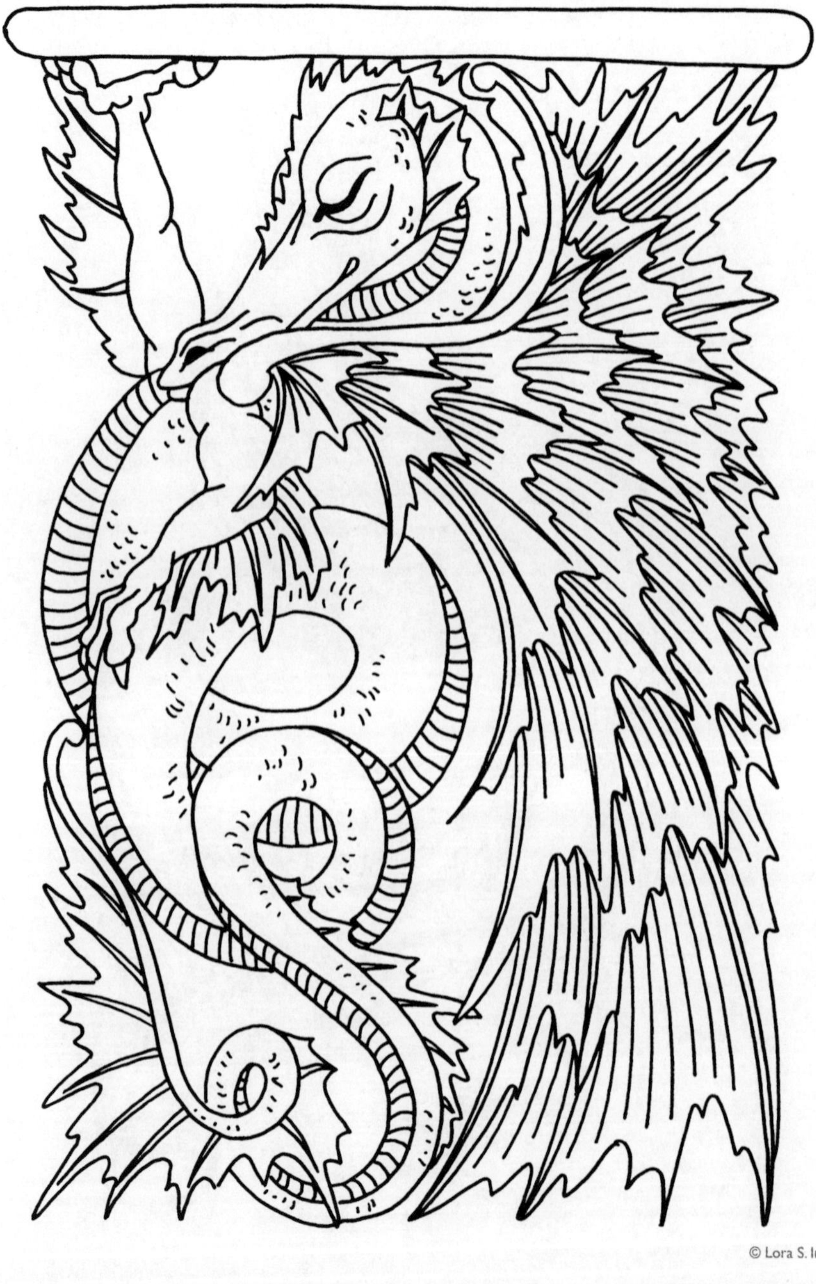

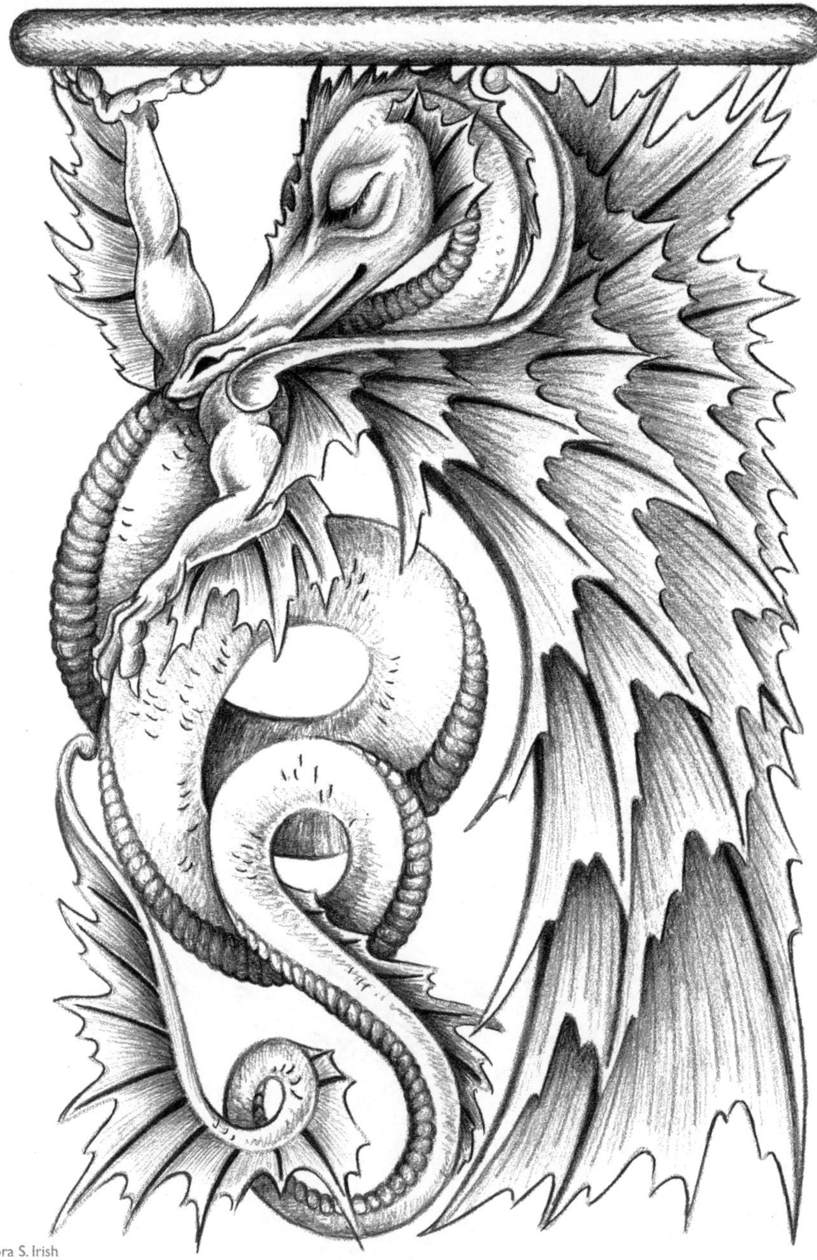

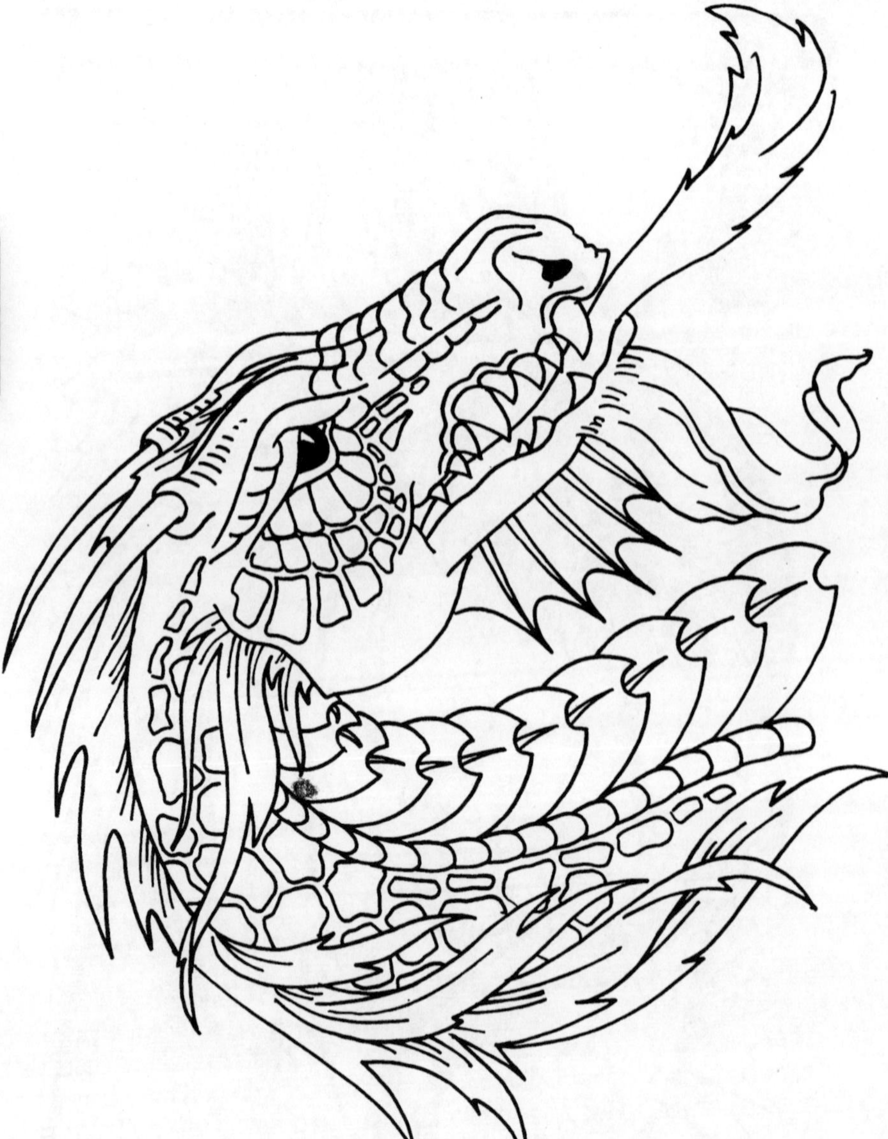

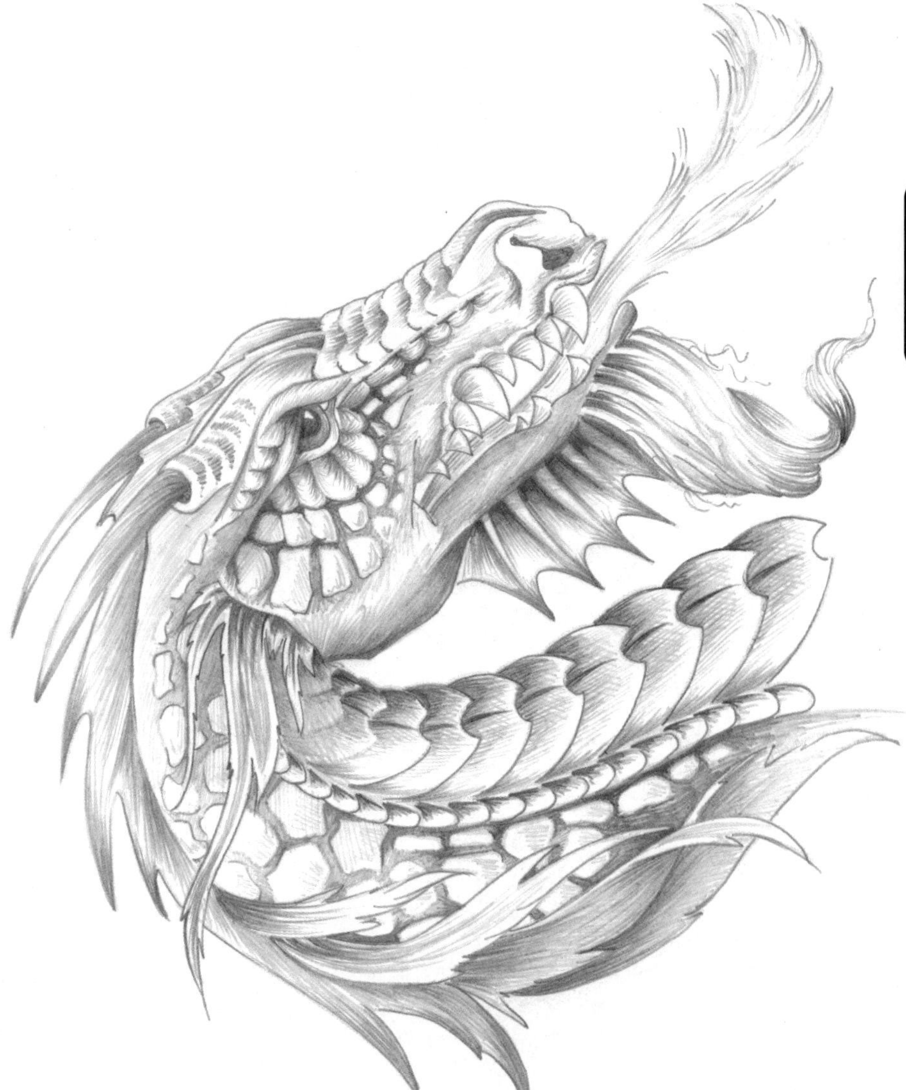

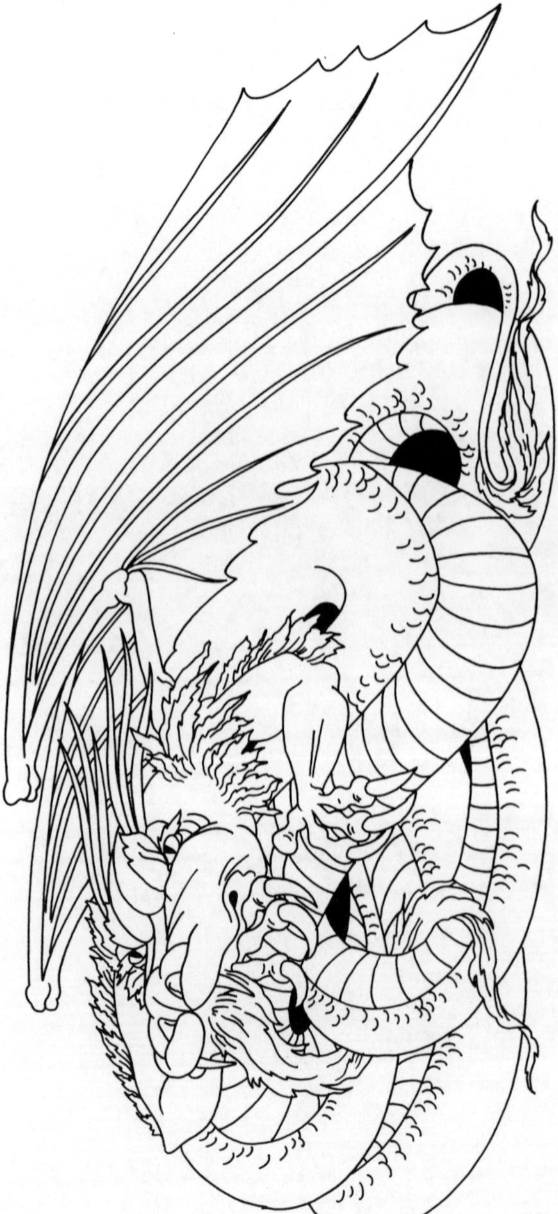

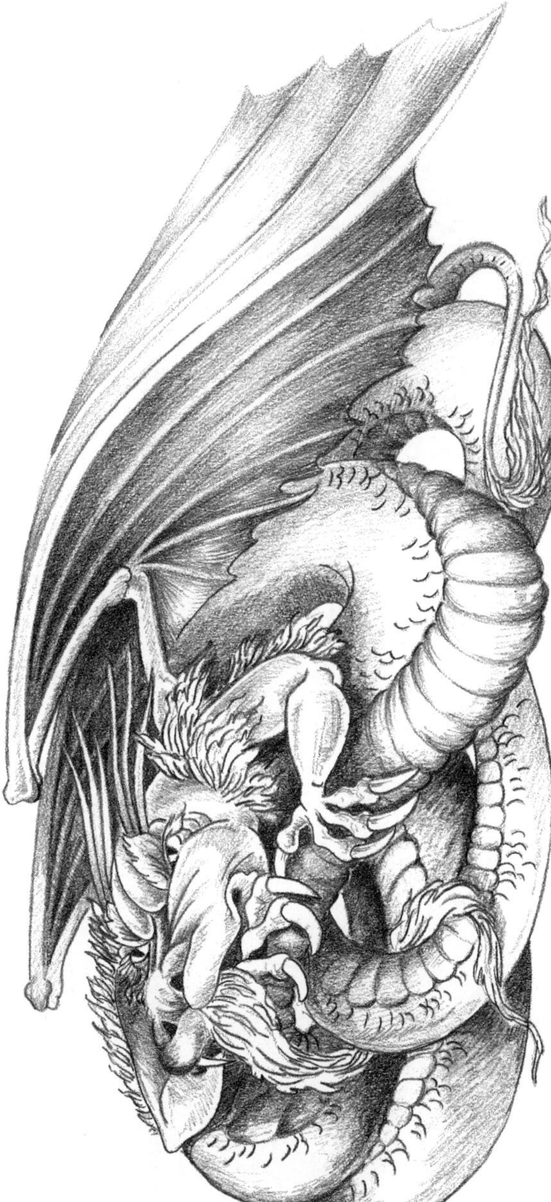

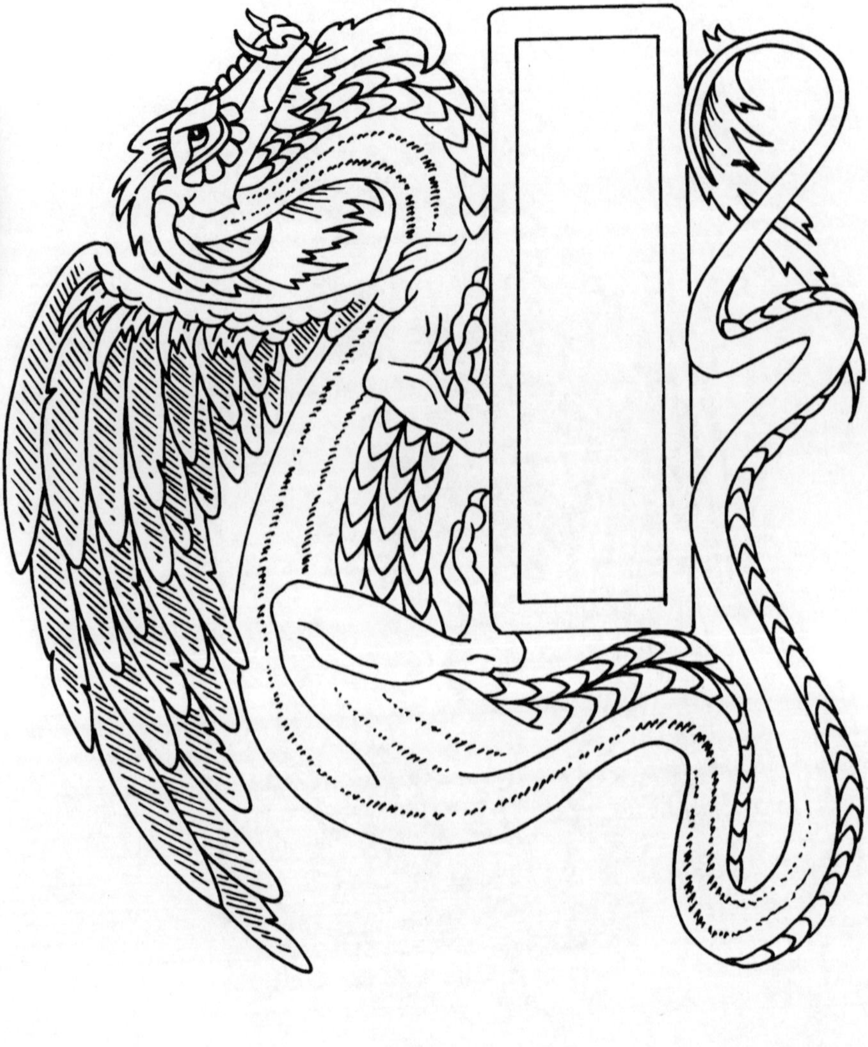

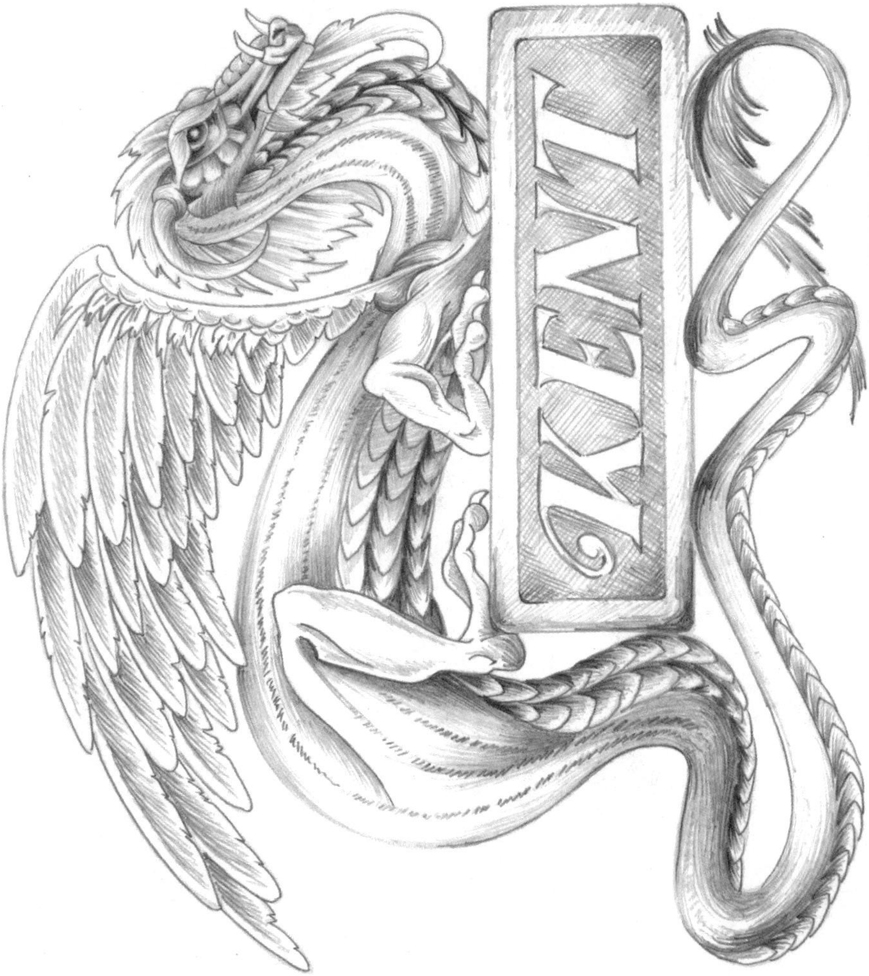

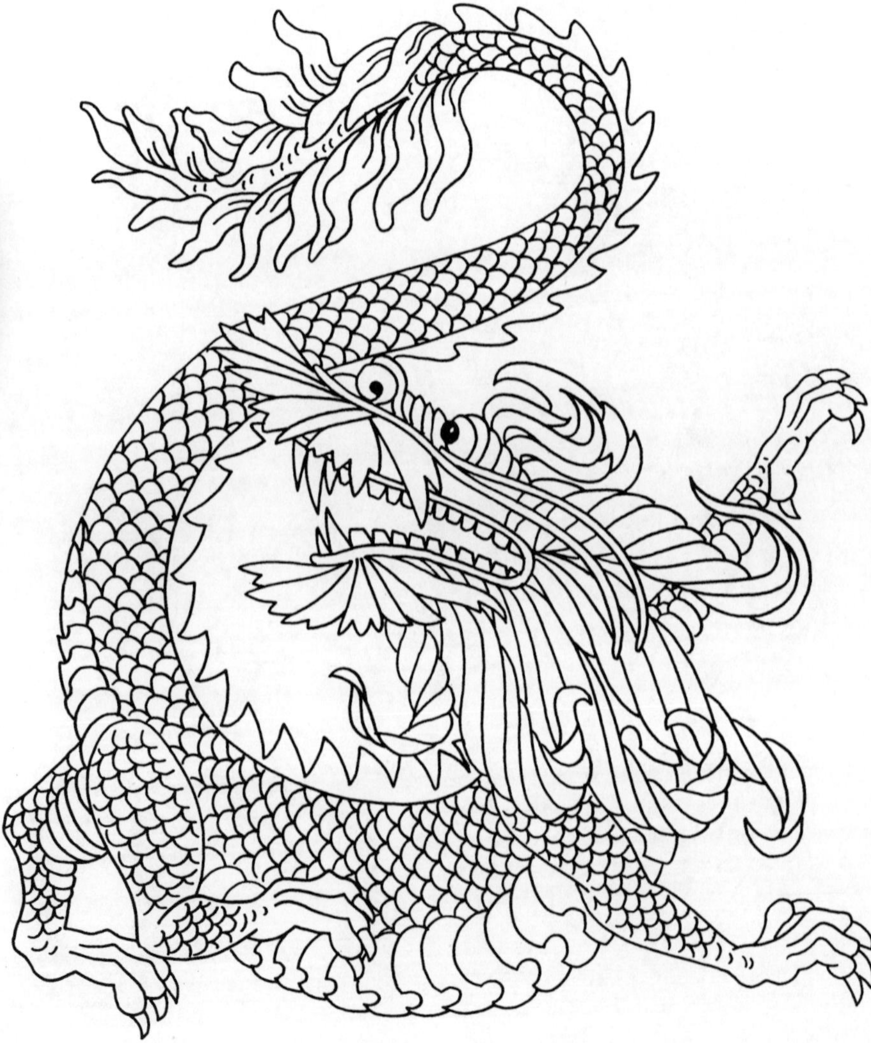

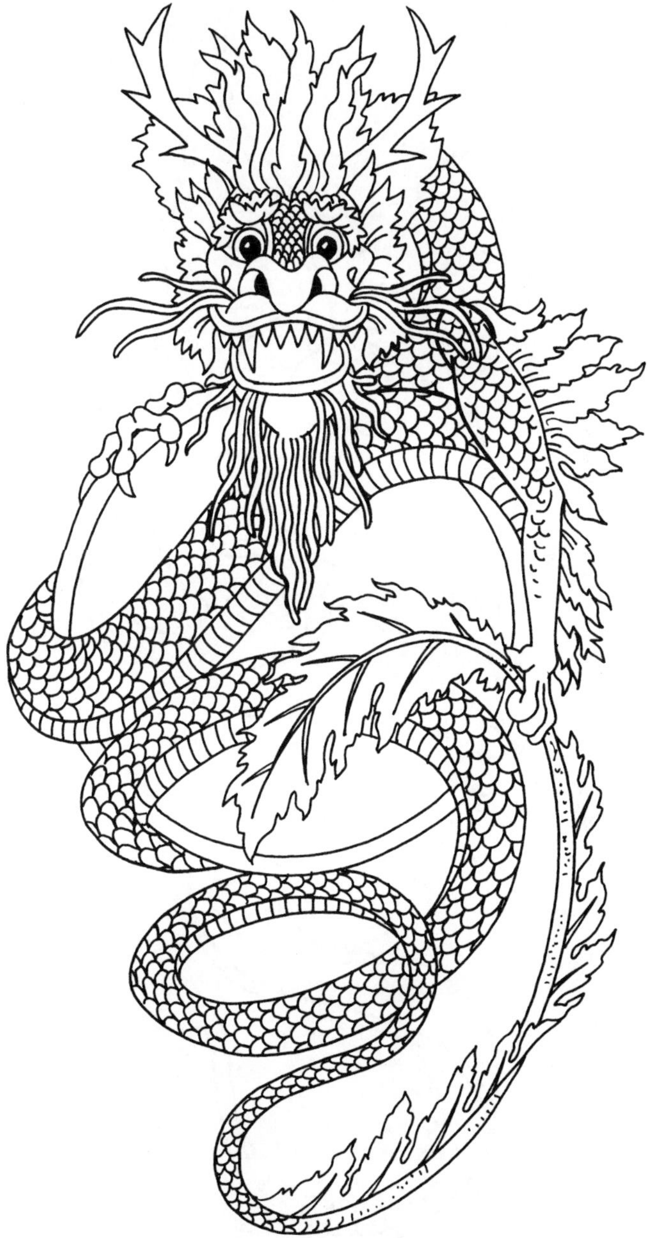

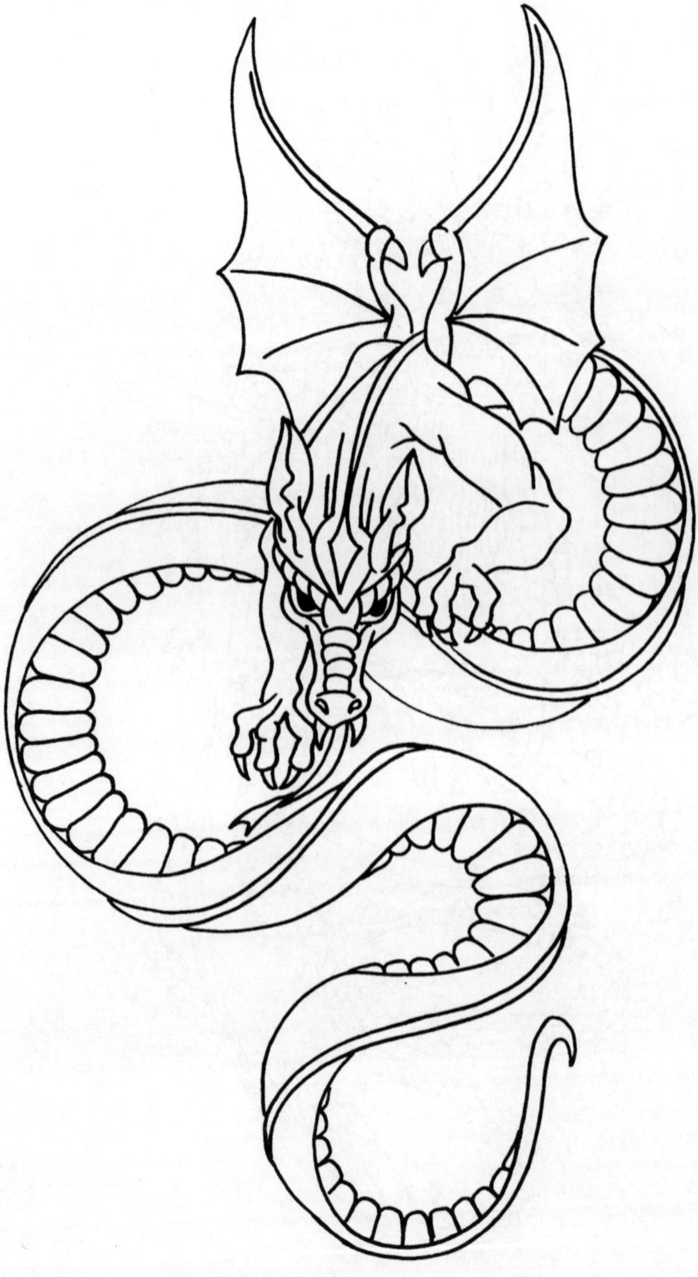

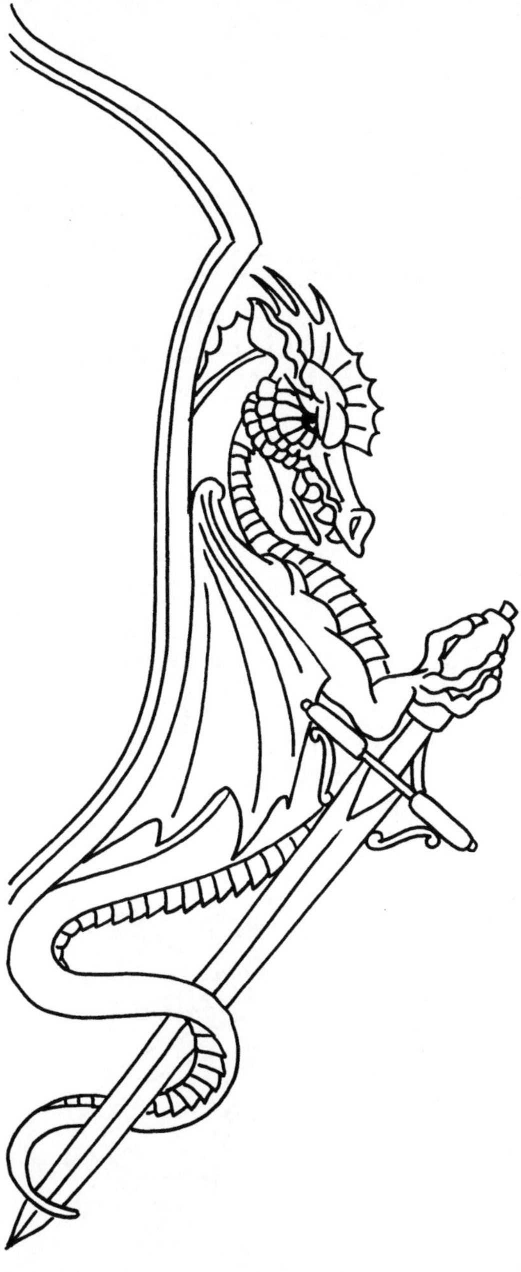

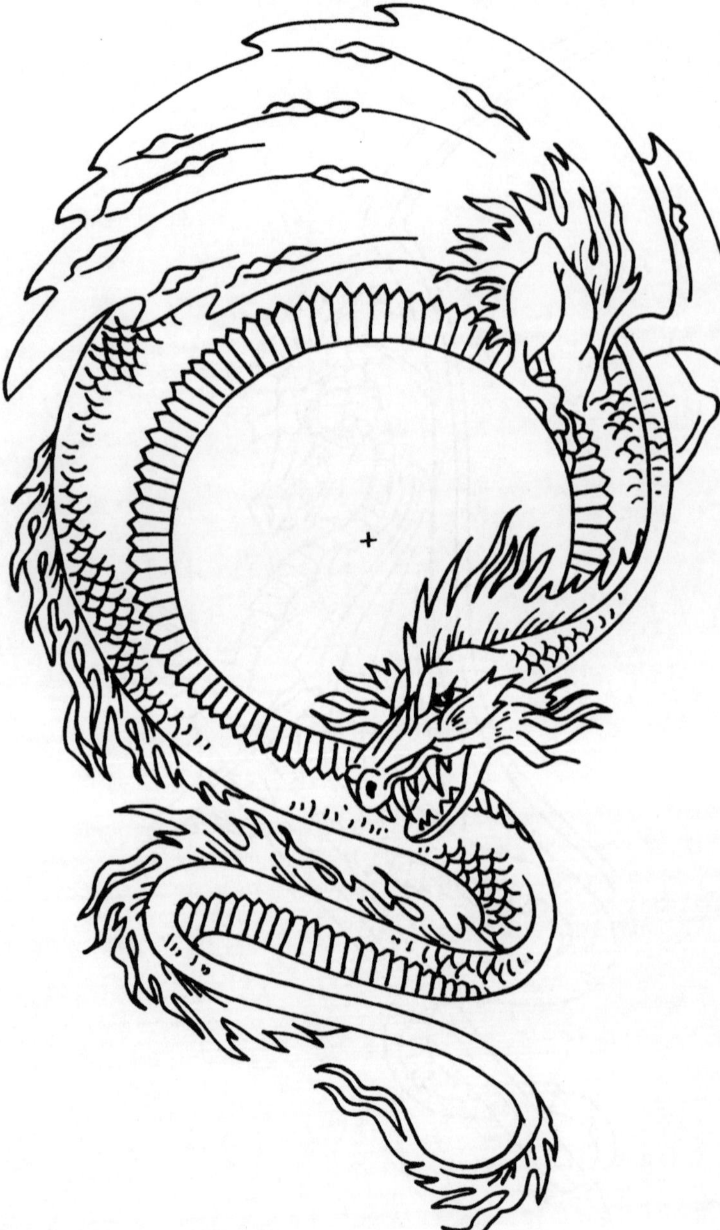

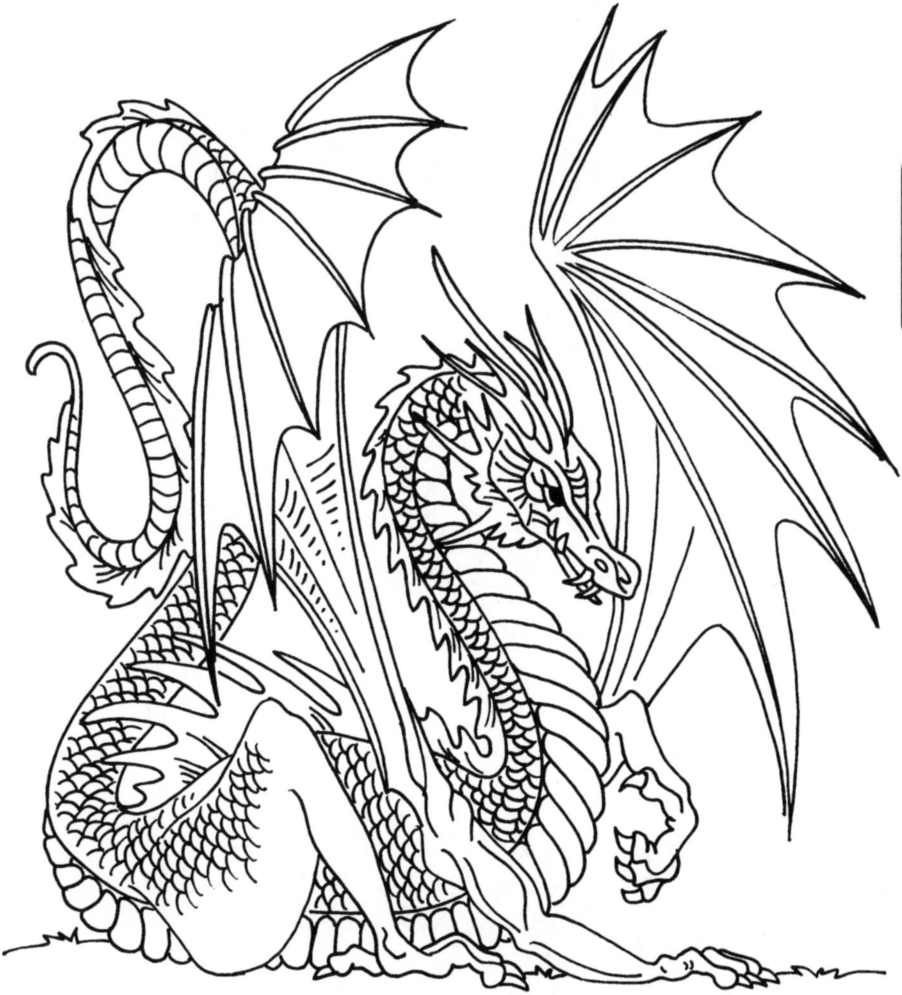

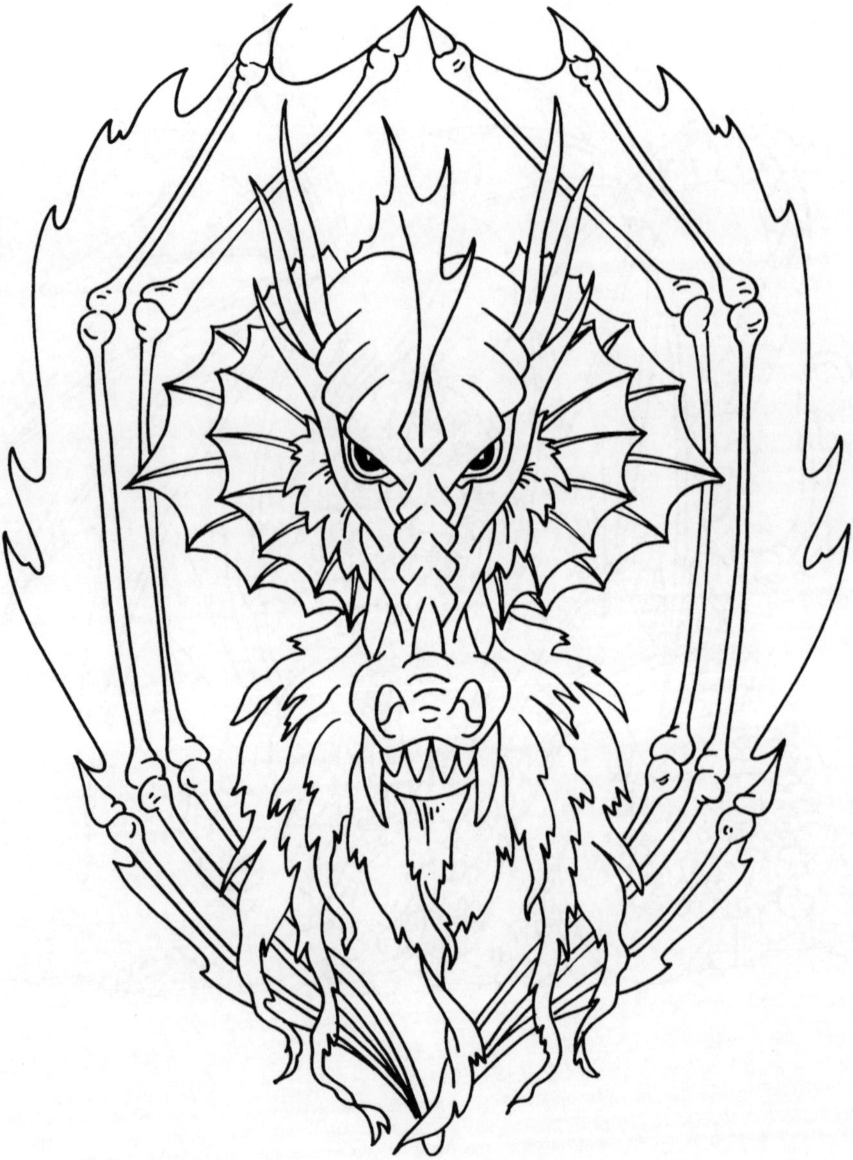

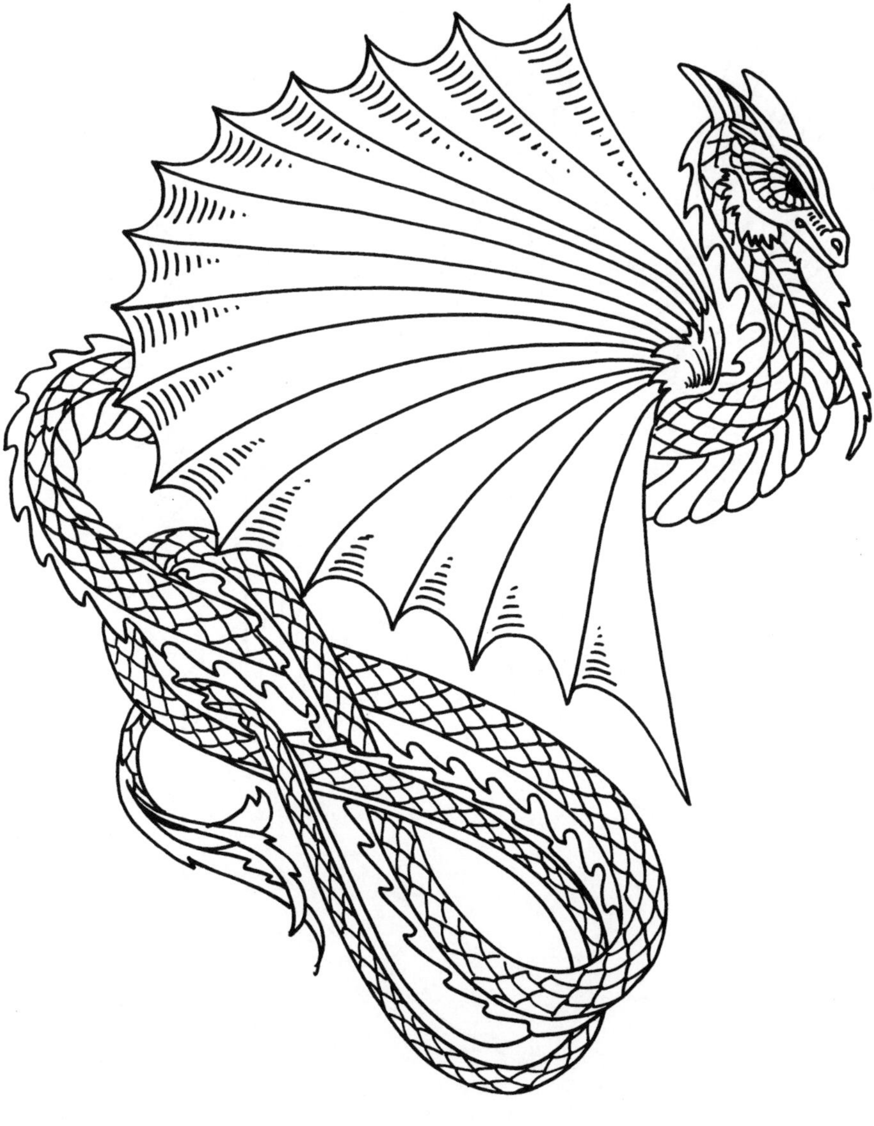

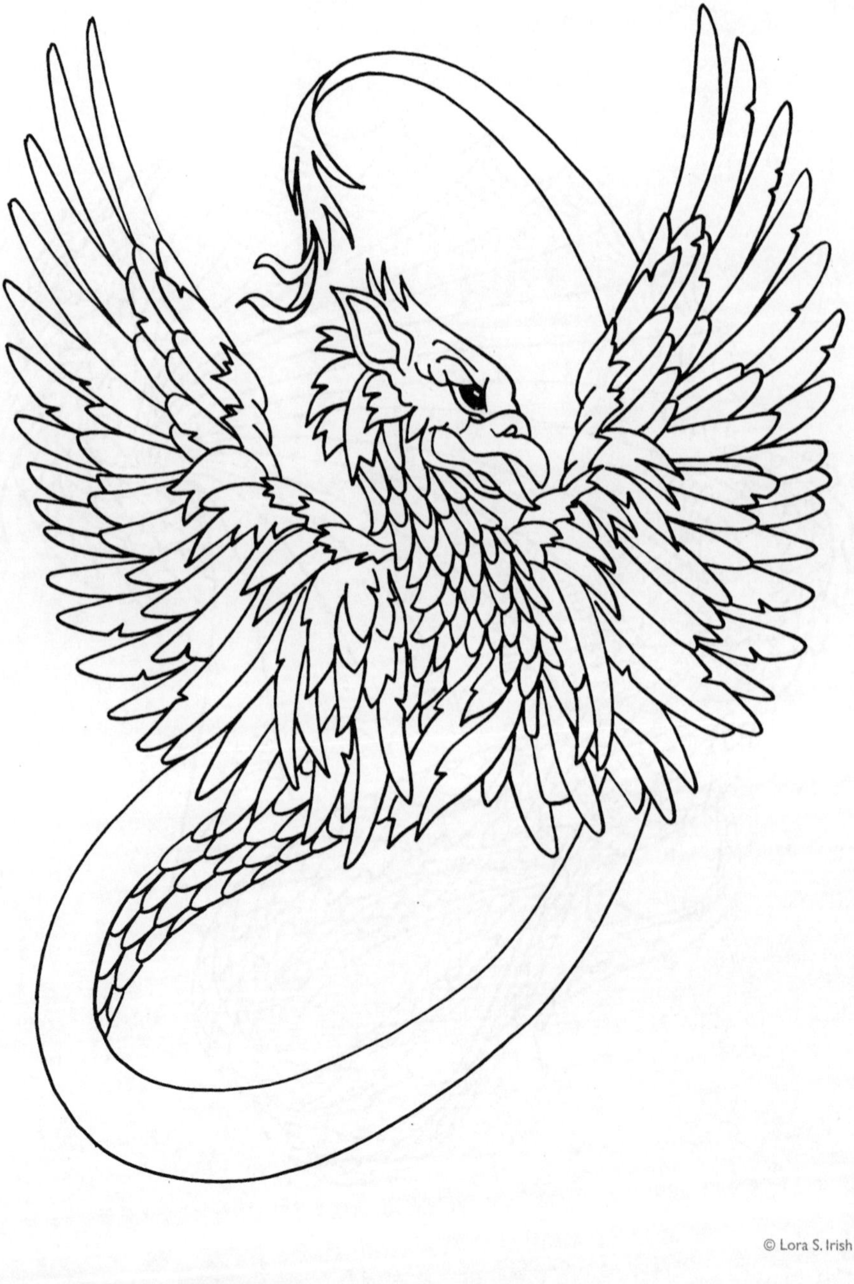

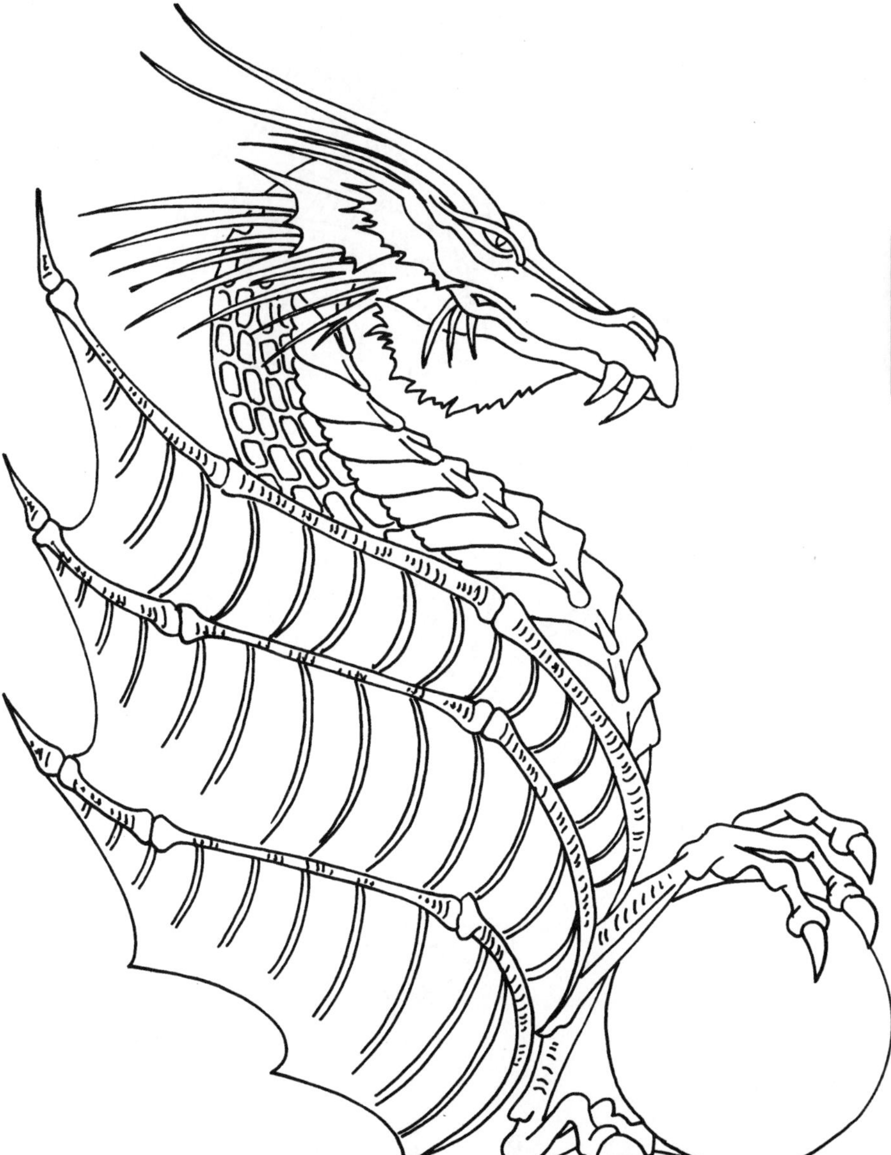

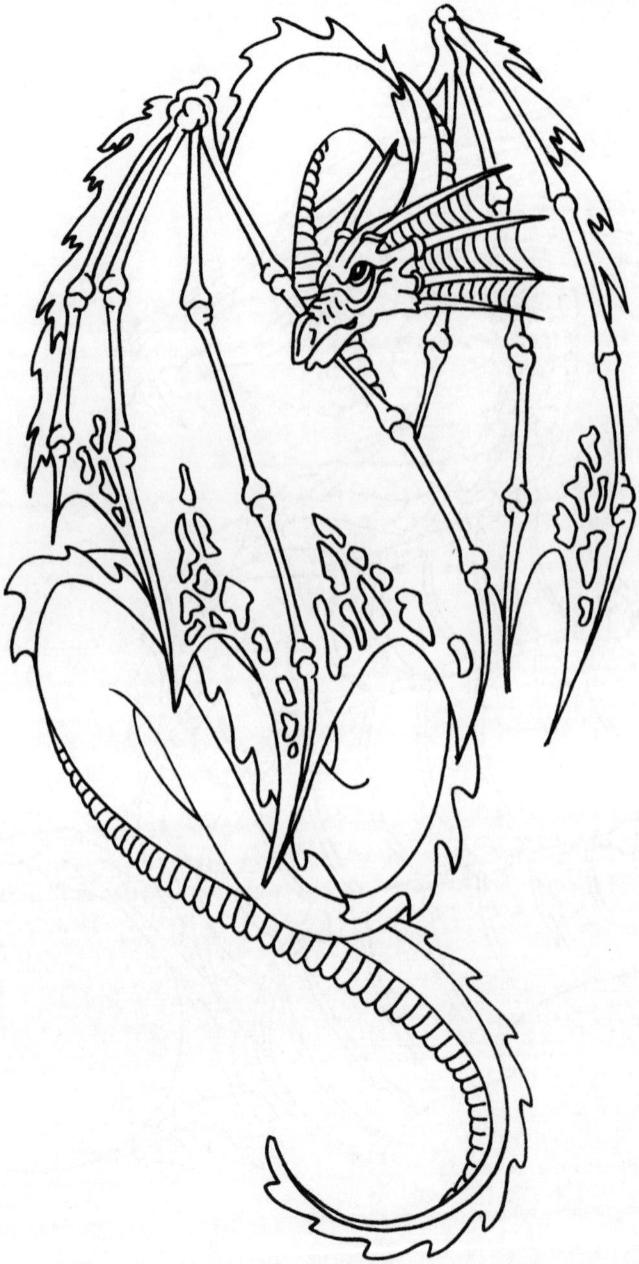

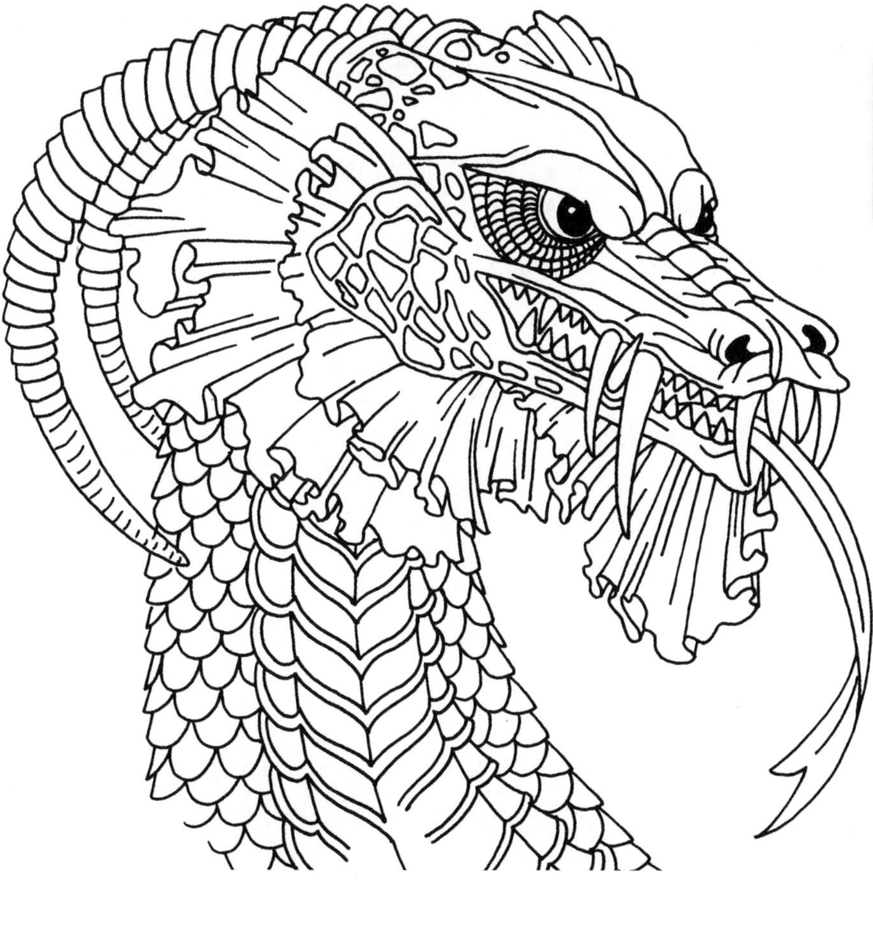

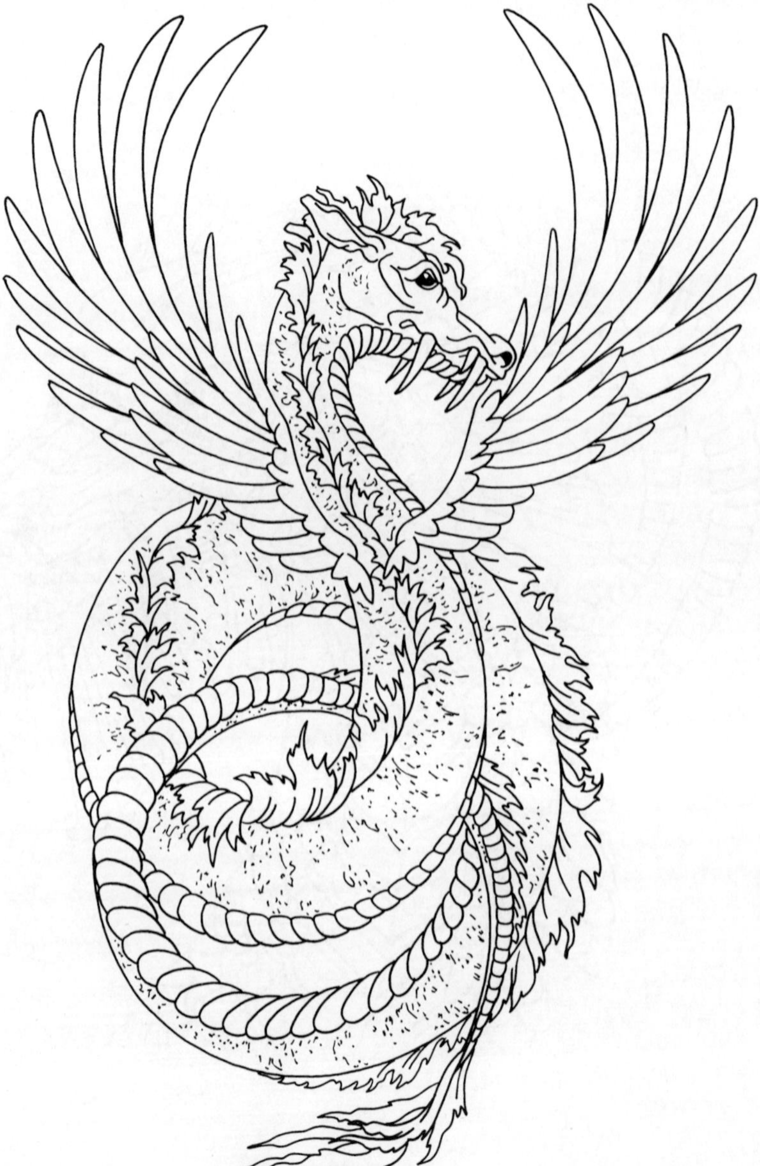

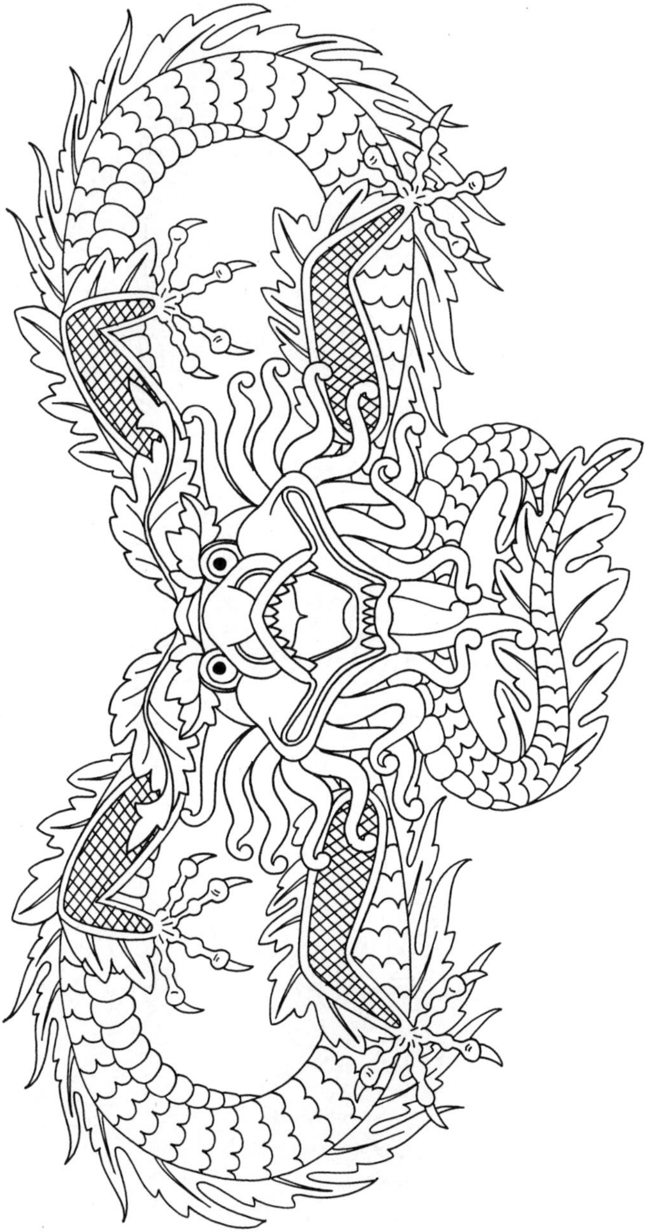

© Lora S. Irish

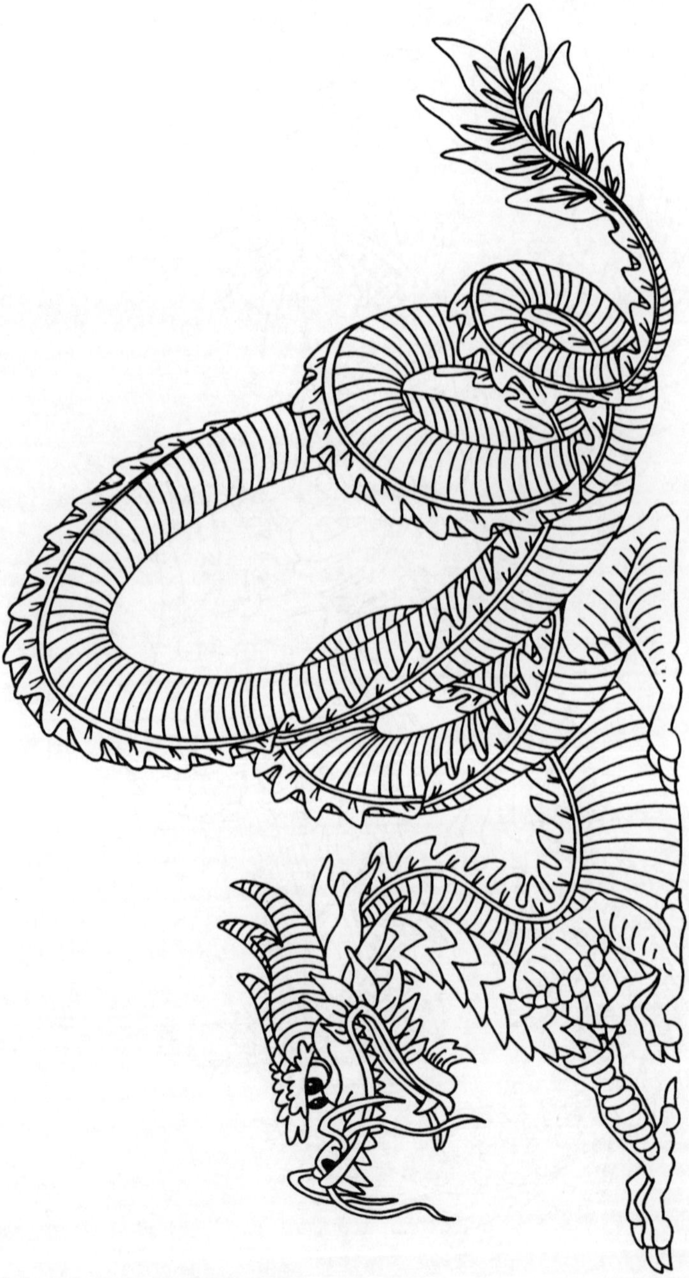

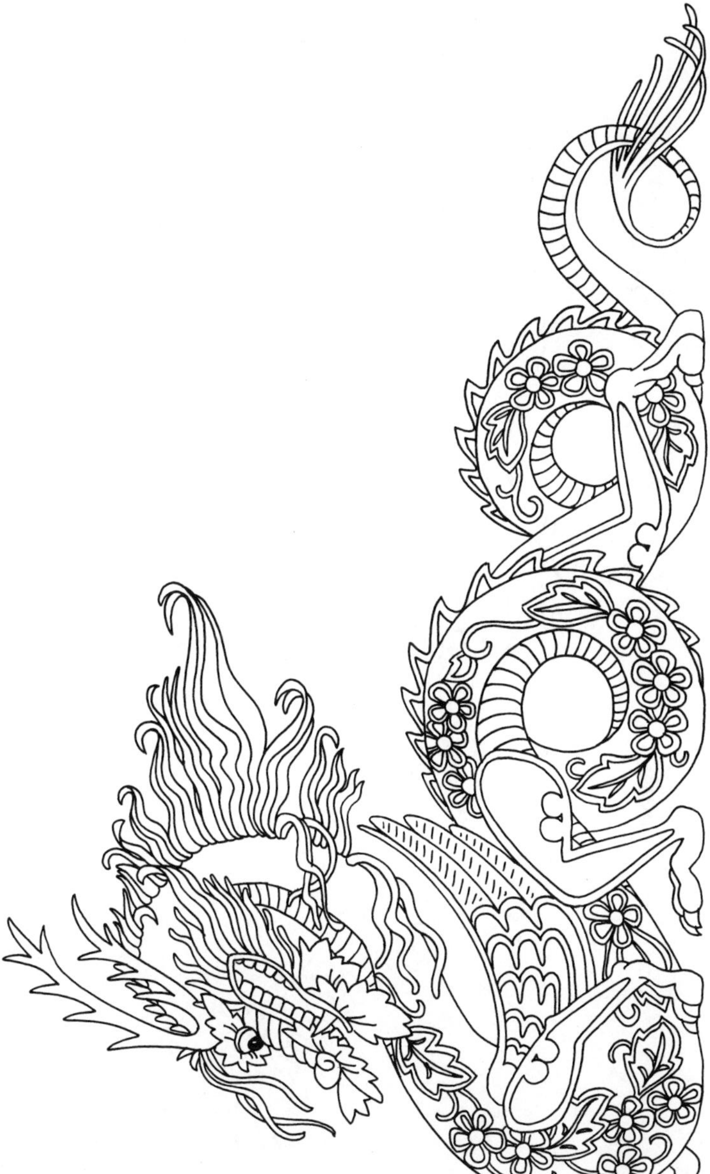

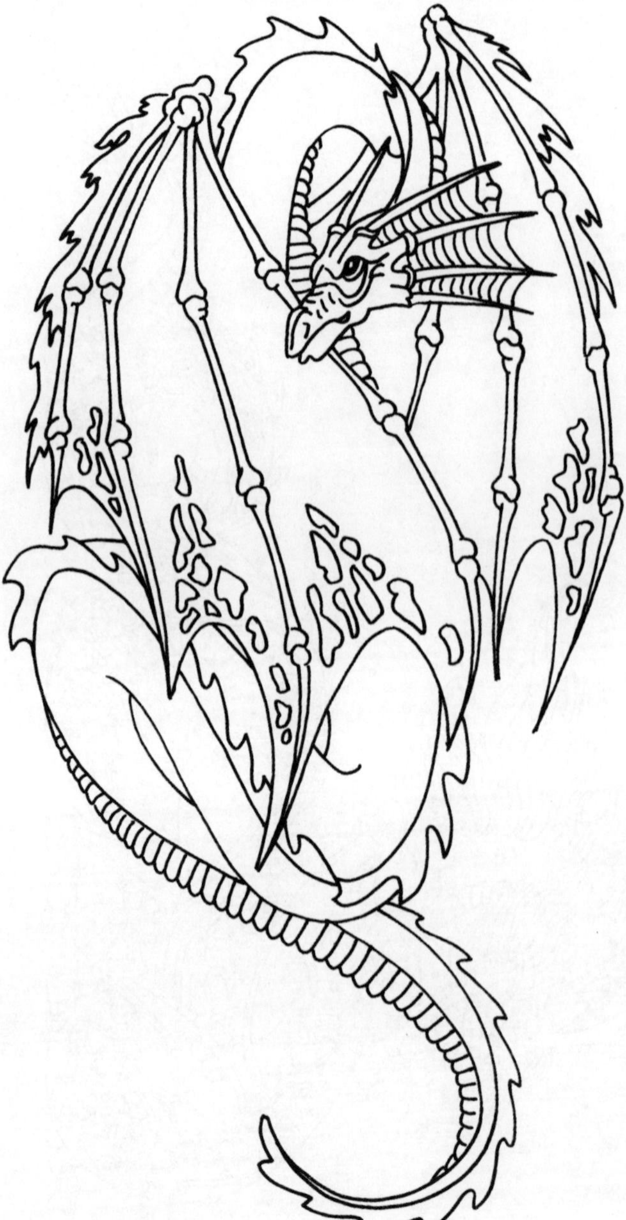

© Lora S. Irish

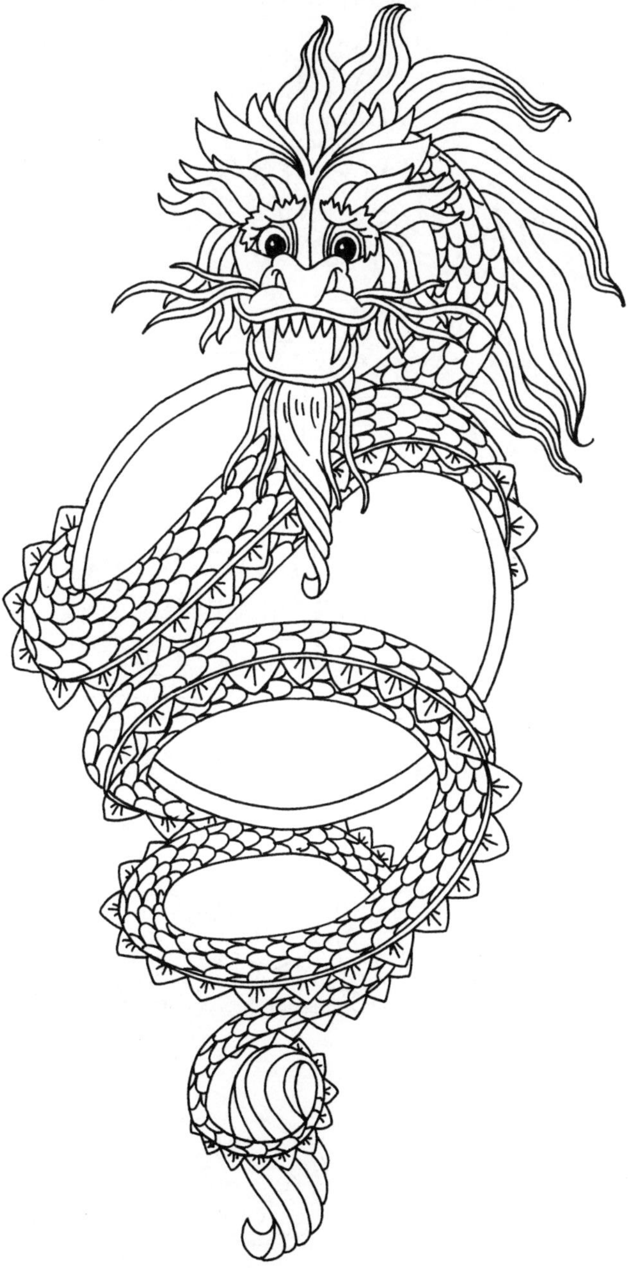

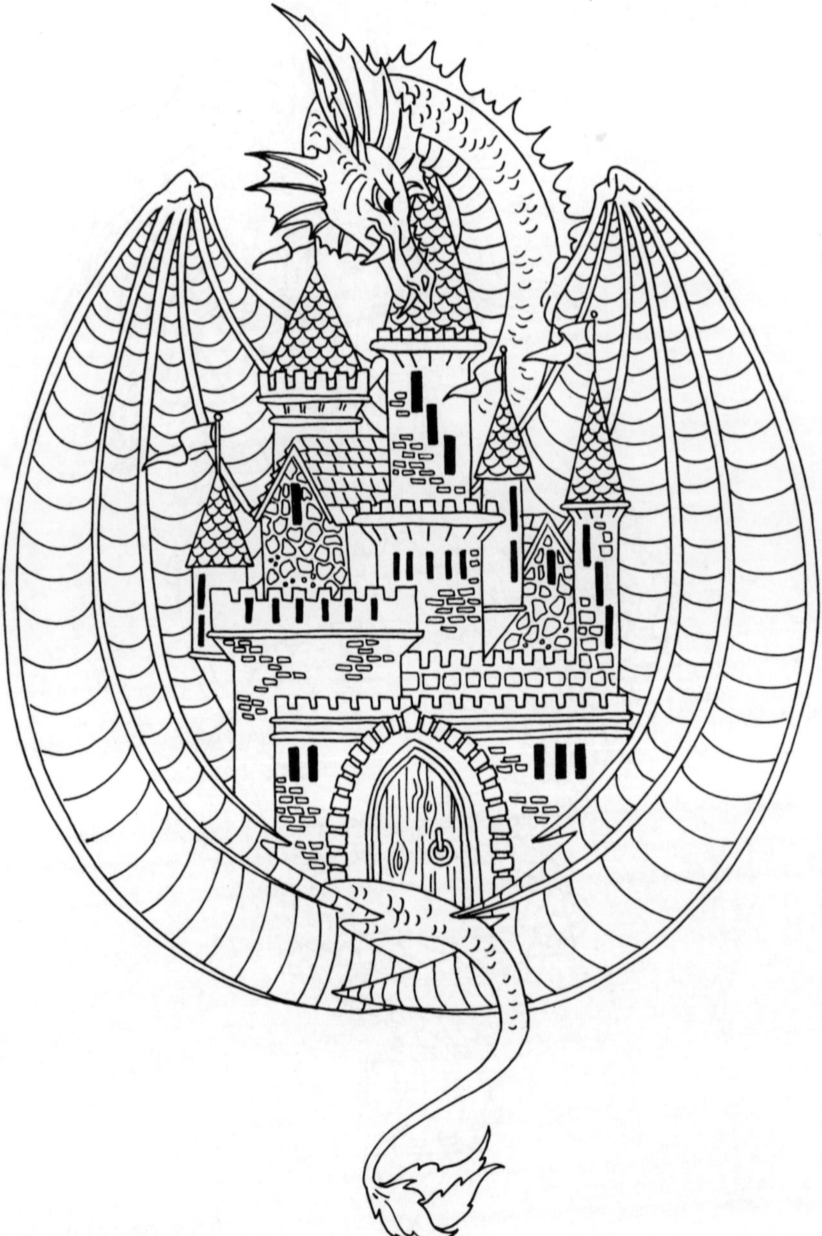

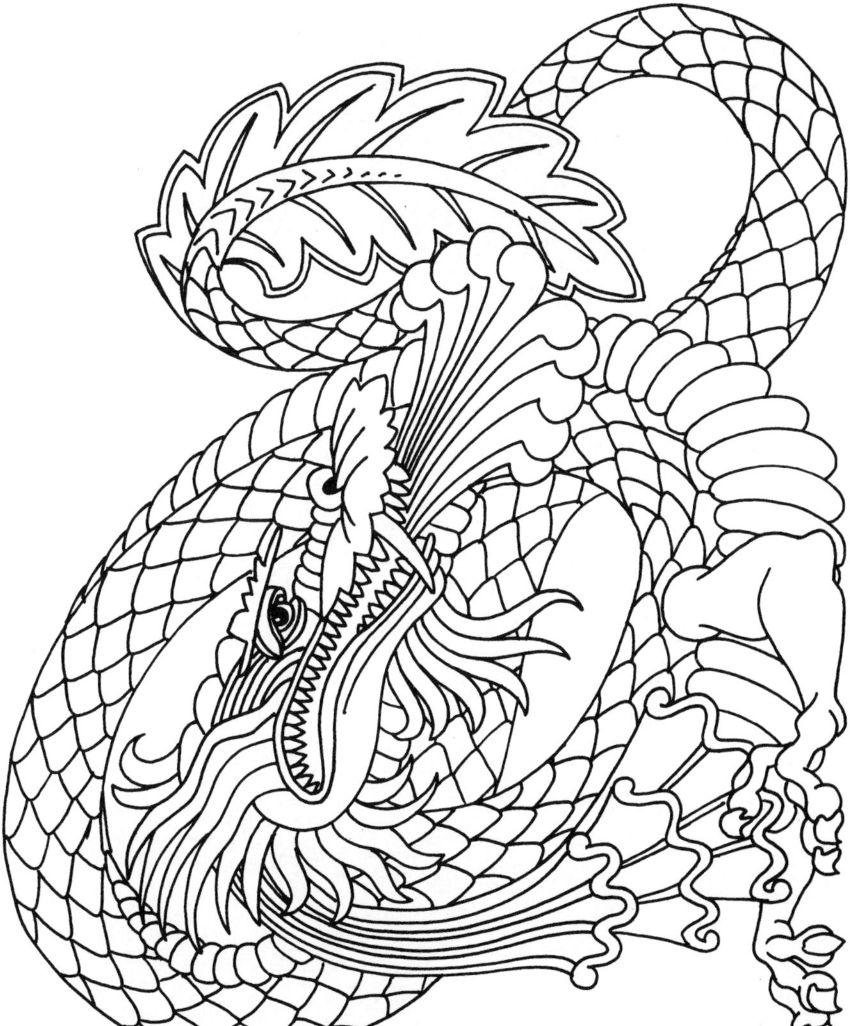

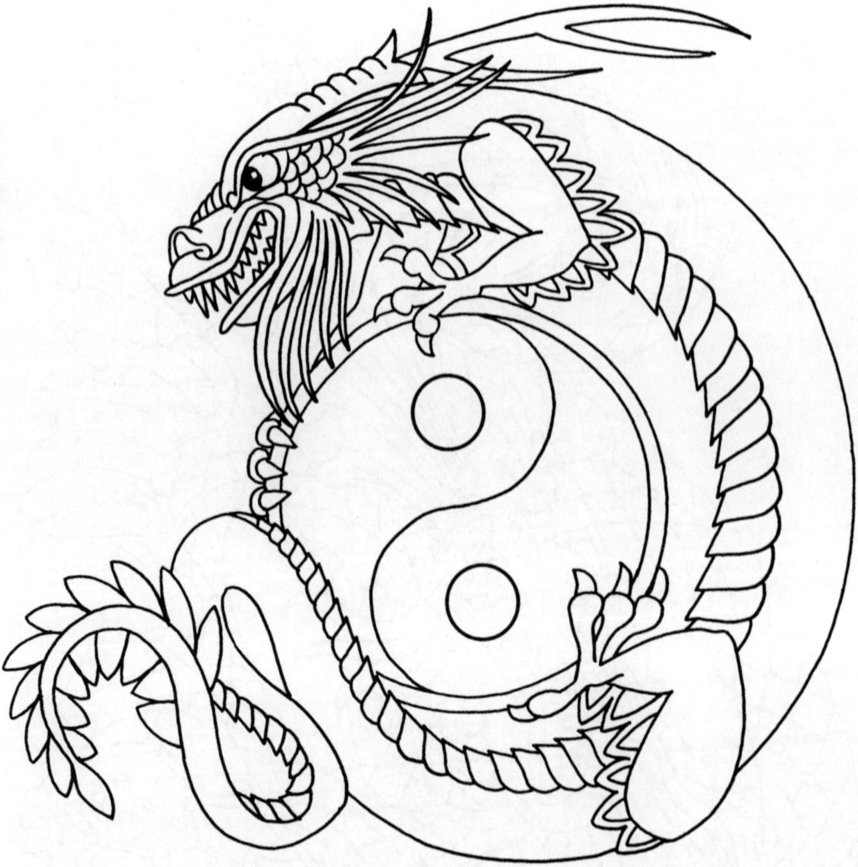

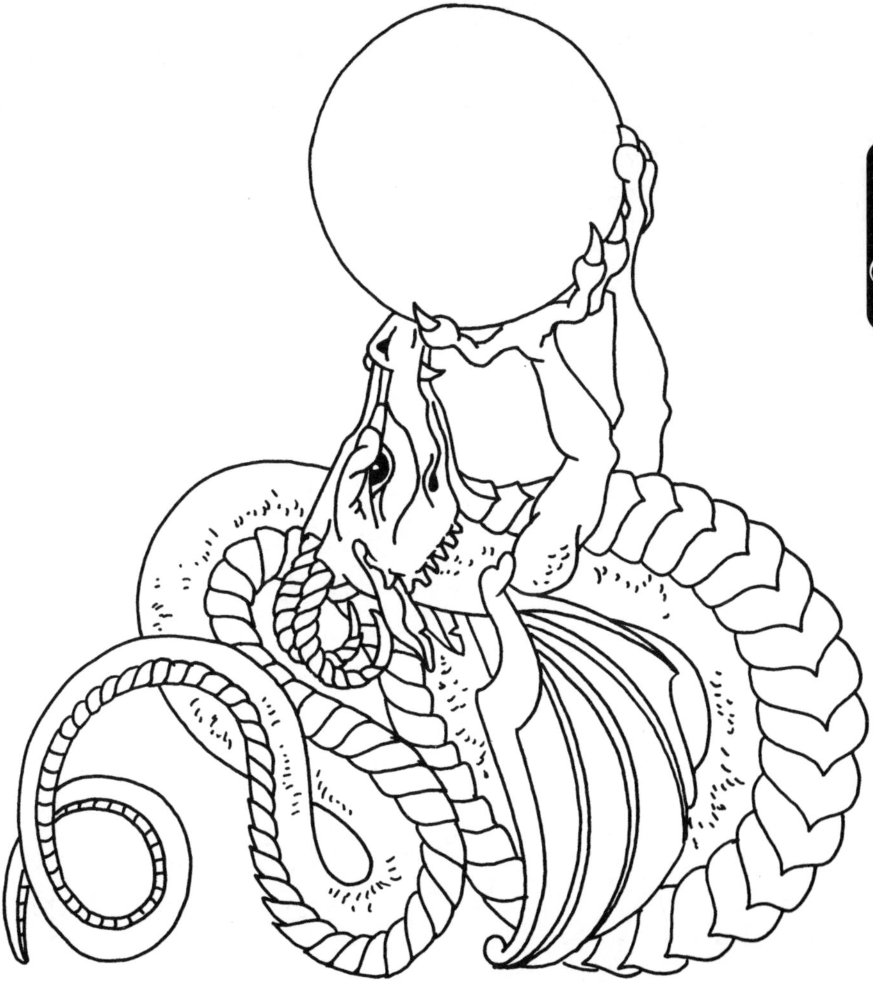

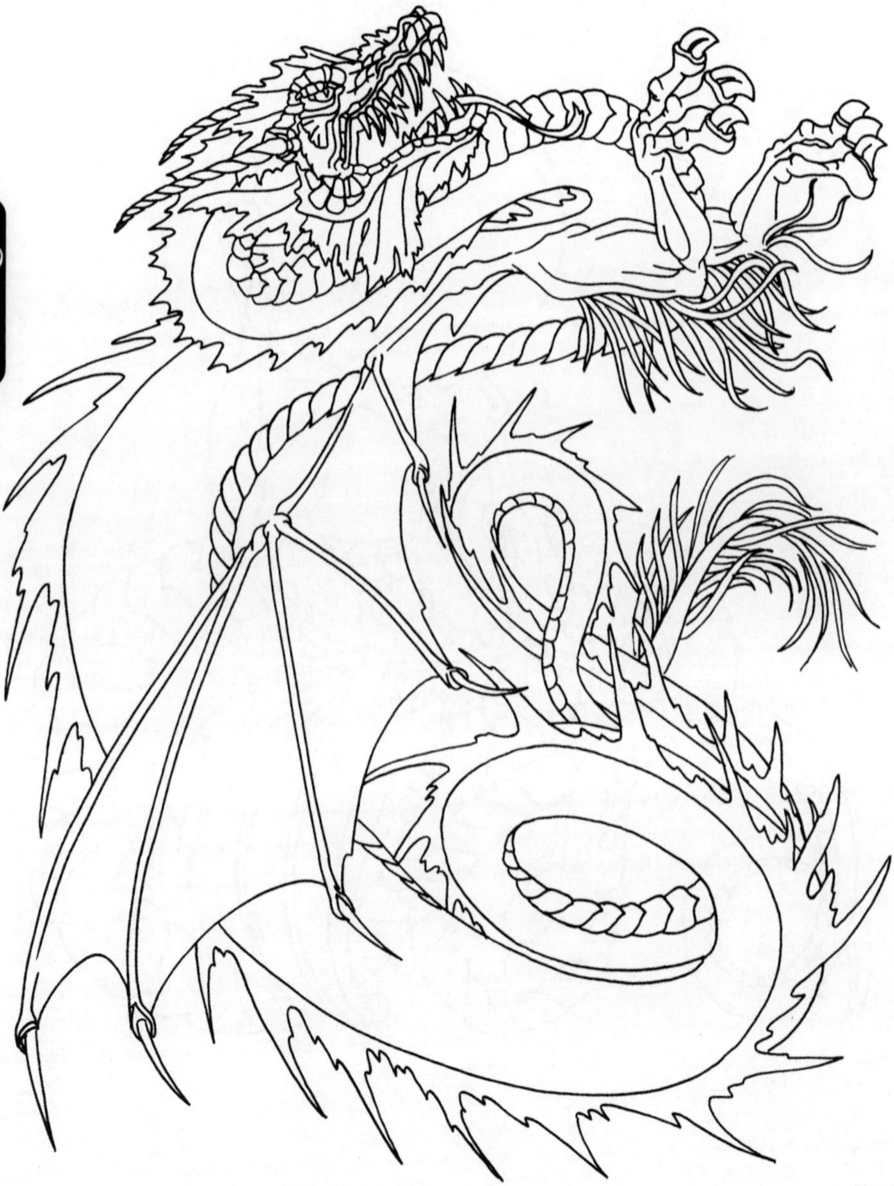

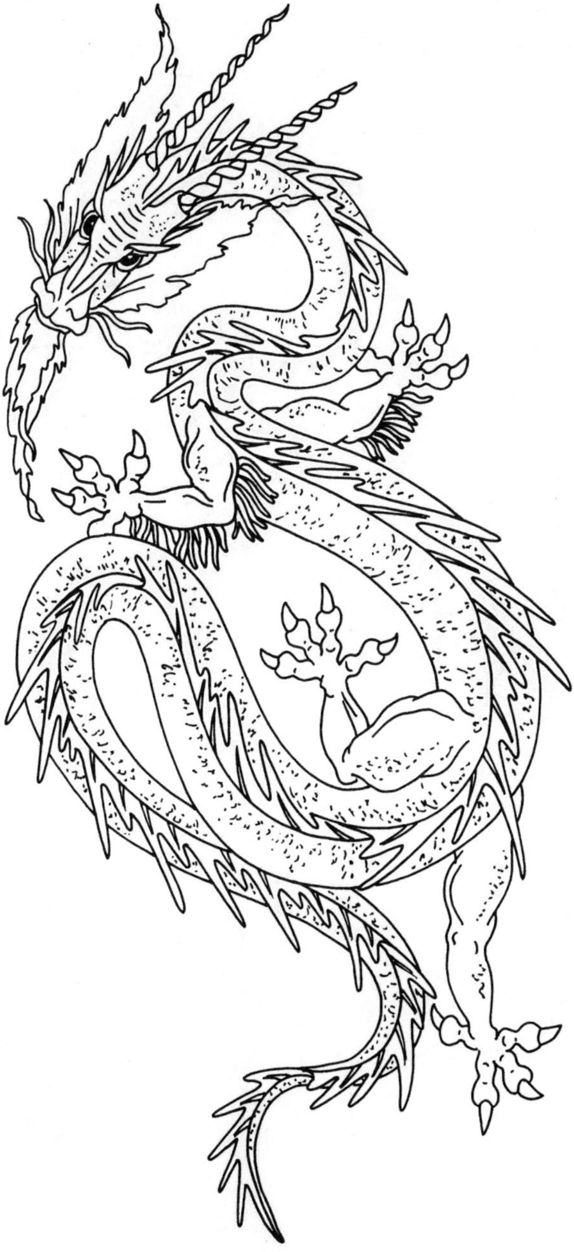

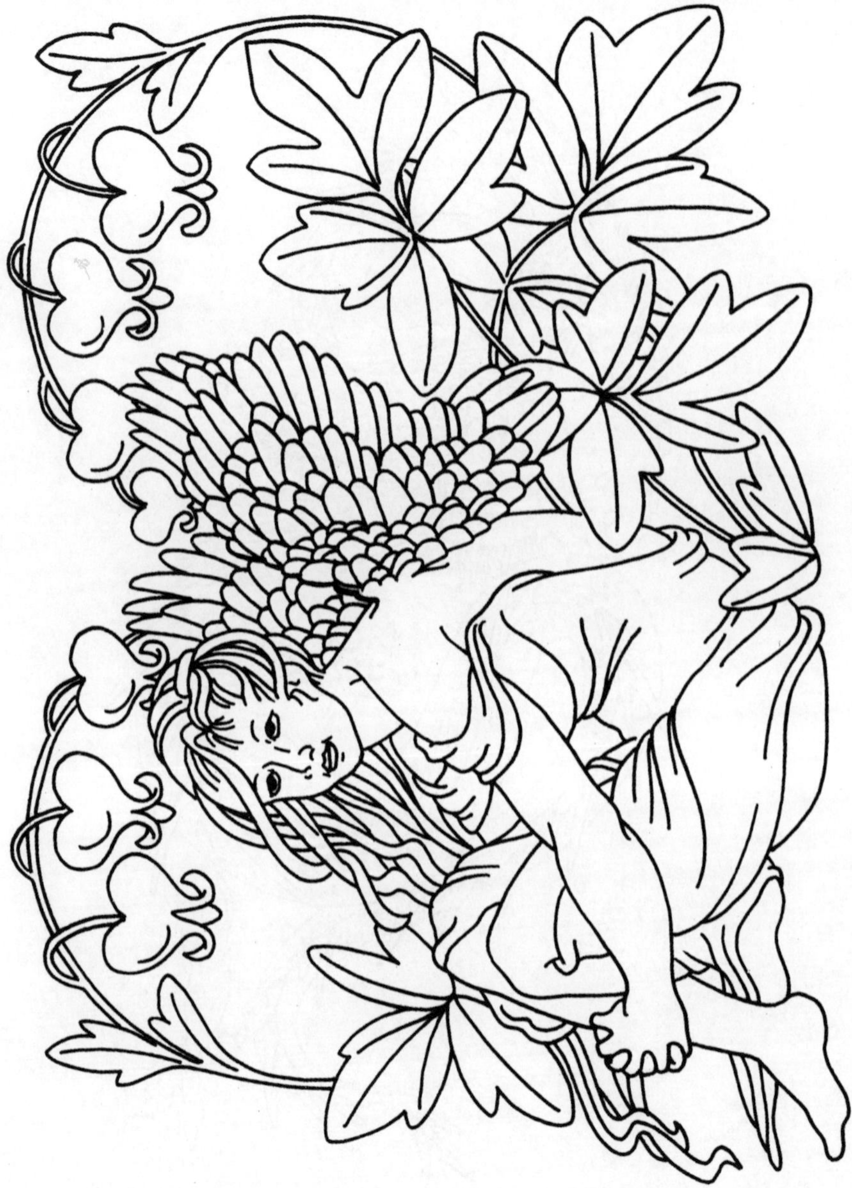

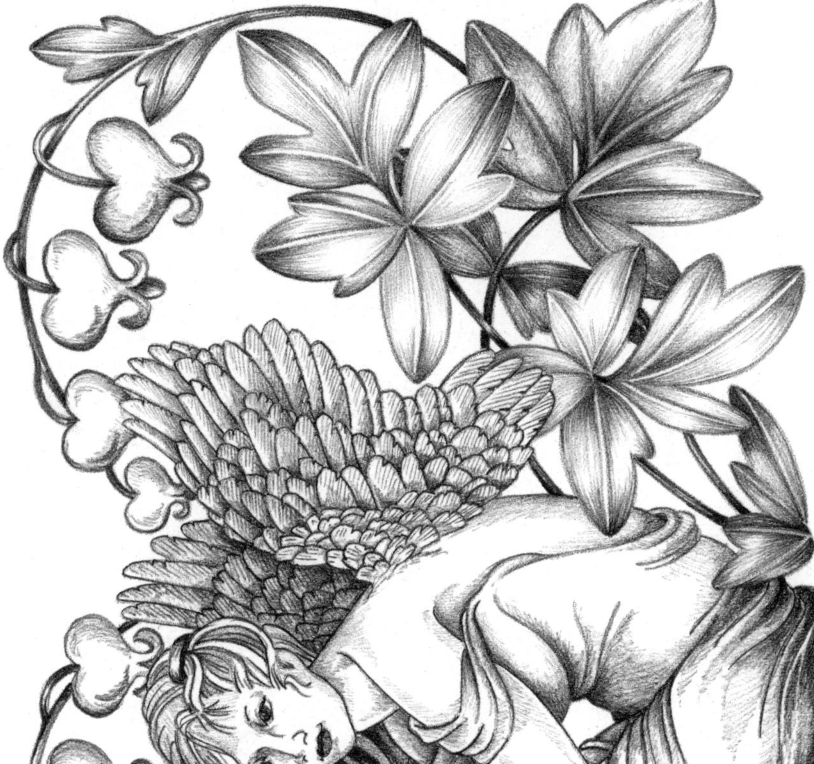

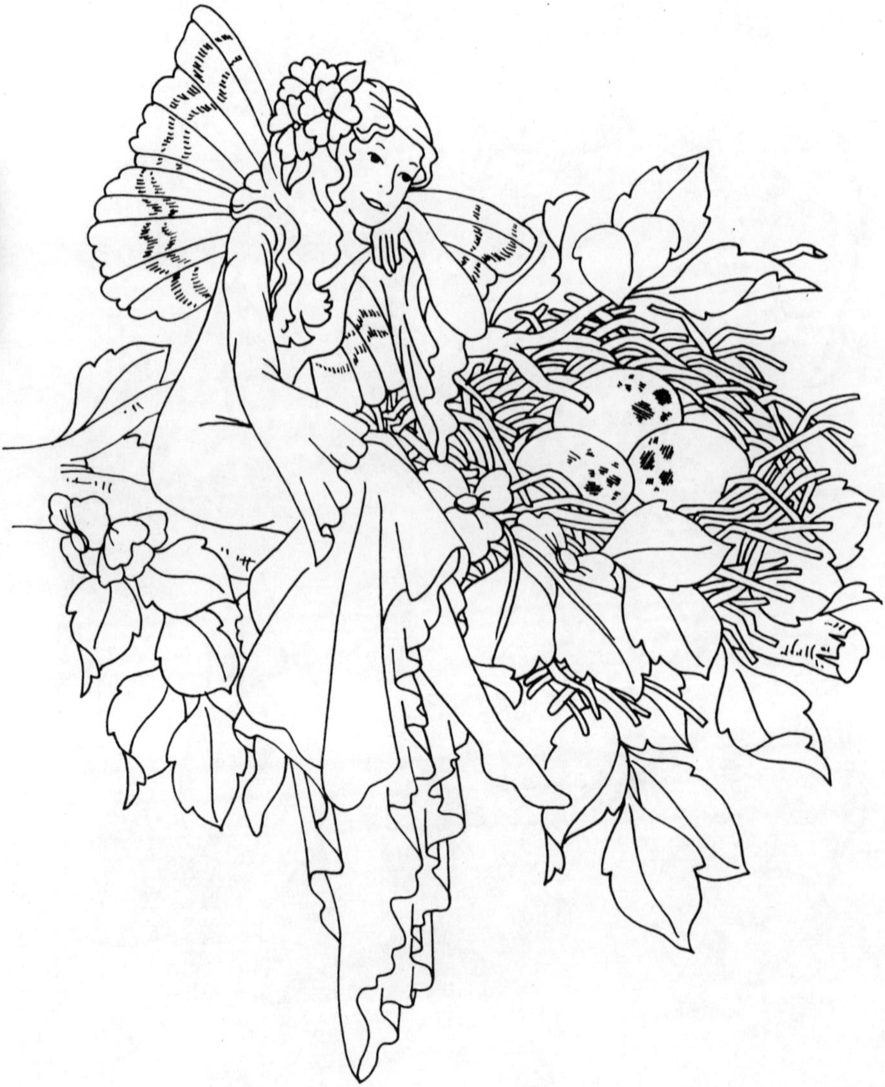

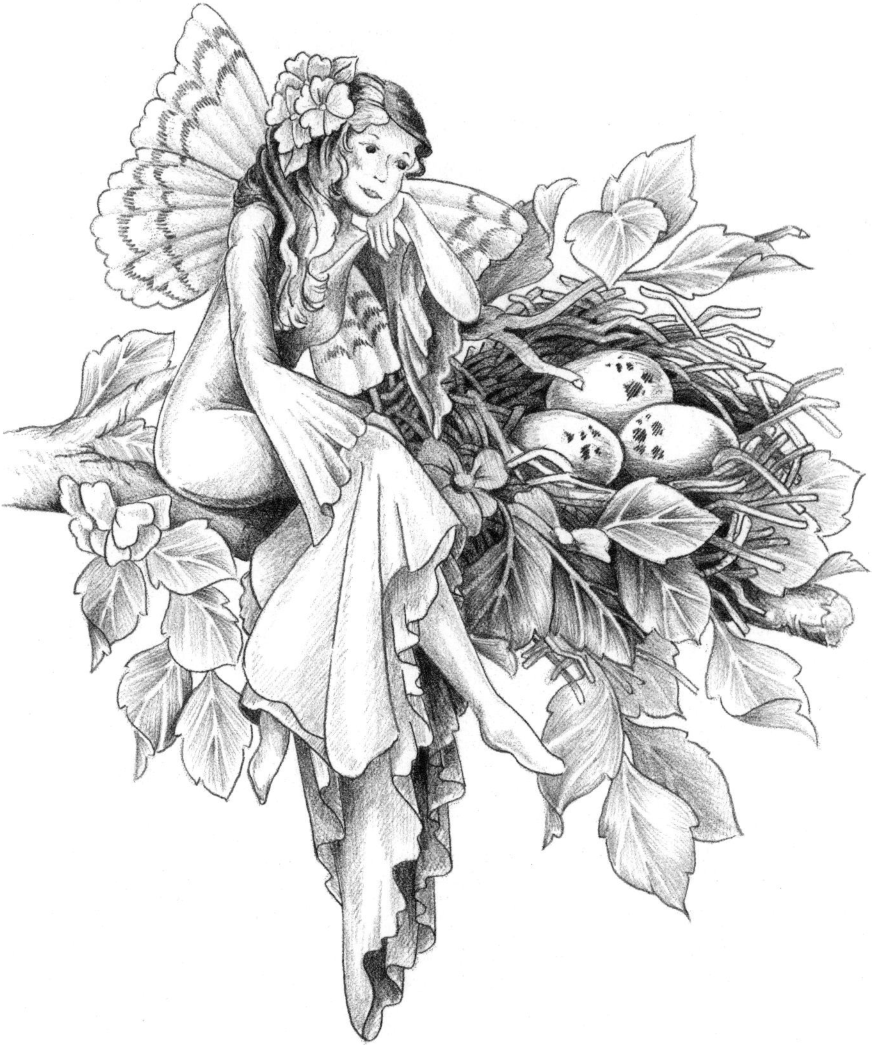

Fantasy

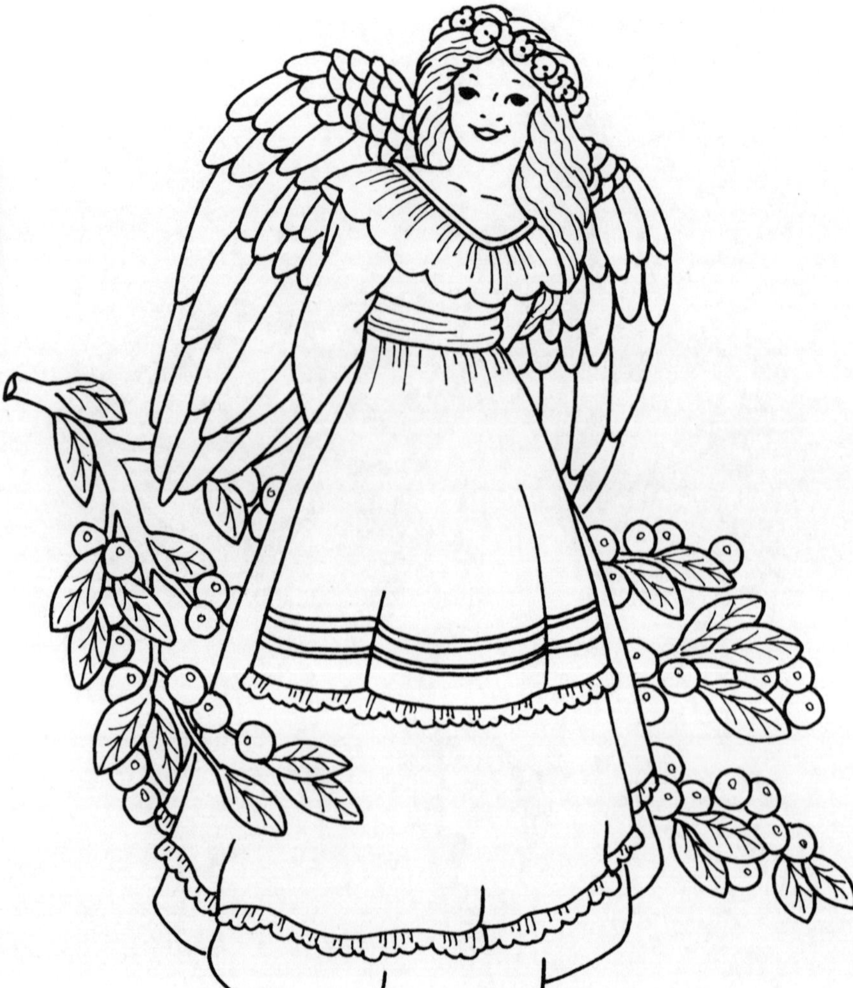

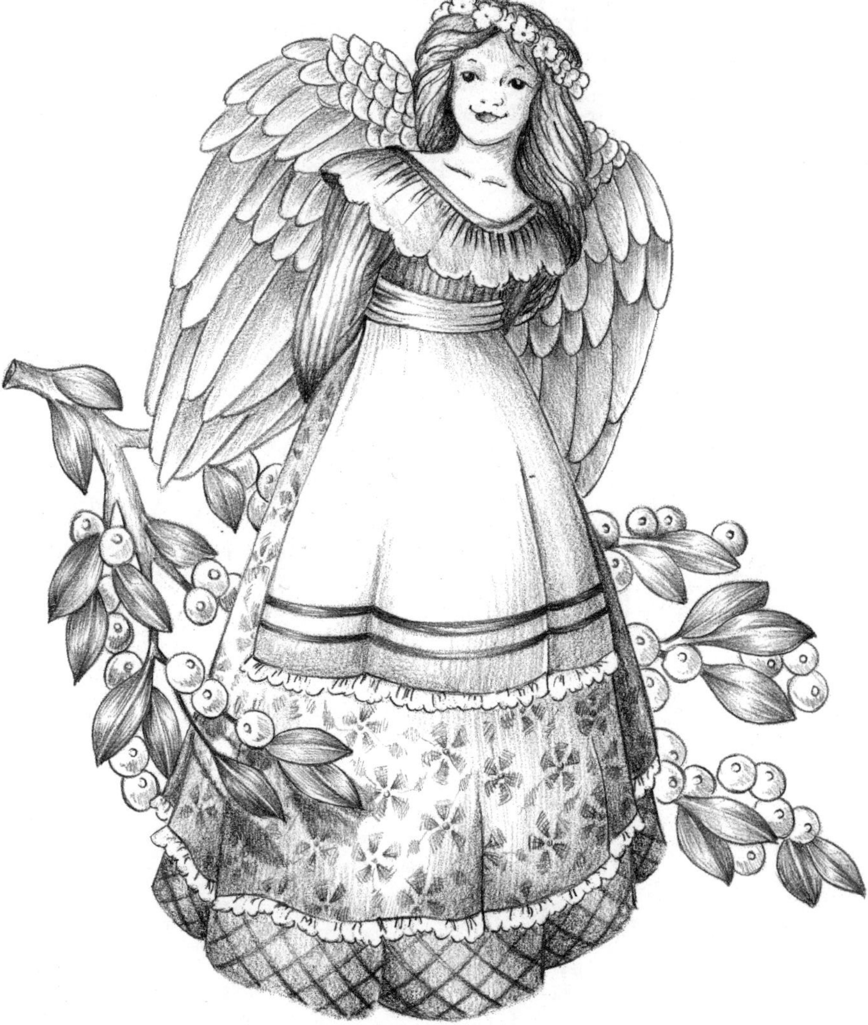

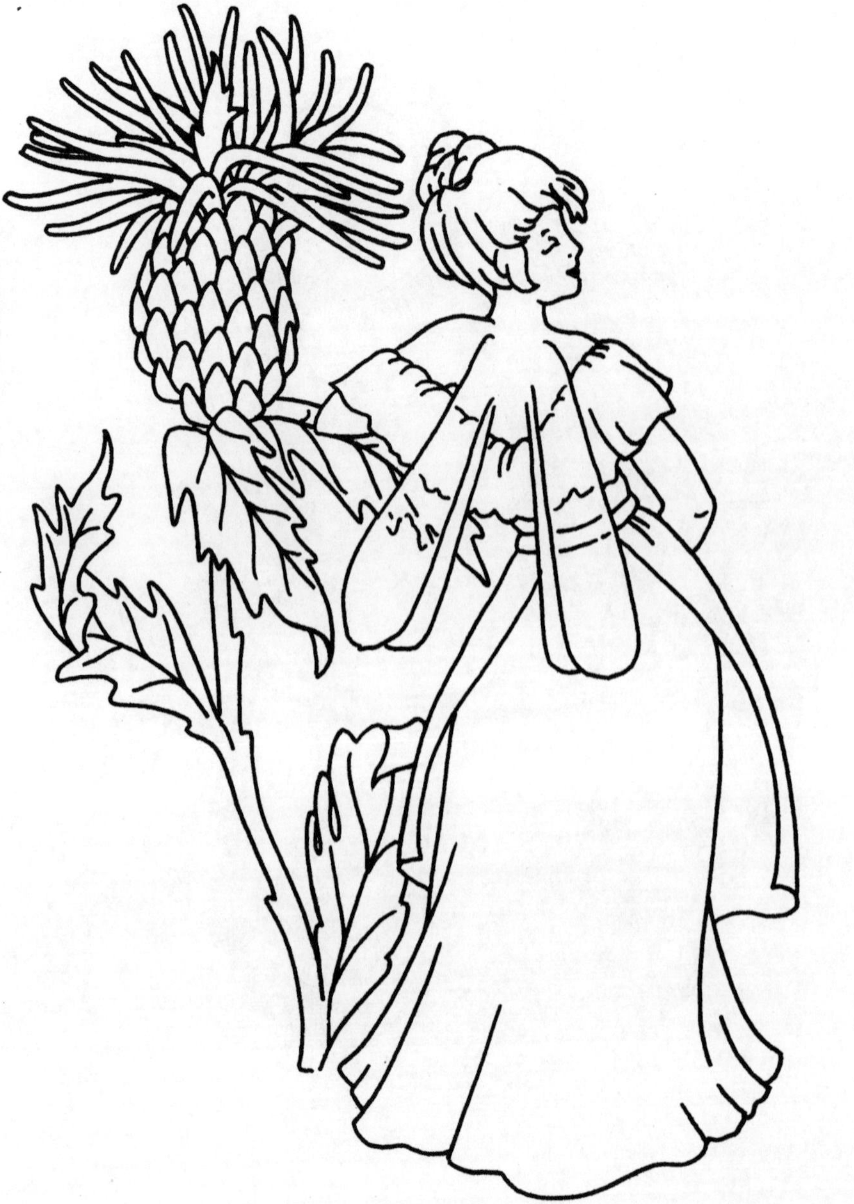

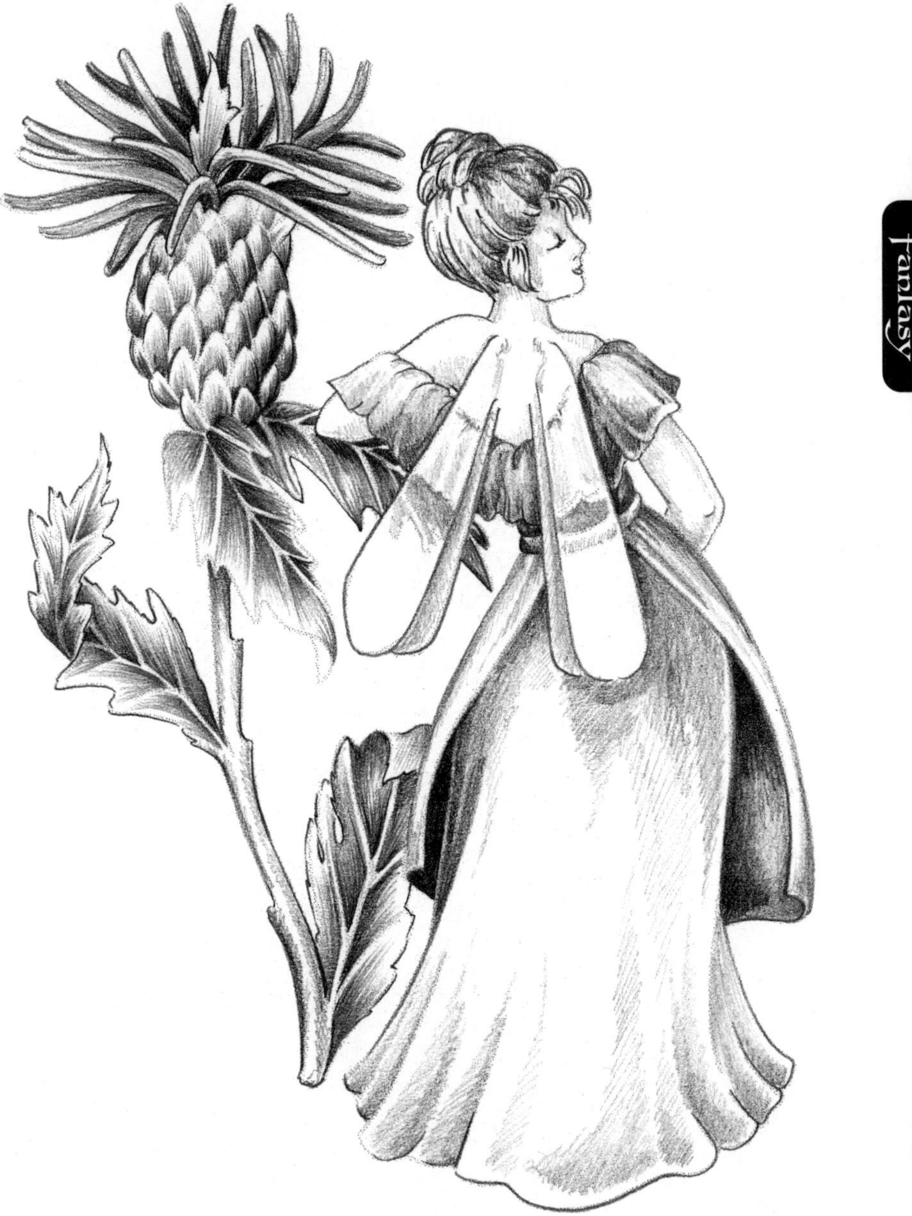

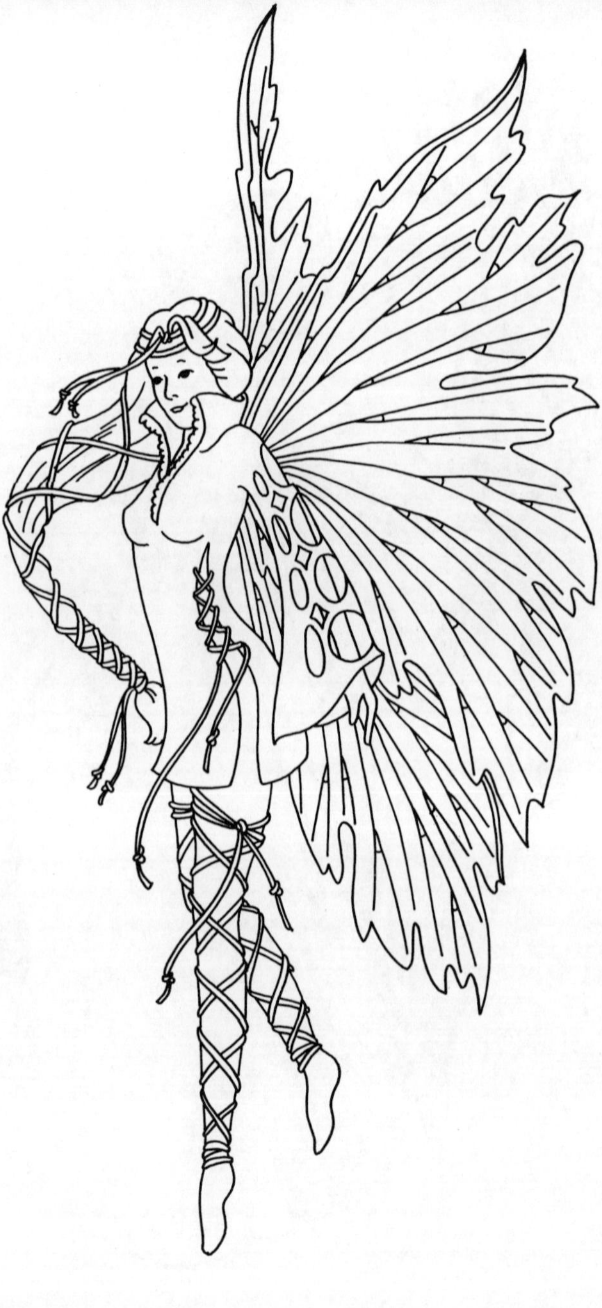

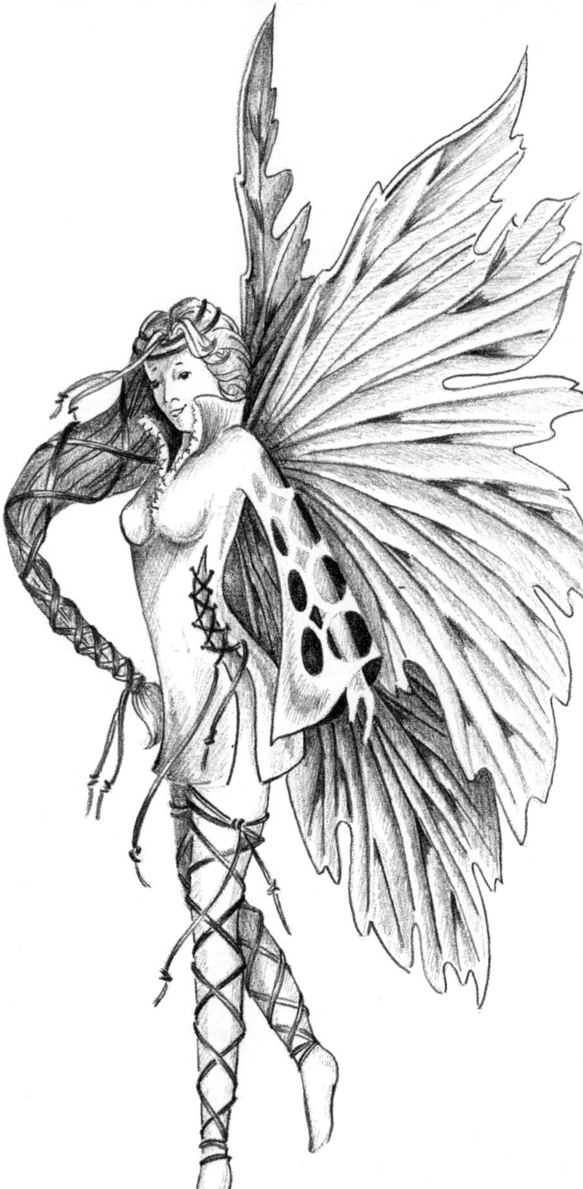

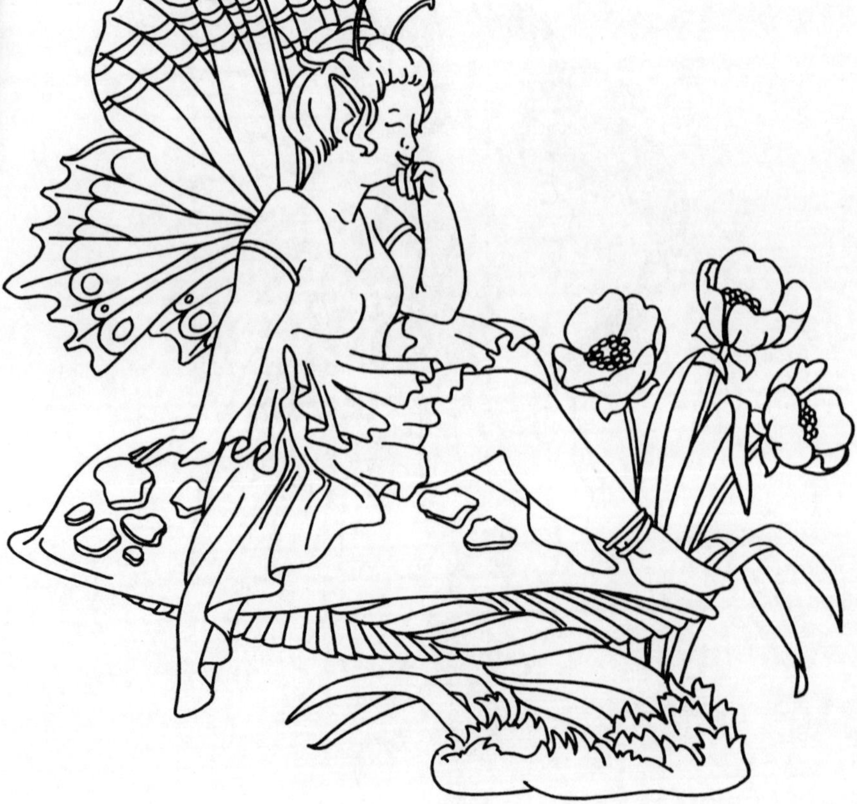

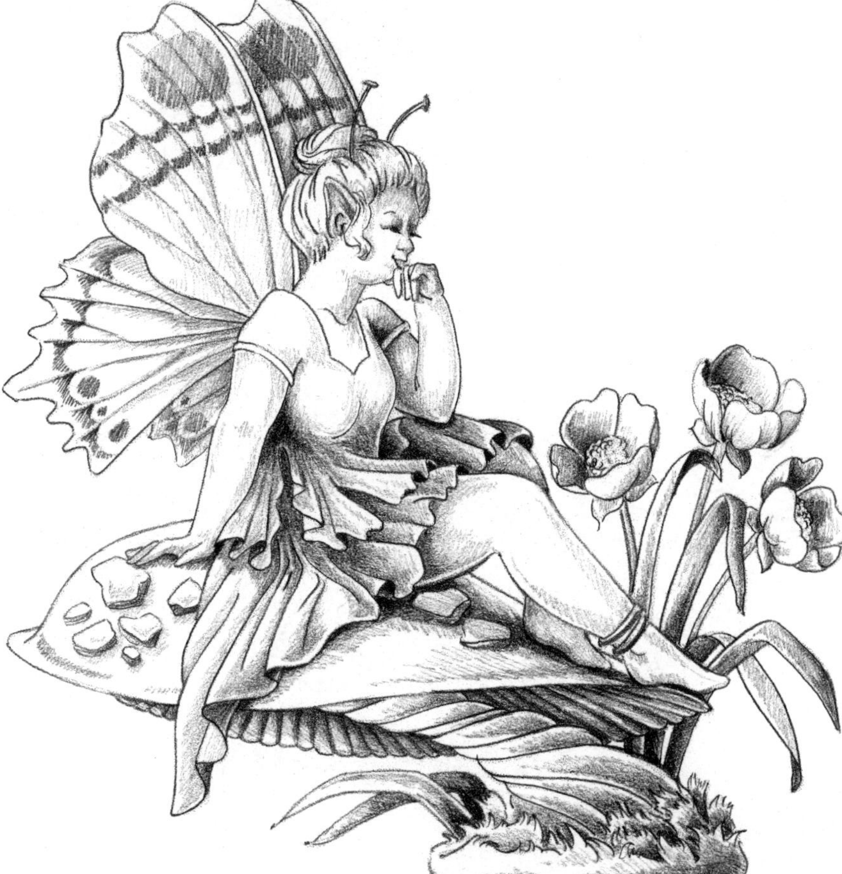

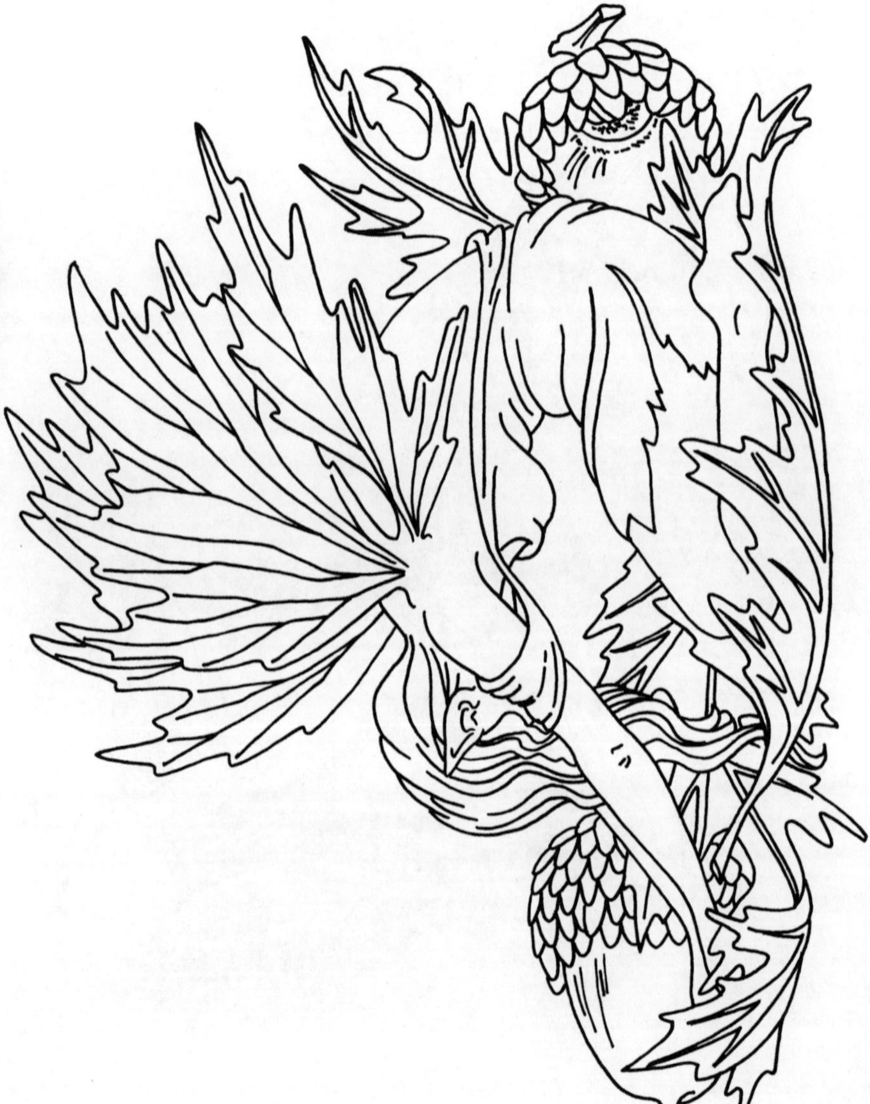

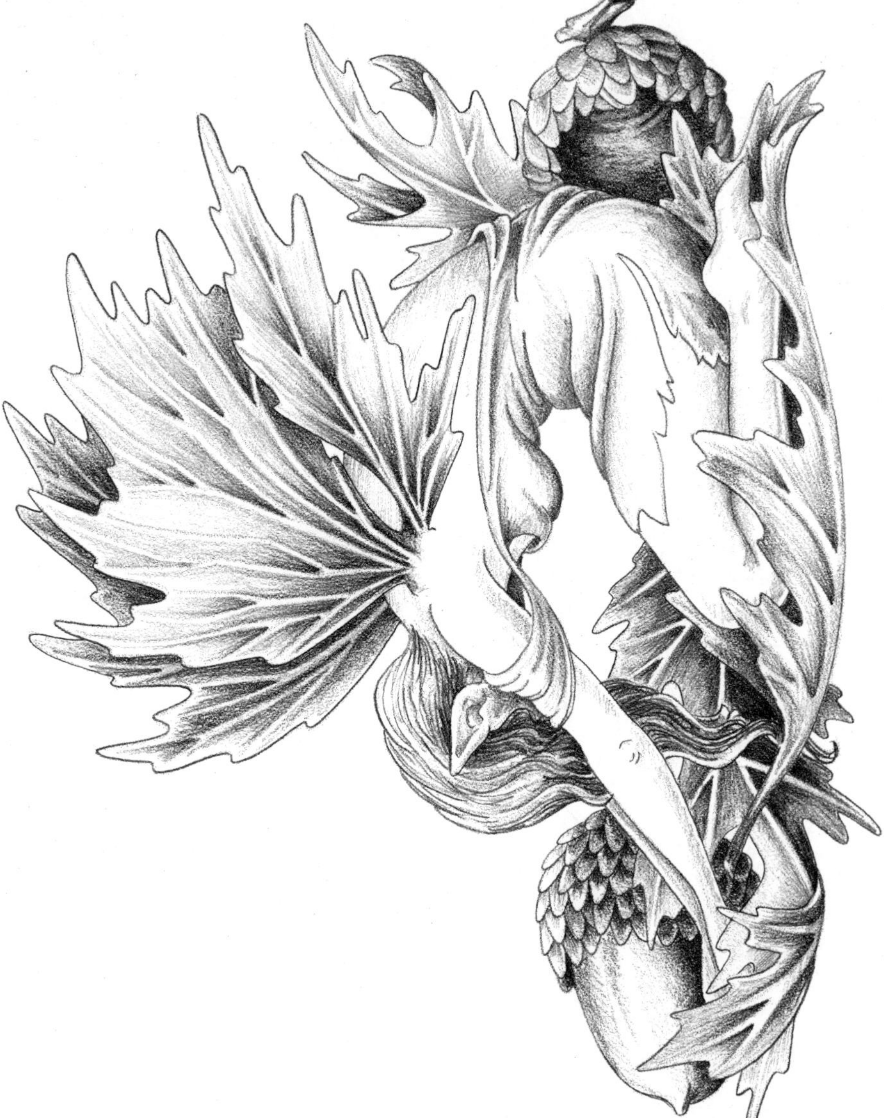

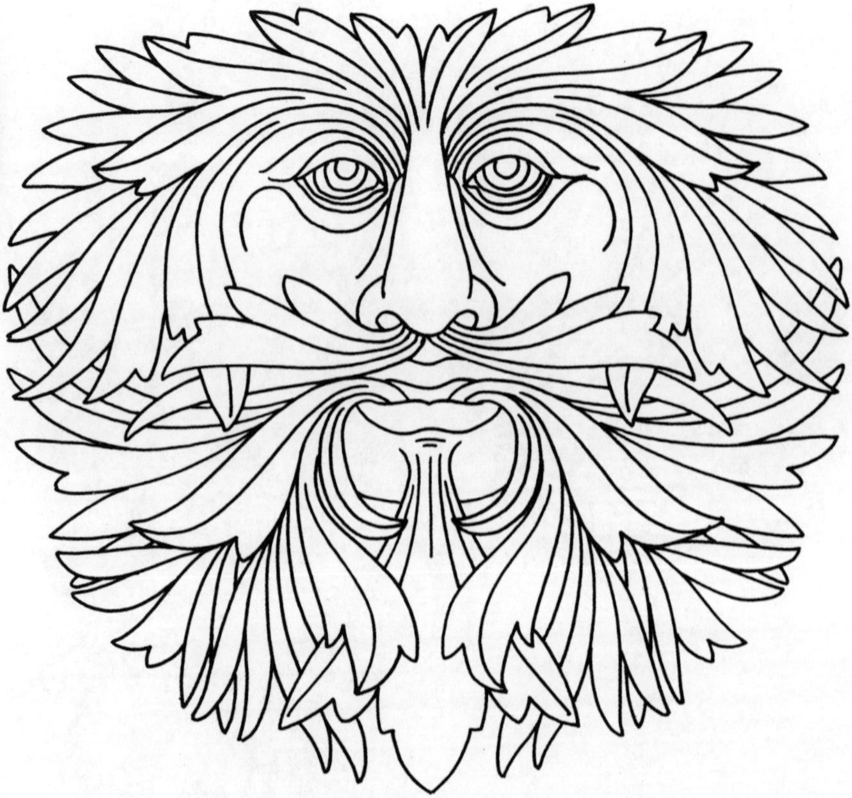

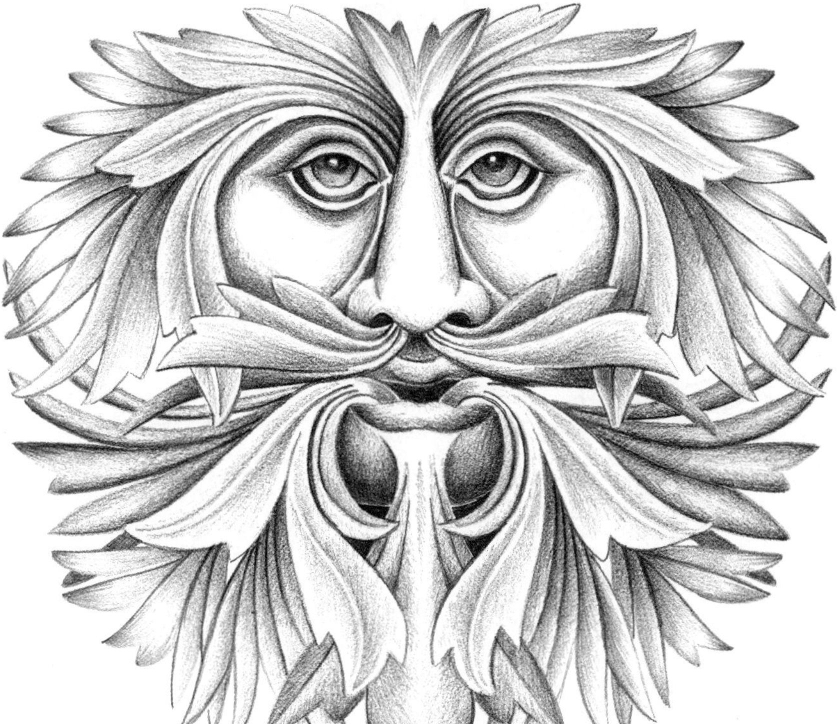

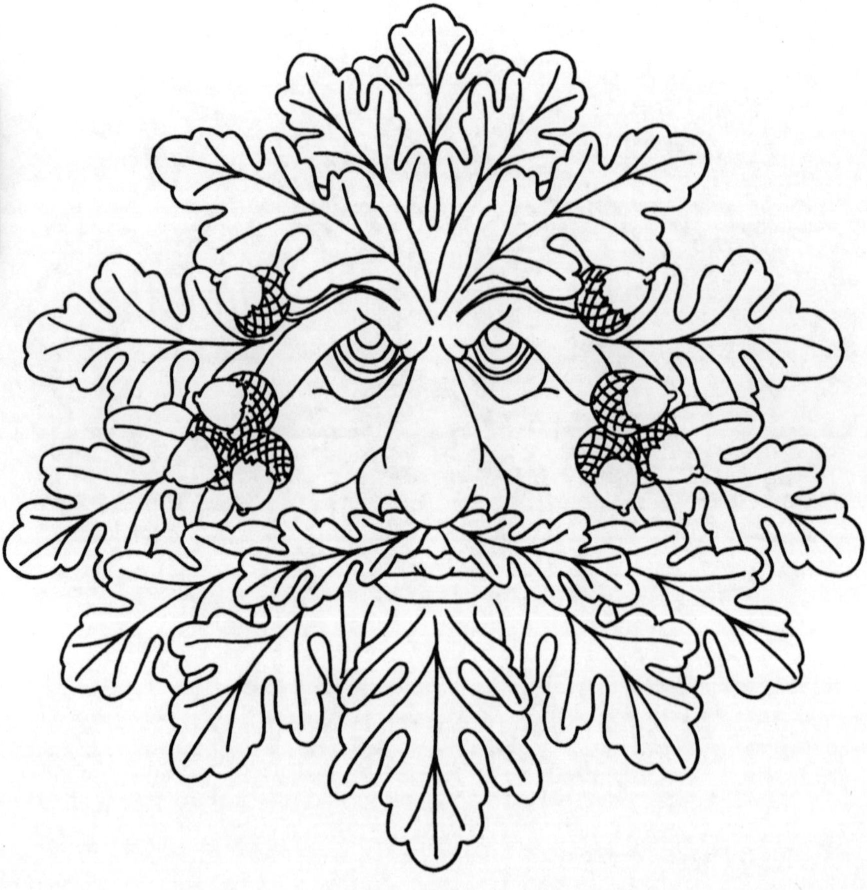

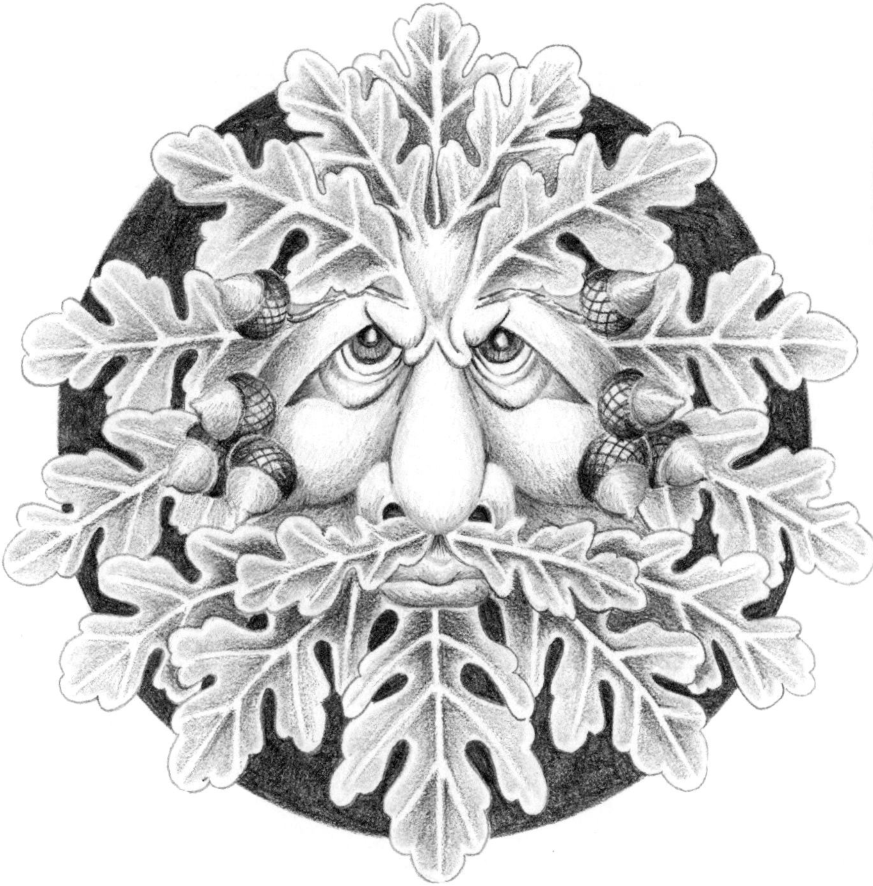

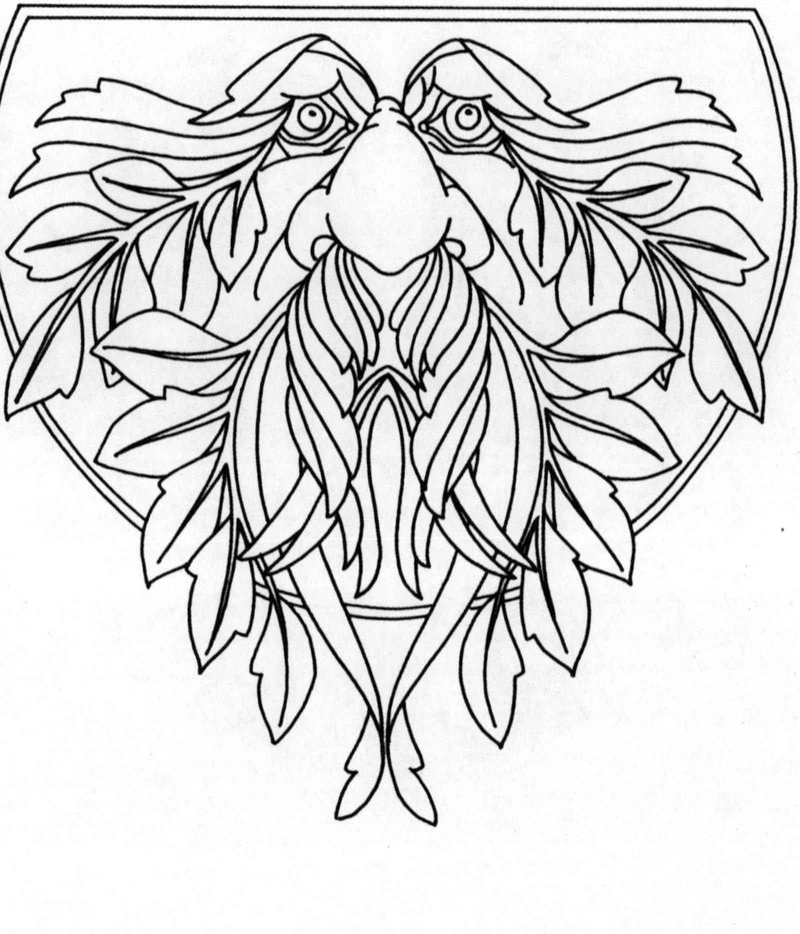

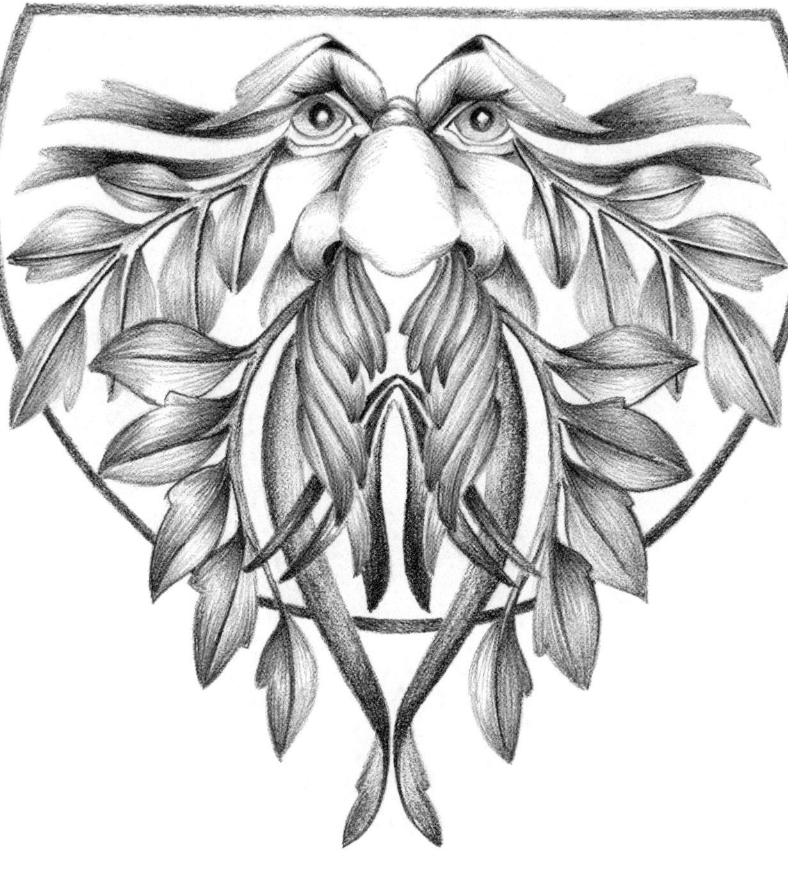

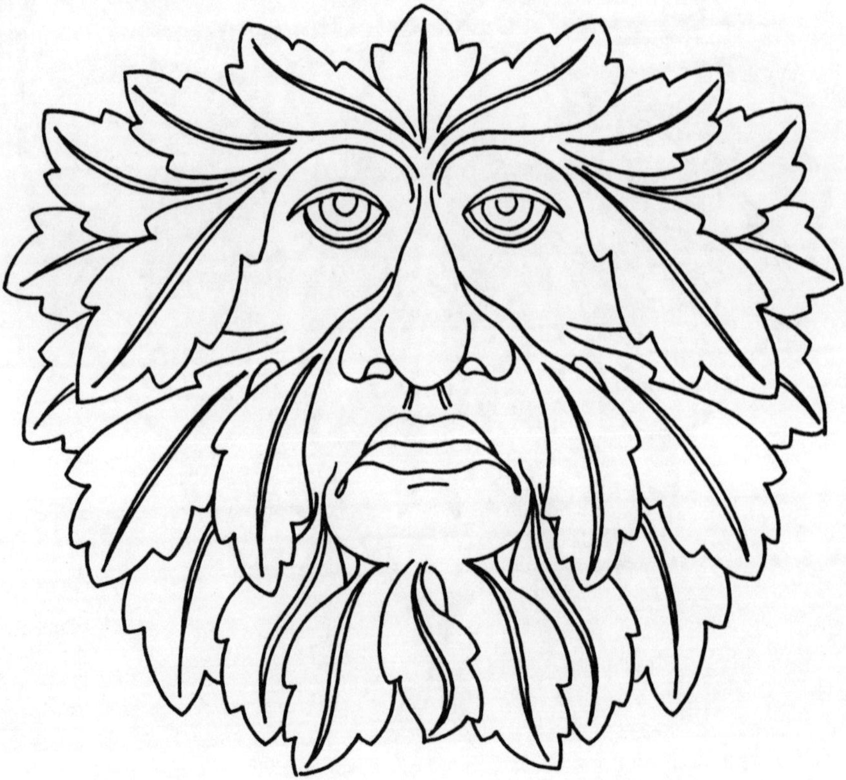

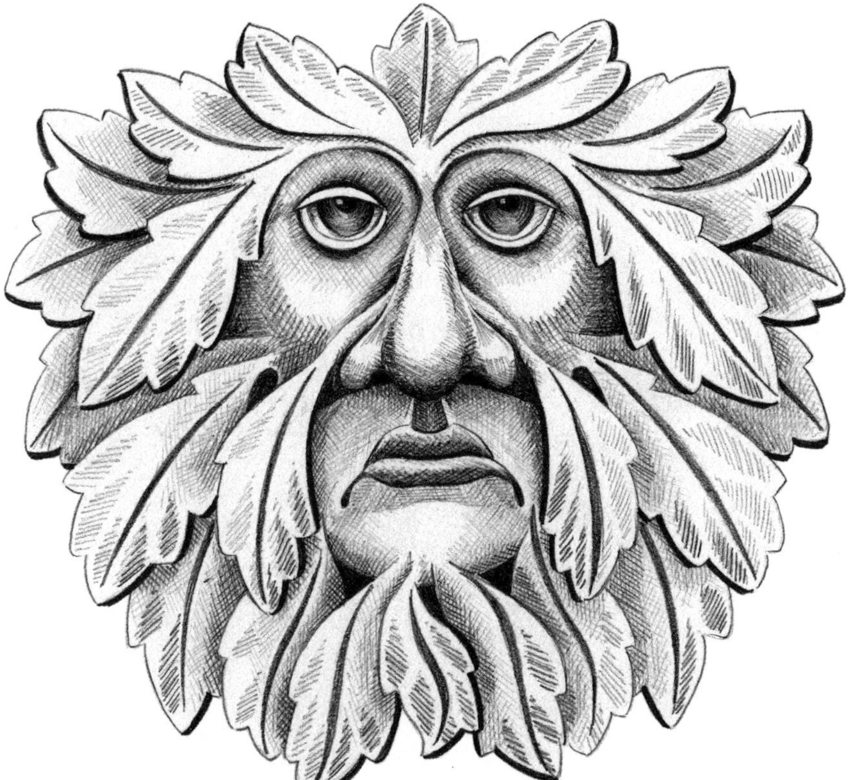

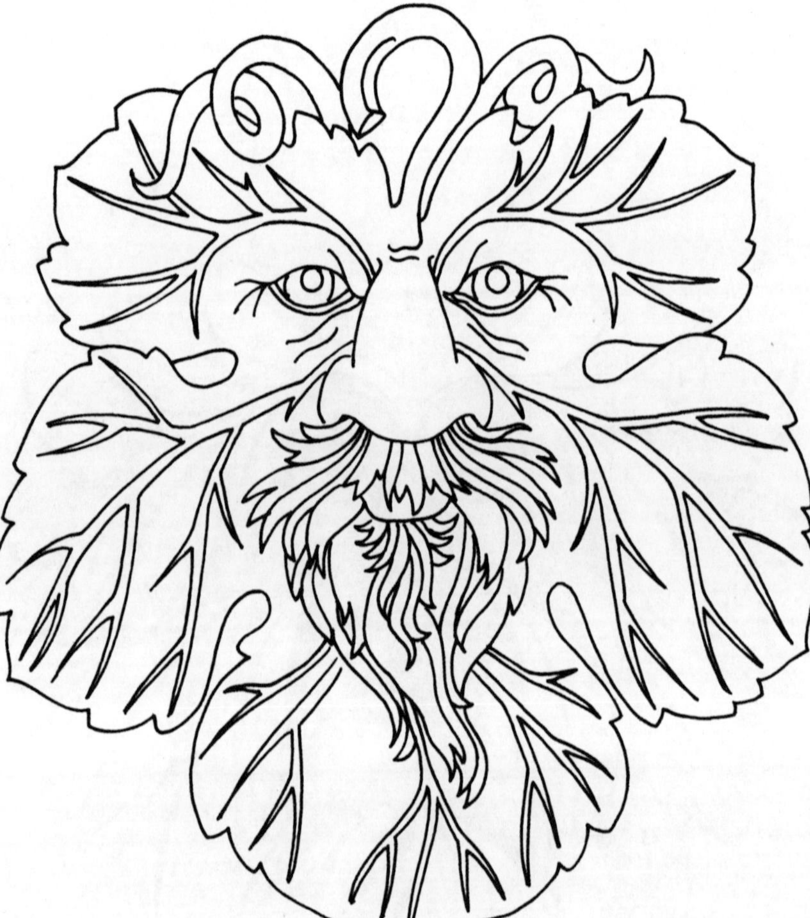

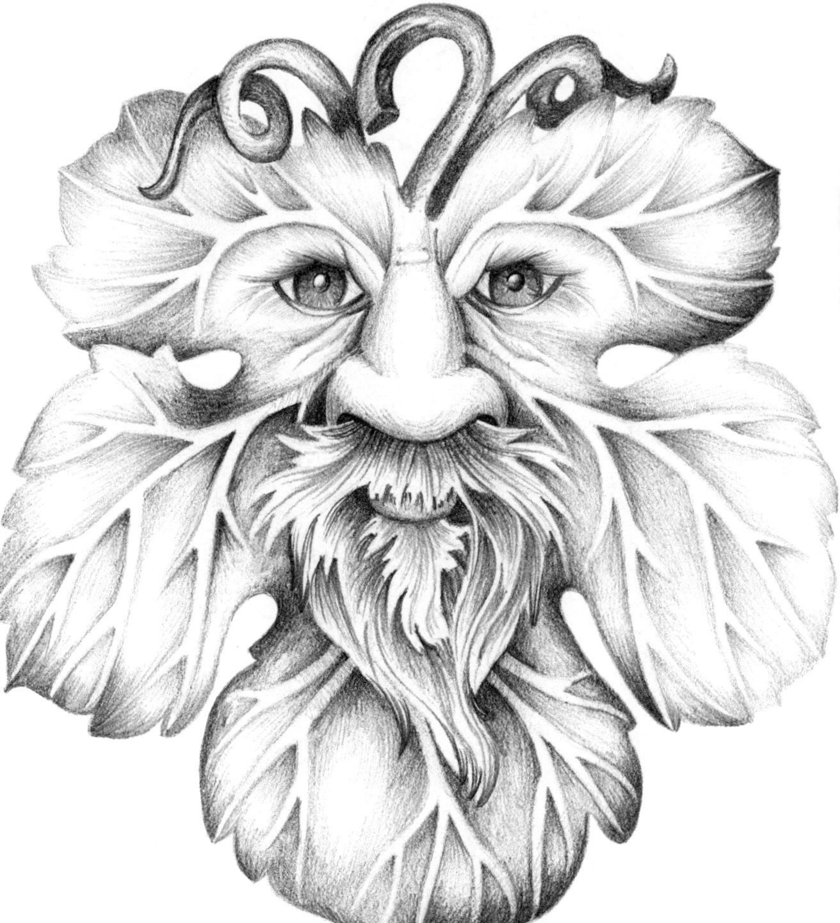

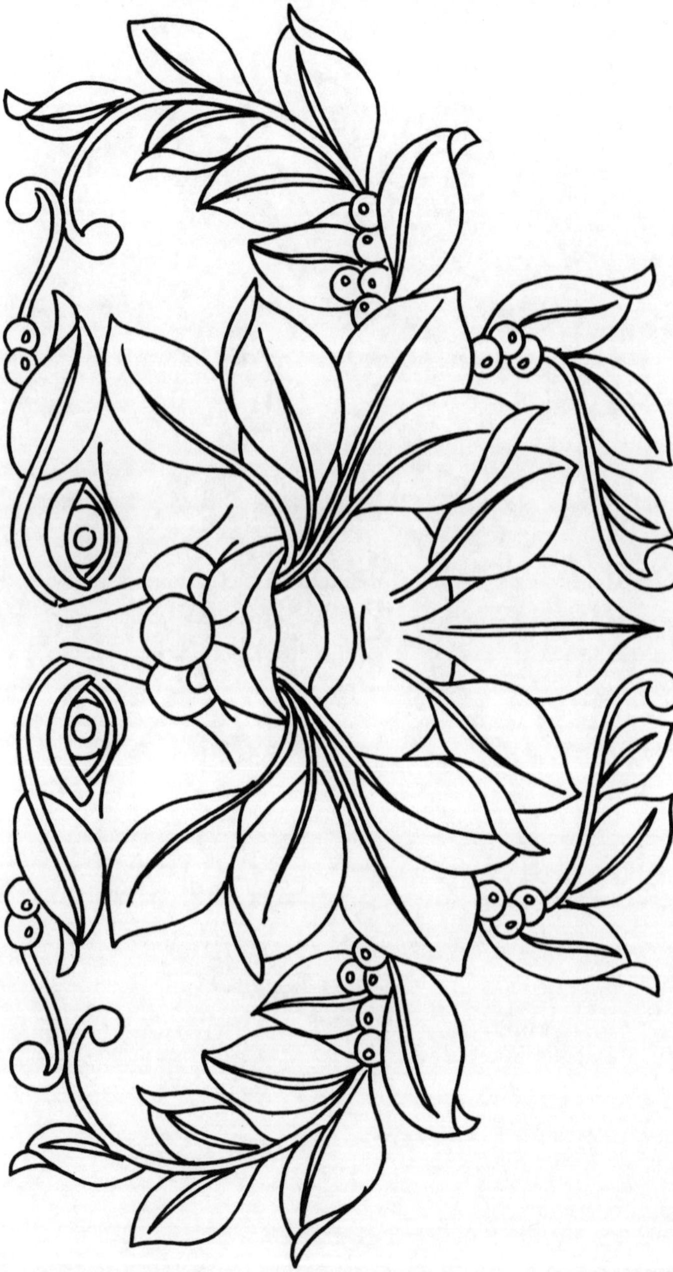

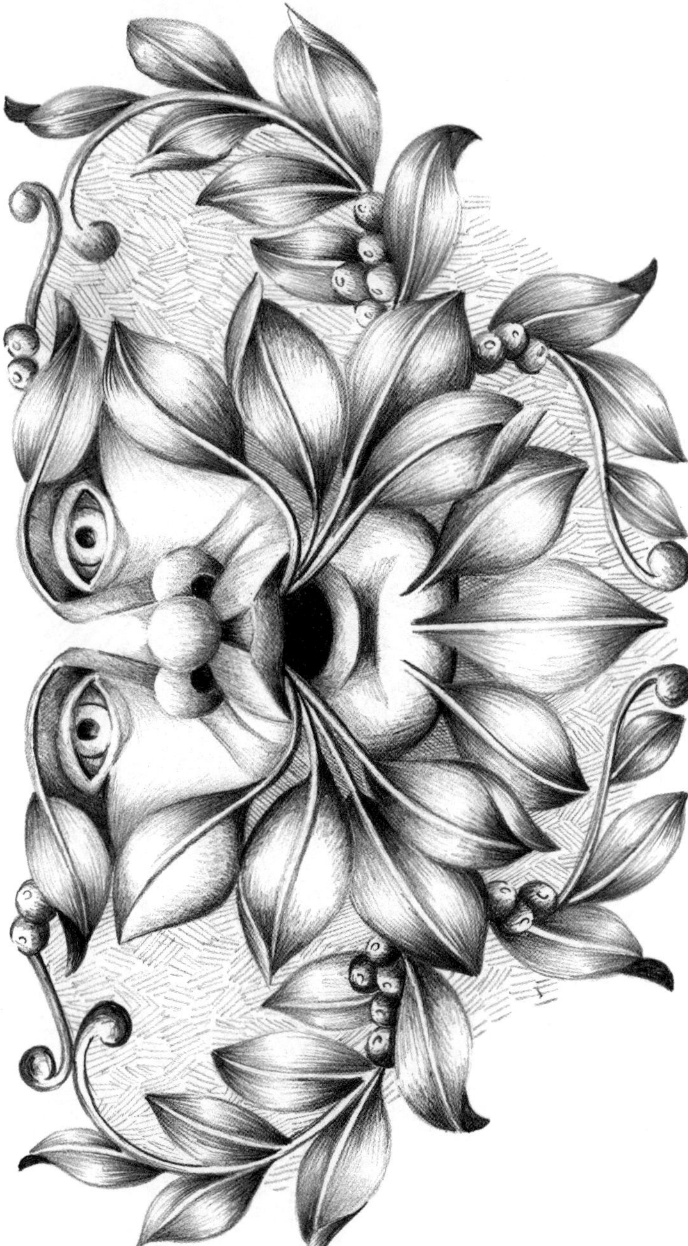

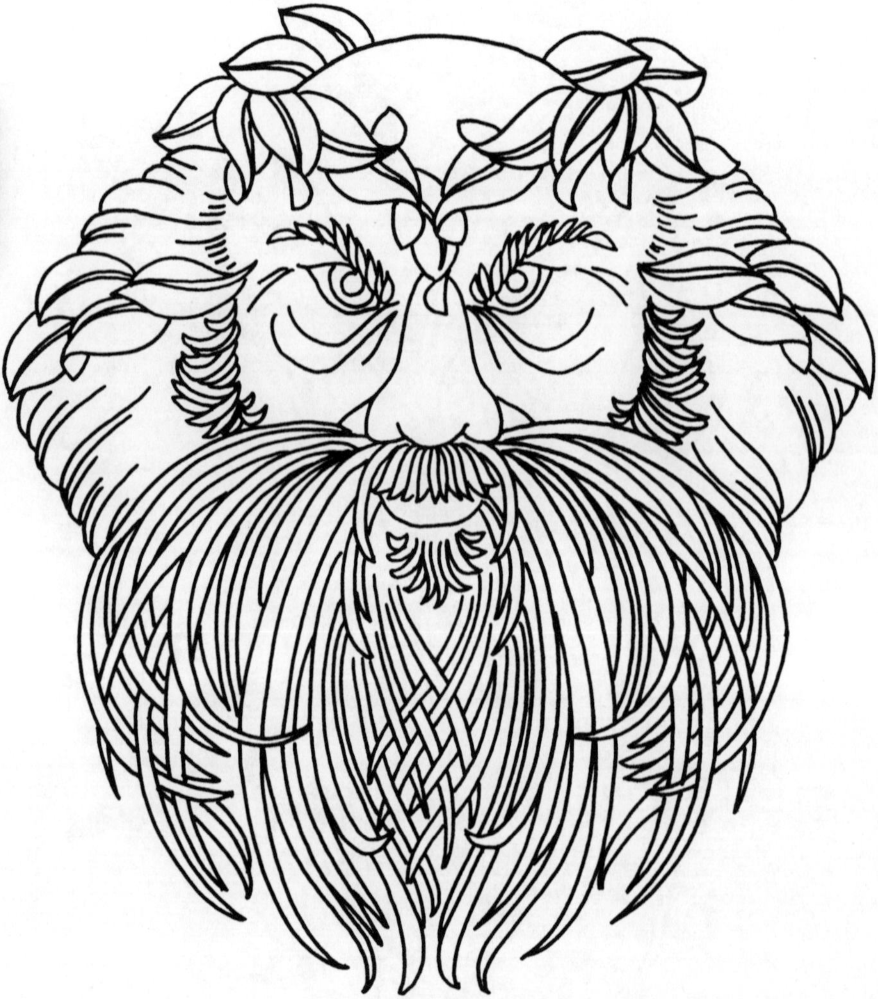

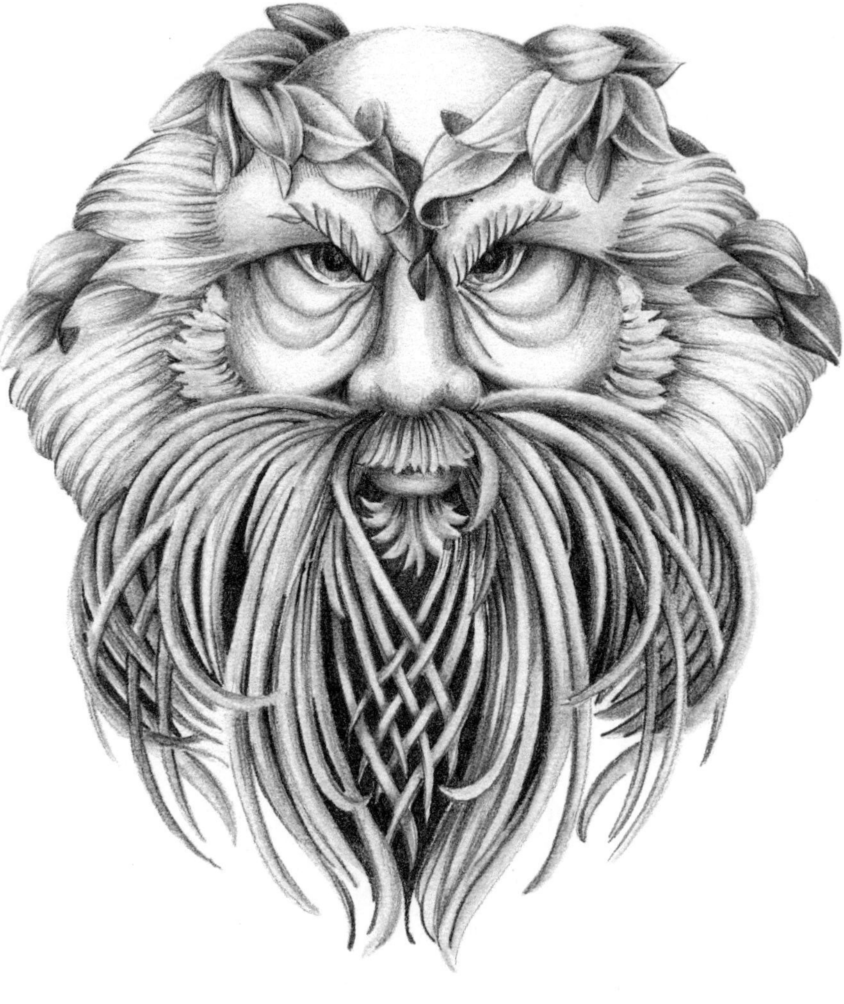

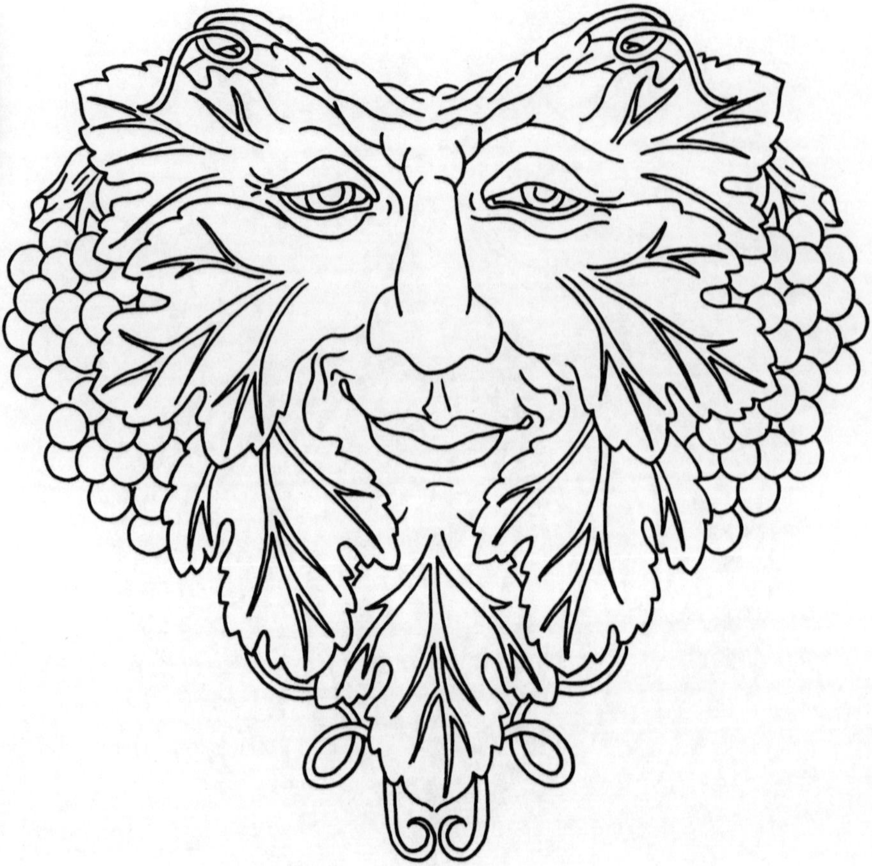

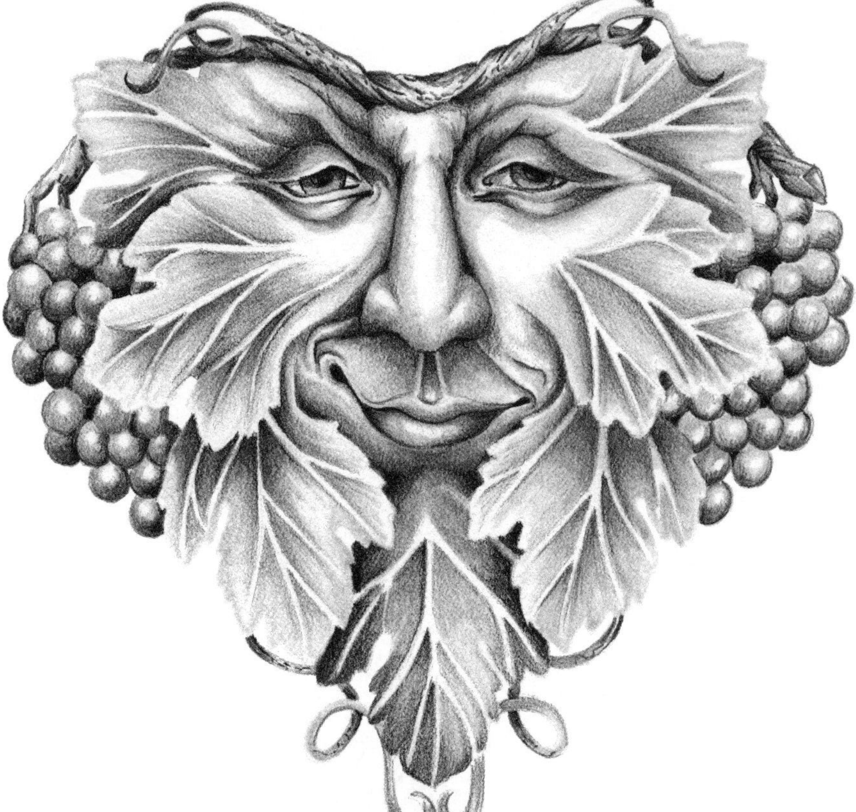

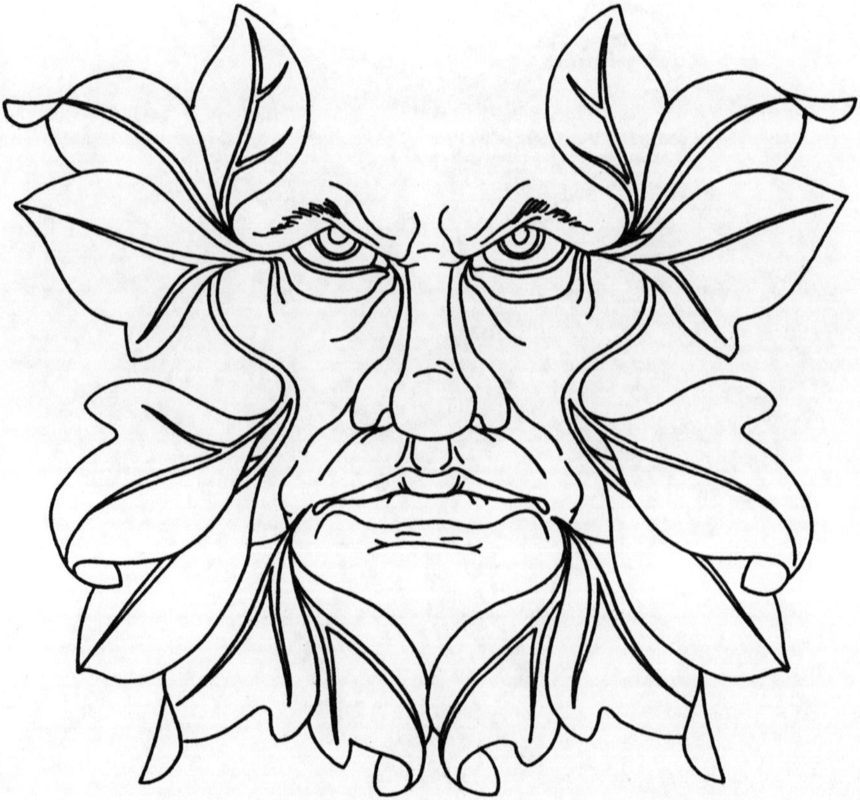

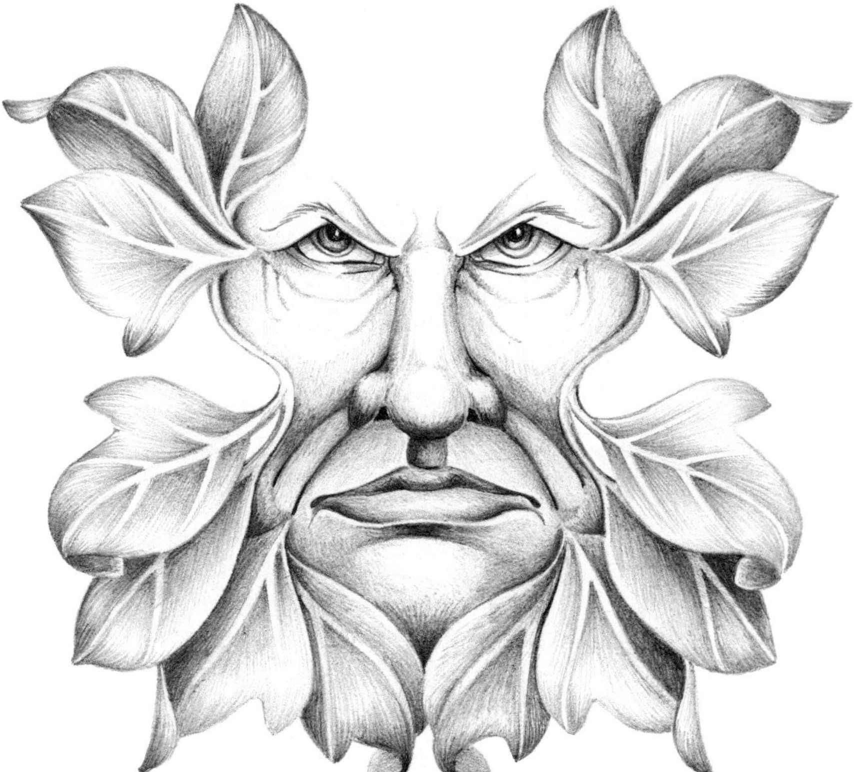

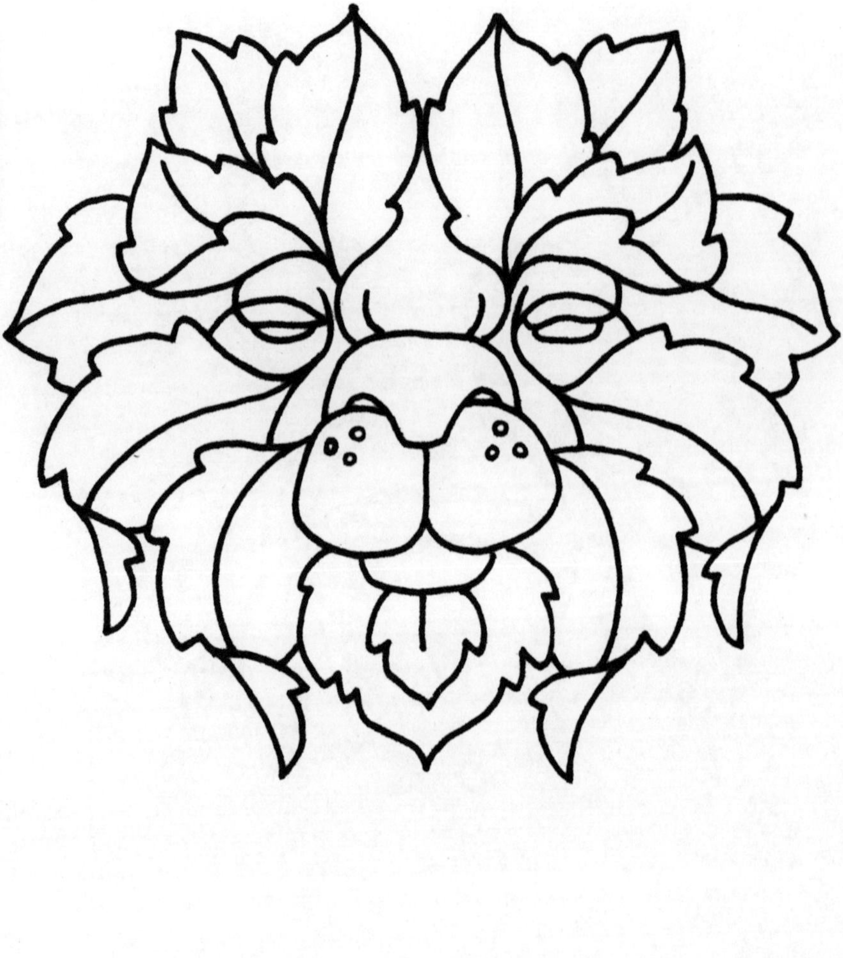

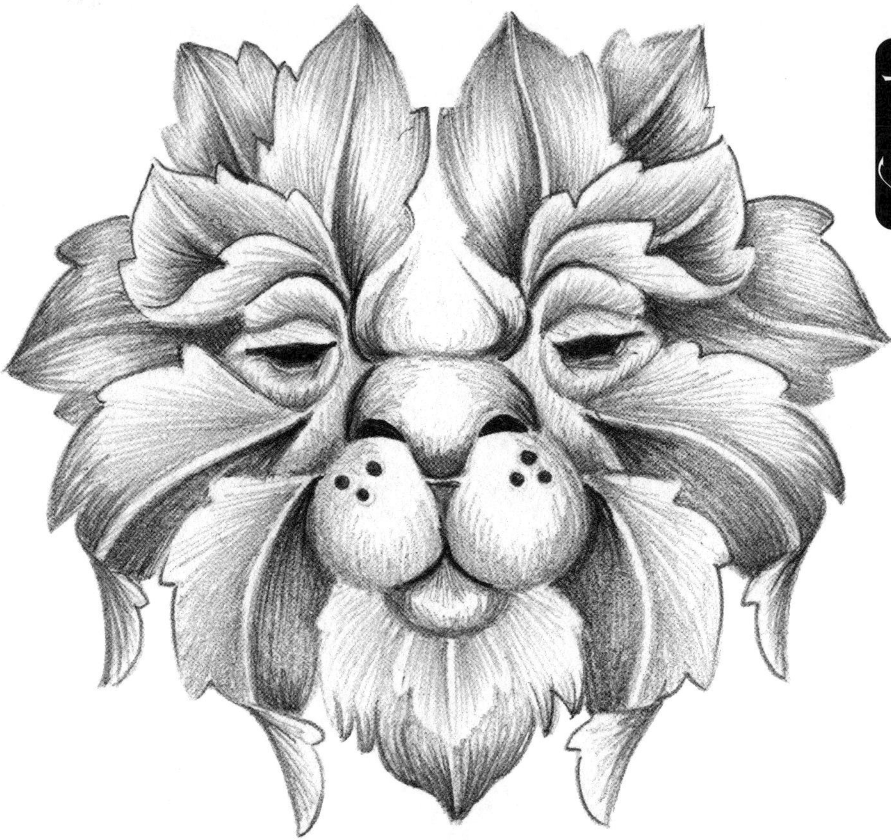

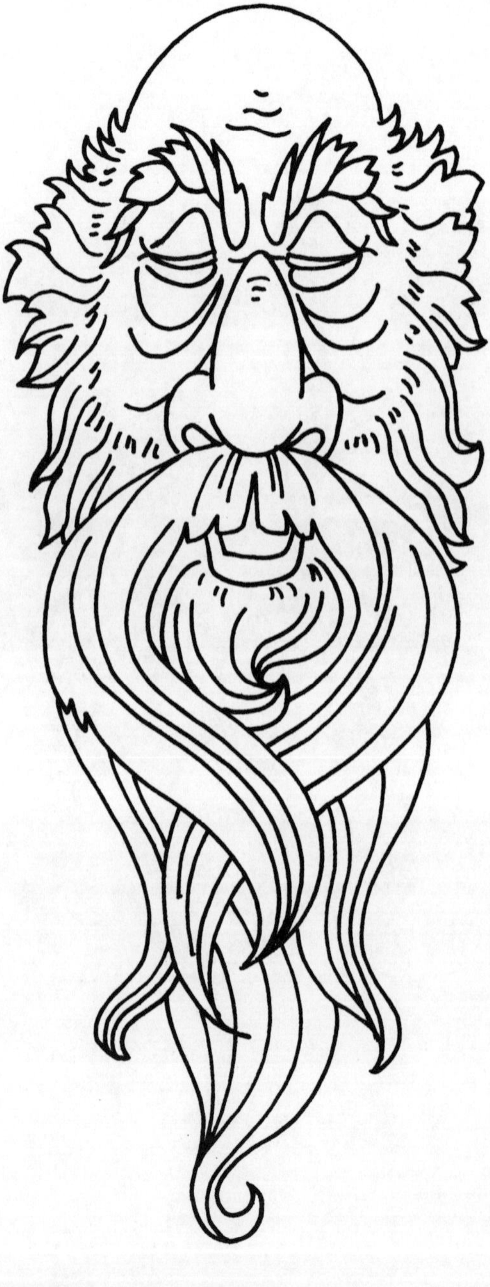

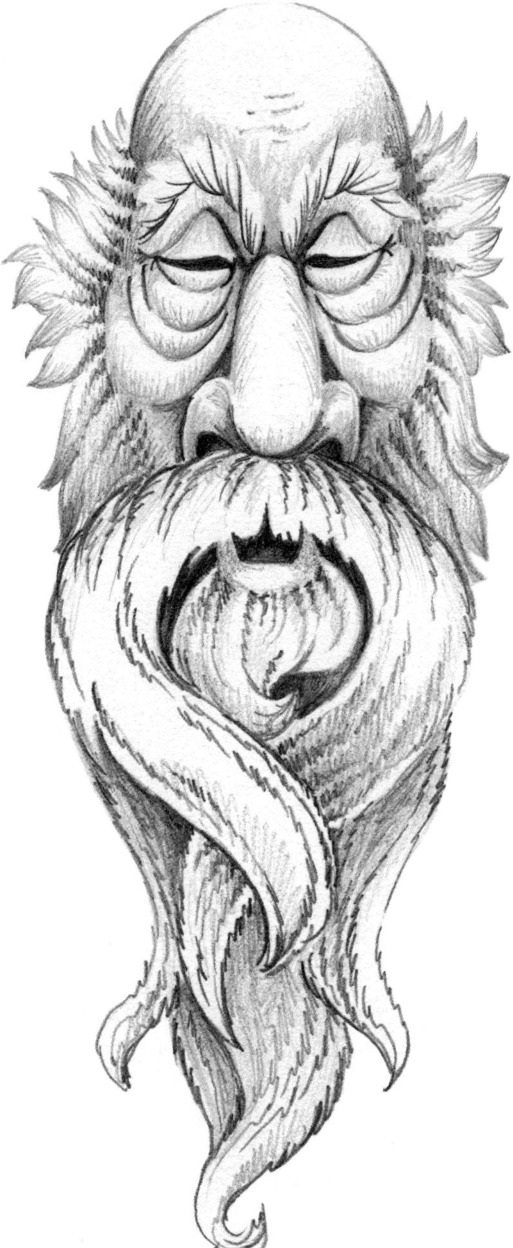

Fantasy

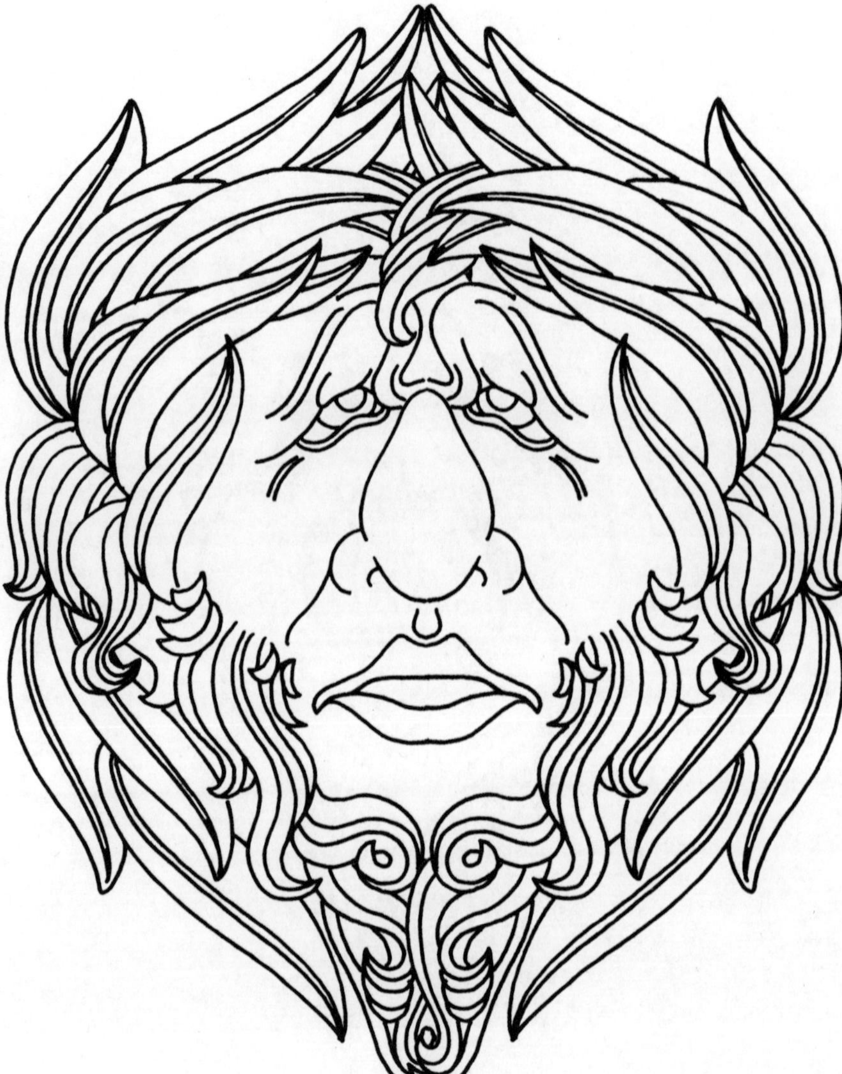

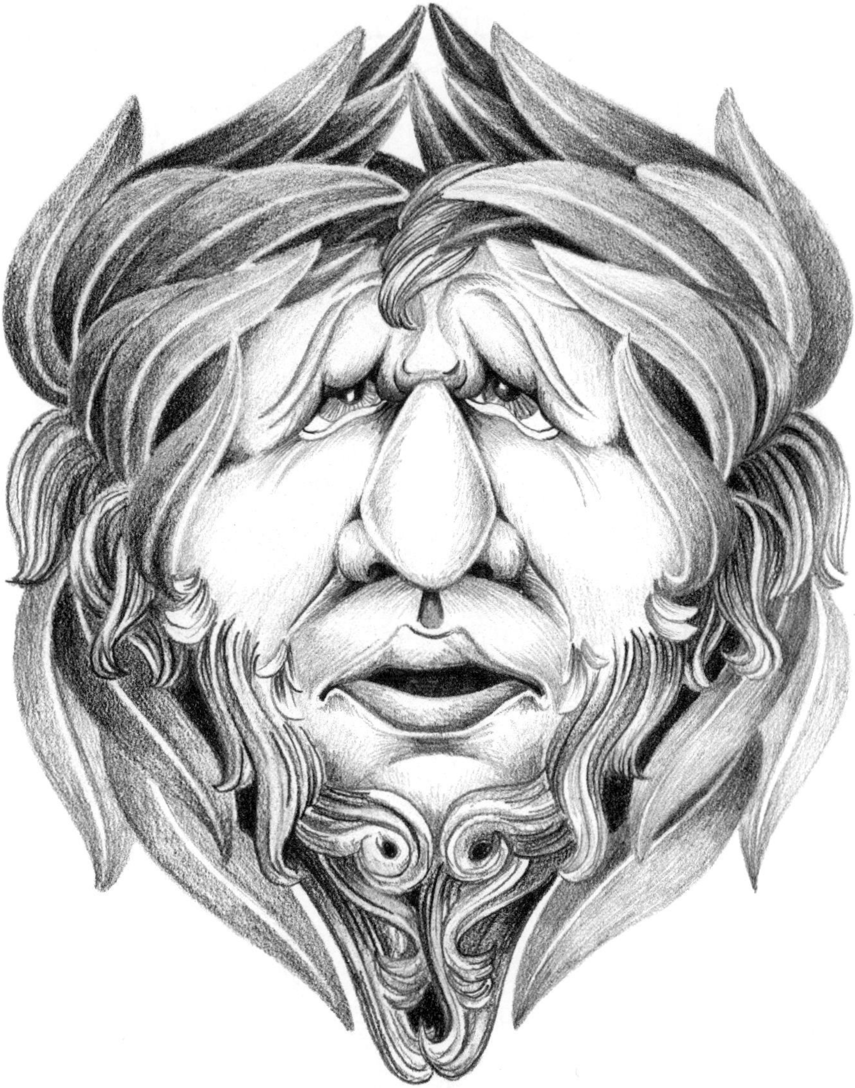

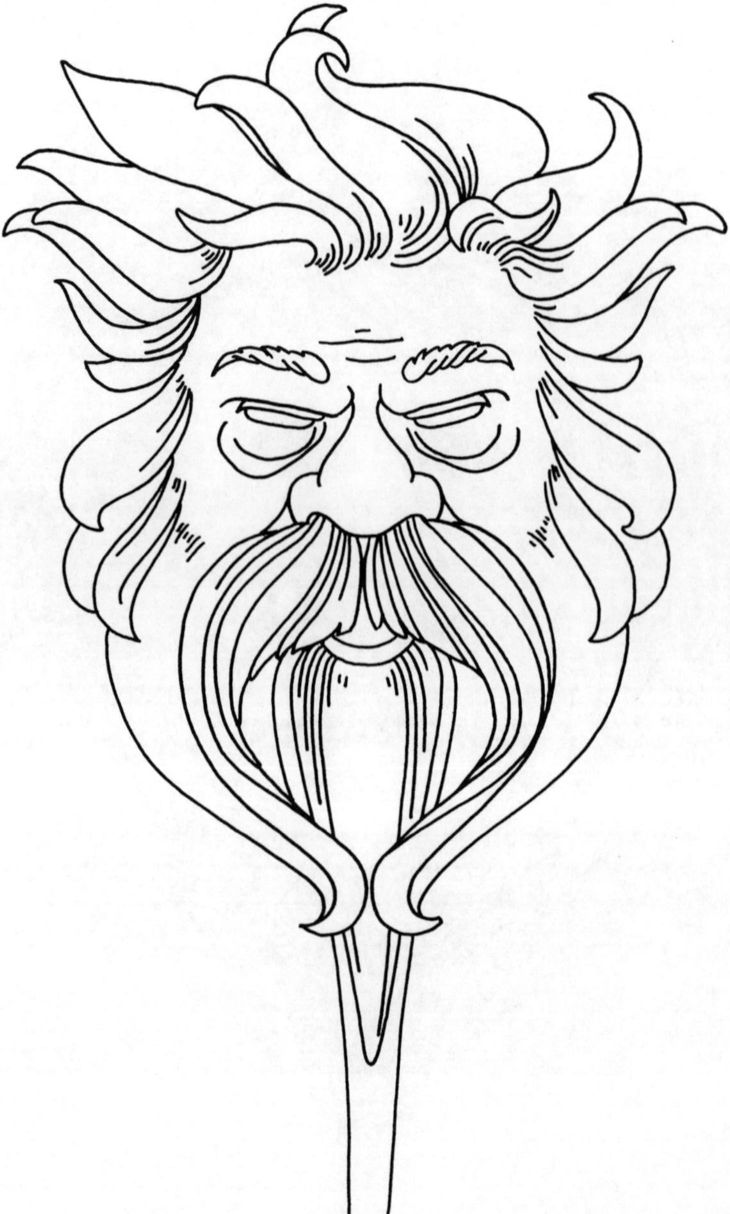

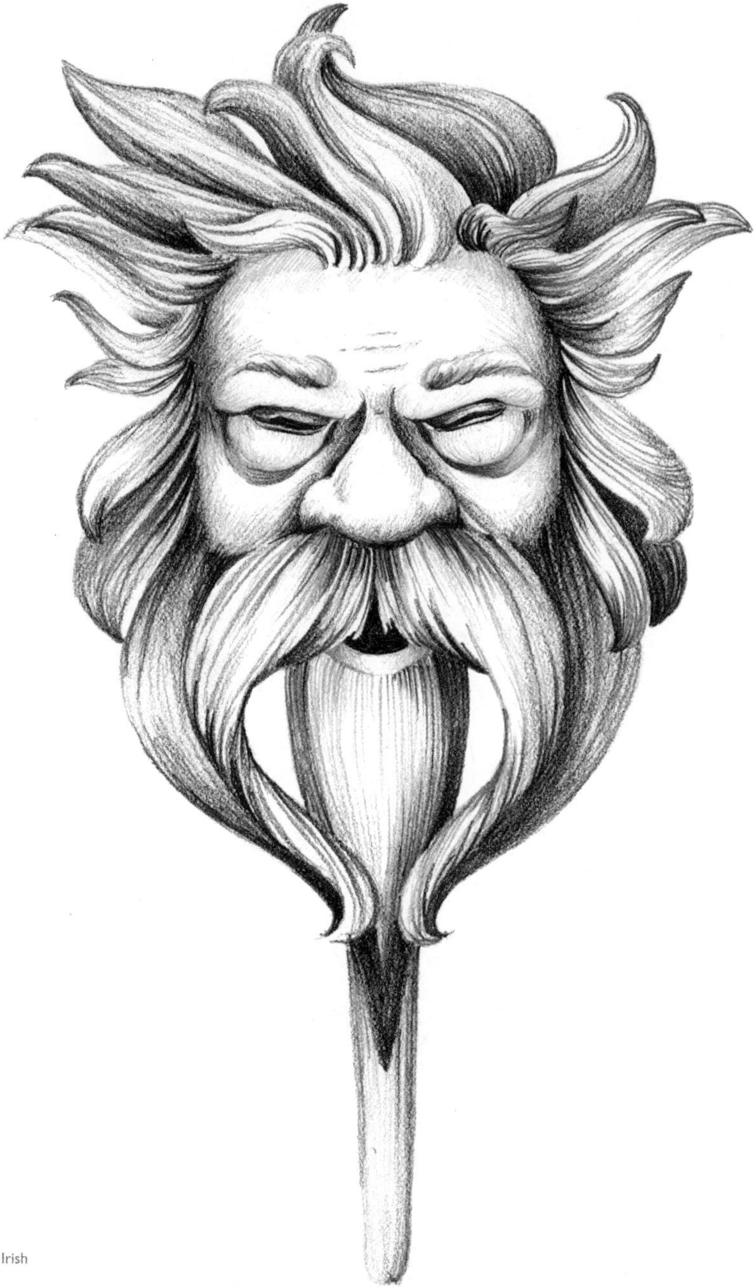

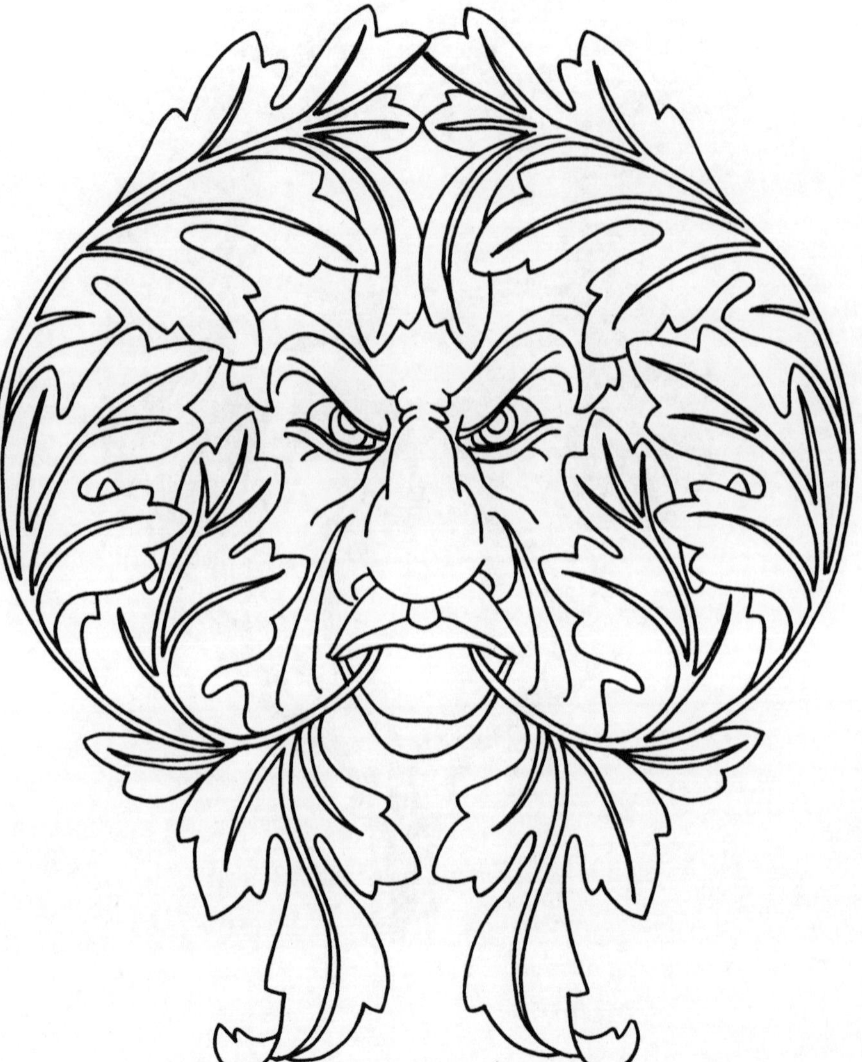

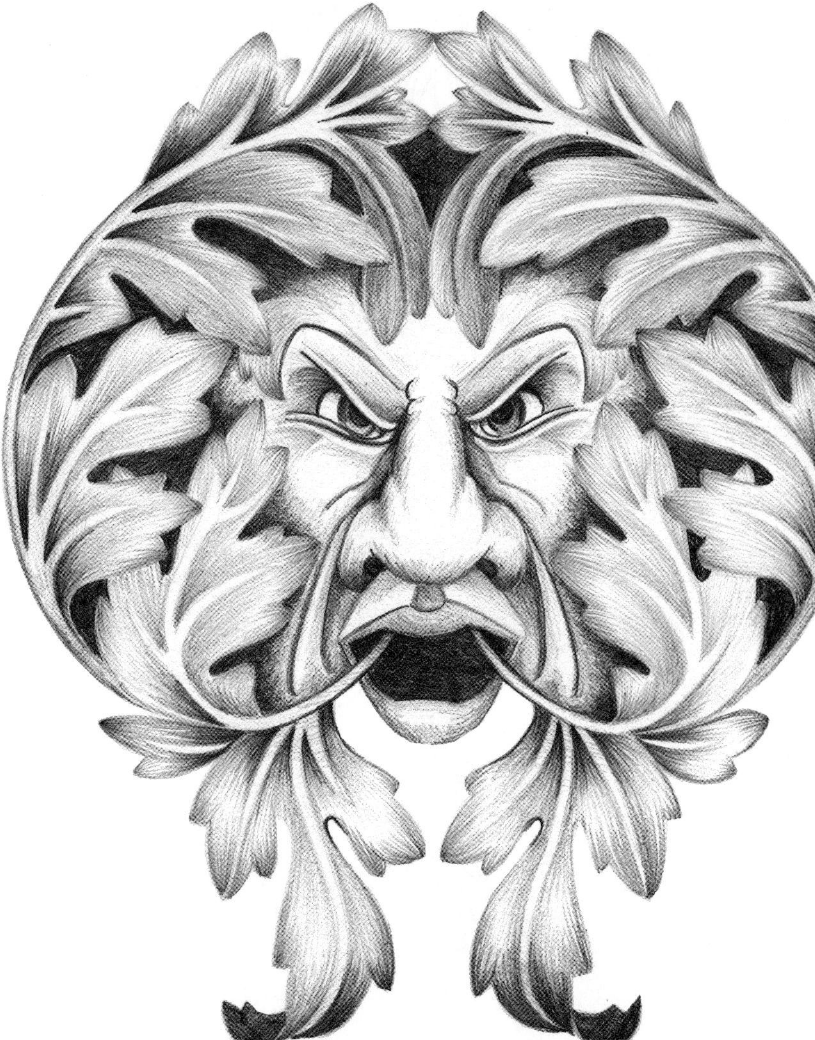

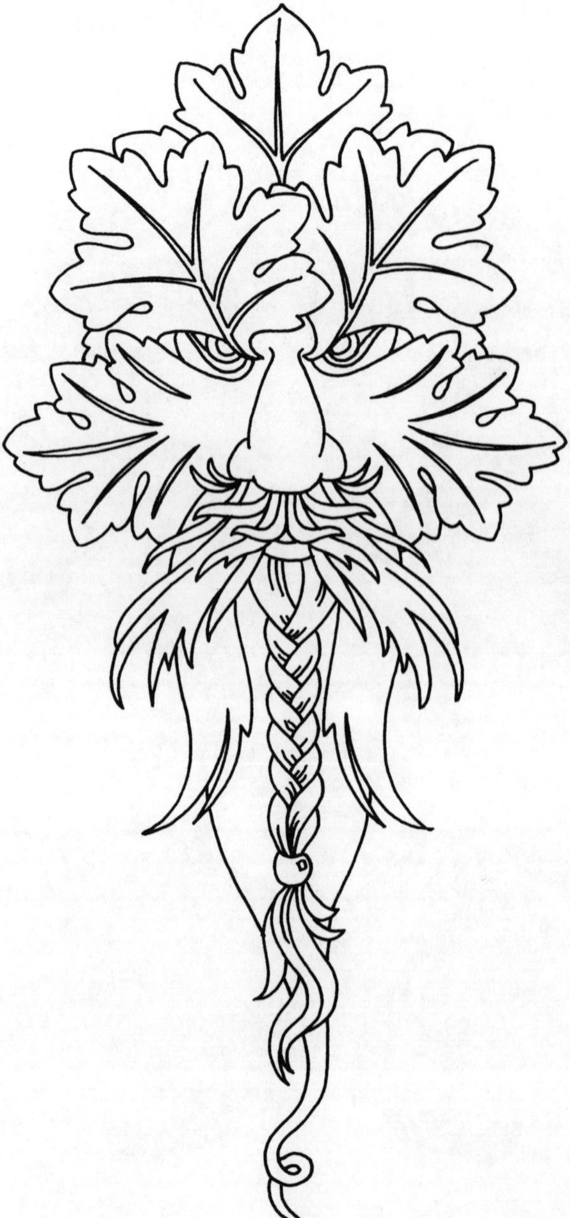

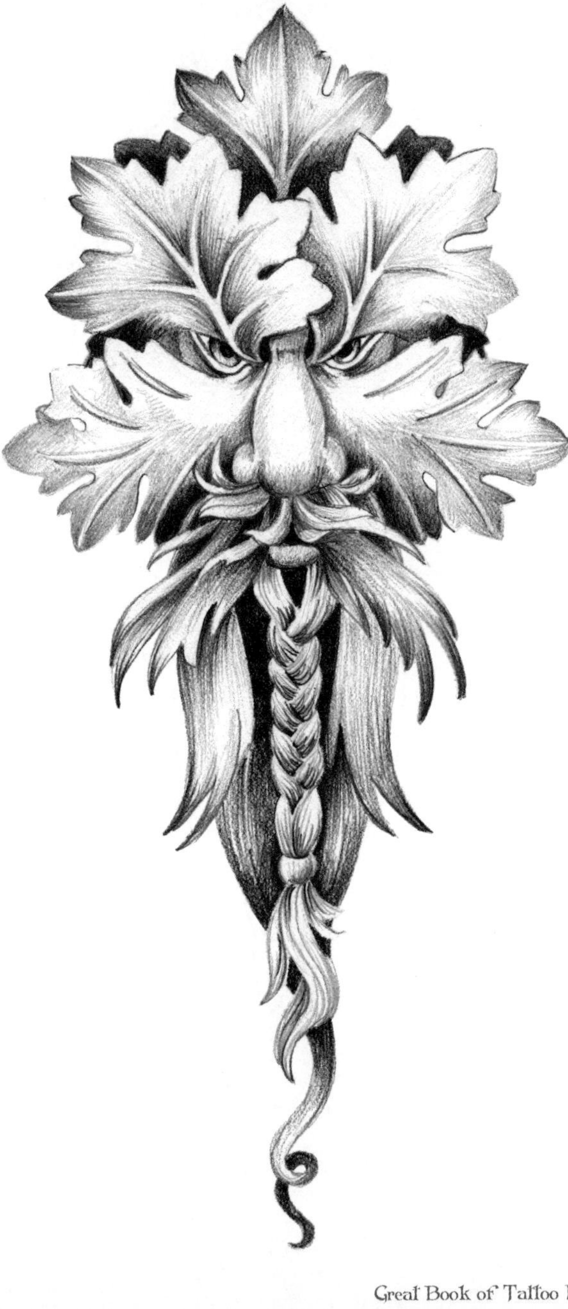

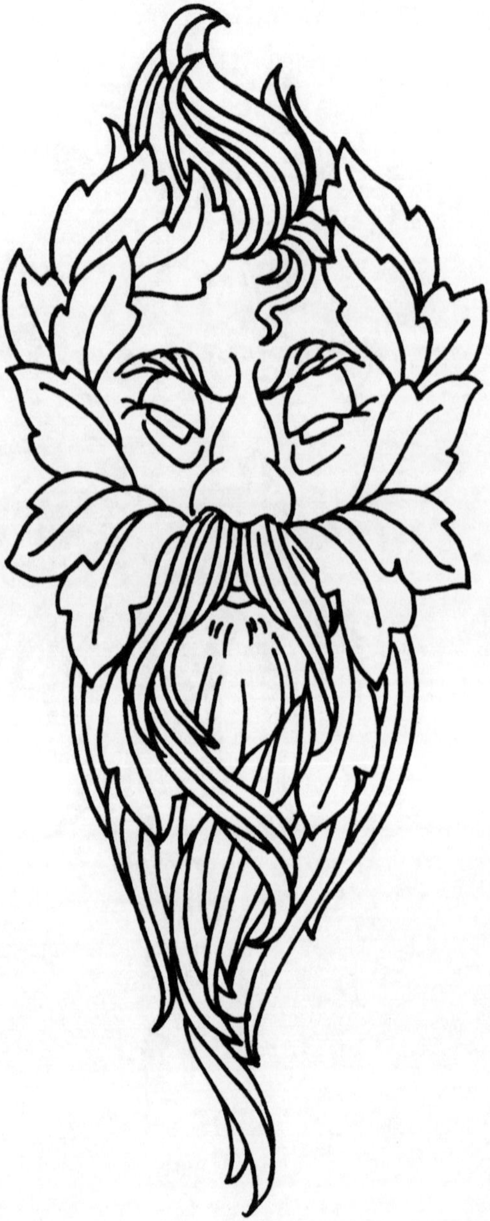

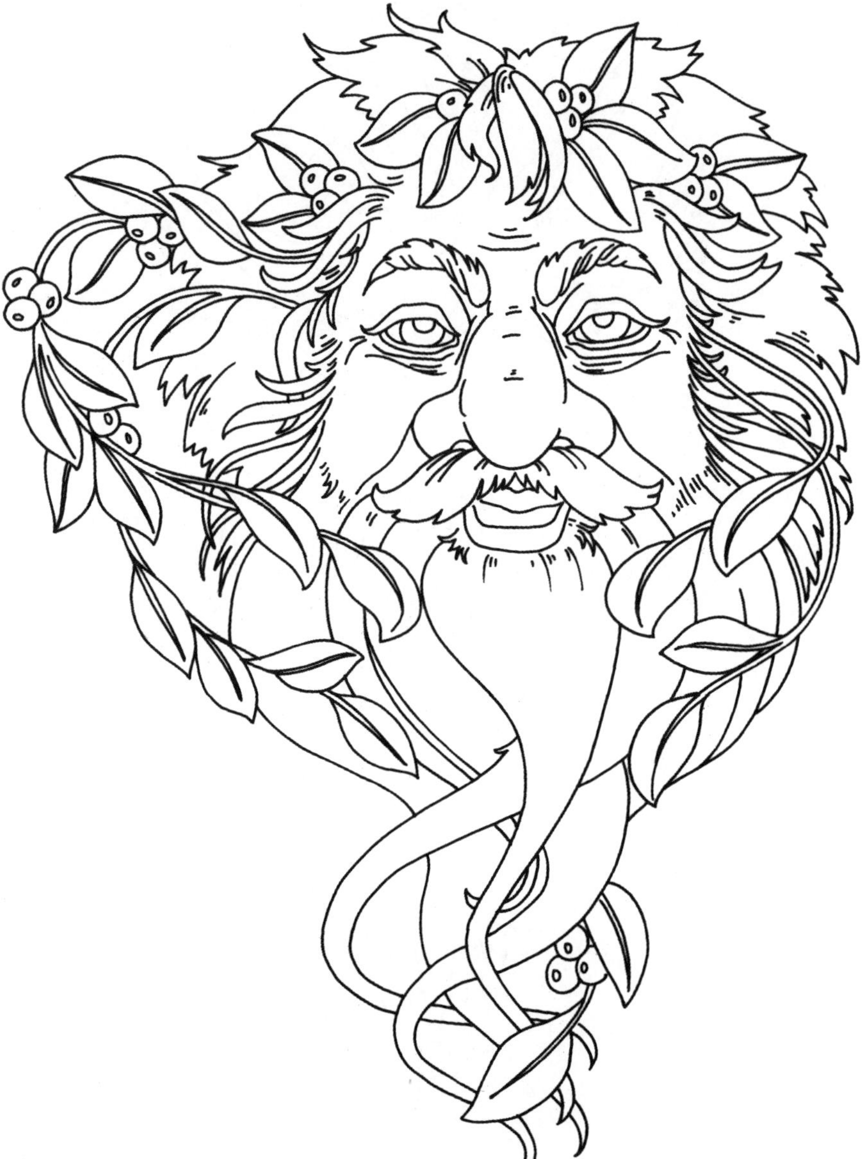

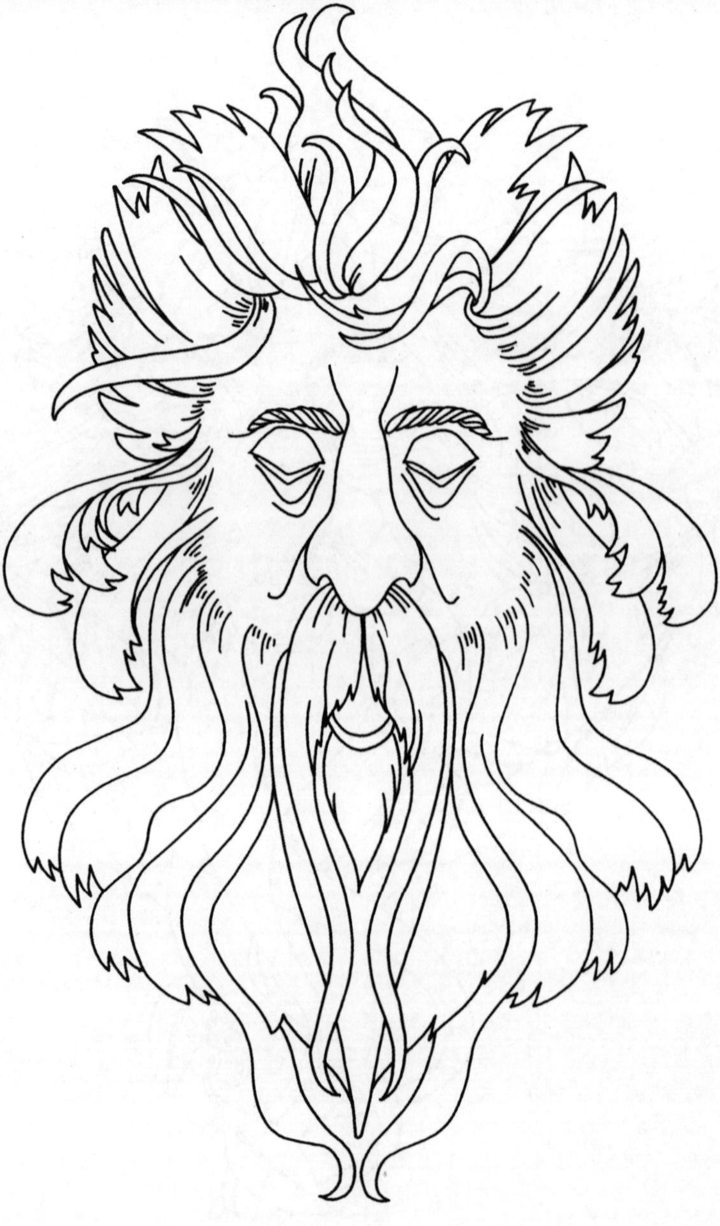

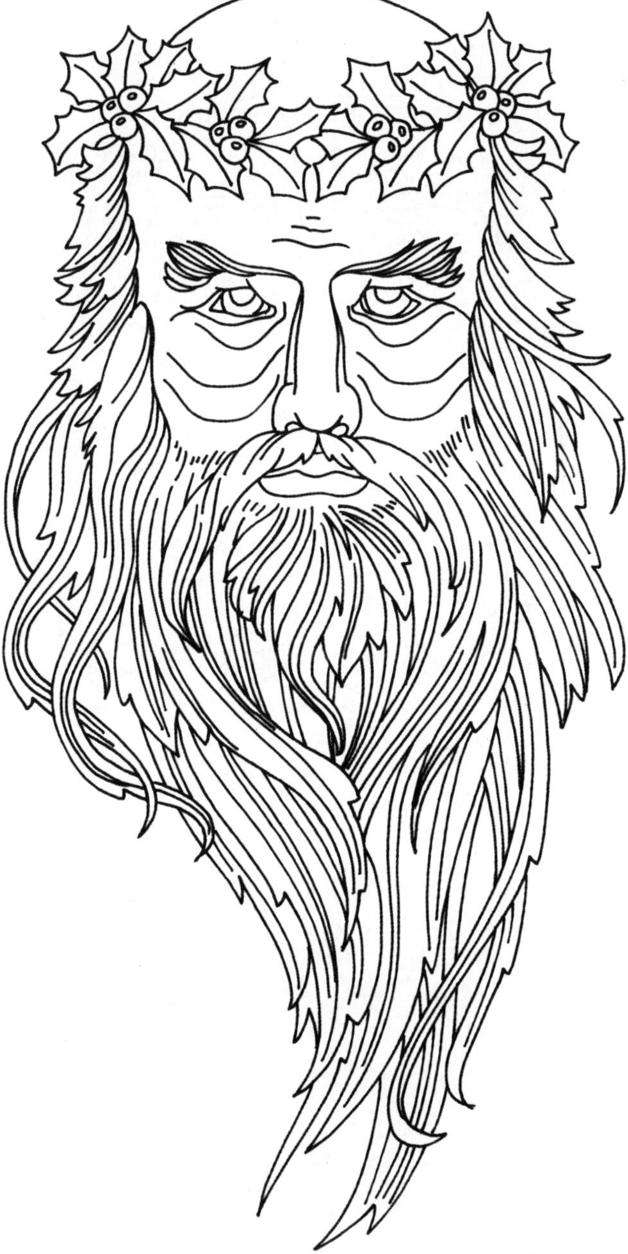

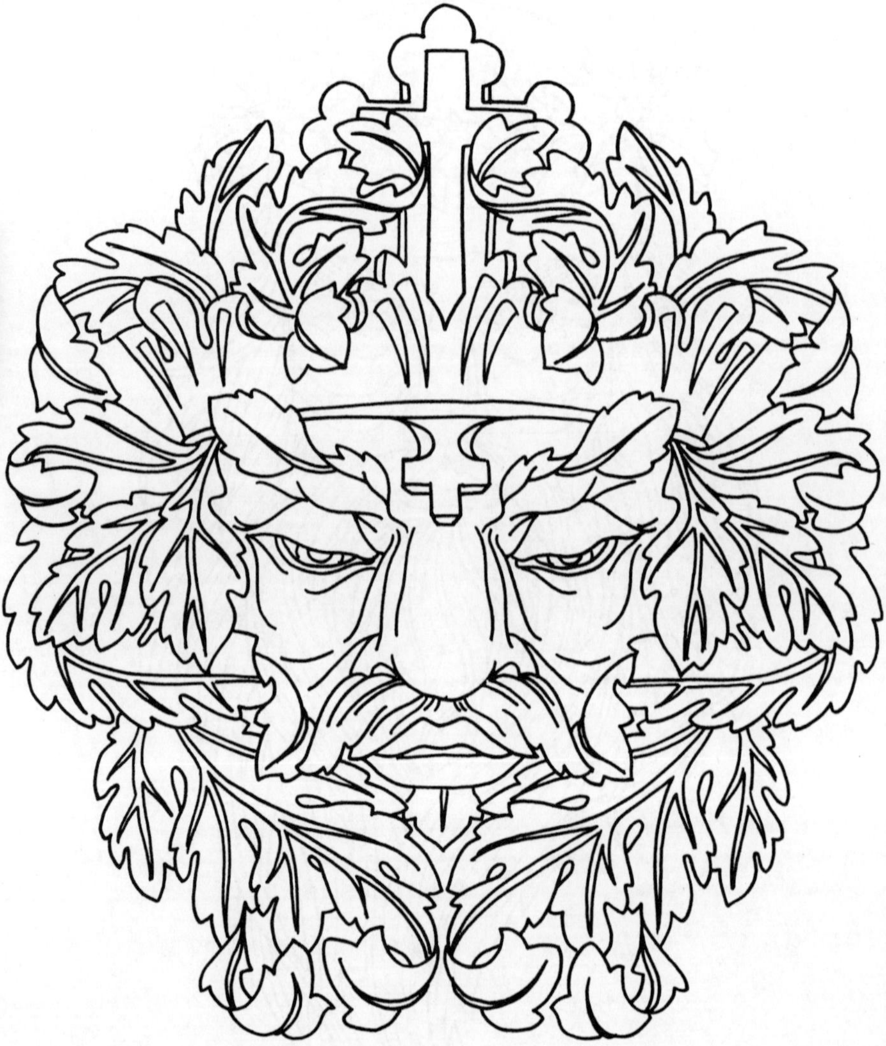

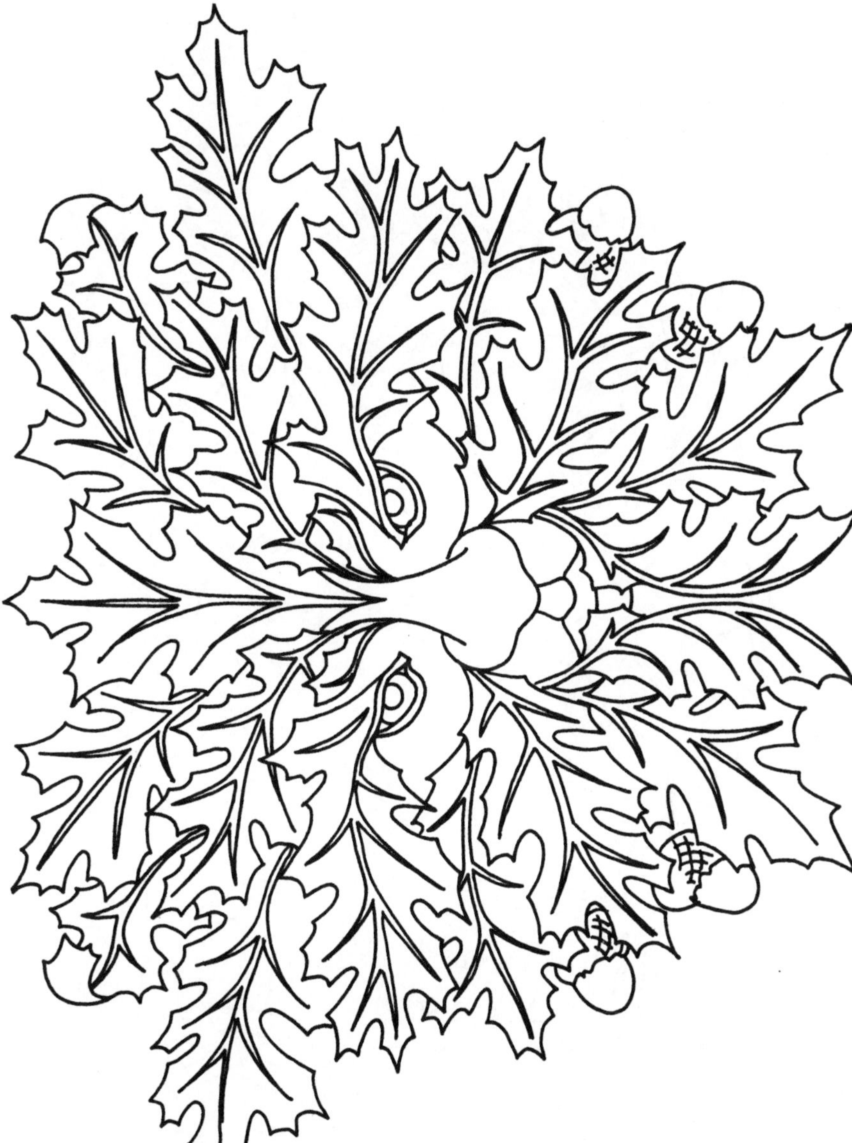

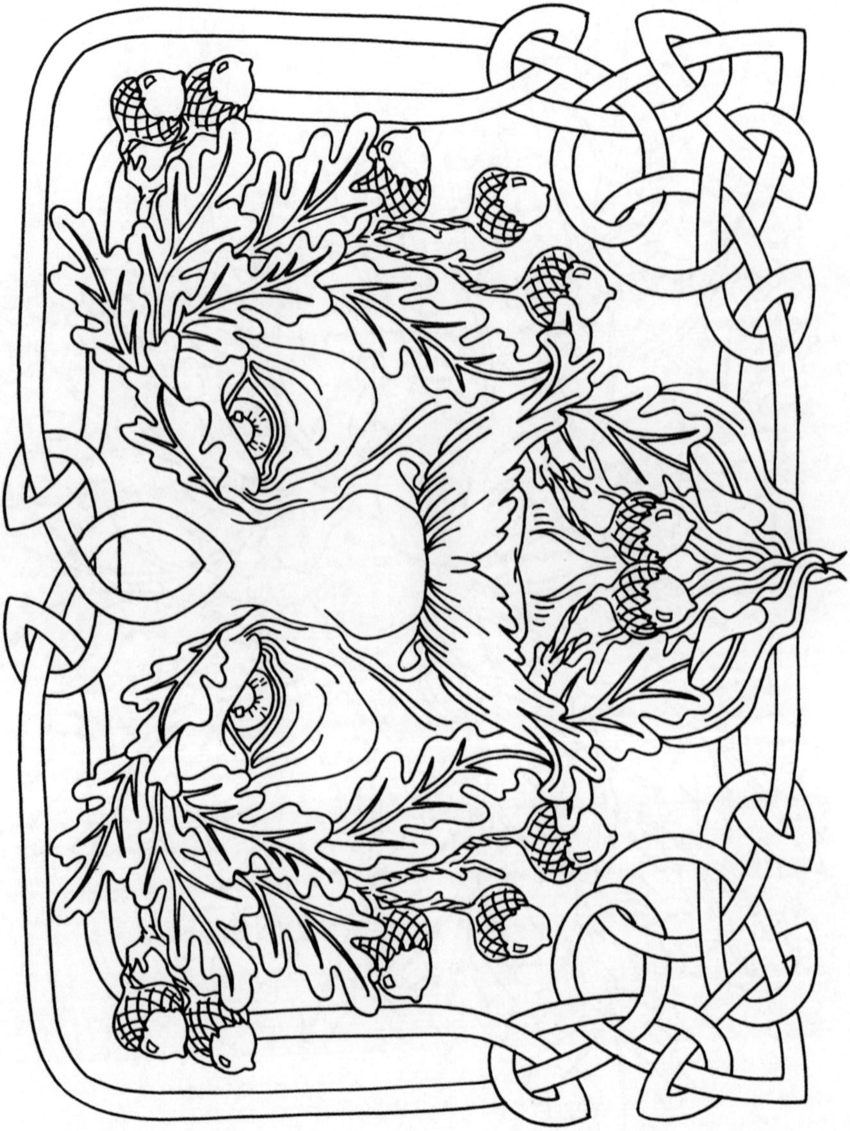

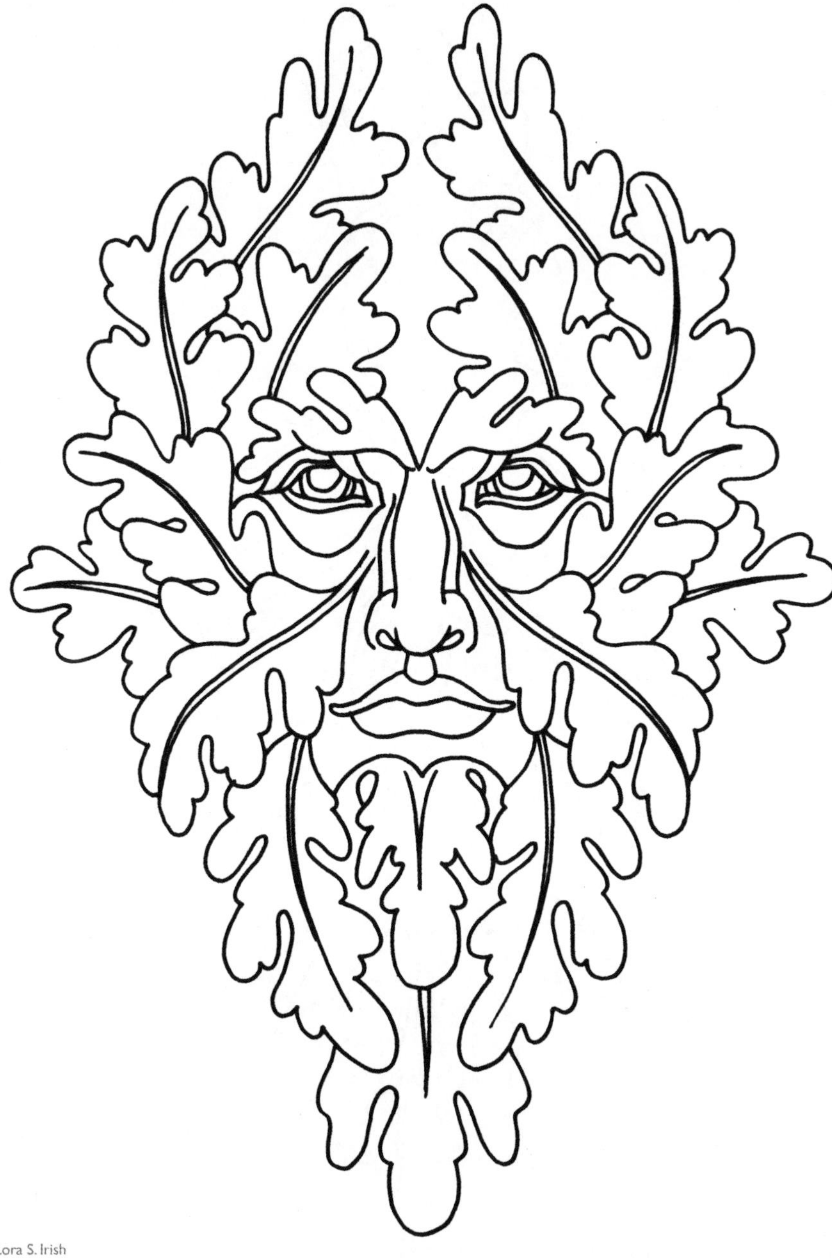

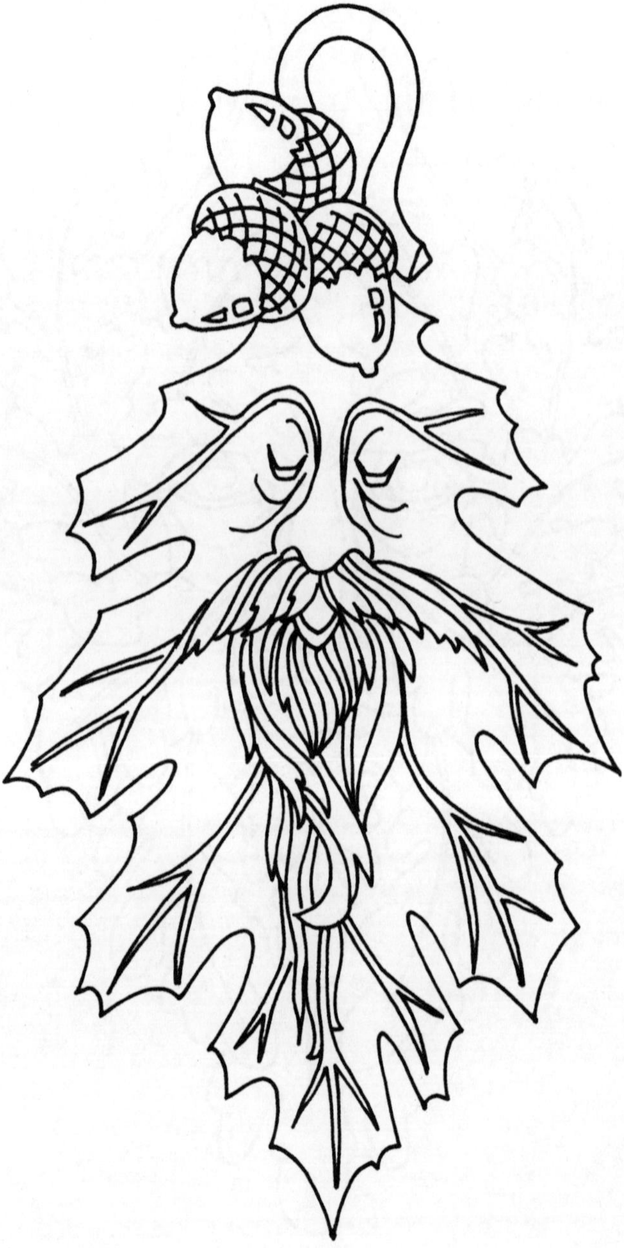

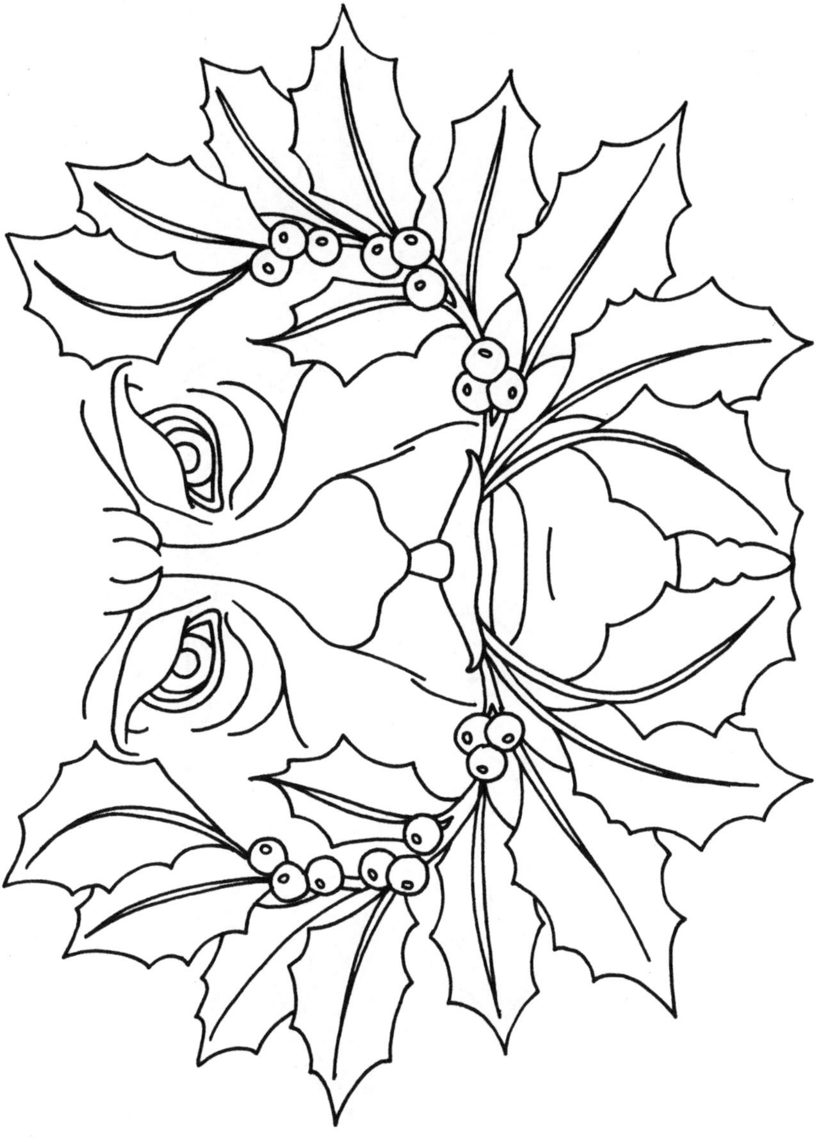

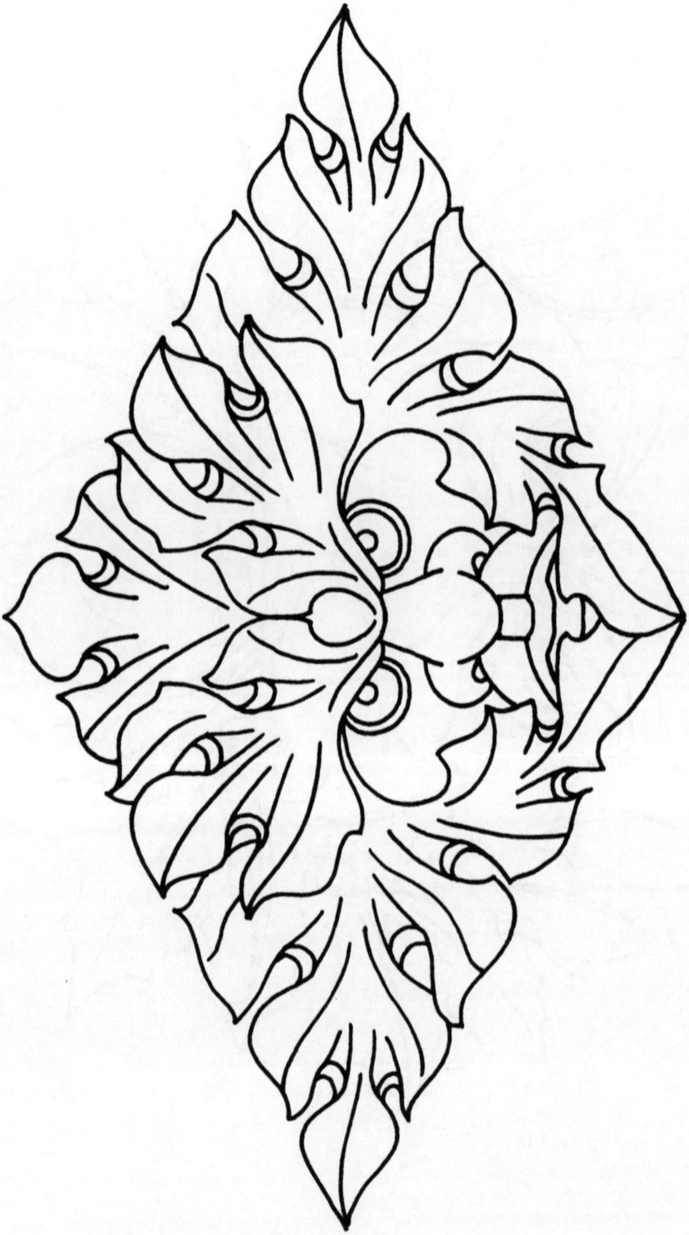

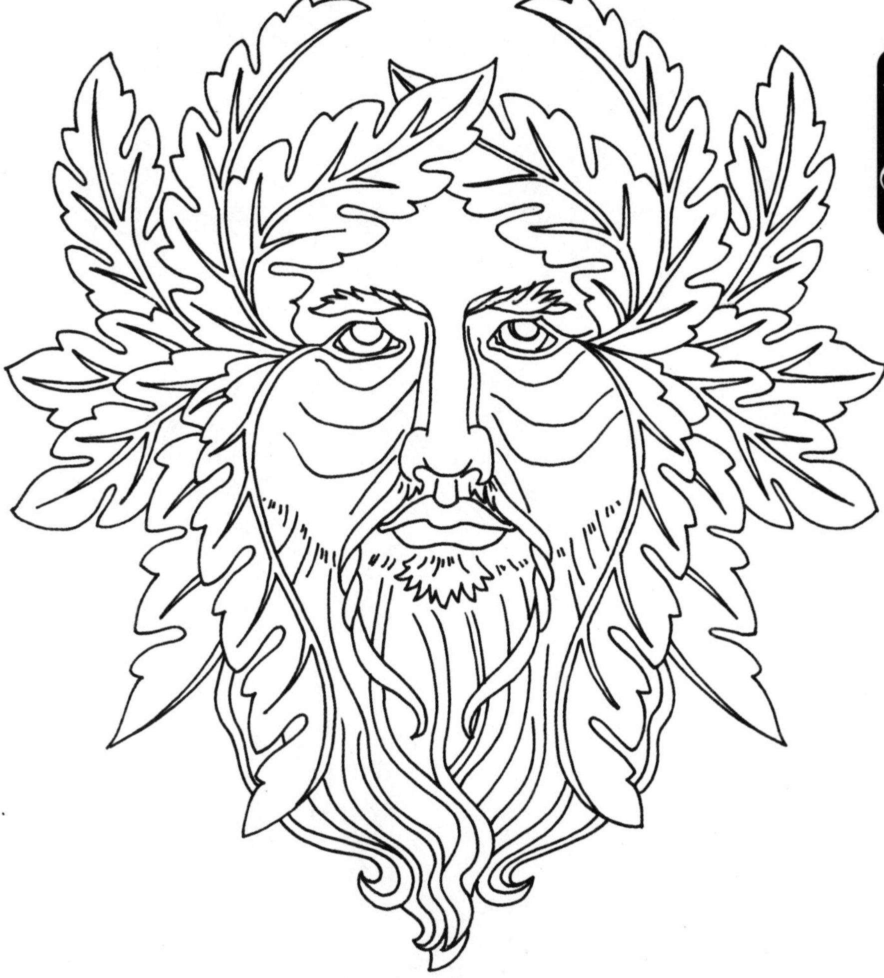

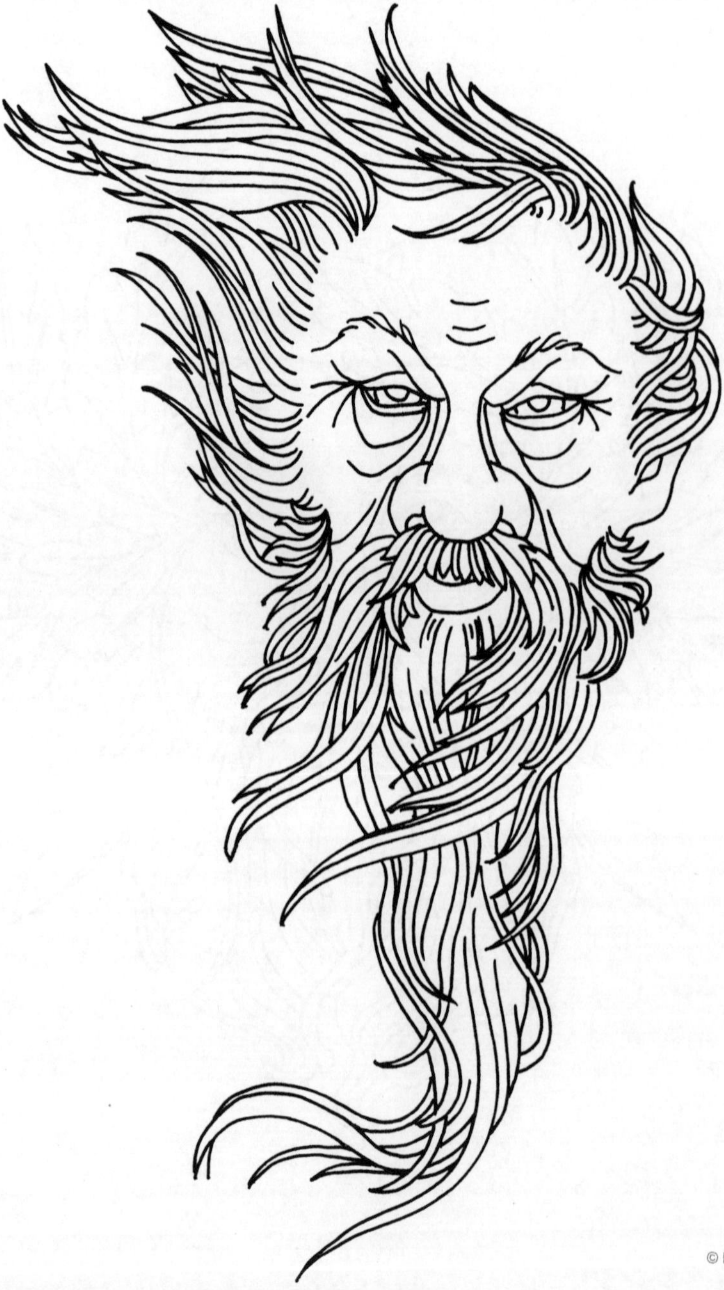

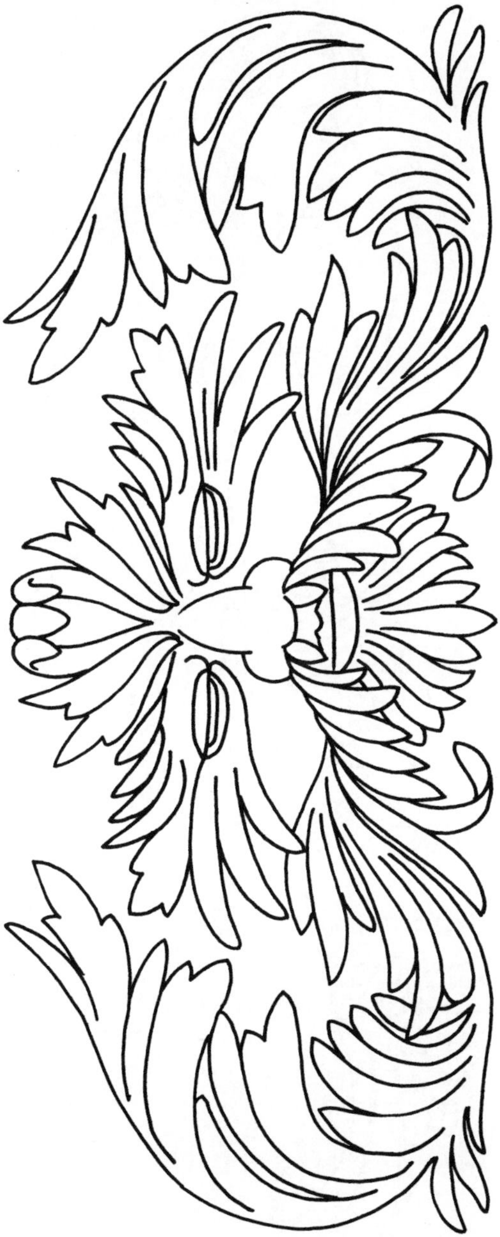

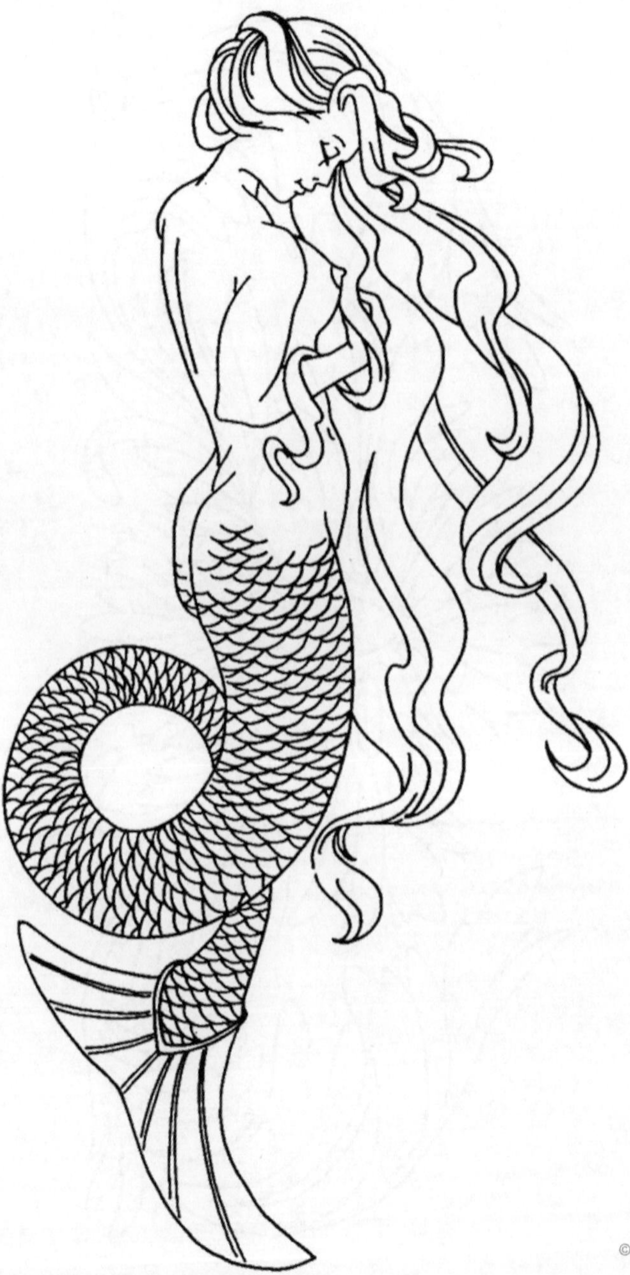

© Lora S. Irish

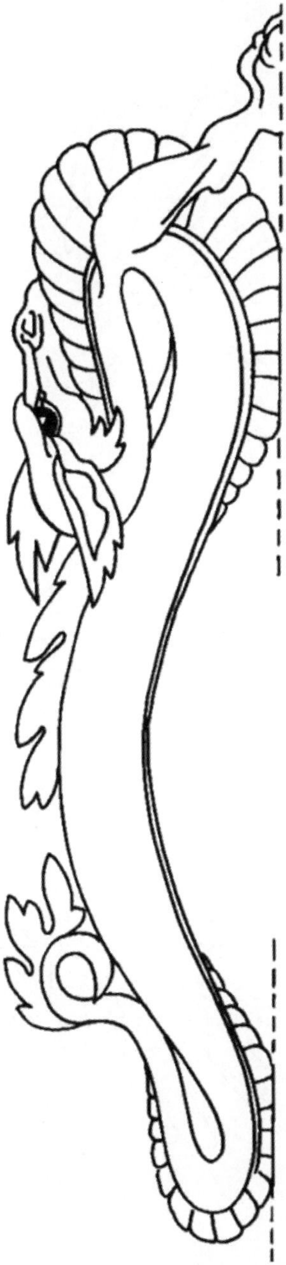

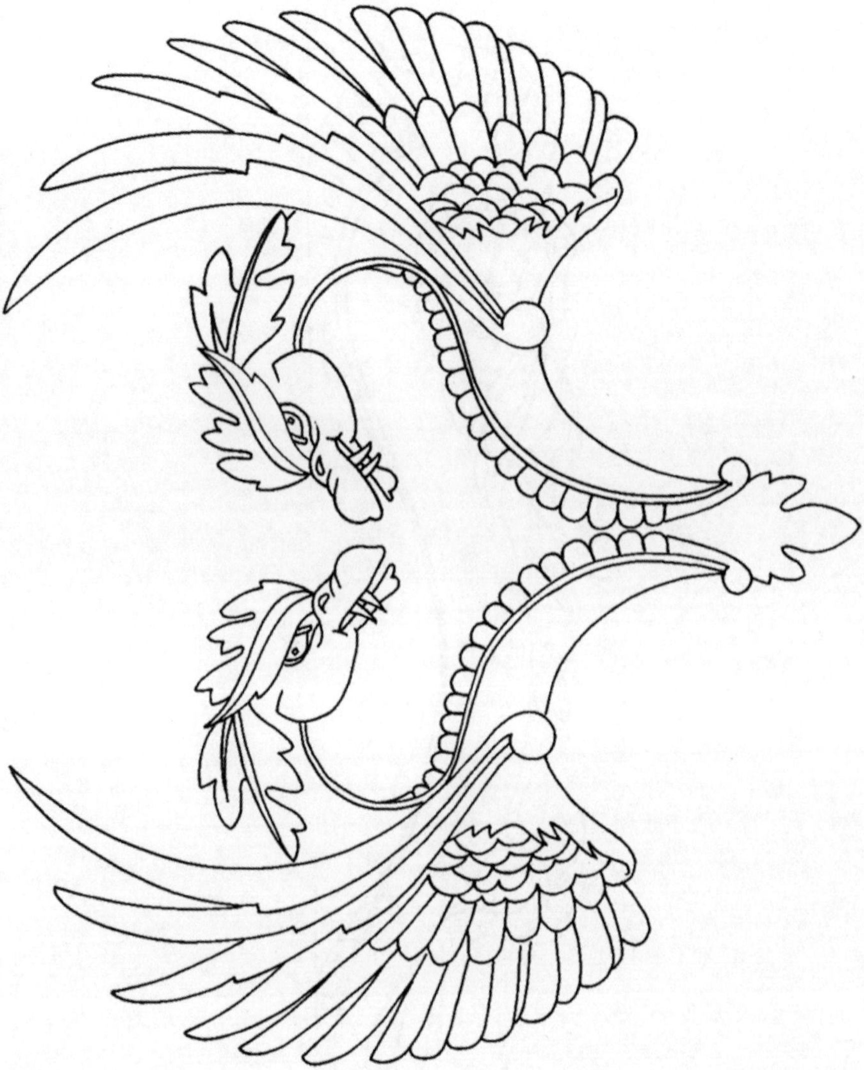

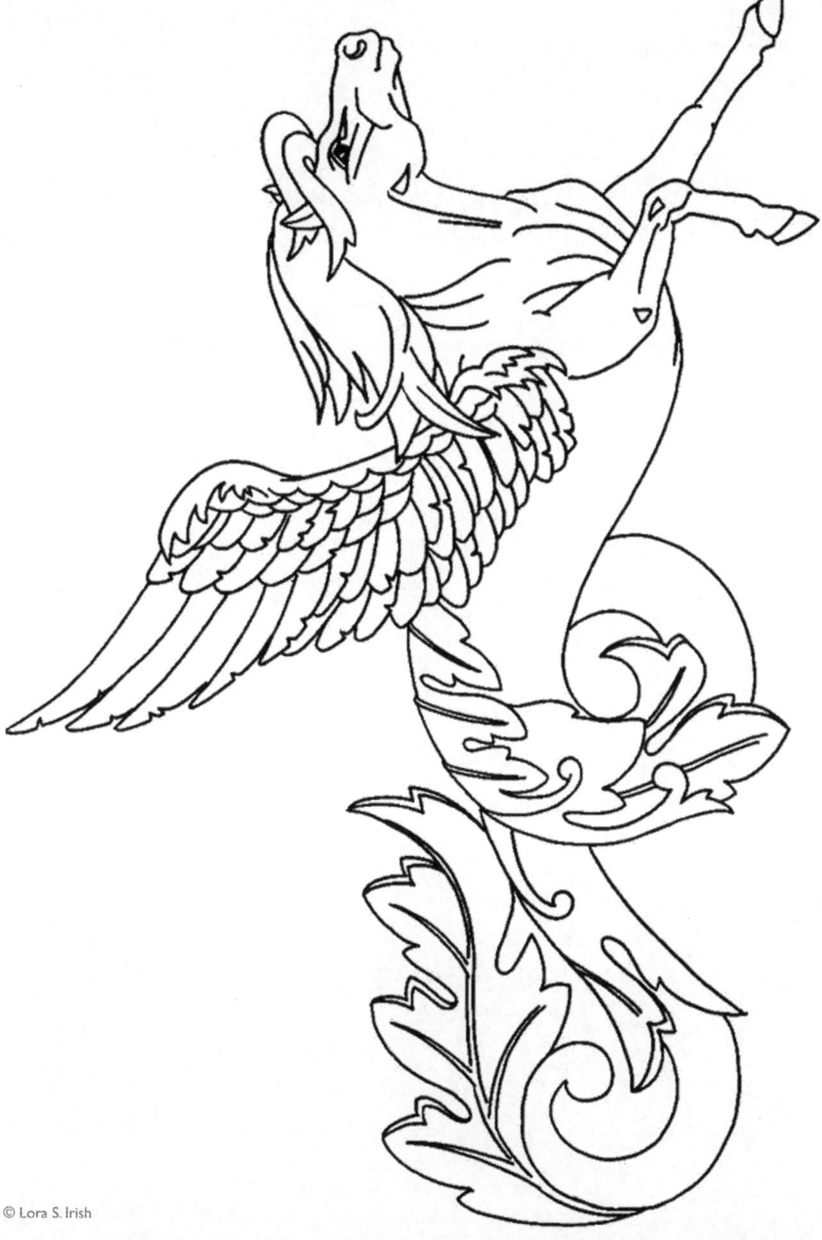

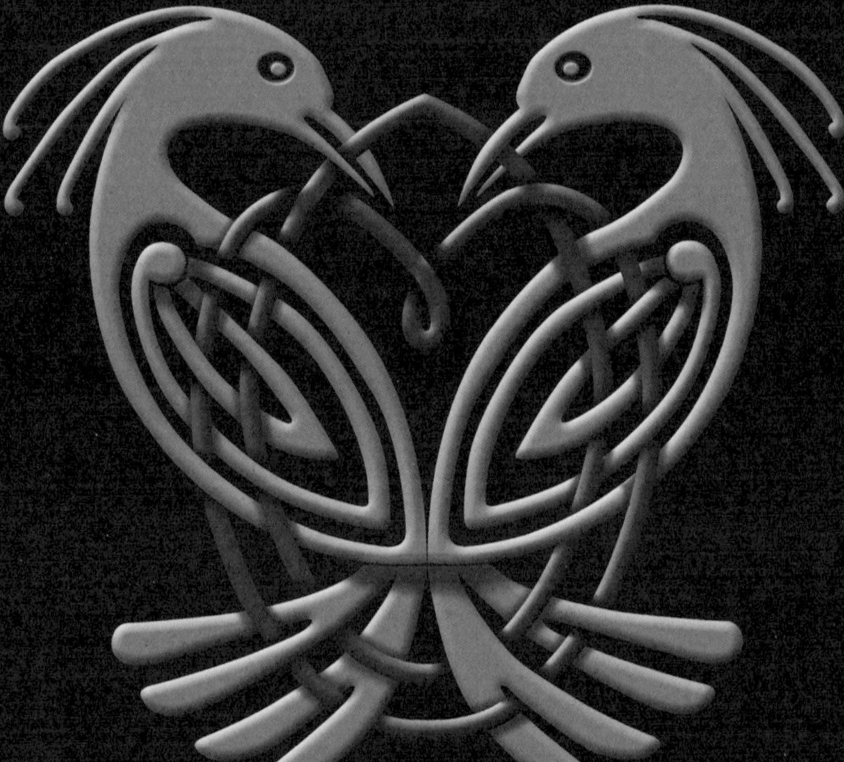

Celtic

Three hundred years of Viking invasions in Ireland, Scotland, Wales, and northern England had a lot to do with the evolution of Celtic art as it exists today. Characterized by intricately woven patterns that are often accented by images of people and animals, these designs may have been created simply for their beauty since no meanings for the patterns and symbols have ever been recorded. What they represent, then, is left to personal interpretation. The continual looping designs, for example, can signify the continuum of life and eternity. The interlaced Celtic knots may represent love and interdependence.

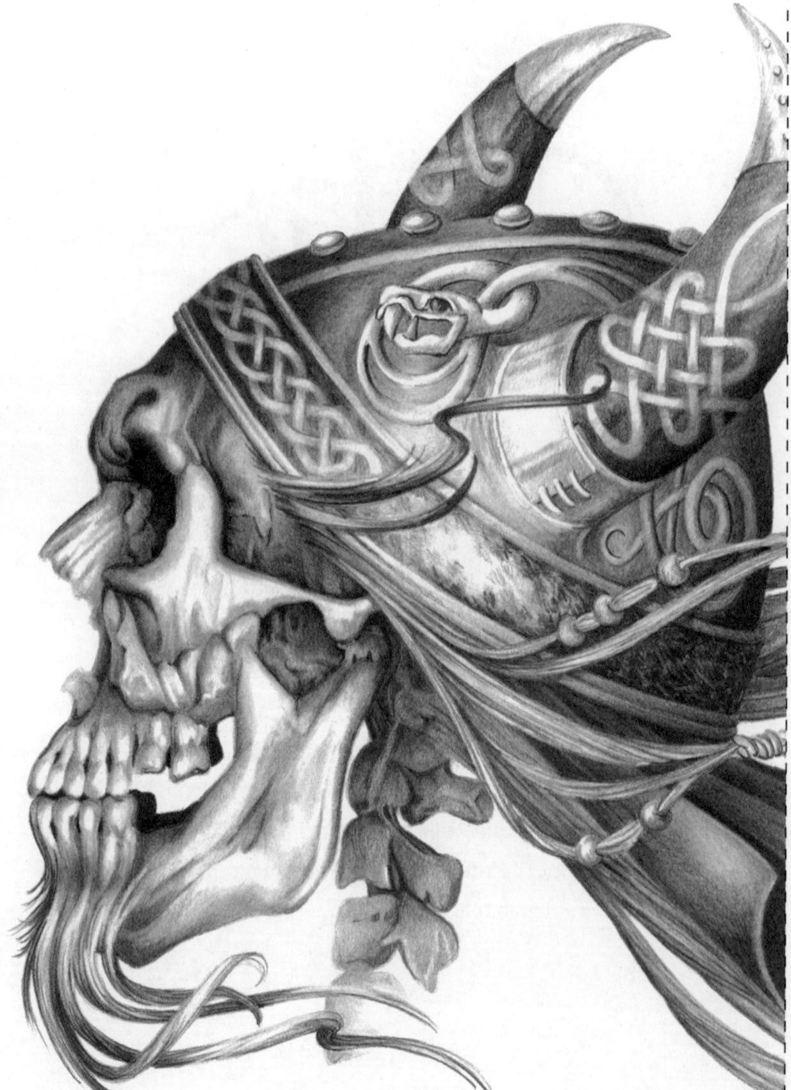

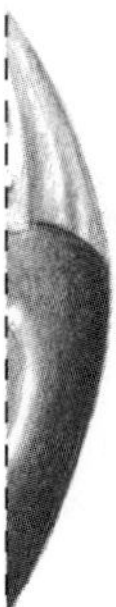

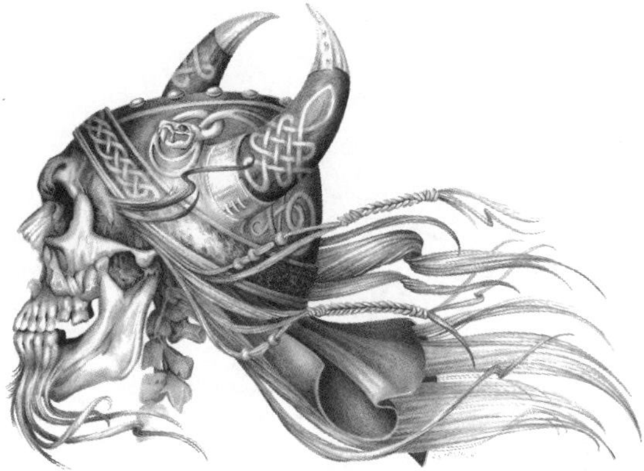

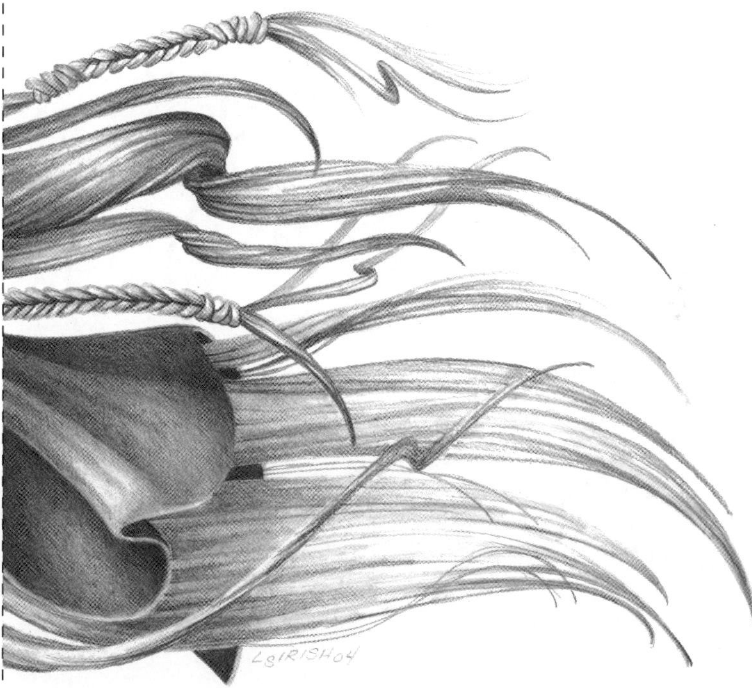
LSIRISH04

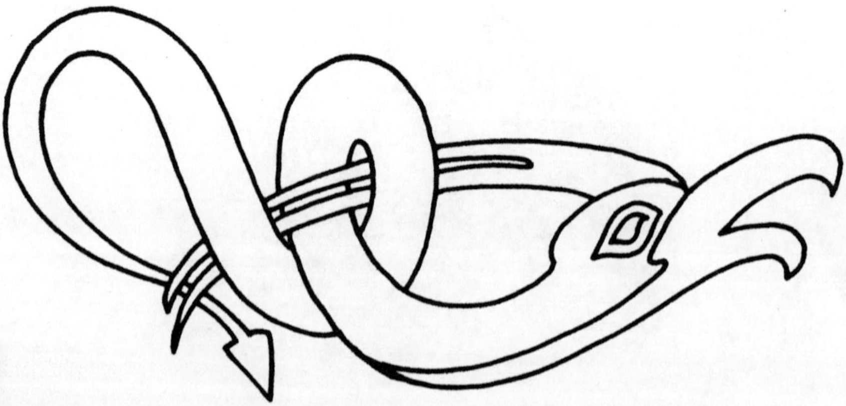

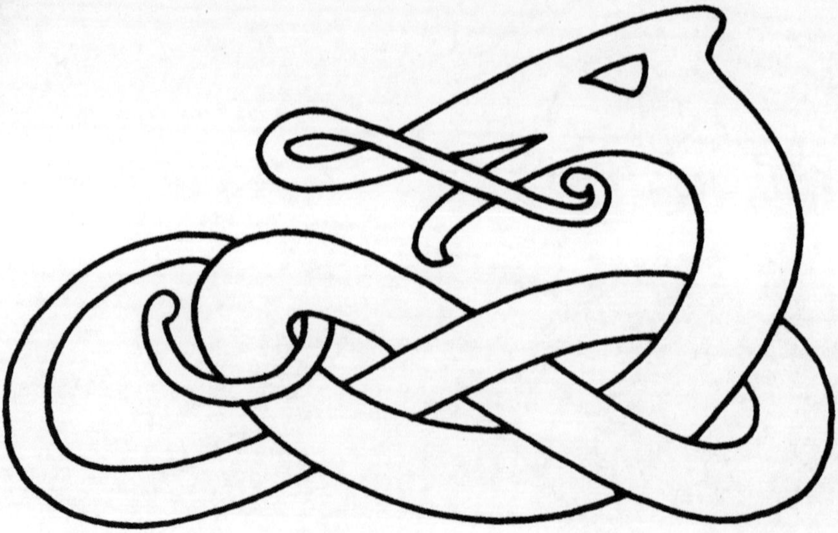

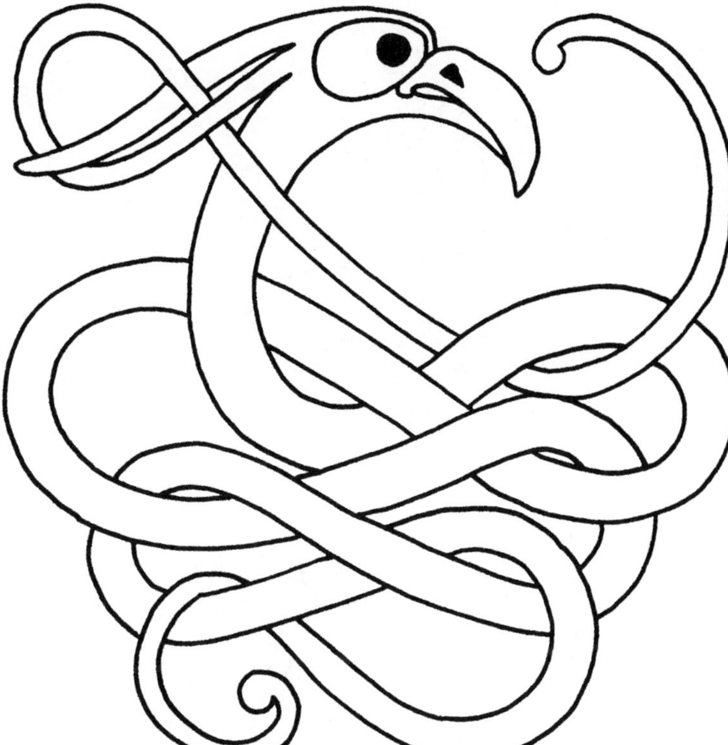

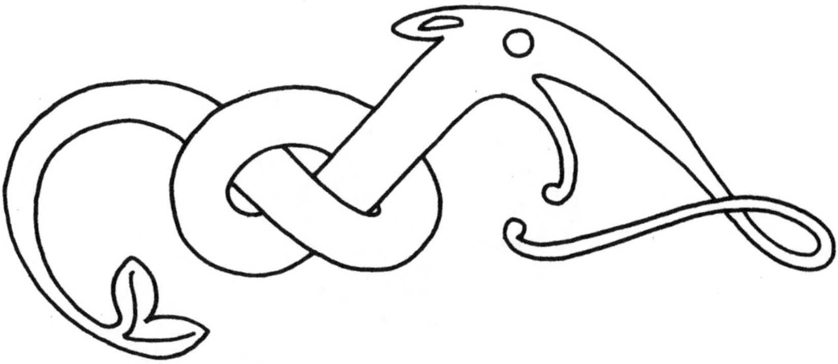

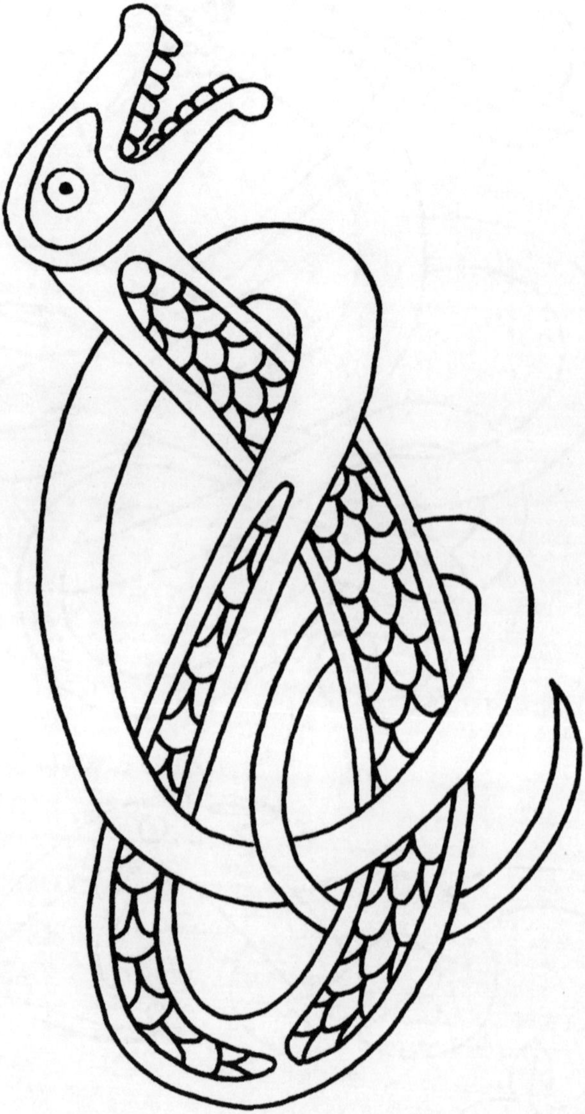

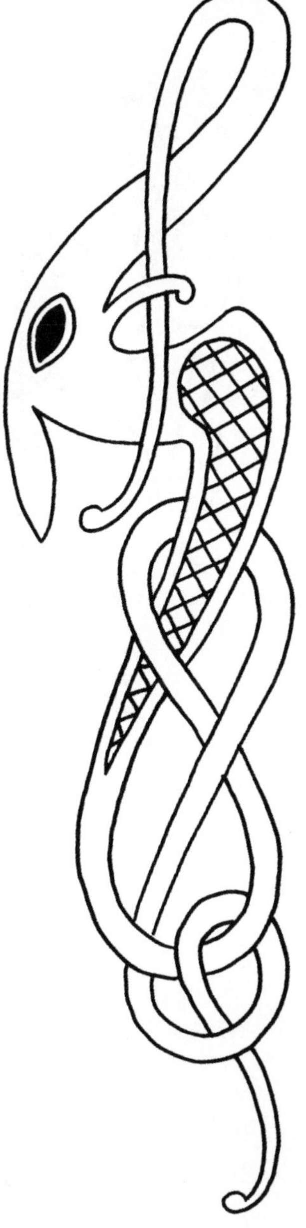

Celtic

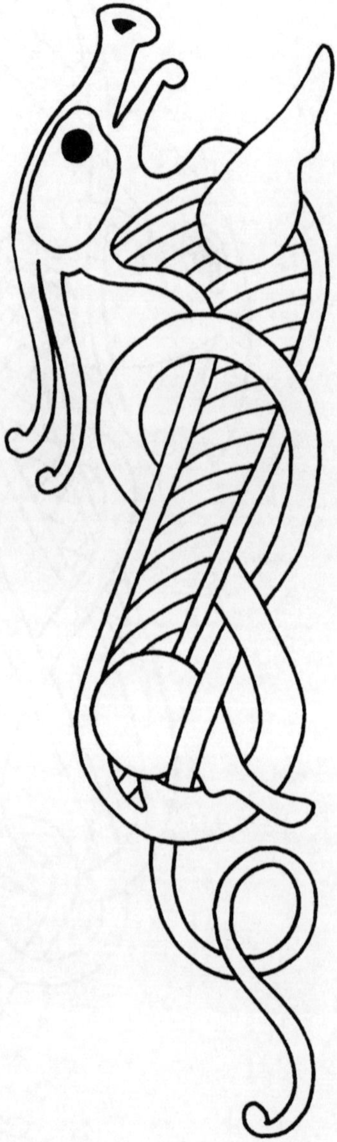

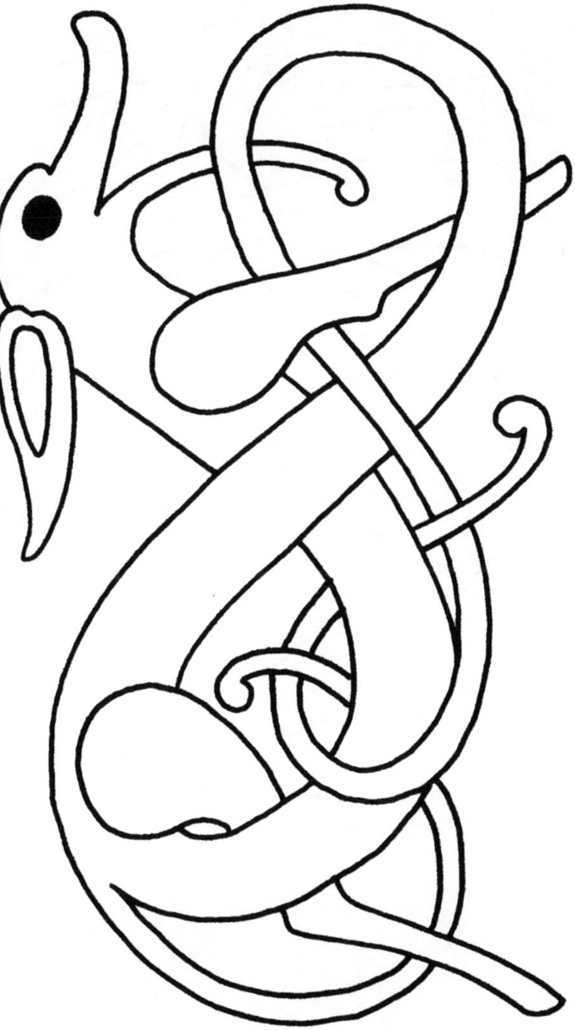

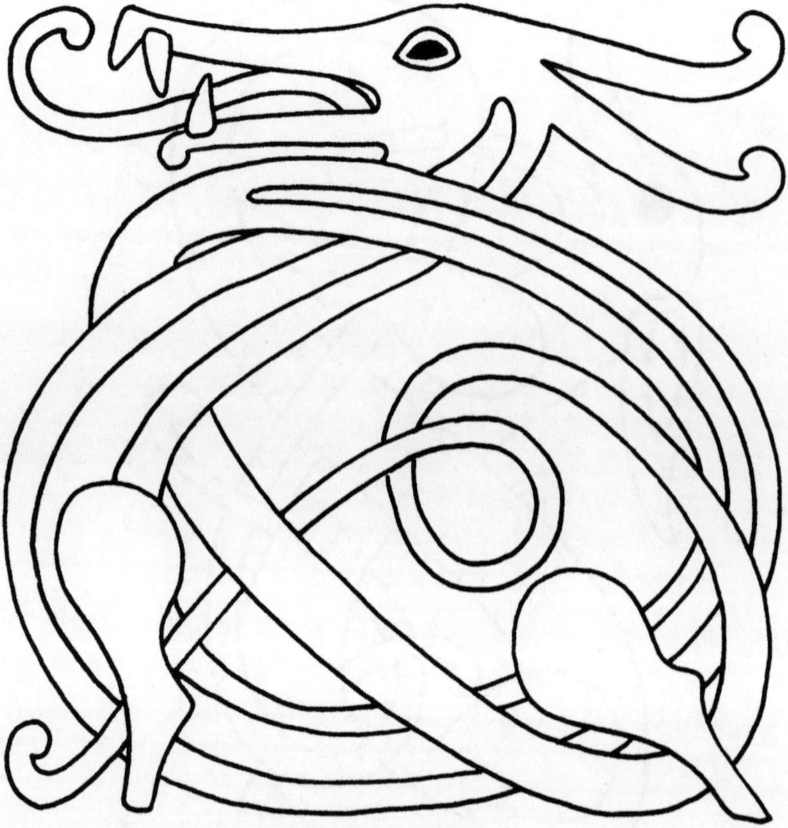

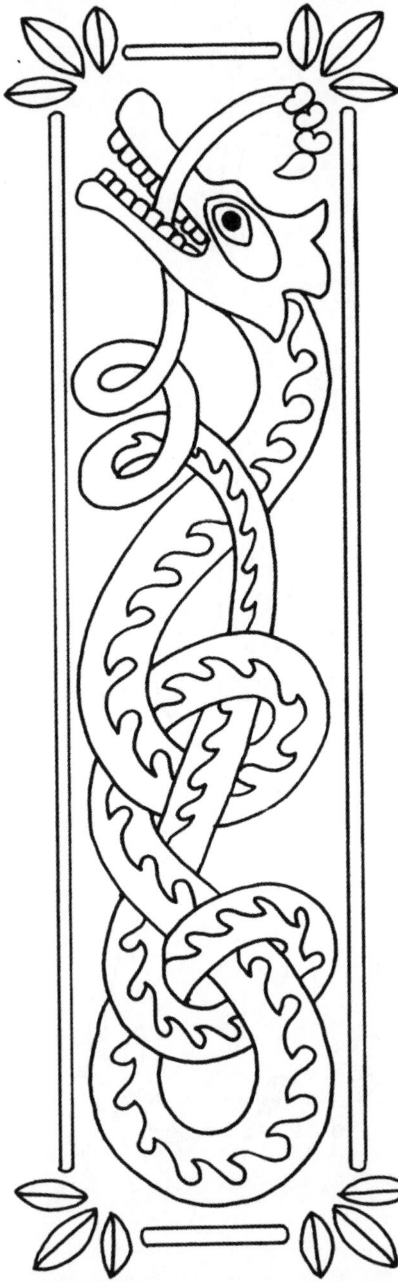

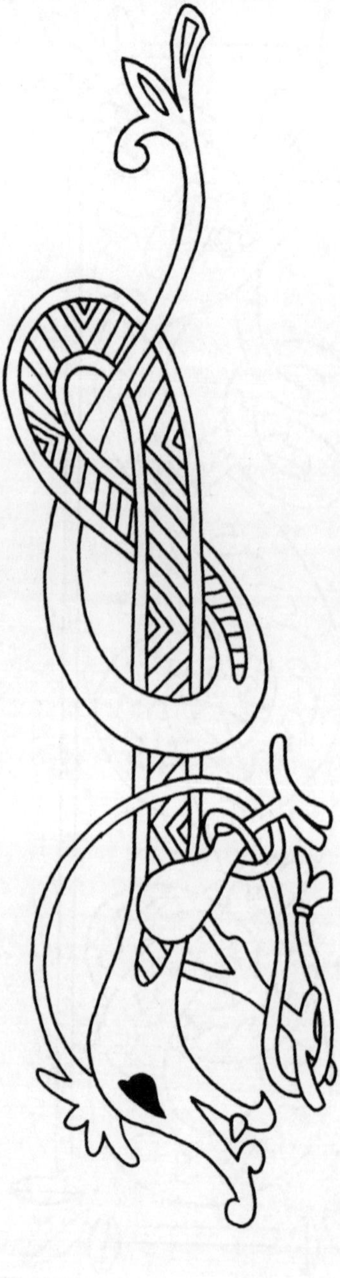

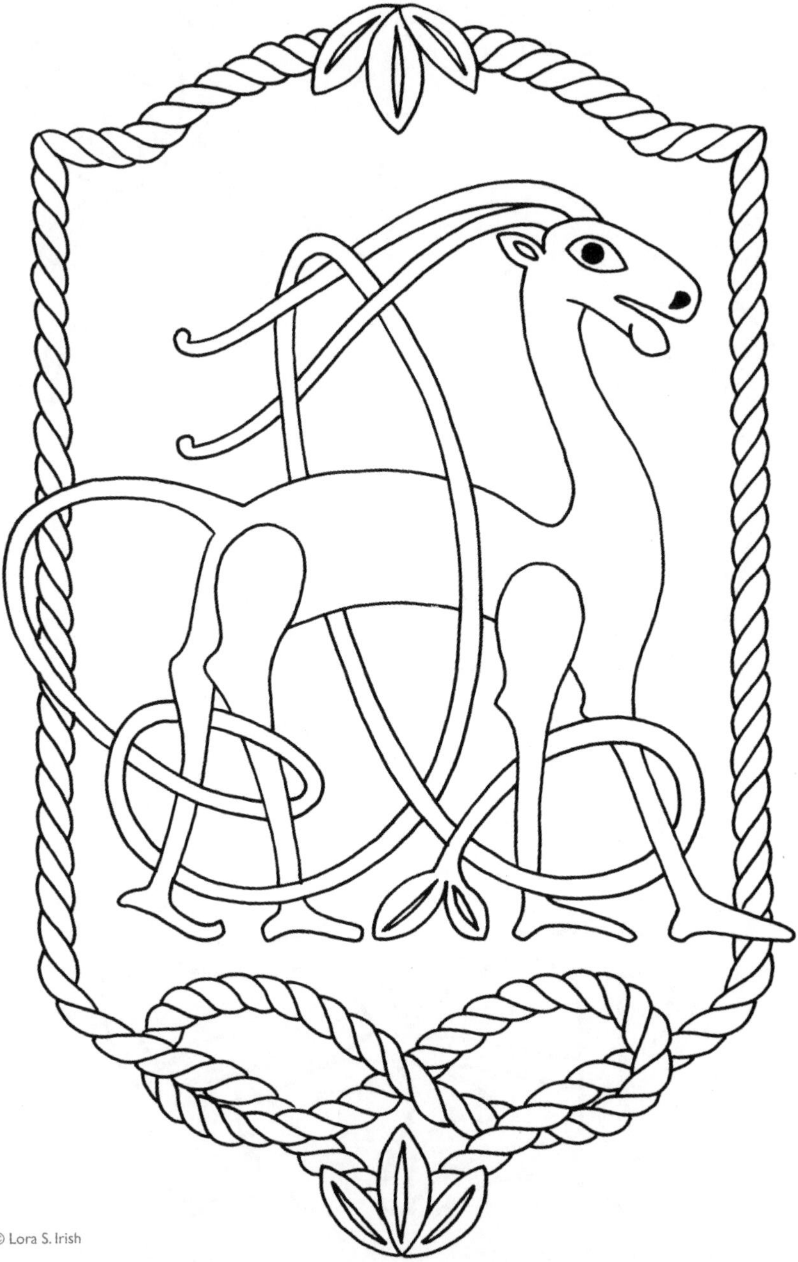

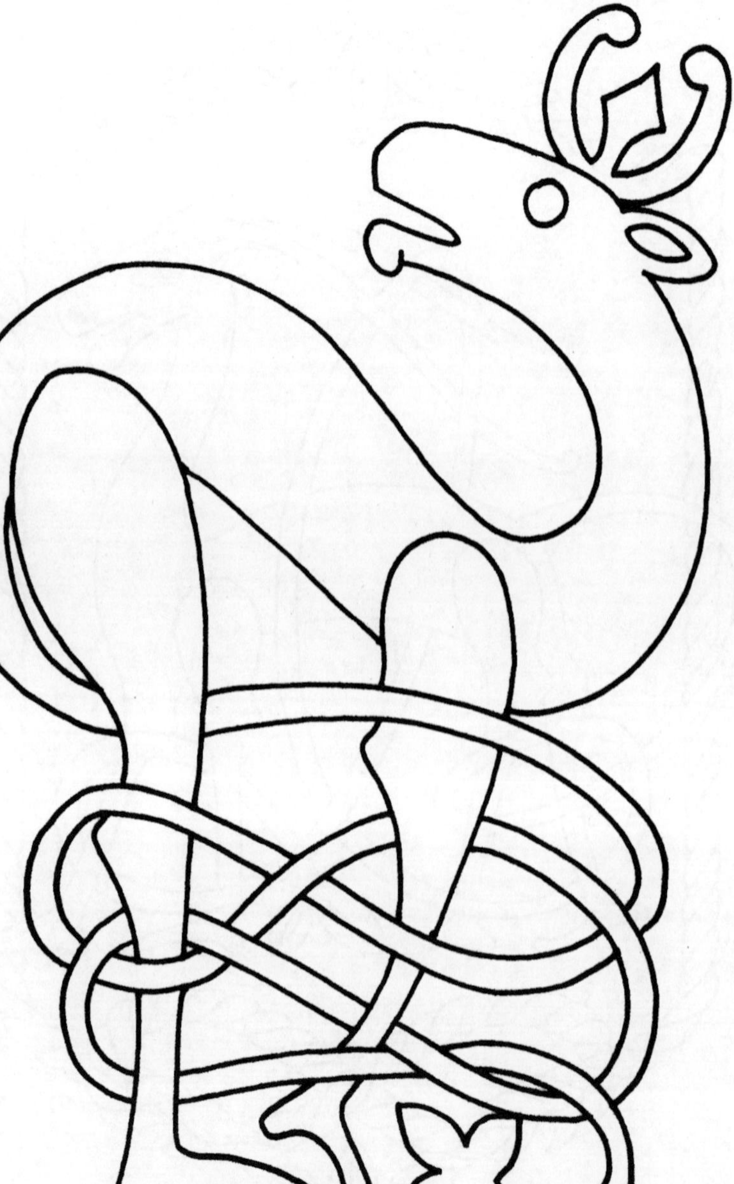

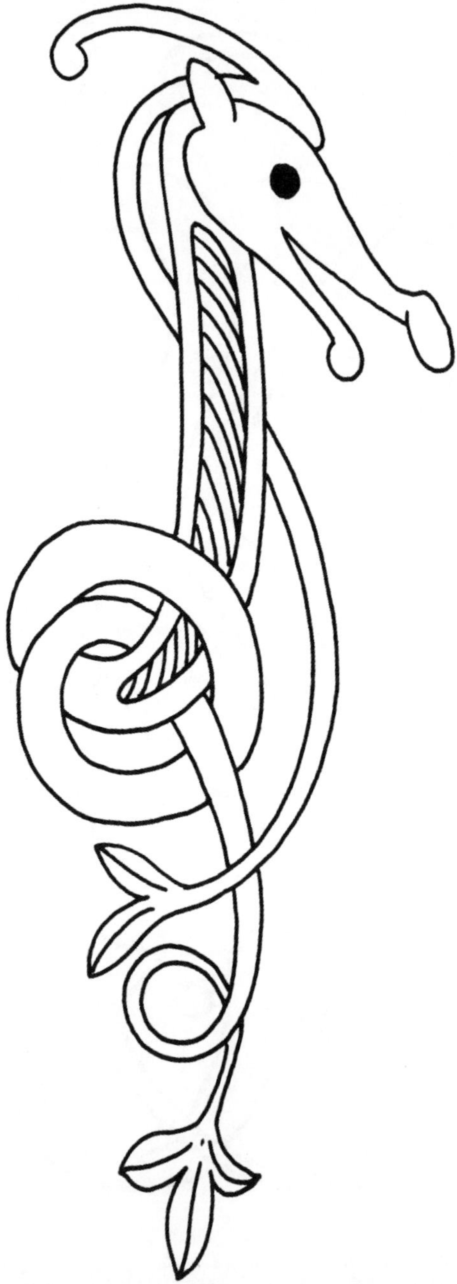

Celtic

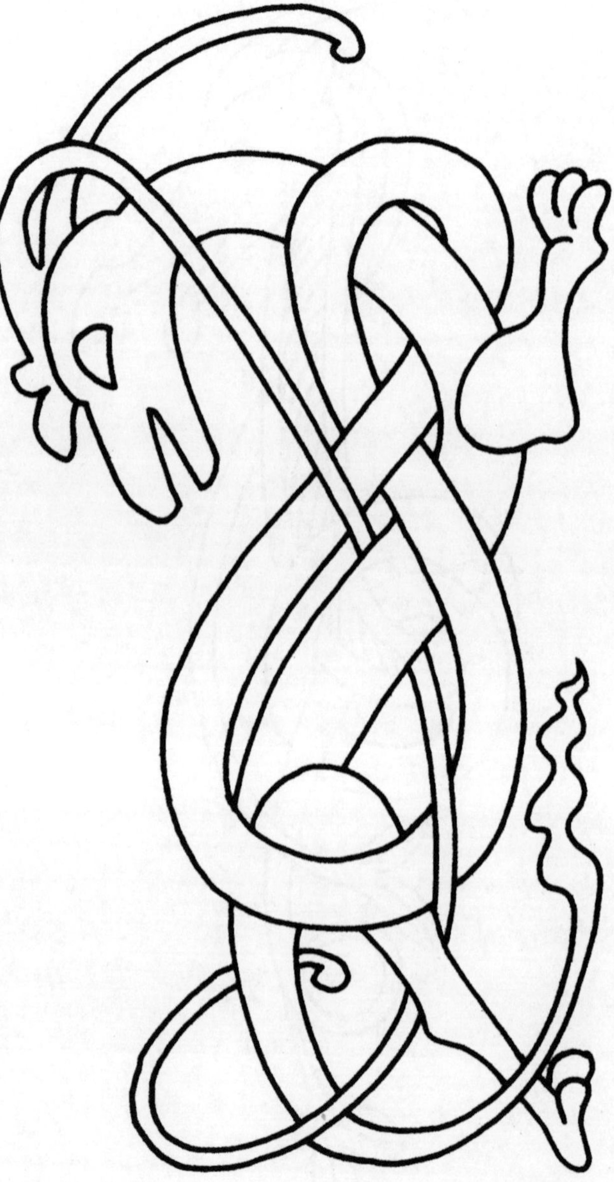

© Lora S. Irish

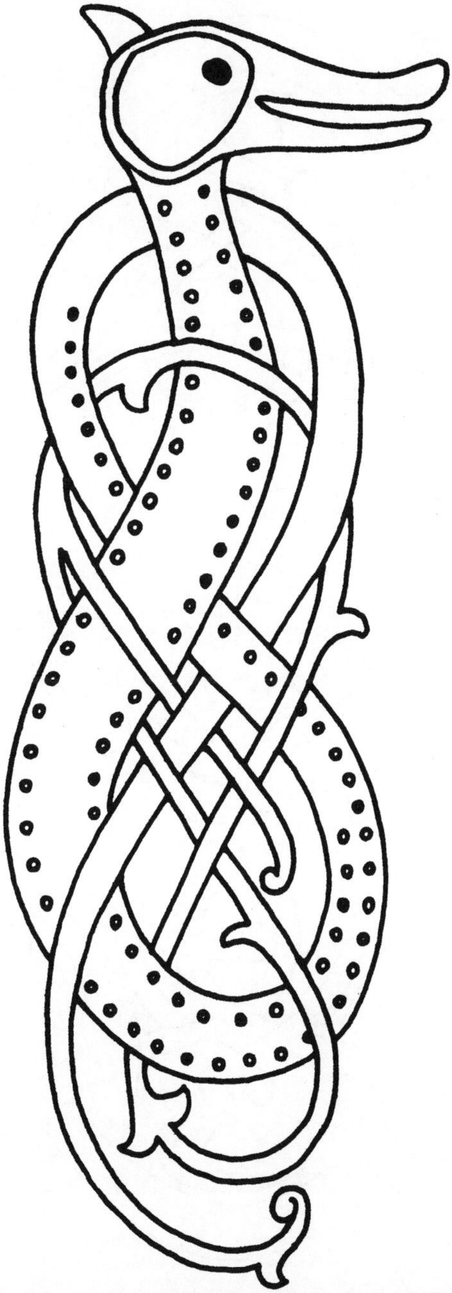

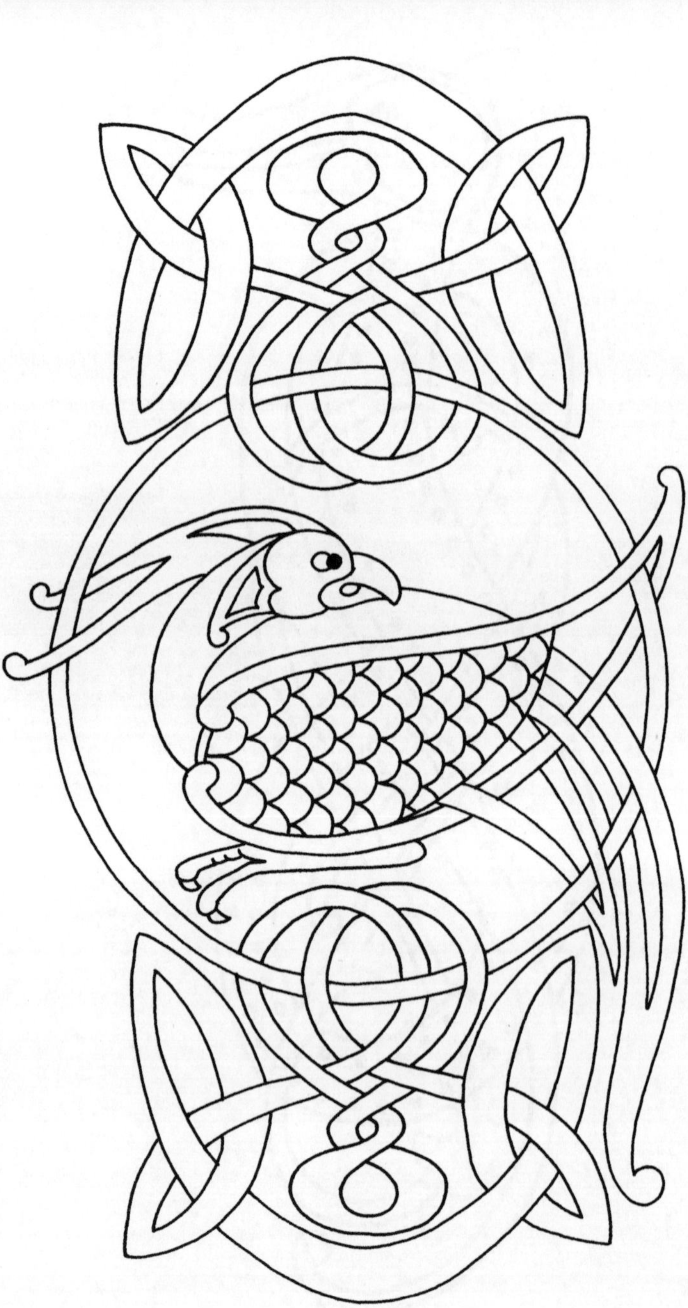

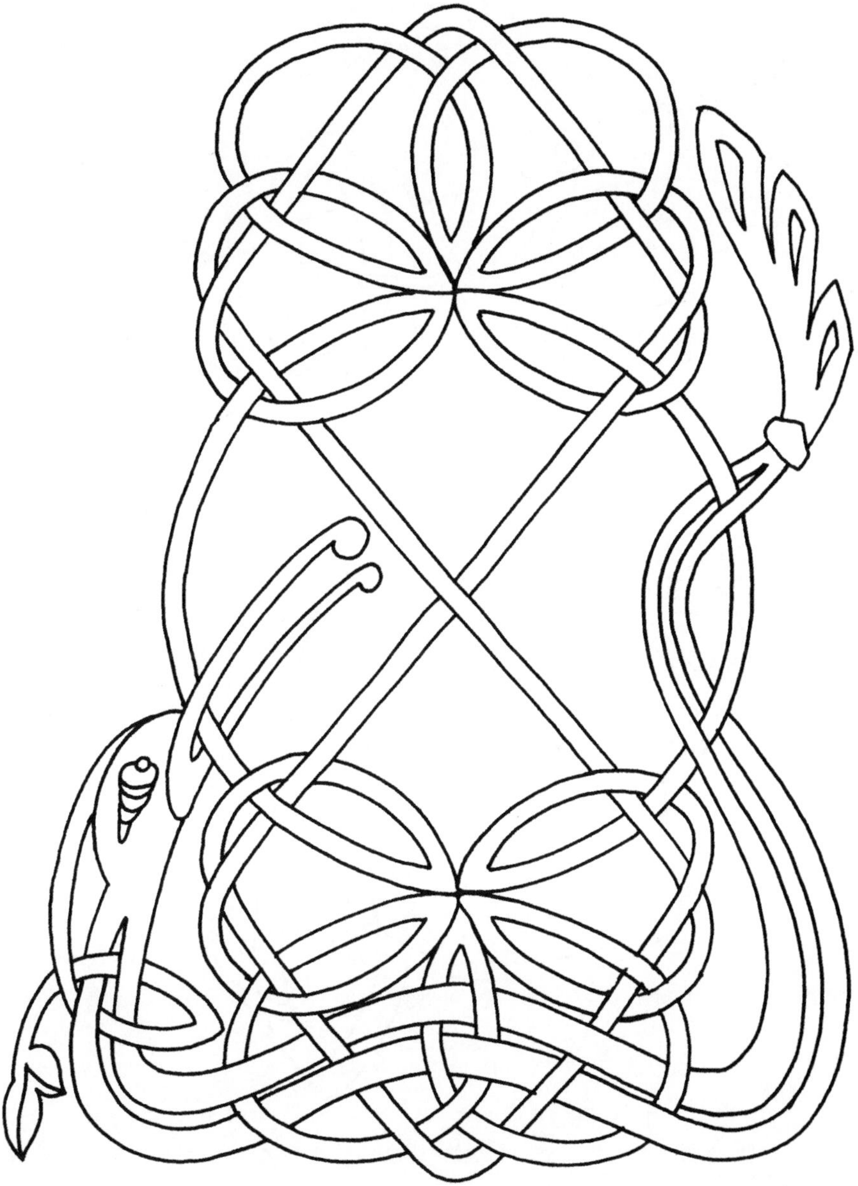

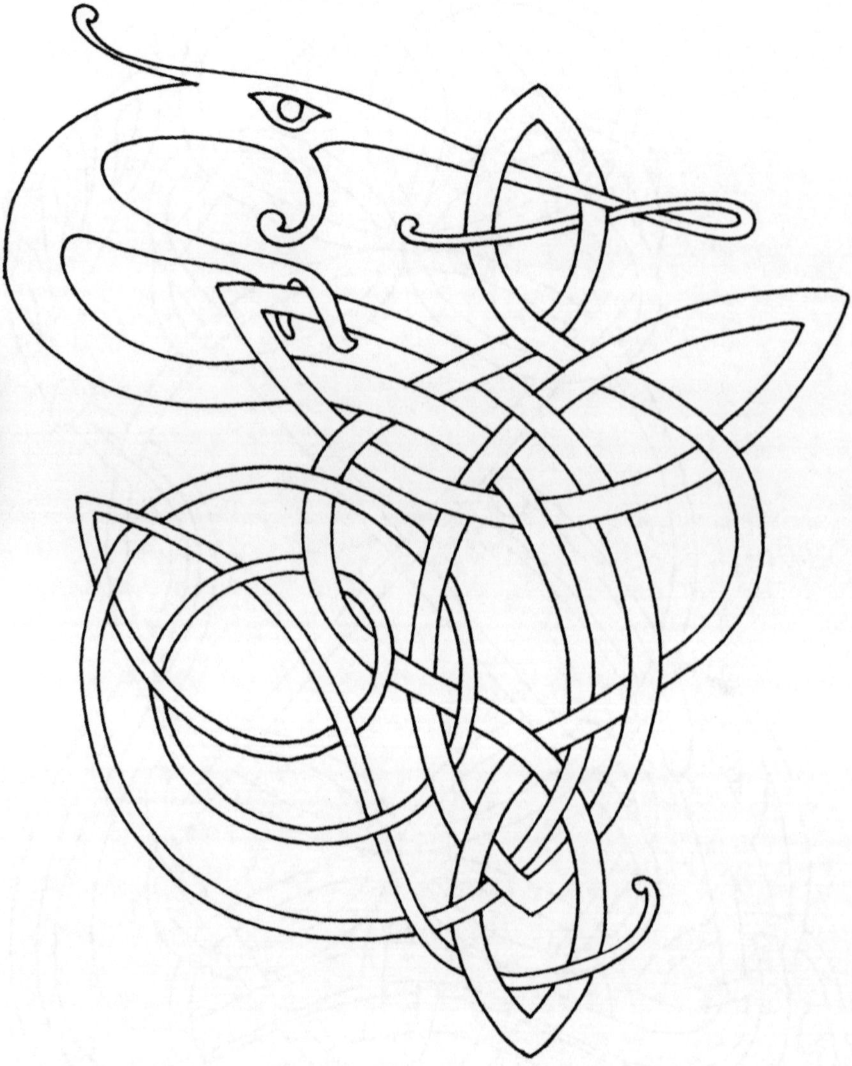

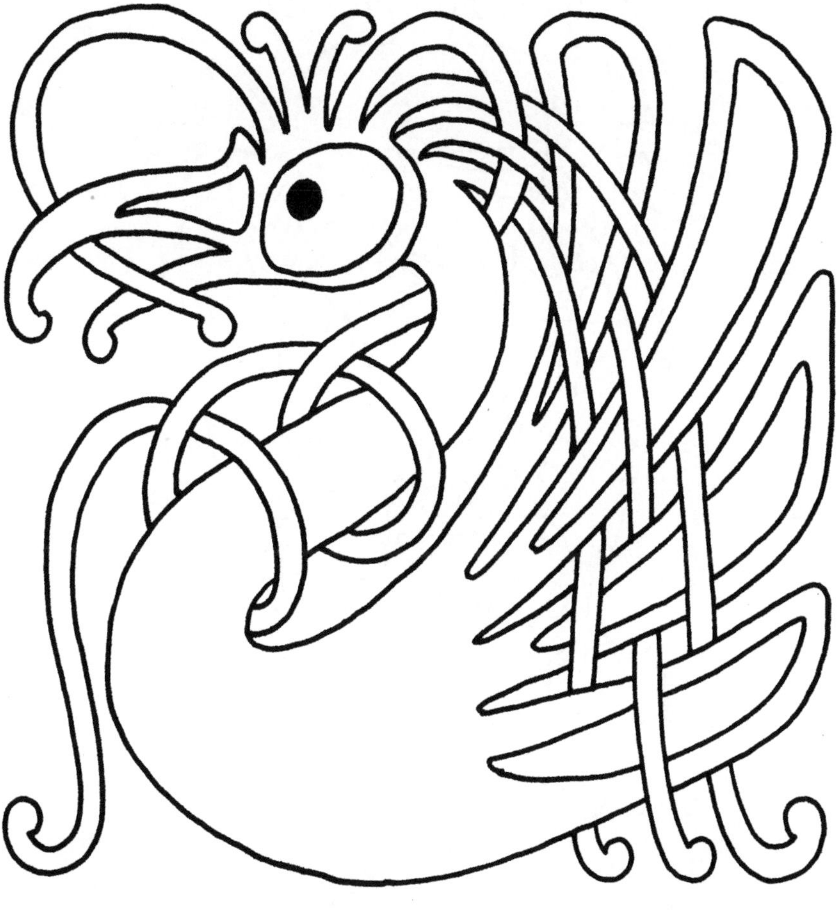

Celtic

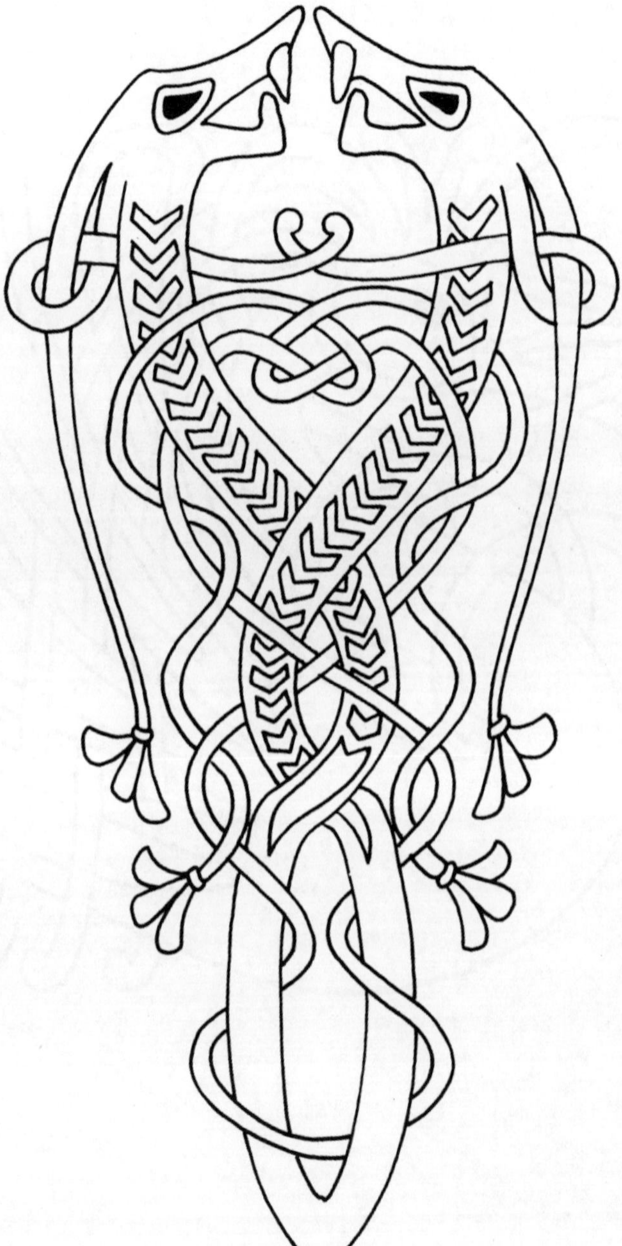

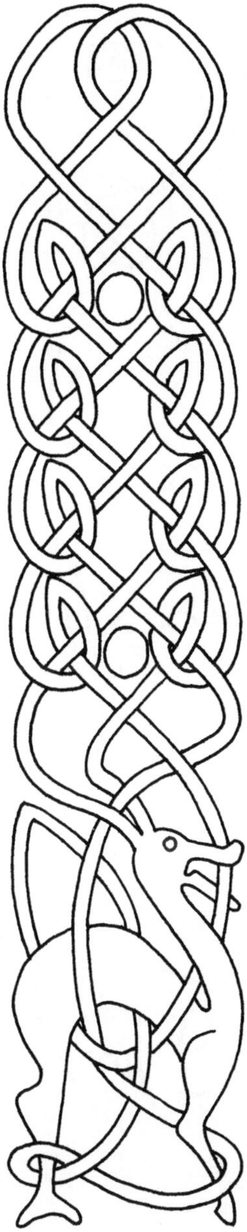

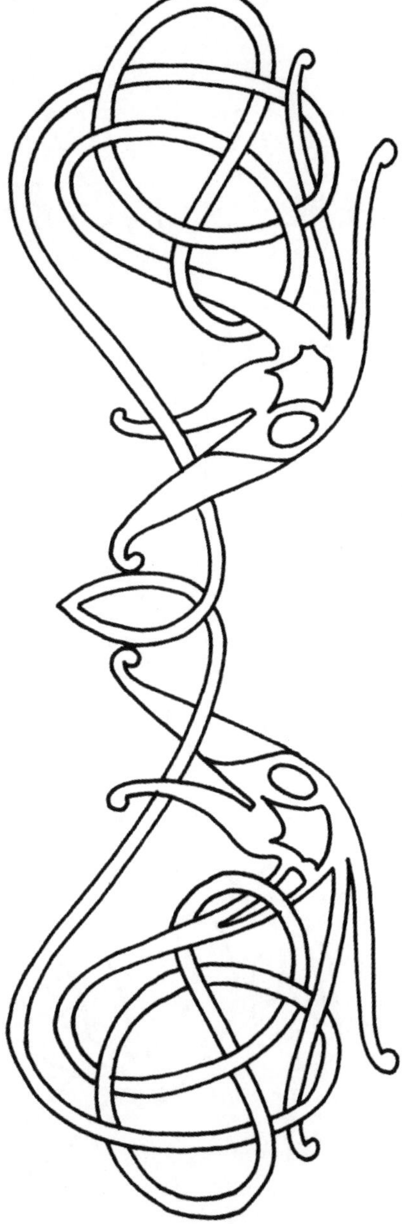

Celtic

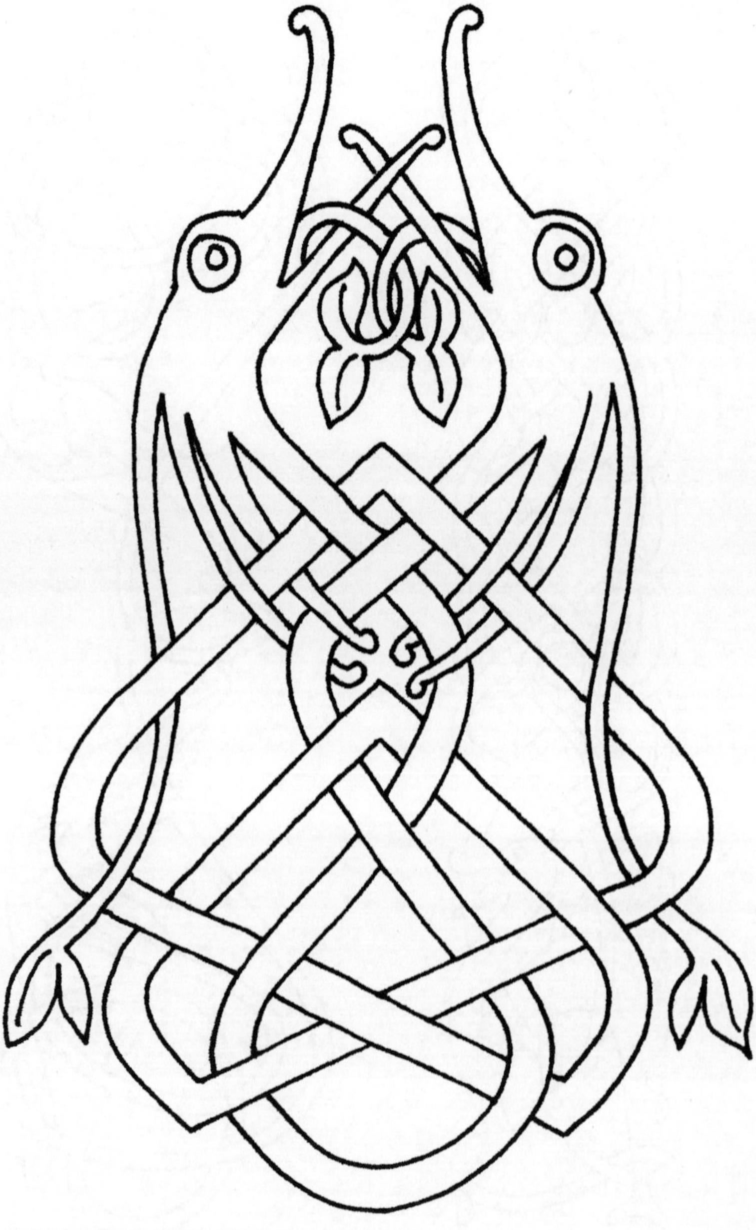

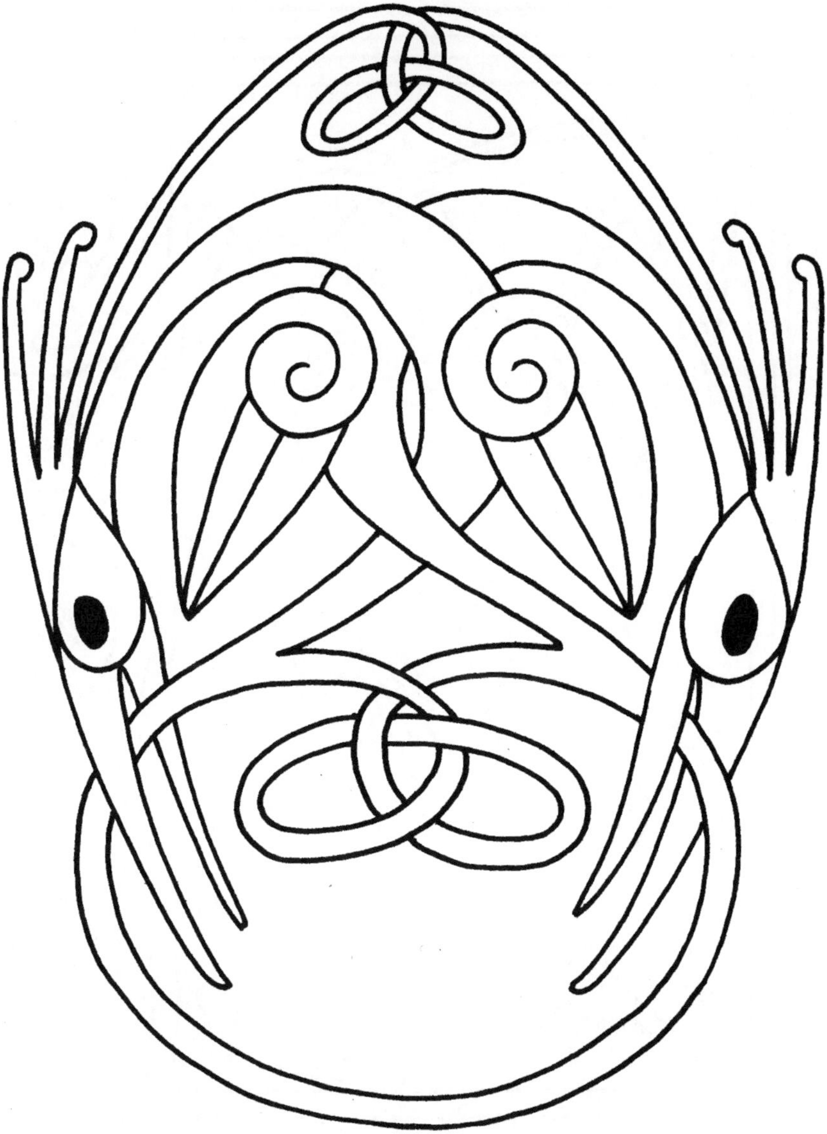

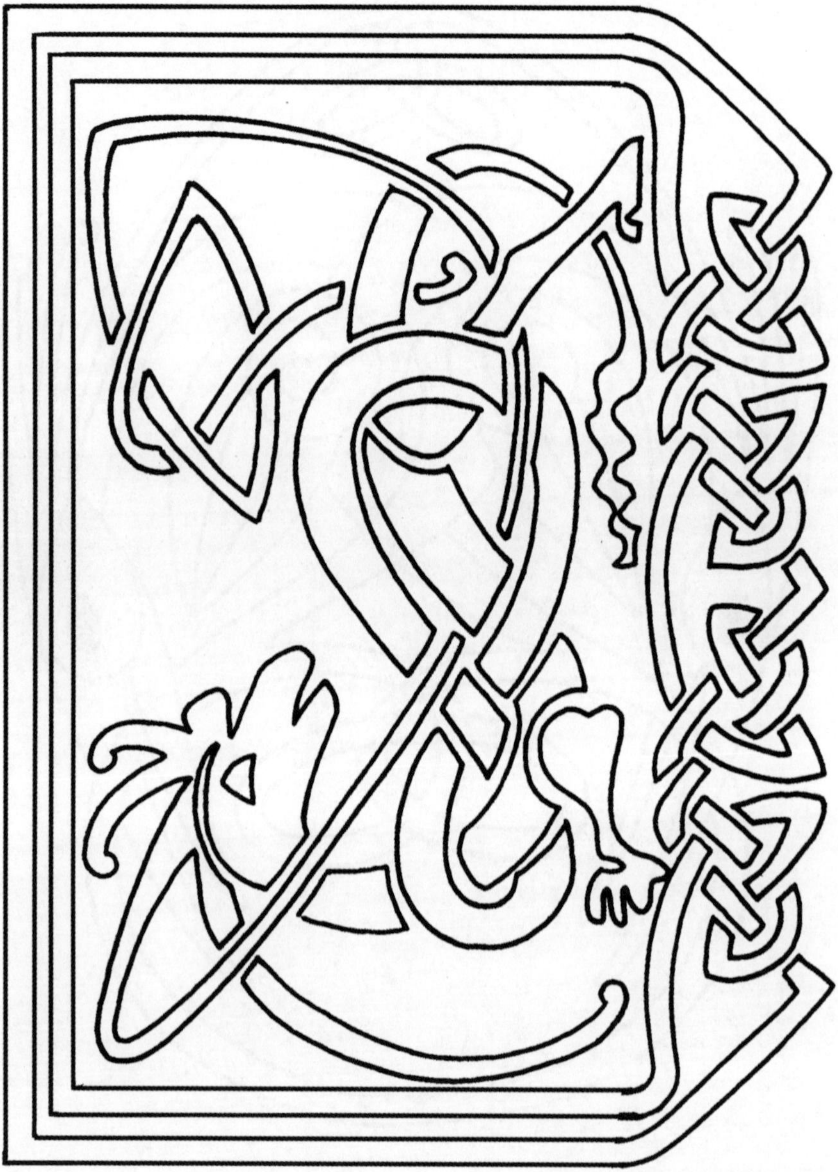

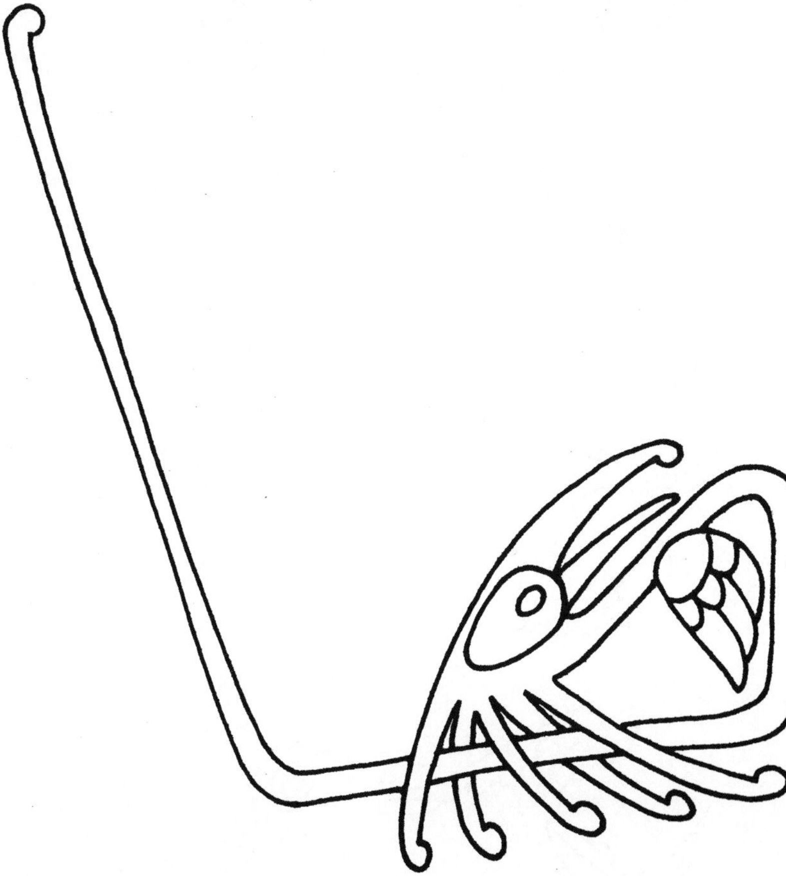

Celtic

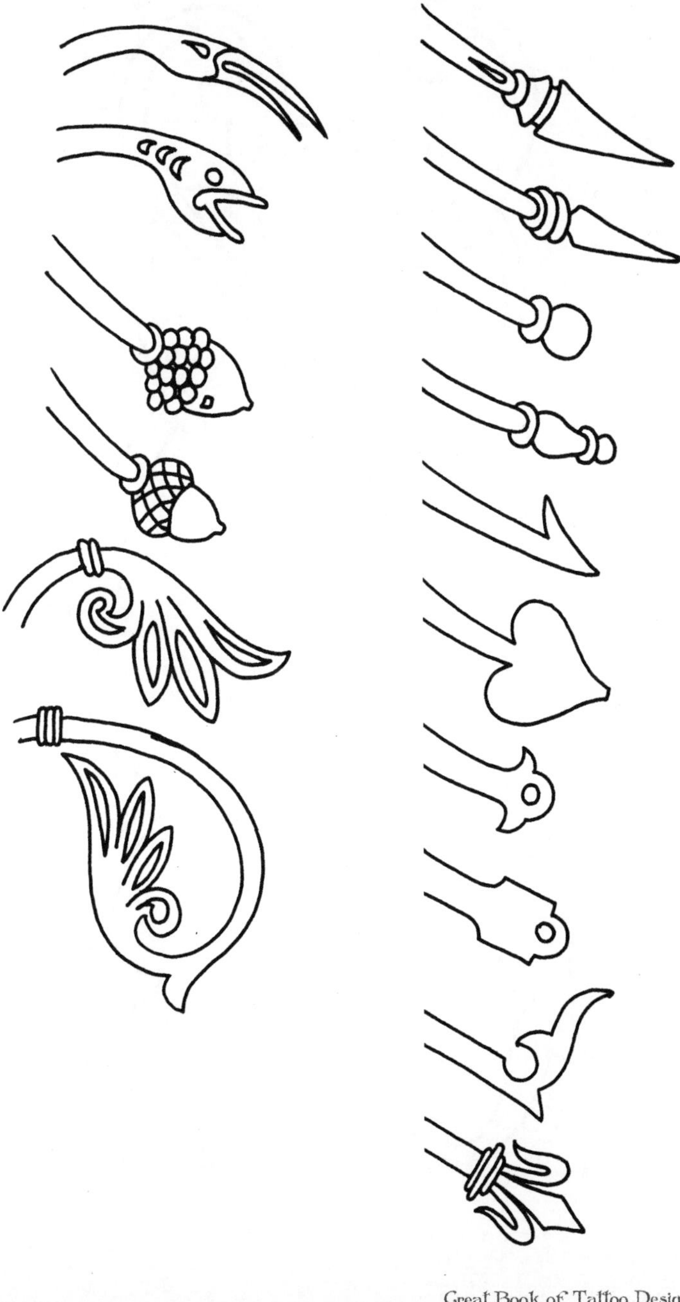

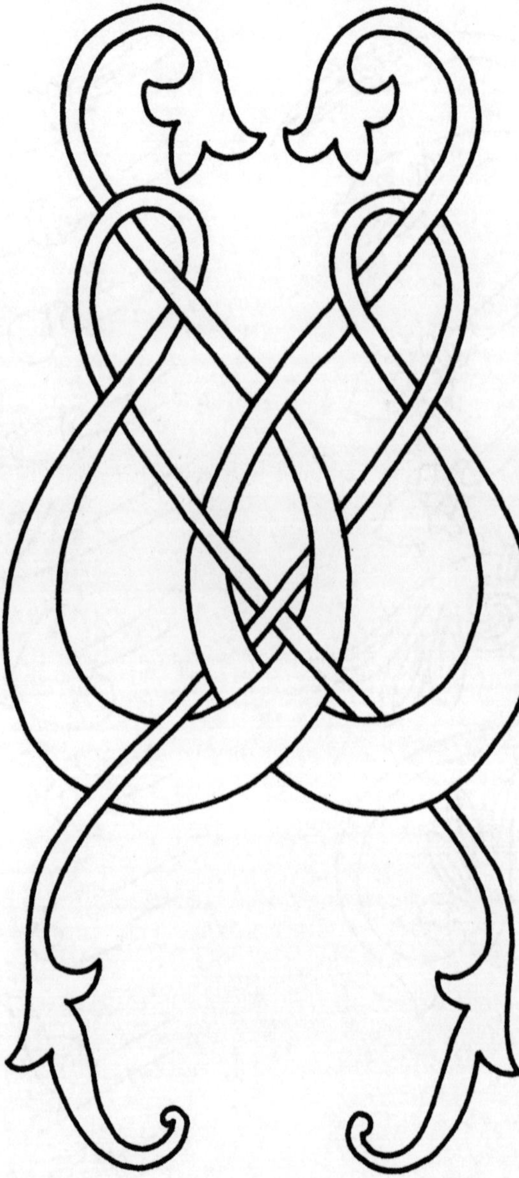

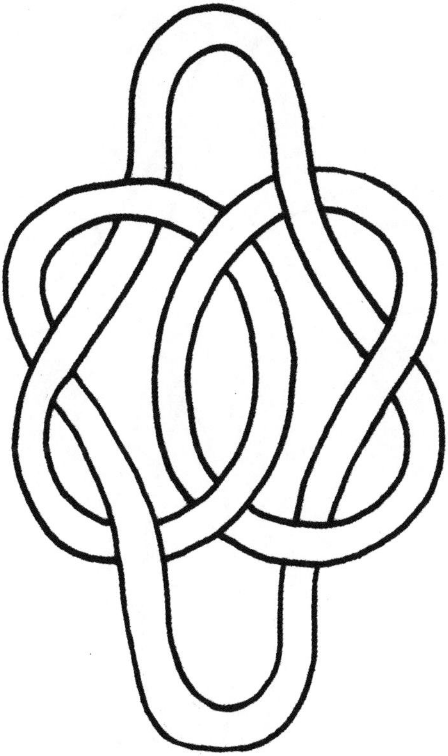

Celtic

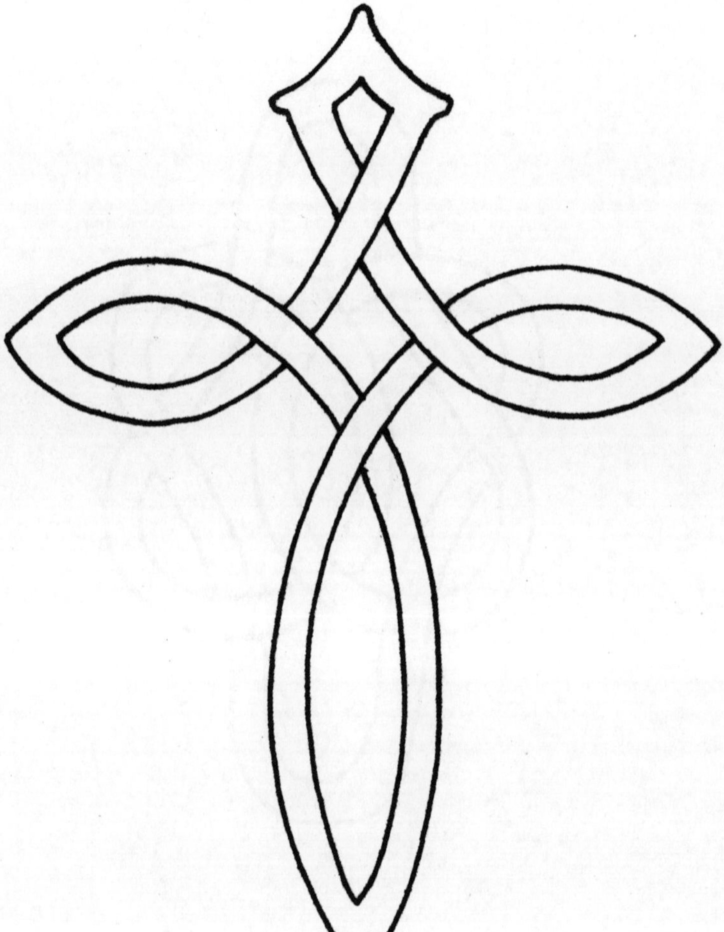

© Lora S. Irish

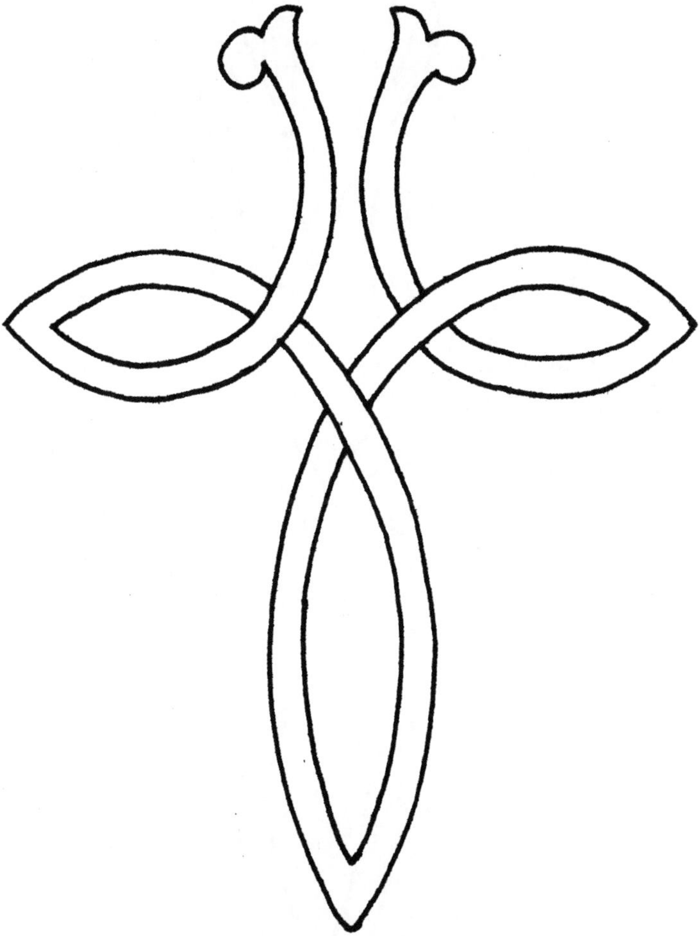

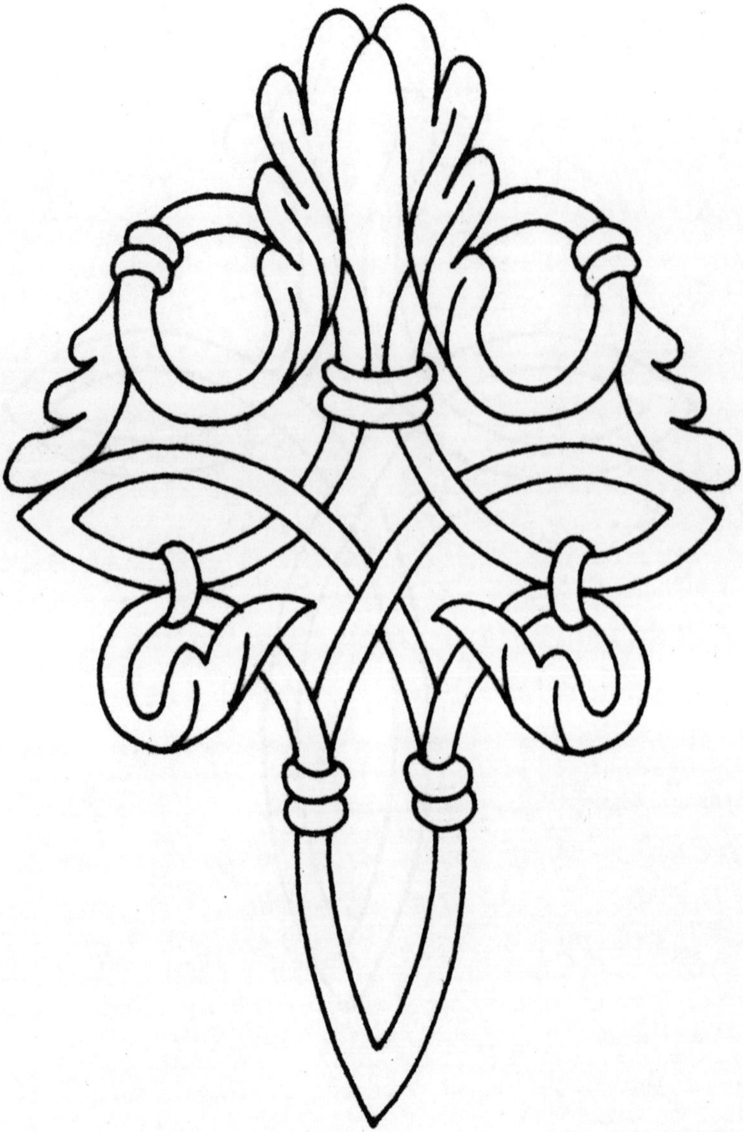

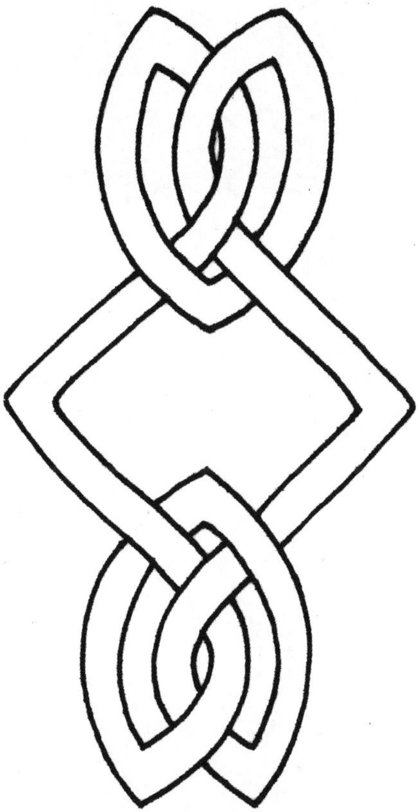

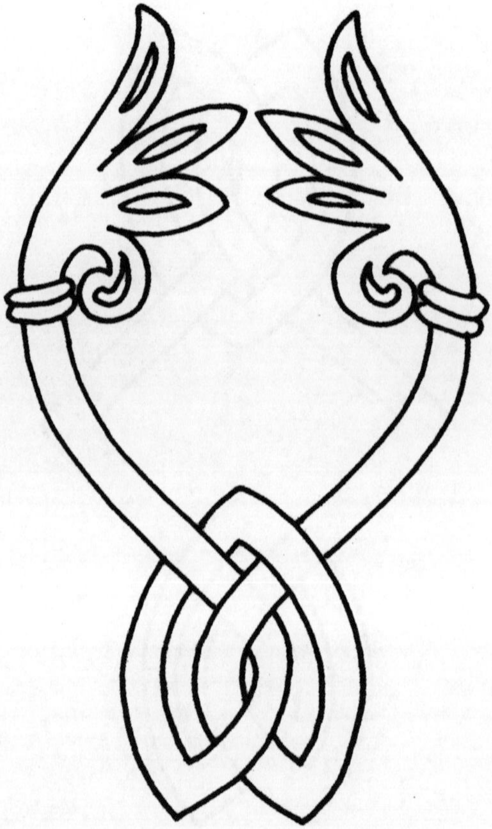

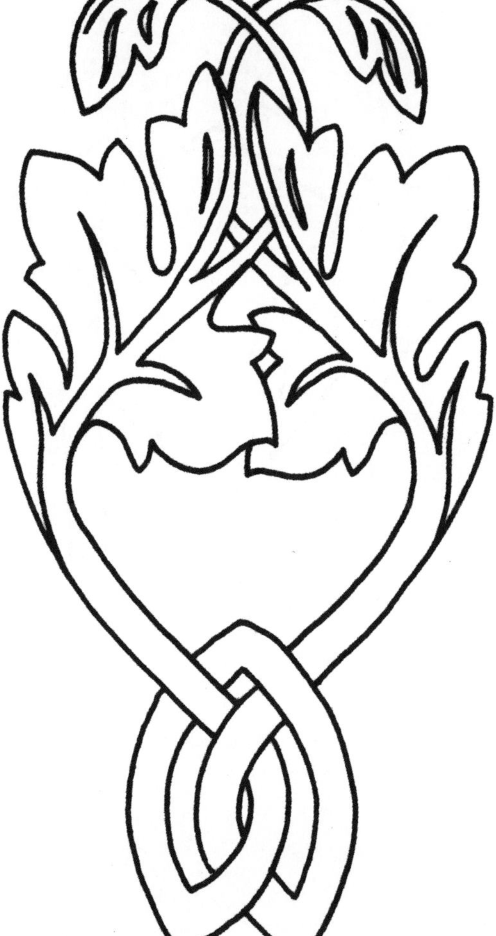

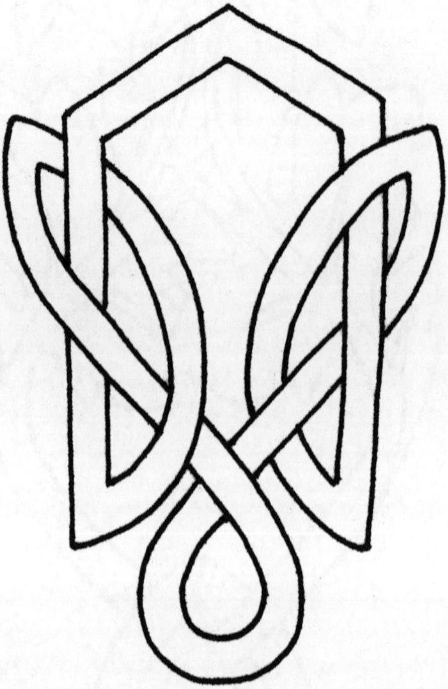

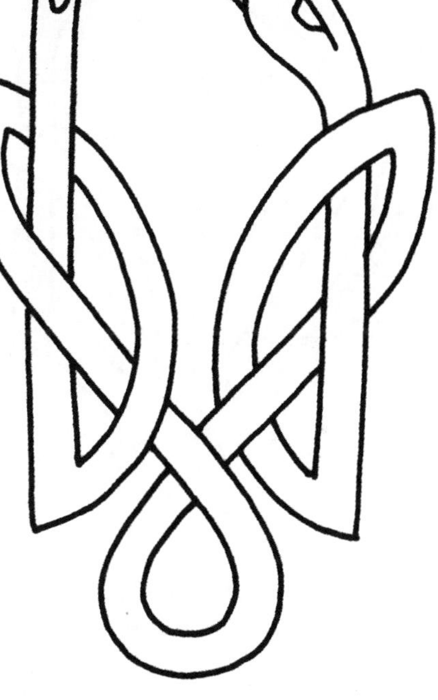

Celtic

© Lora S. Irish

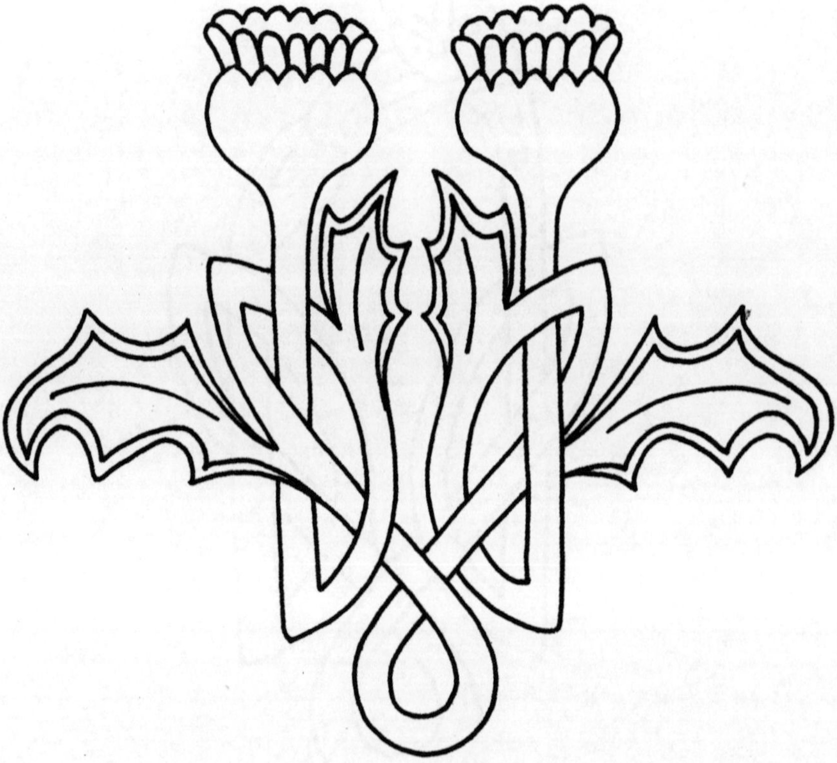

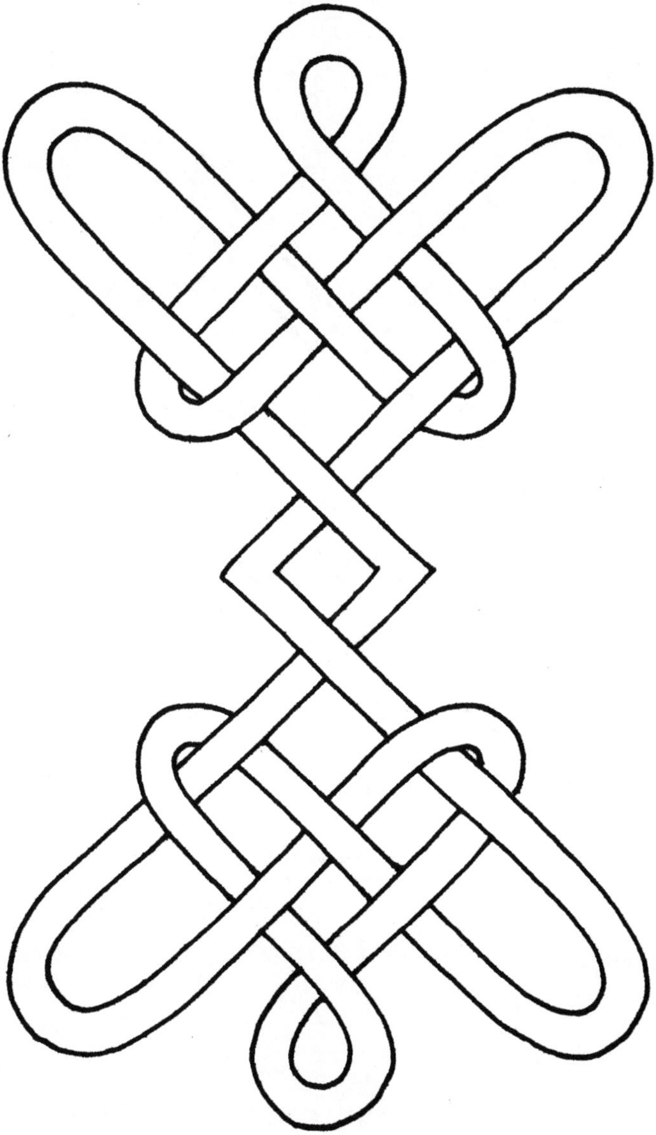

Celtic

Celtic

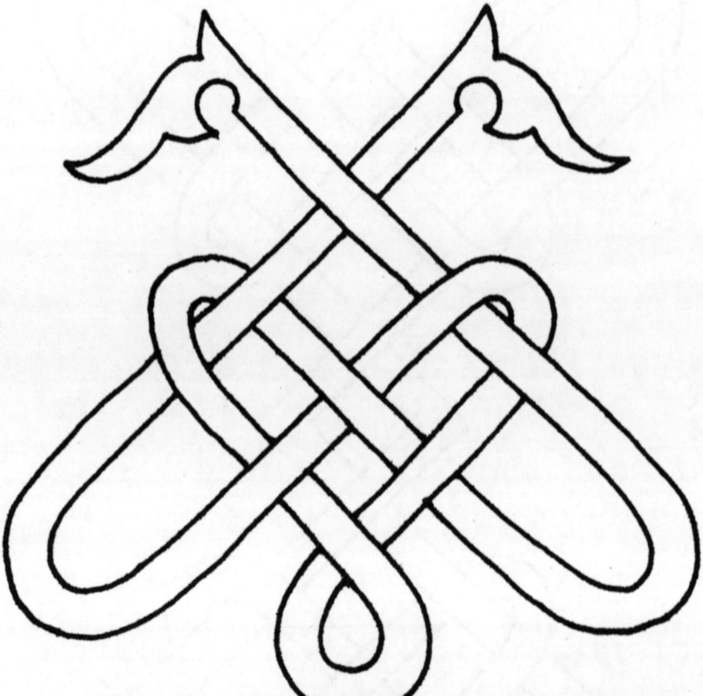

© Lora S. Irish

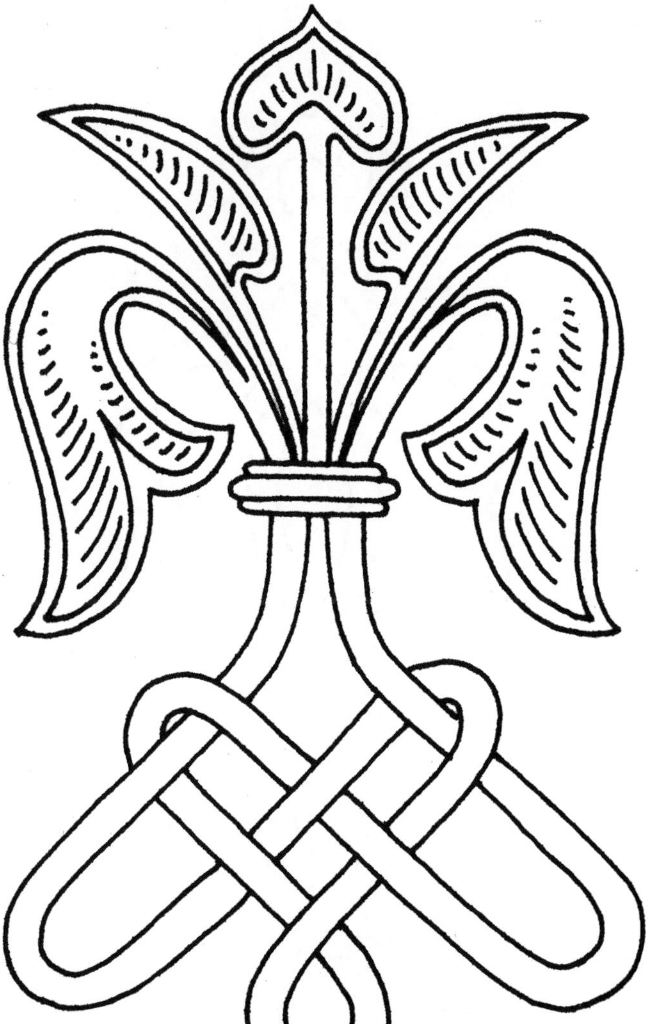

Celtic

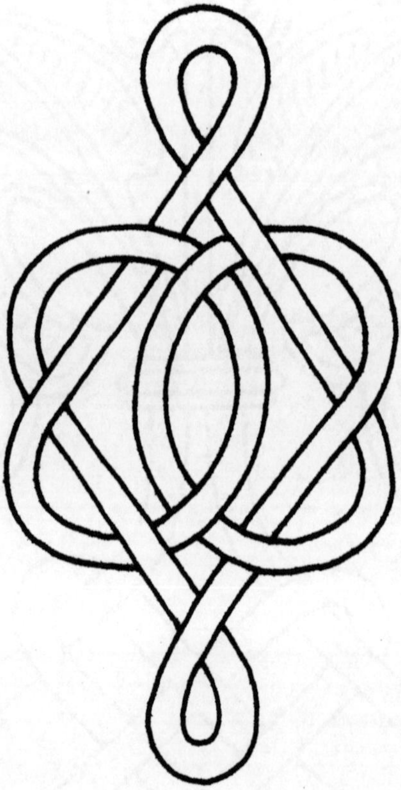

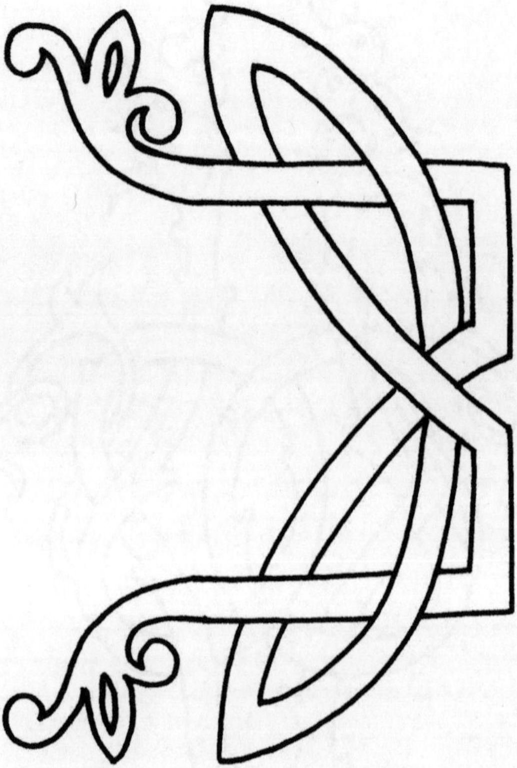

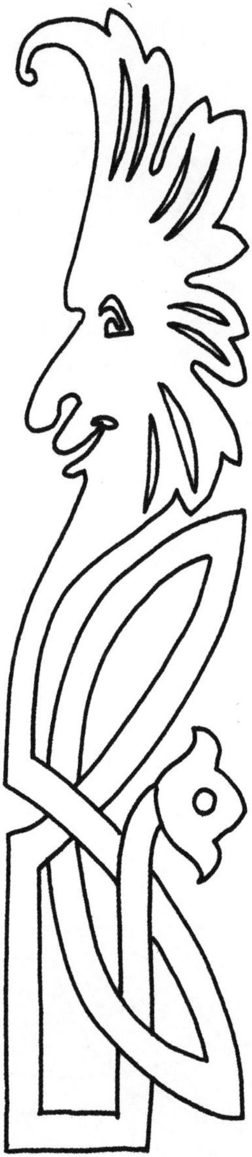

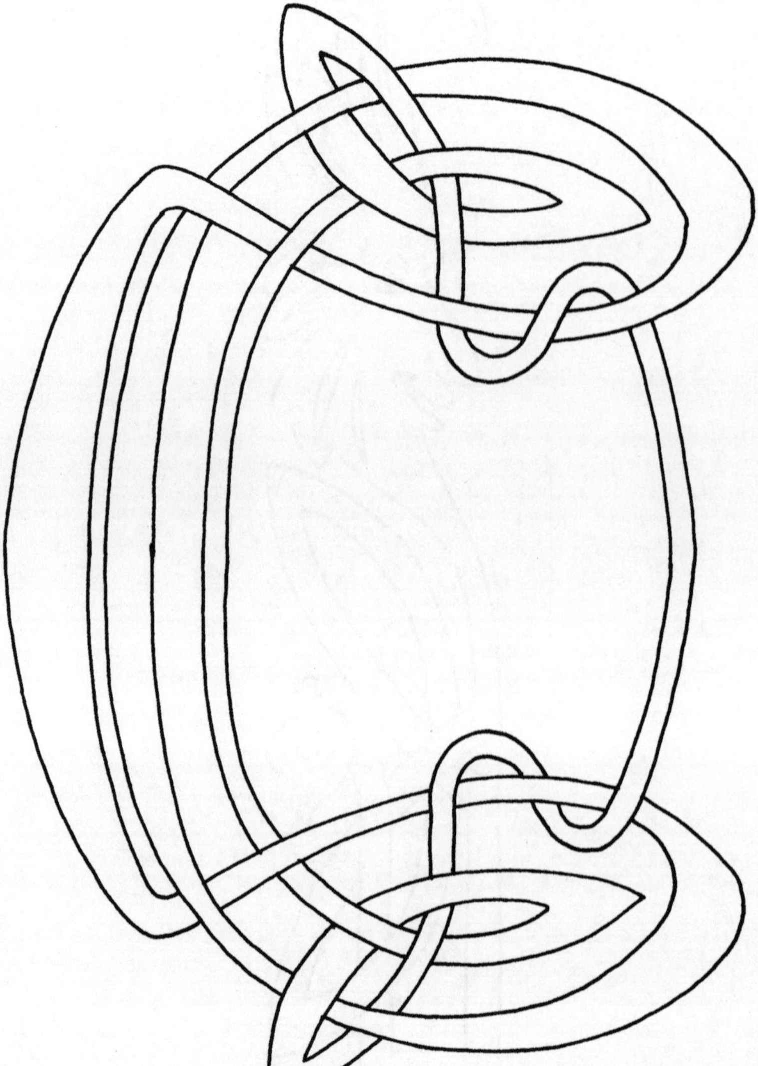

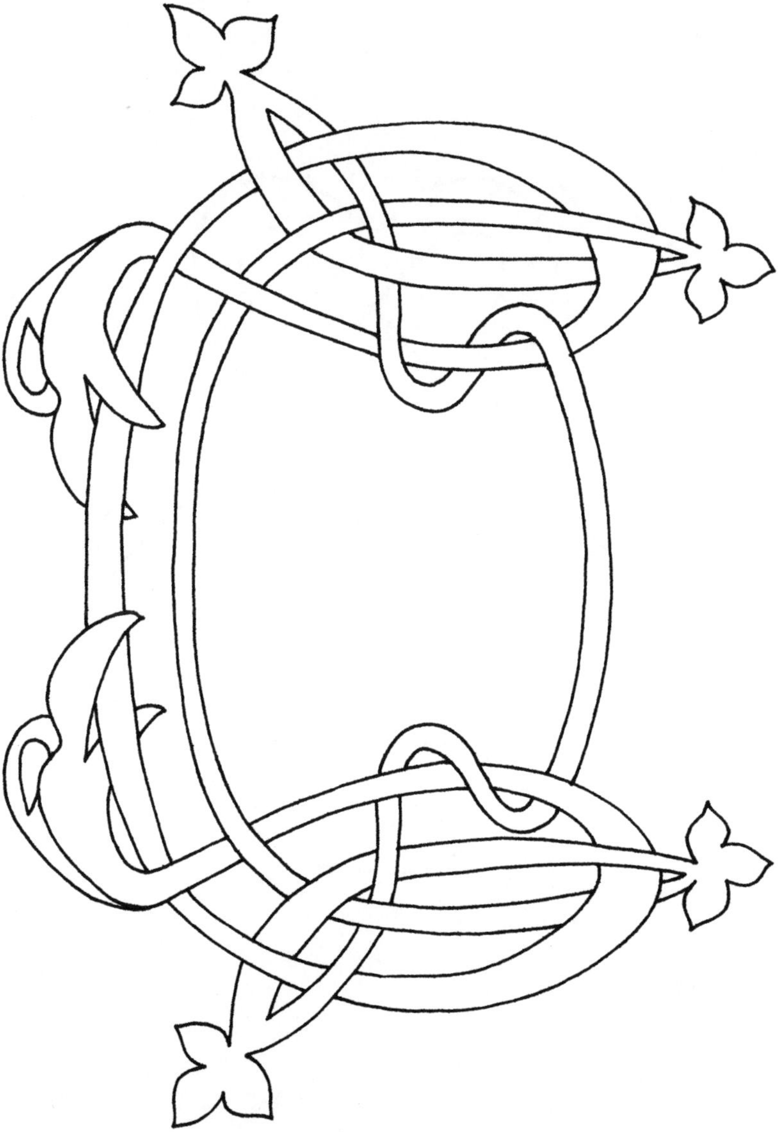

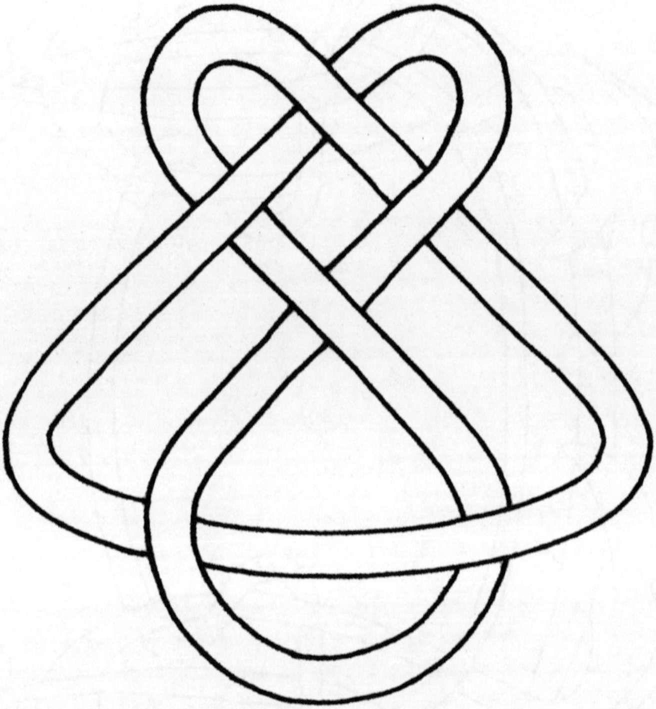

© Lora S. Irish

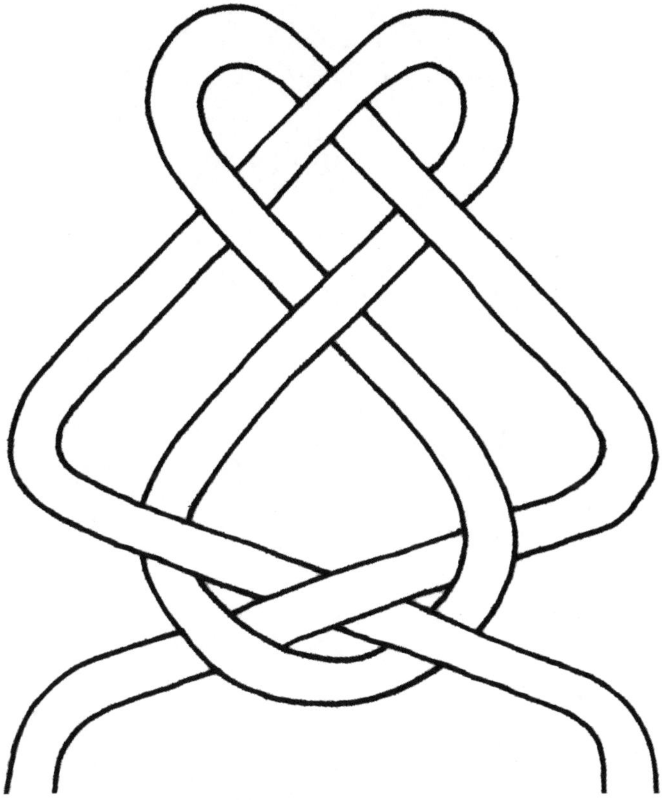

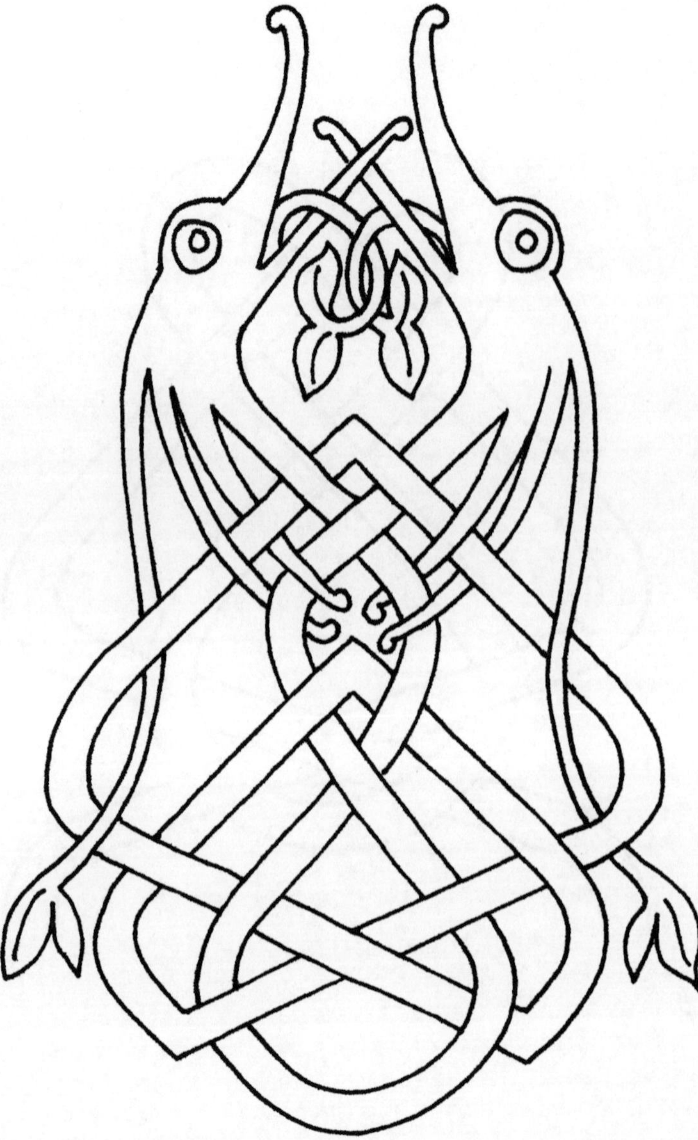

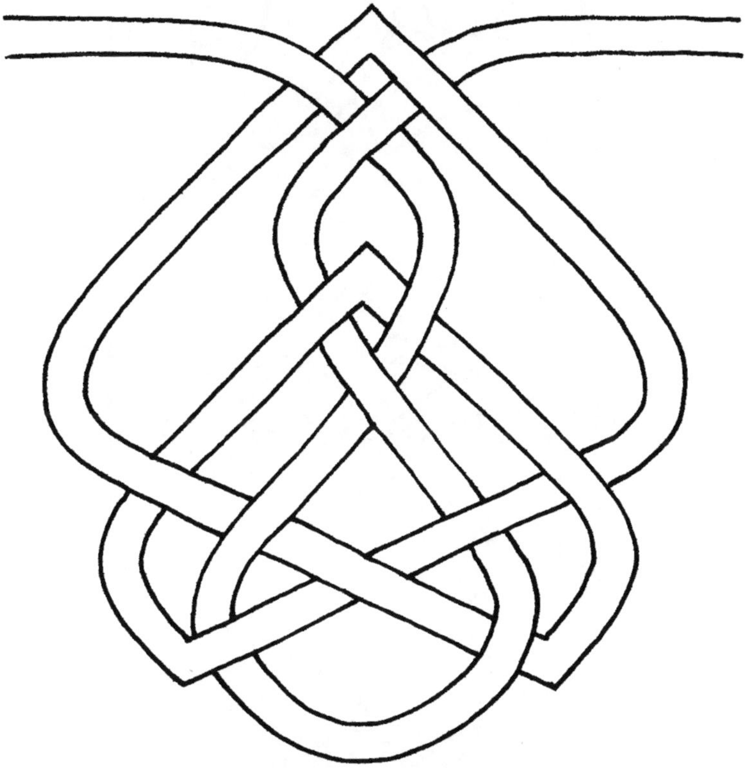

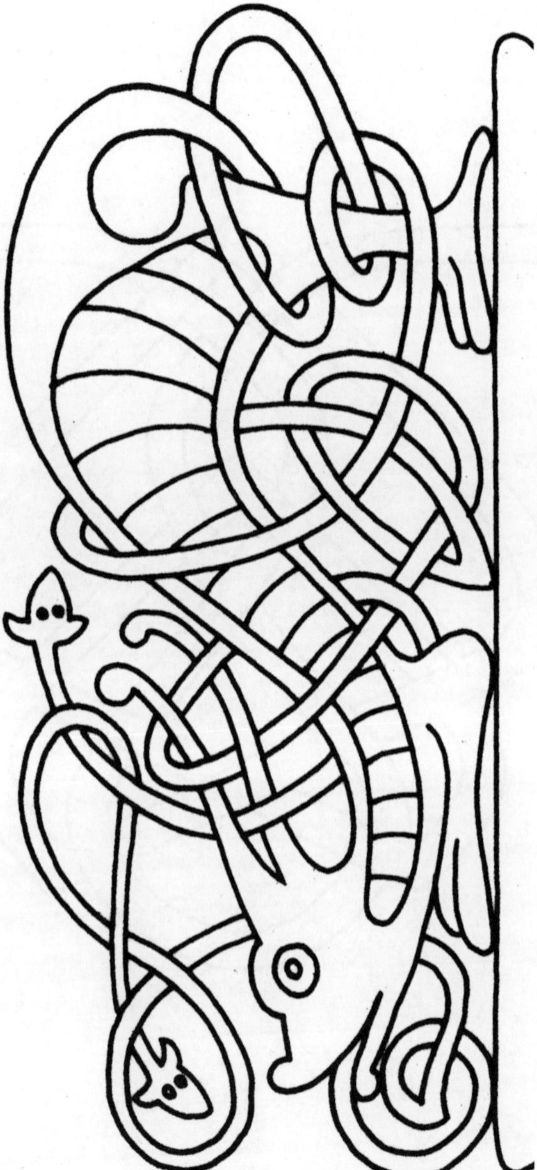

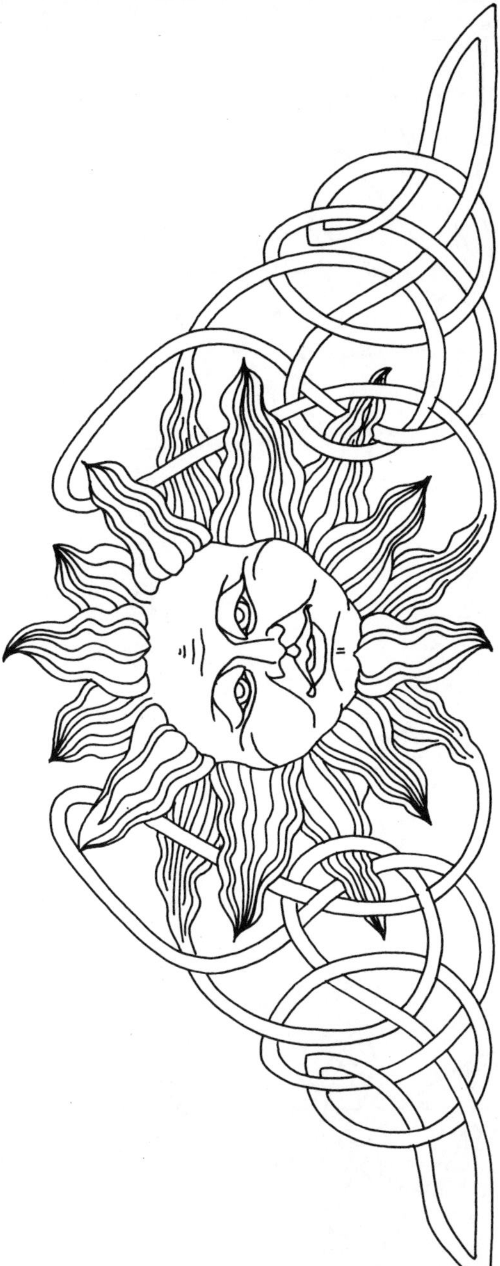

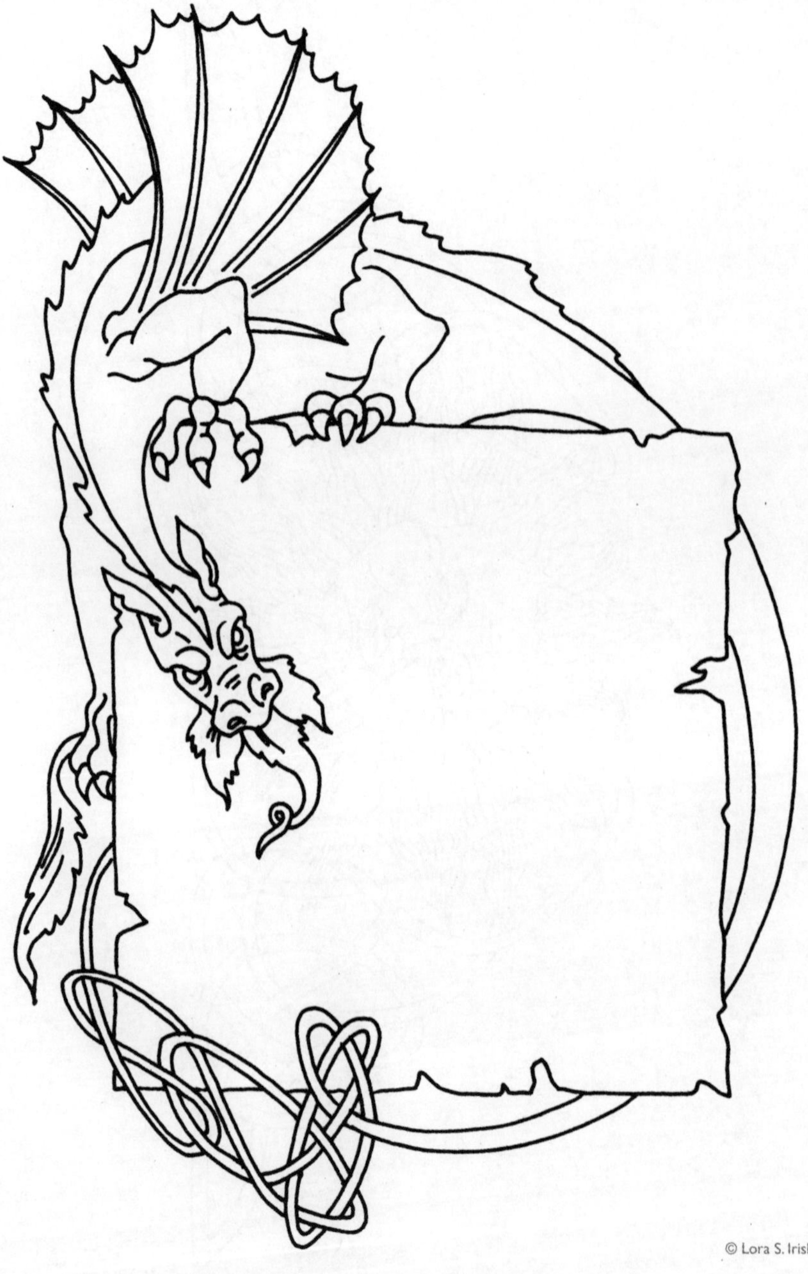

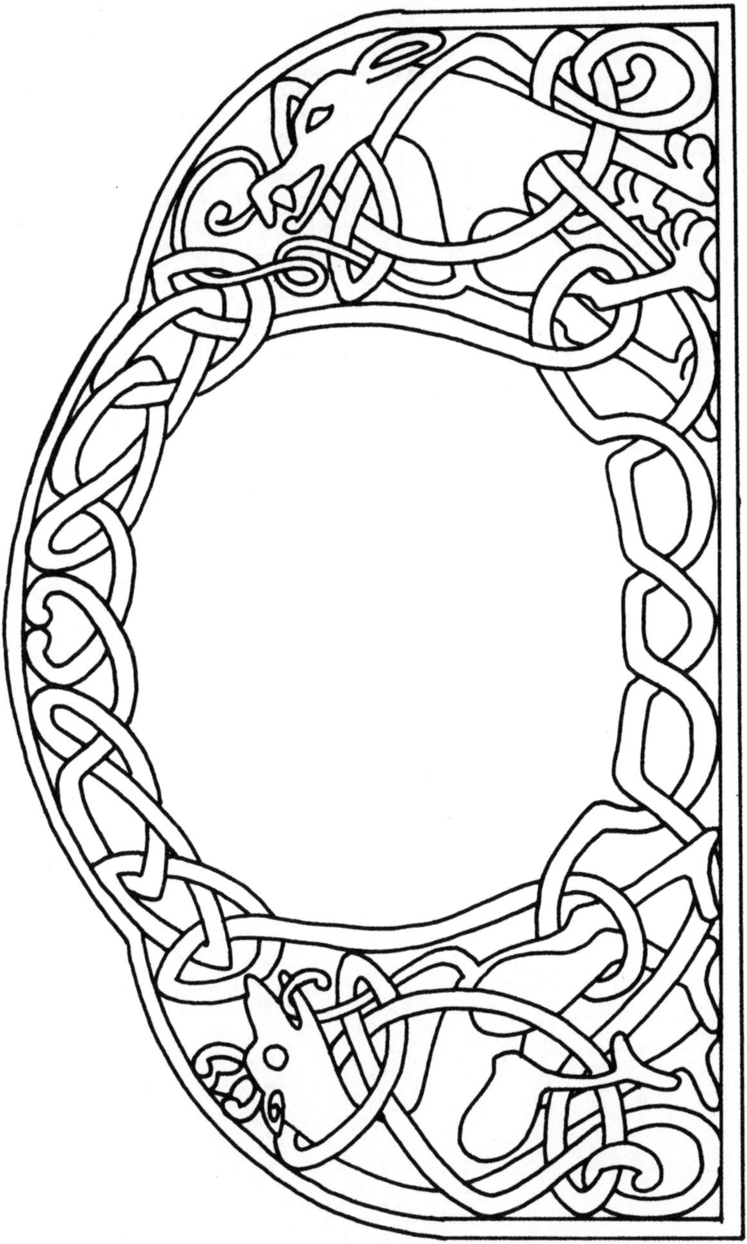

Celtic

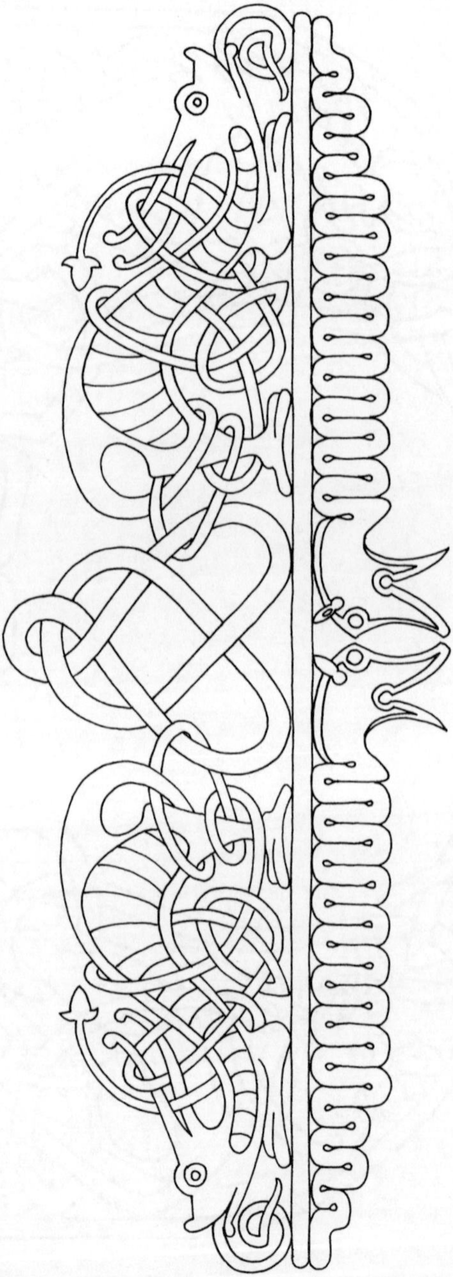

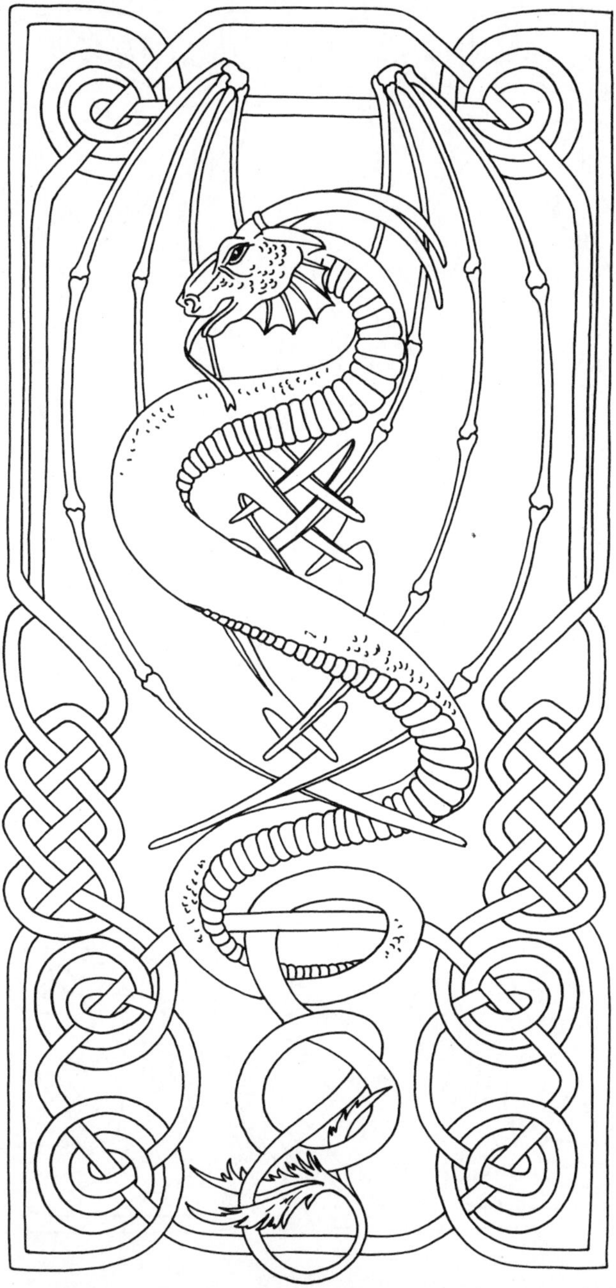

Celtic

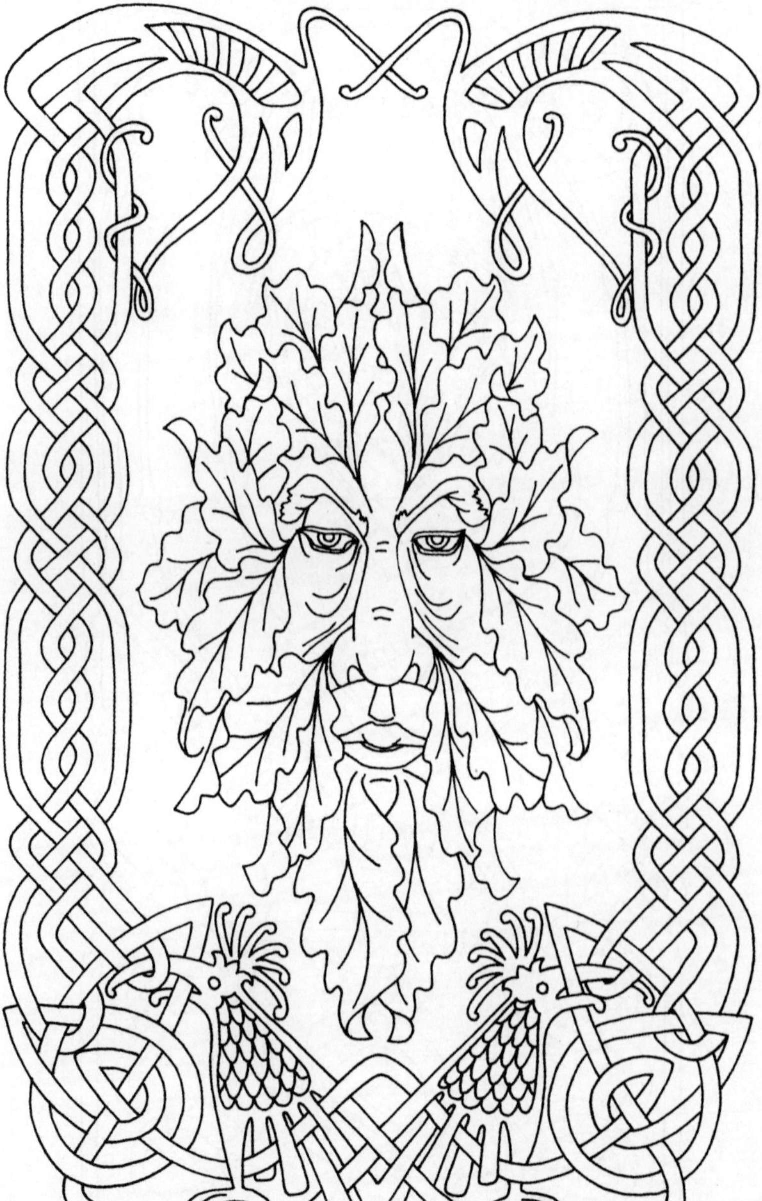

© Lora S. Irish

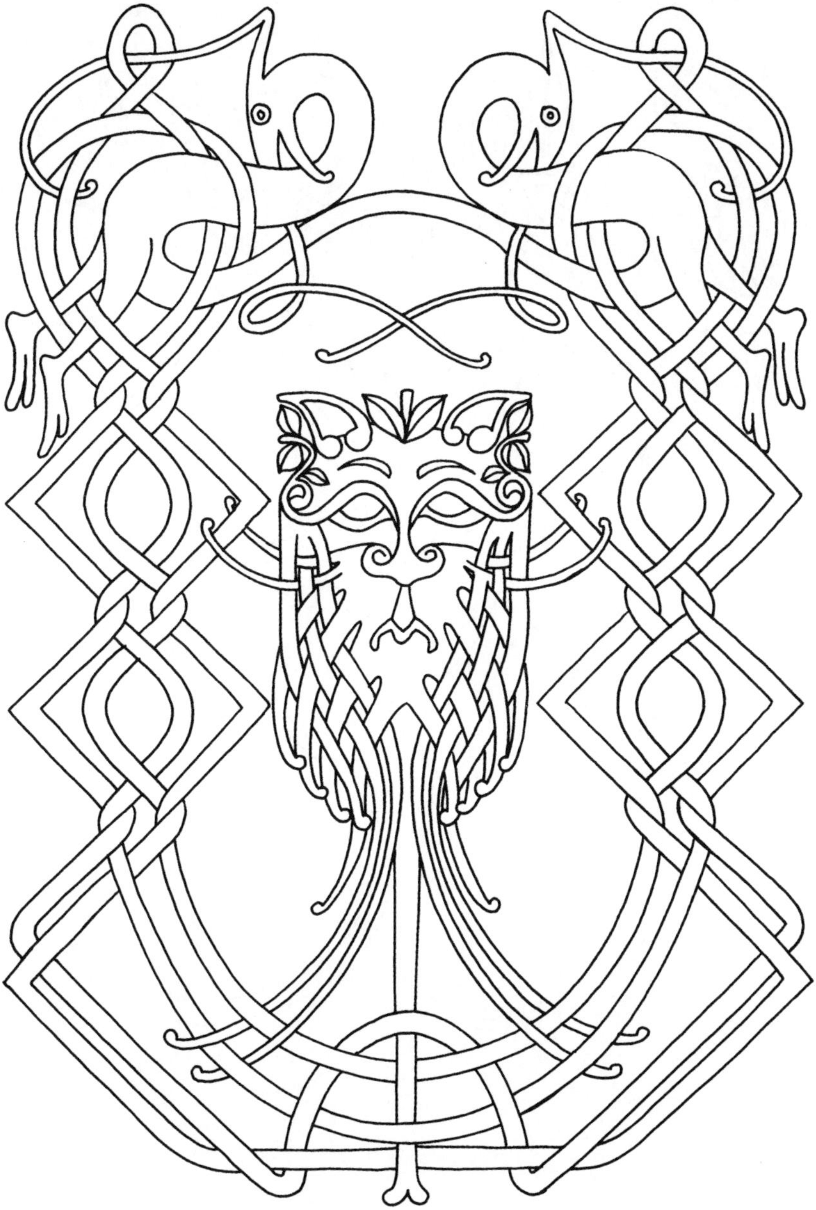

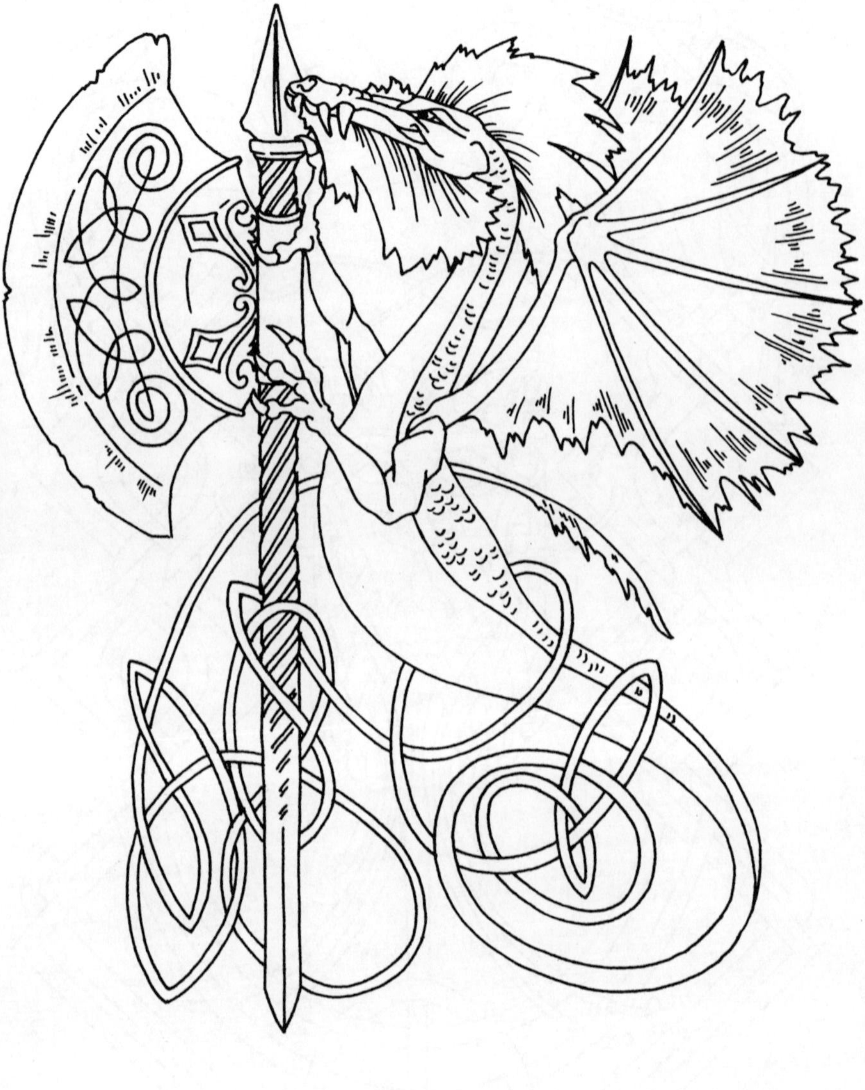

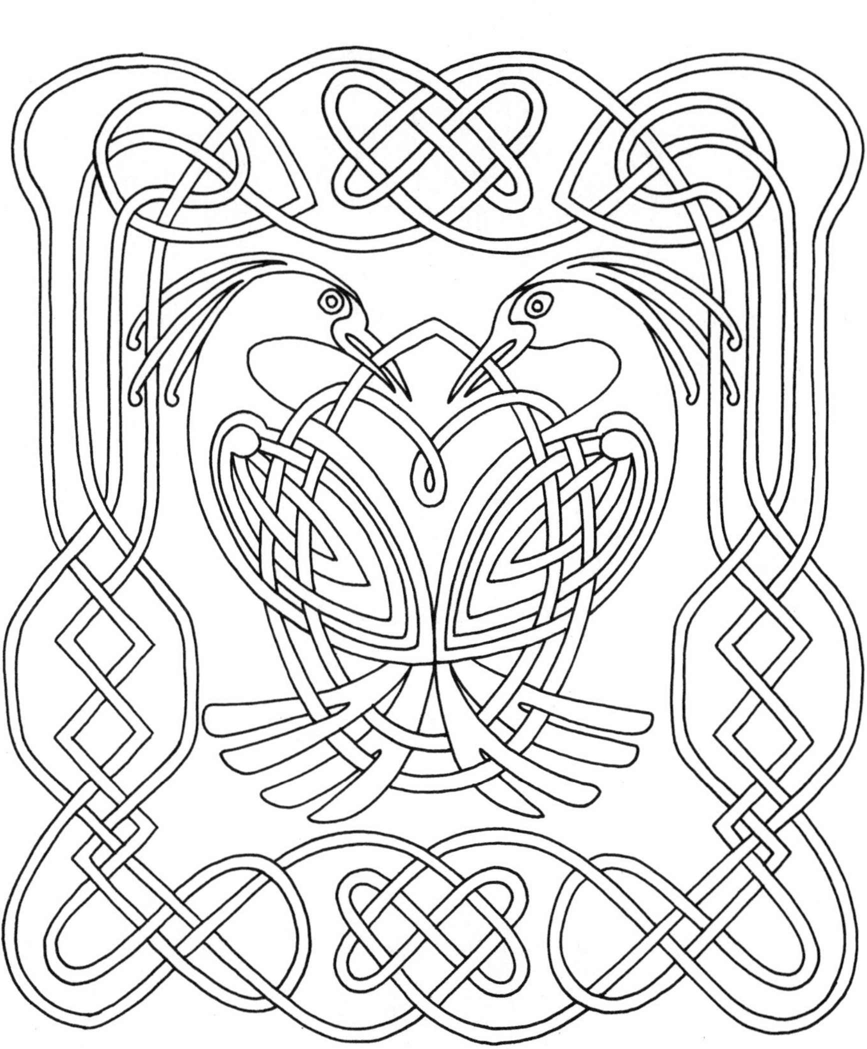

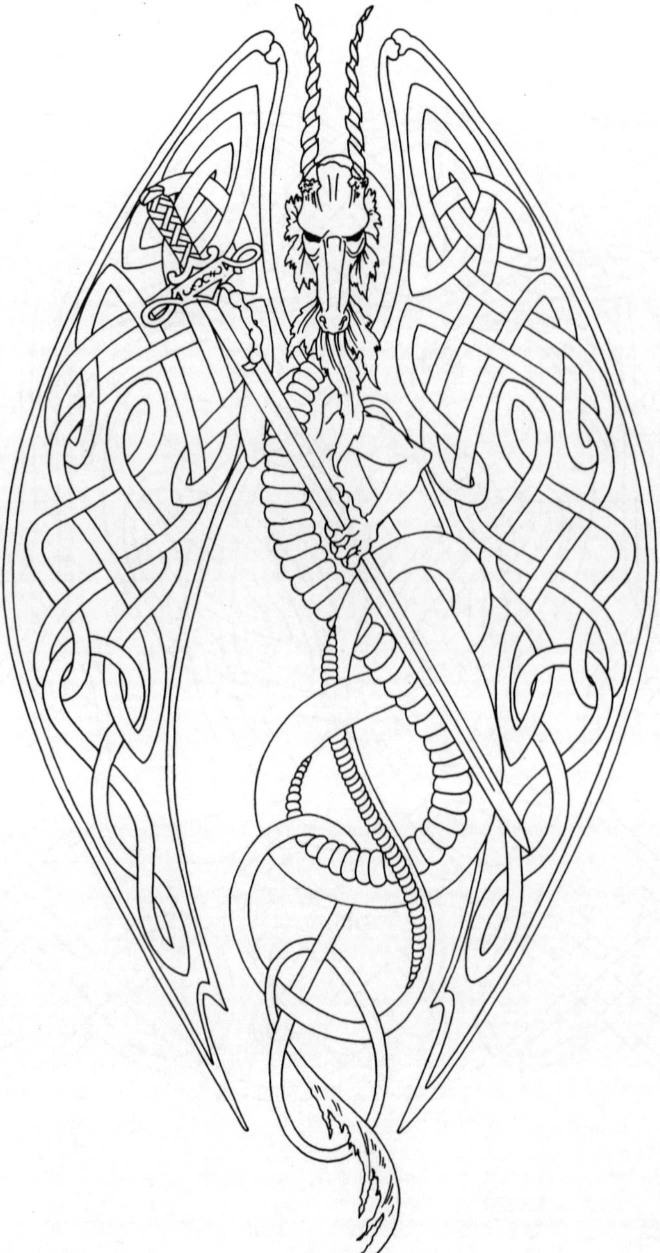

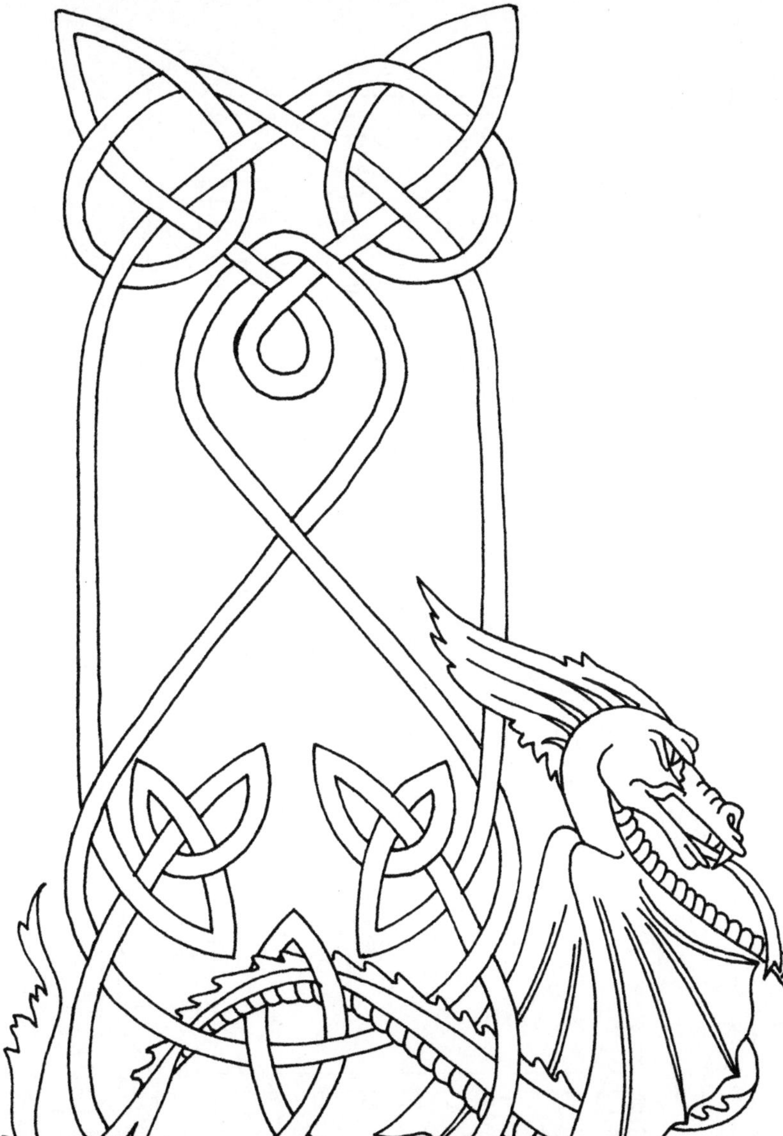

Celtic

Celtic

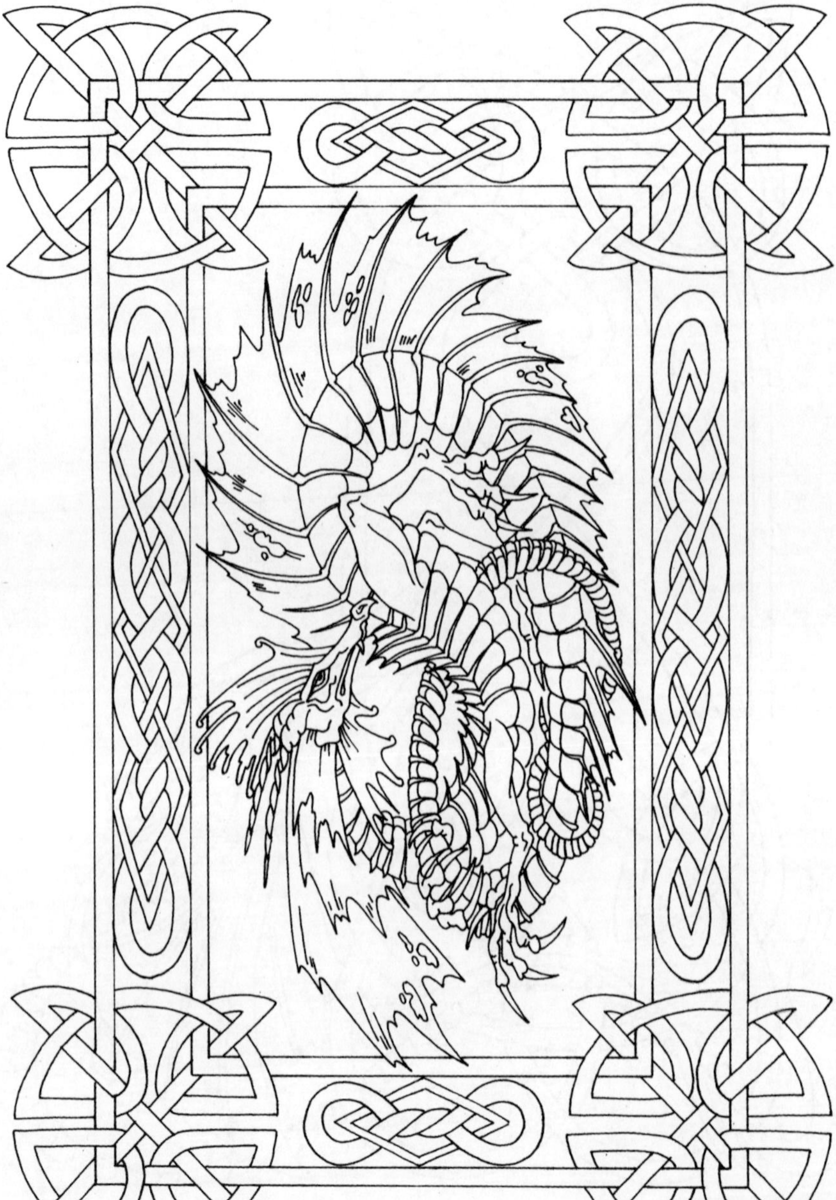

© Lora S. Irish

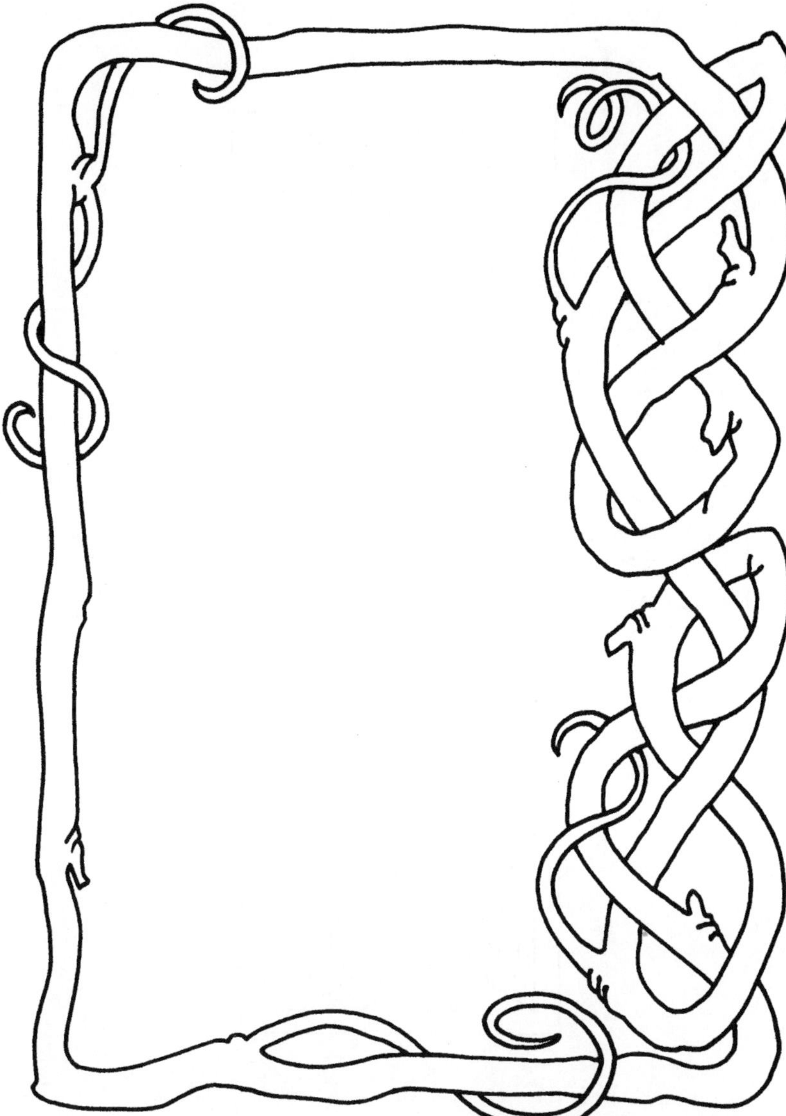

Celtic

Celtic

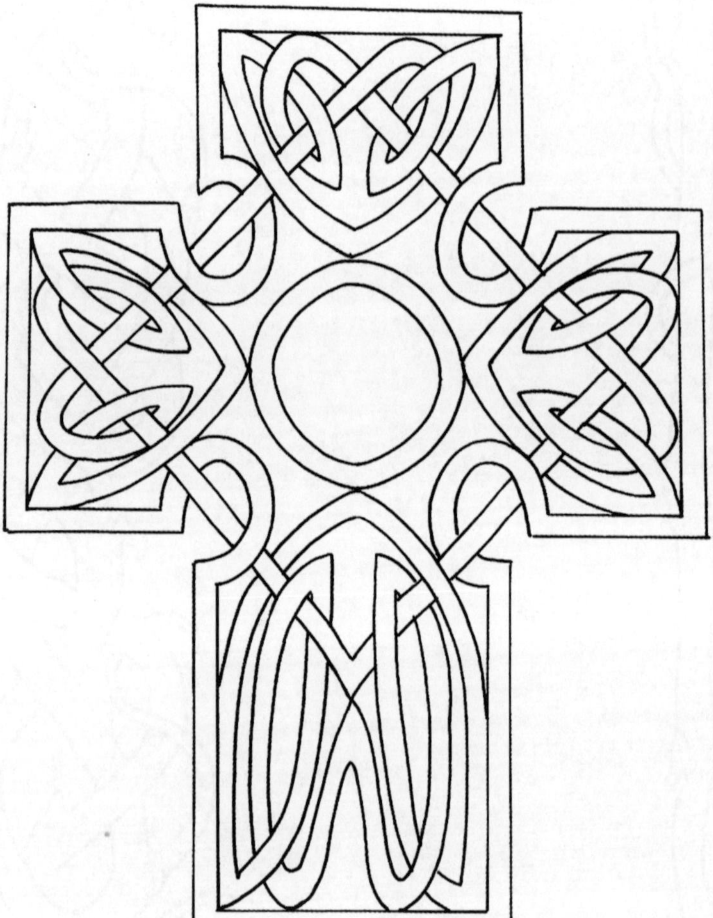

© Lora S. Irish

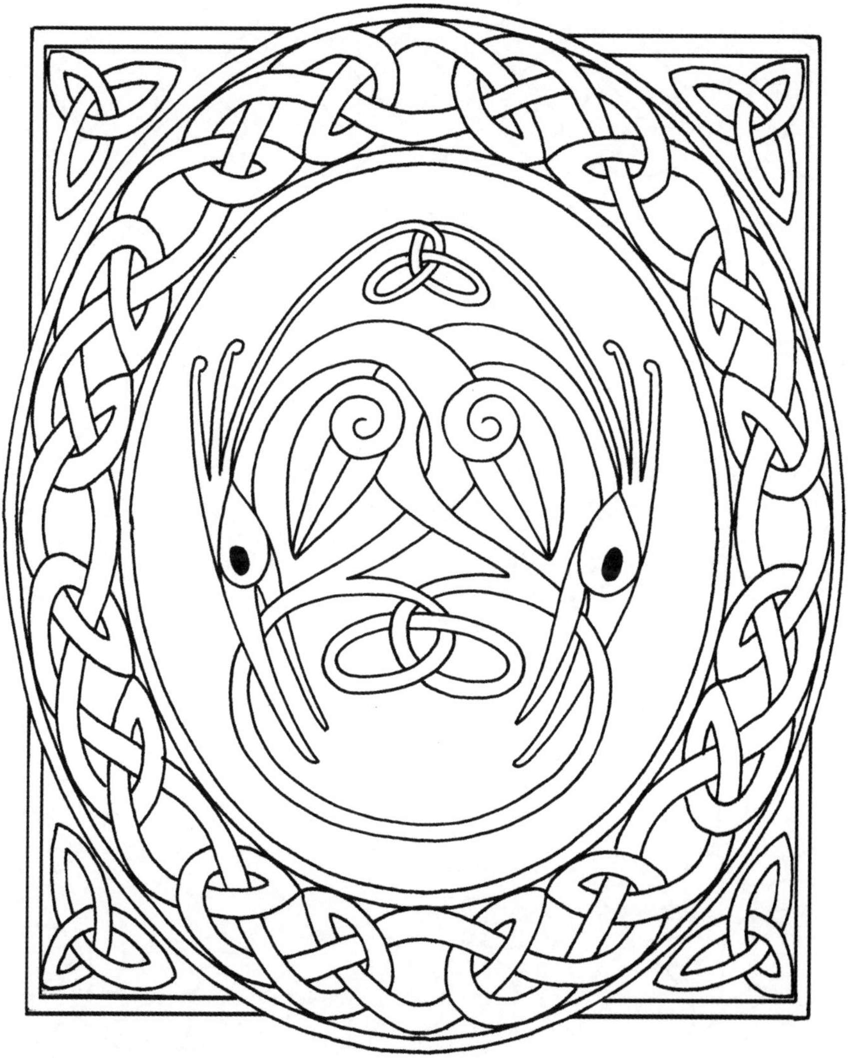

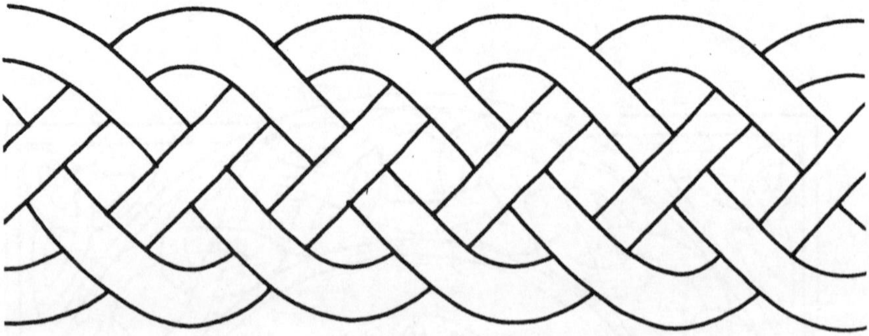

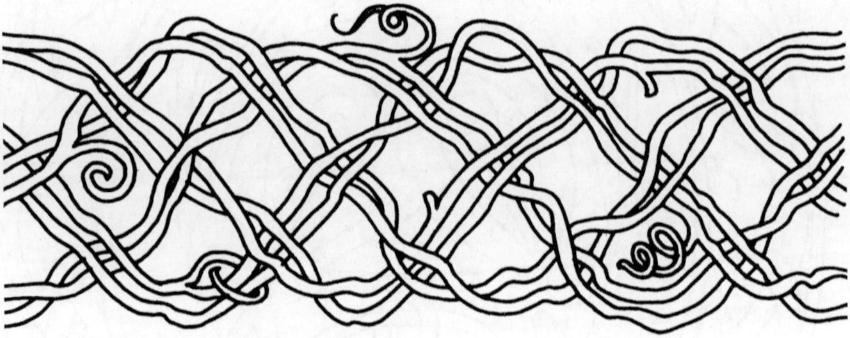

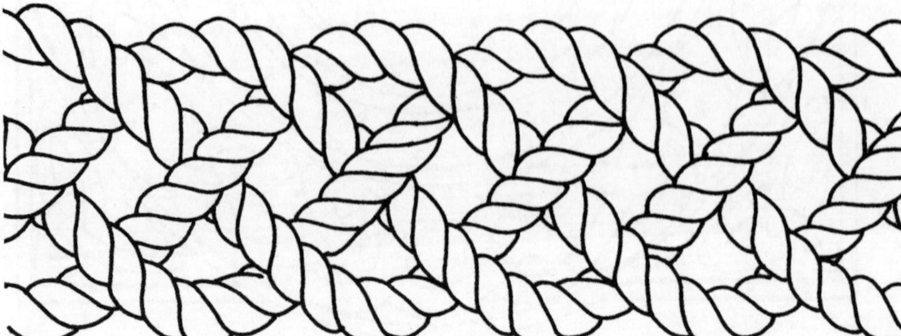

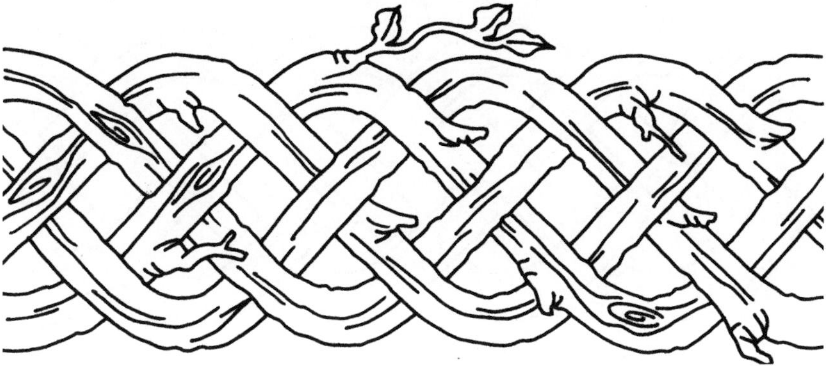

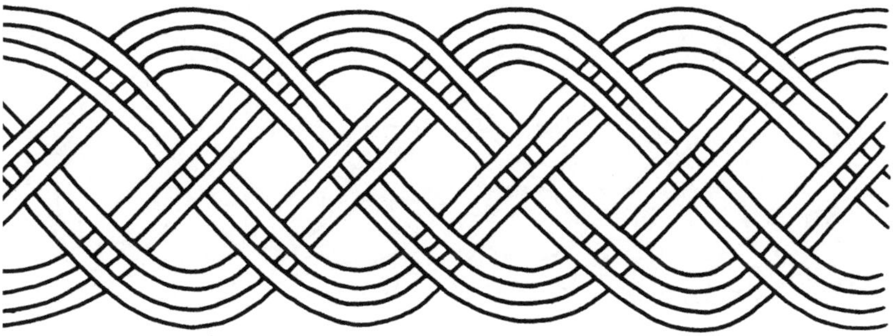

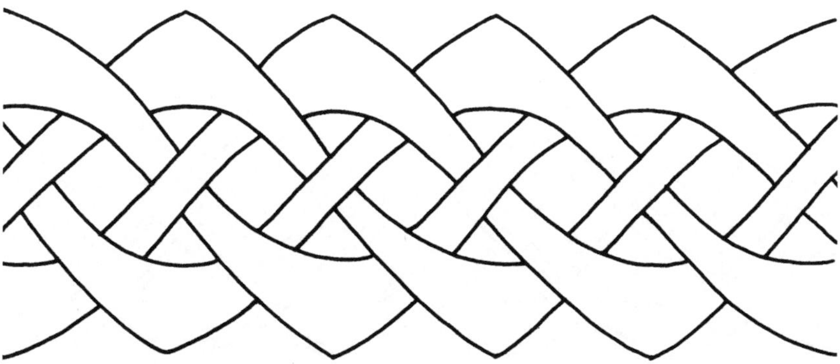

Celtic

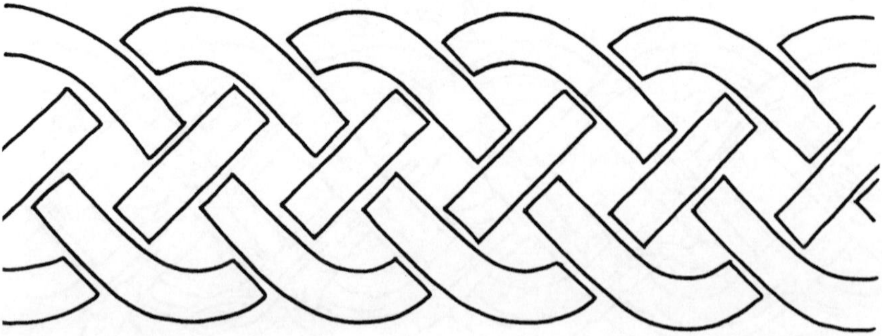

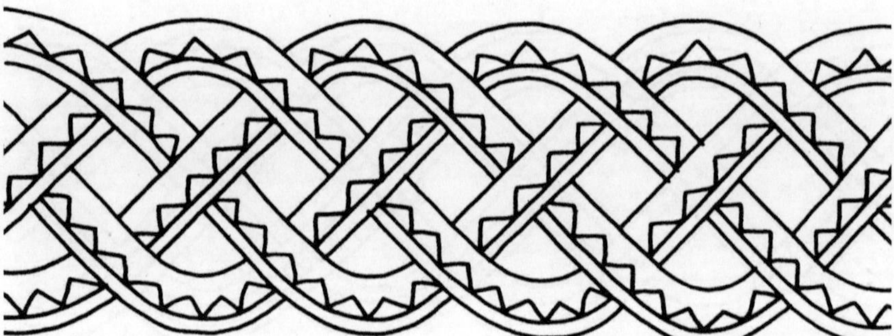

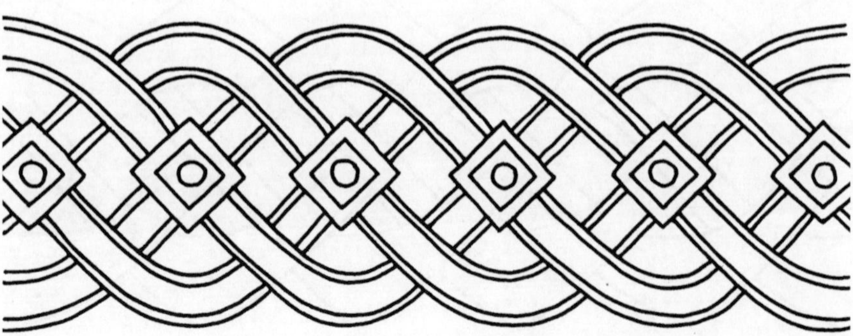

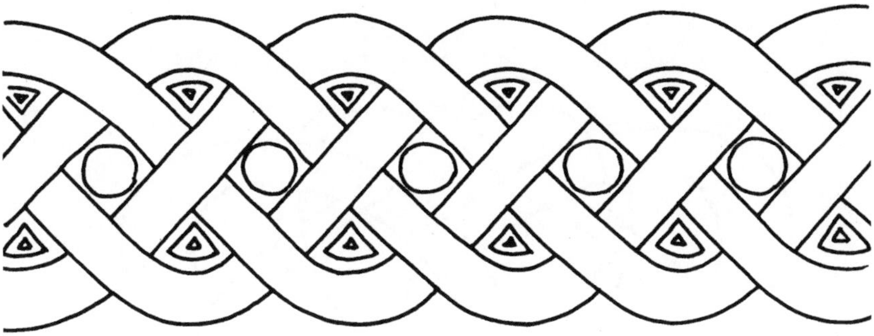

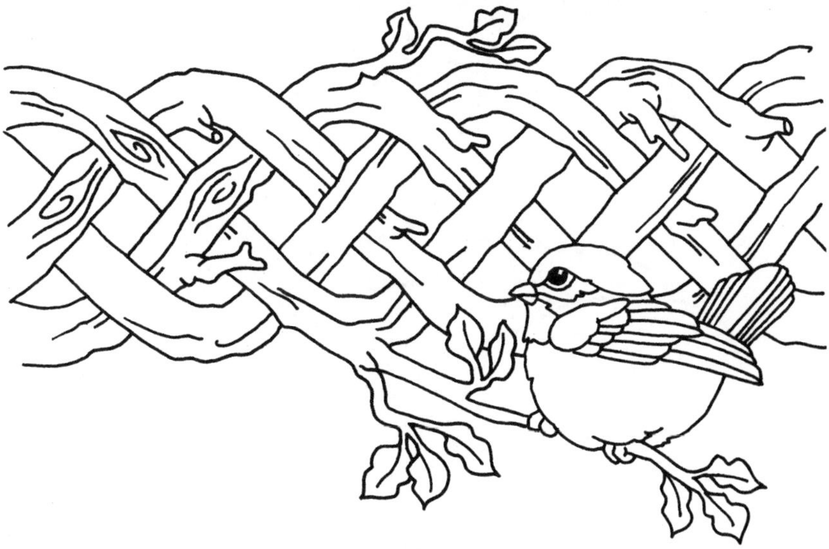

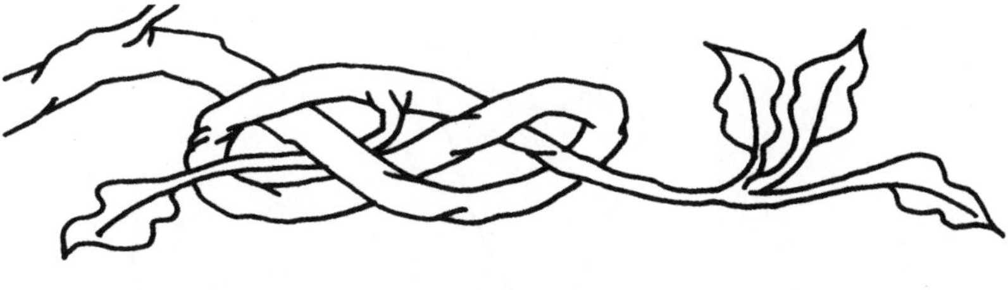

Celtic

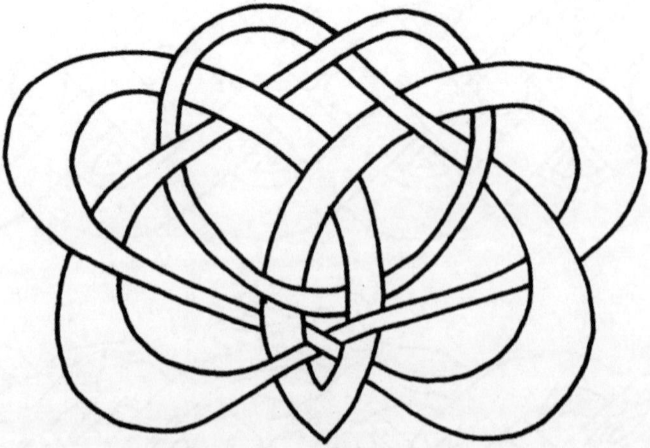

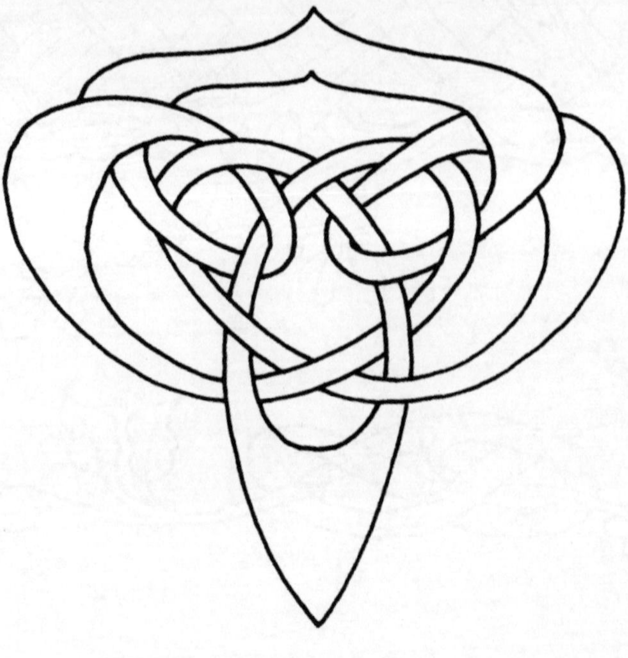

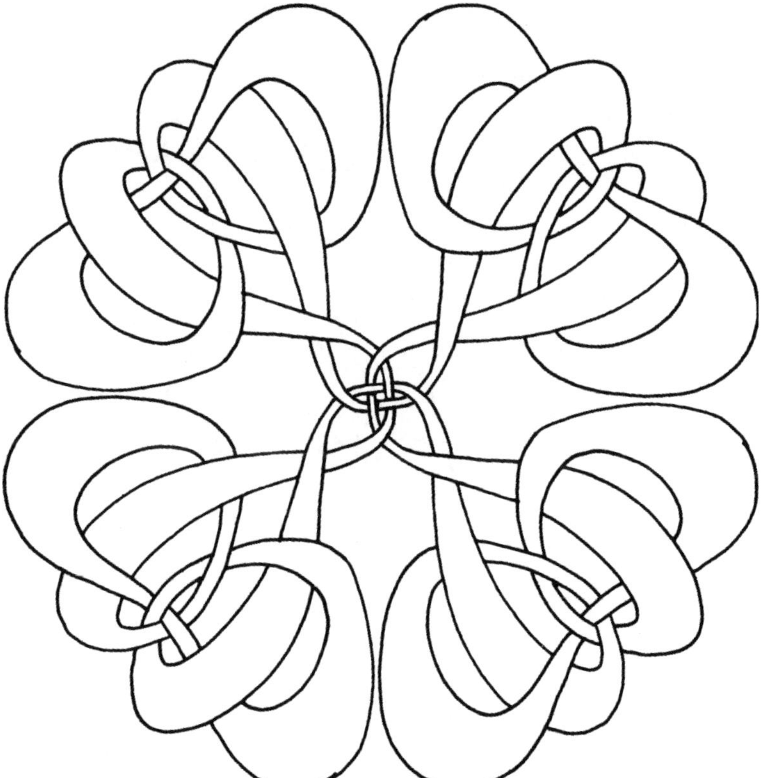

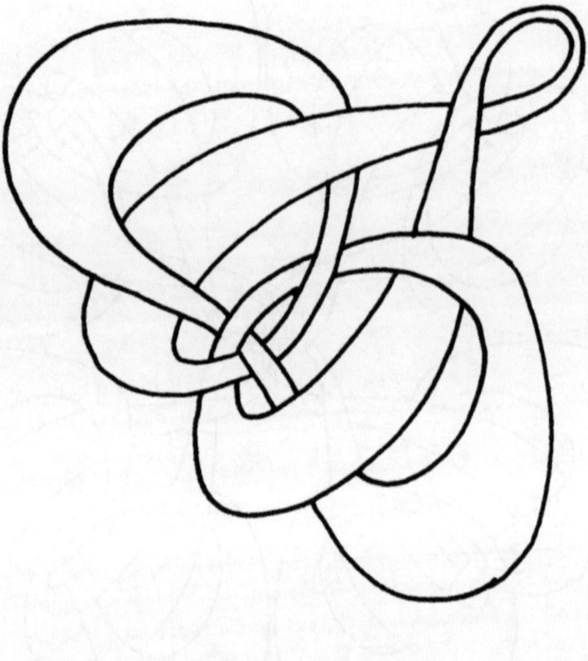

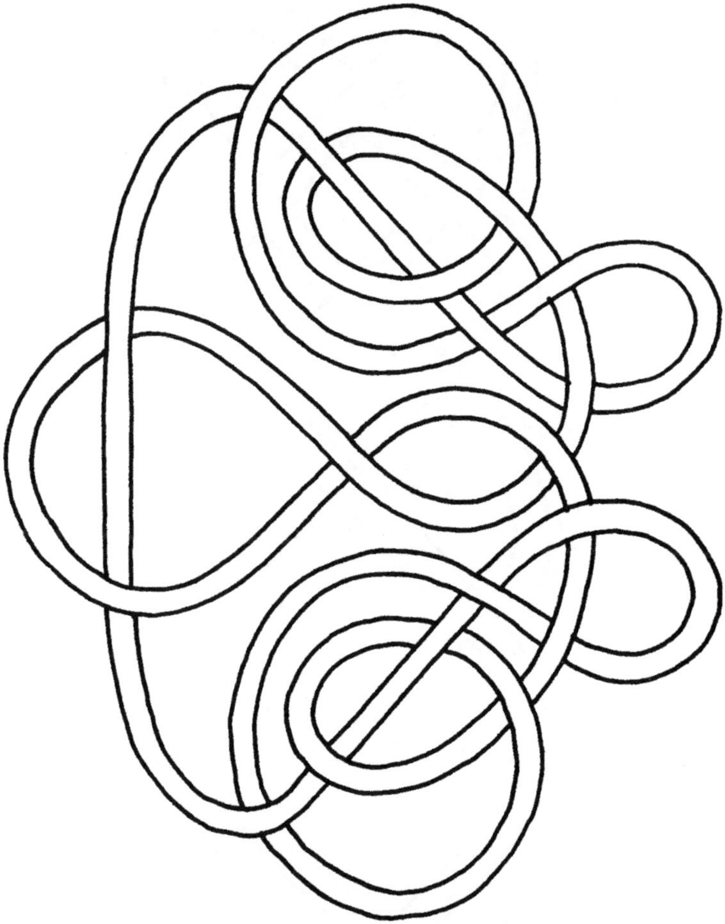

Celtic

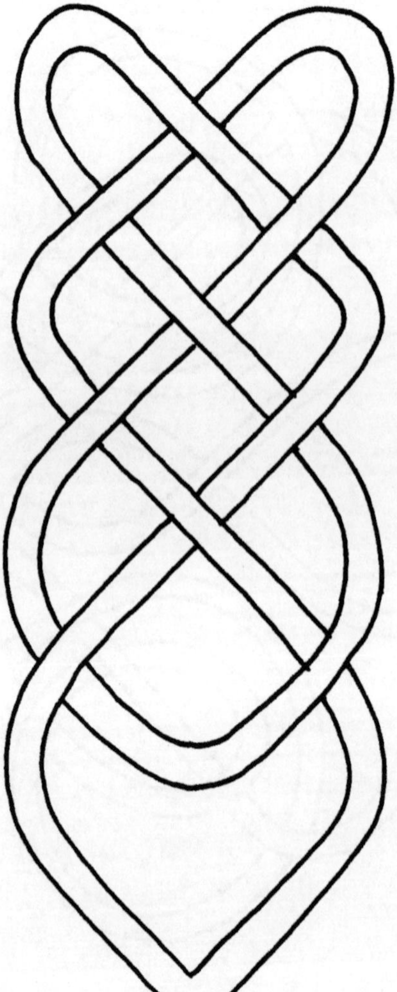

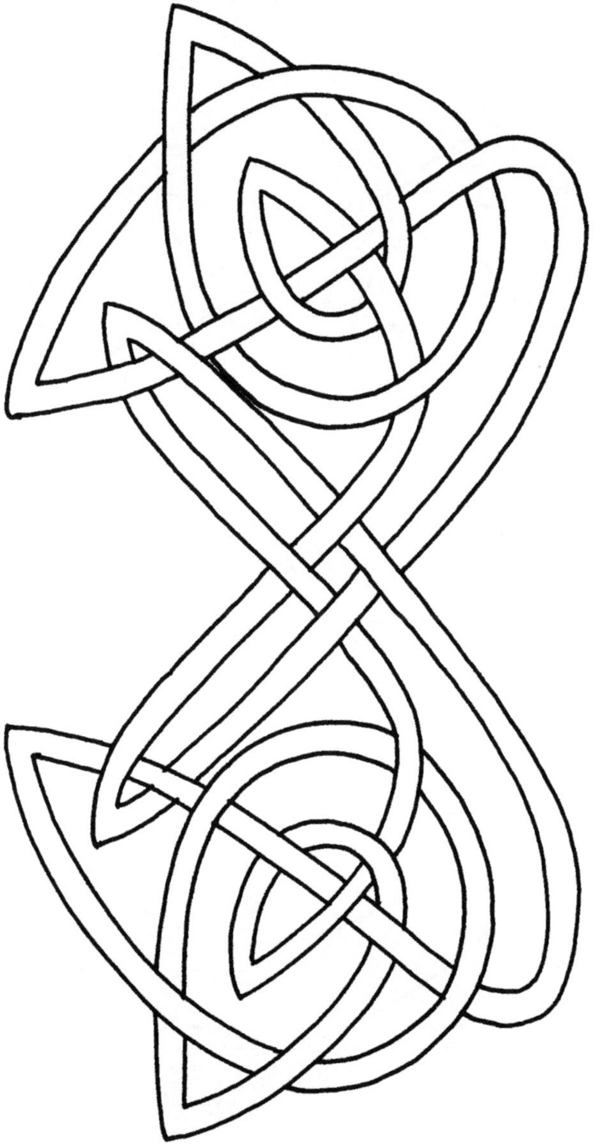

Celtic

© Lora S. Irish

Celtic

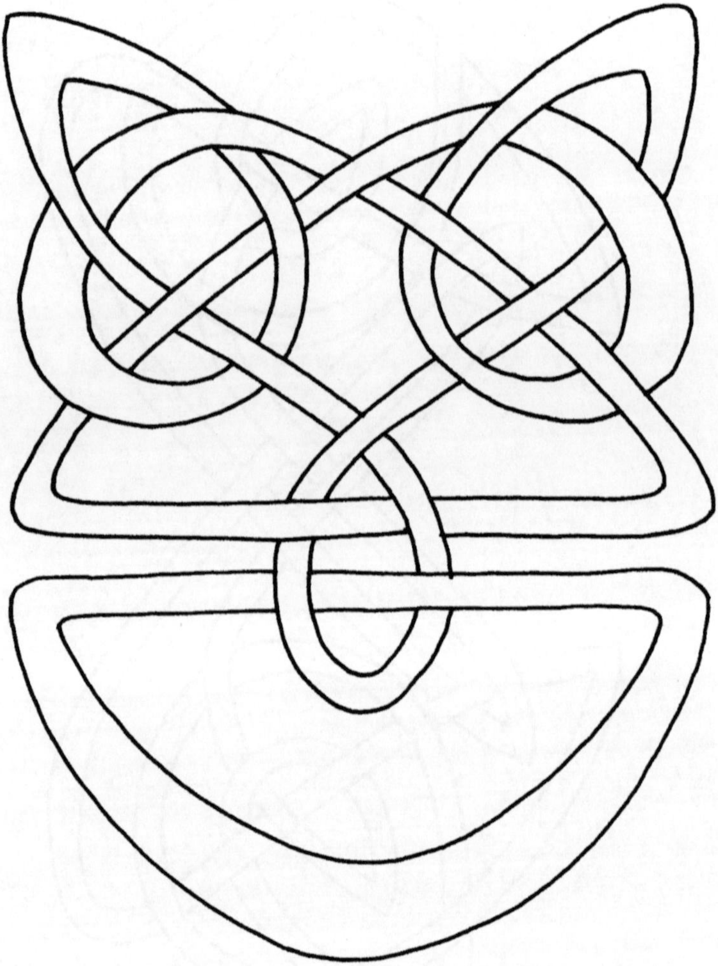

© Lora S. Irish

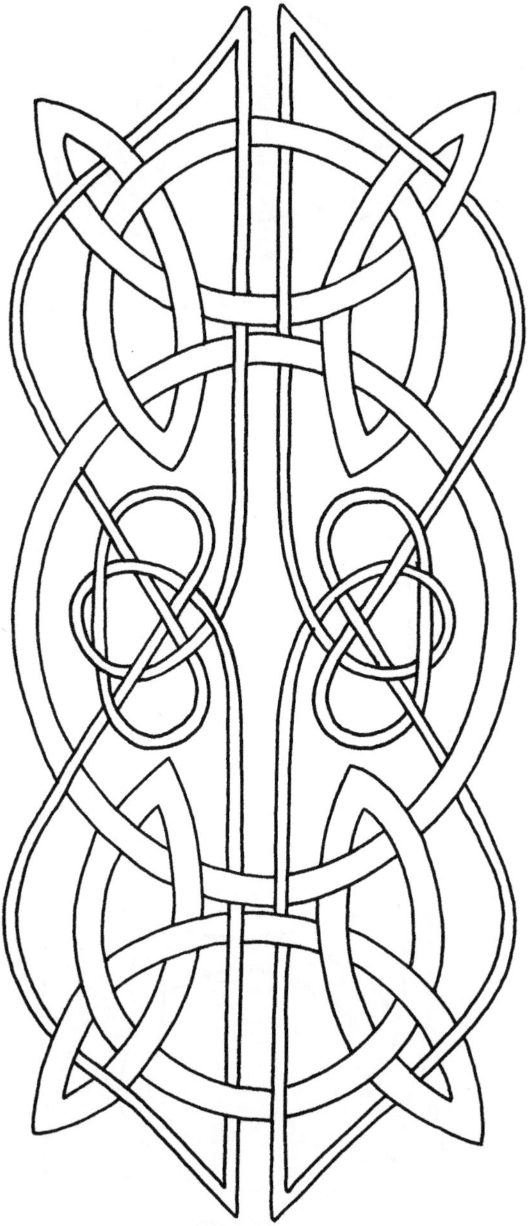

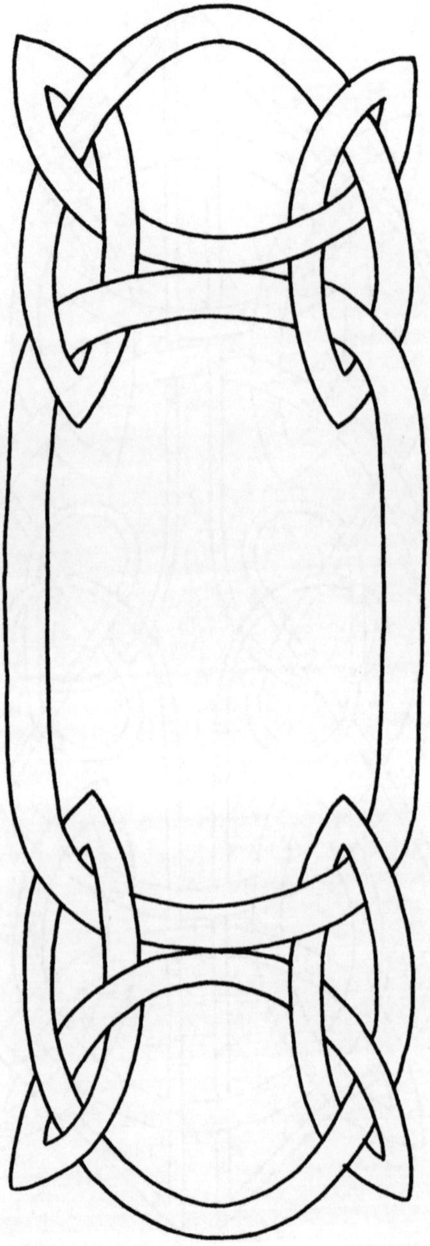

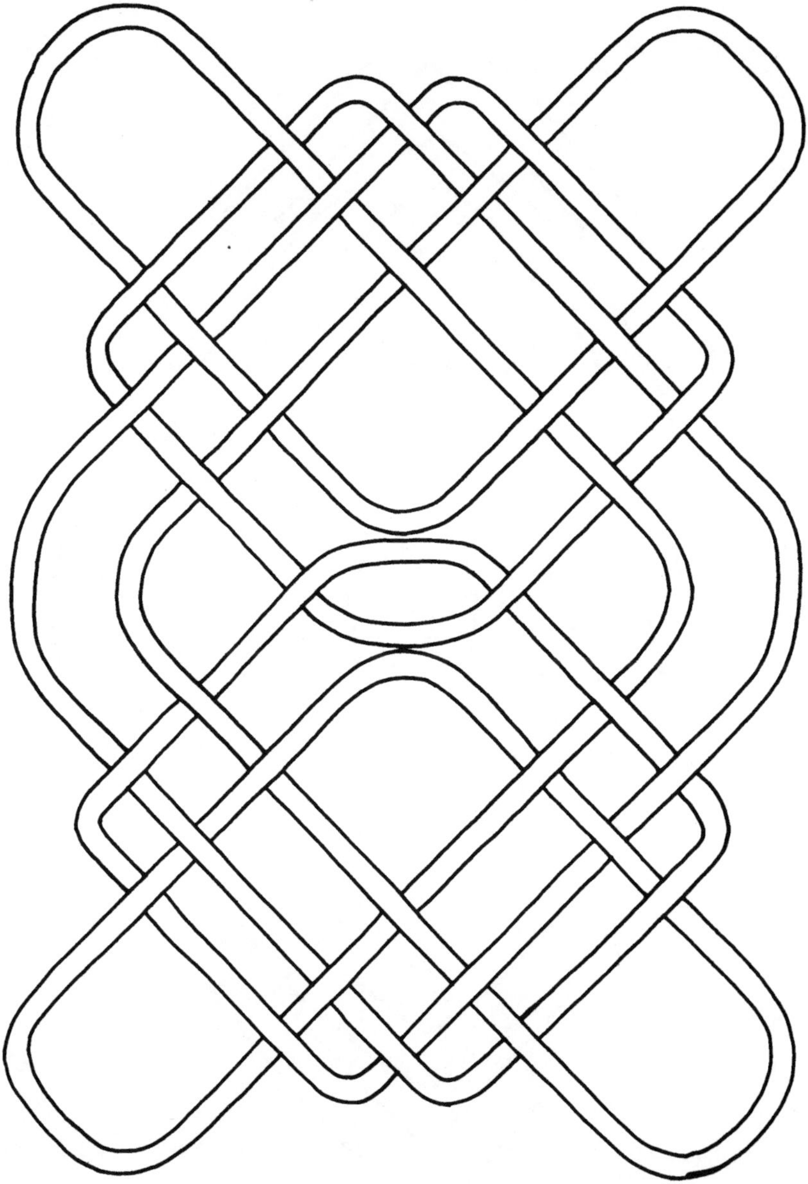

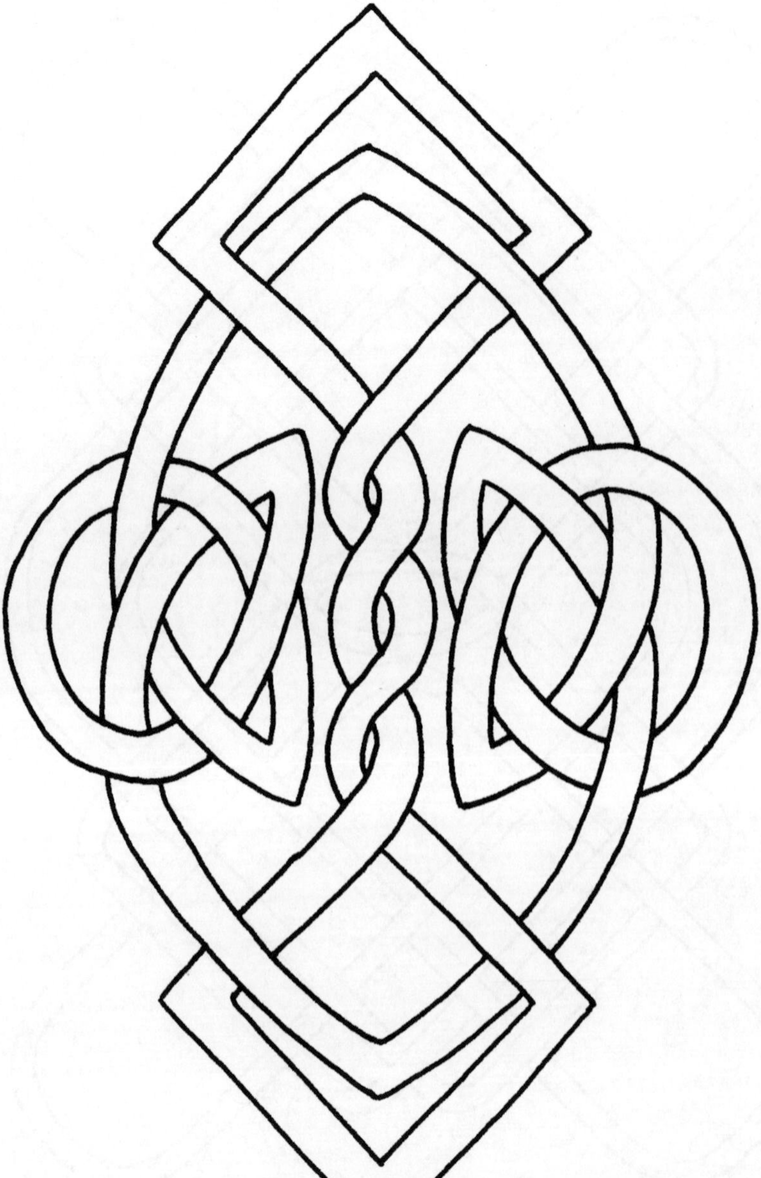

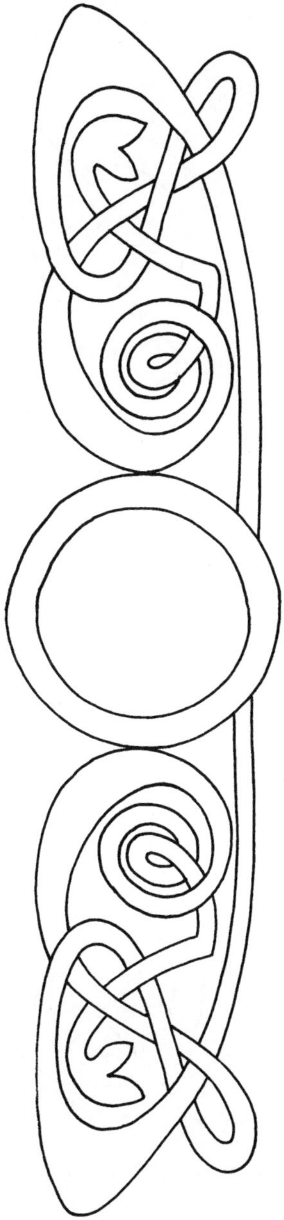

Celtic

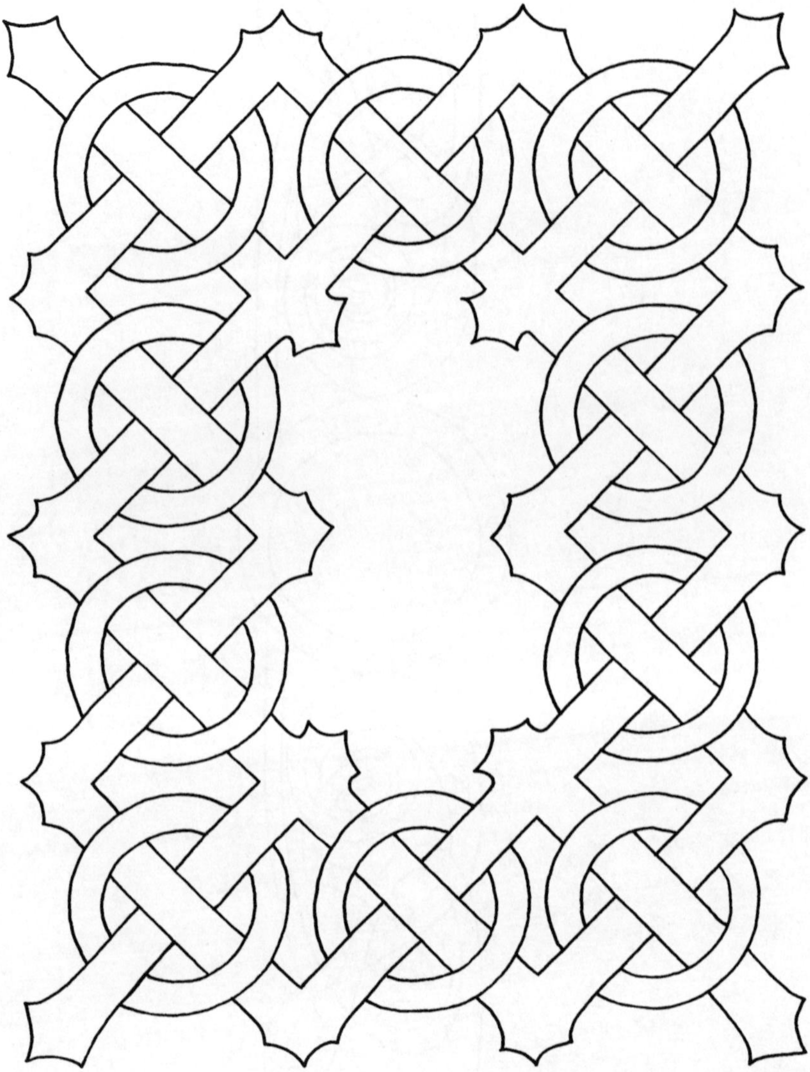

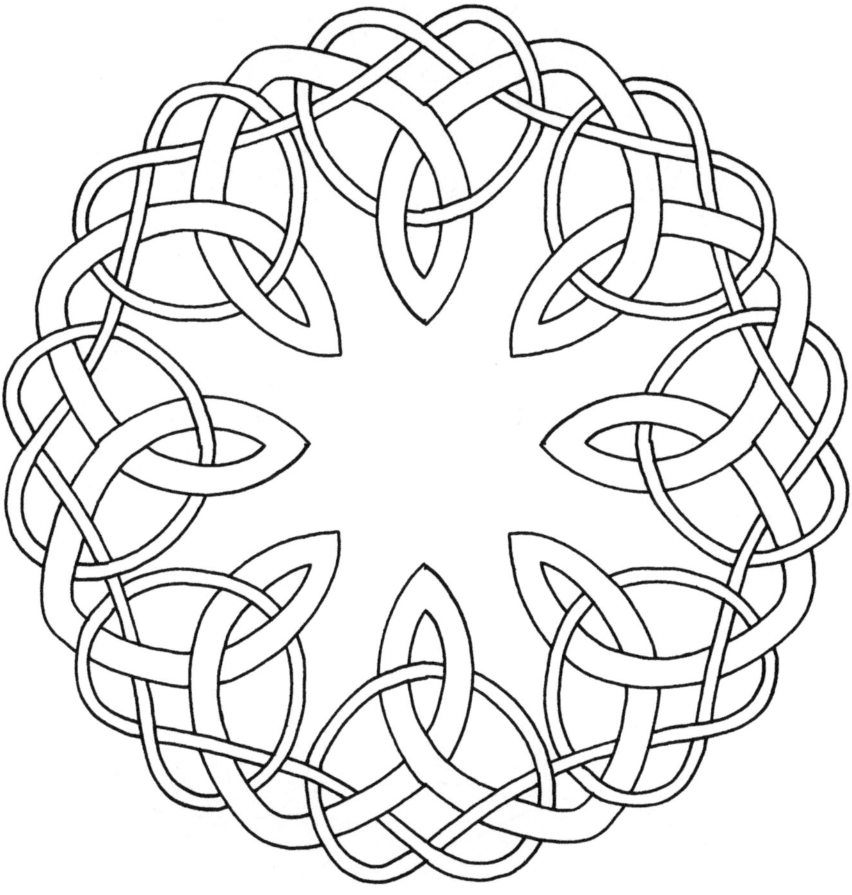

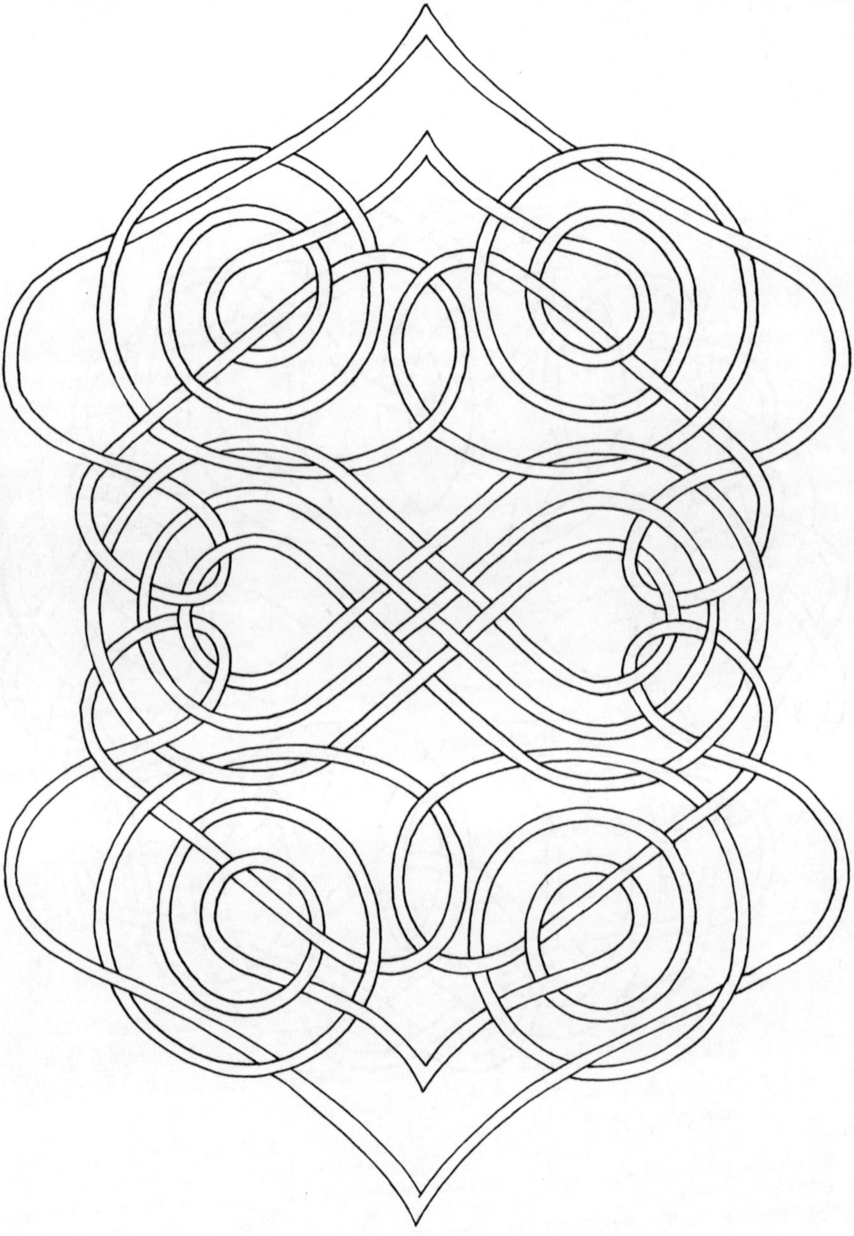

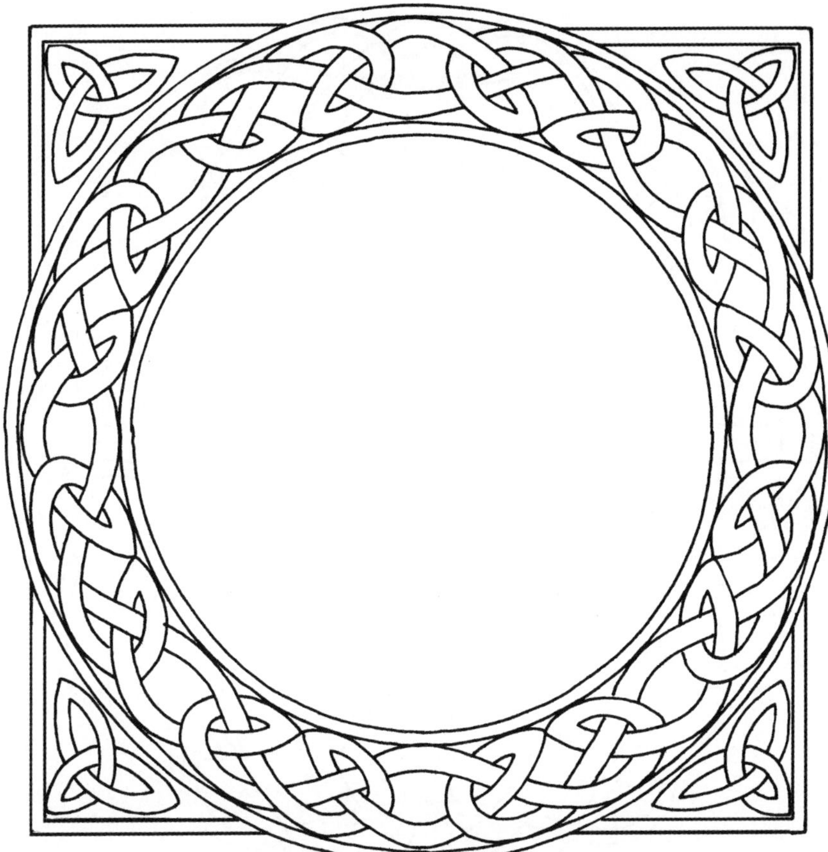

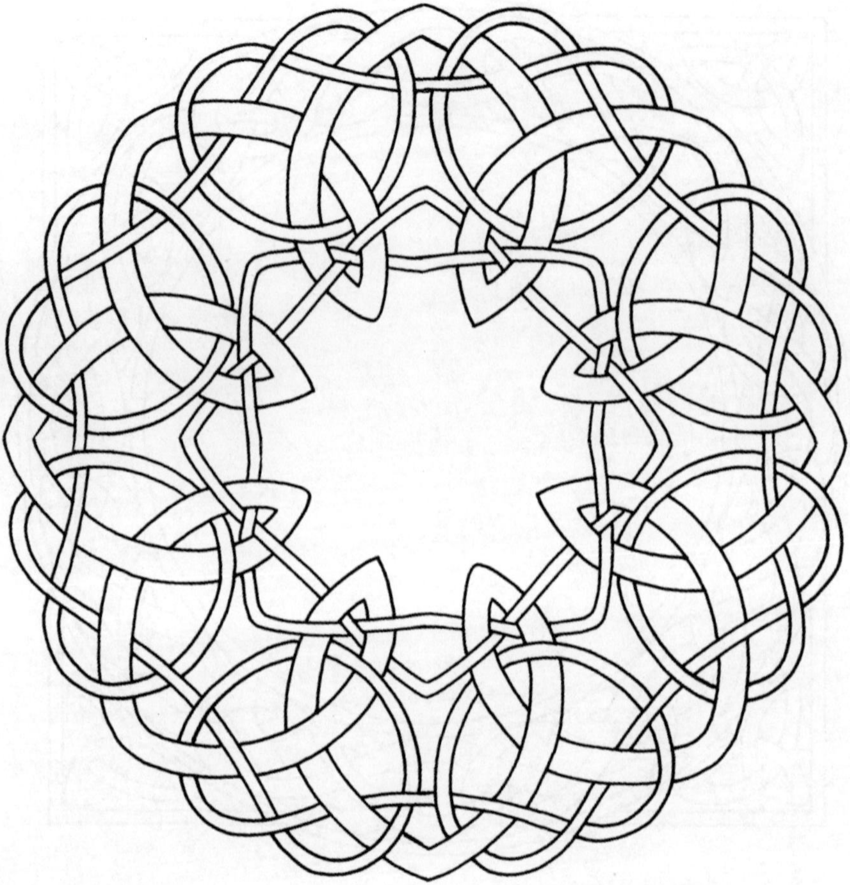

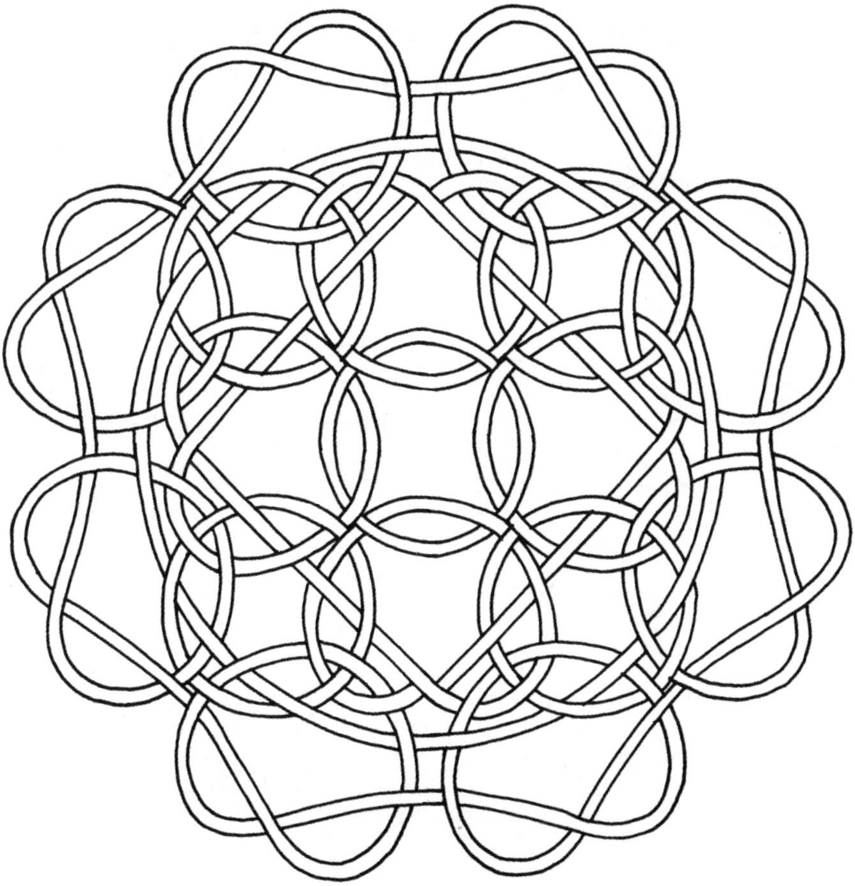

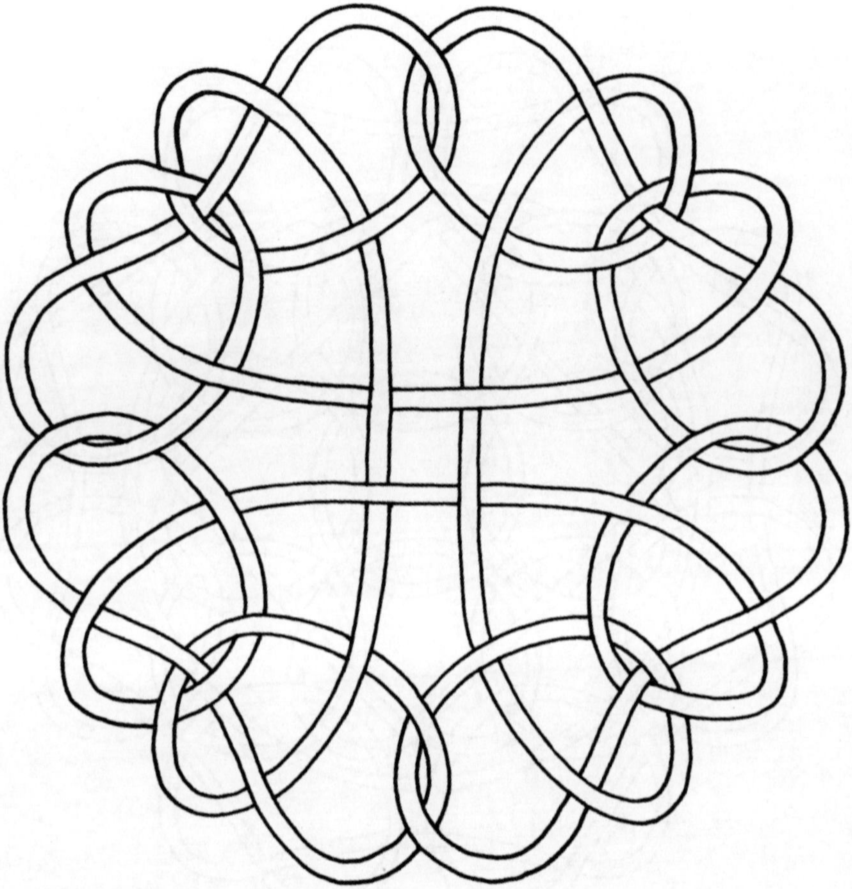

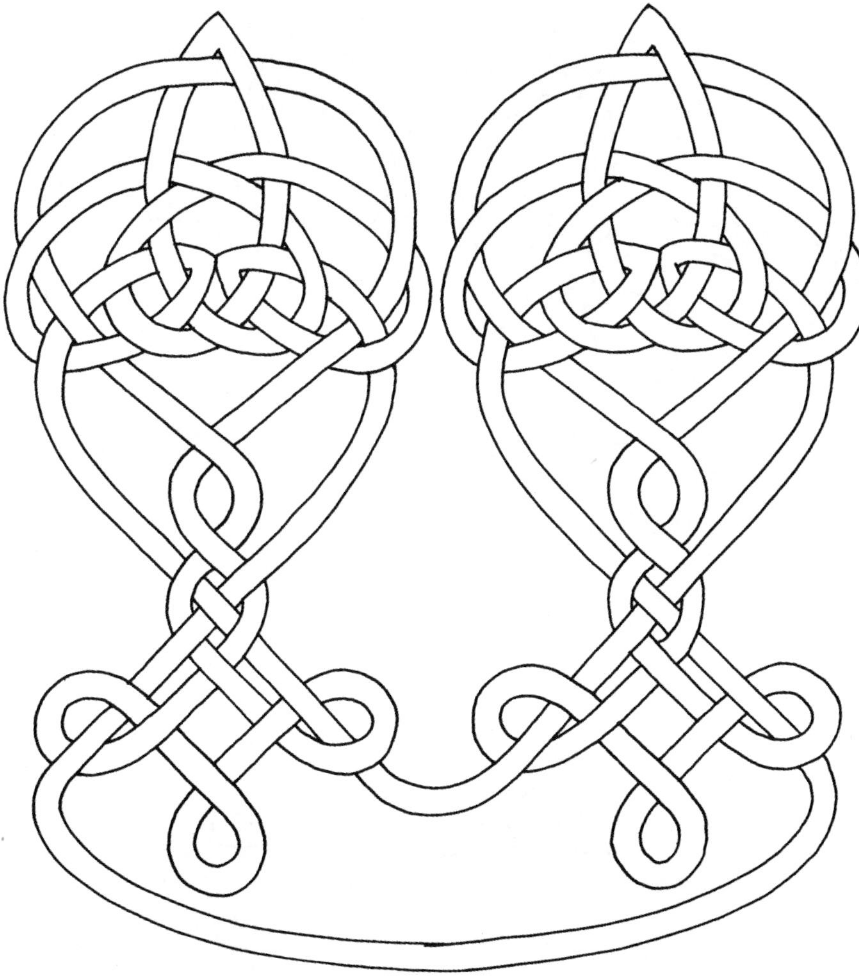

Celtic

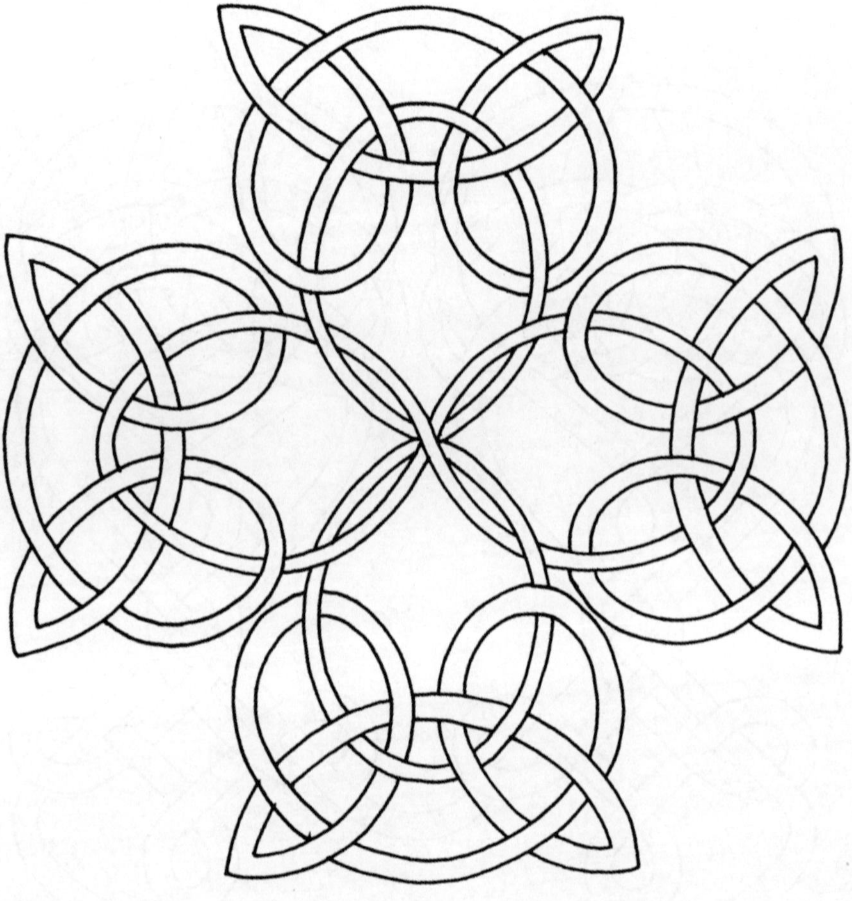

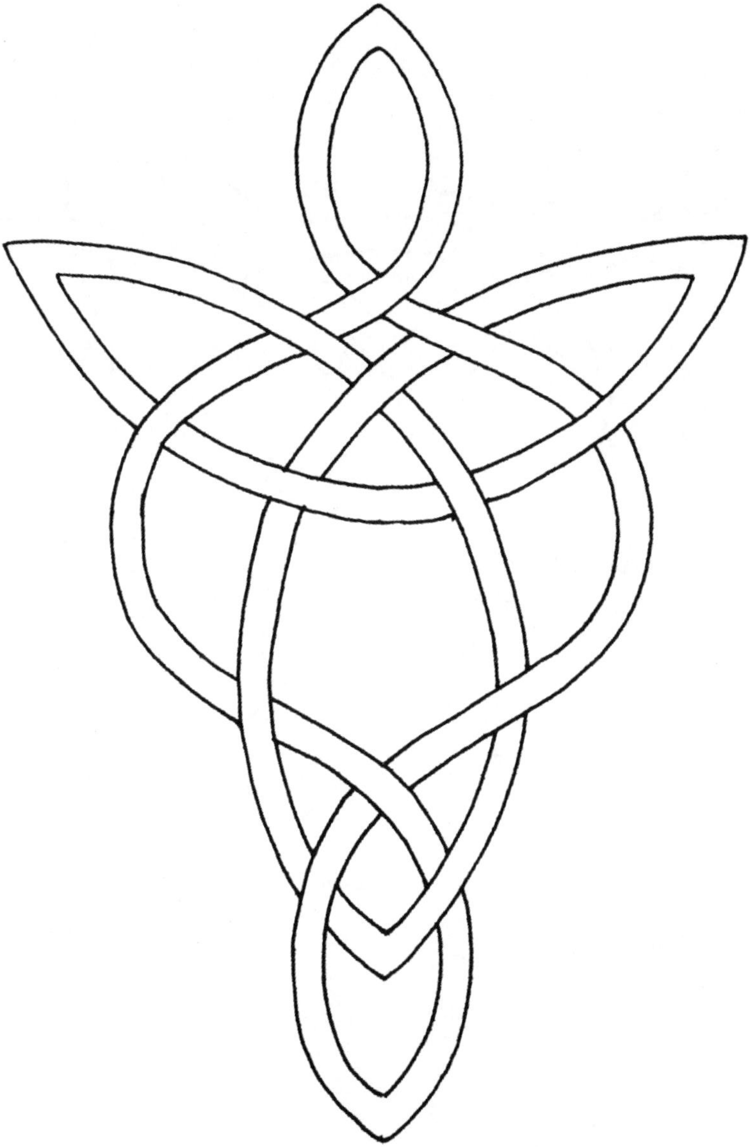

Celtic

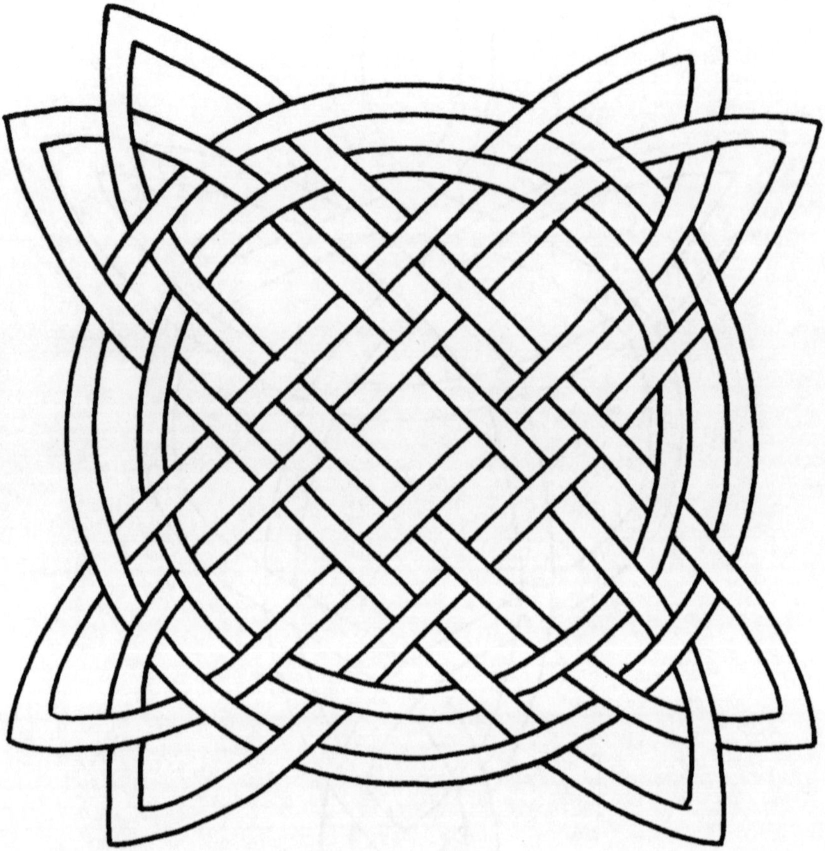

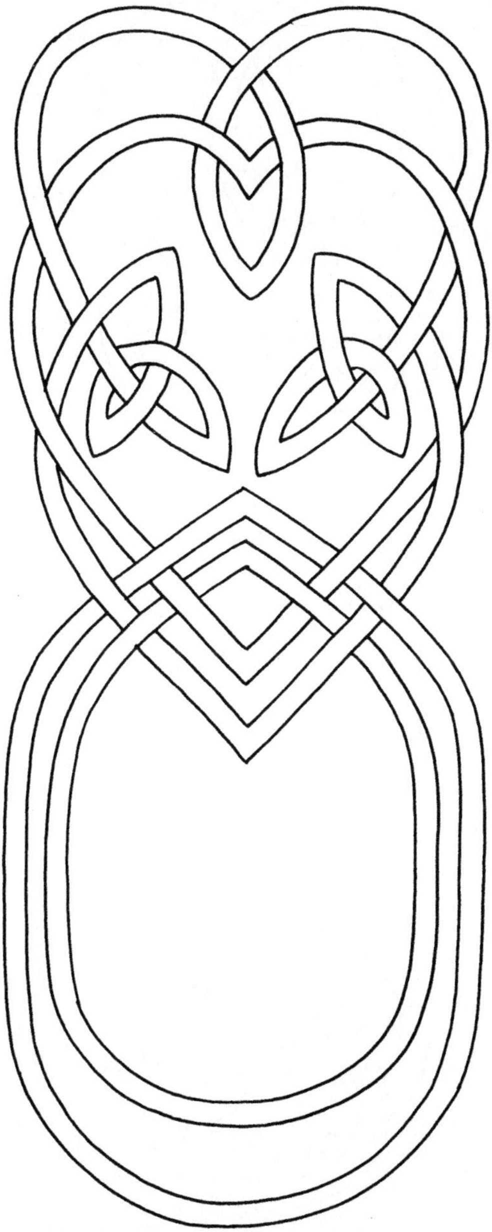

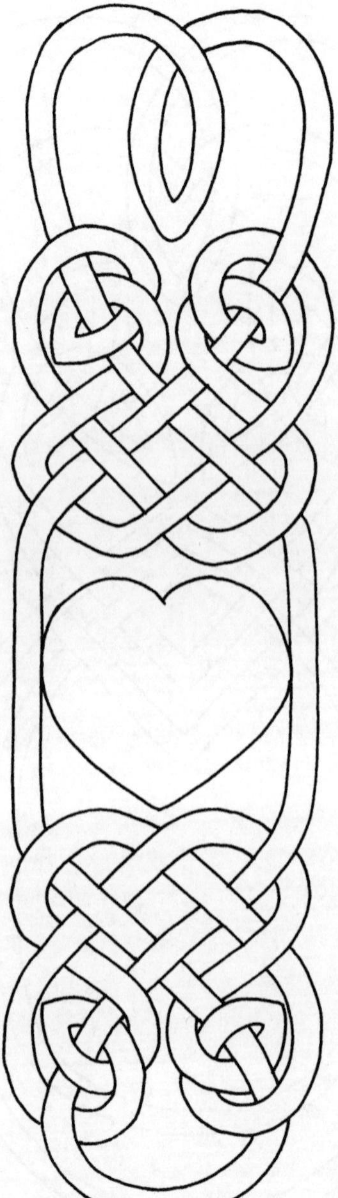

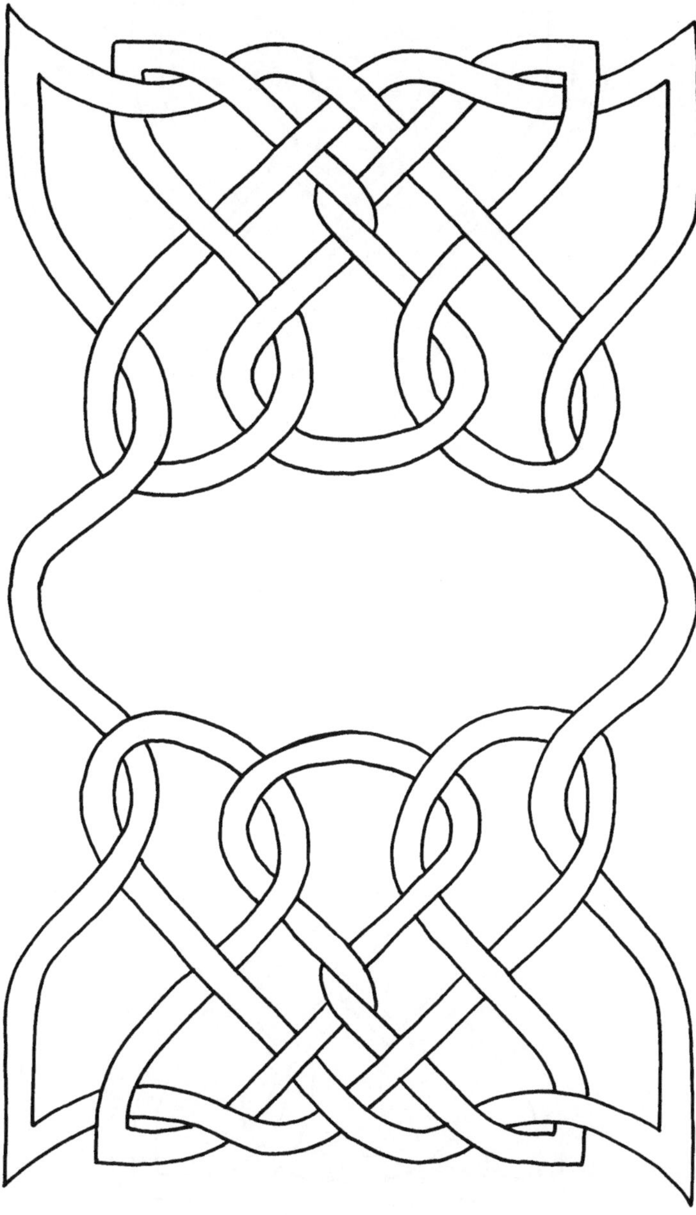

Celtic

Celtic

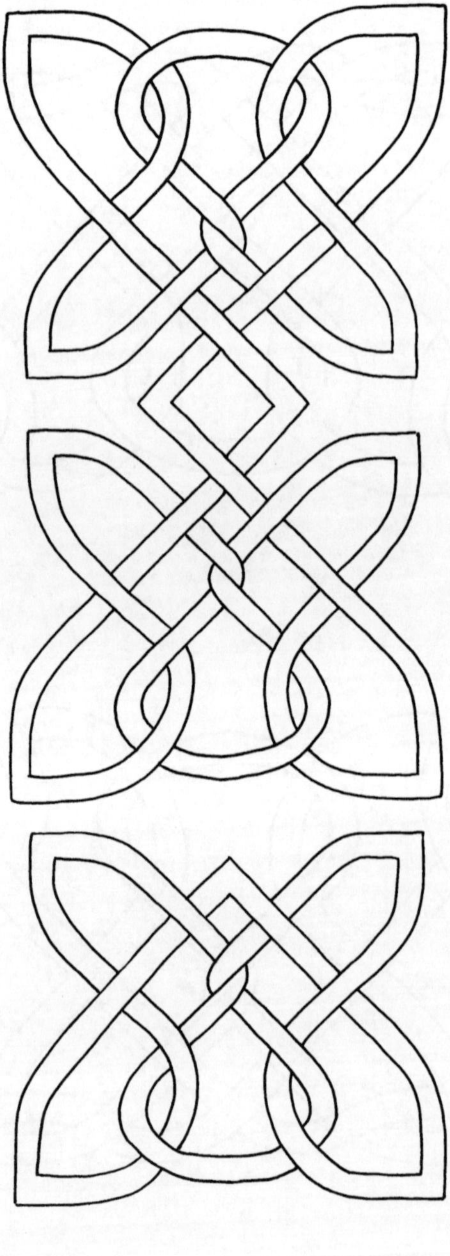

© Lora S. Irish

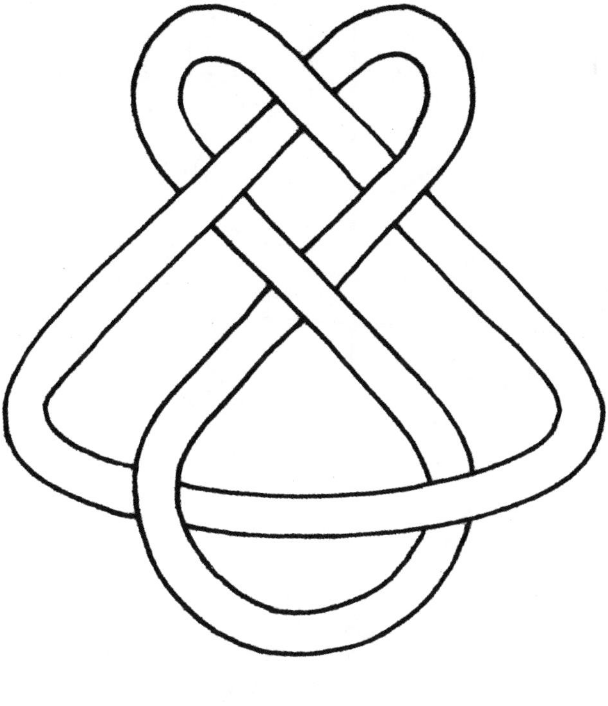

Celtic

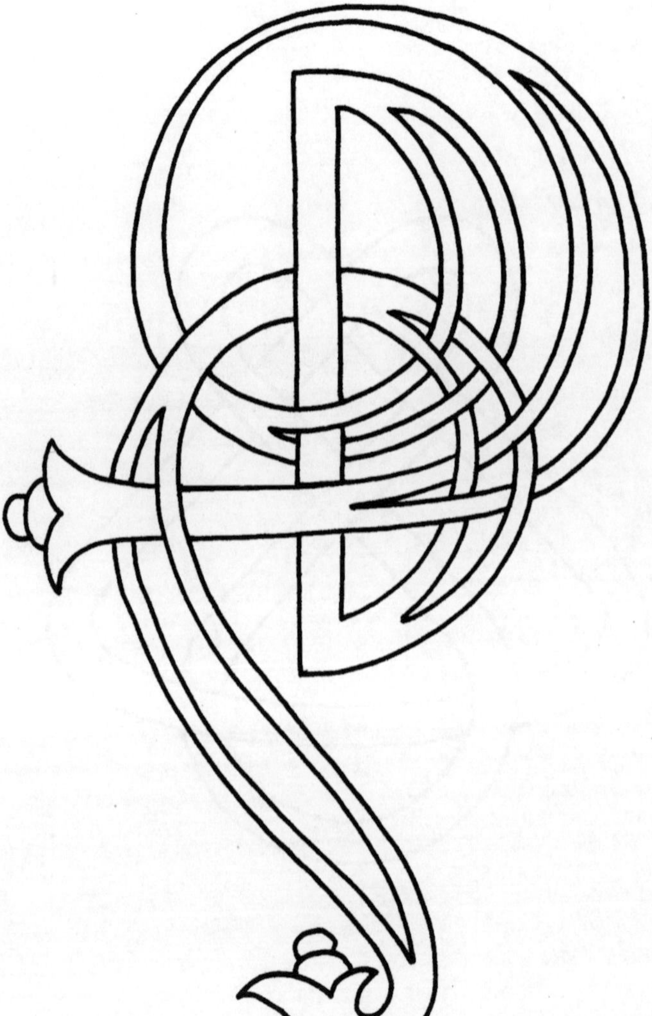

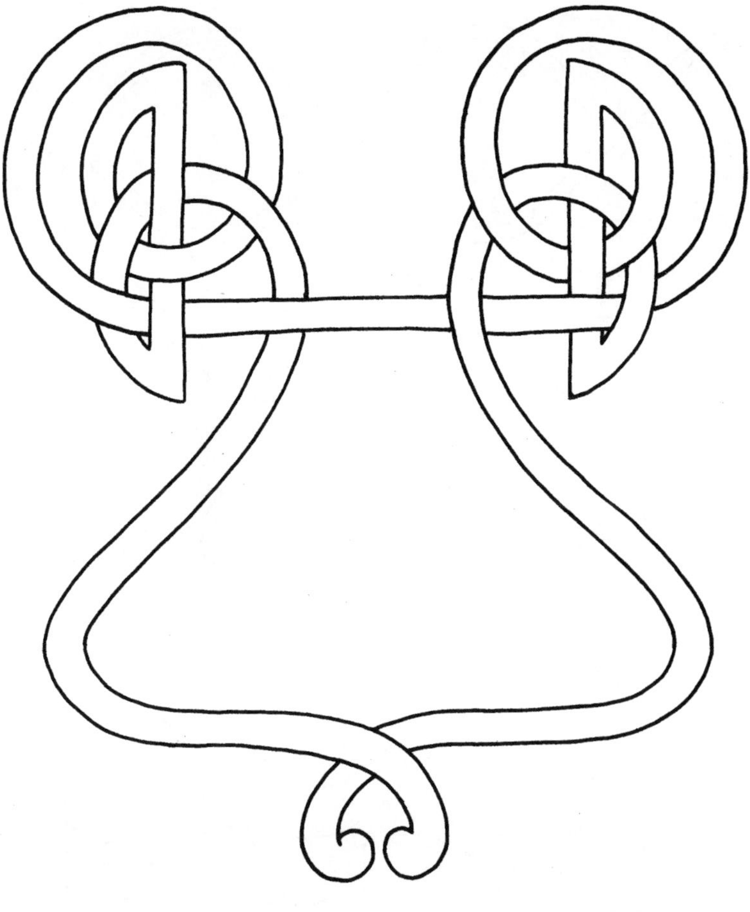

Celtic

© Lora S. Irish

Celtic

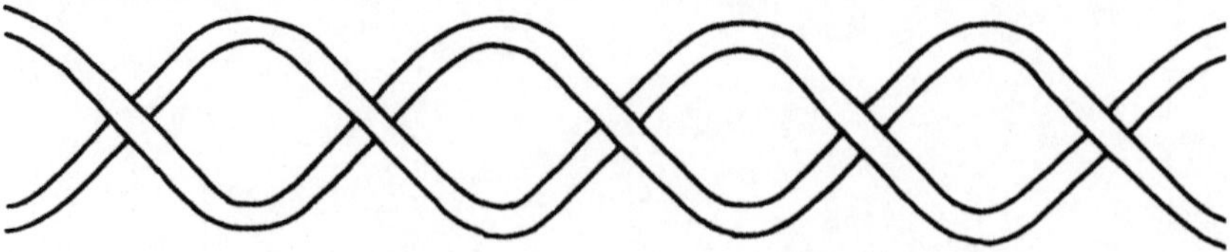

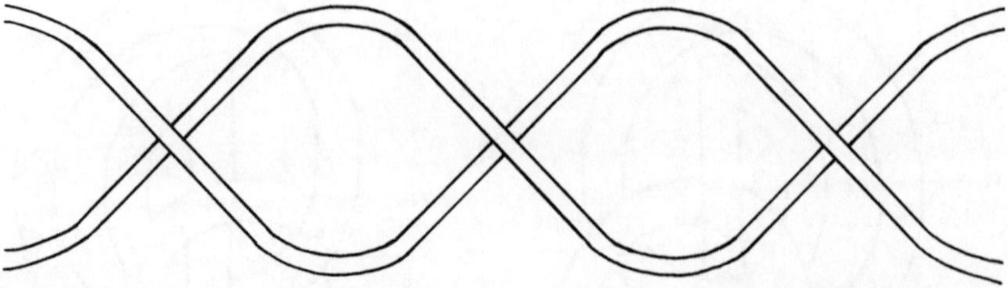

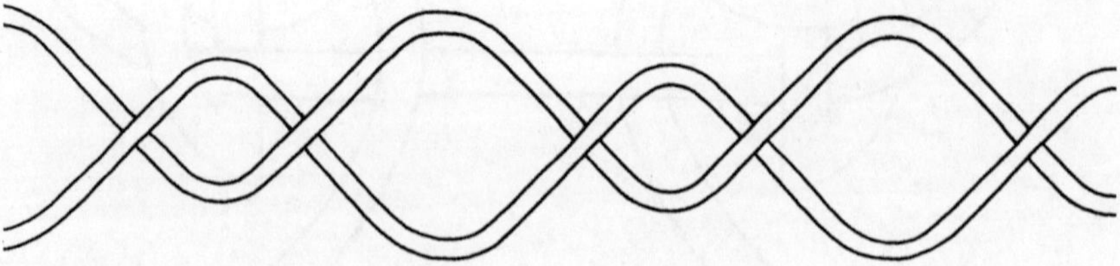

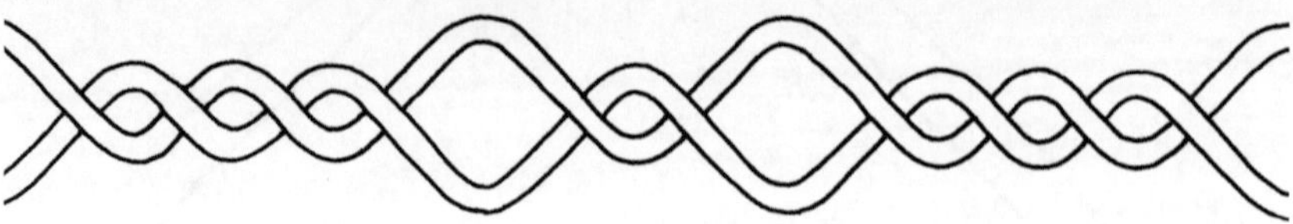

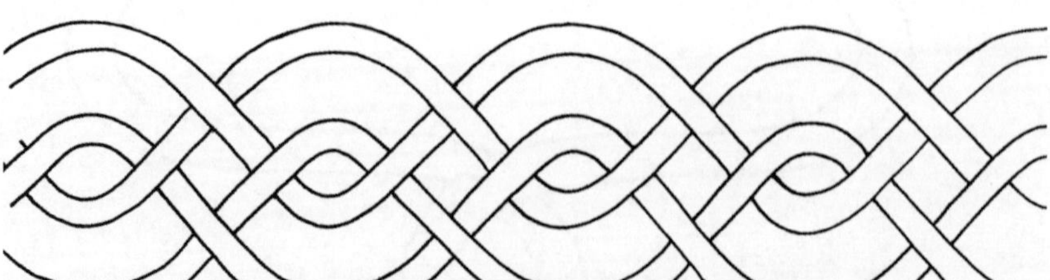

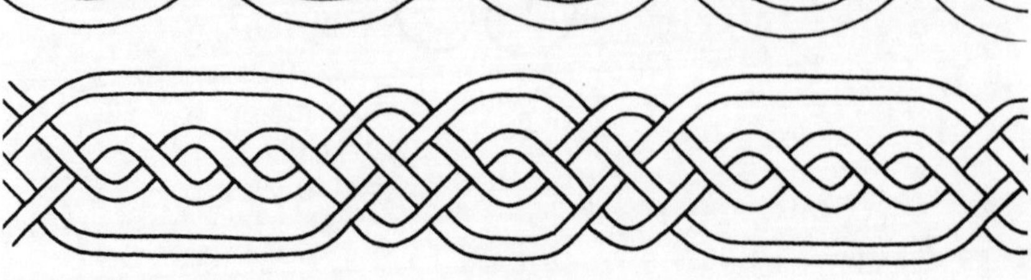

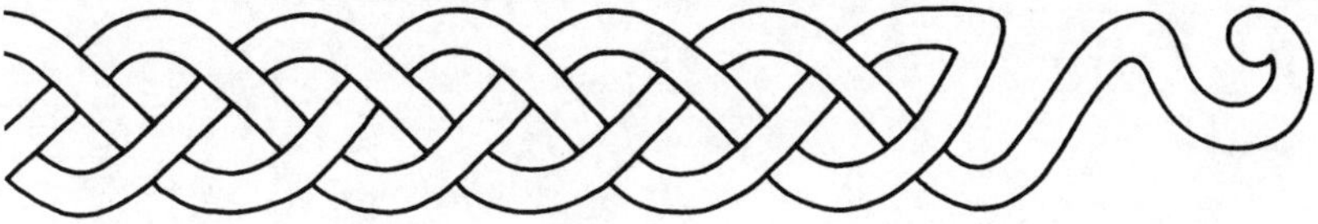

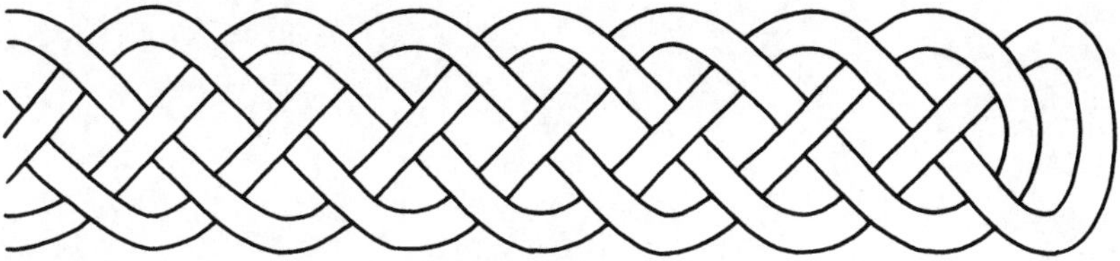

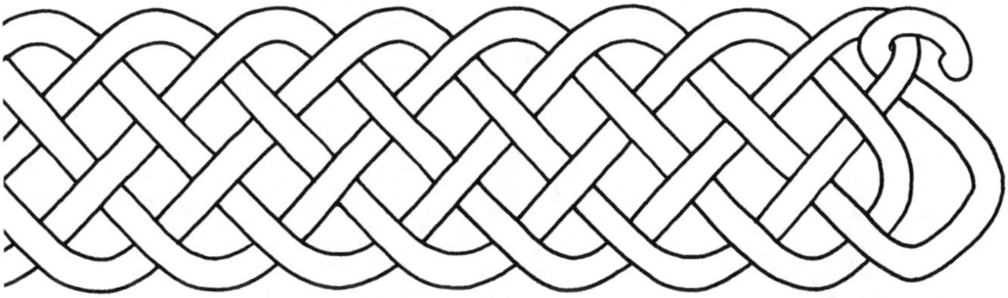

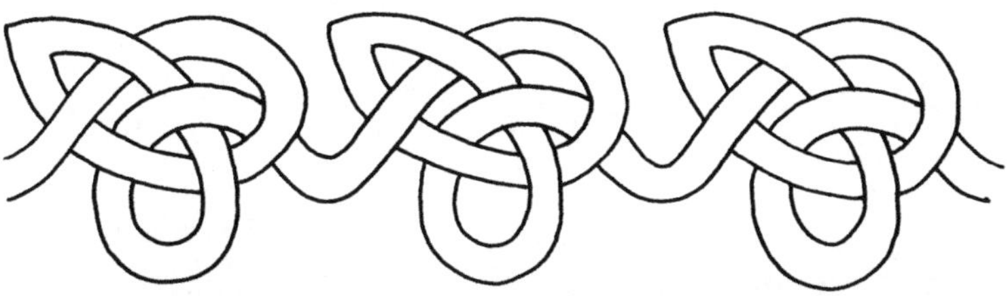

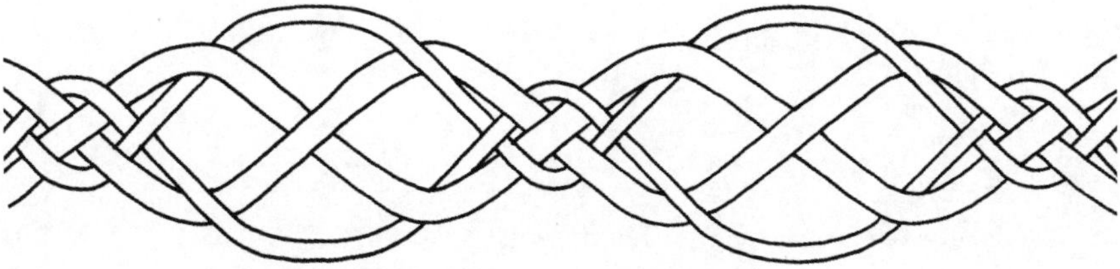

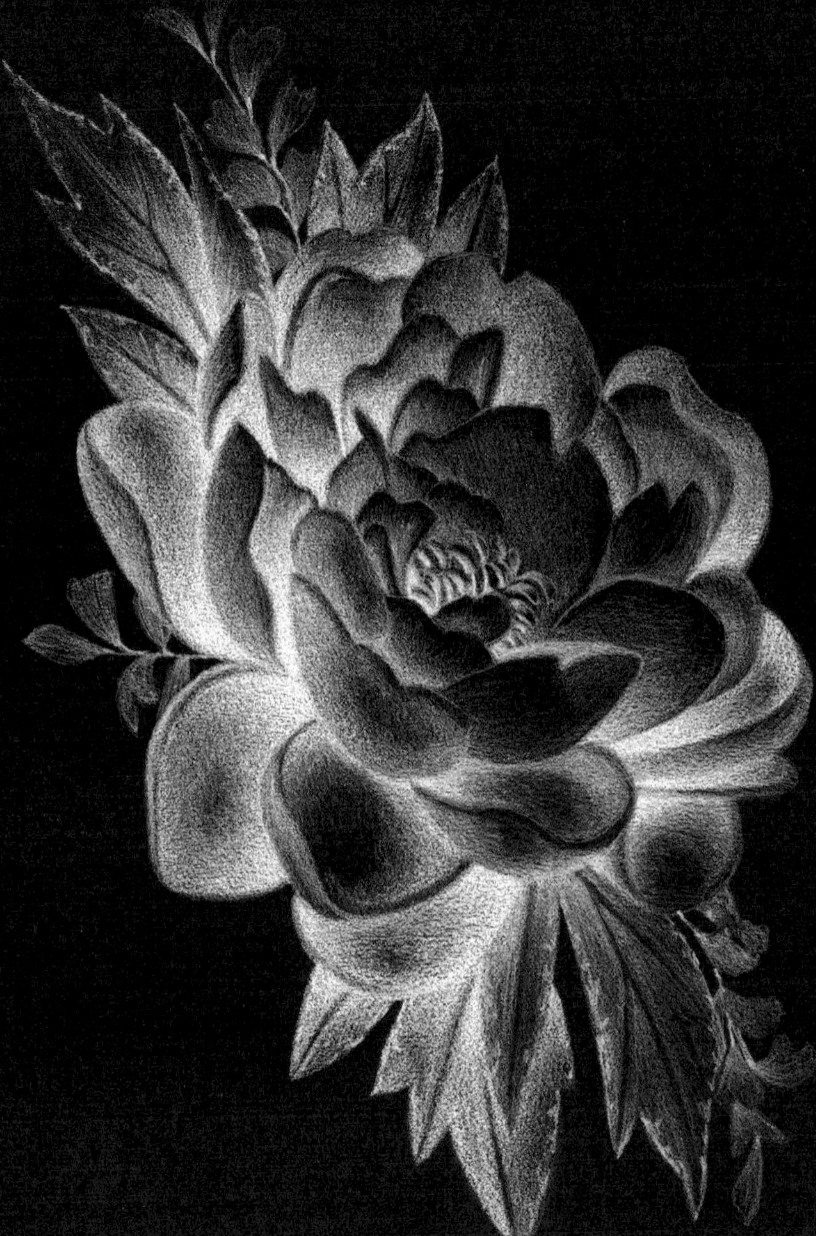

Floral

In the art world, a rose is not just a rose. Red roses commonly represent love and passion; white roses, virginity and purity; yellow roses, jealousy and infidelity. Then there is the carnation, a metaphor for betrothal; the chrysanthemum, a symbol of optimism and long life; the daisy, a sign of innocence; the iris, a representation of death as well as faith, valor, and wisdom; the lily, a mark of purity, innocence, and the Virgin Mary; the daffodil, a symbol of unrequited love; the marigold, a mark of happiness; the morning glory, a representation of the transience of life; and the violet, a sign of faithfulness, humility, and chastity.

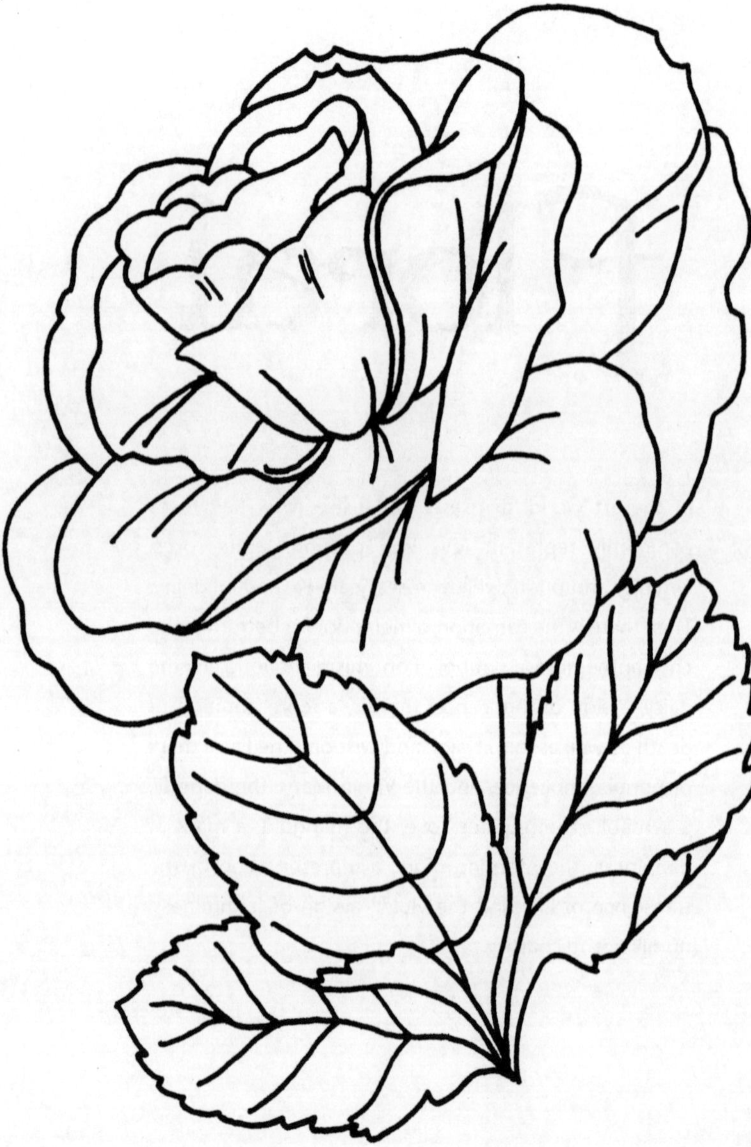

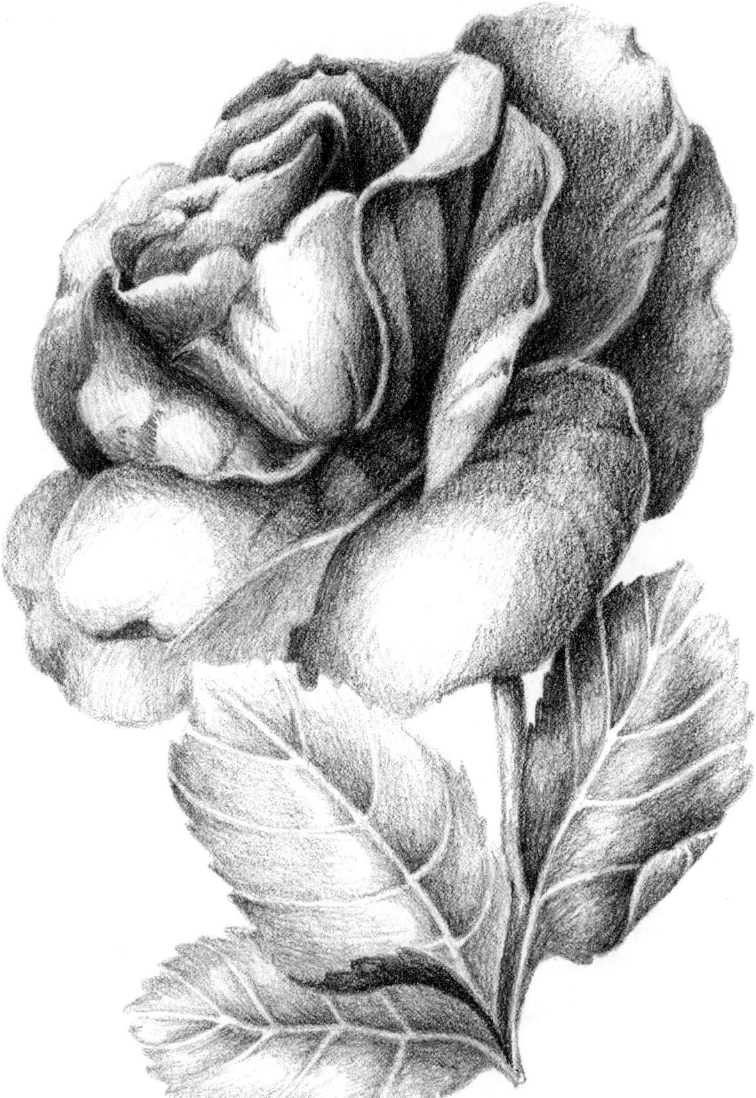

Floral

Floral

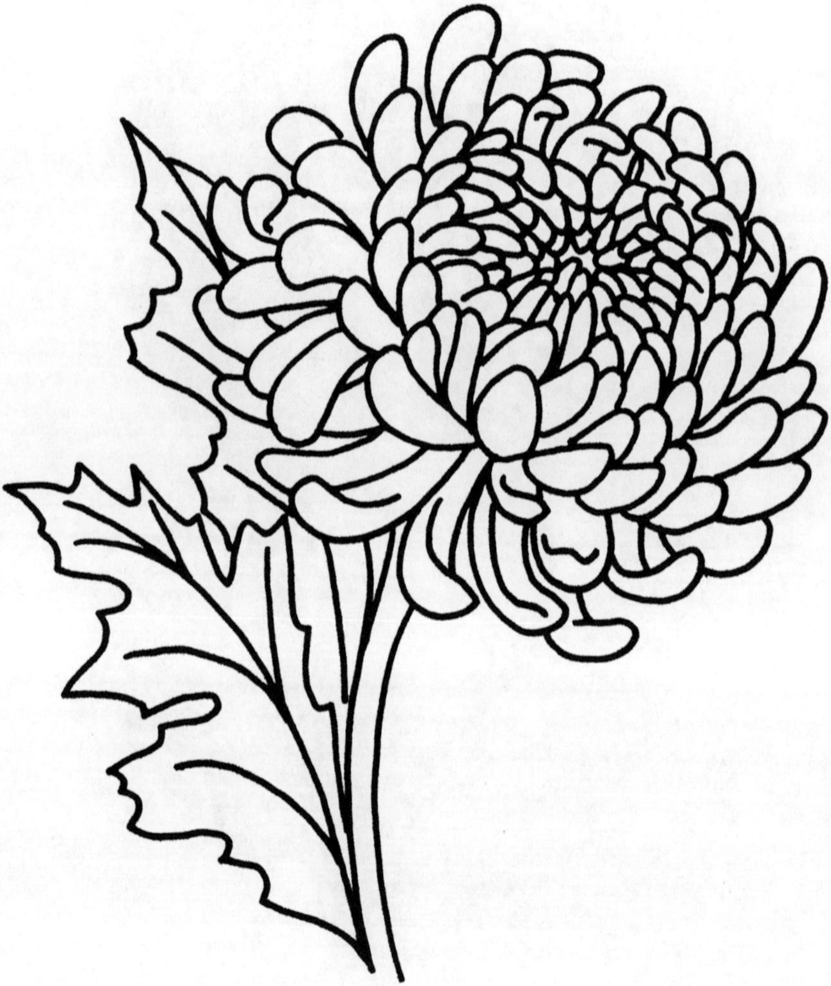

© Lora S. Irish

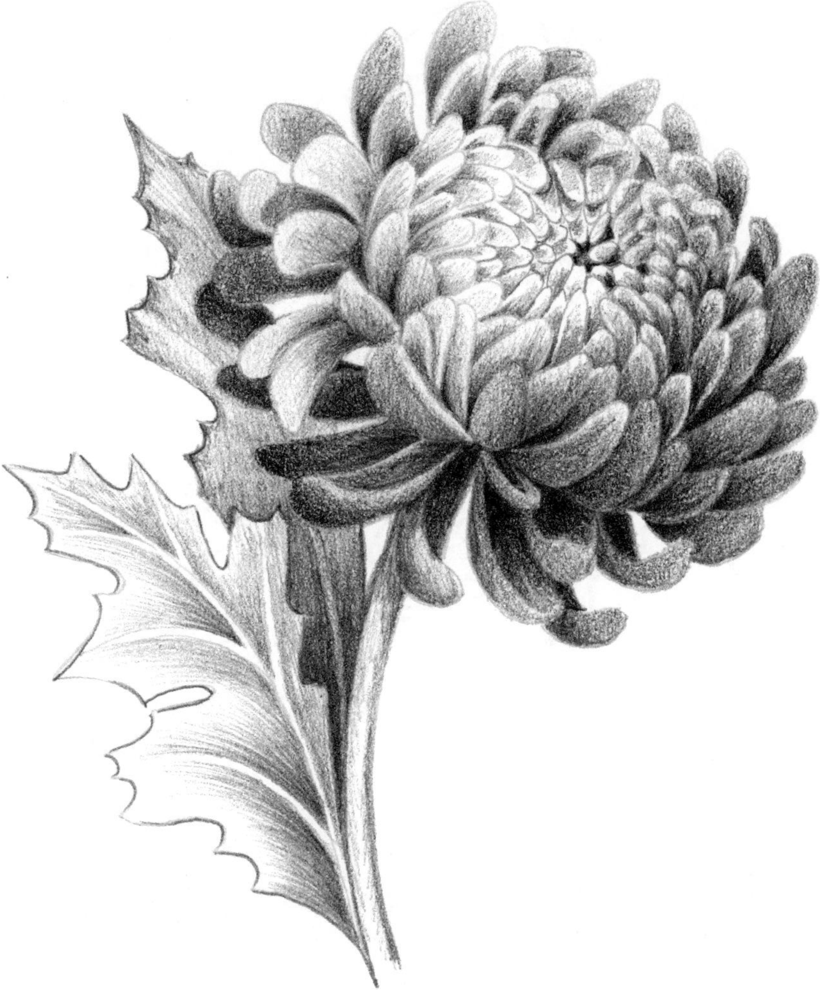

Floral

Floral

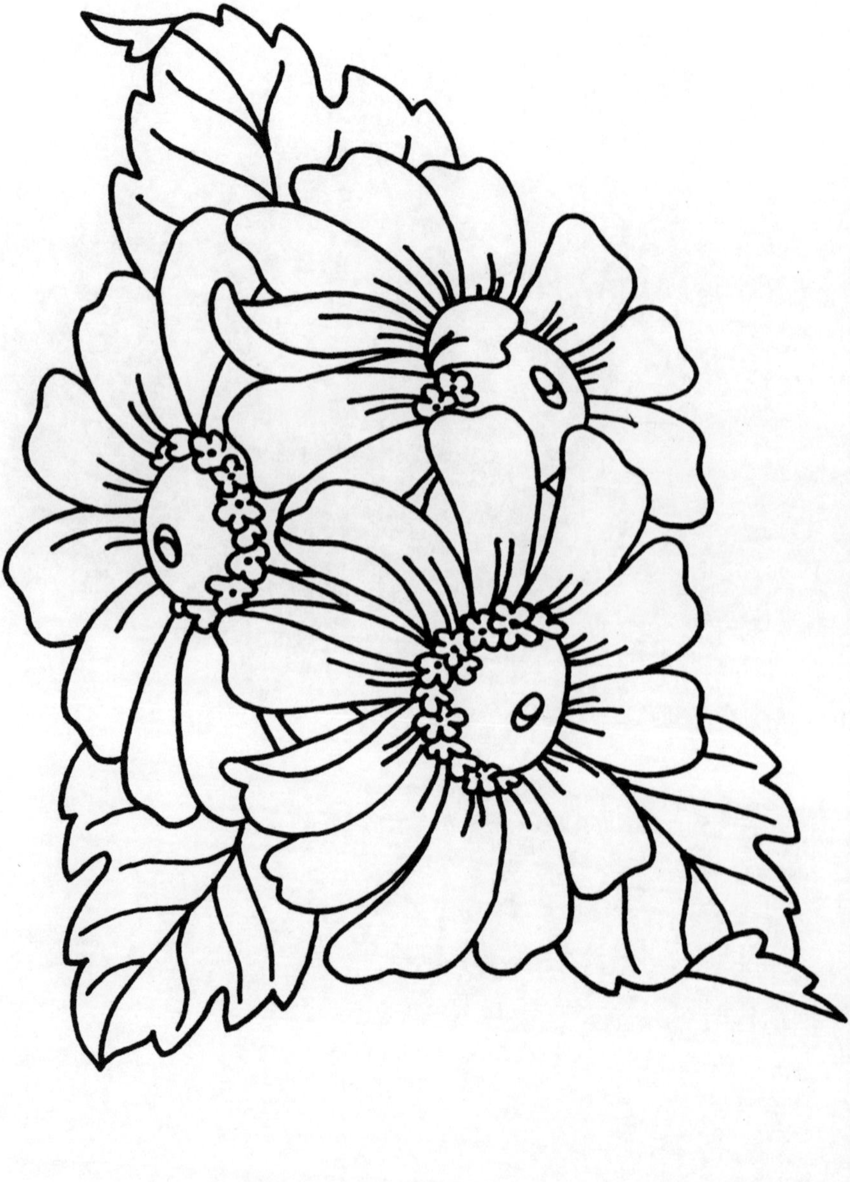

© Lora S. Irish

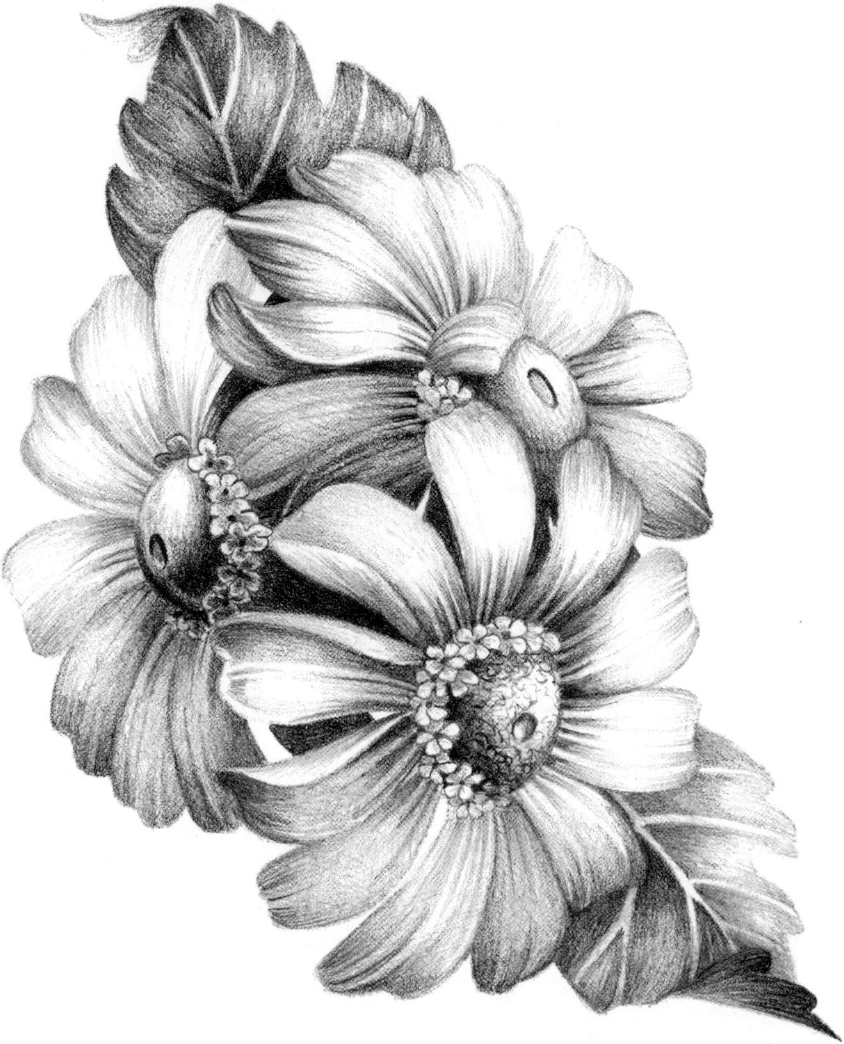

Floral

© Lora S. Irish

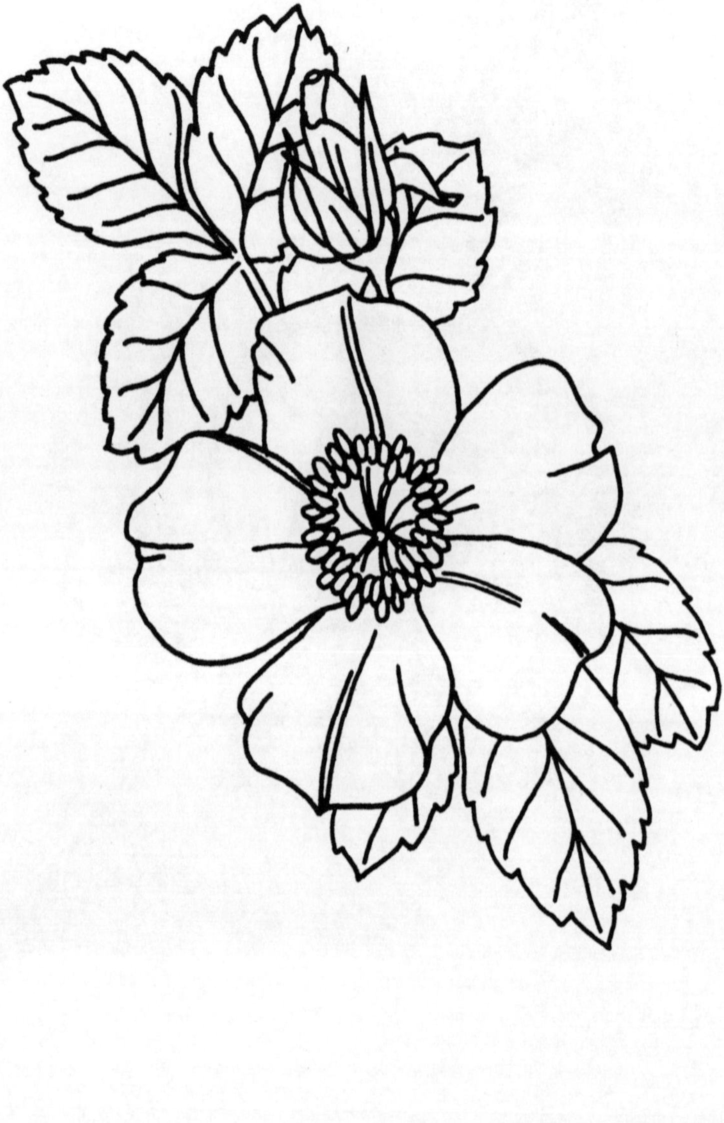

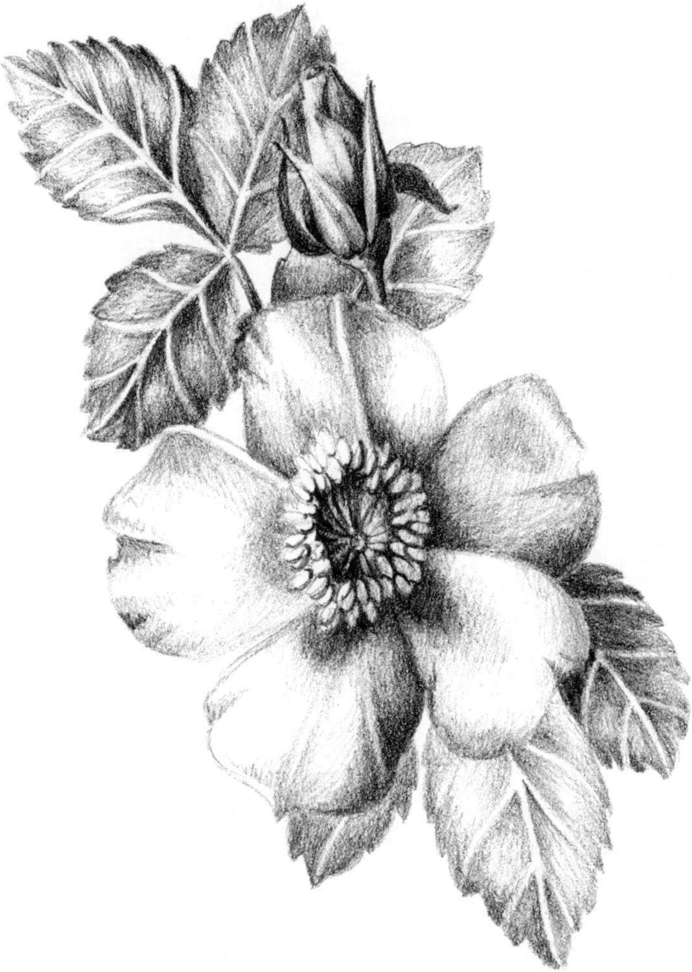

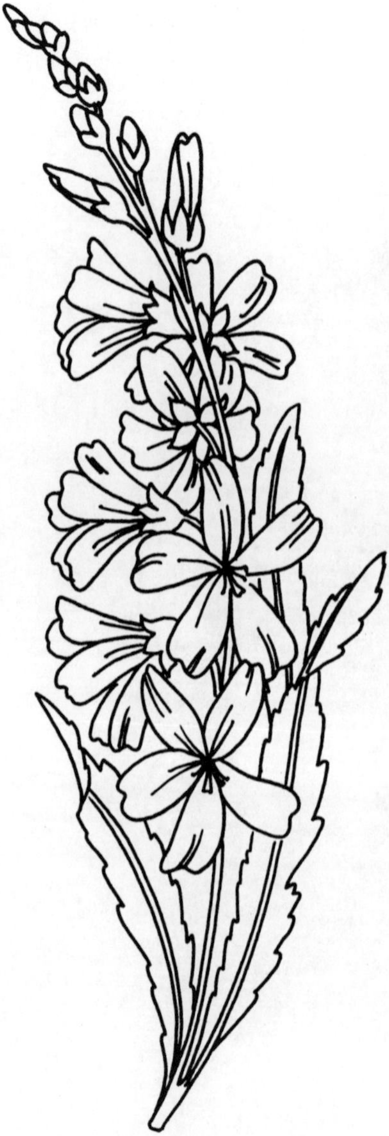

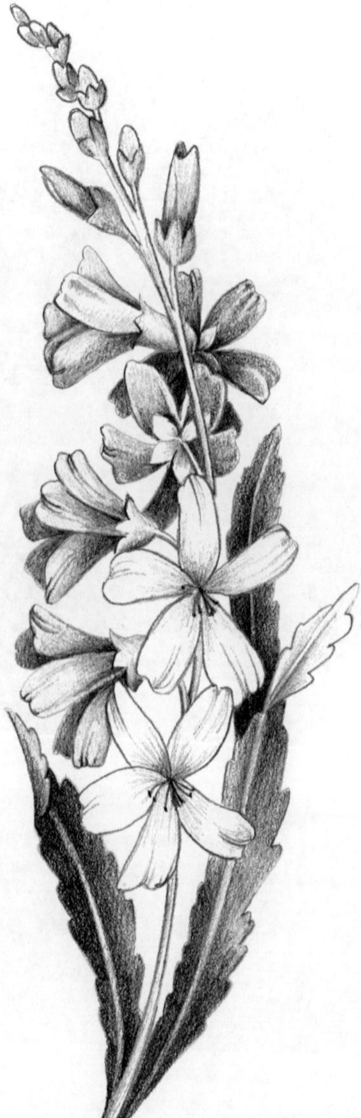

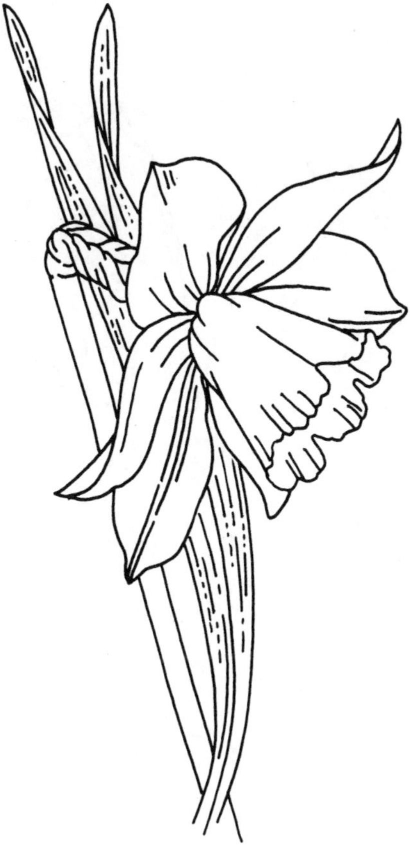

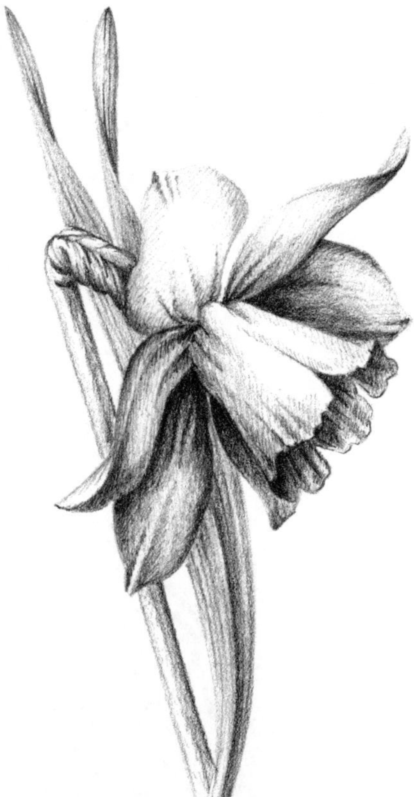

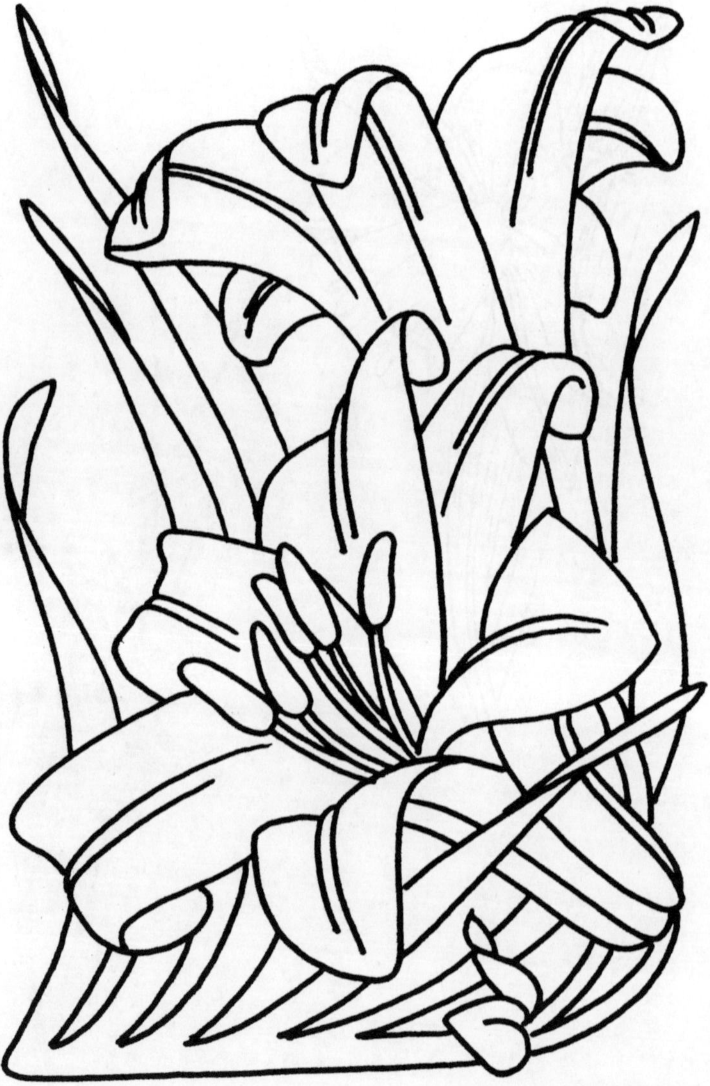

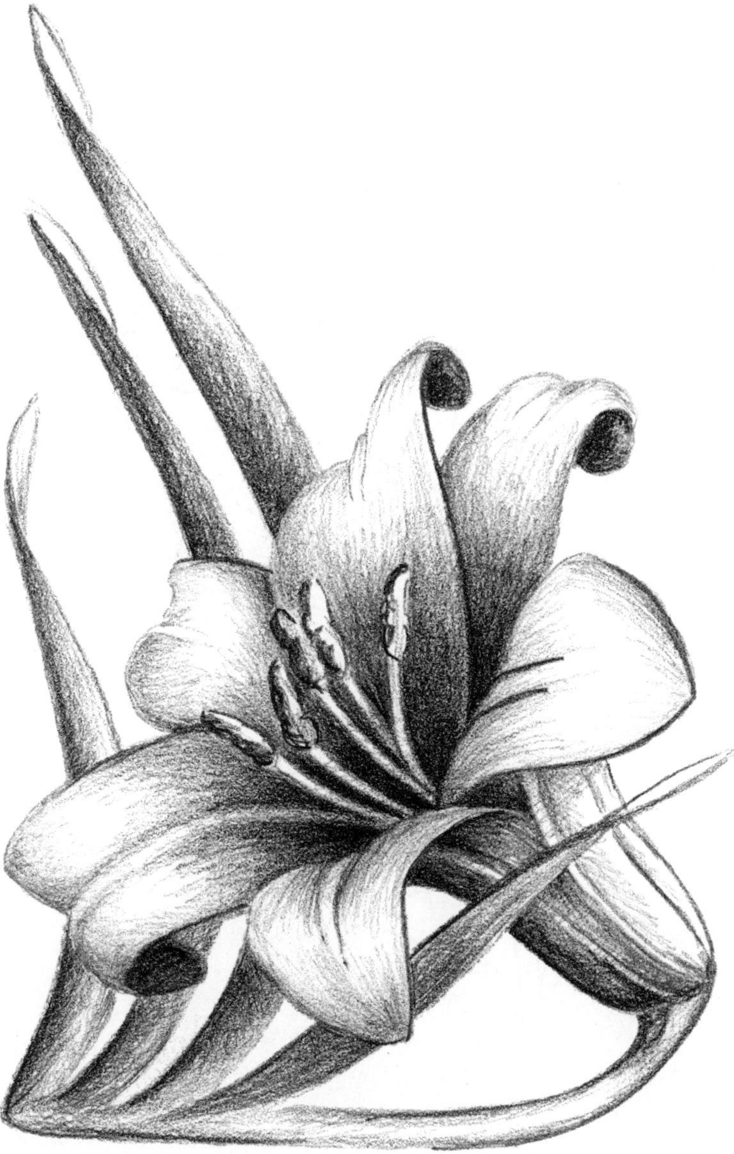

© Lora S. Irish

Floral

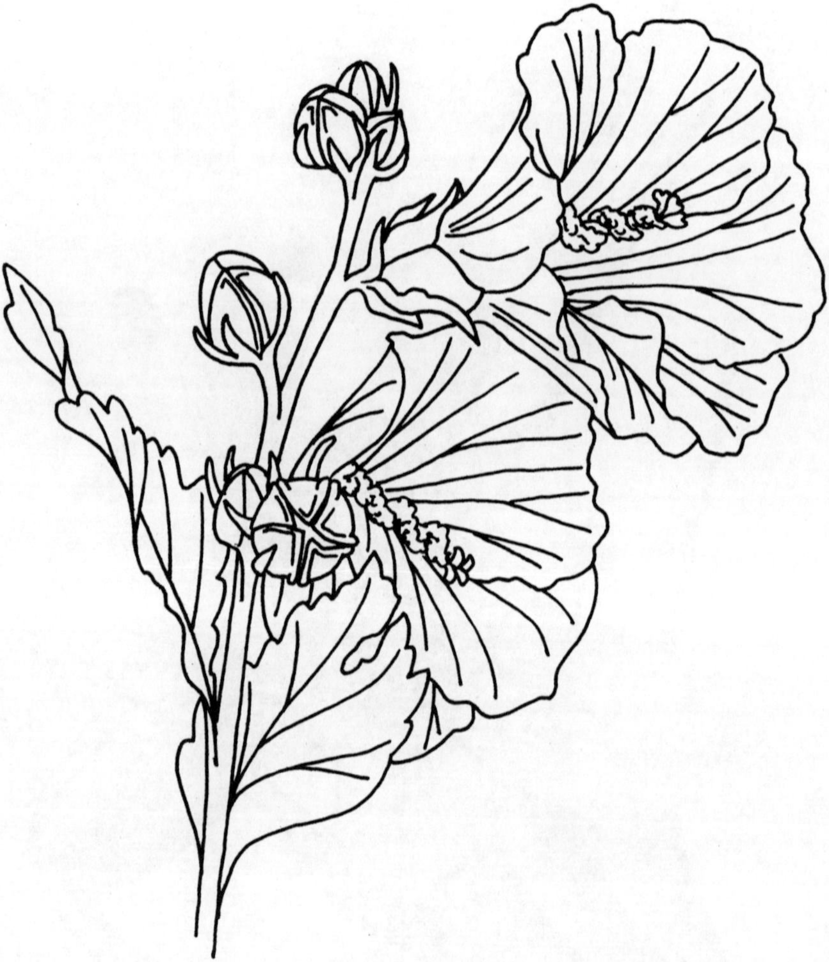

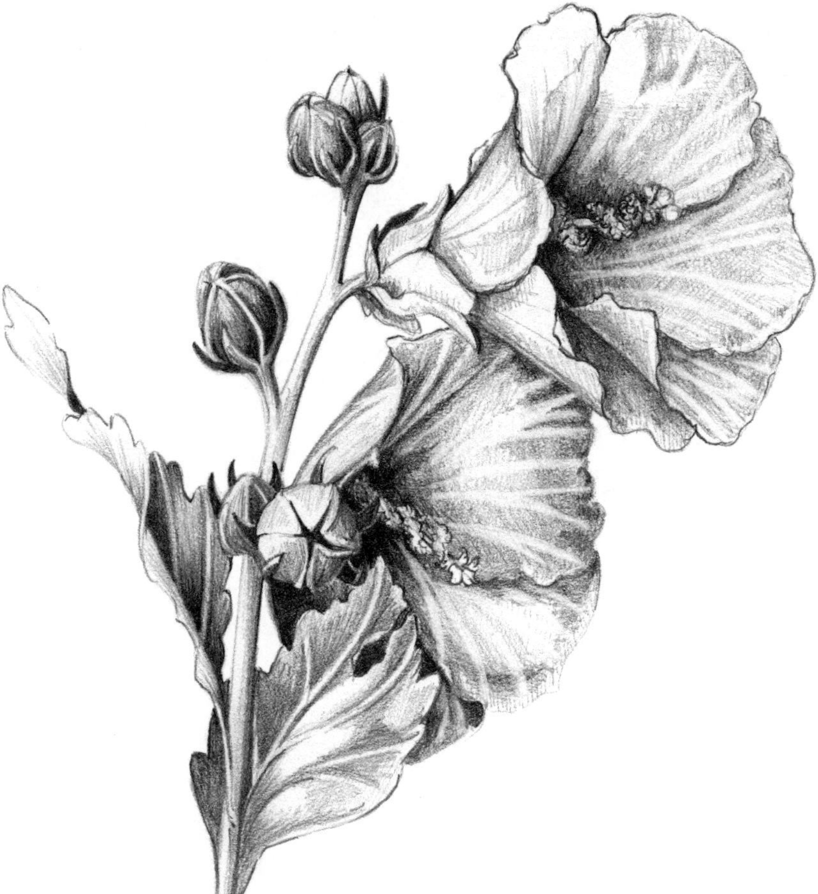

Floral

Floral

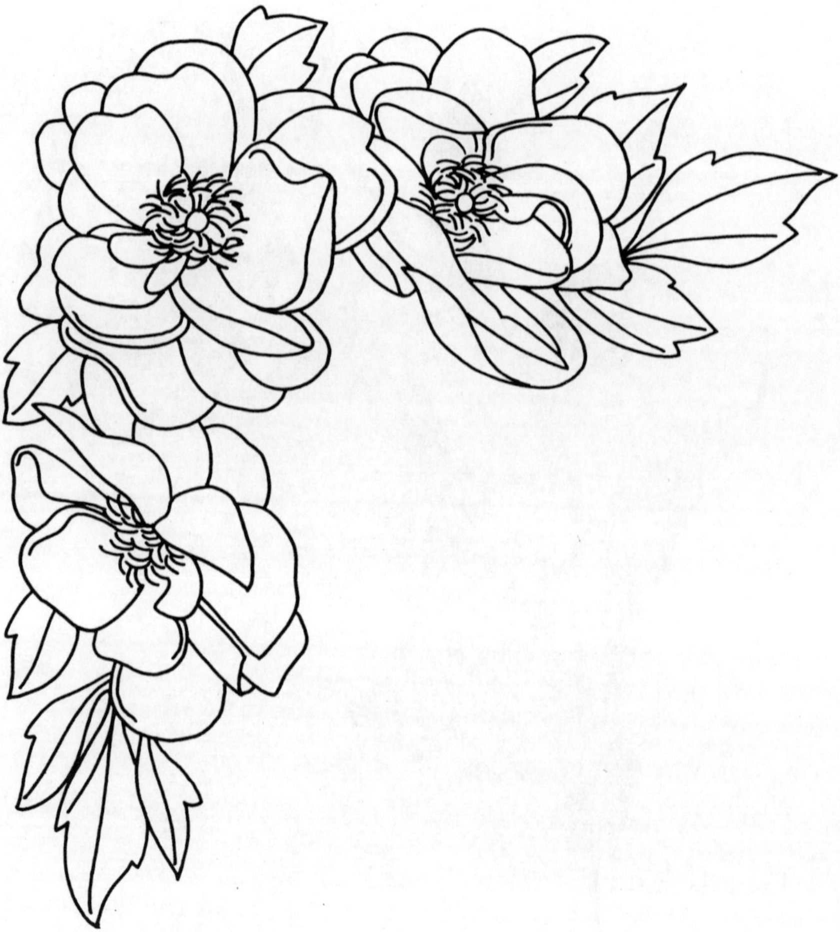

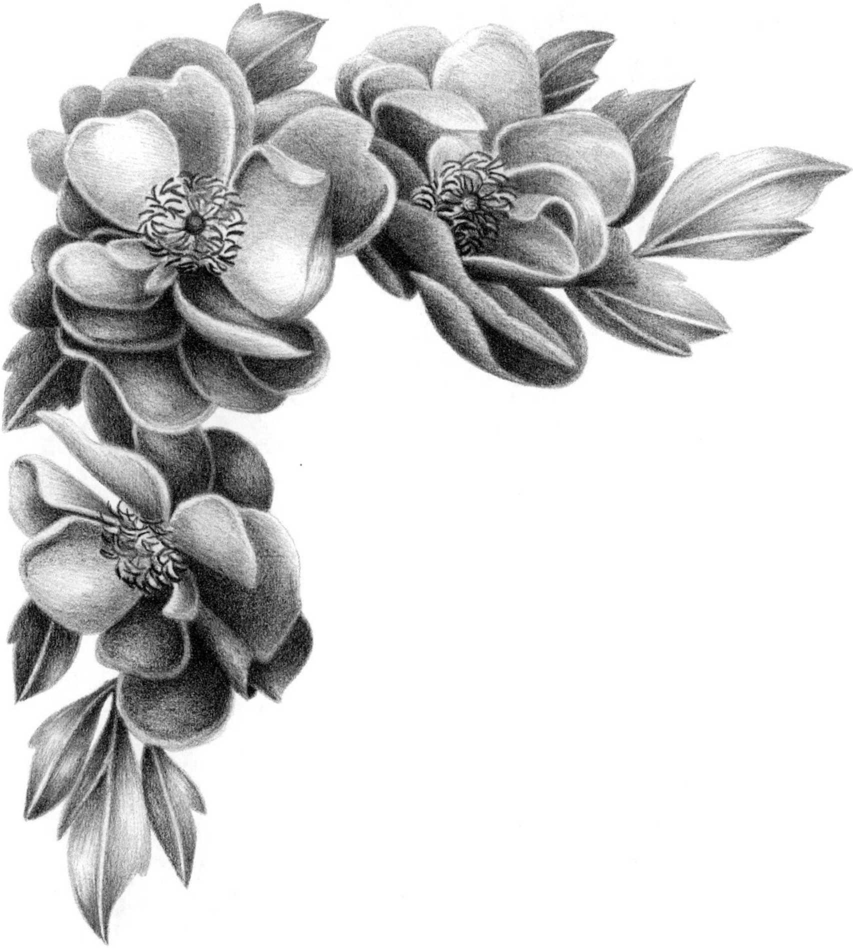

Floral

© Lora S. Irish

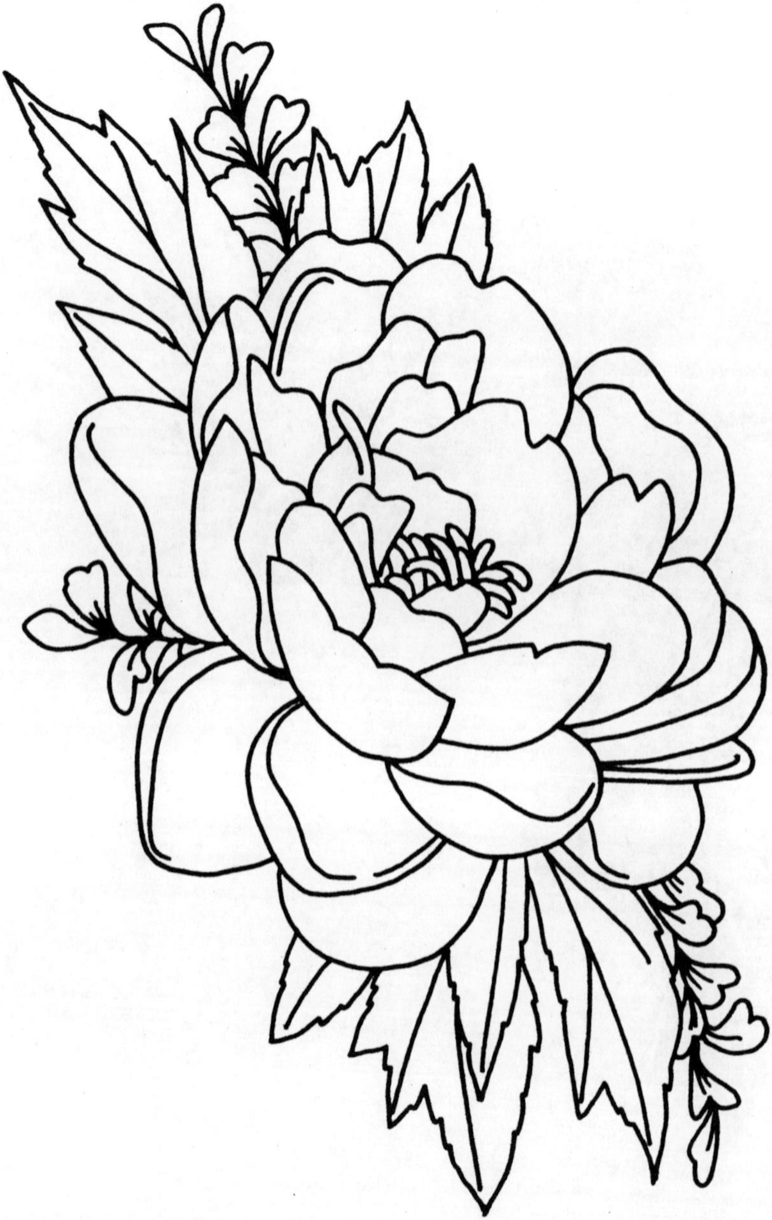

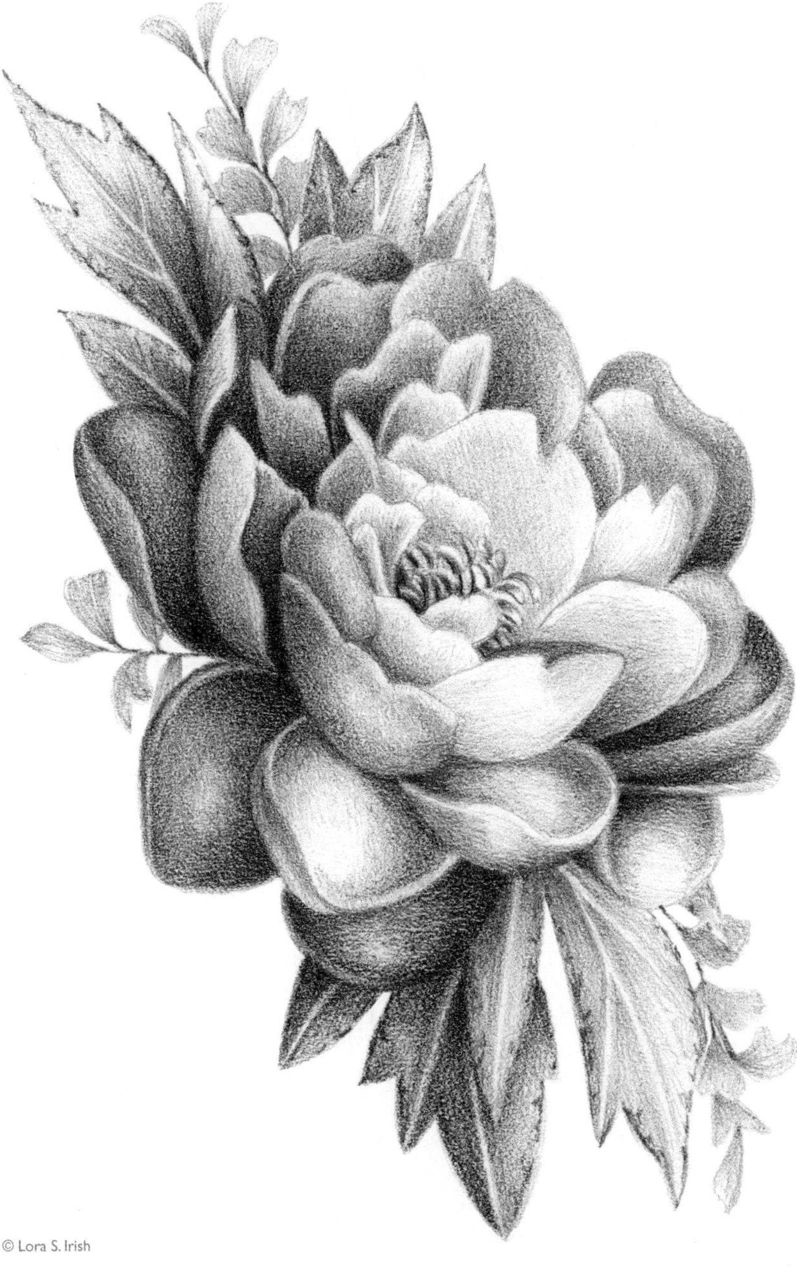

Floral

© Lora S. Irish

Floral

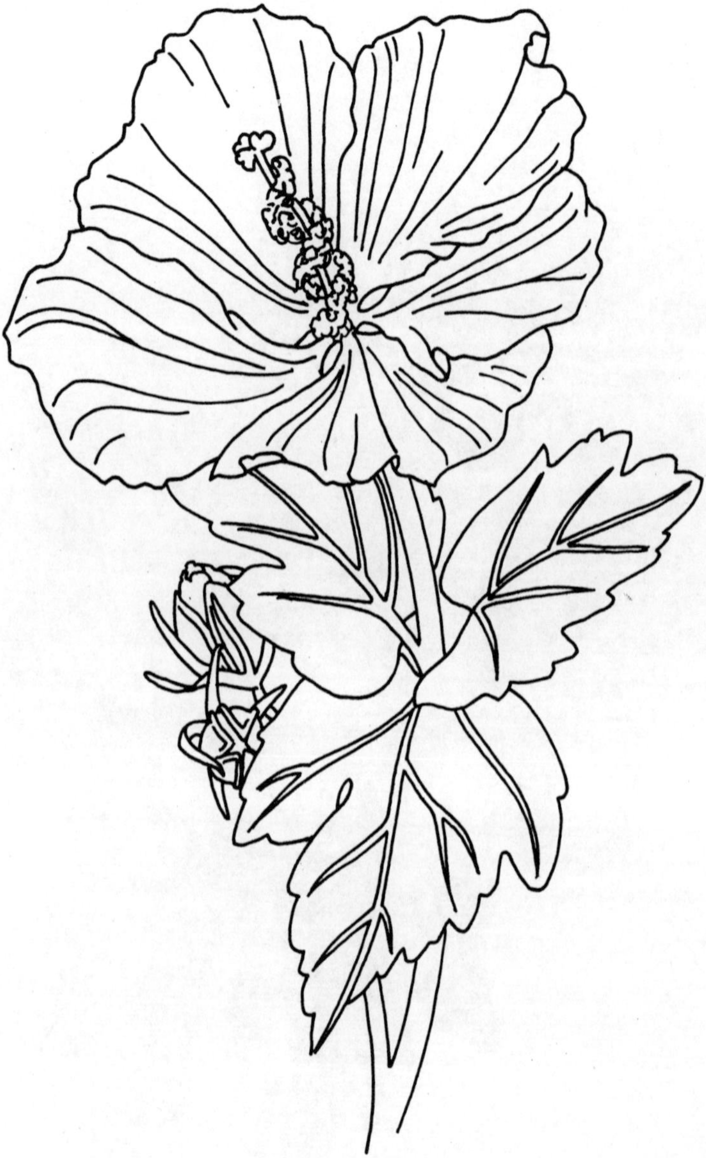

© Lora S. Irish

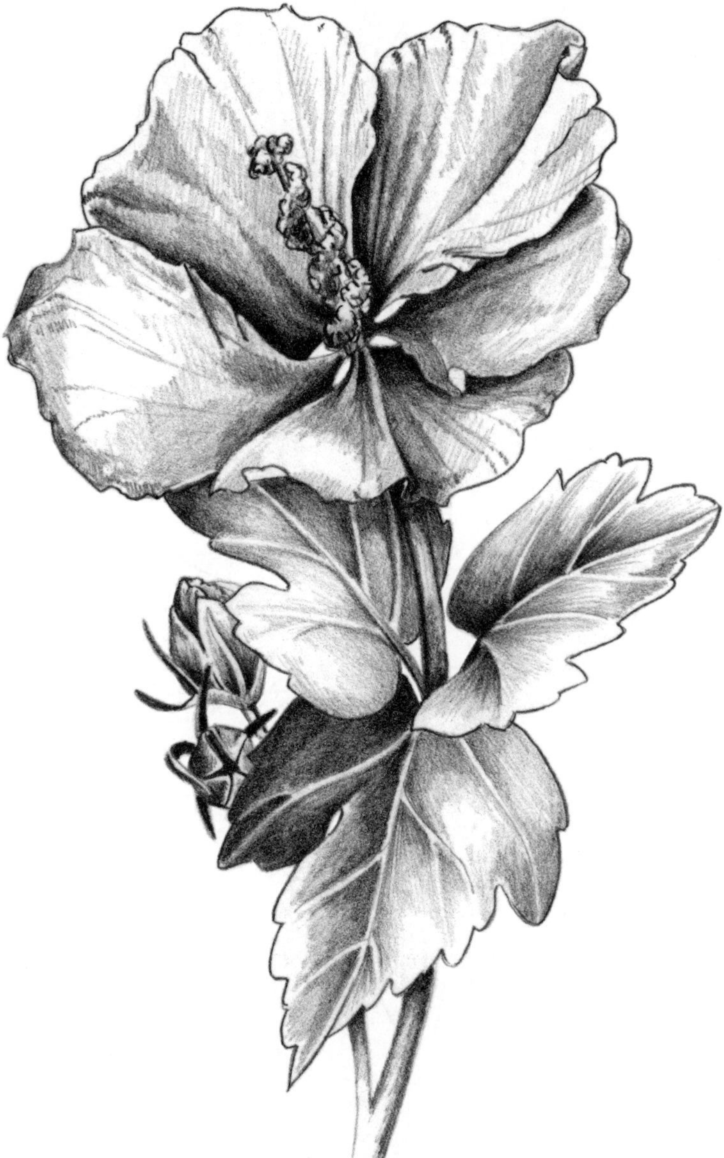

Floral

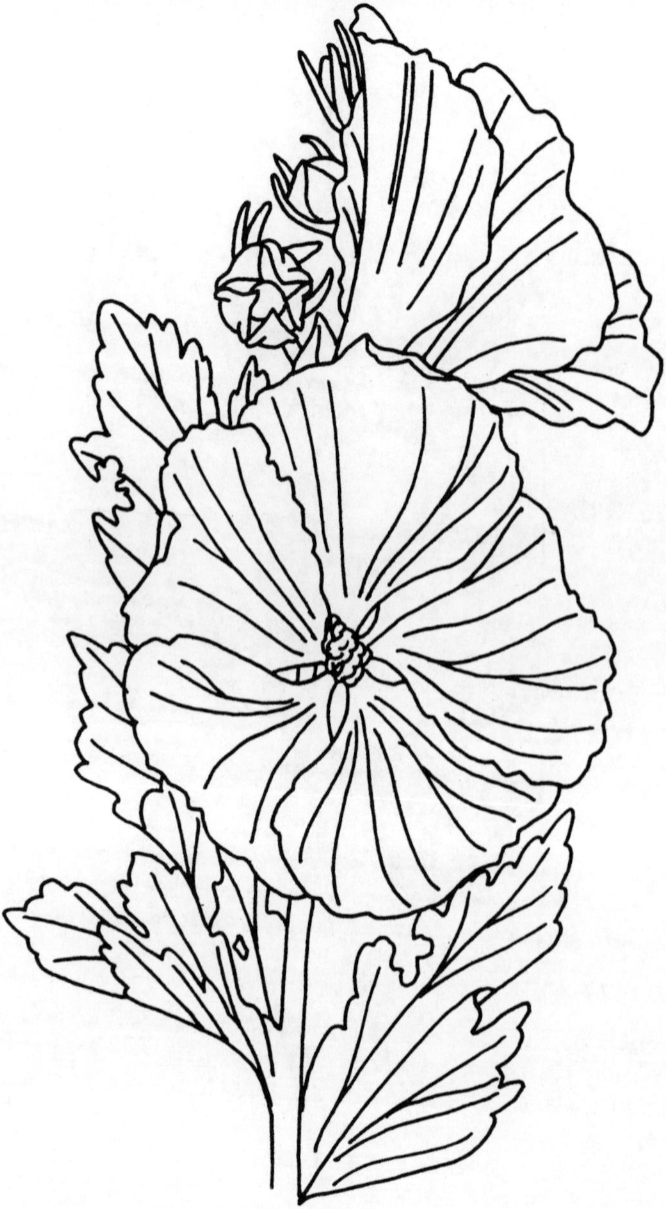

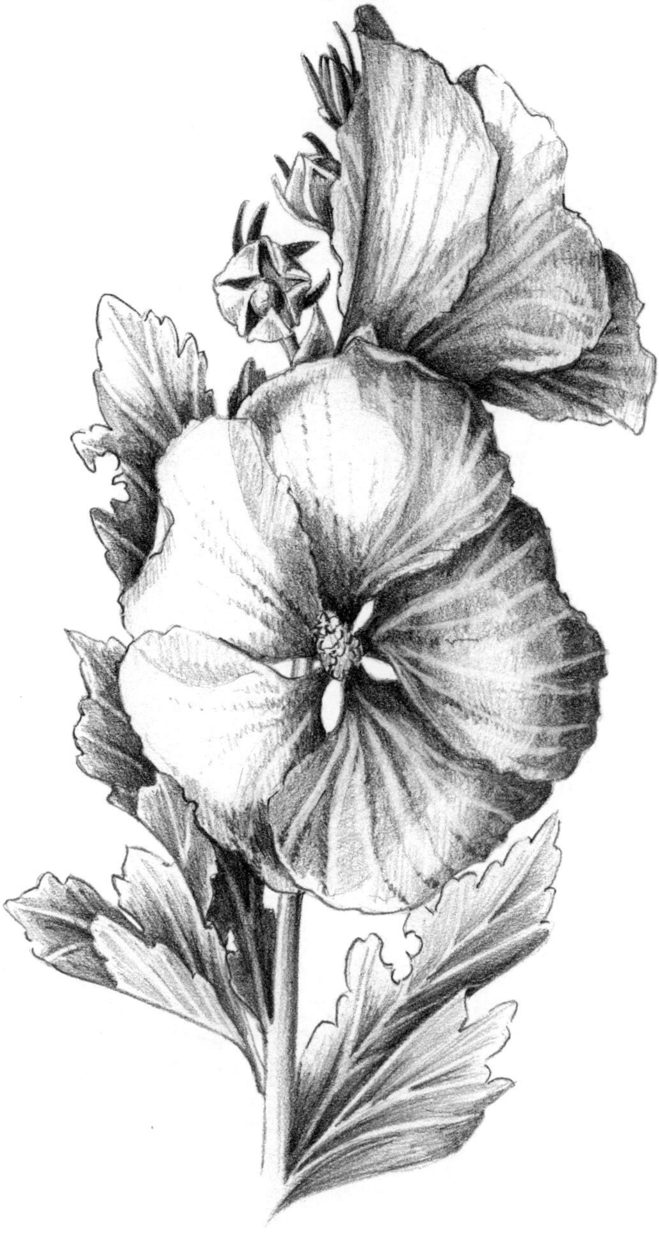

Floral

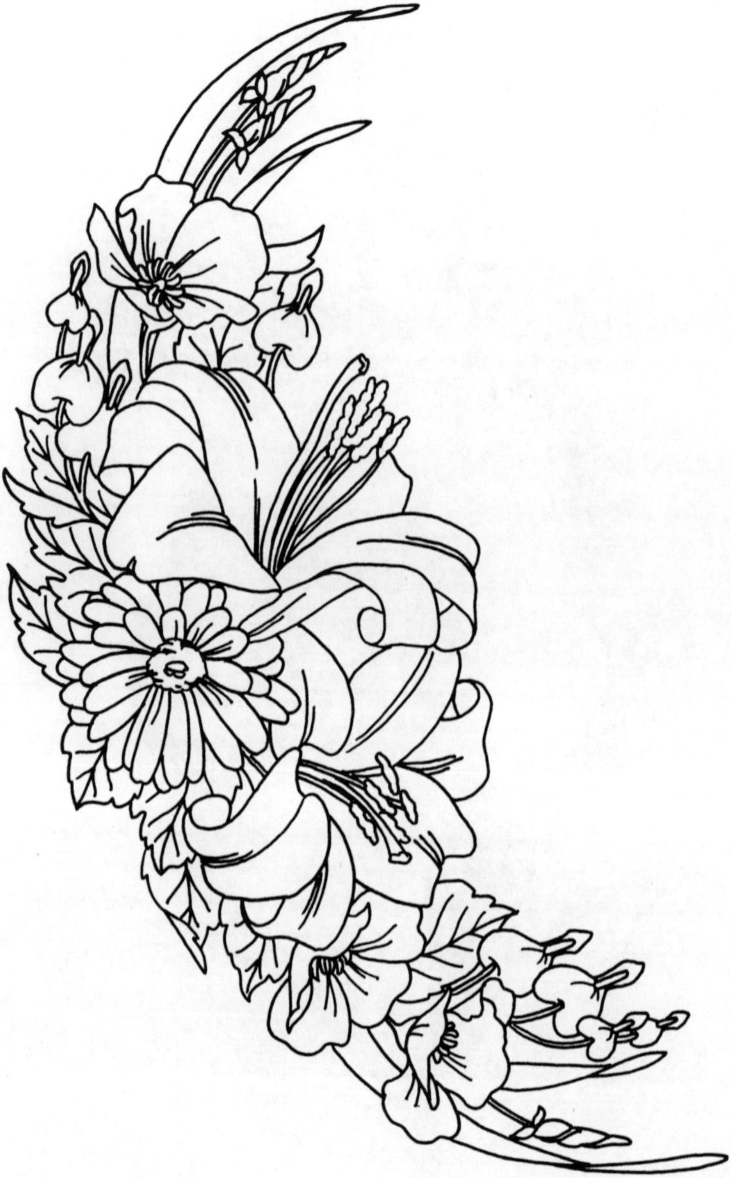

© Lora S. Irish

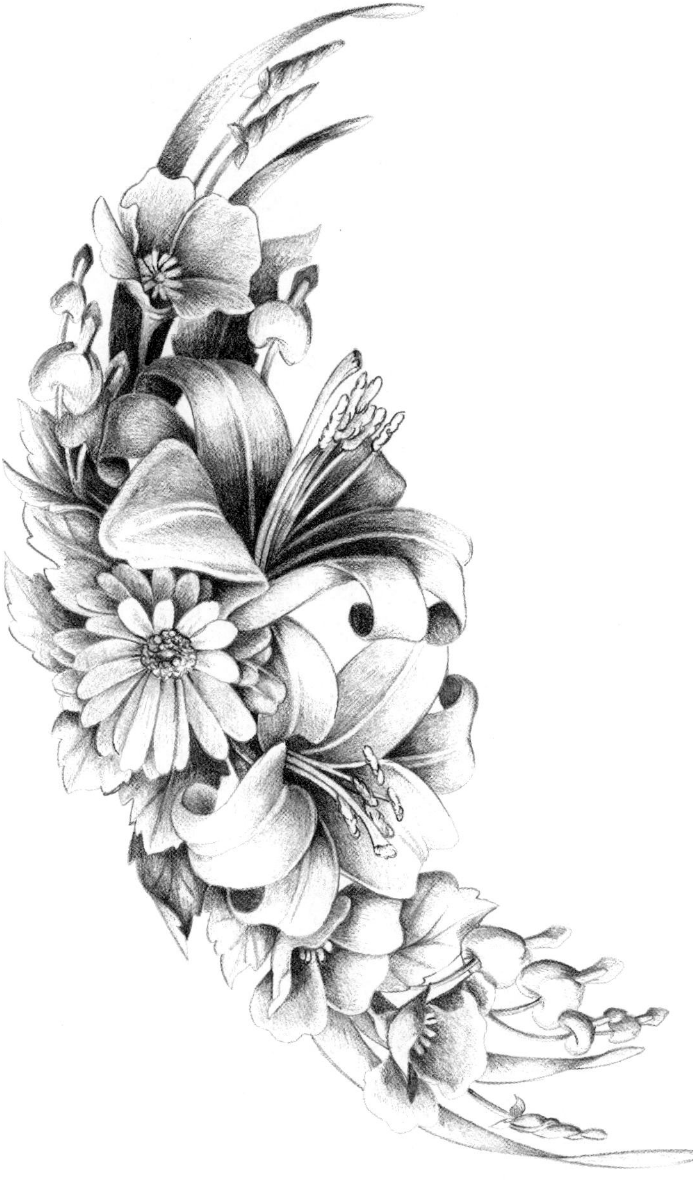

Floral

© Lora S. Irish

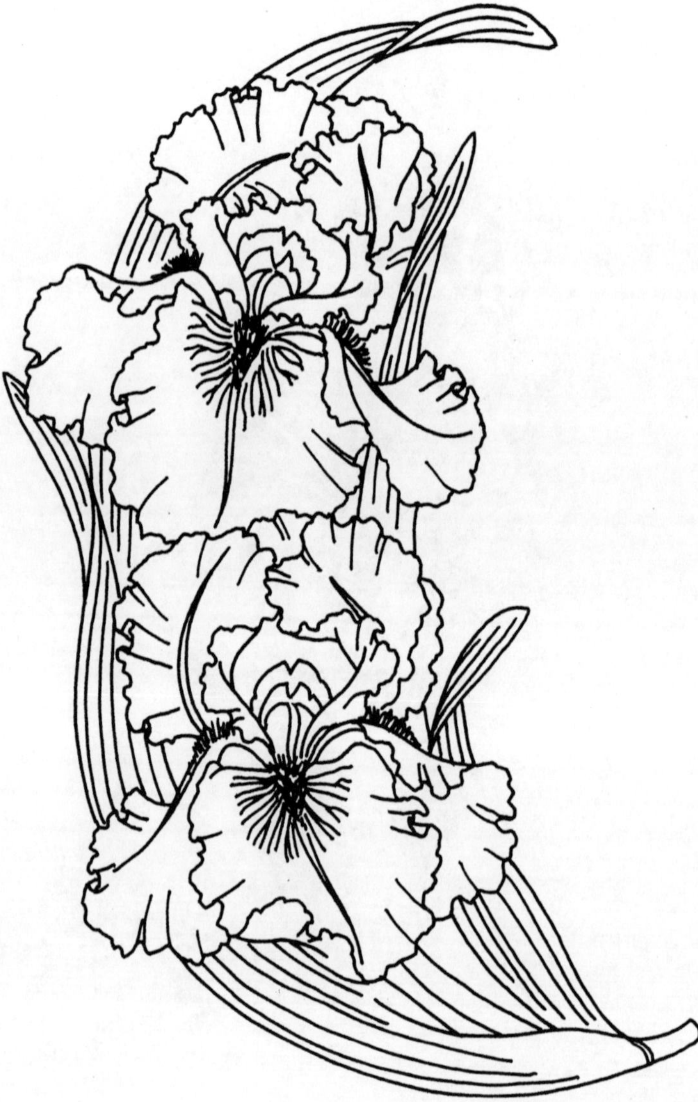

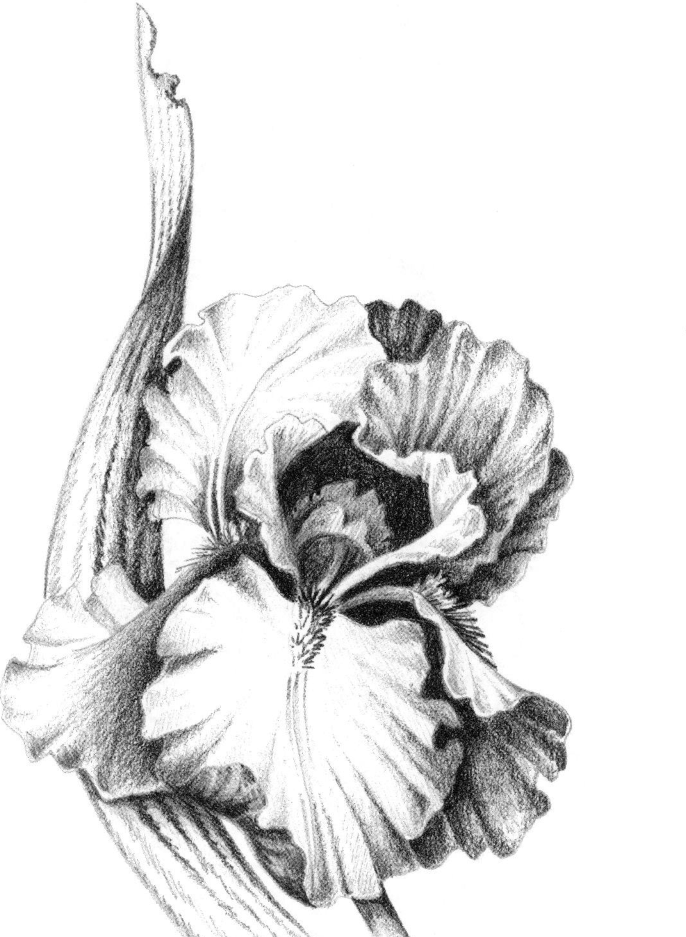

Floral

© Lora S. Irish

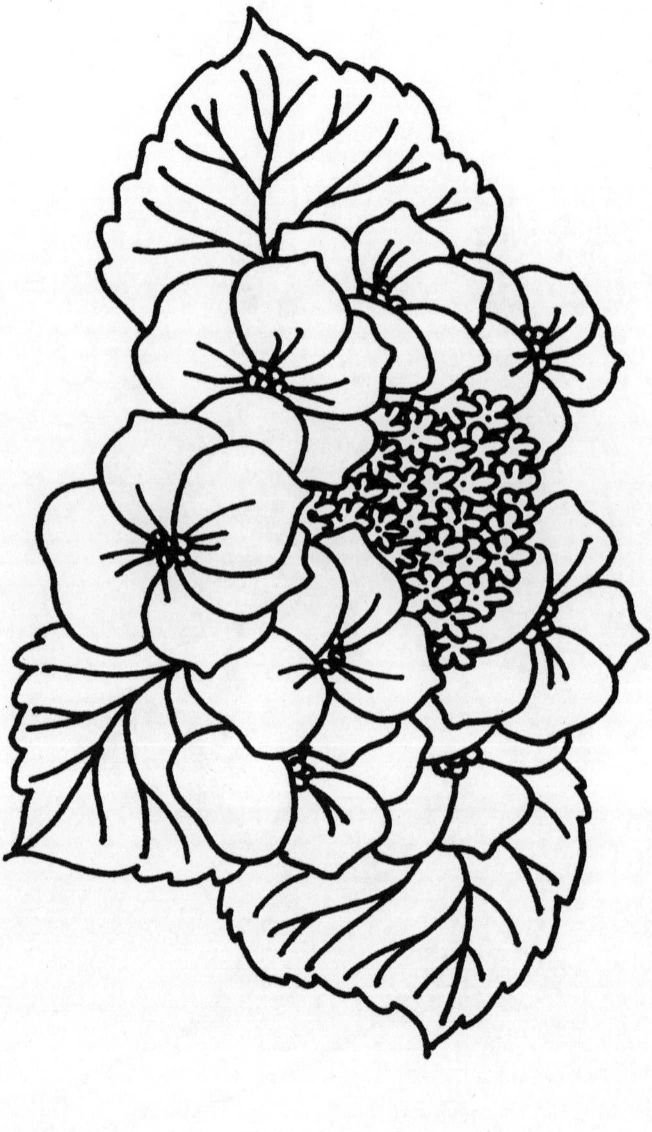

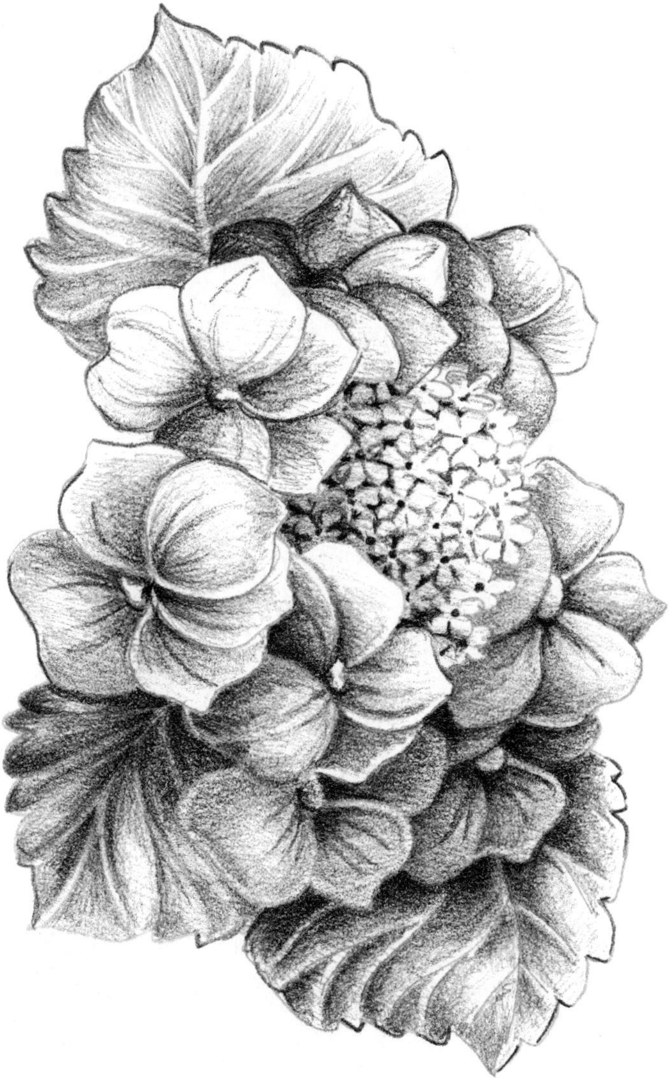

Floral

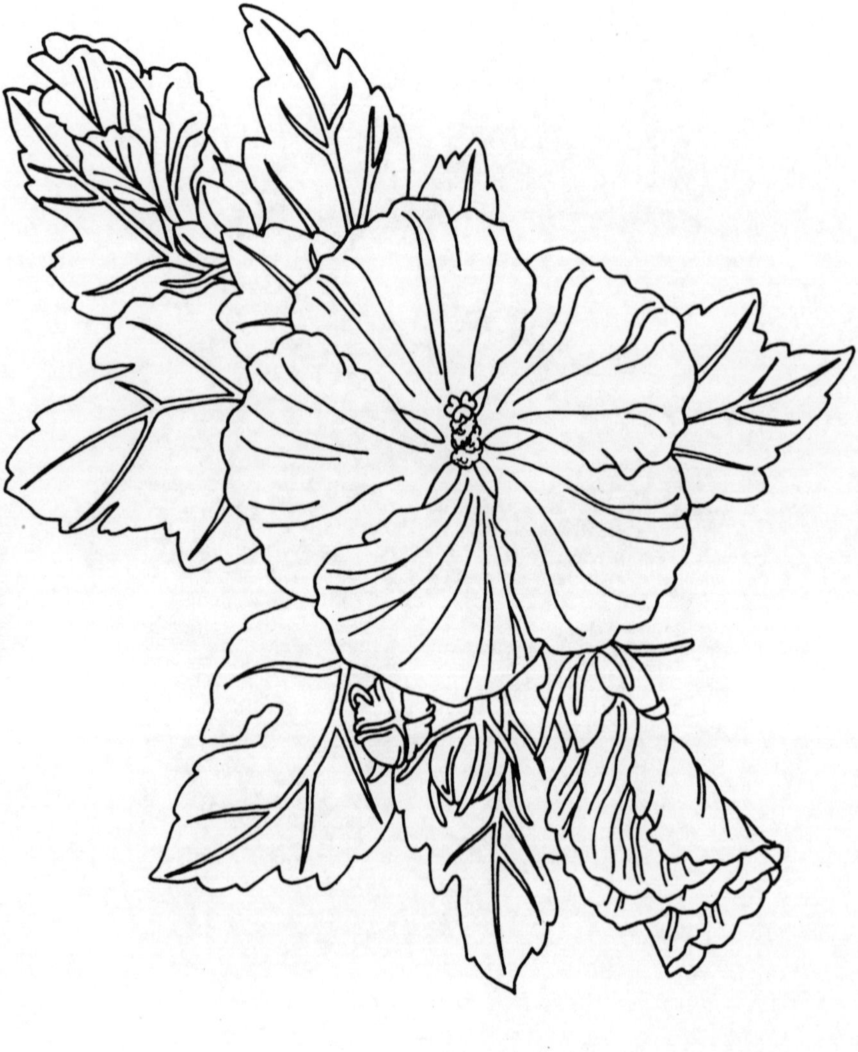

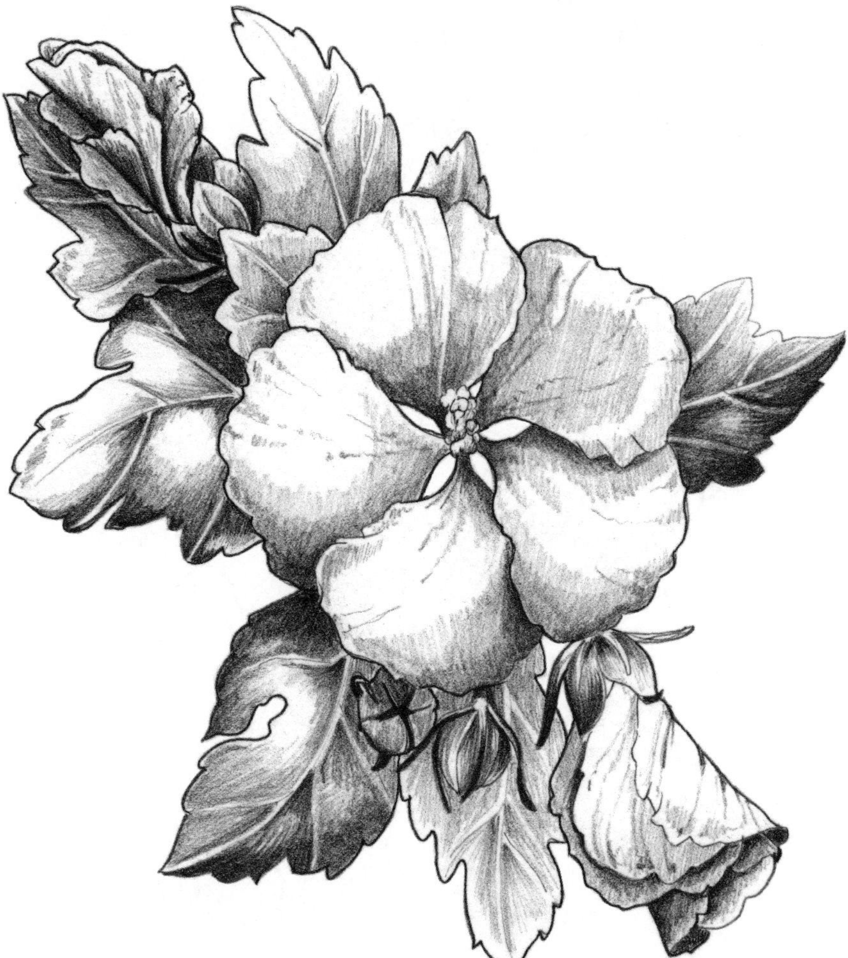

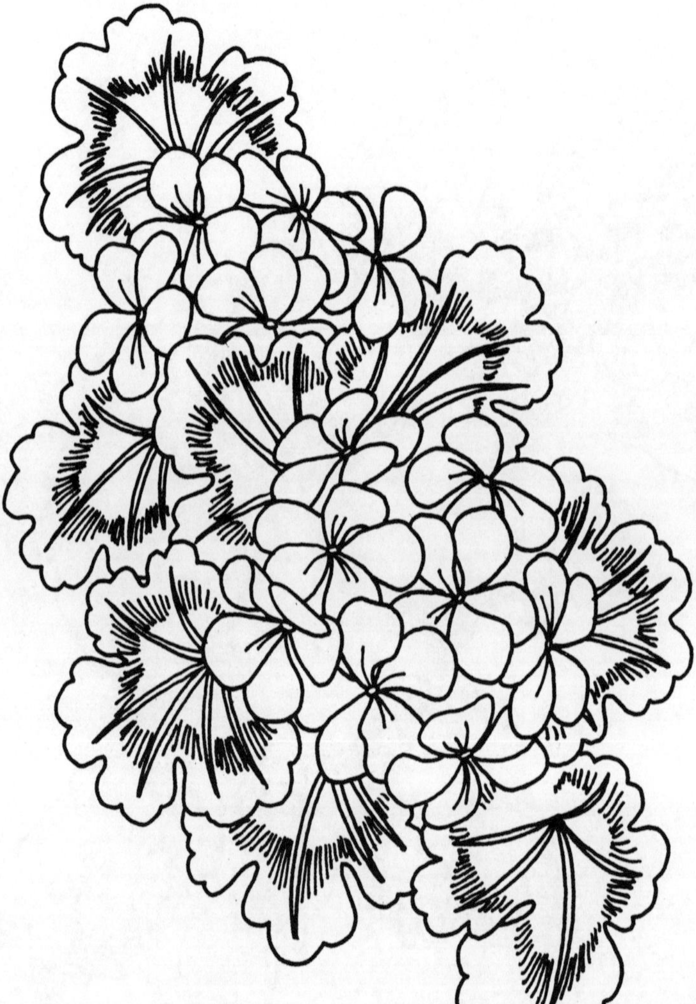

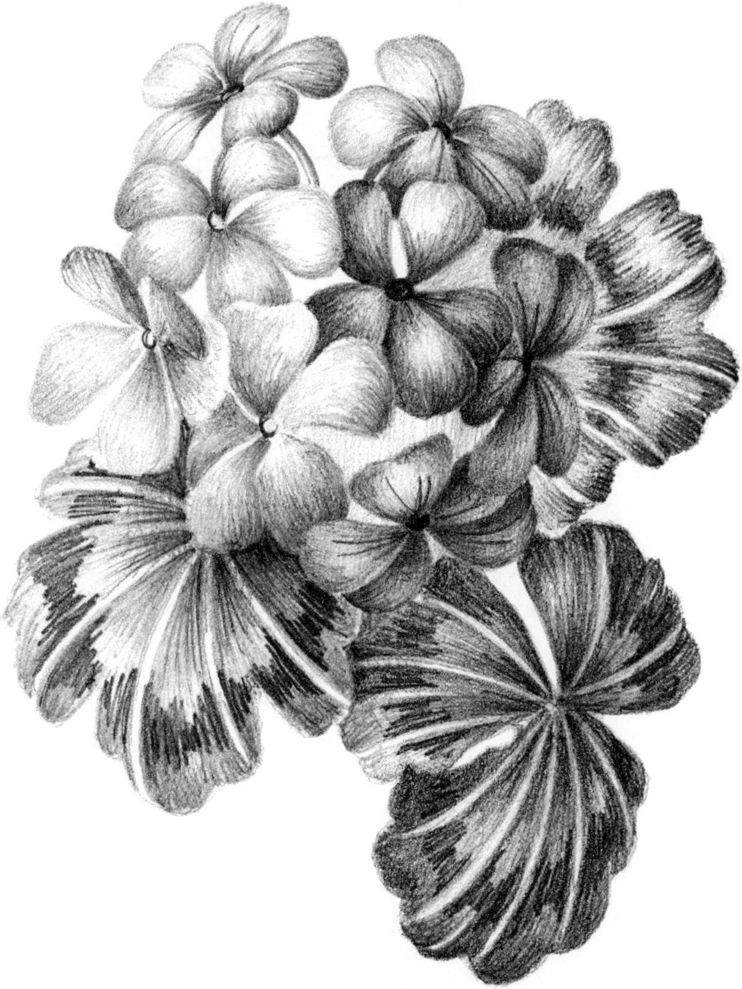

Floral

Floral

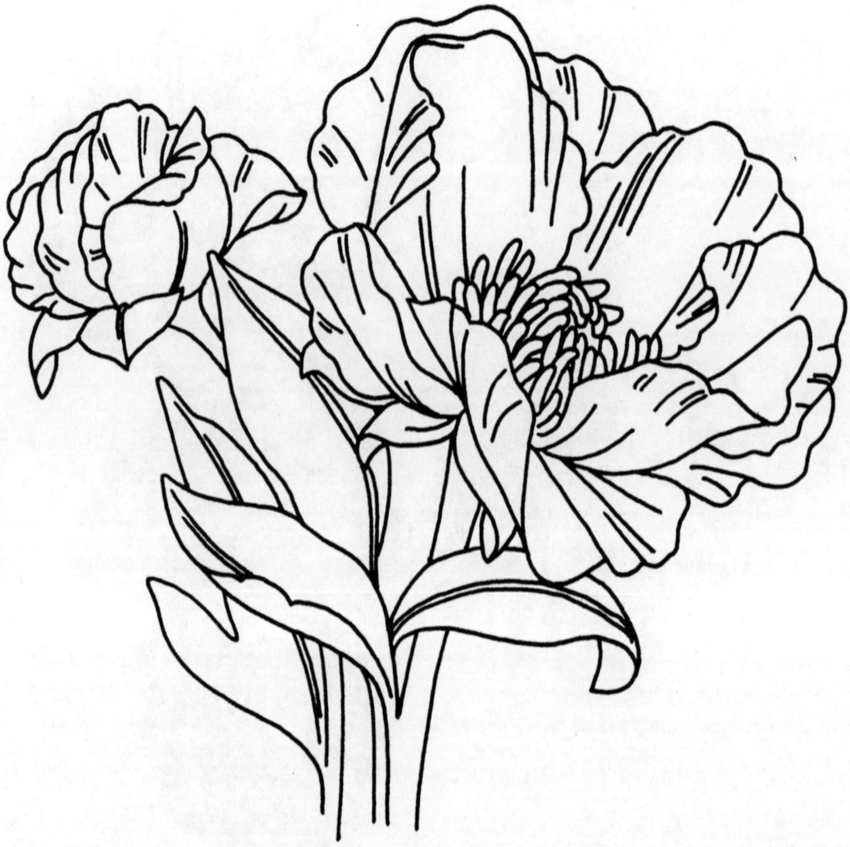

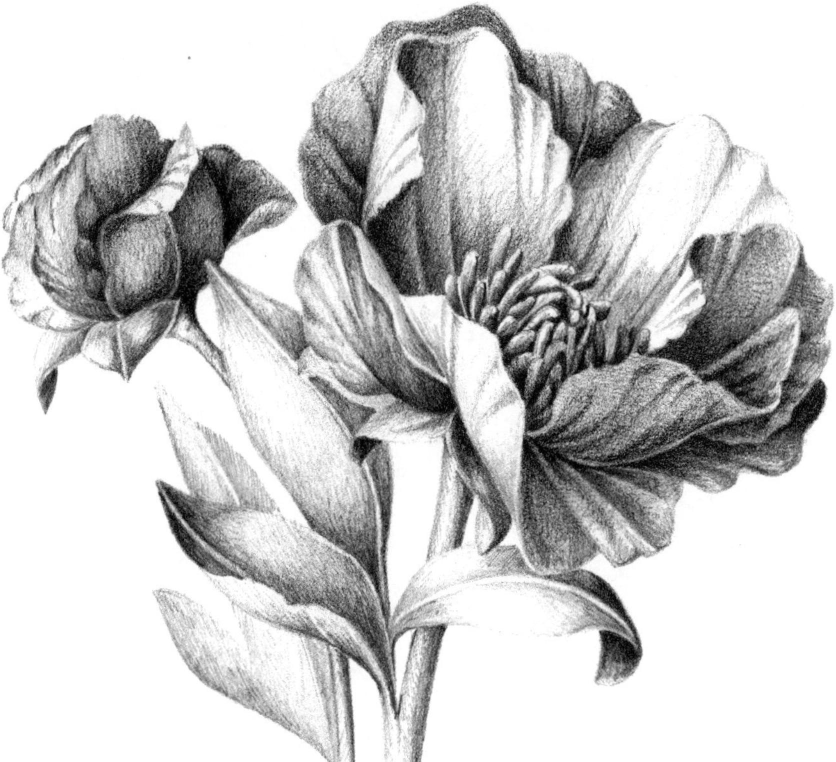

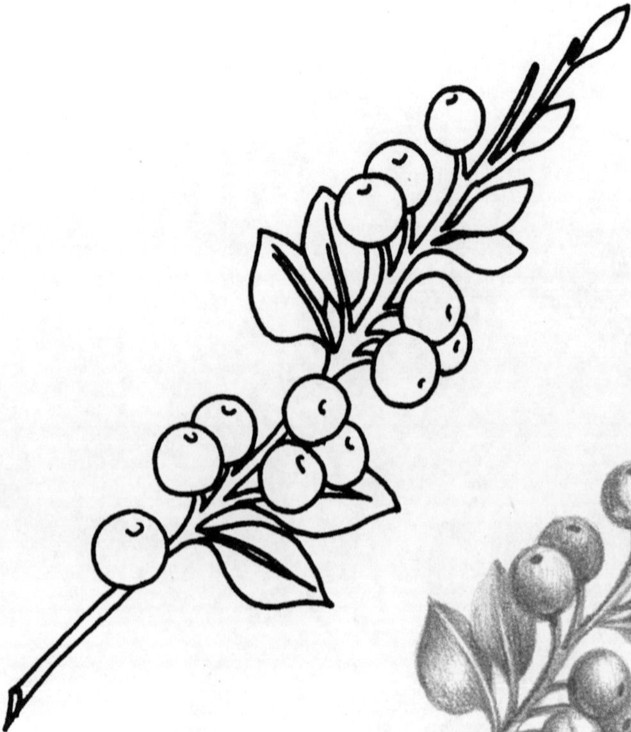

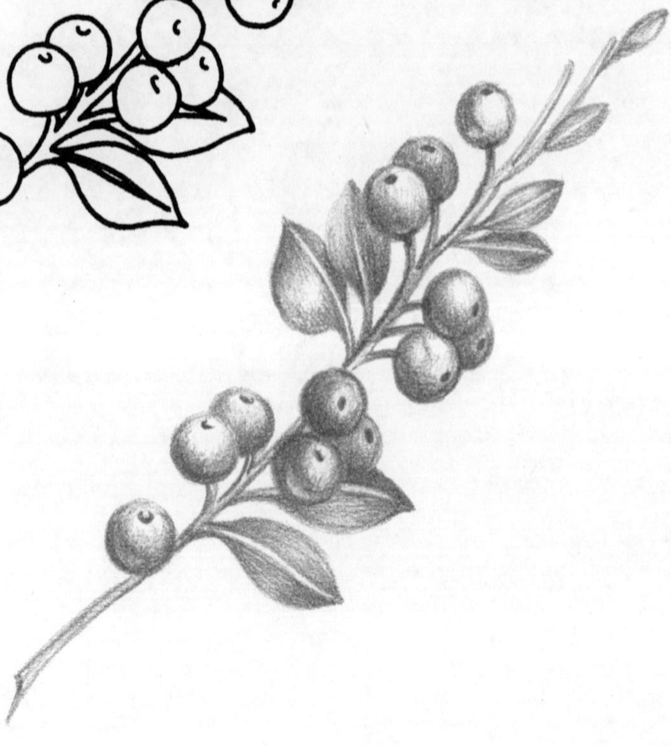

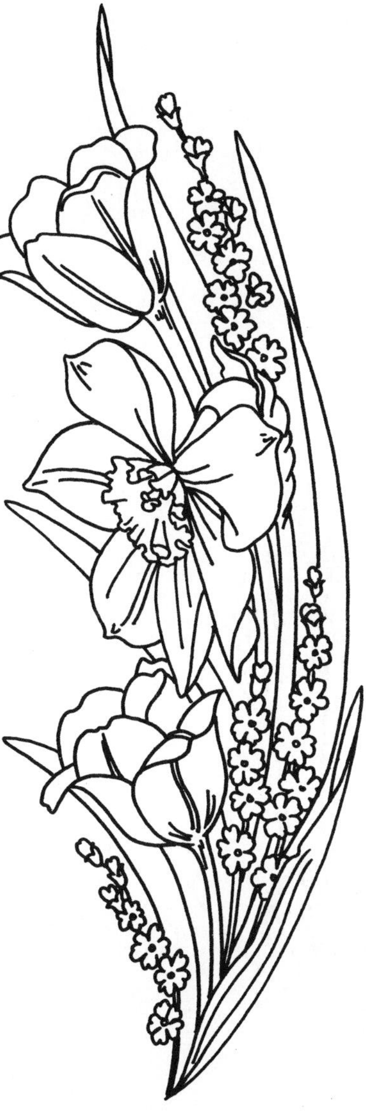

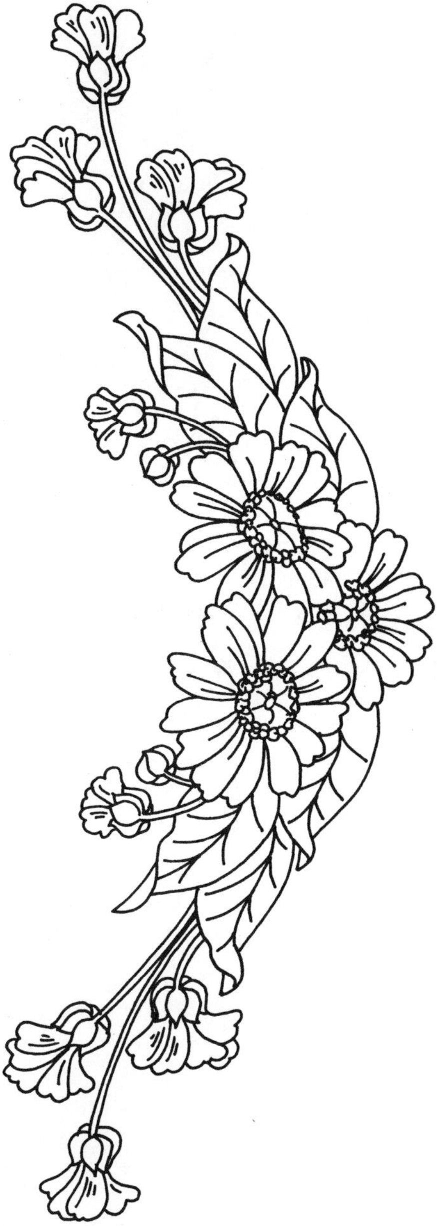

Floral

Floral

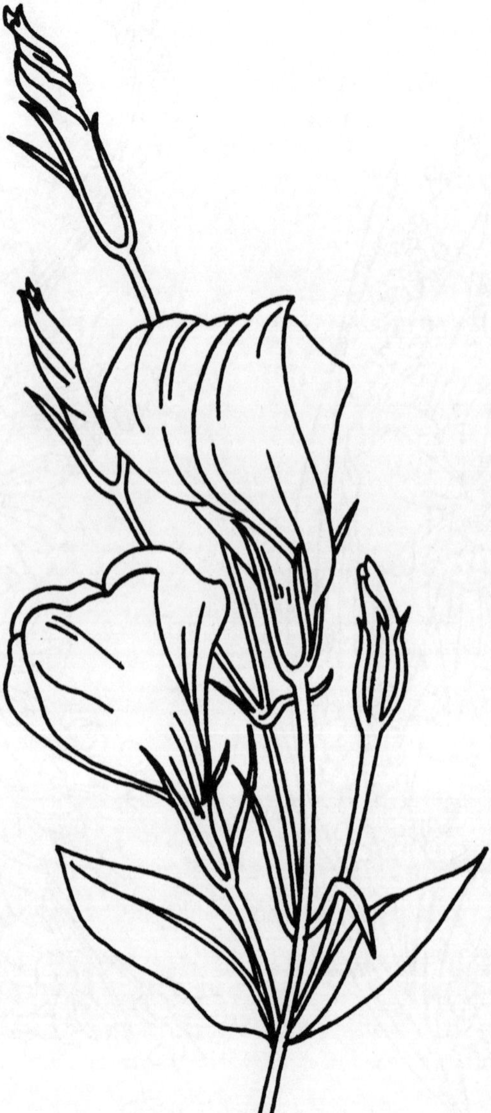

© Lora S. Irish

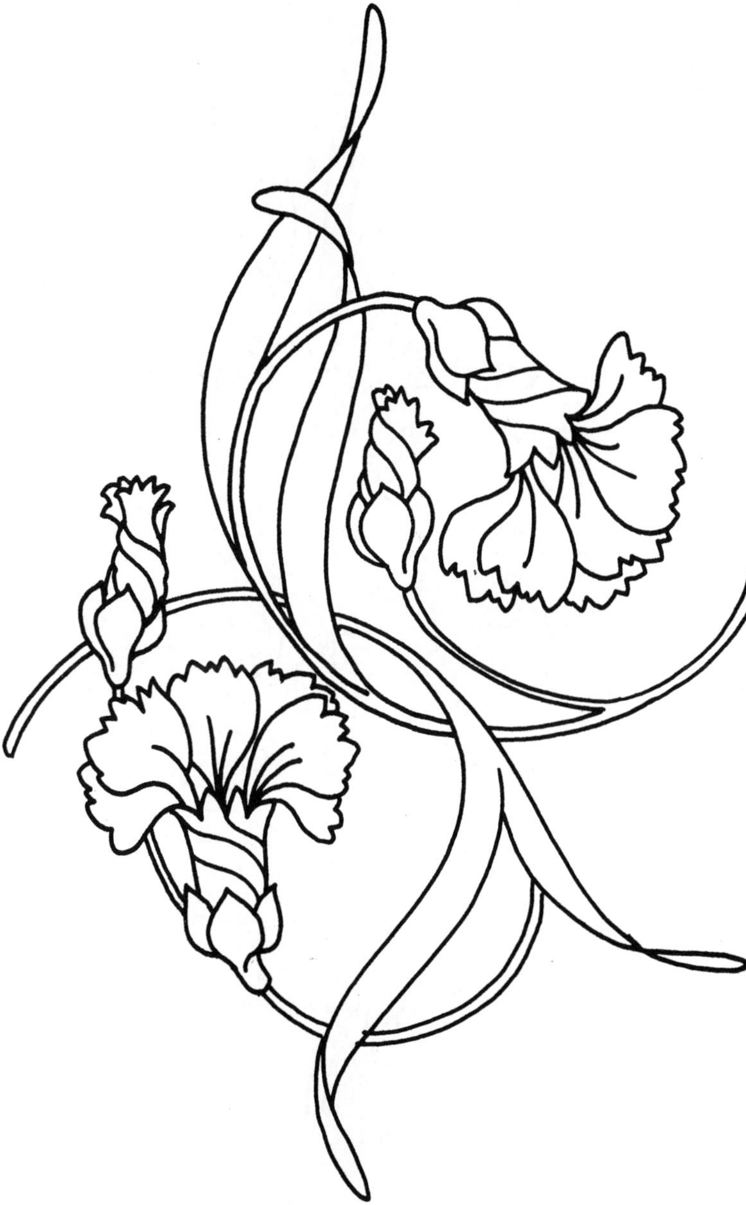

Floral

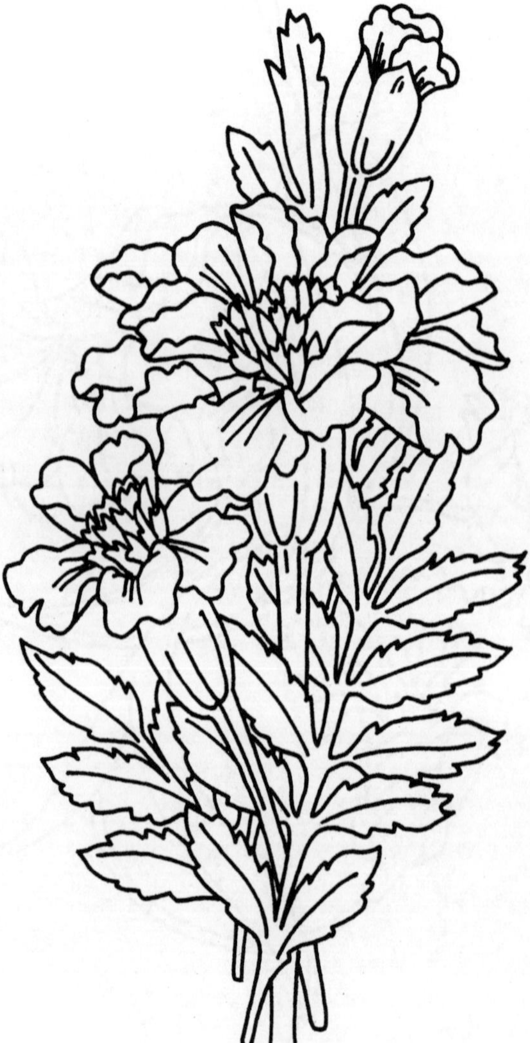

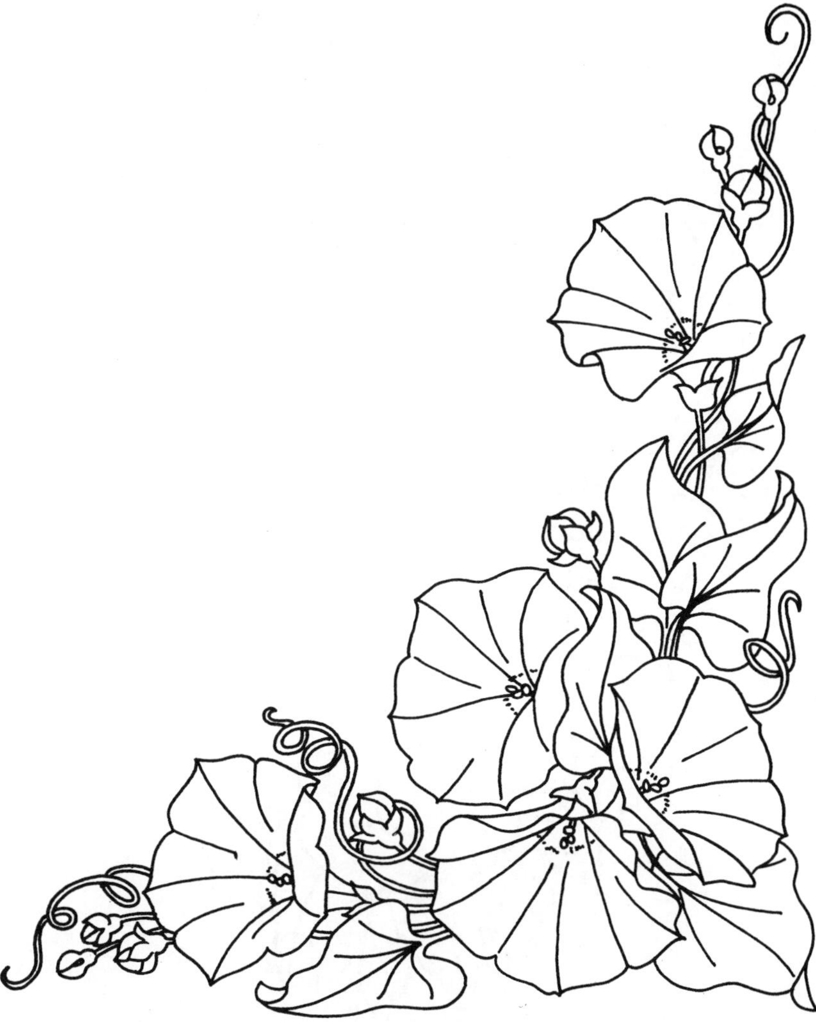

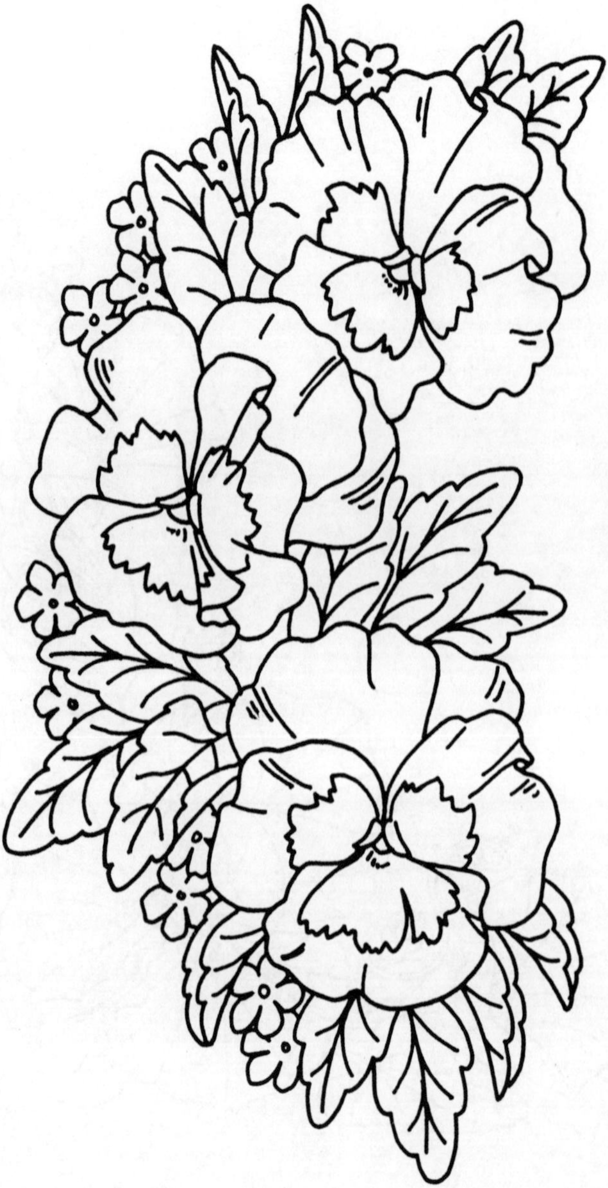

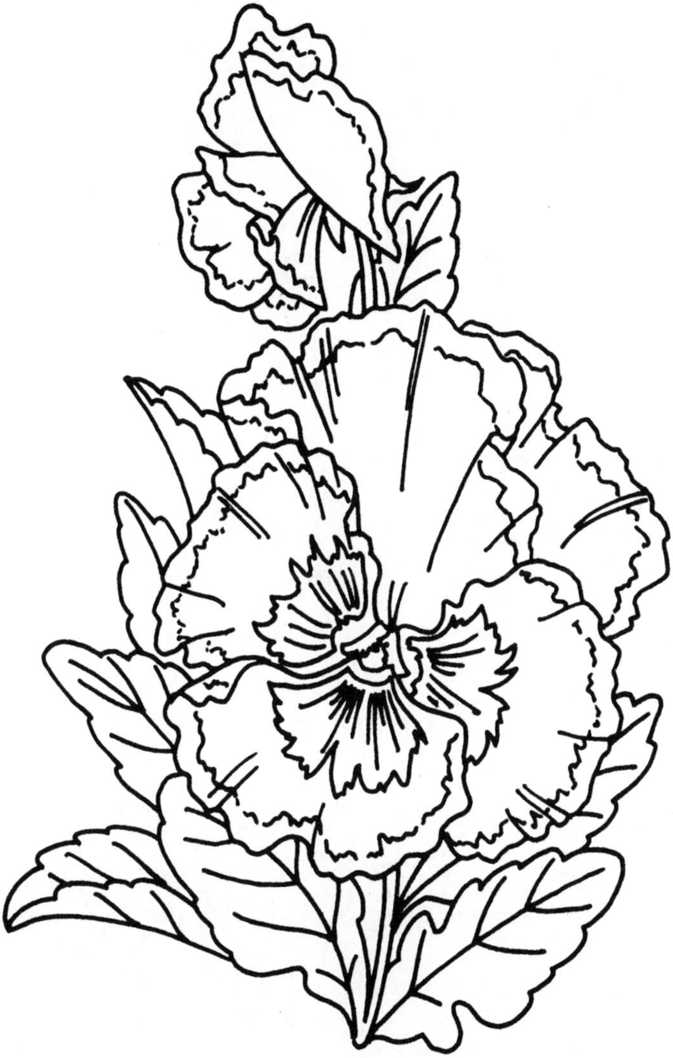

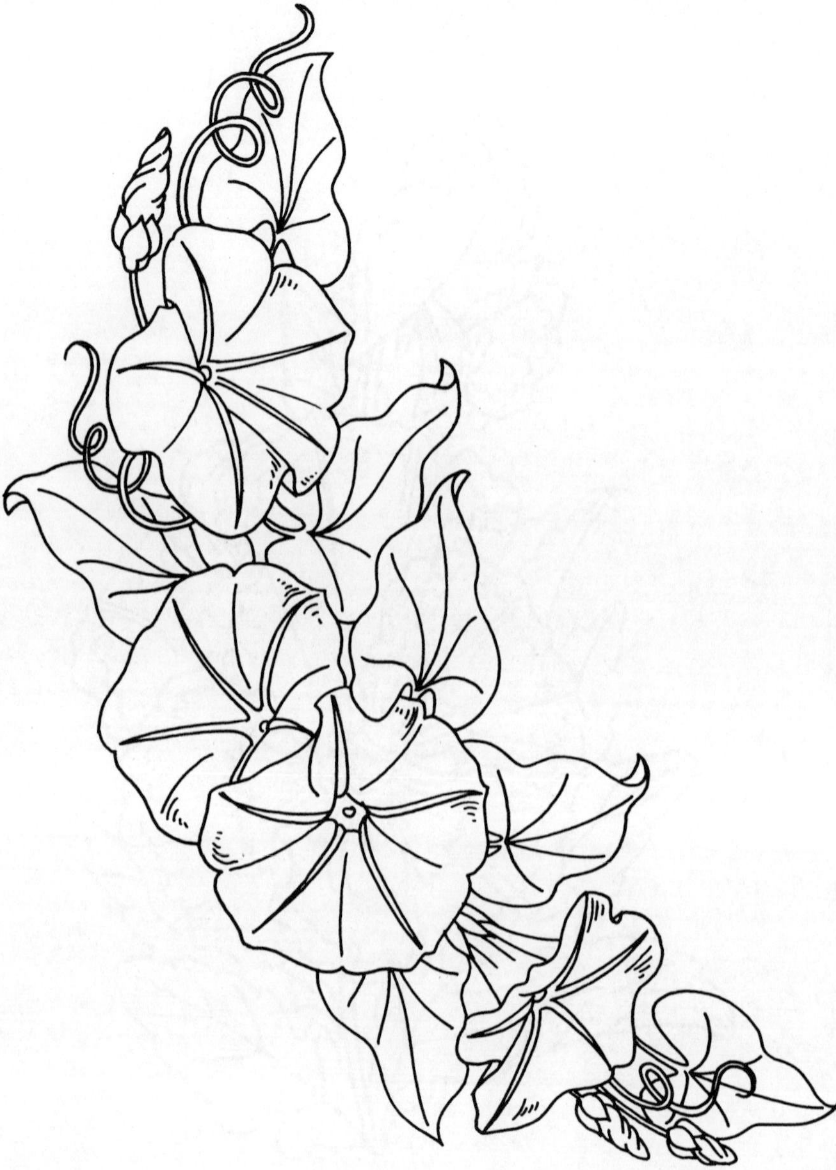

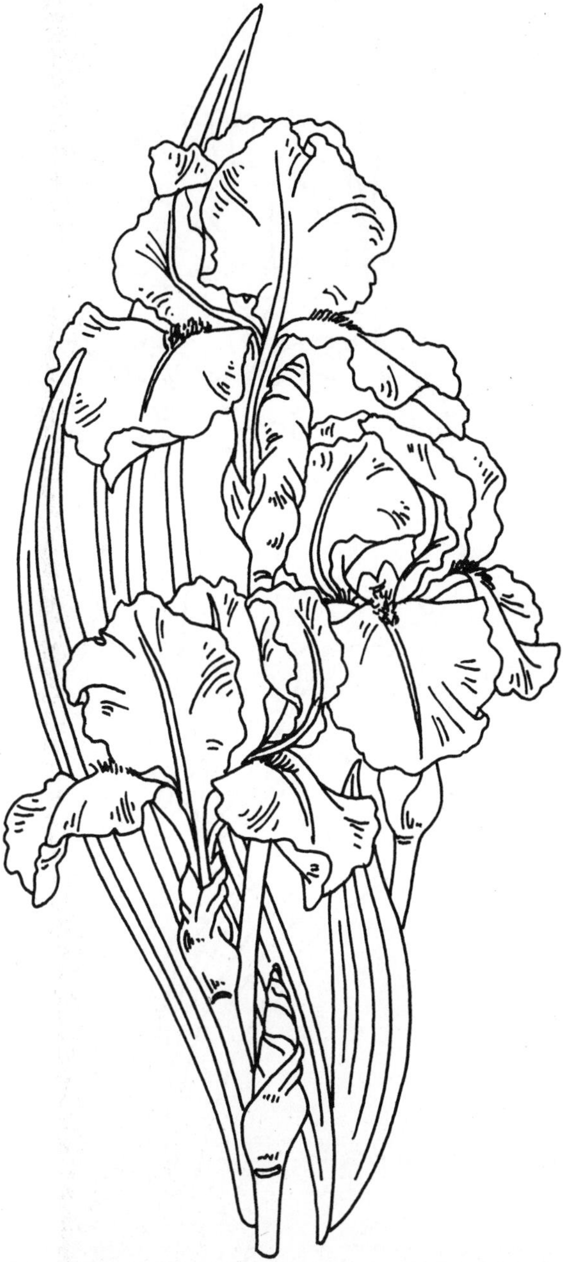

© Lora S. Irish

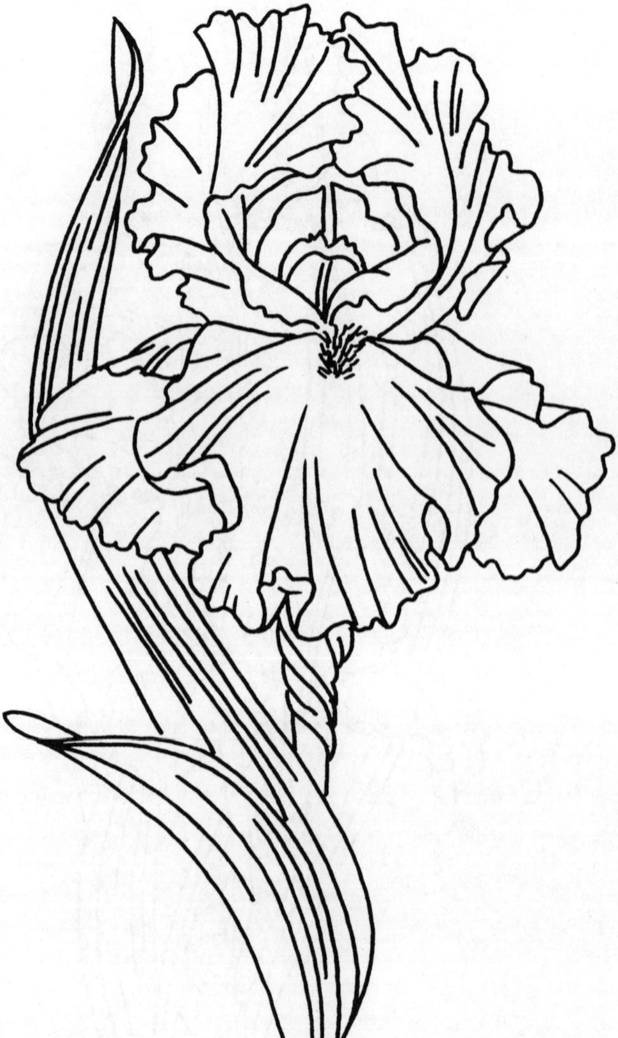

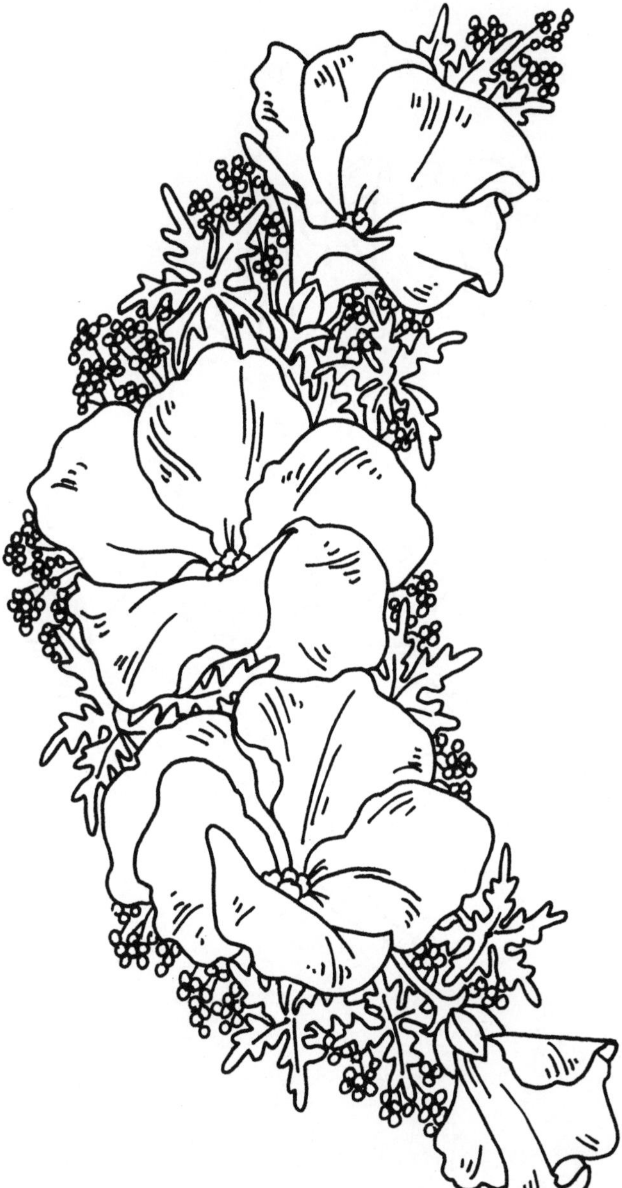

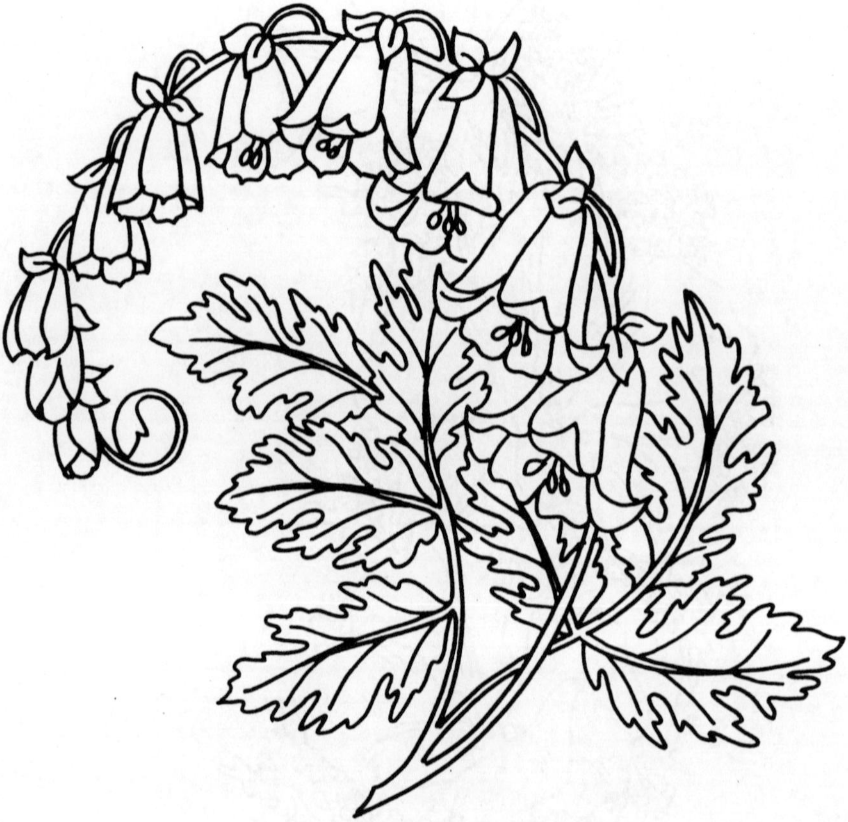

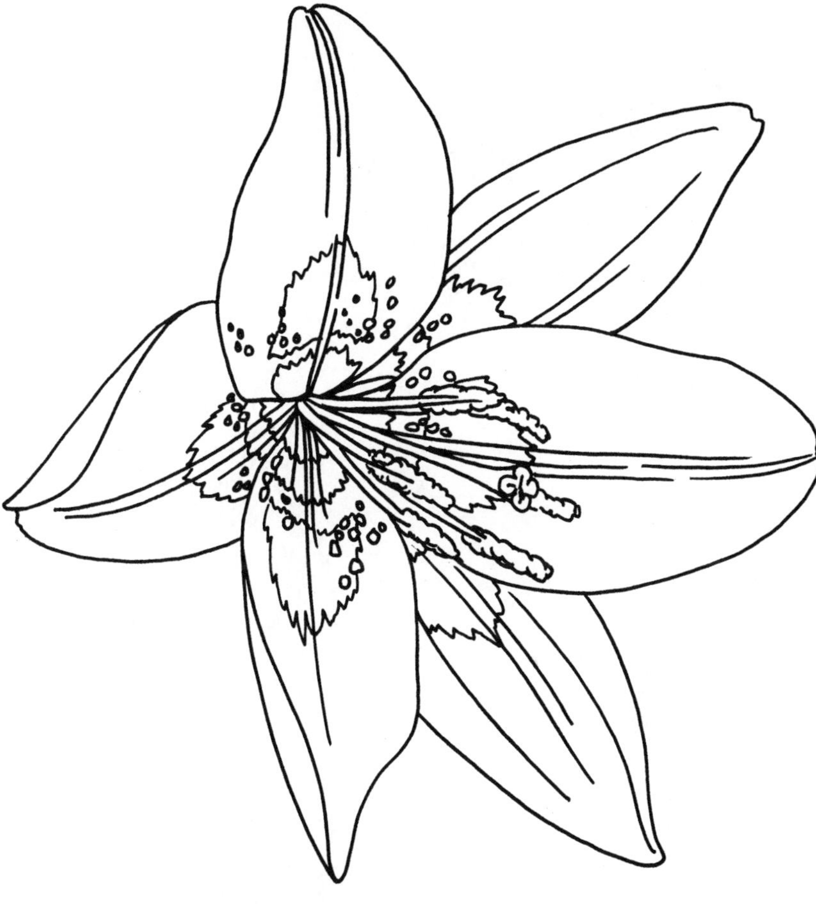

Floral

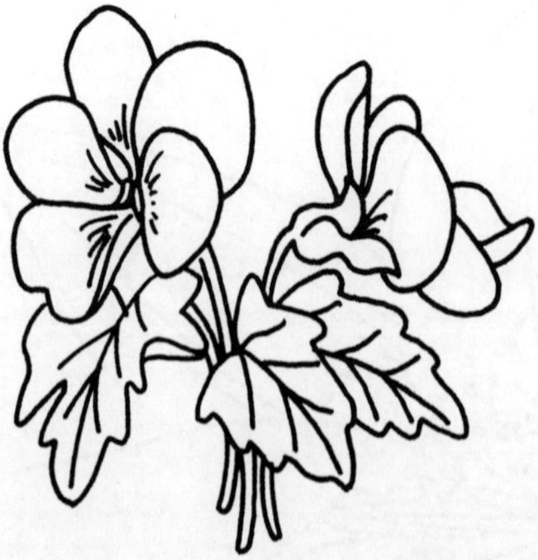

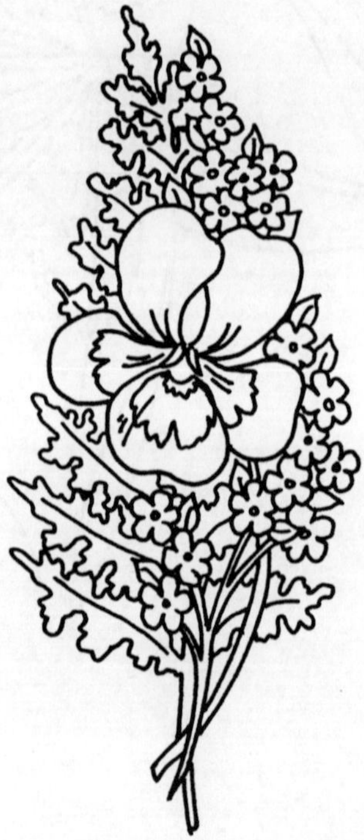

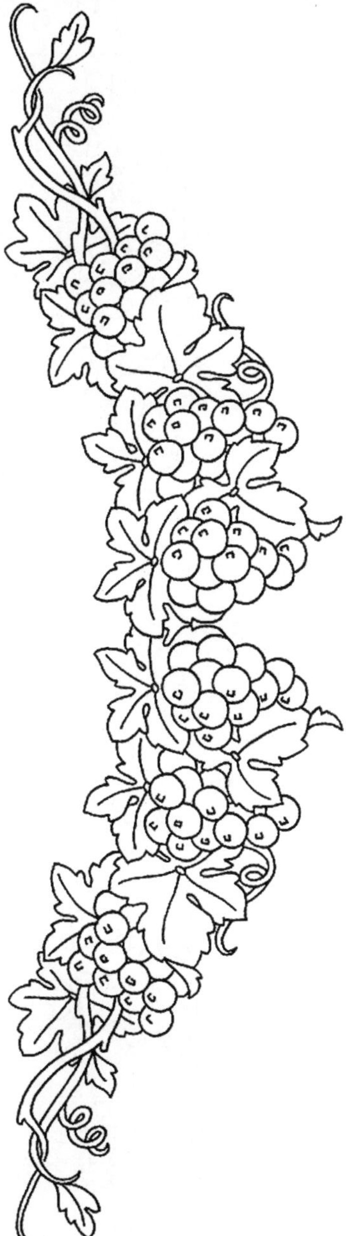

Floral

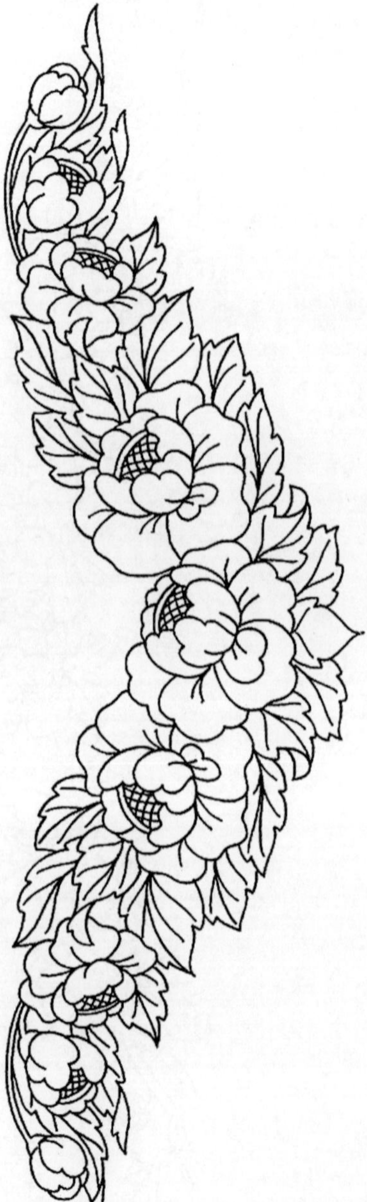

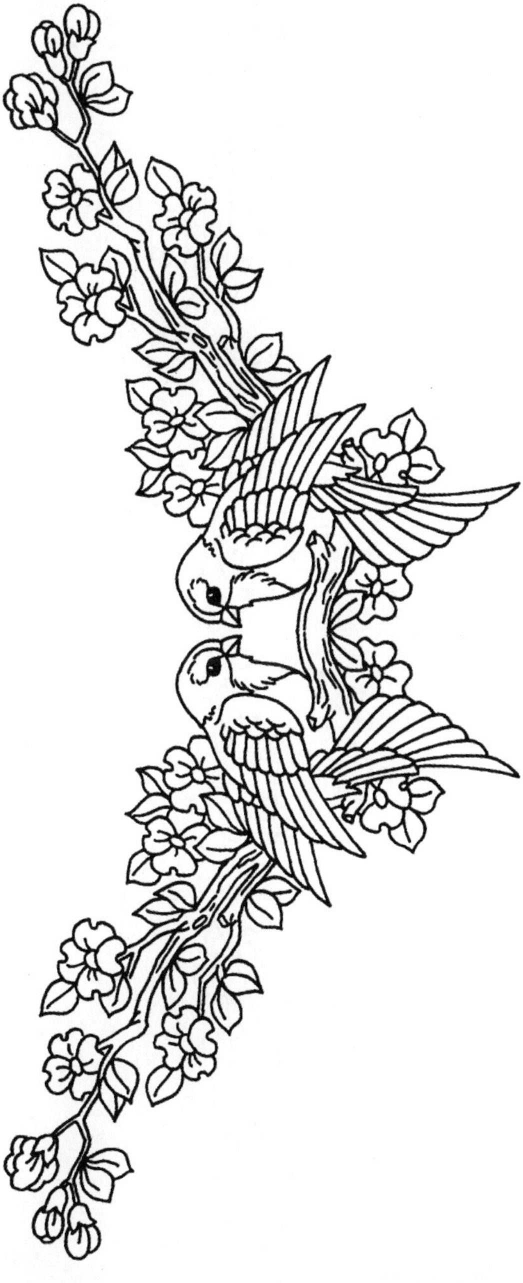

Floral

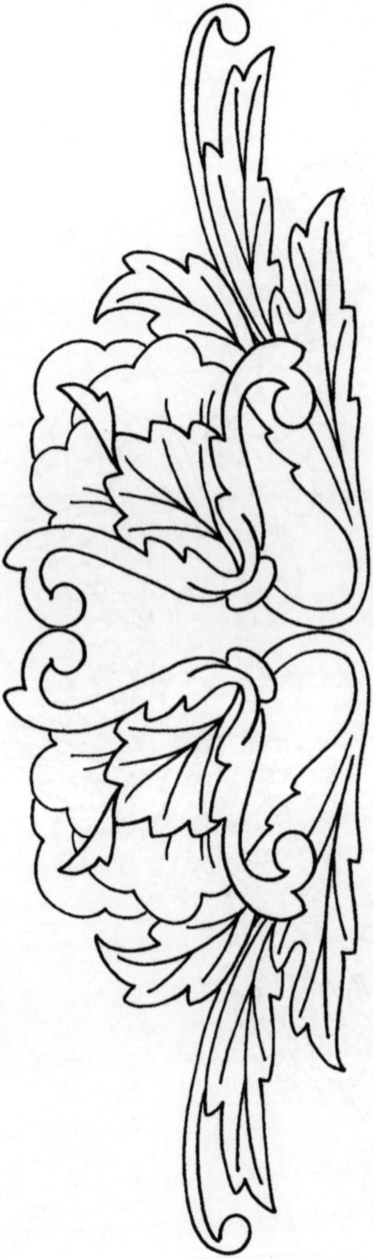

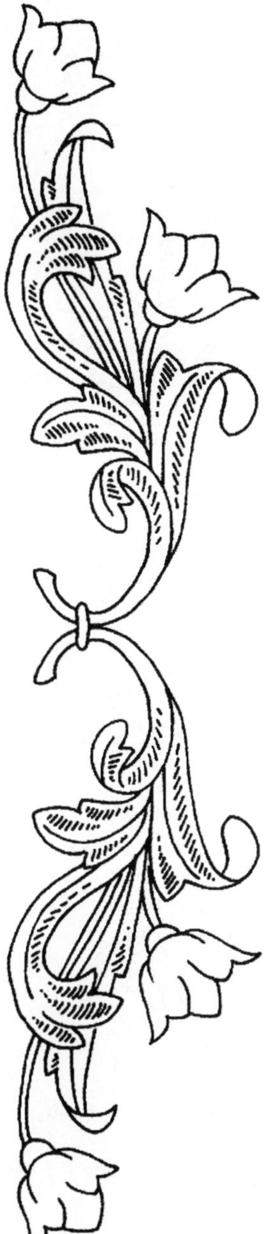

Floral

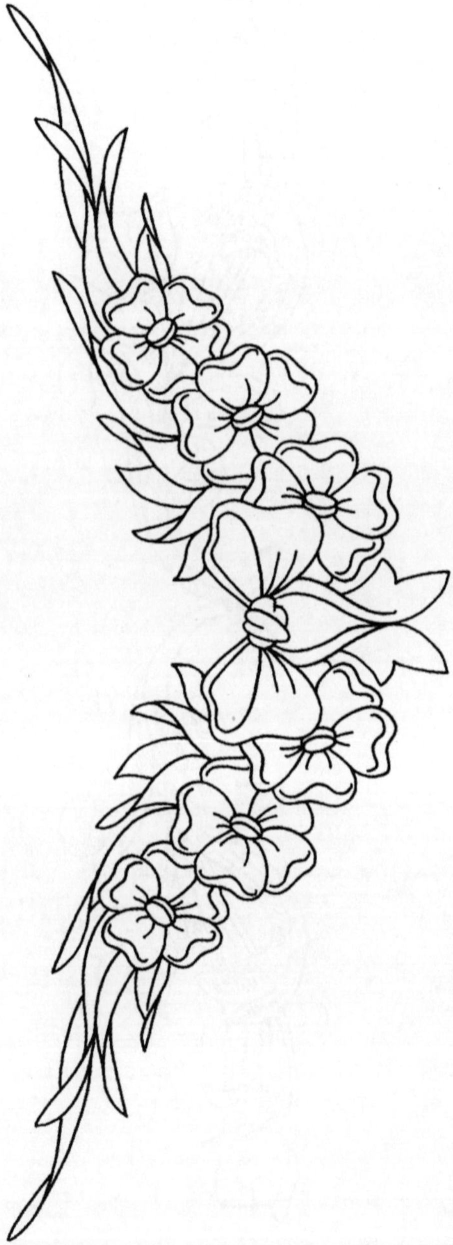

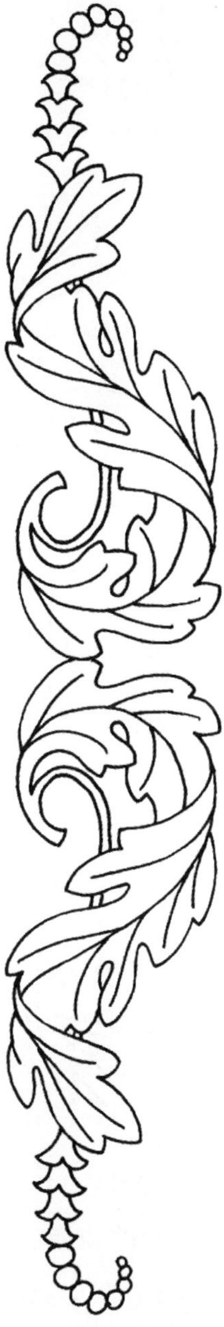

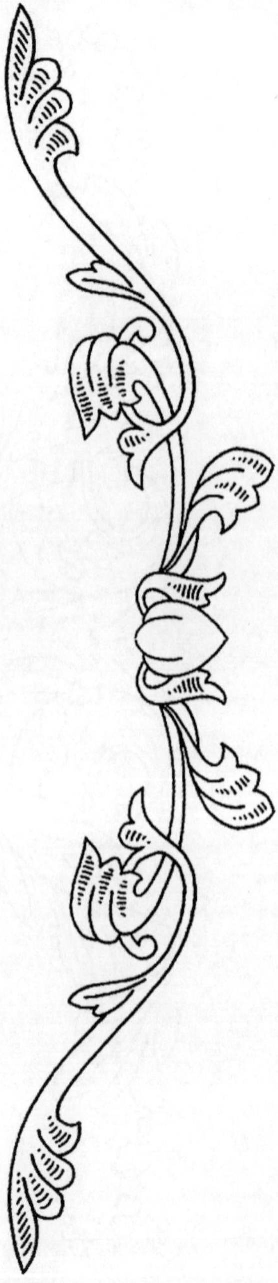

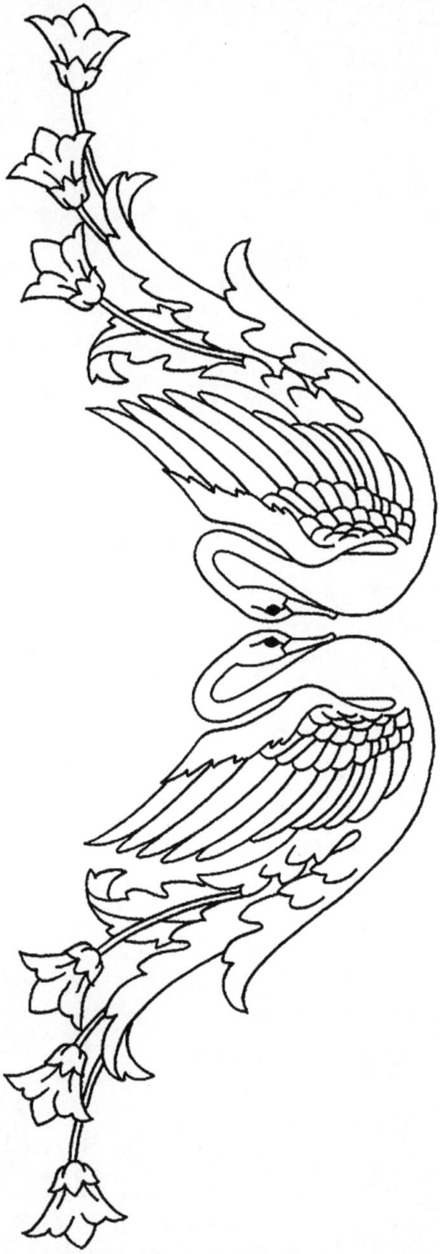

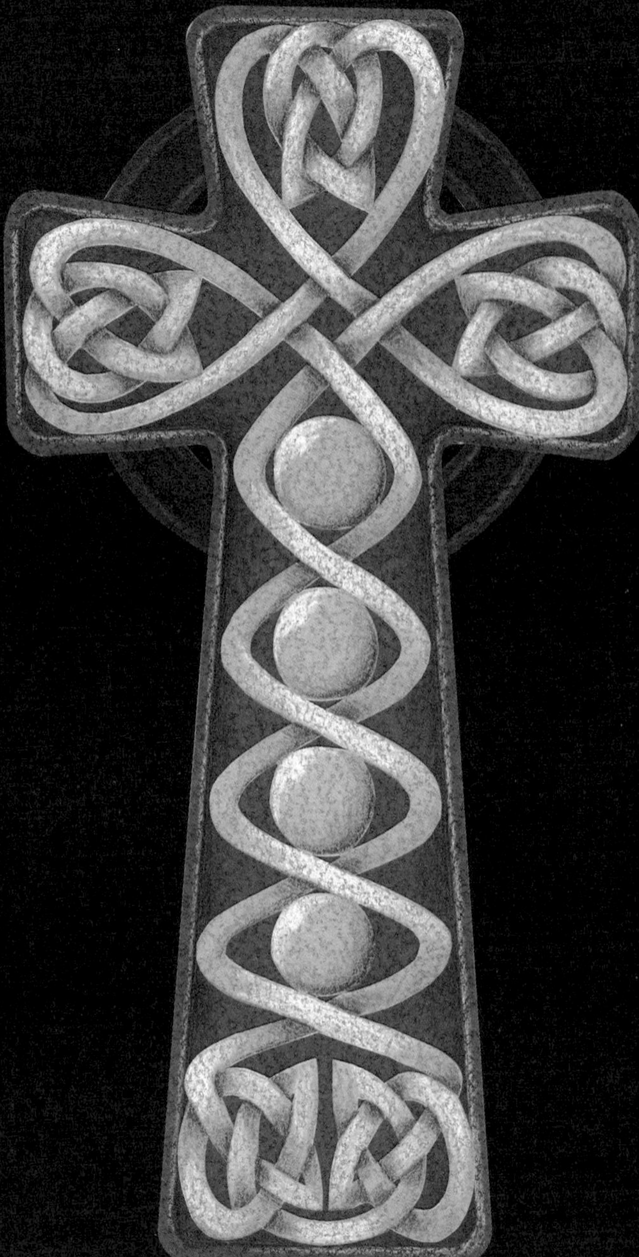

Symbols

From Celtic crosses to ships, symbols can make a powerful statement about who you are and what you believe. The Celtic cross, for example, is an emblem of the Christian faith, and its characteristic circle, a metaphor for eternity. Angels represent good and evil spirits; unicorns stand for power, purification, healing, wisdom, renewal, and eternal life. The eagle signifies ingenuity, its wings represent protection, and its gripping talons ruin to evildoers. In Christianity, it also represents salvation, redemption, and resurrection.

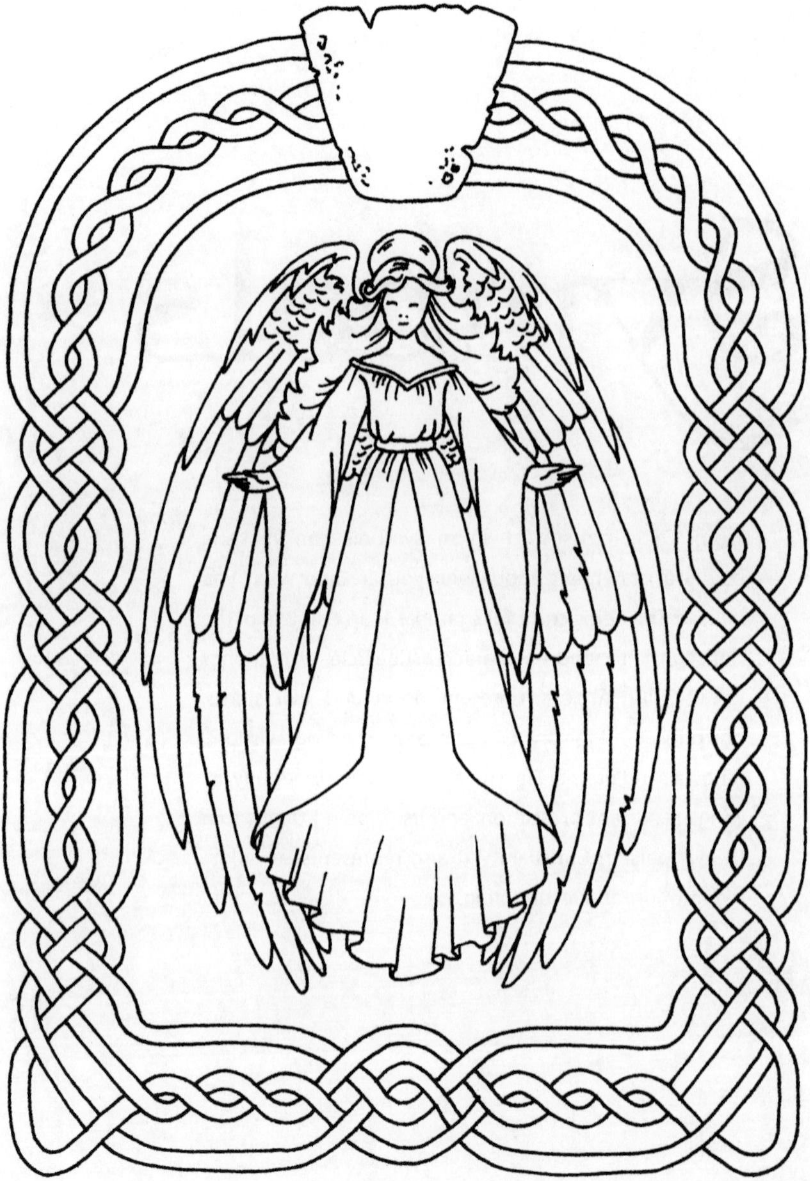

© Lora S. Irish

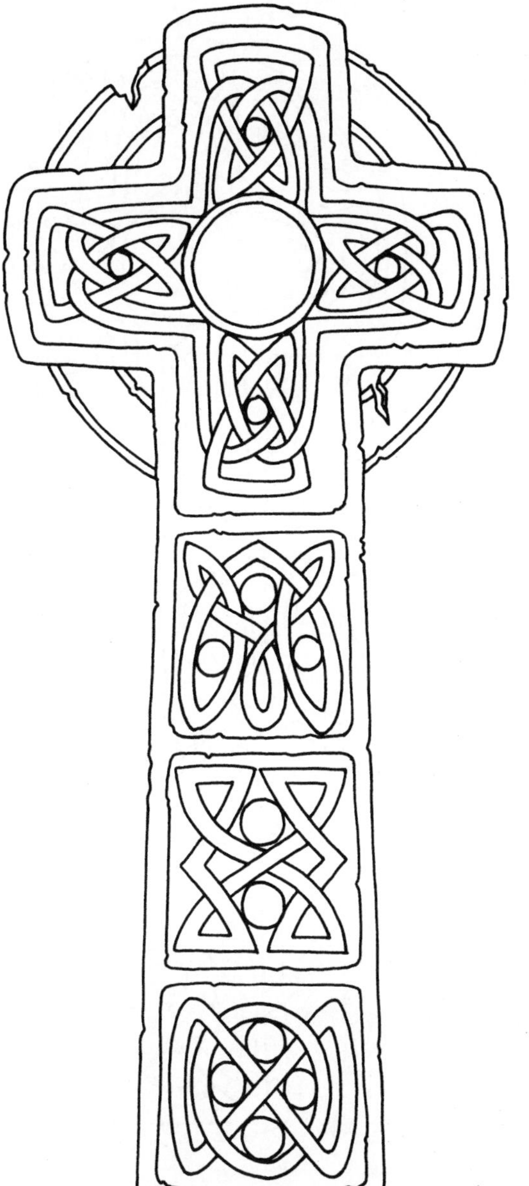

Symbols

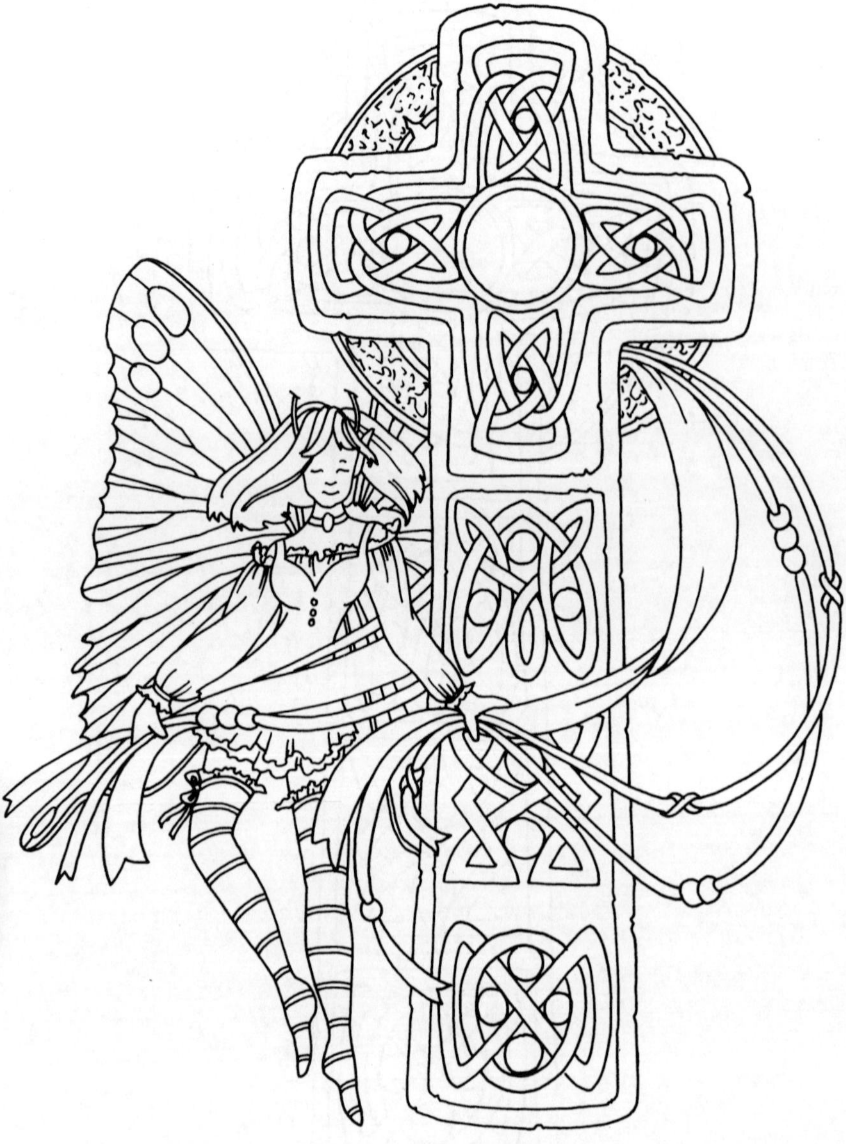

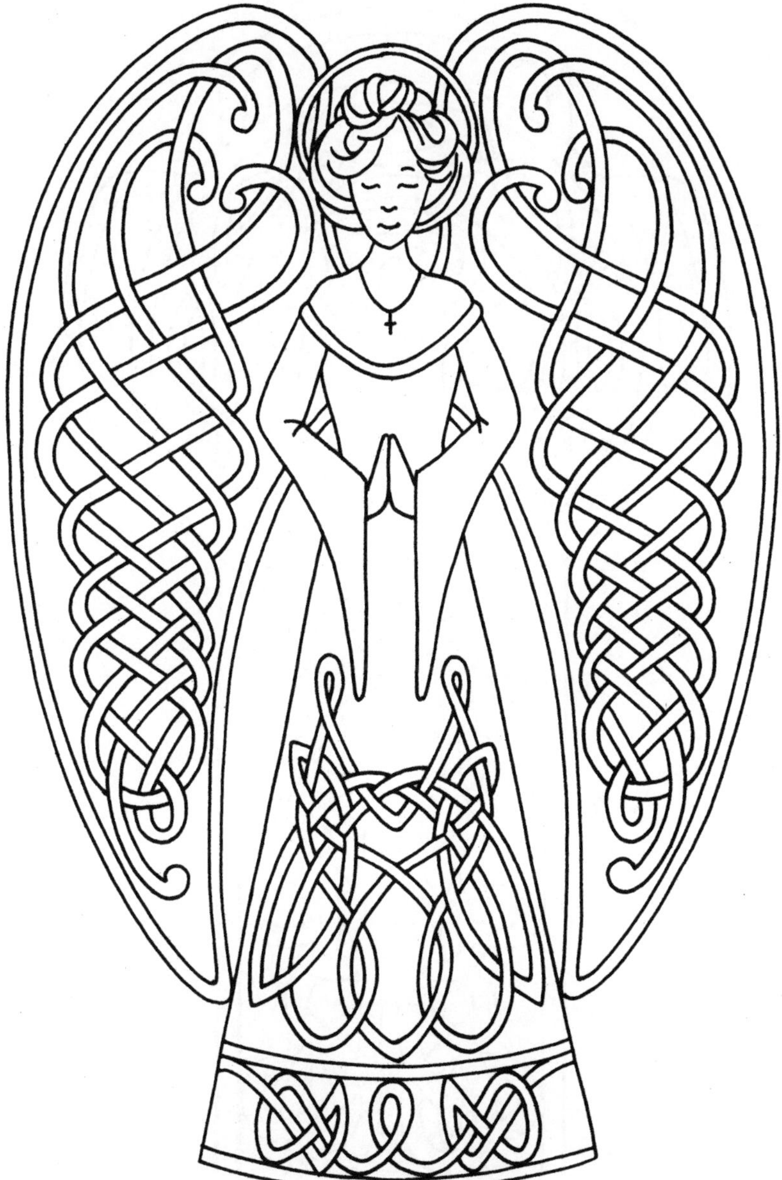

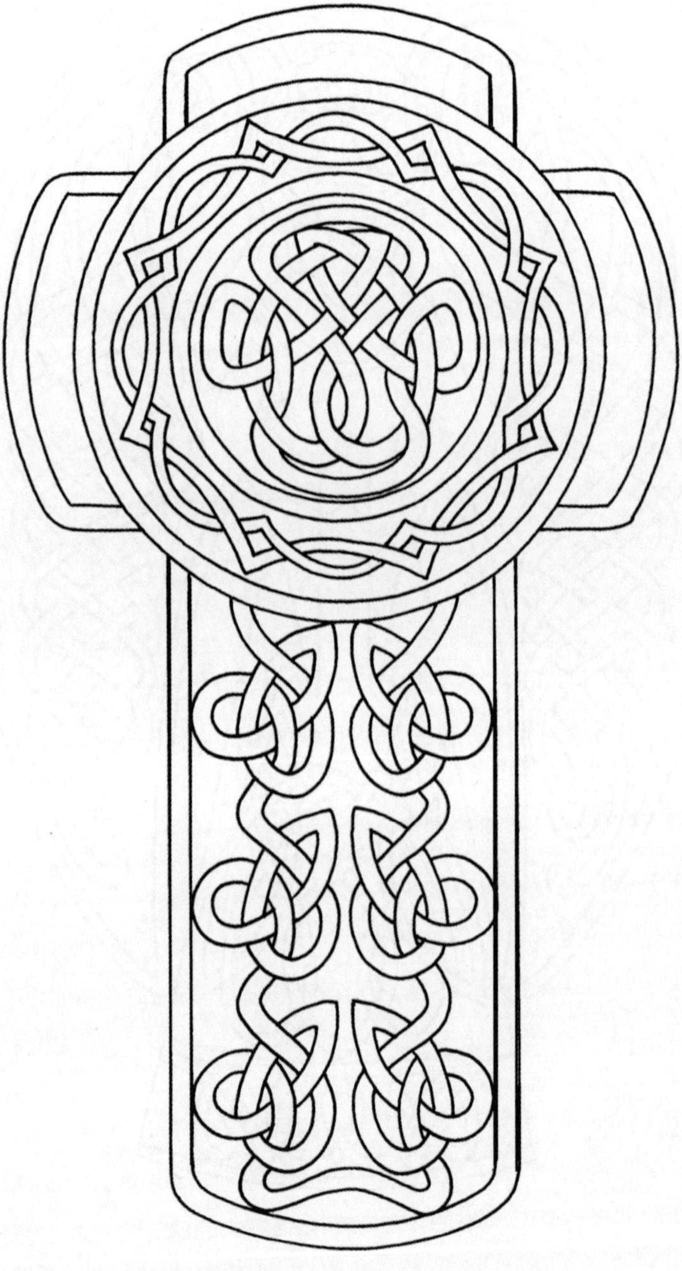

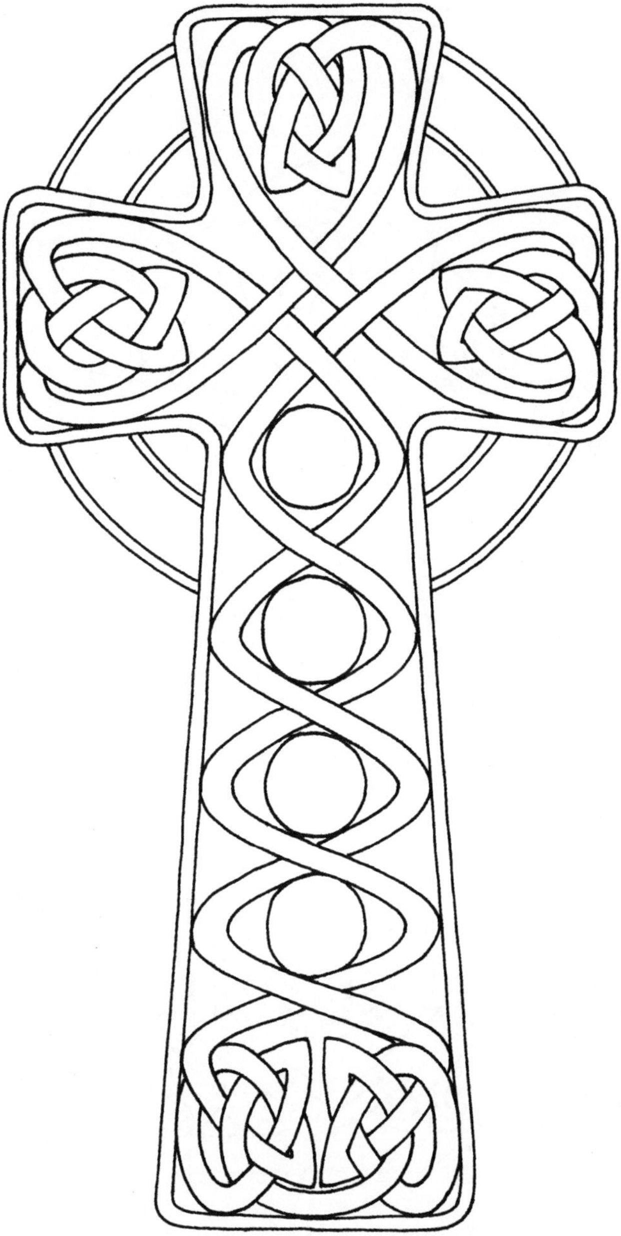

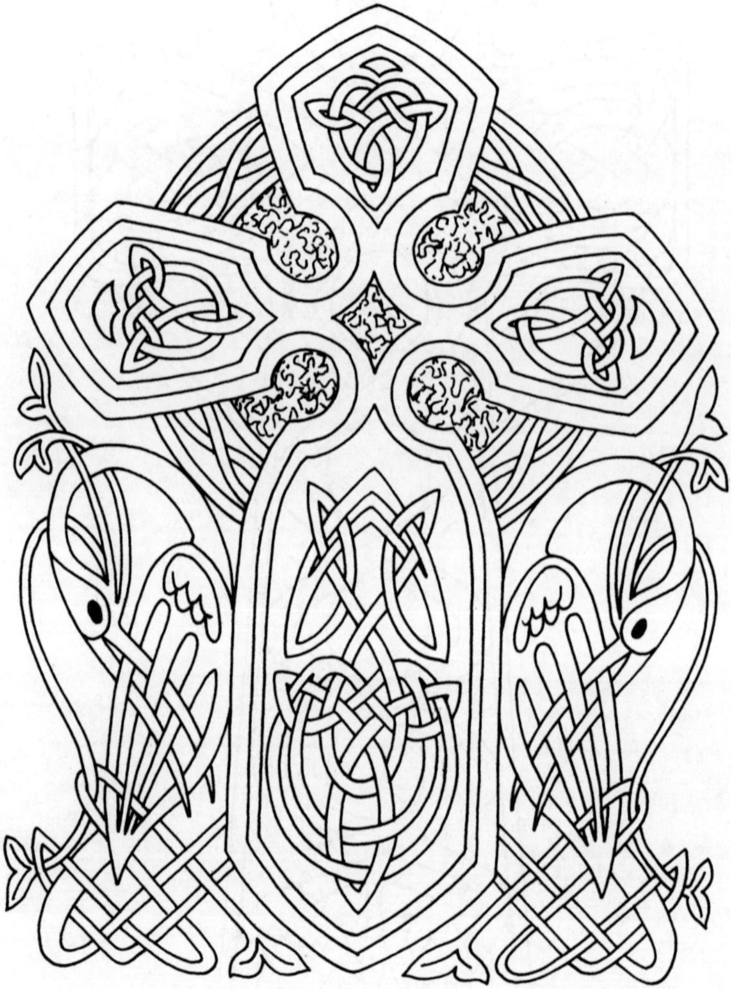

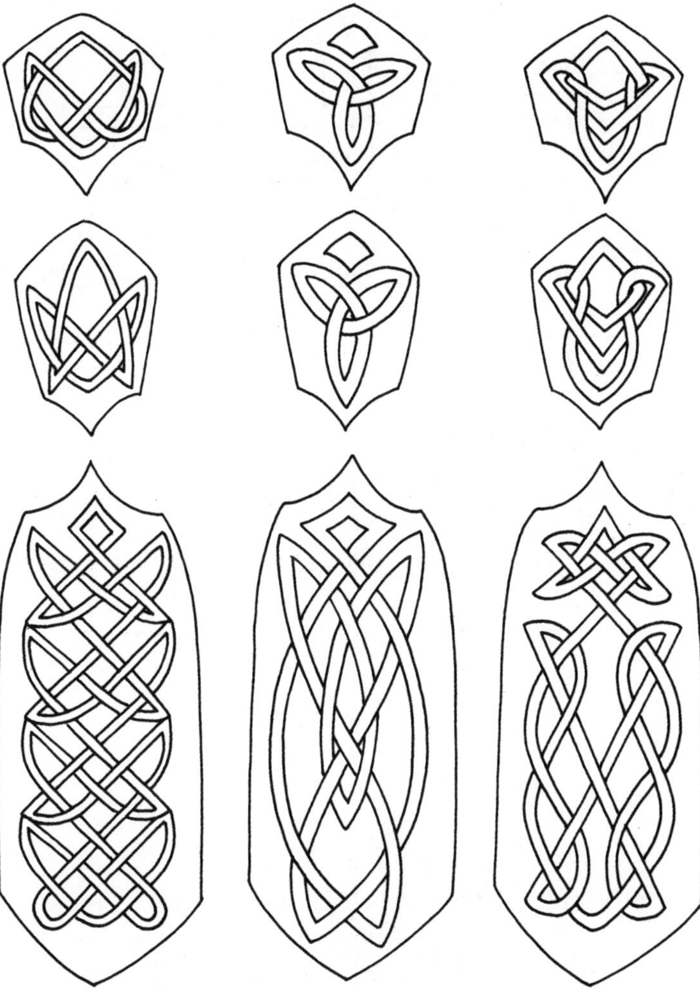

Note: The patterns on this page can be used with the cross on the previous page.

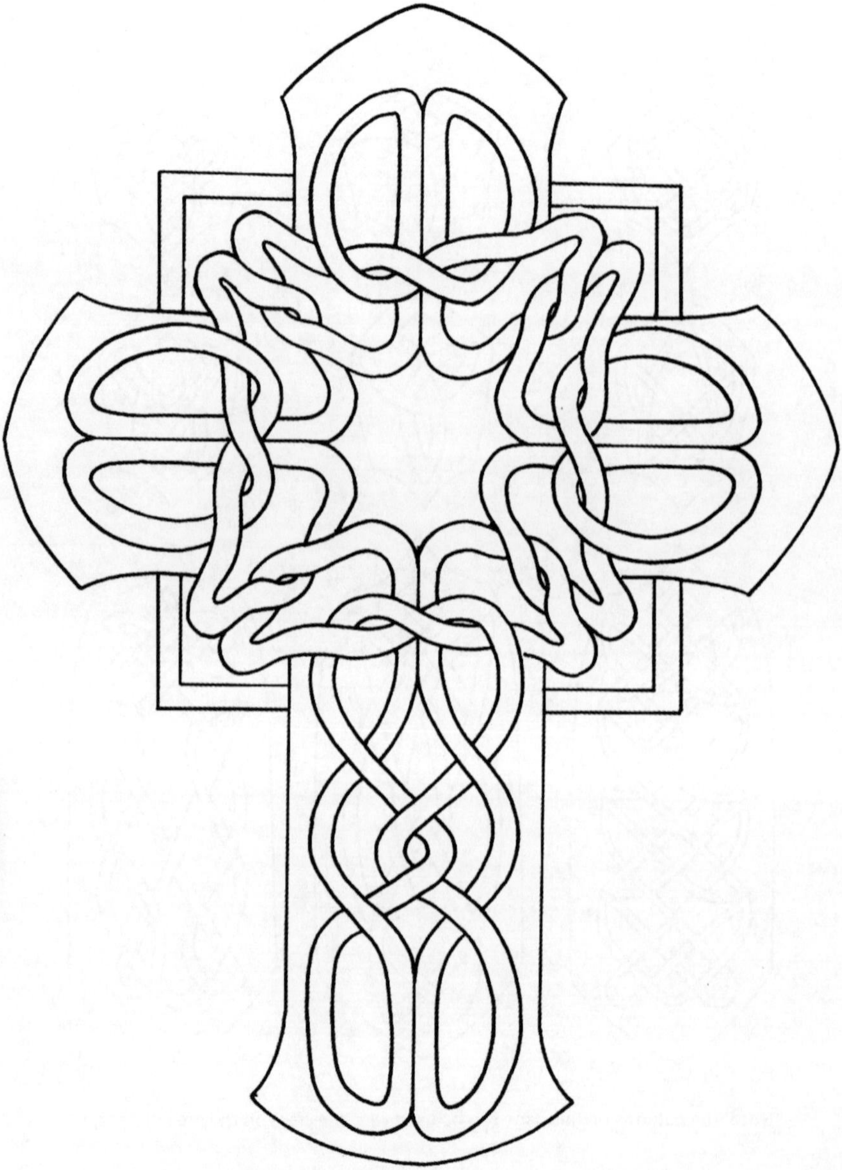

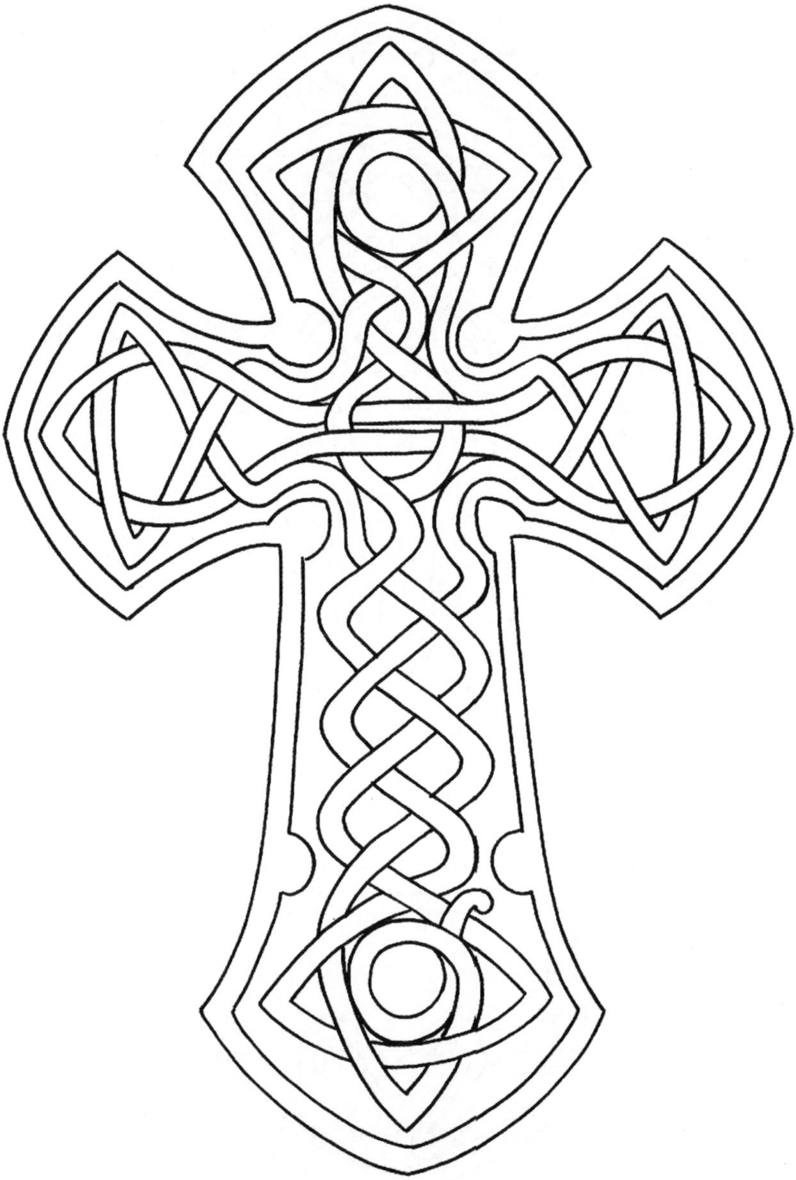

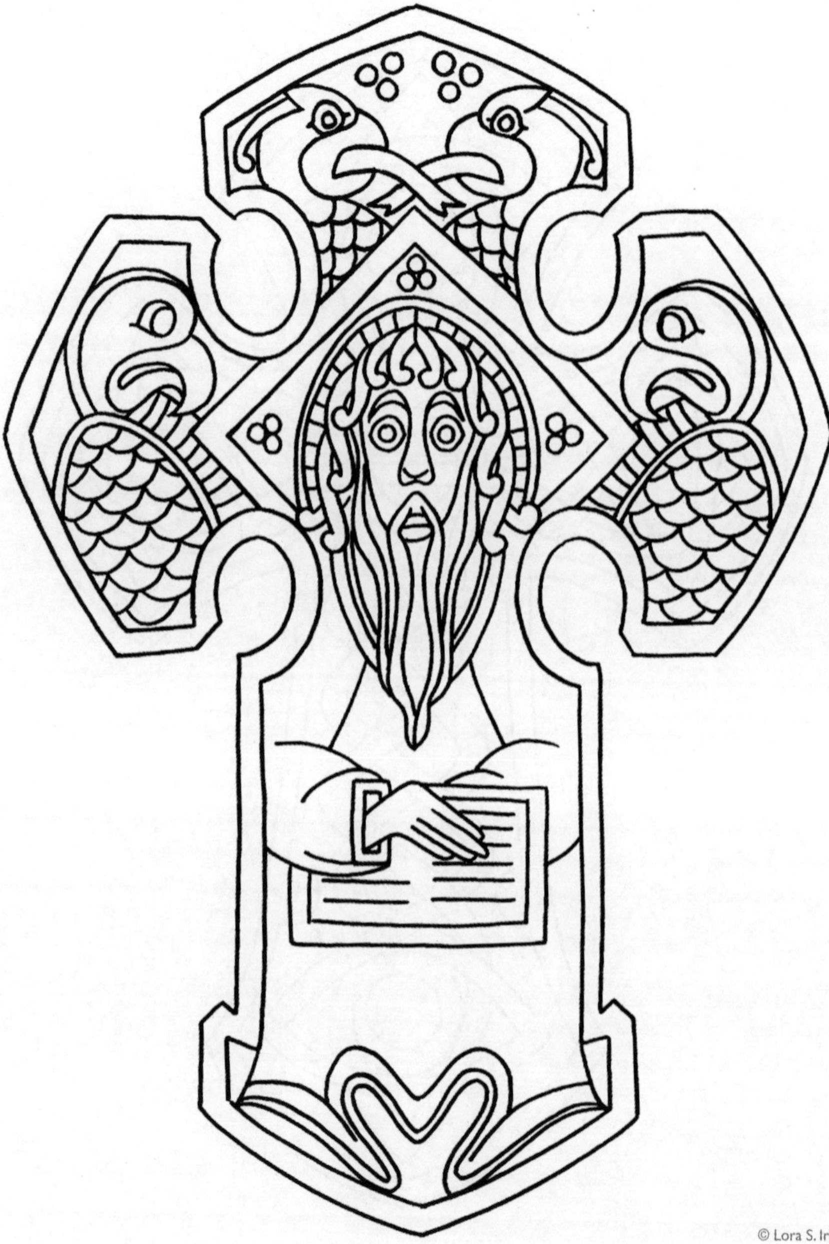

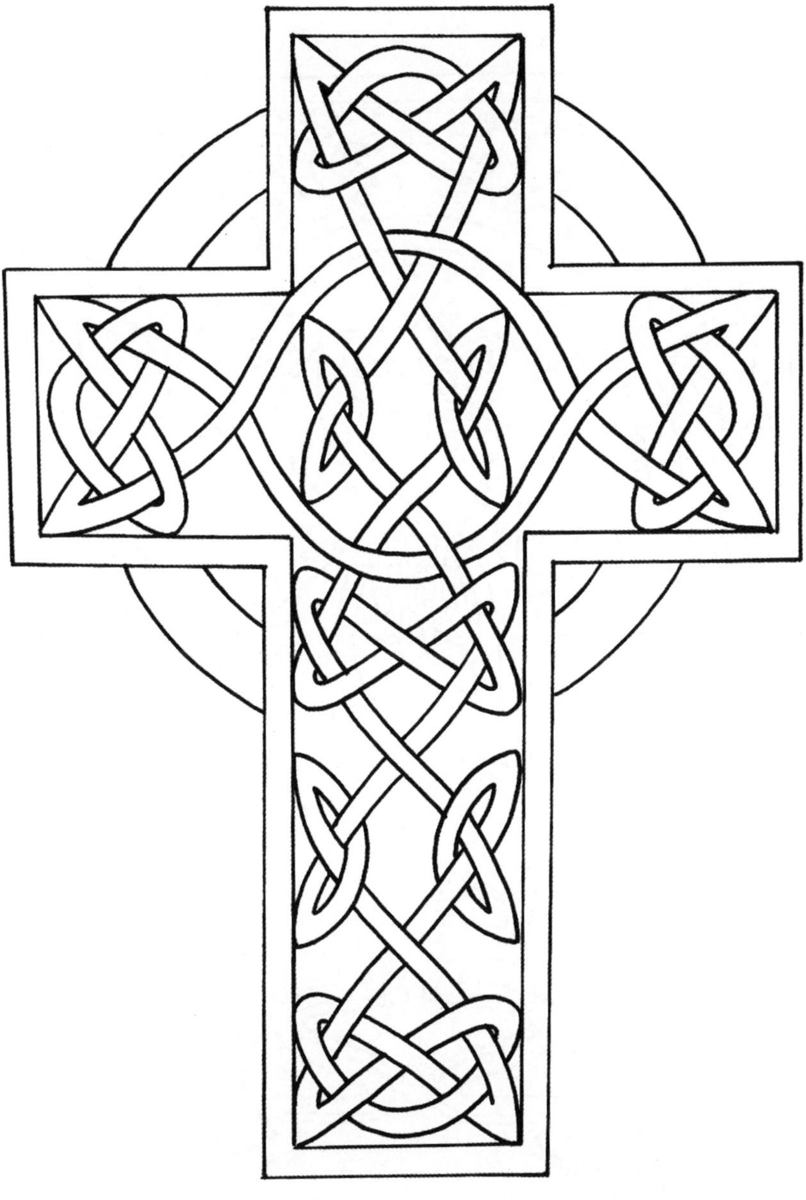

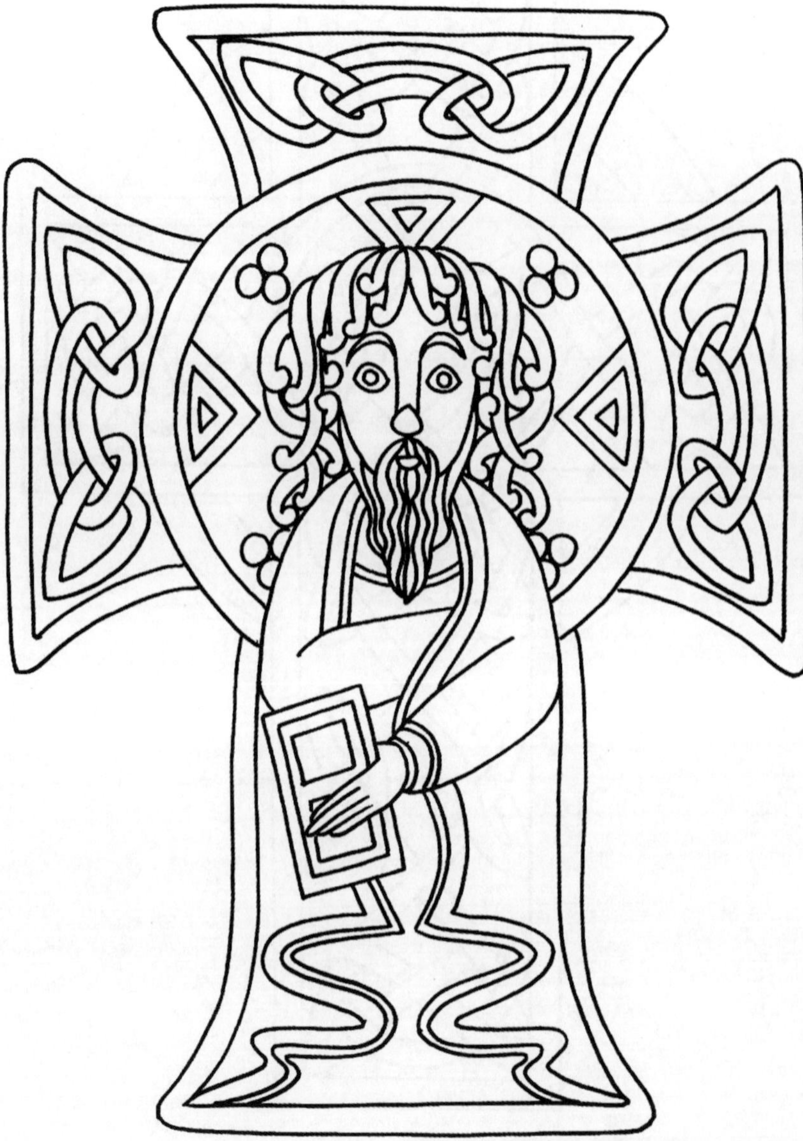

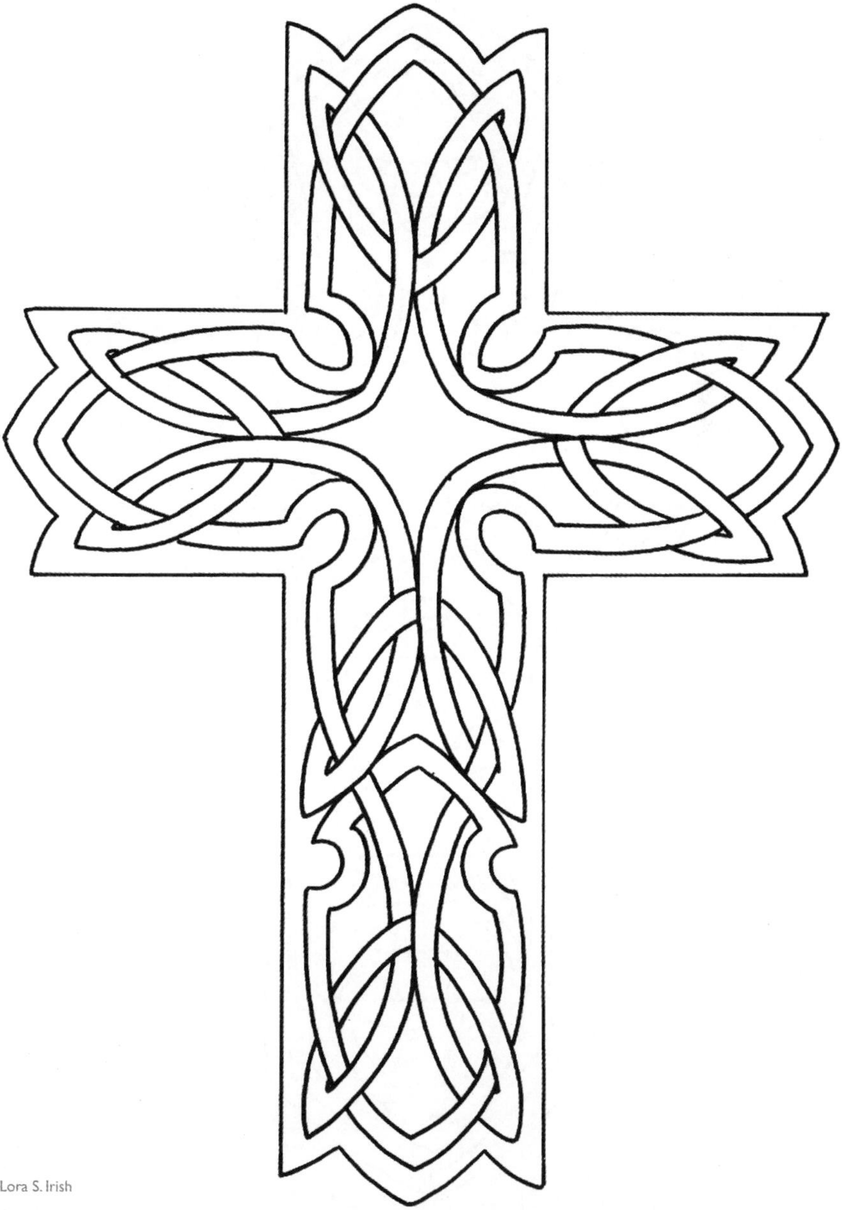

Symbols

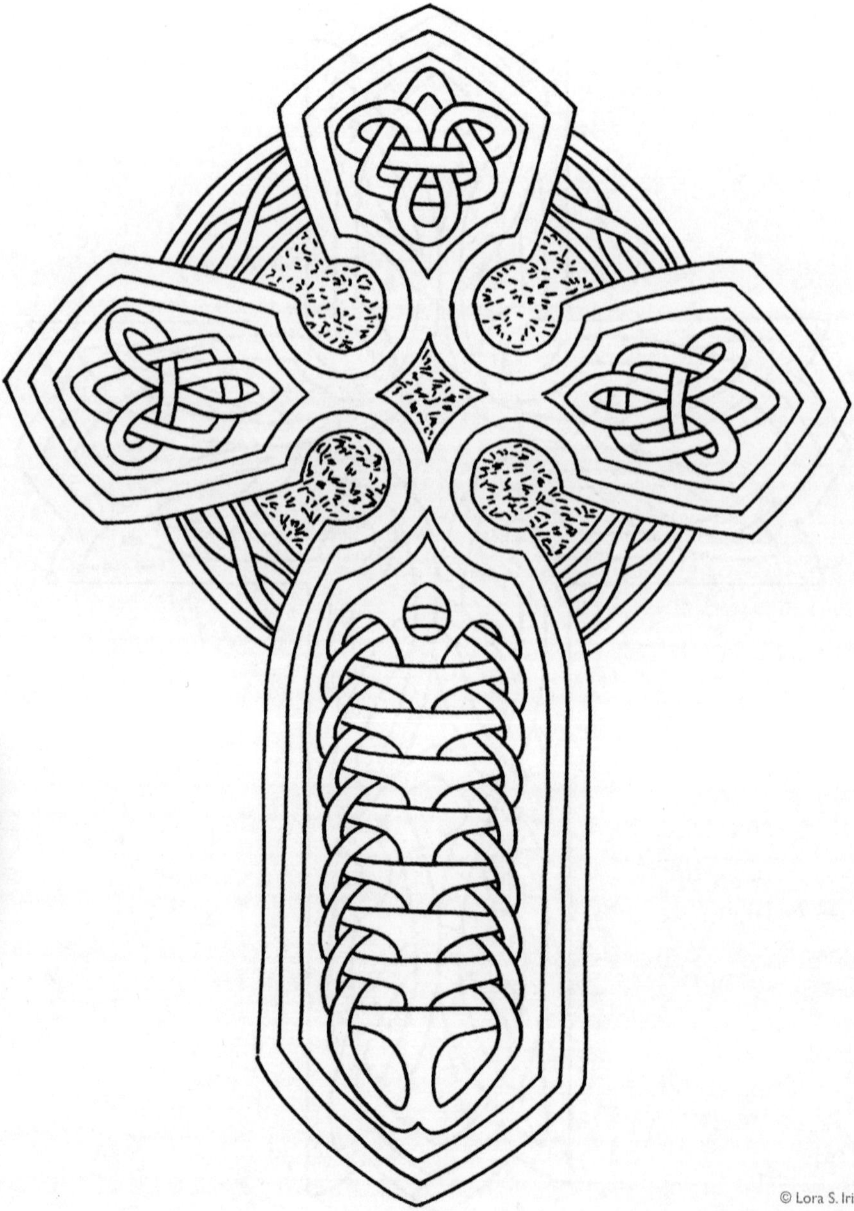

© Lora S. Irish

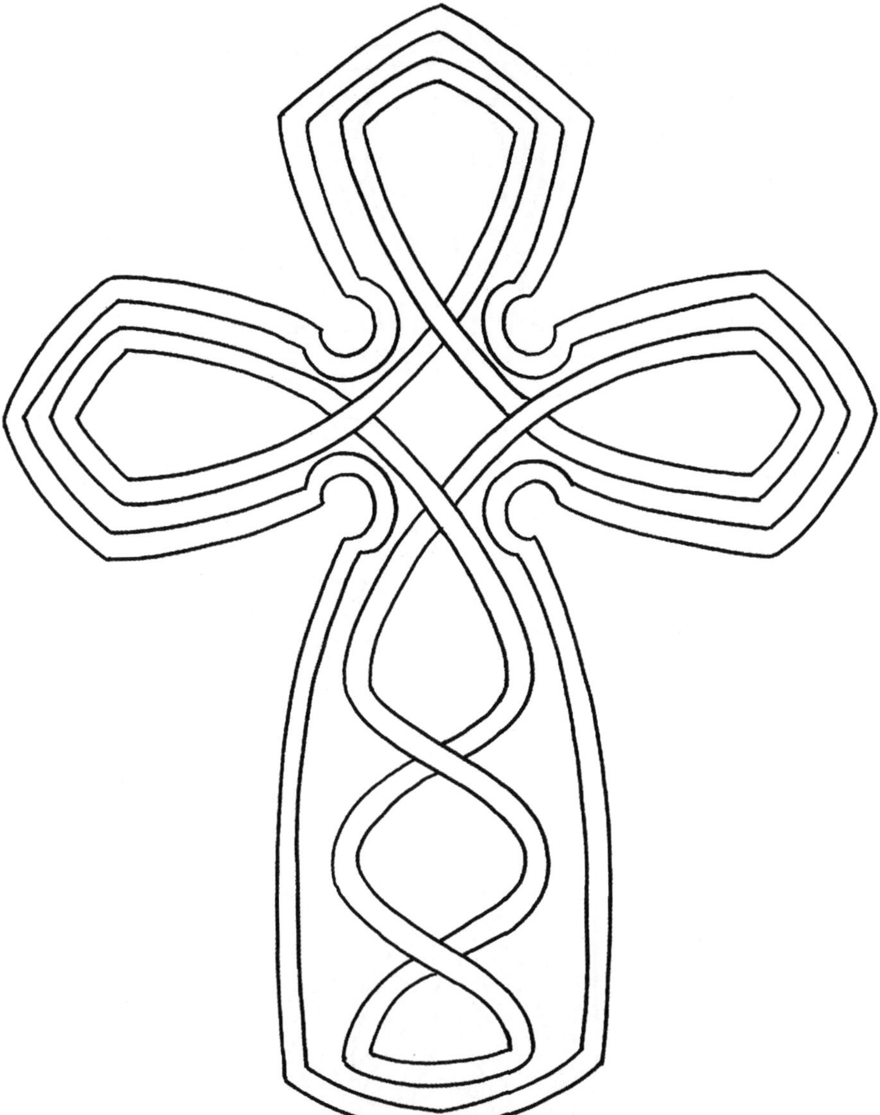

Symbols

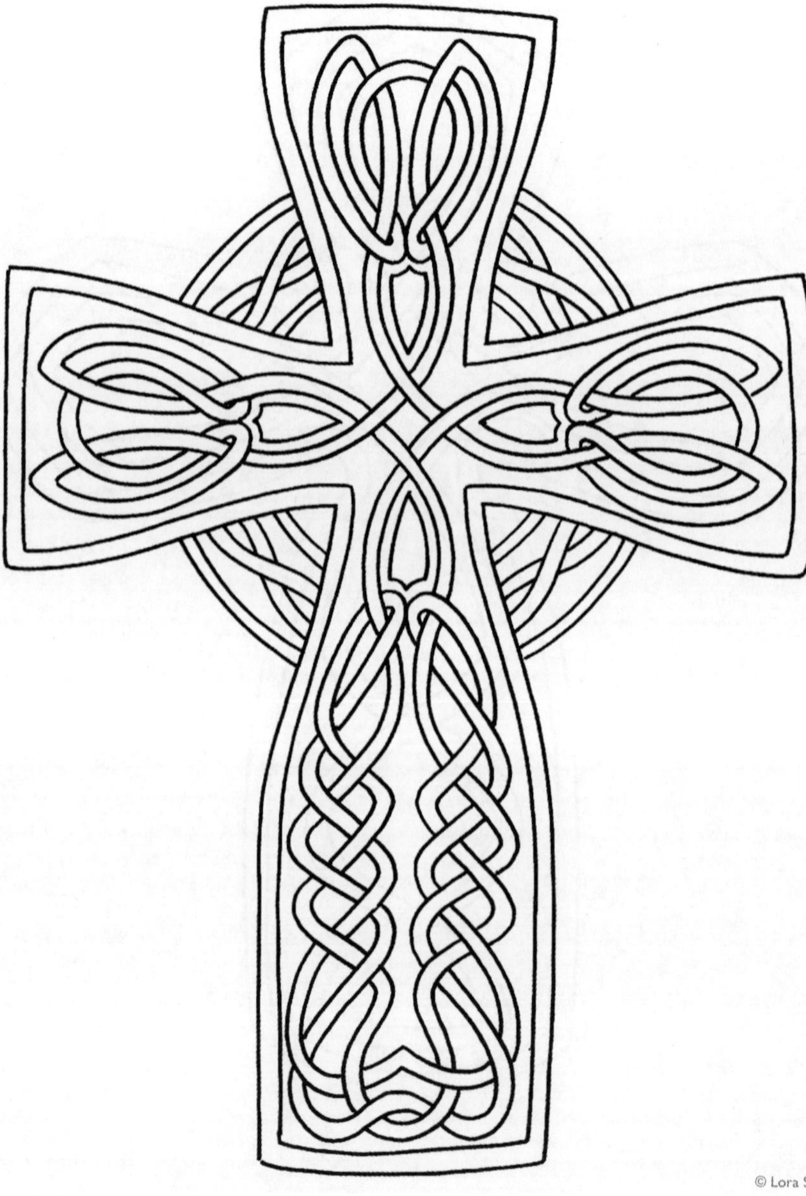

© Lora S. Irish

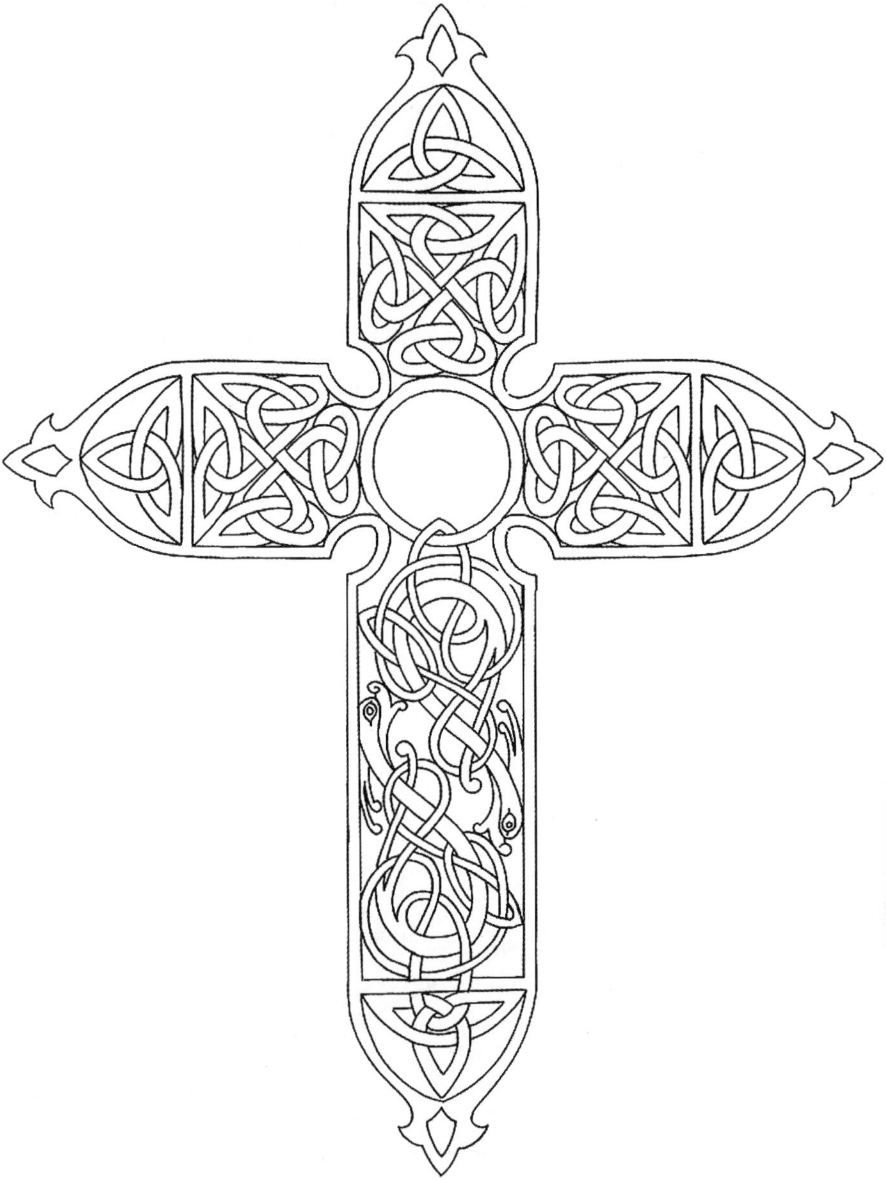

Symbols

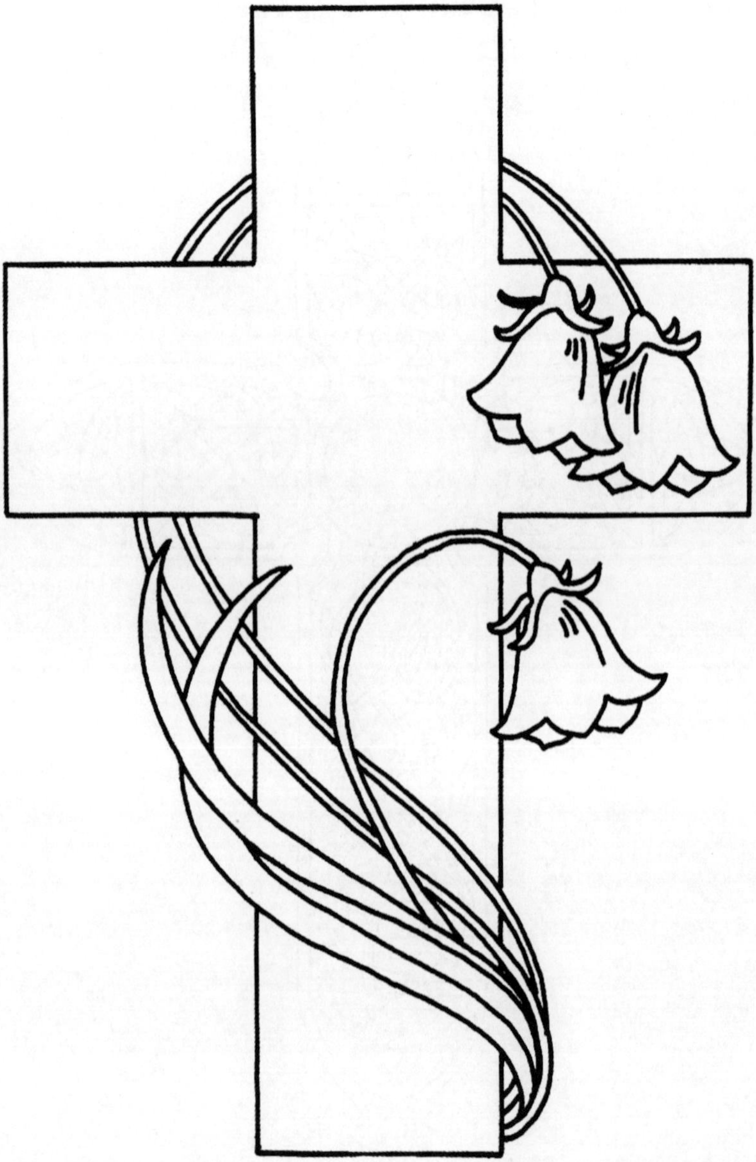

© Lora S. Irish

Symbols

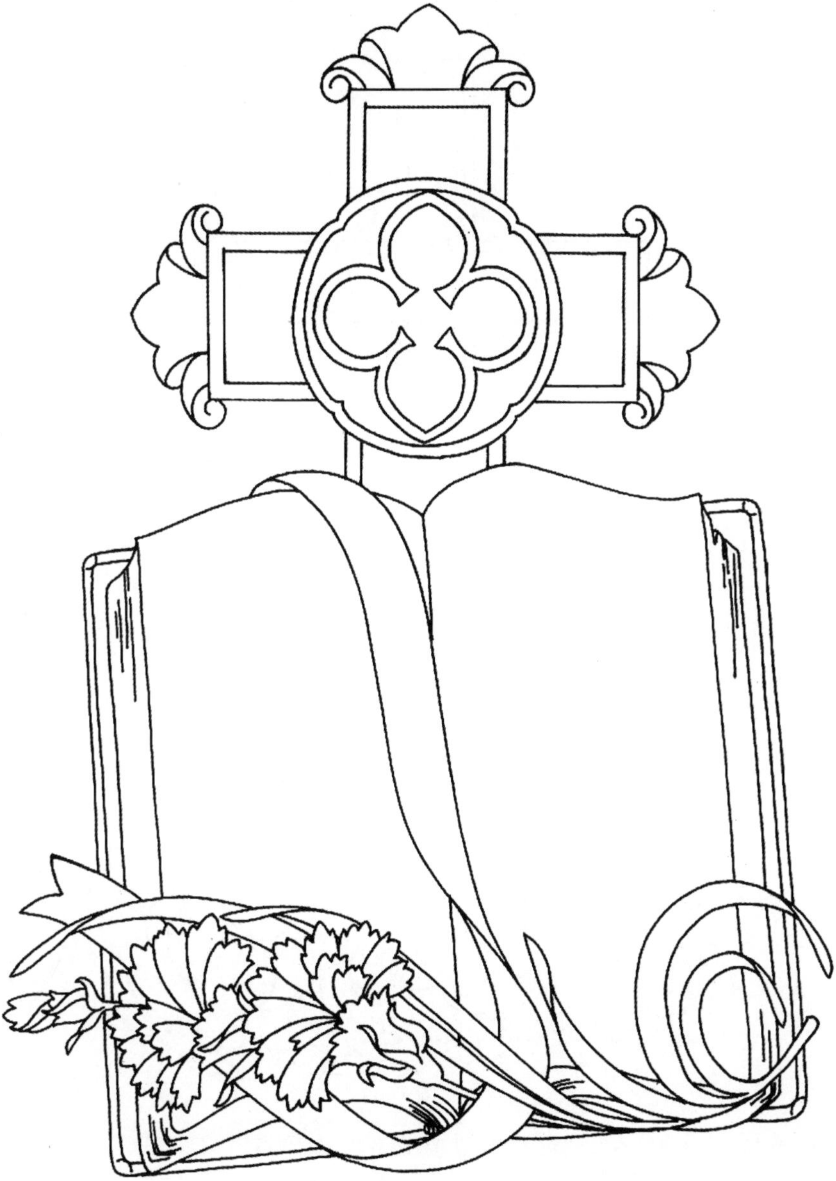

Symbols

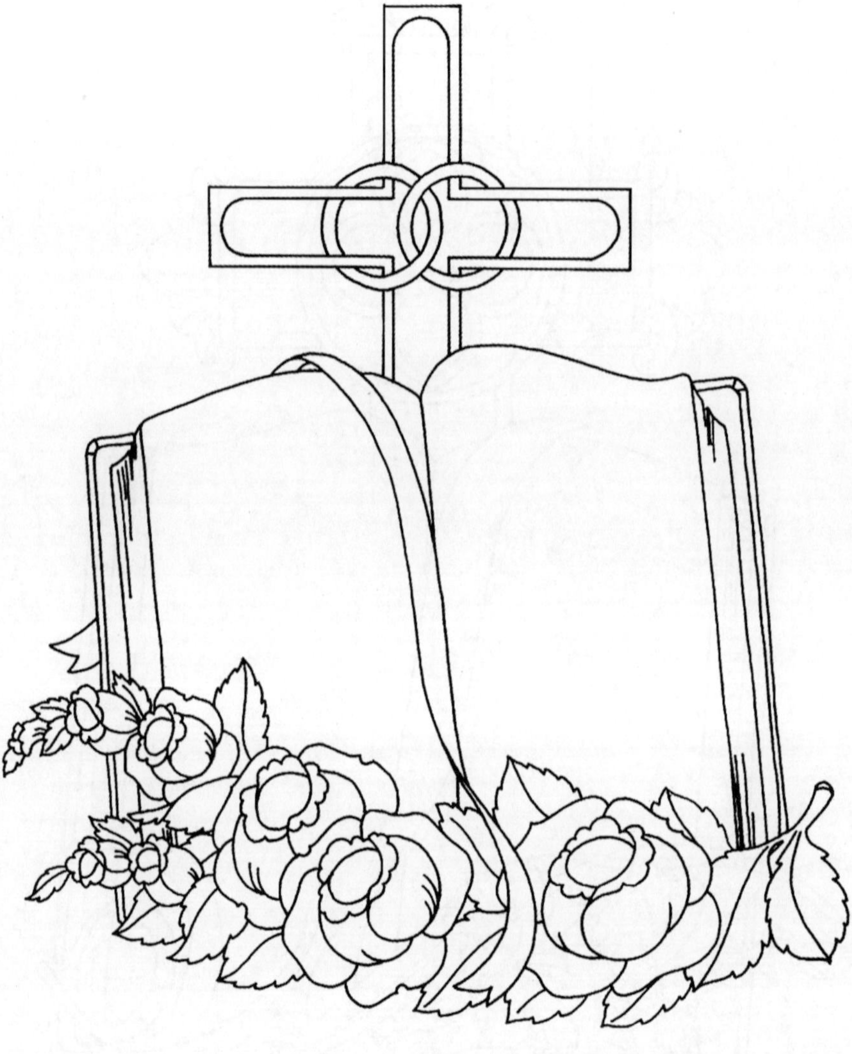

Symbols

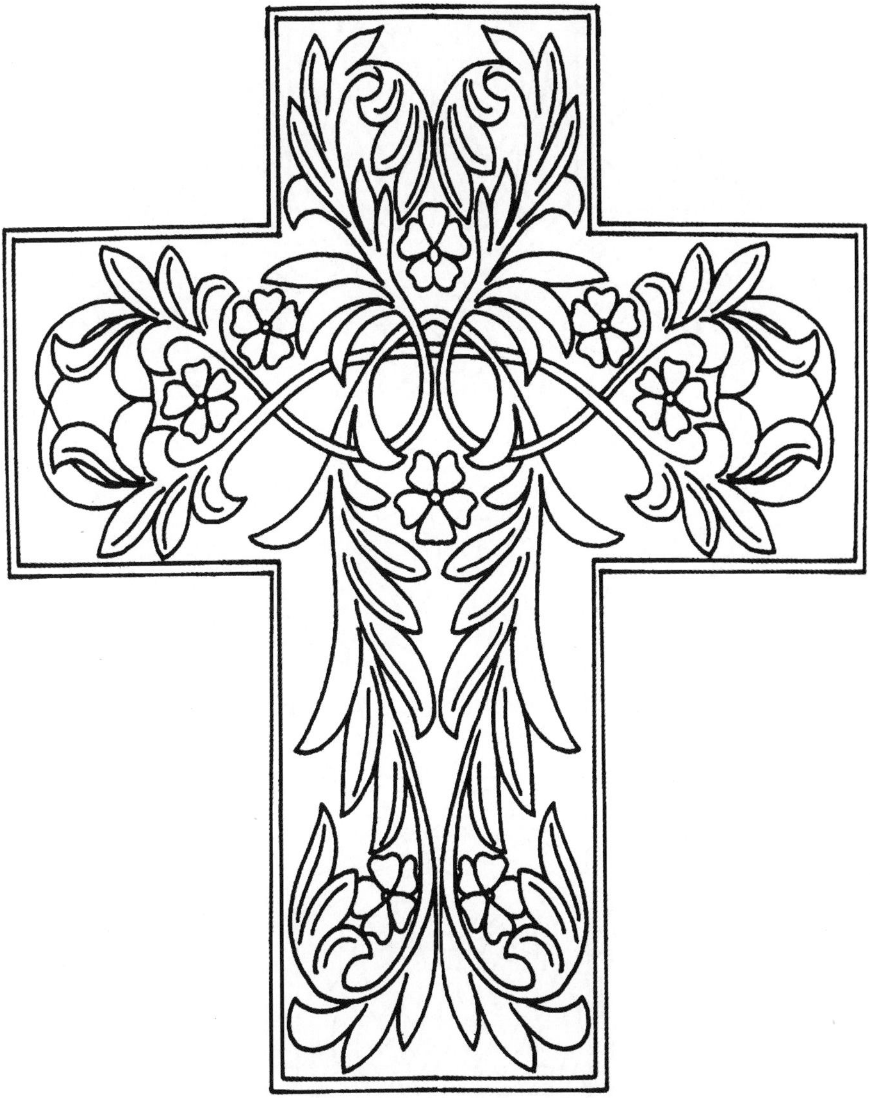

Symbols

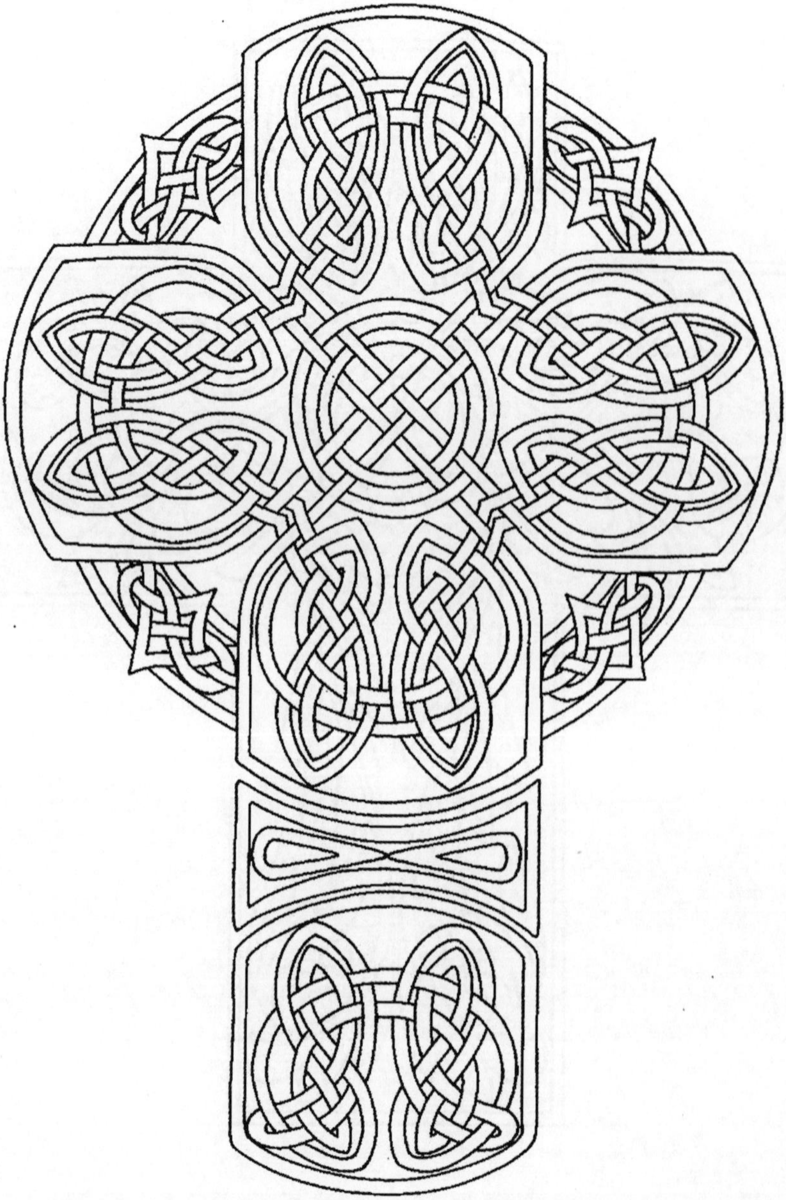

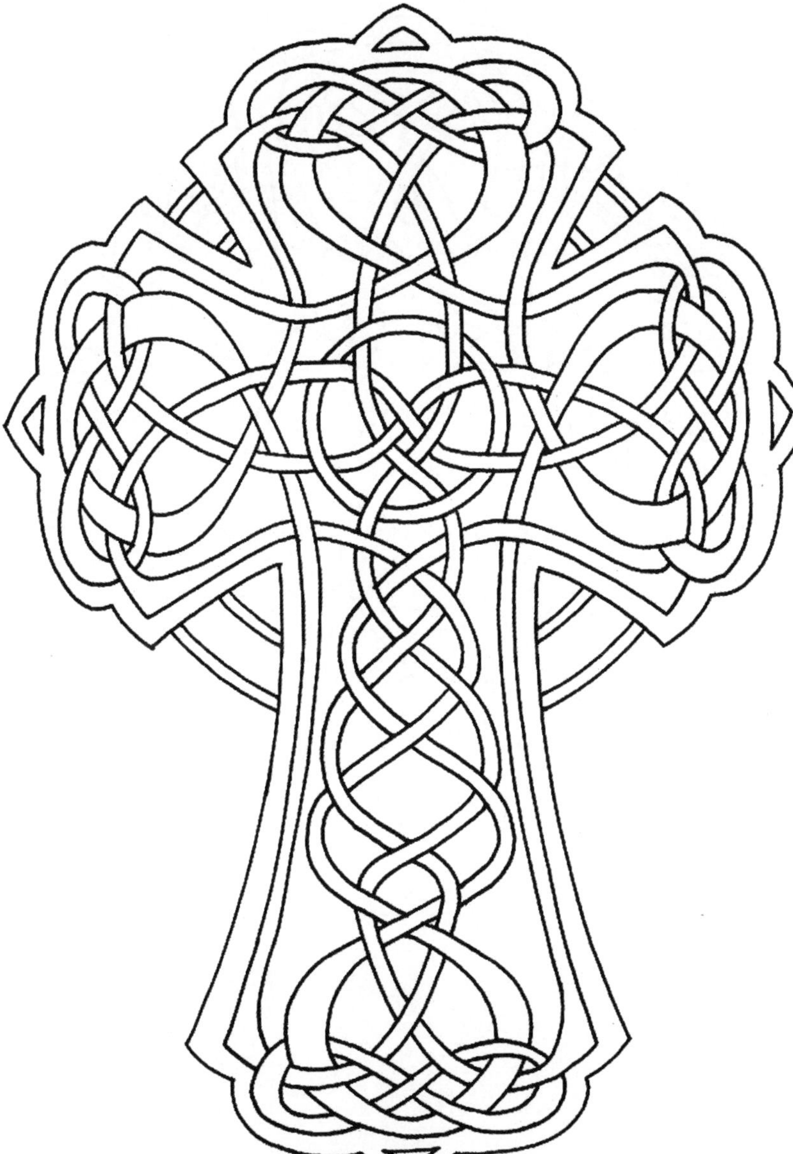

Symbols

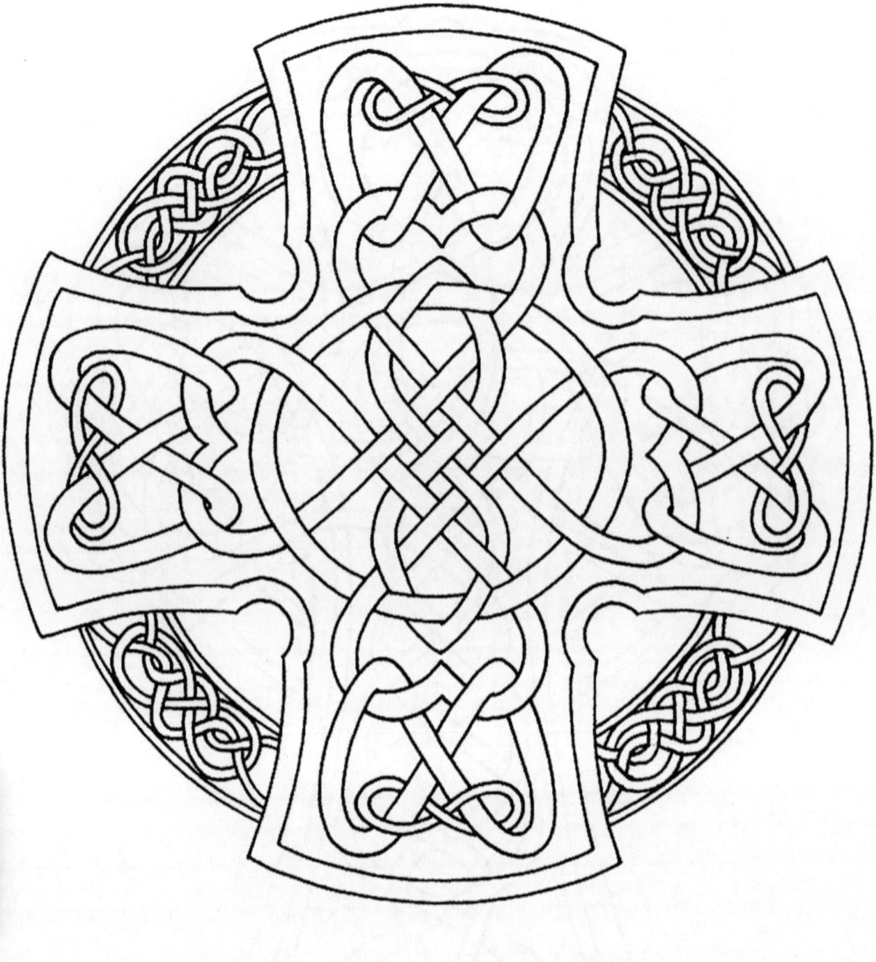

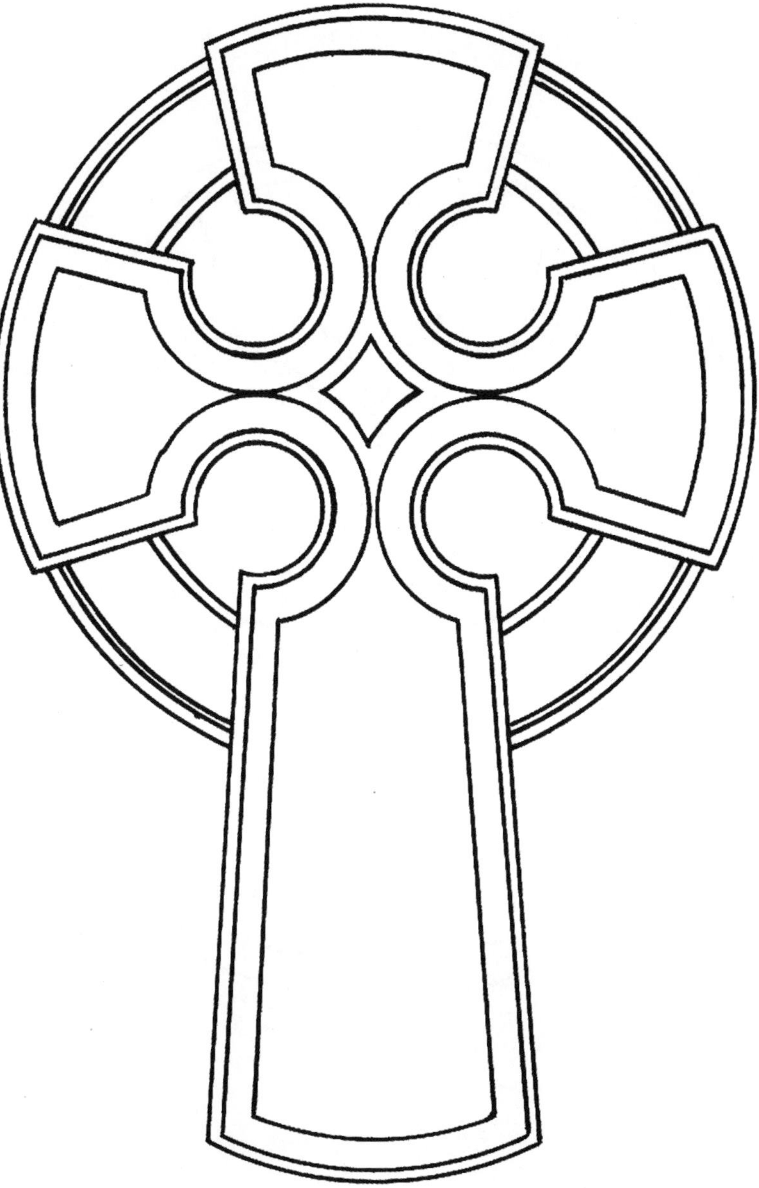

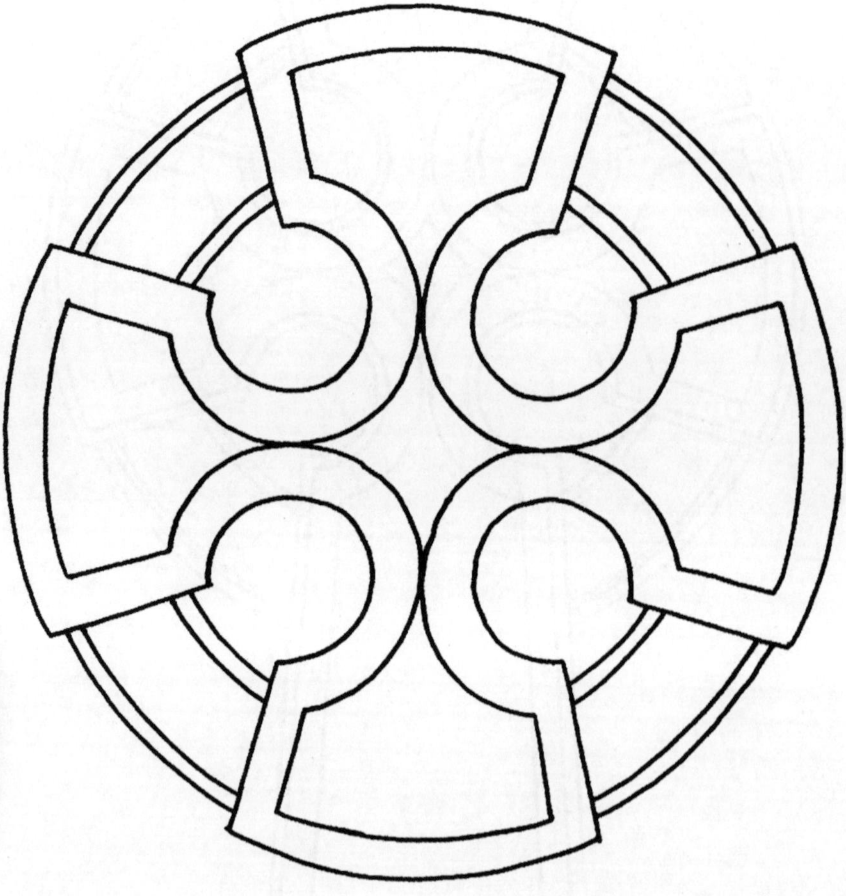

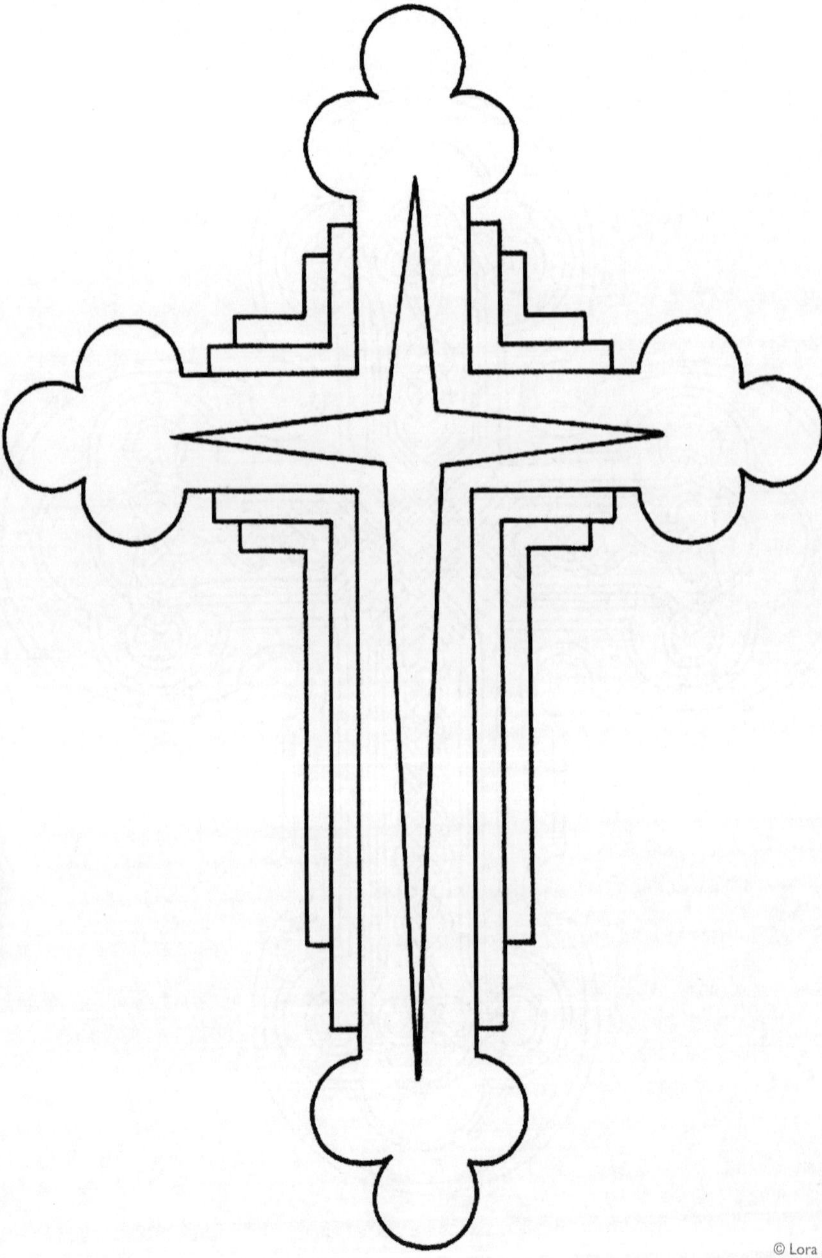

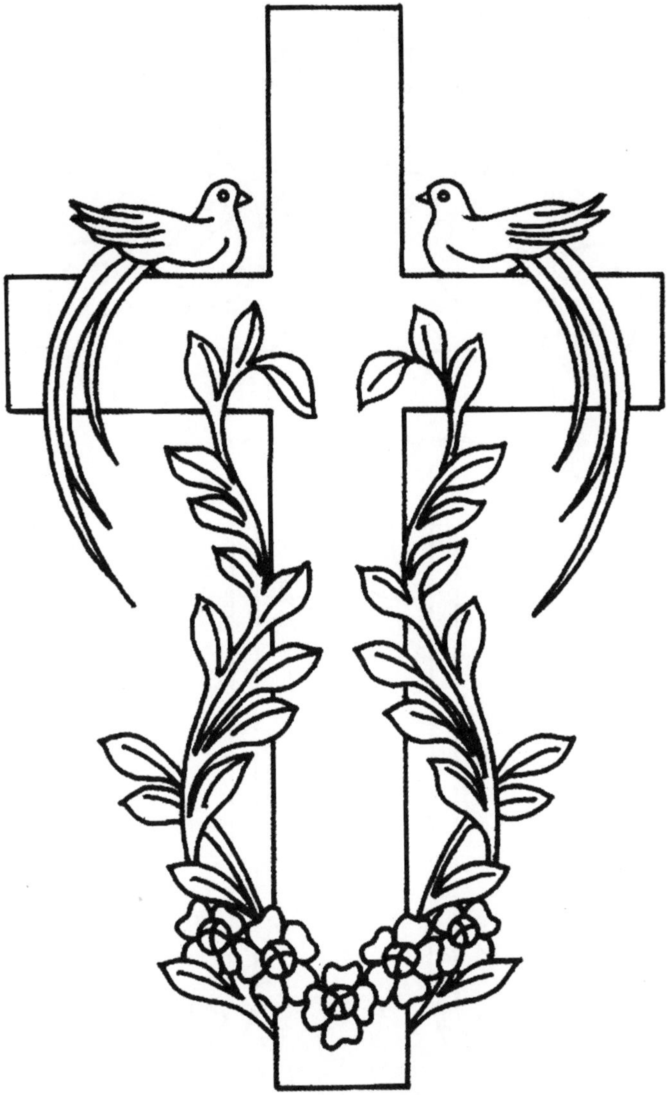

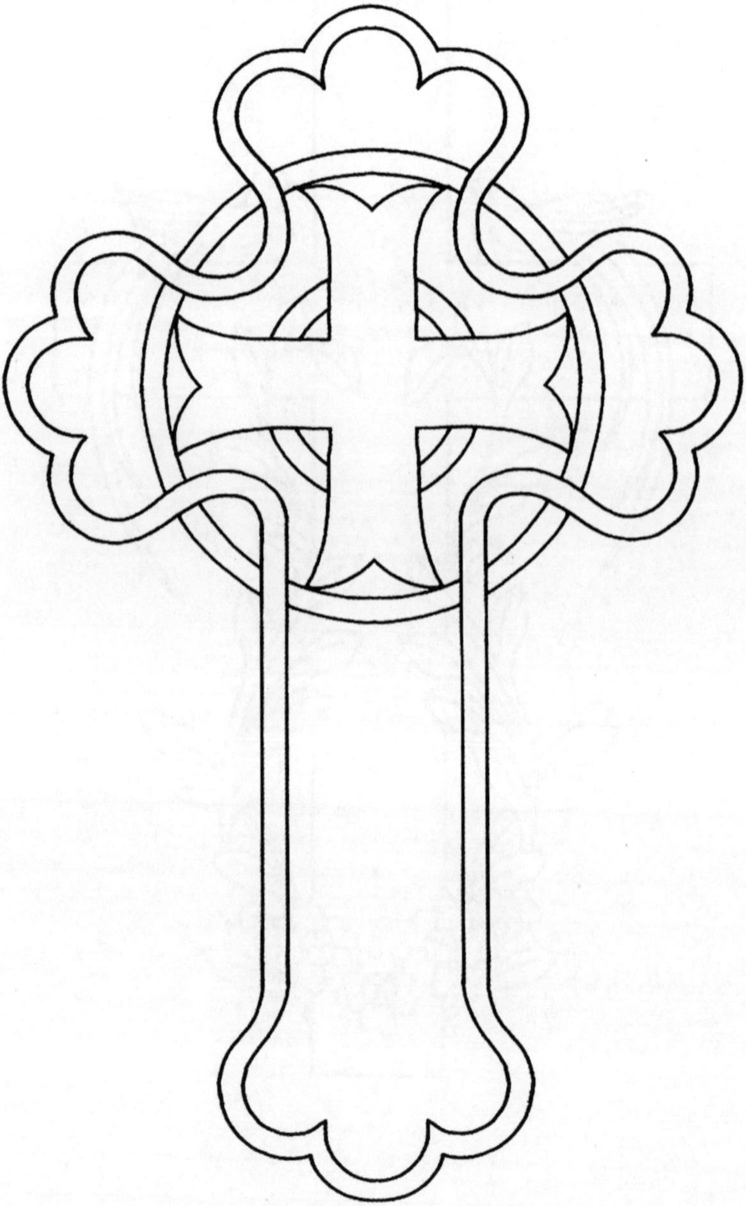

Symbols

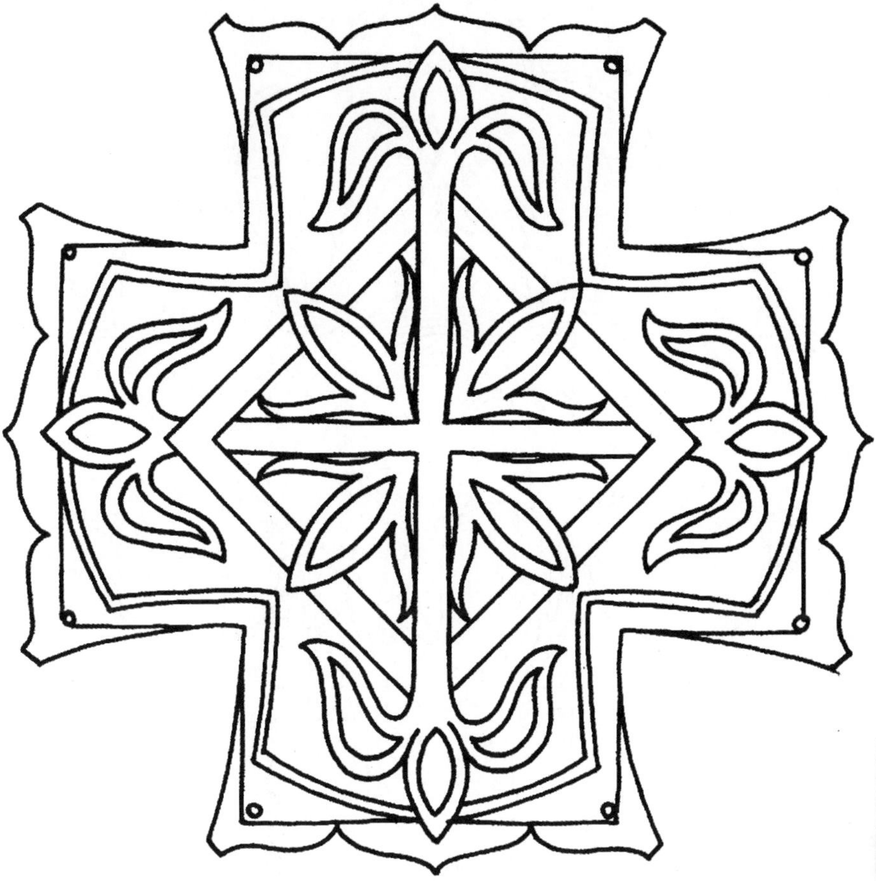

Symbols

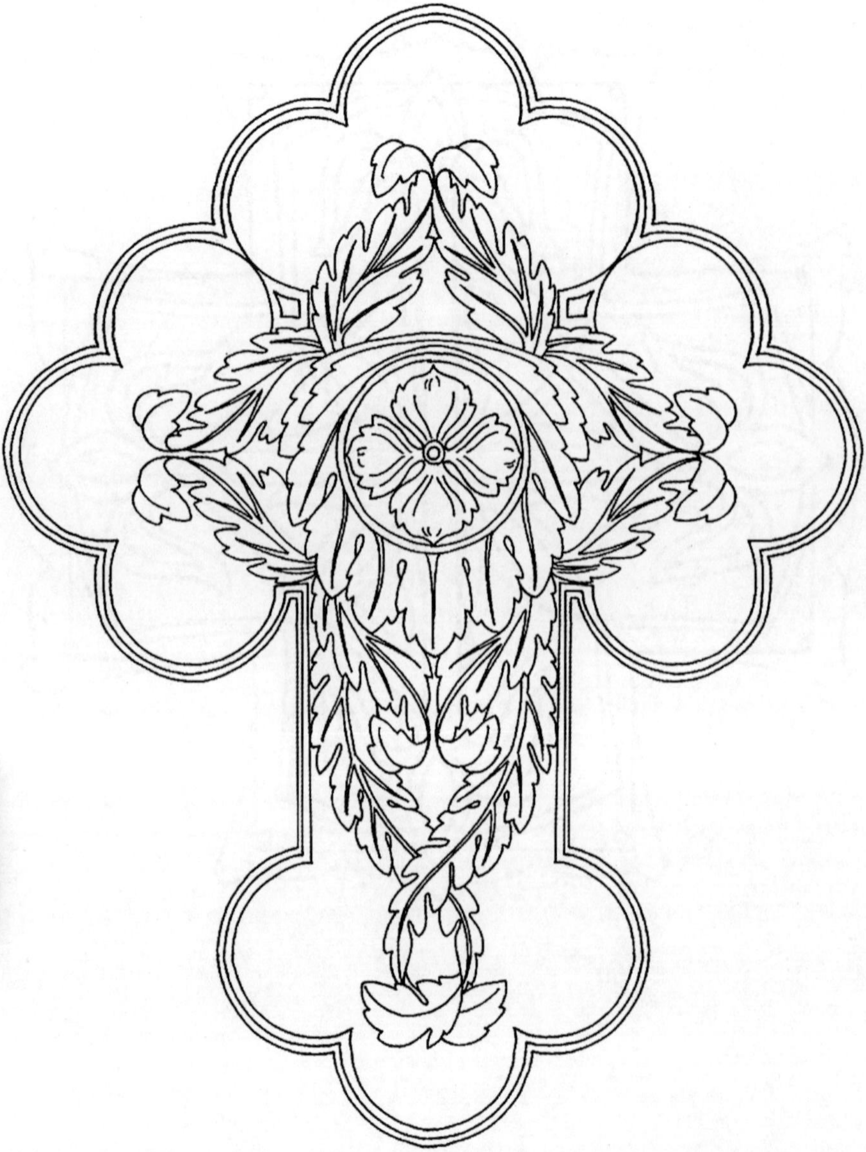

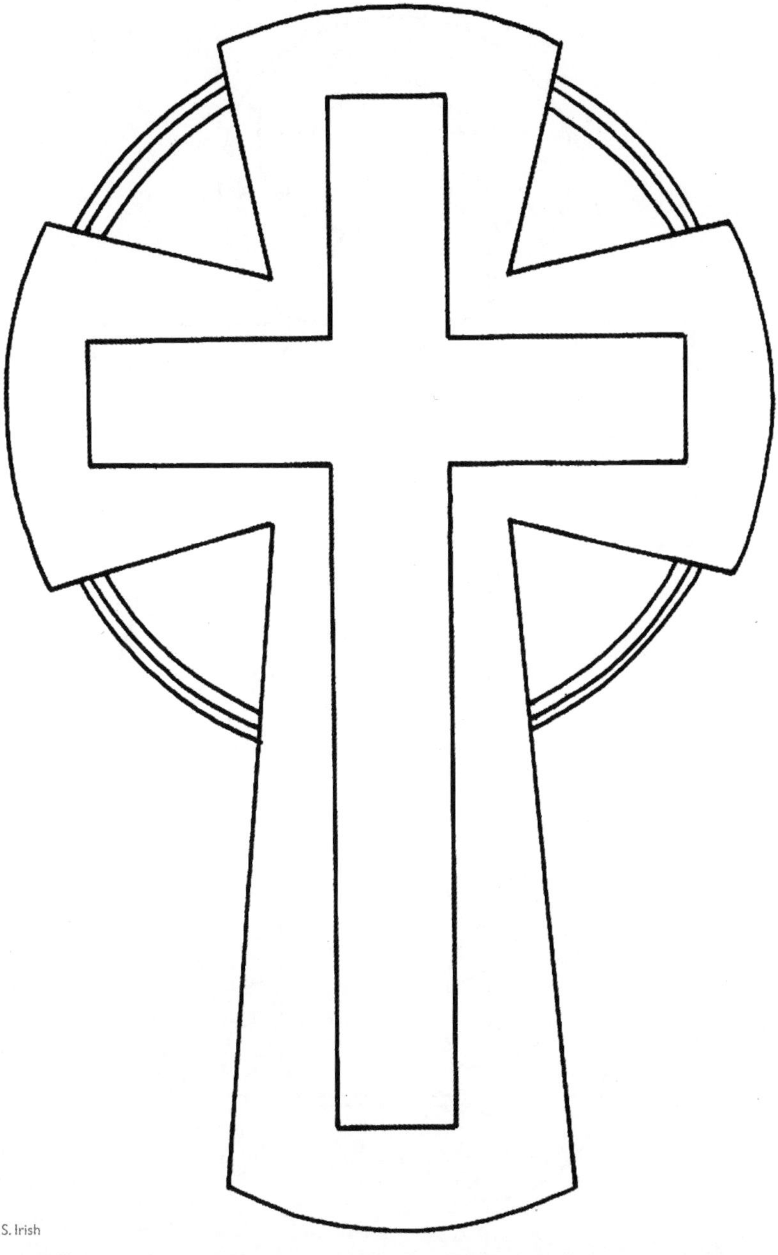

Symbols

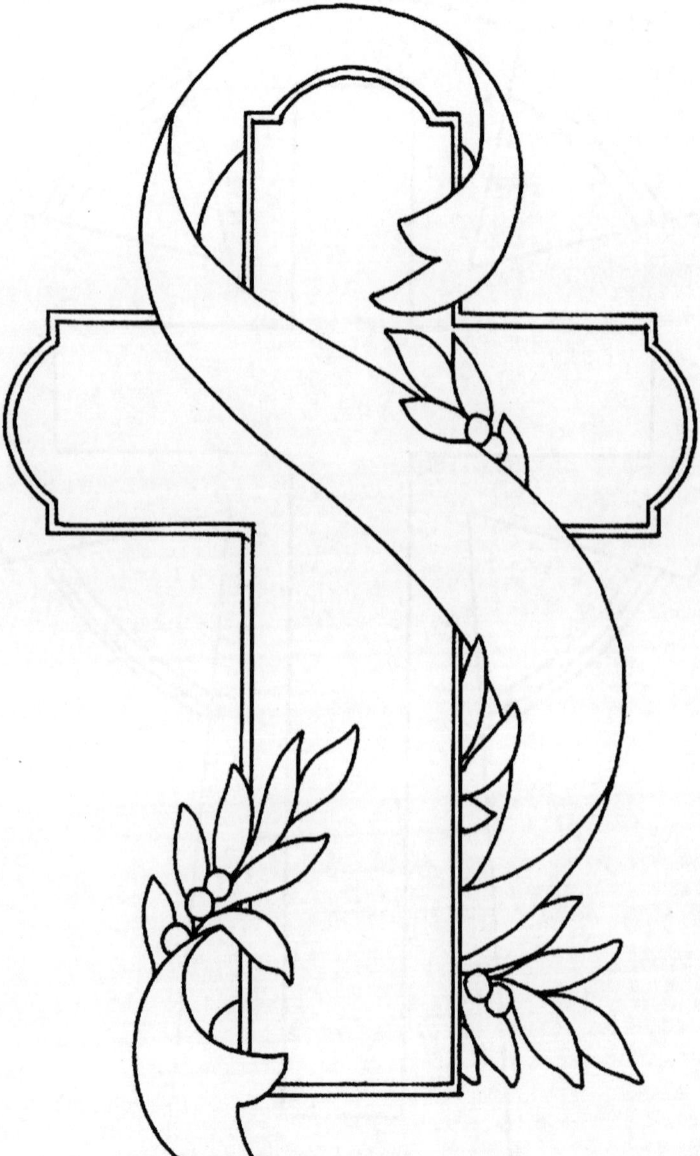

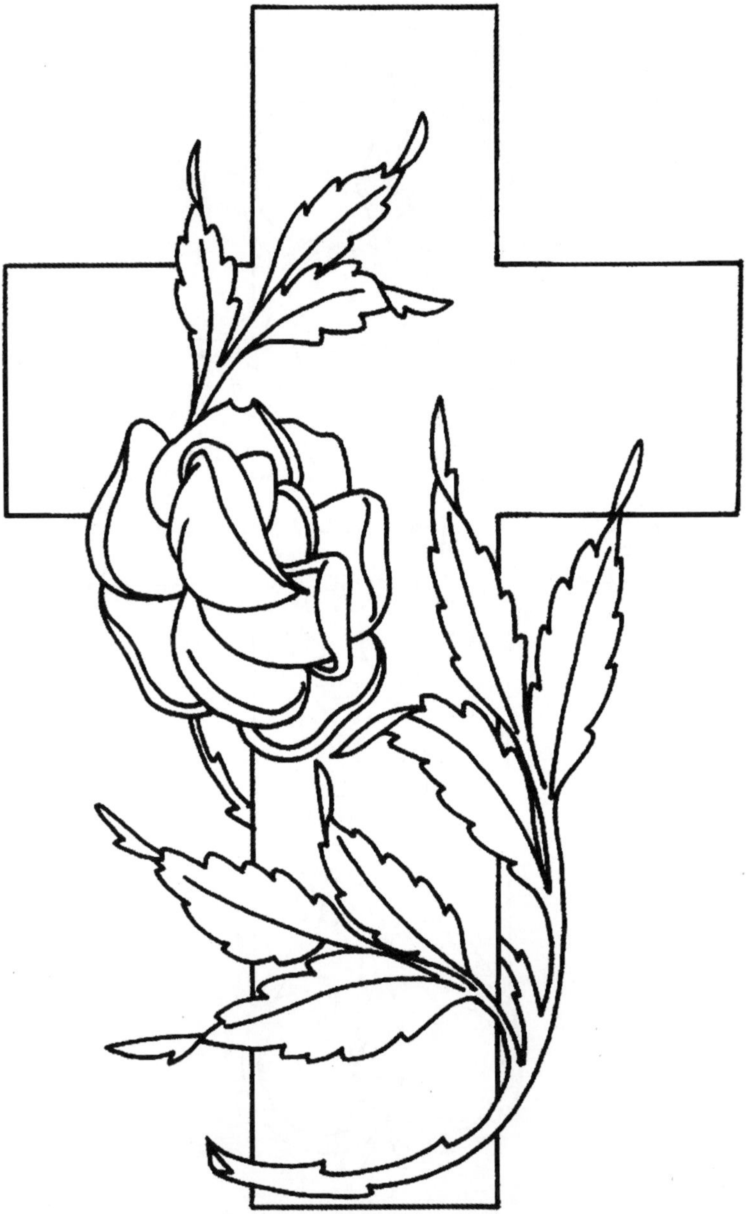

Symbols

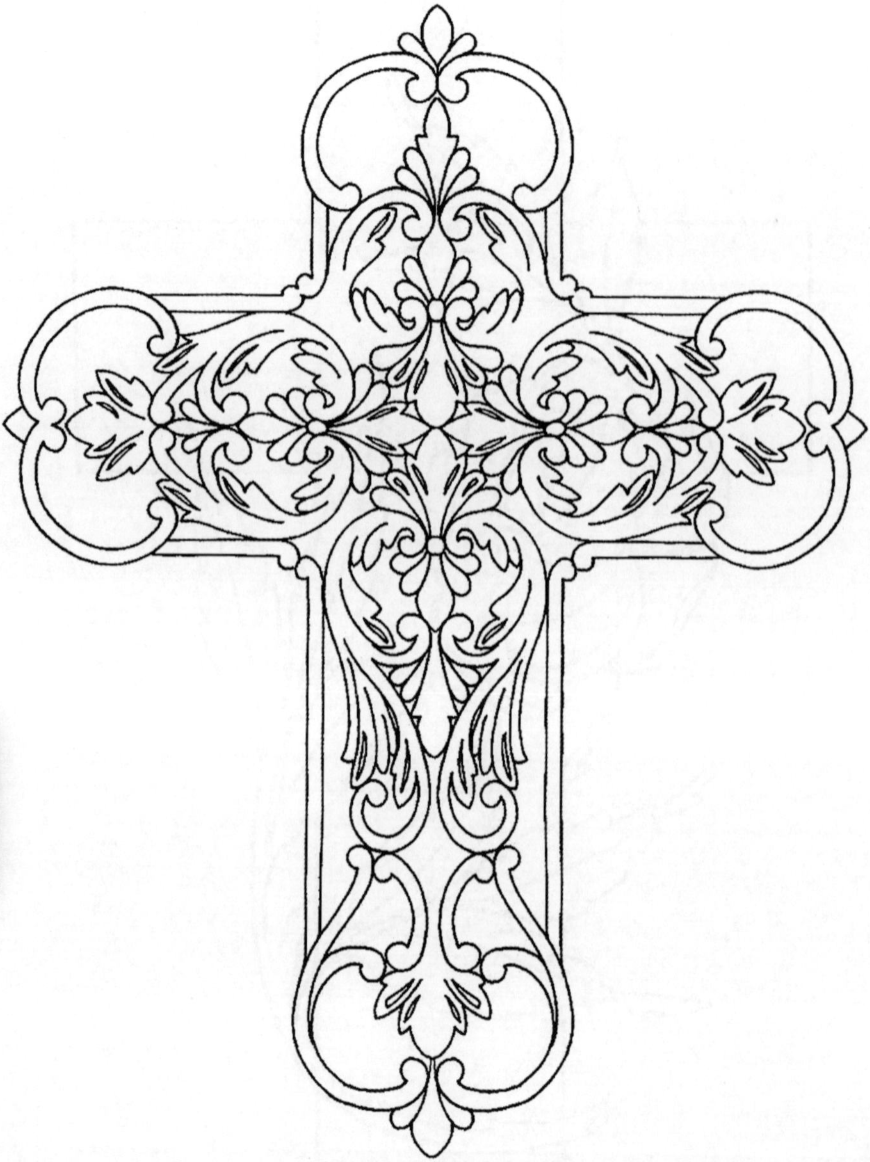

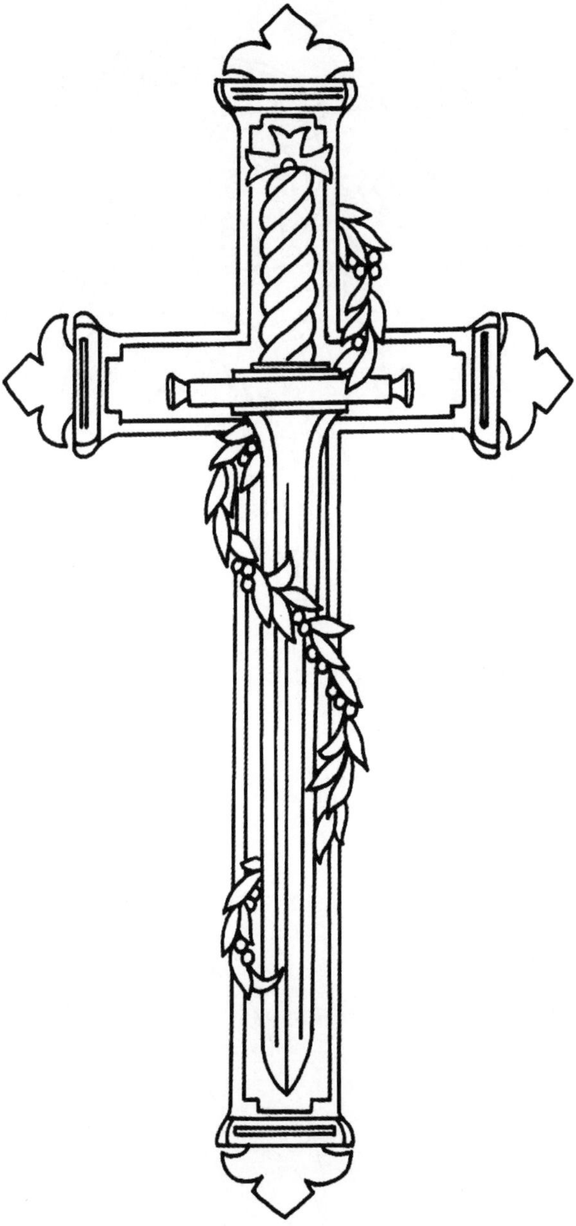

Symbols

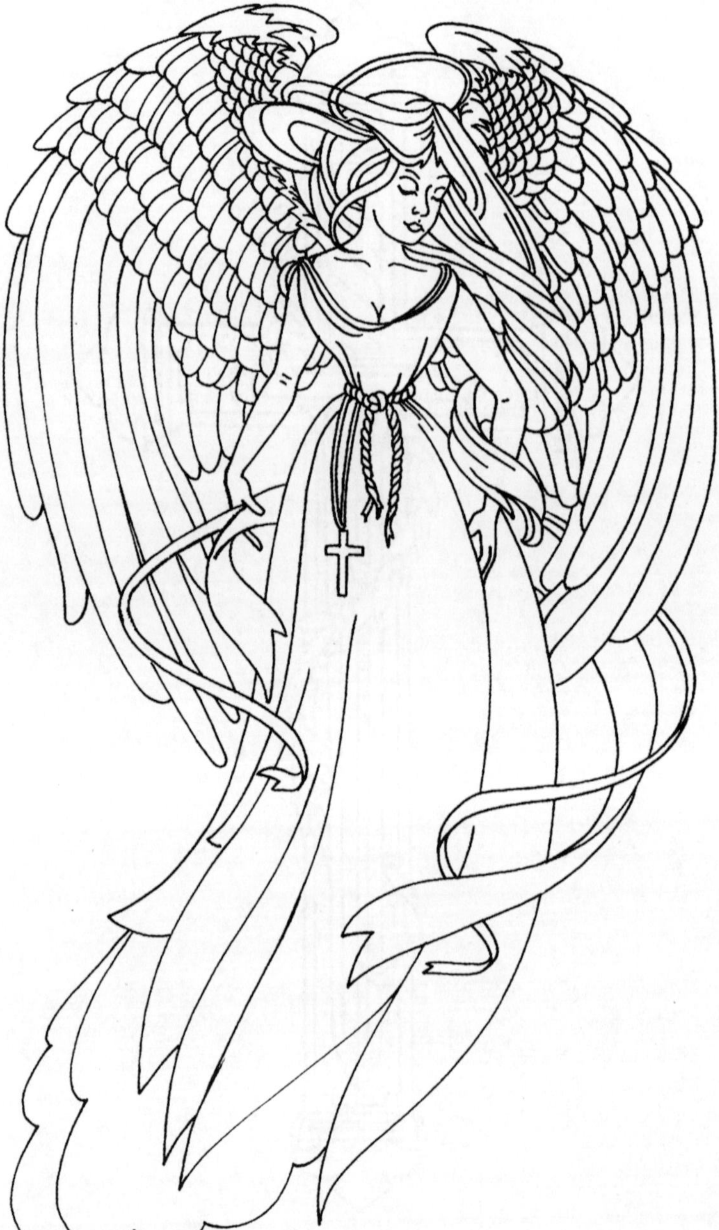

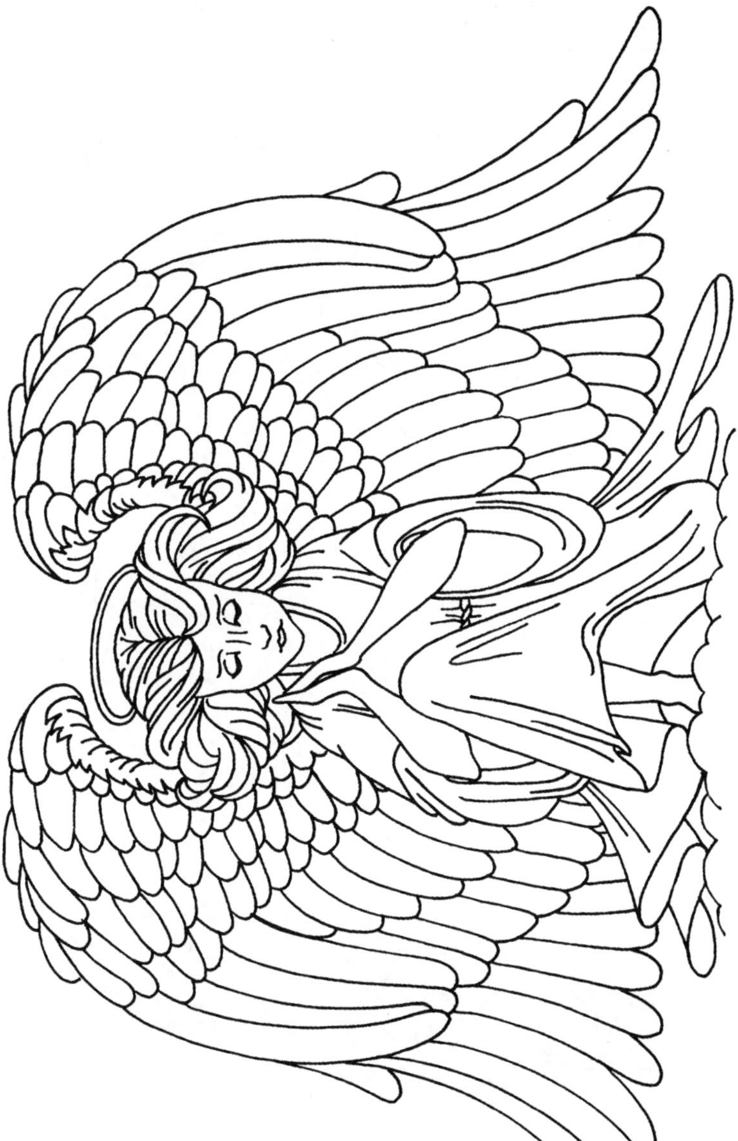

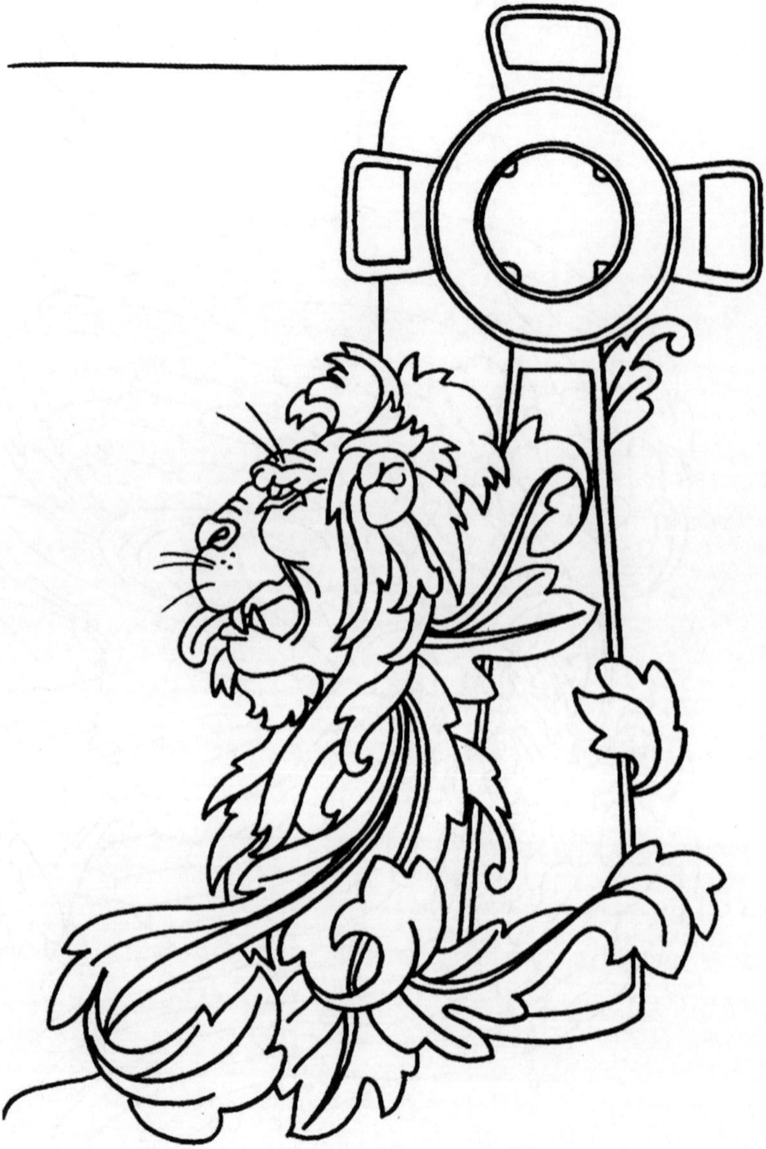

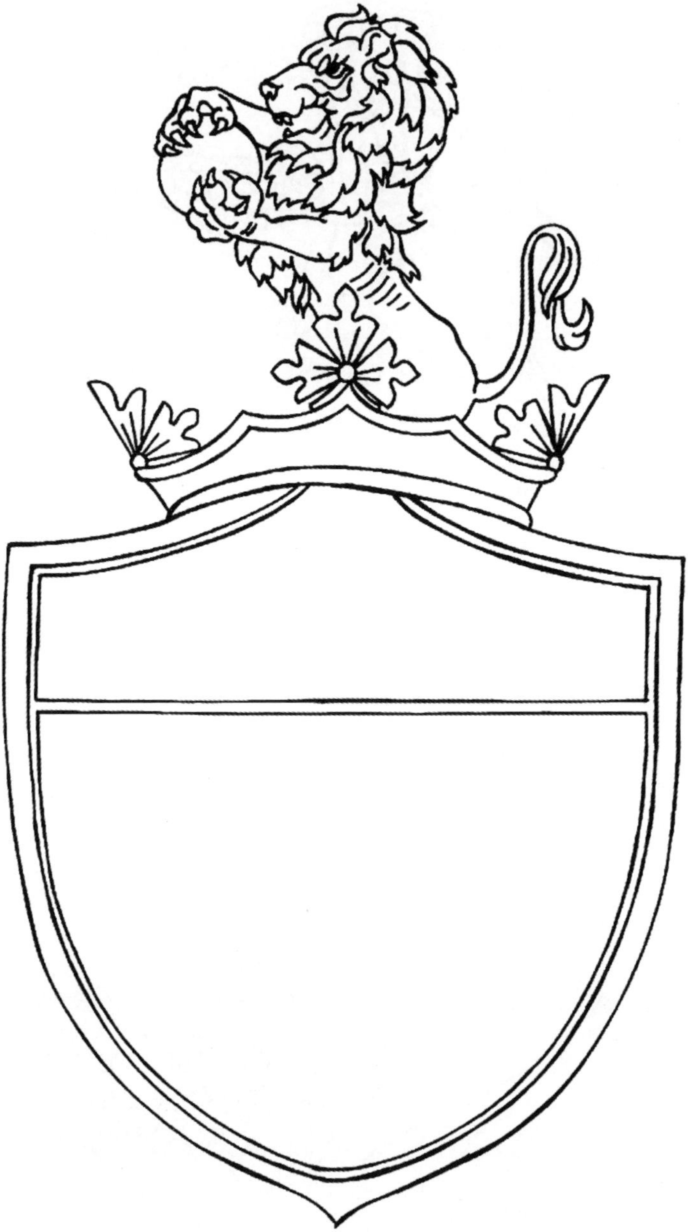

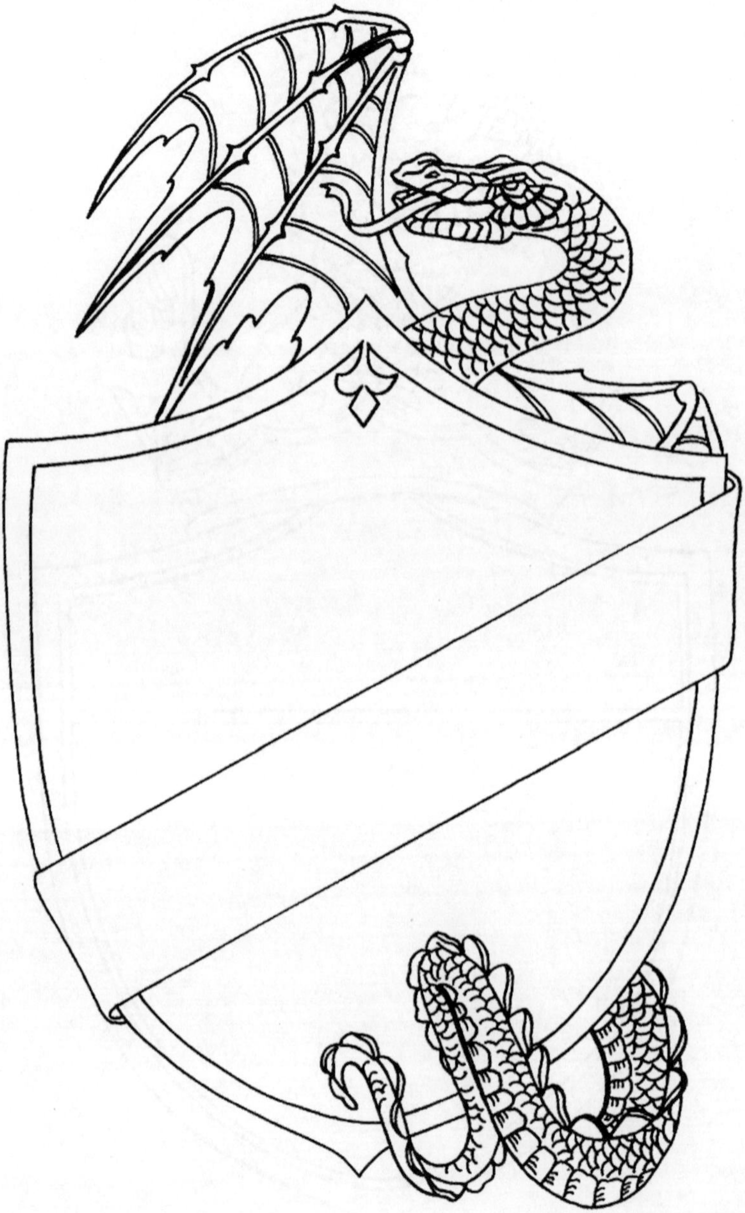

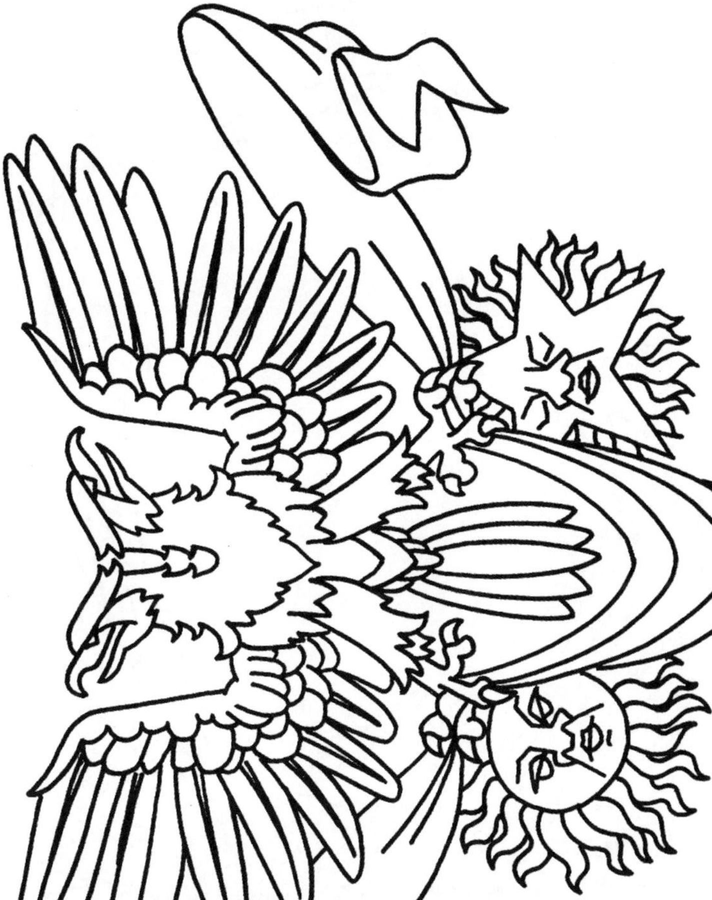

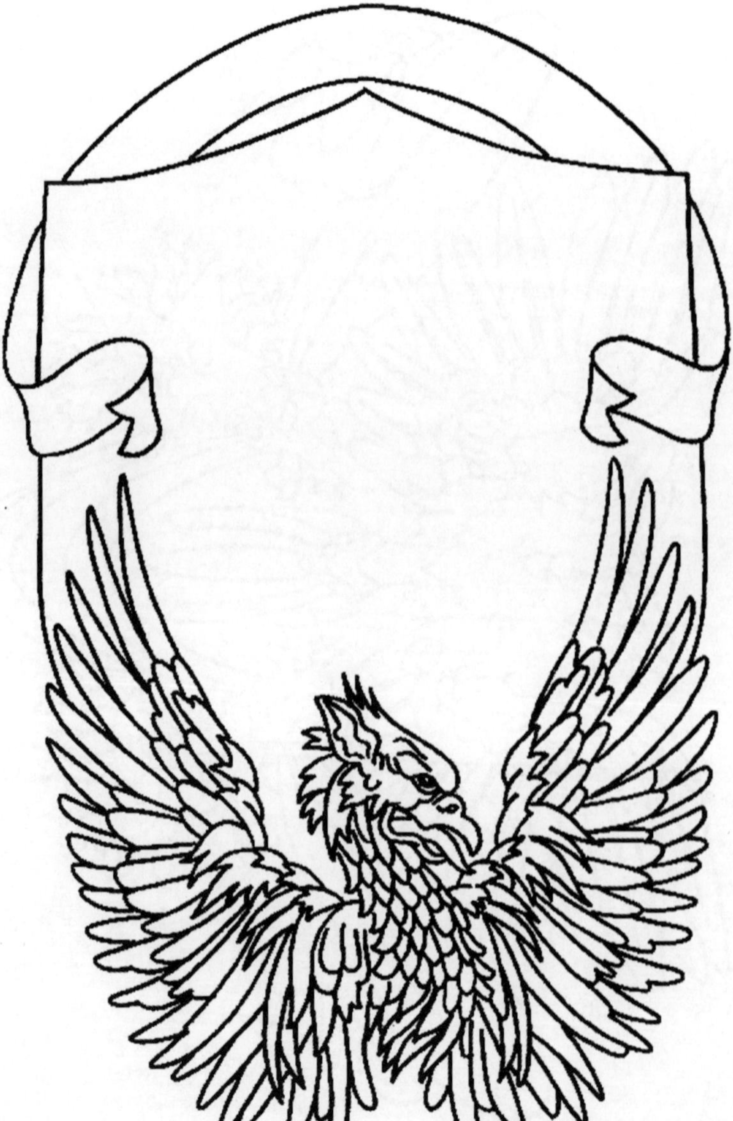

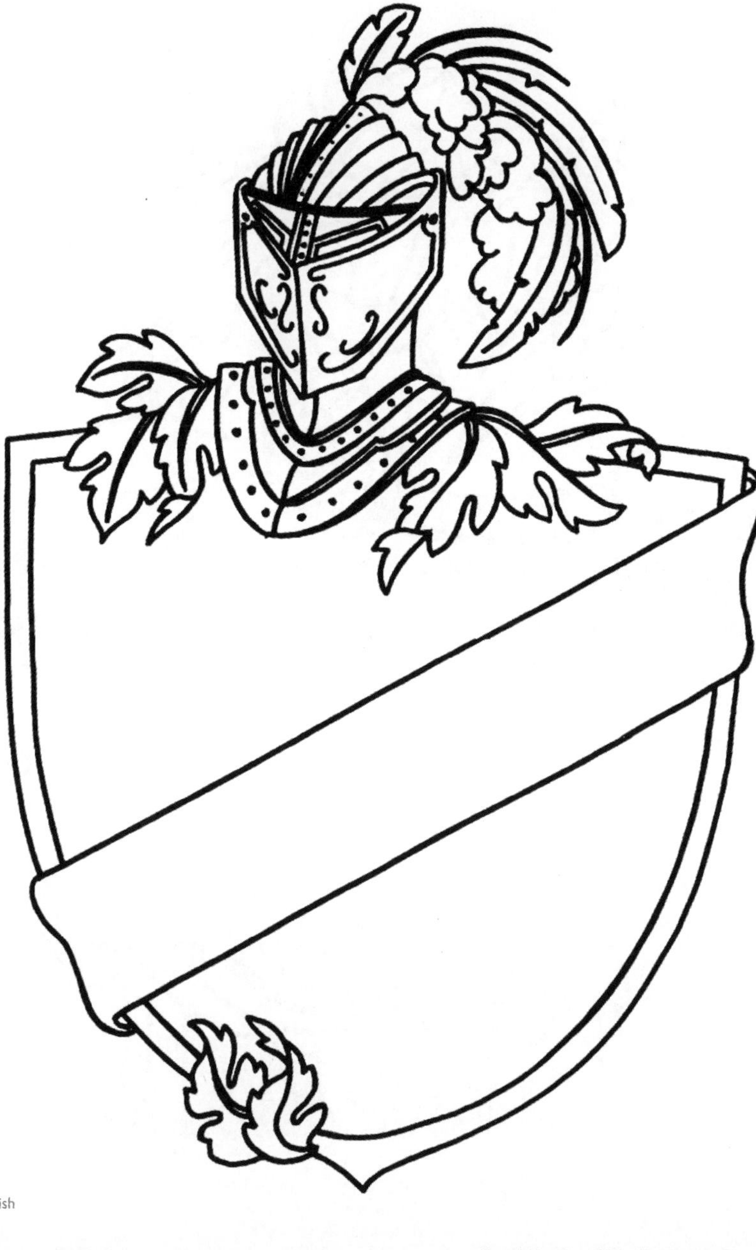

Symbols

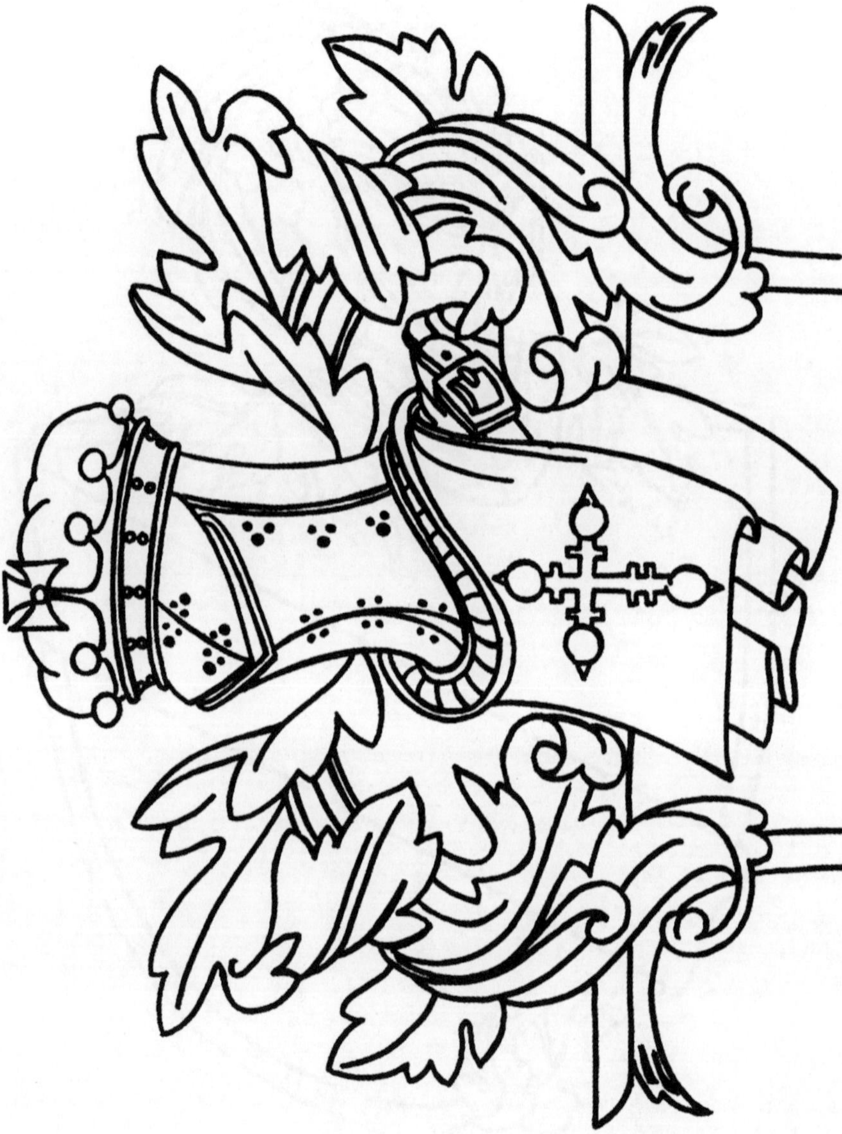

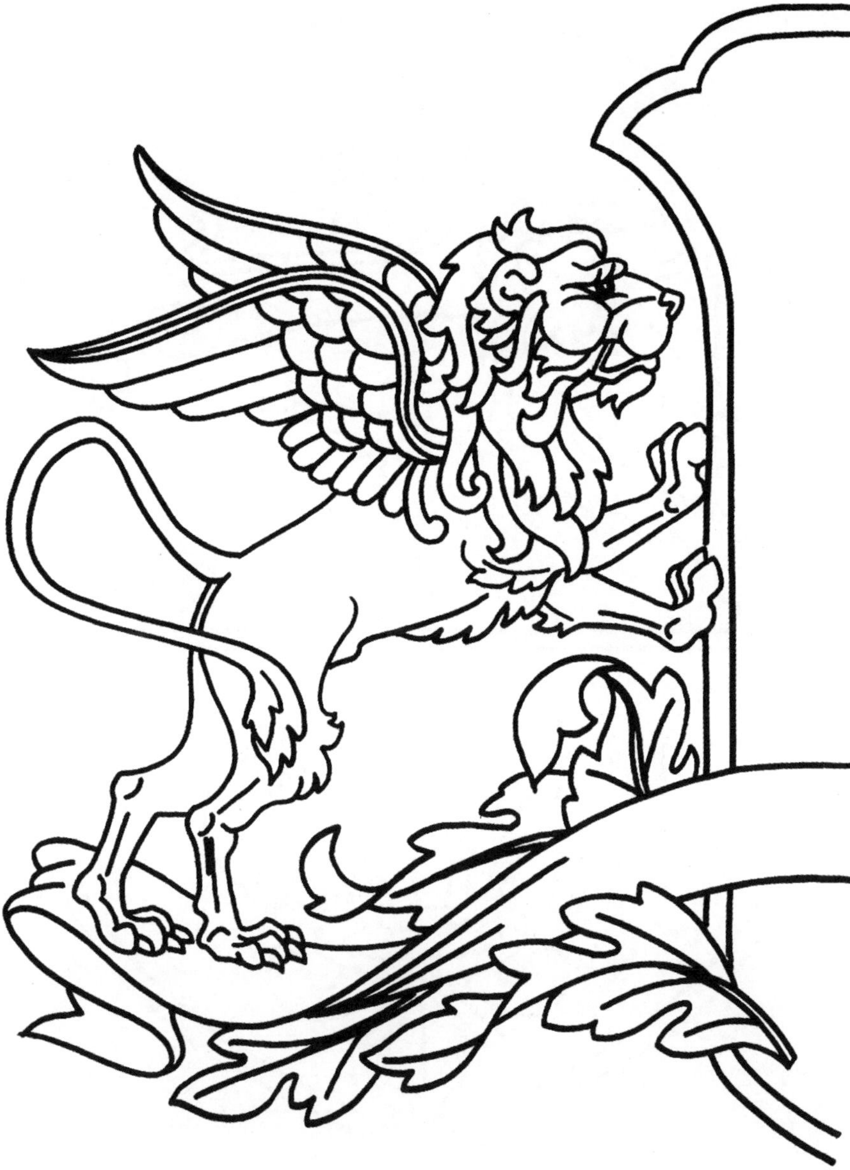

Symbols

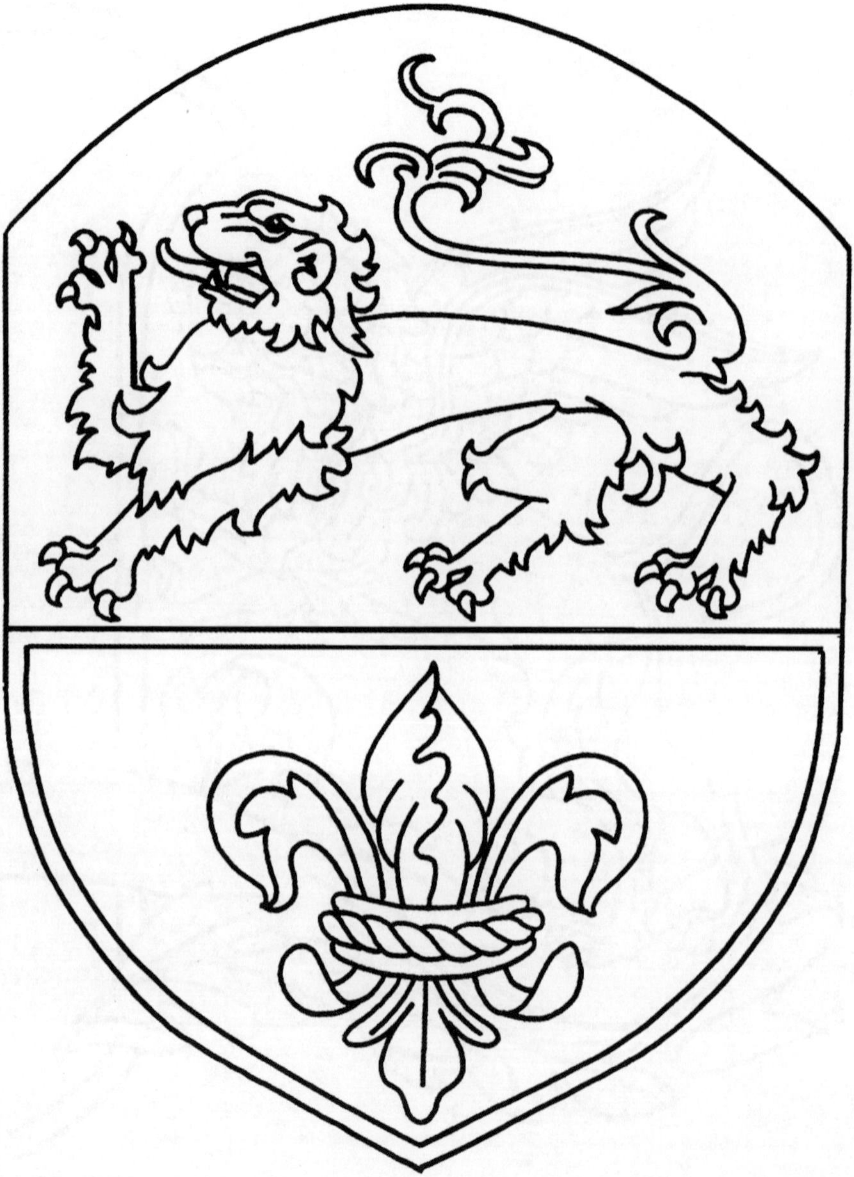

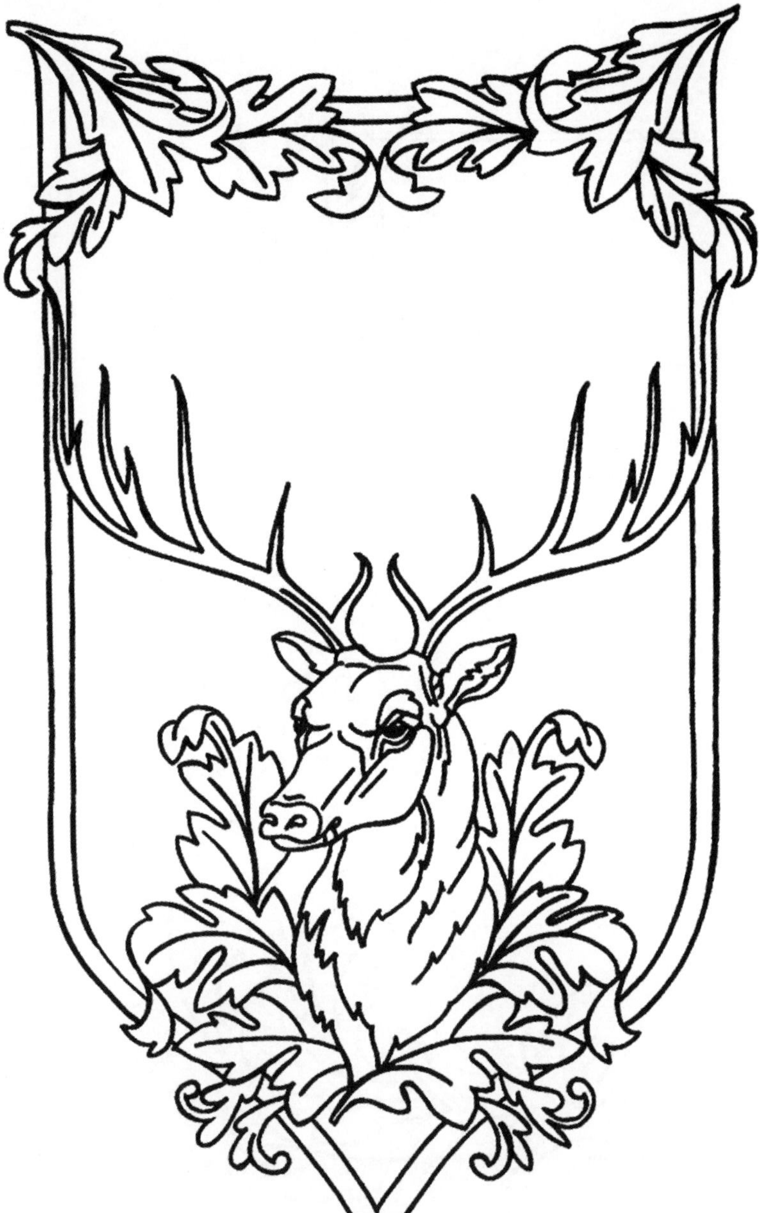

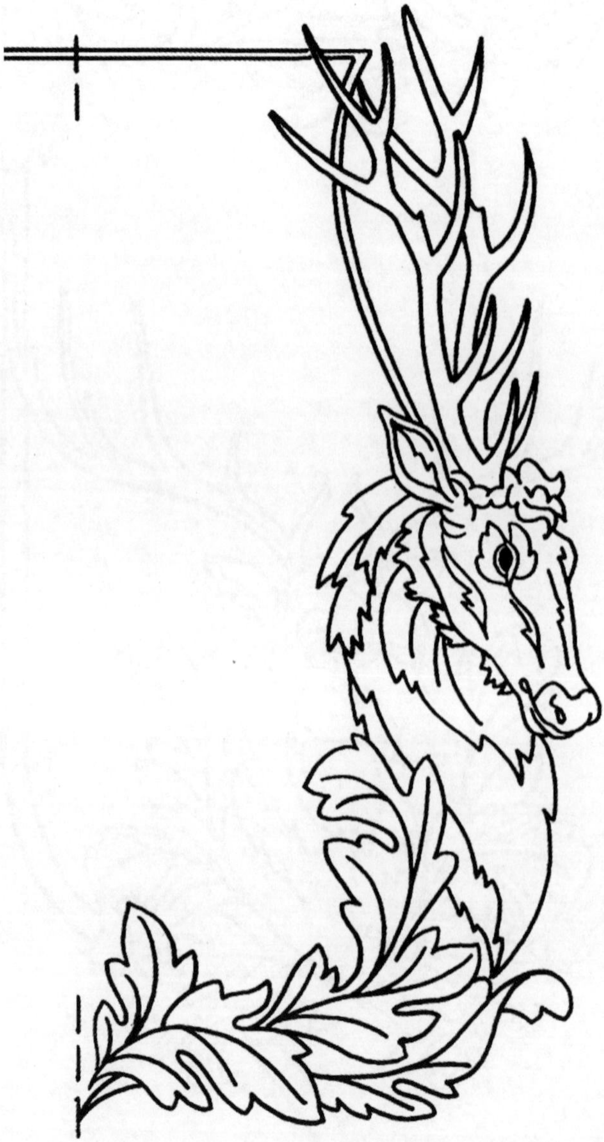

Symbols

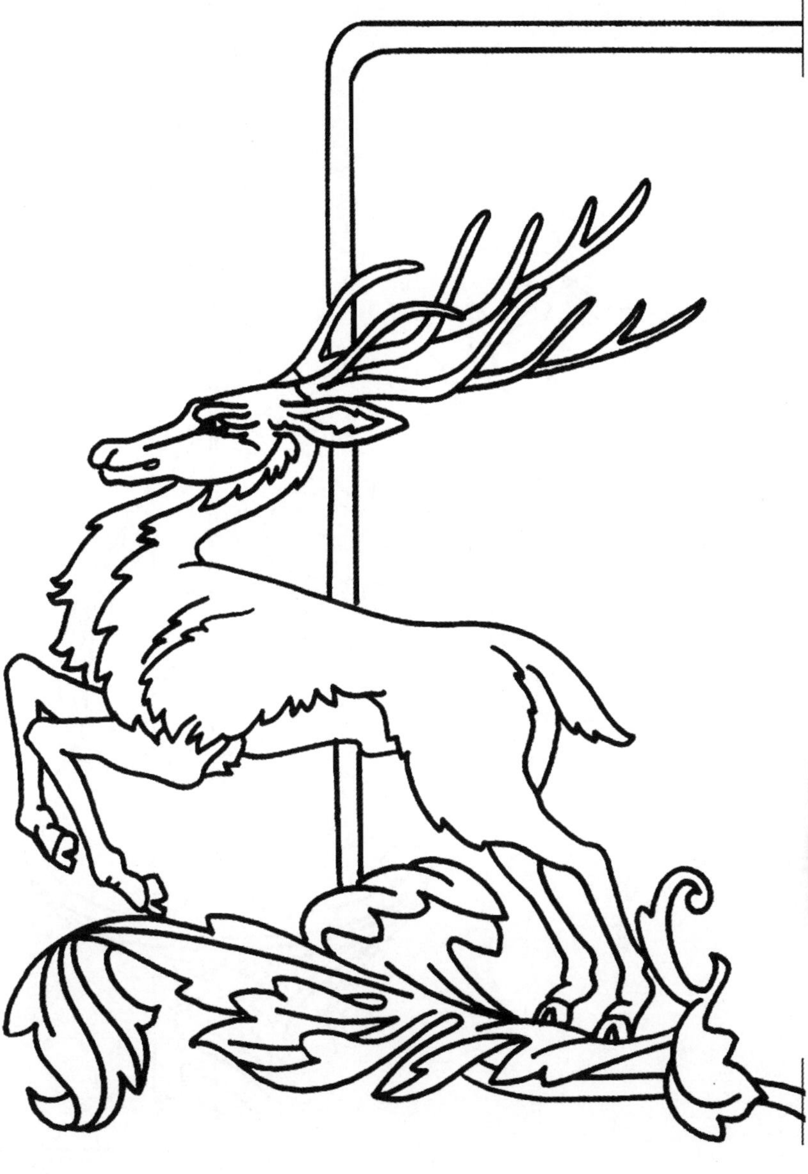

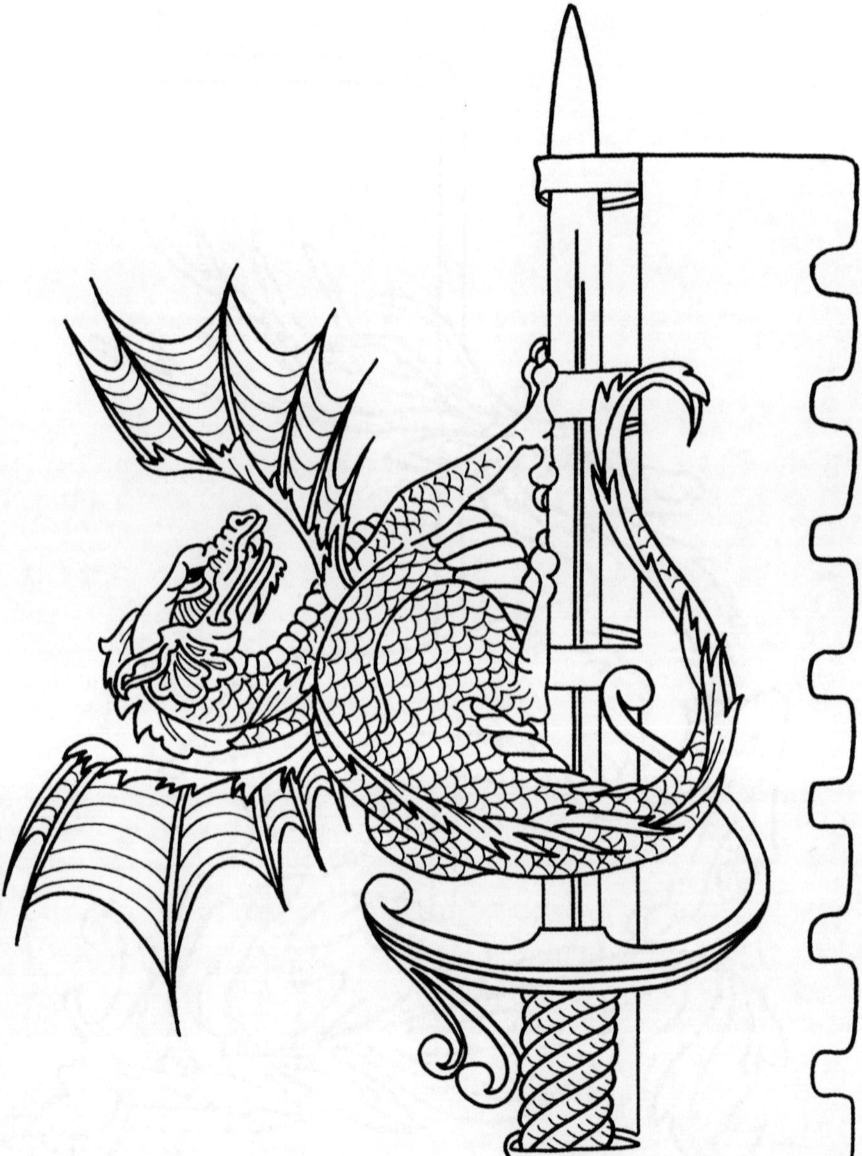

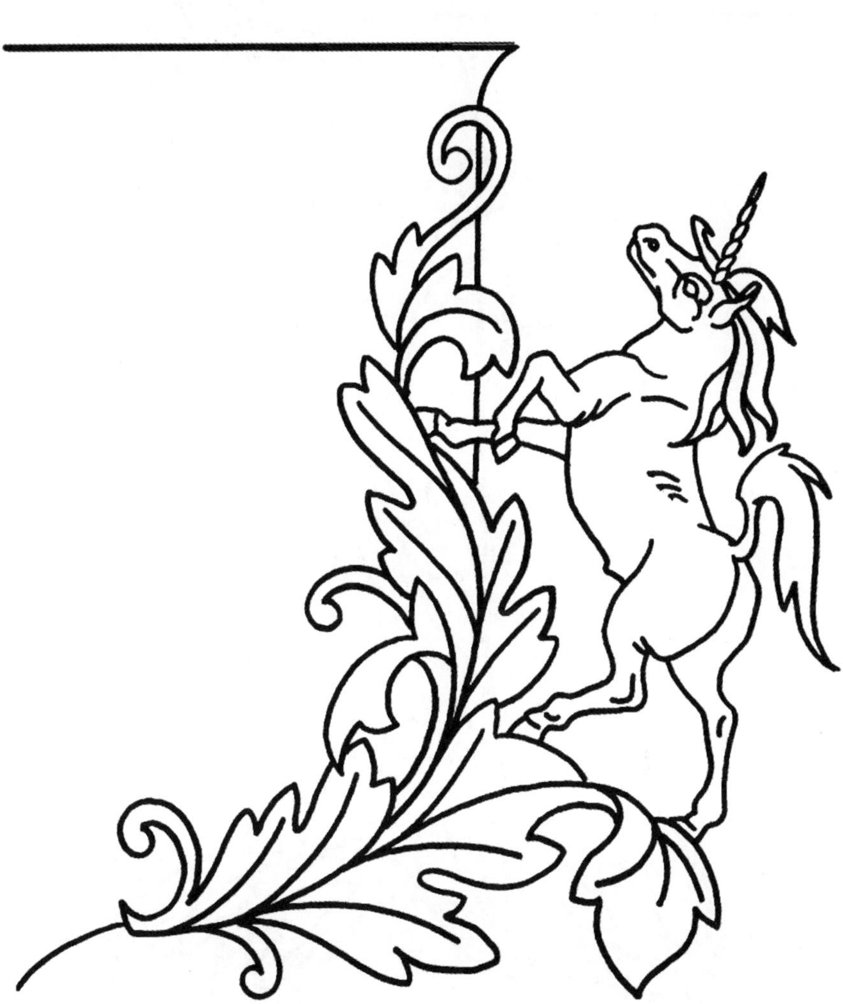

Symbols

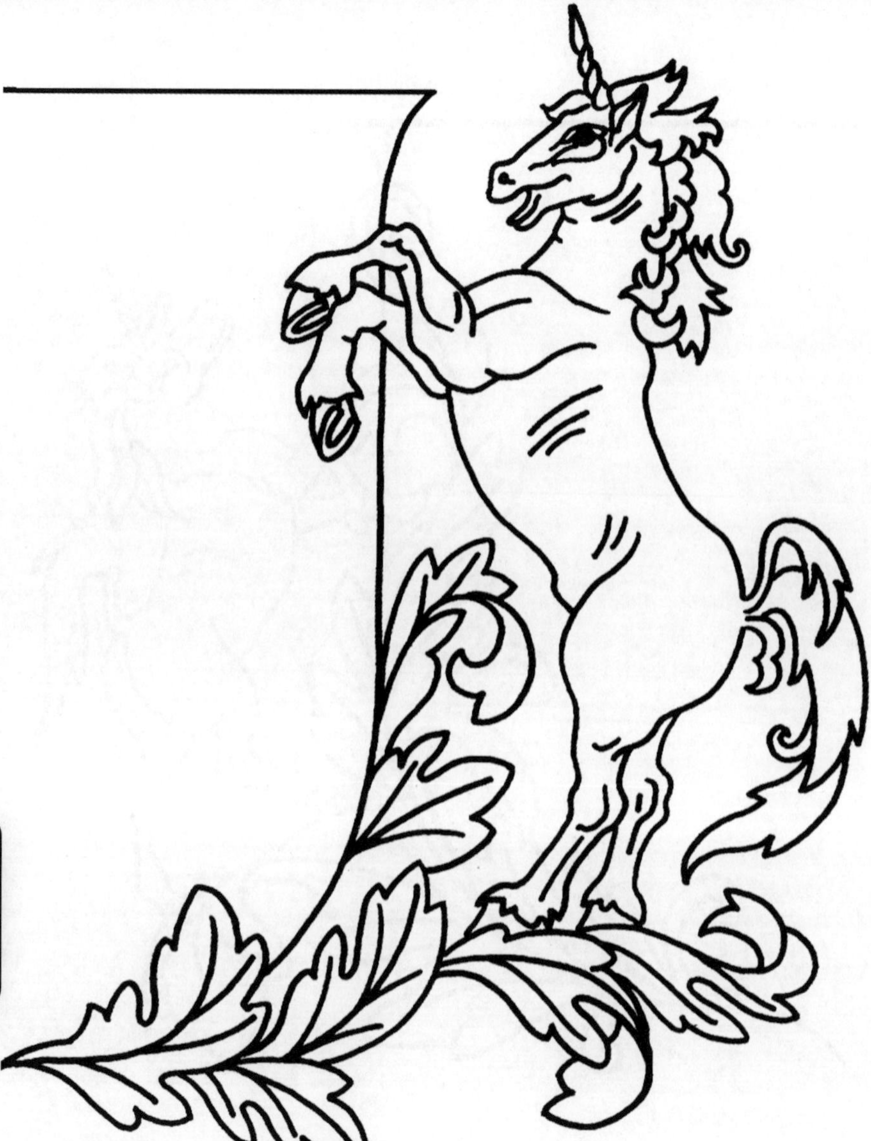

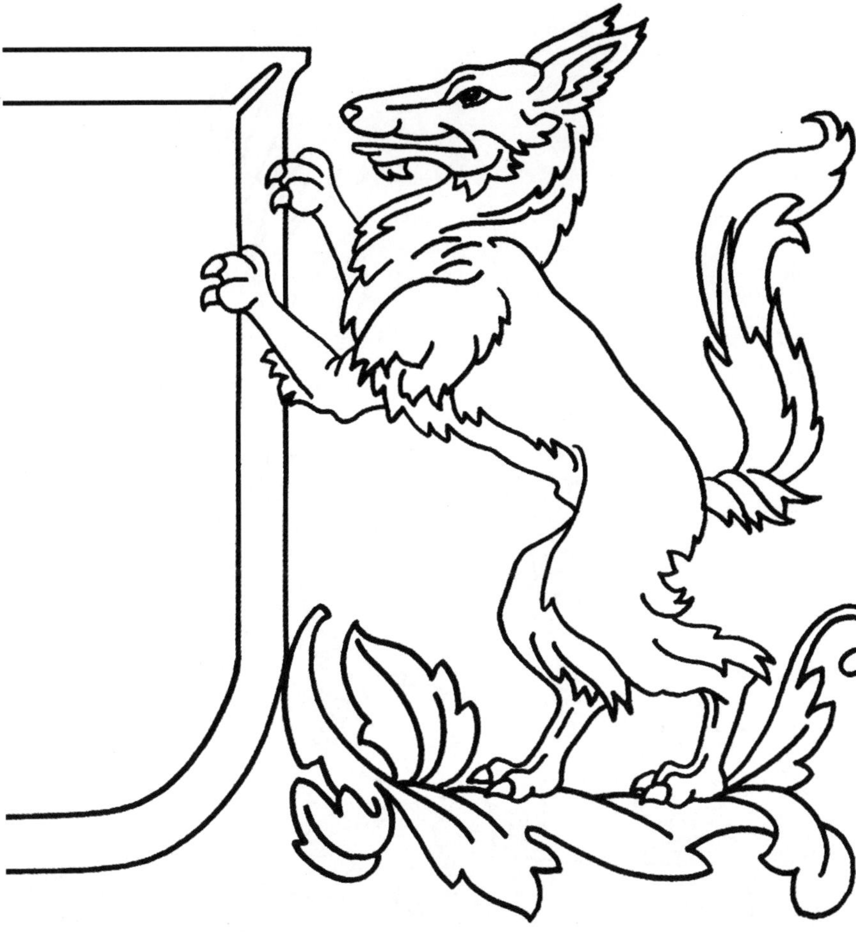

Symbols

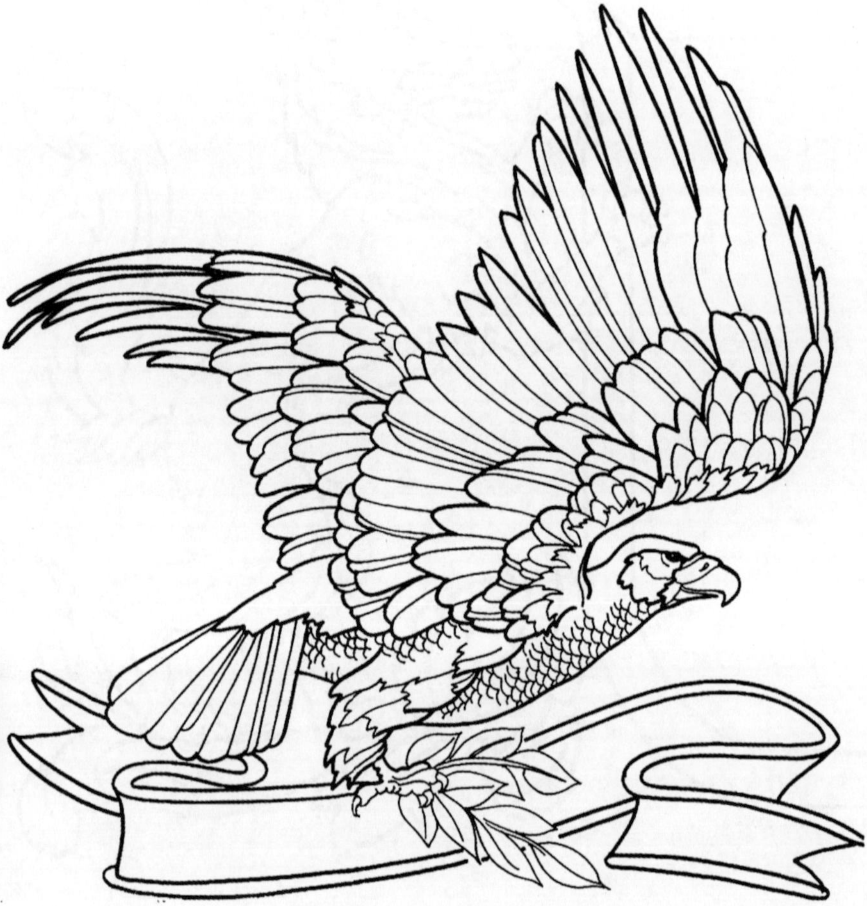

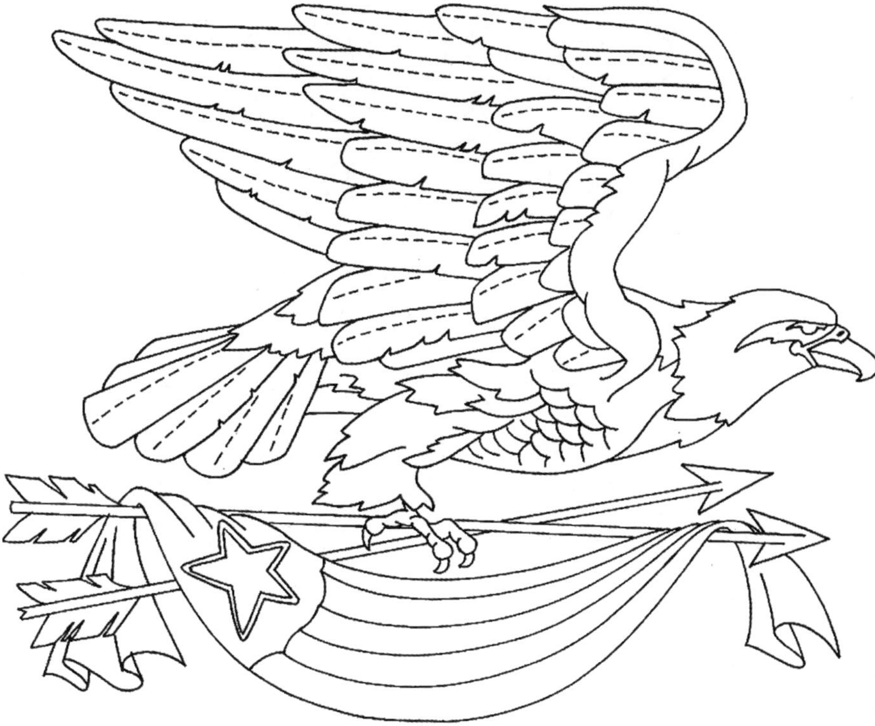

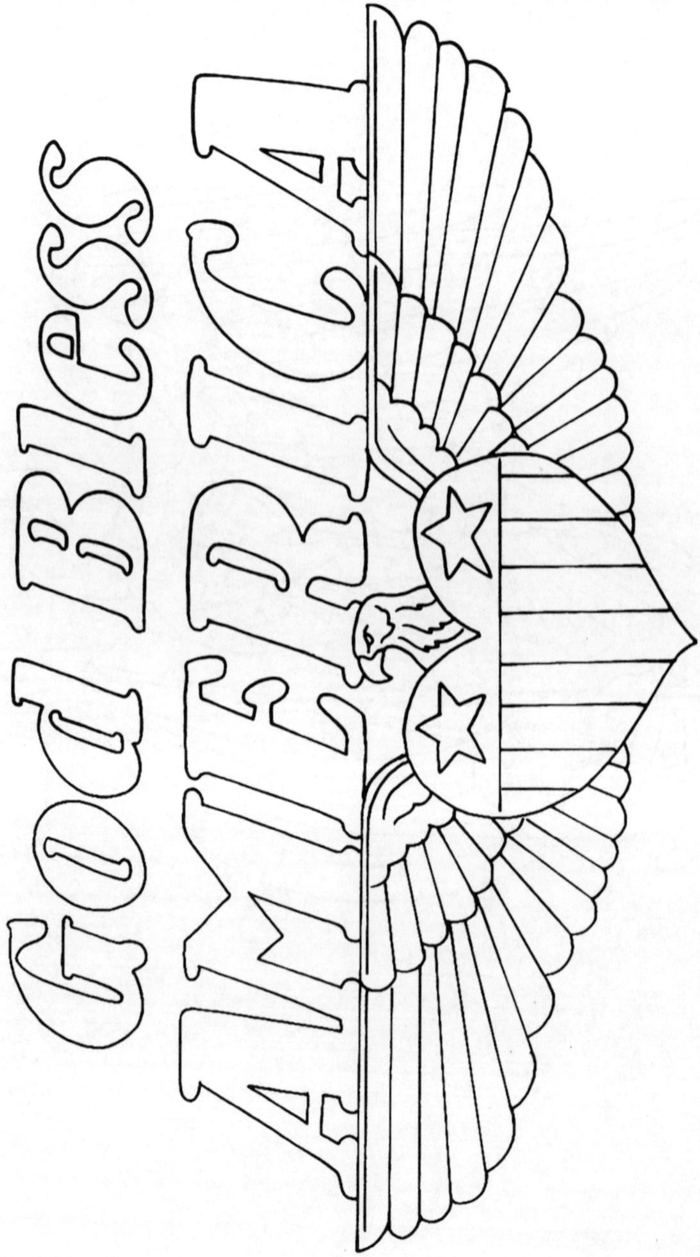
God Bless
America

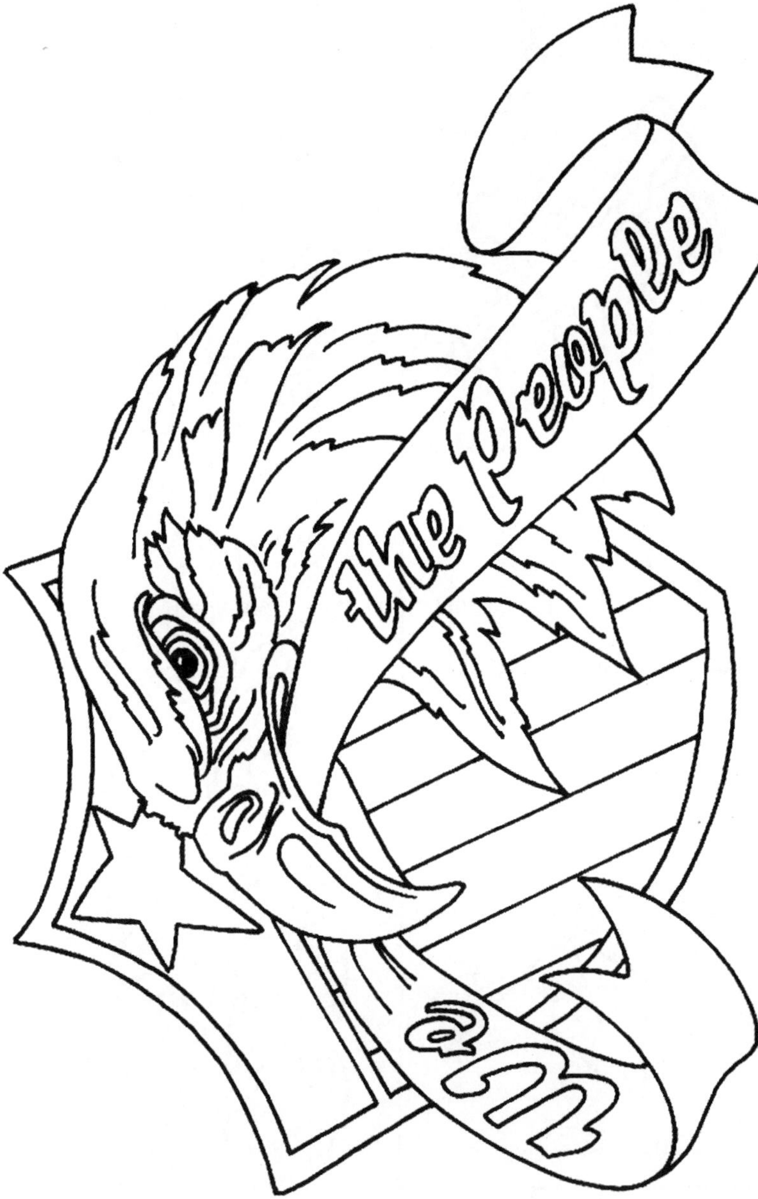
We
the People

Symbols

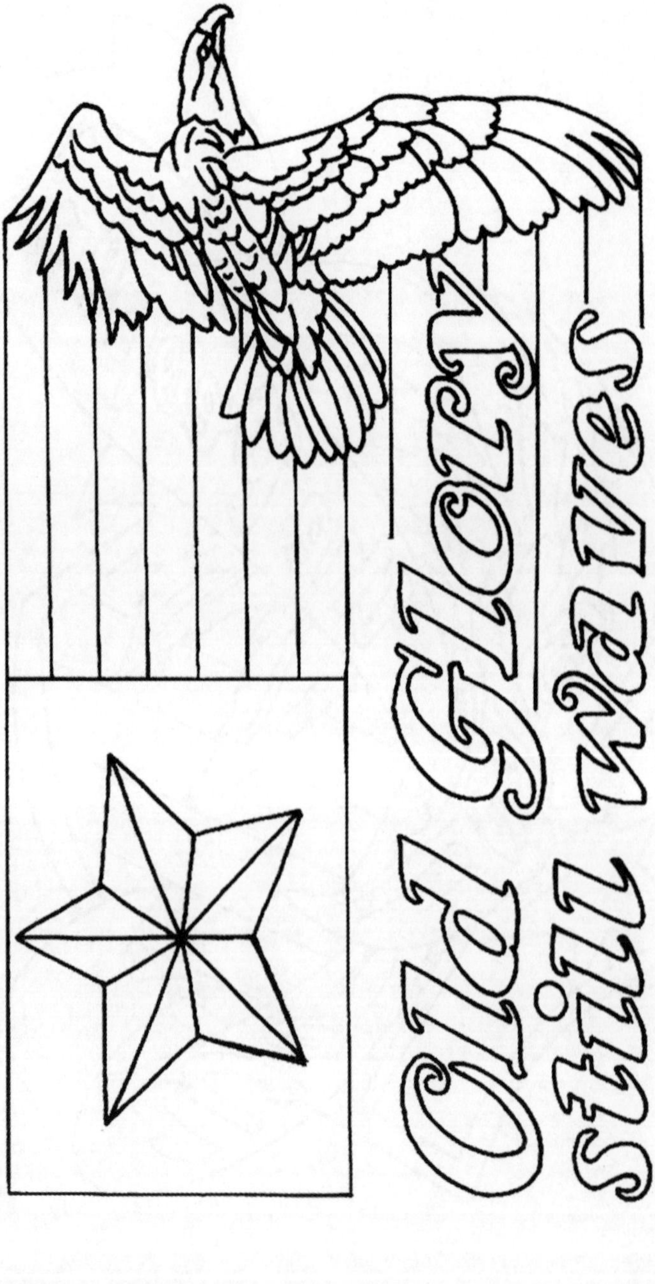

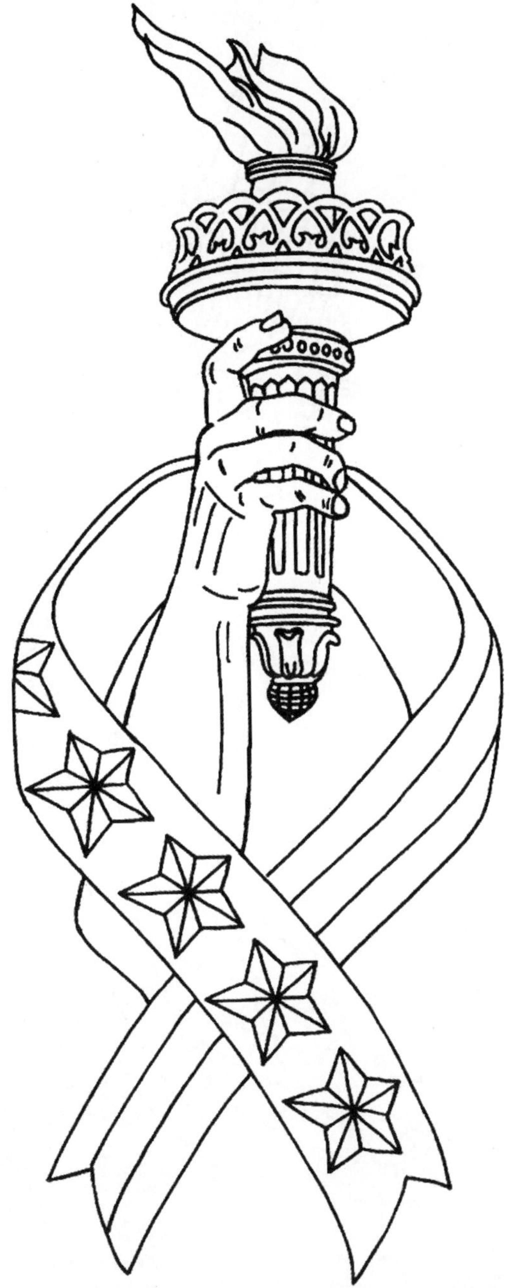

Symbols

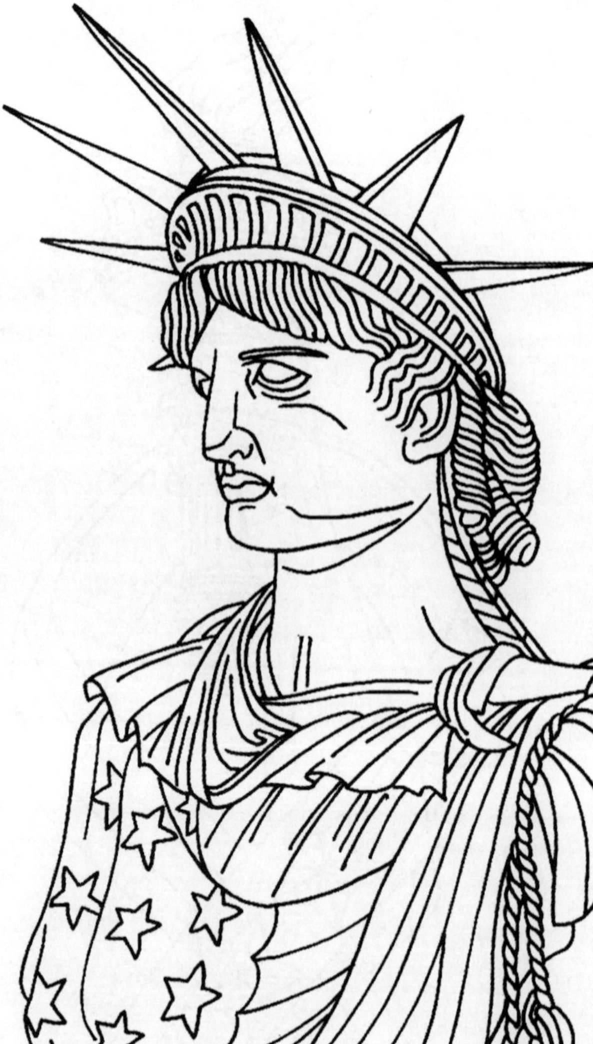

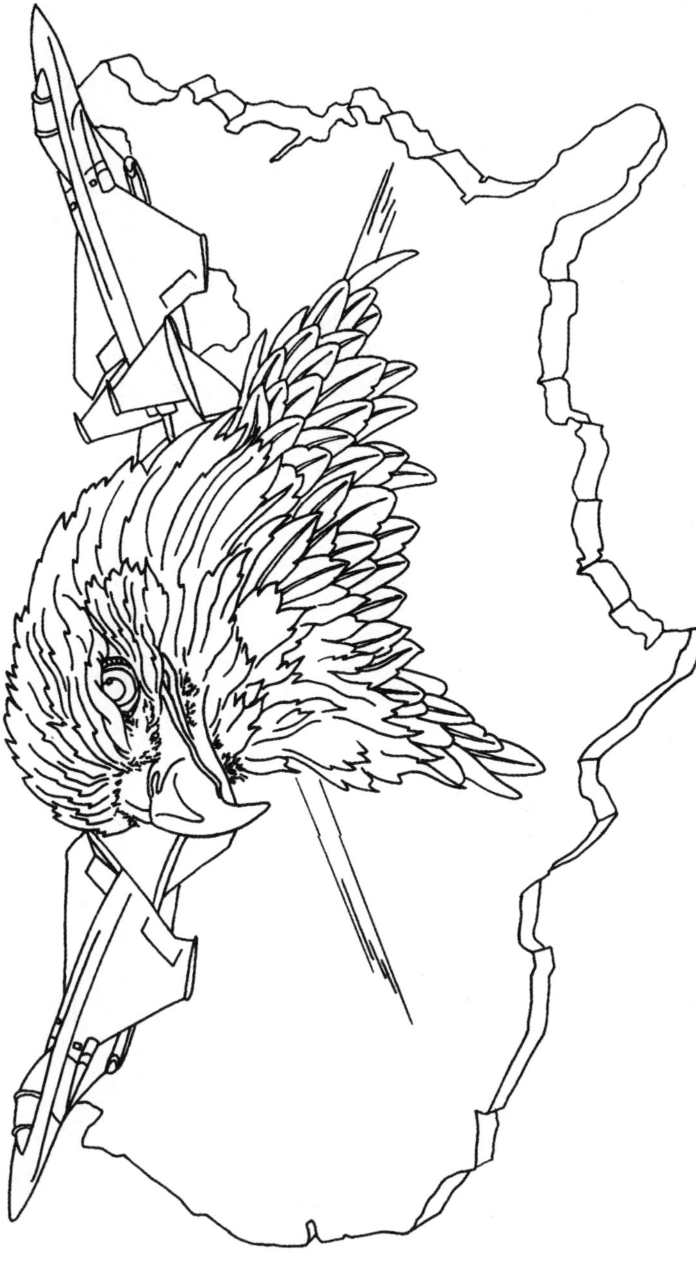

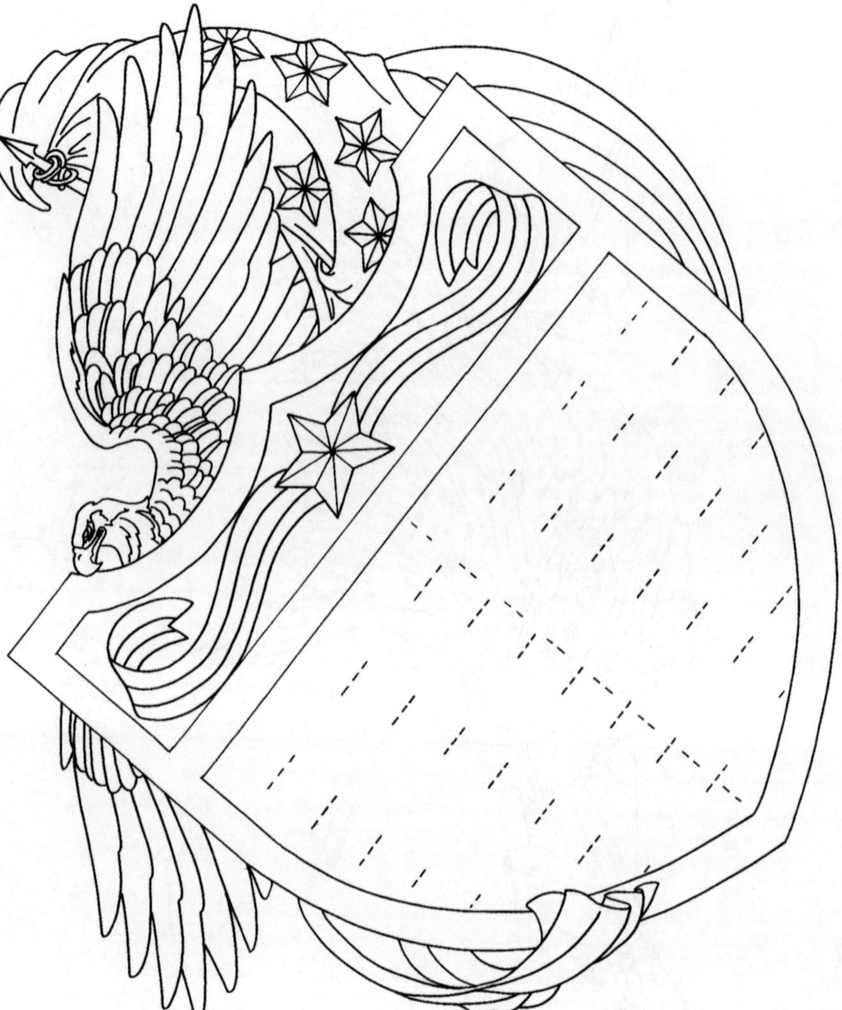

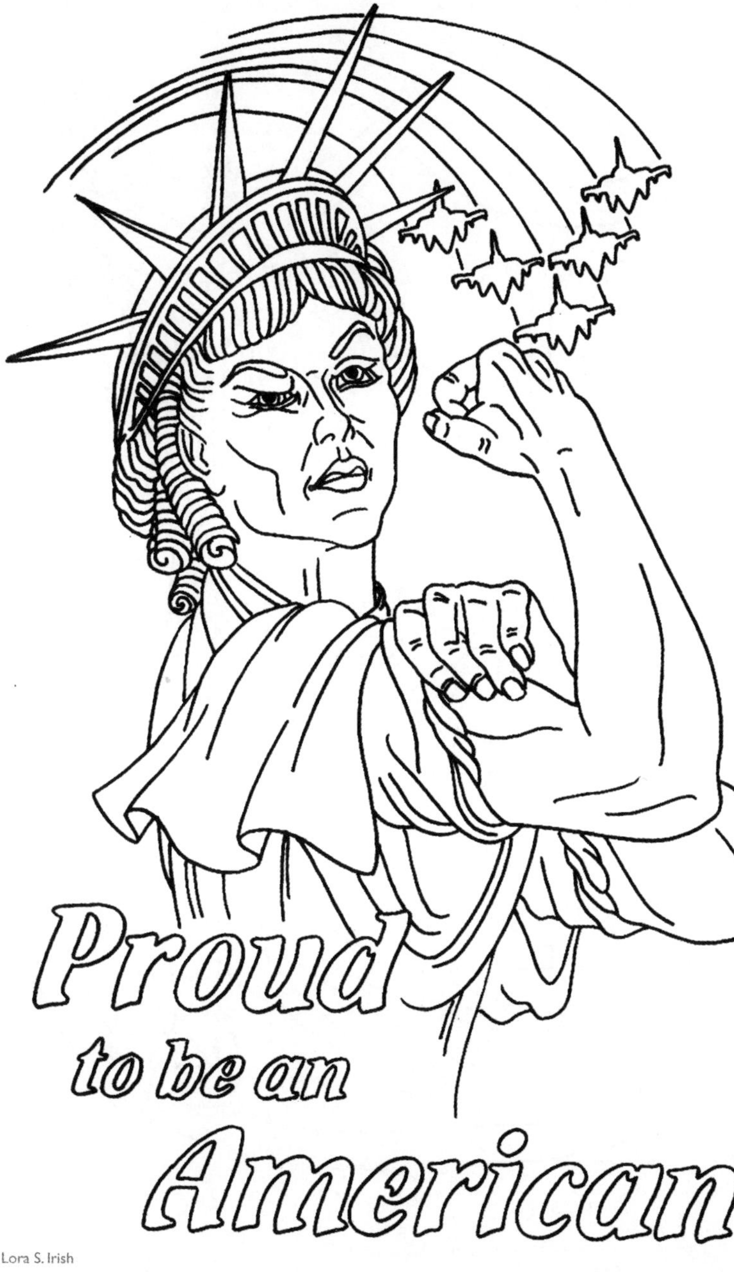
Proud
to be an
American

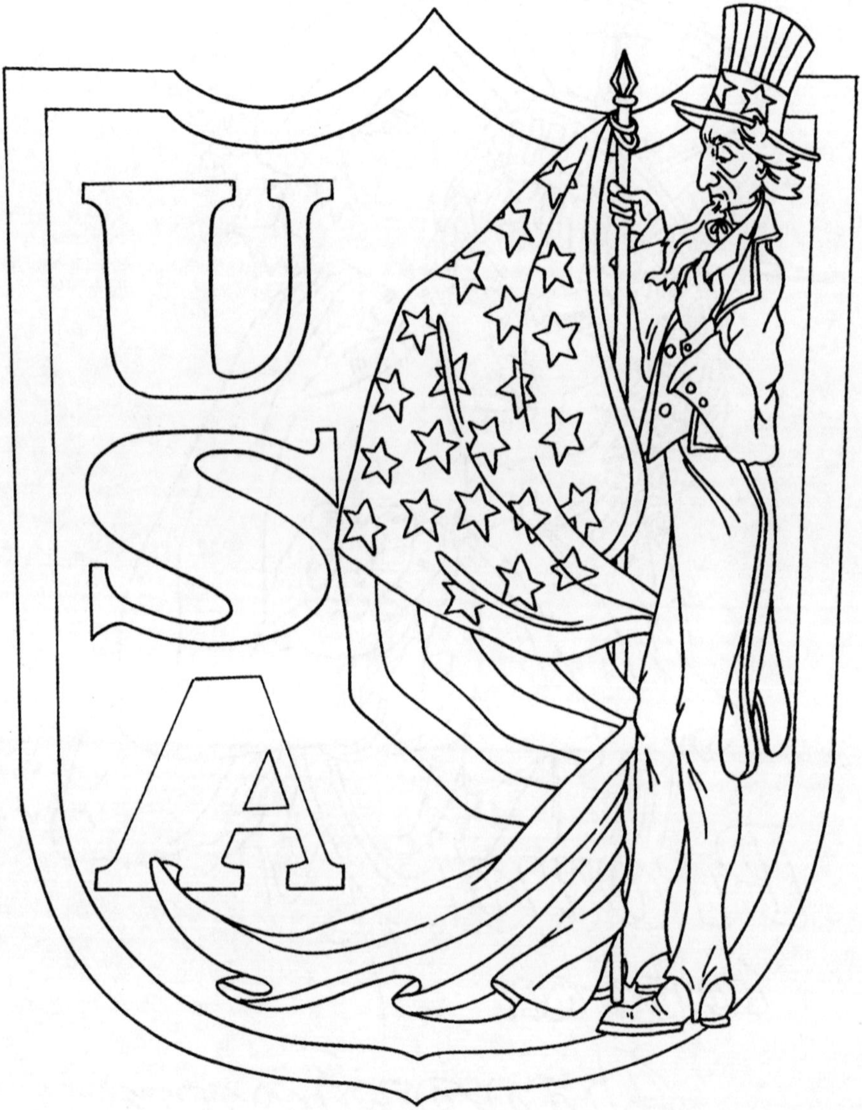
USA

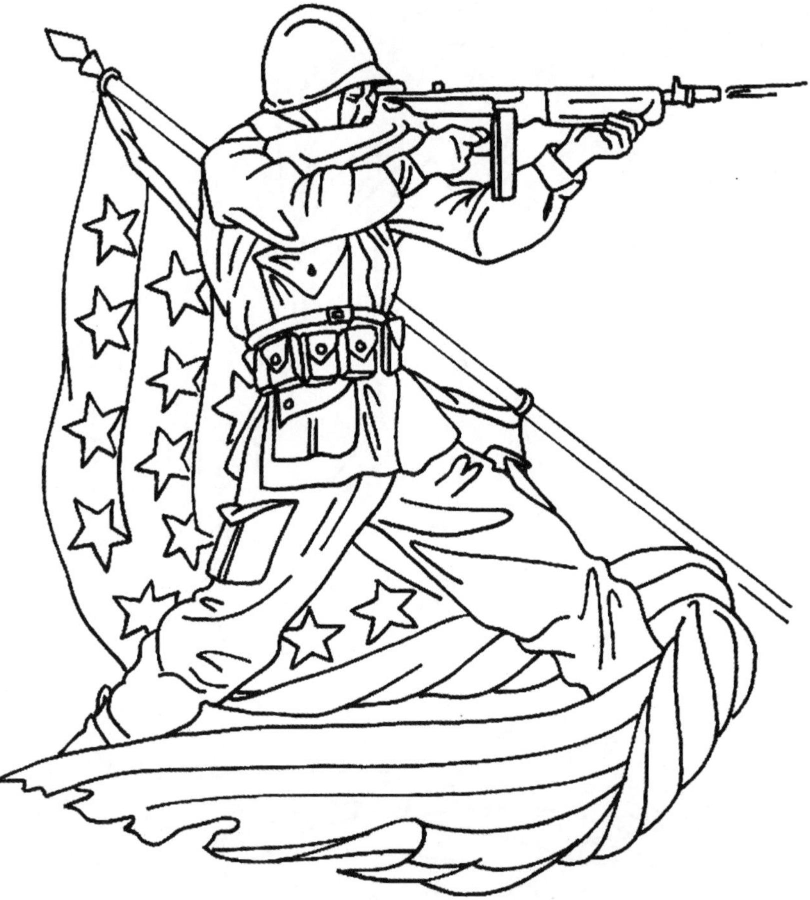

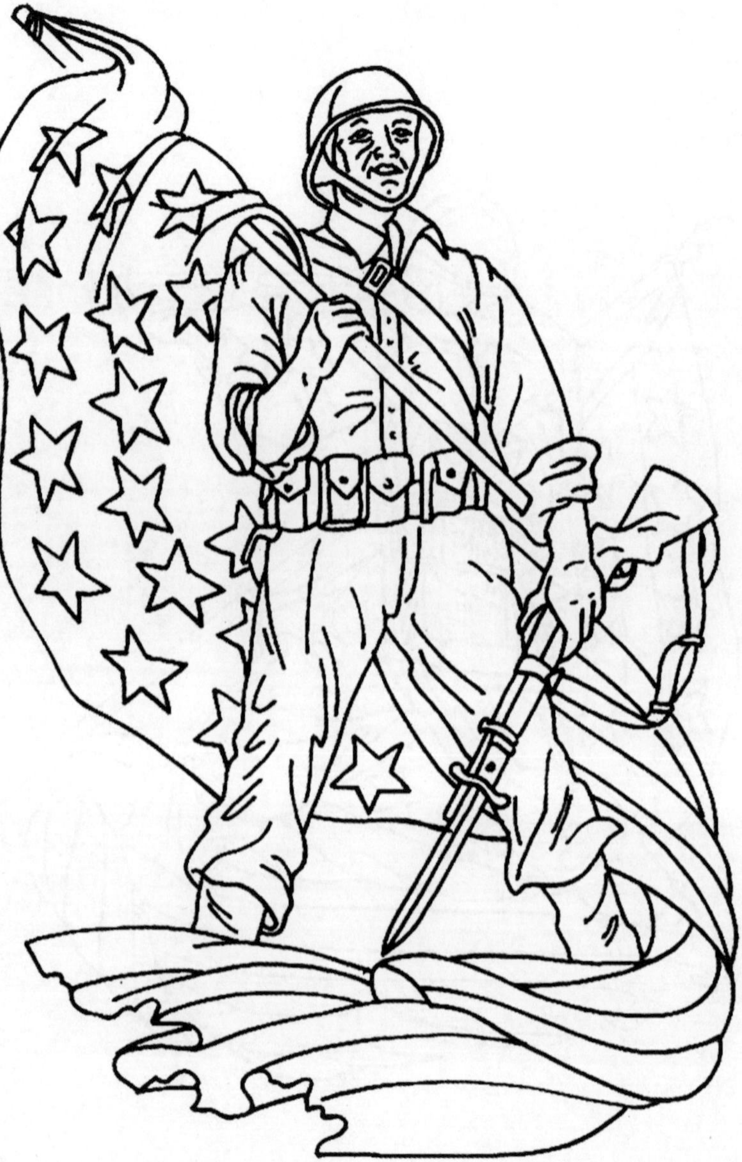

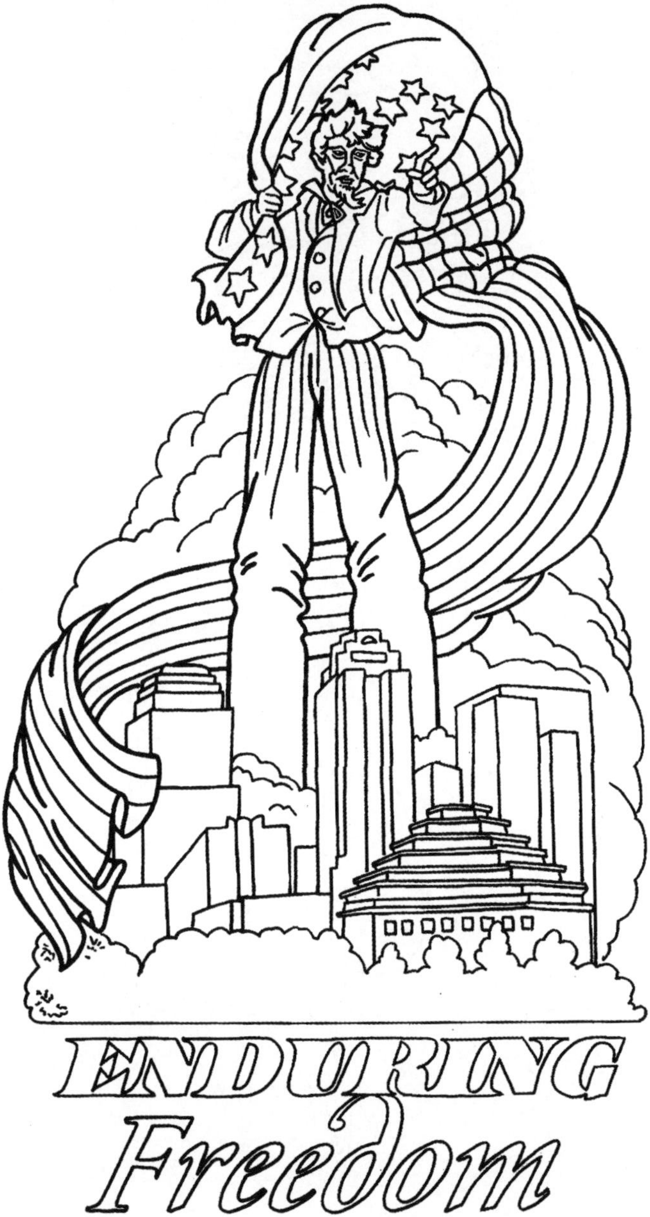
ENDURING
Freedom

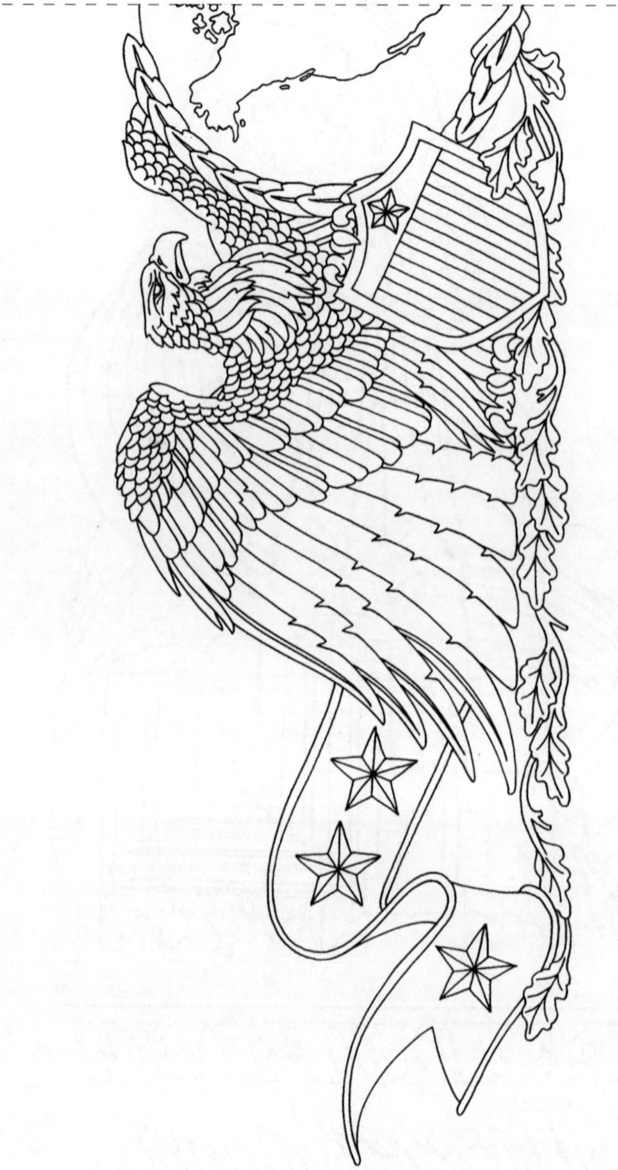

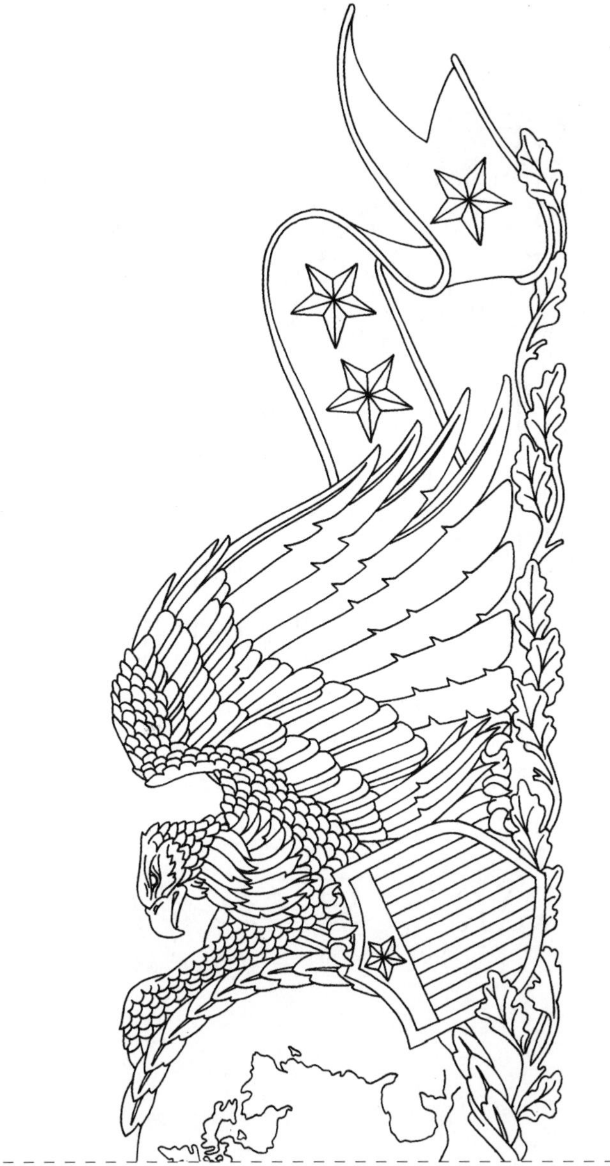

Symbols

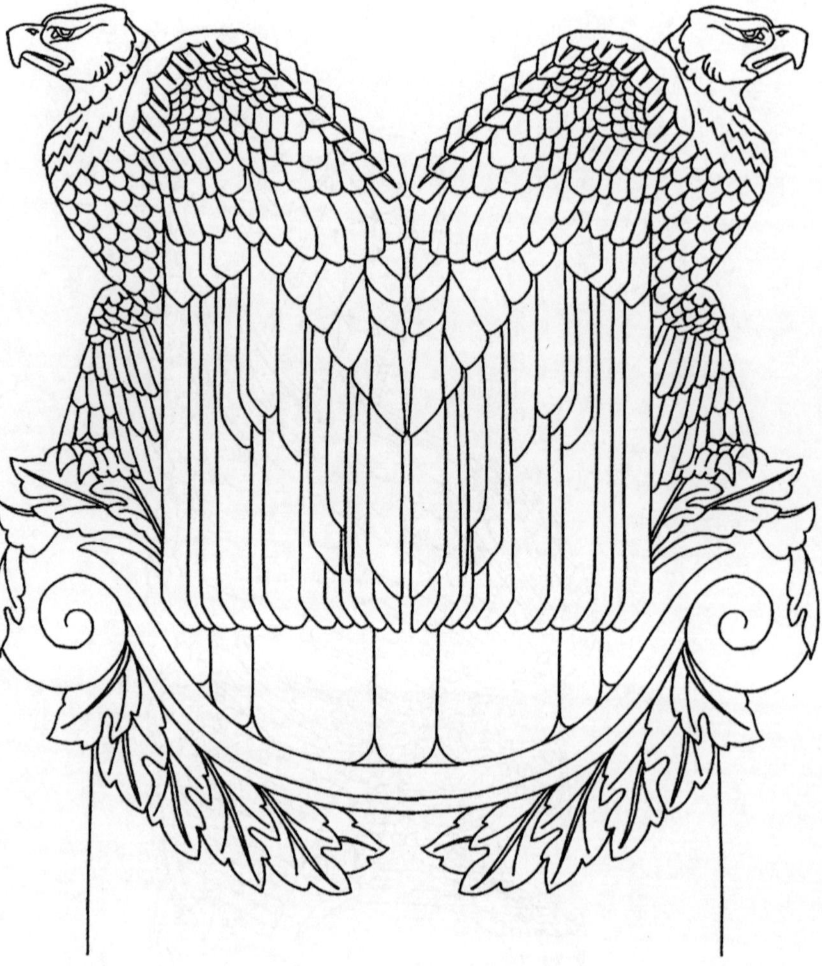

© Lora S. Irish

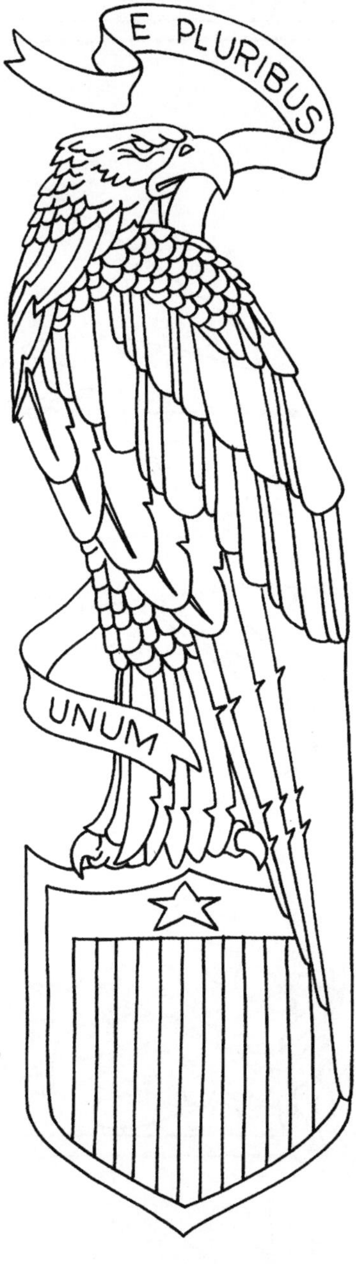
E PLURIBUS
UNUM

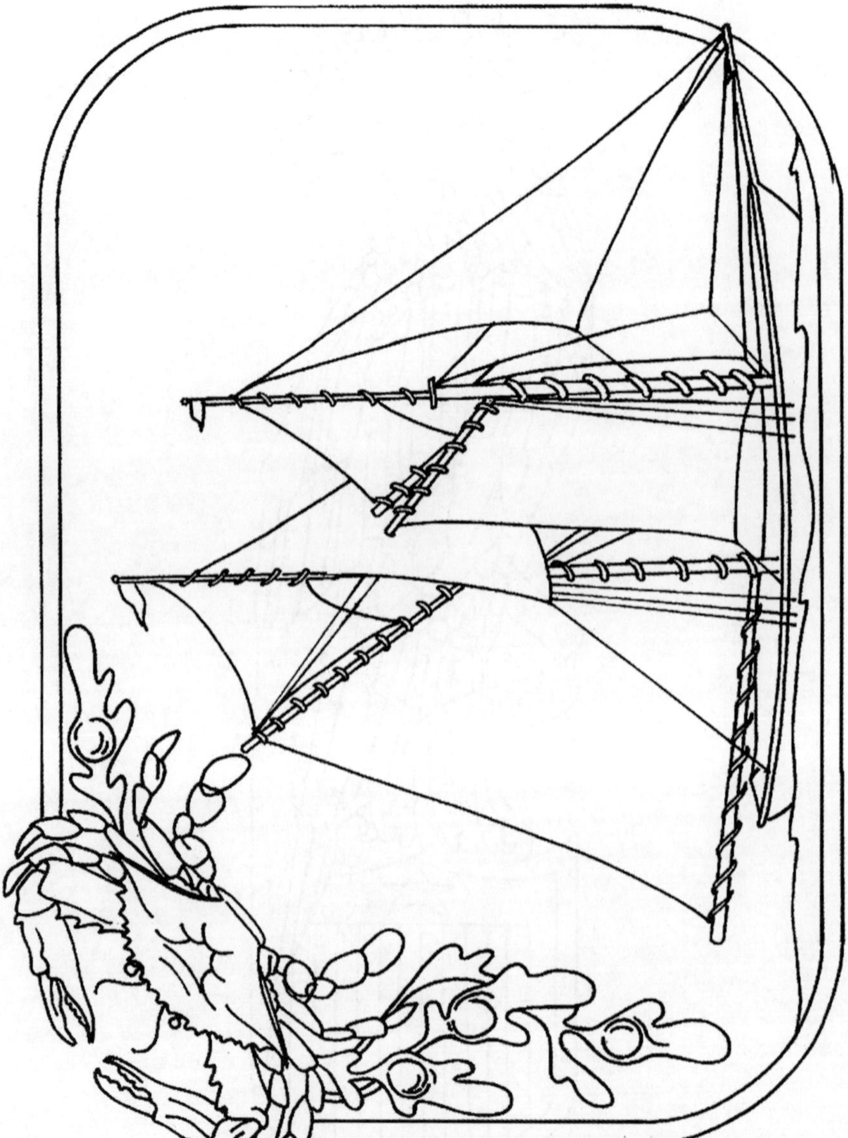

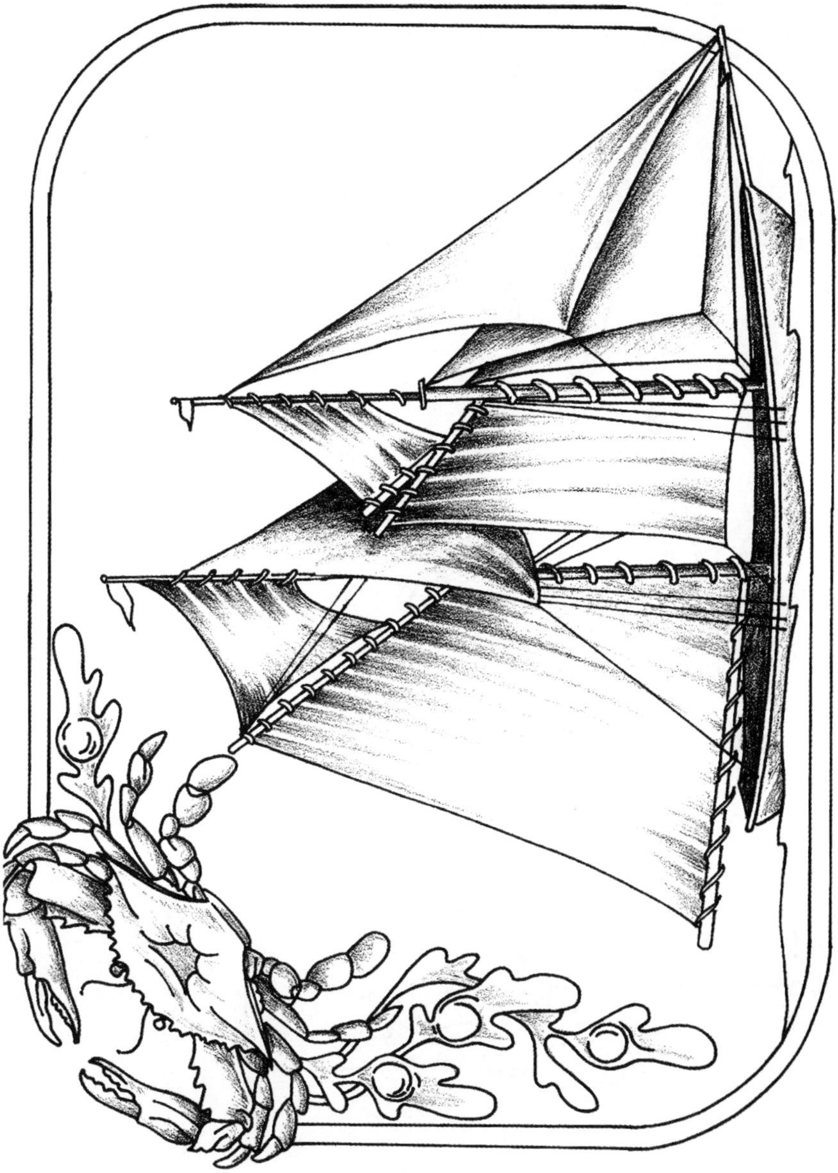

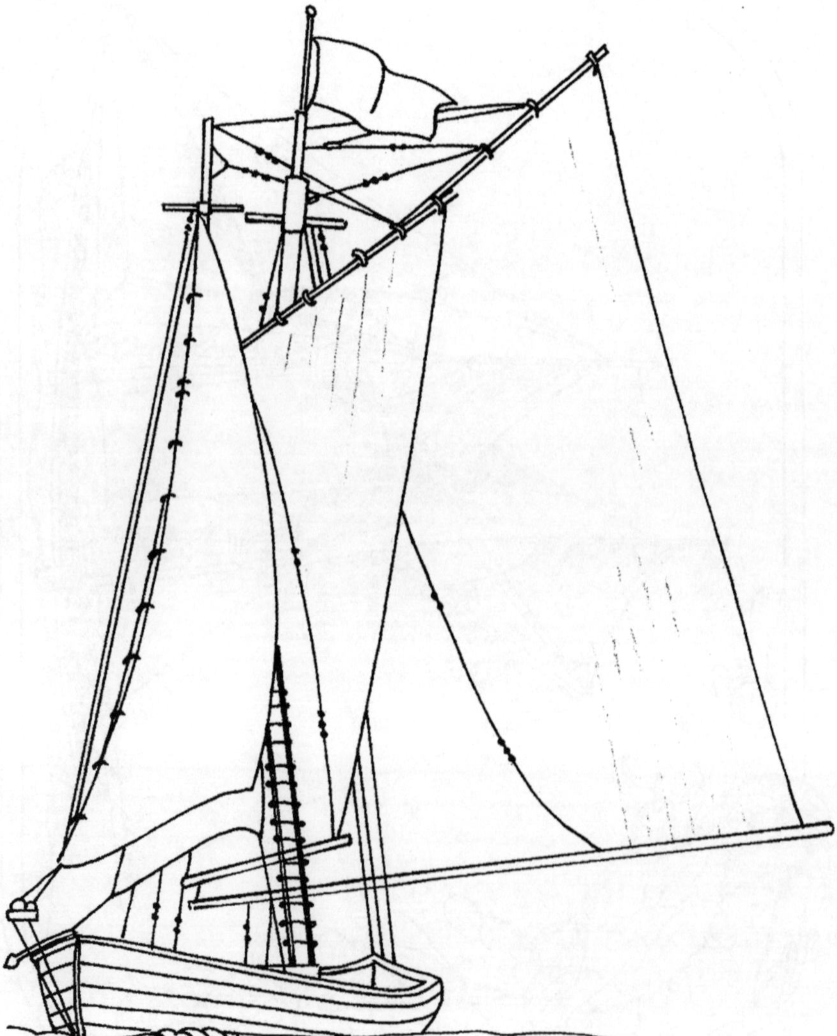

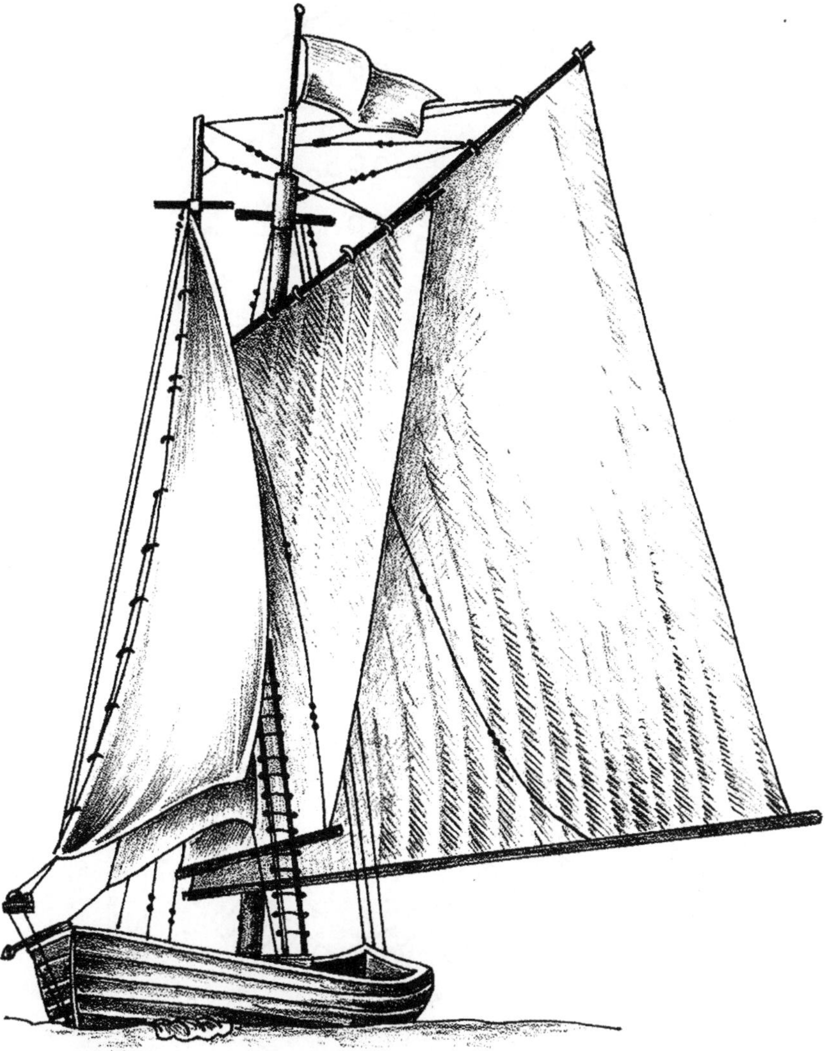

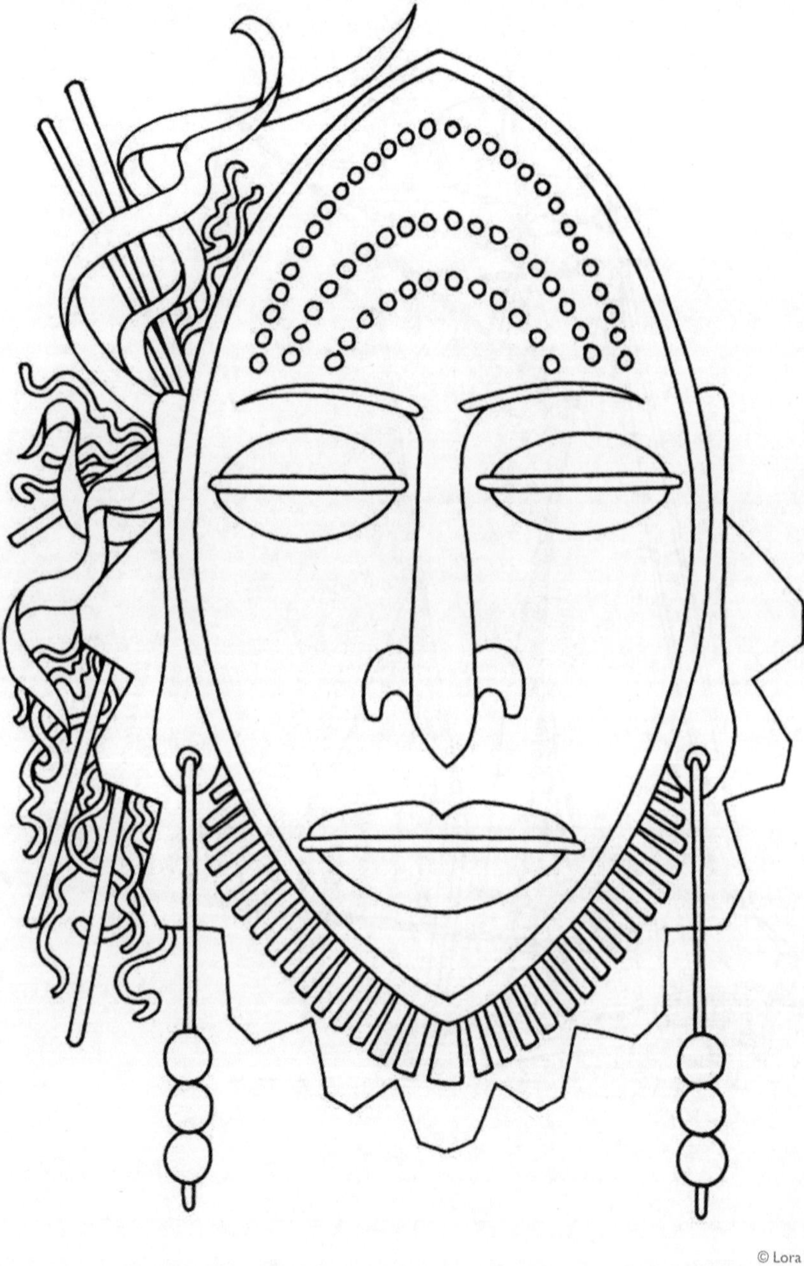

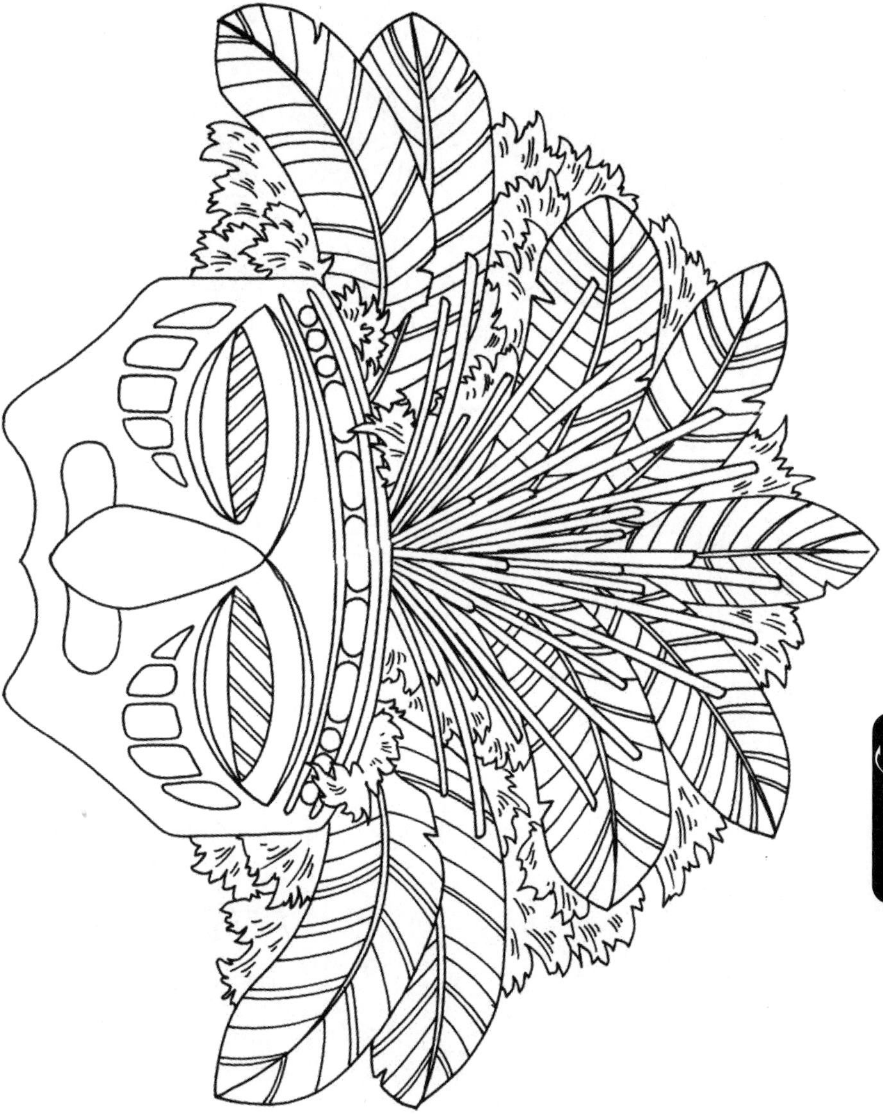

Symbols

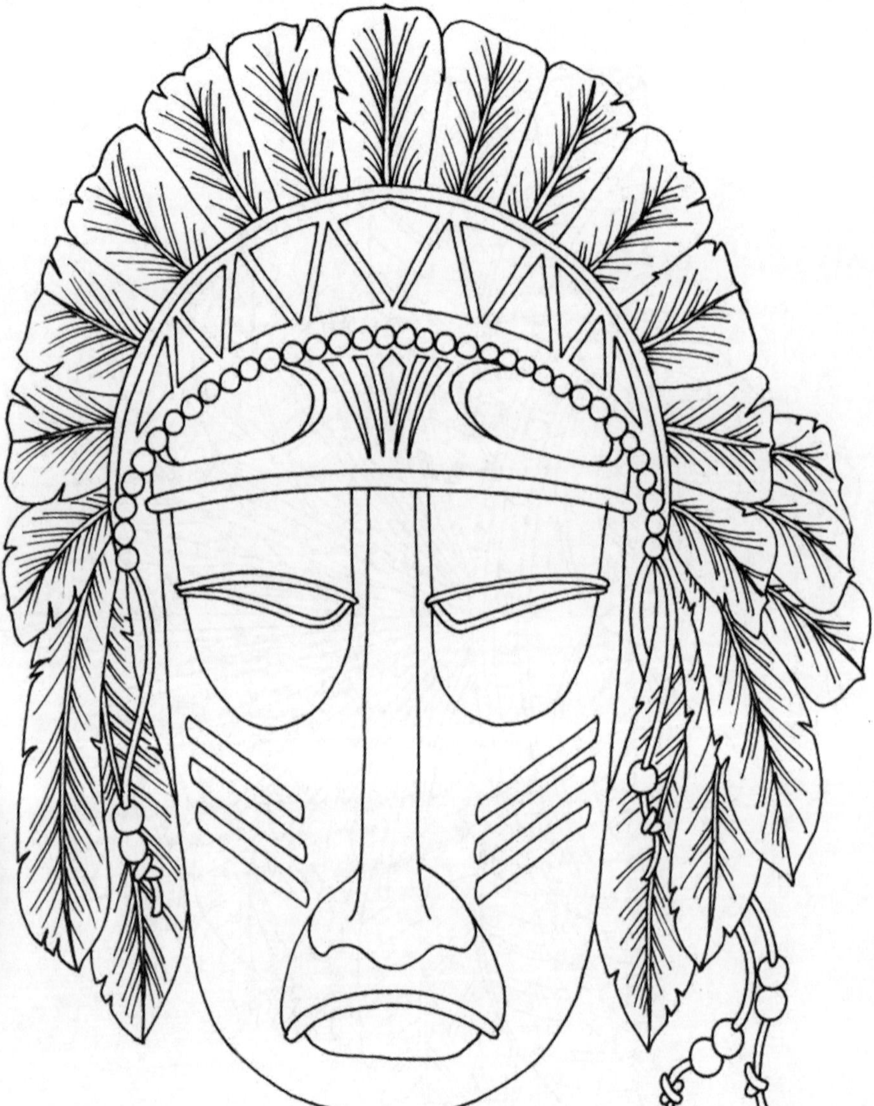

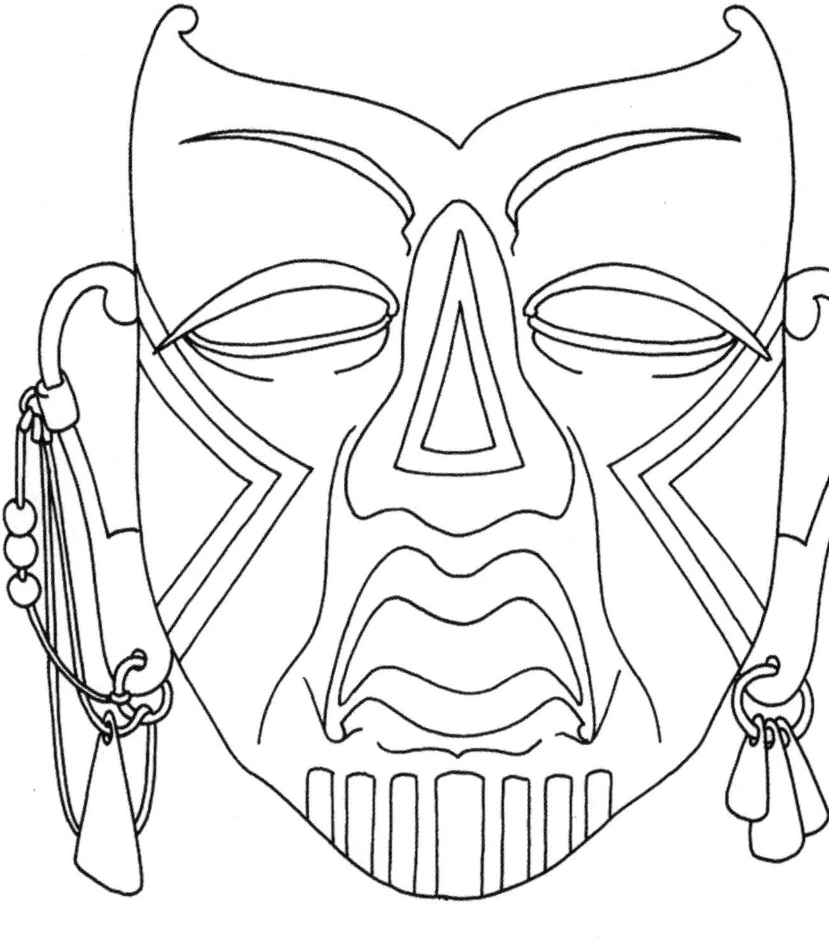

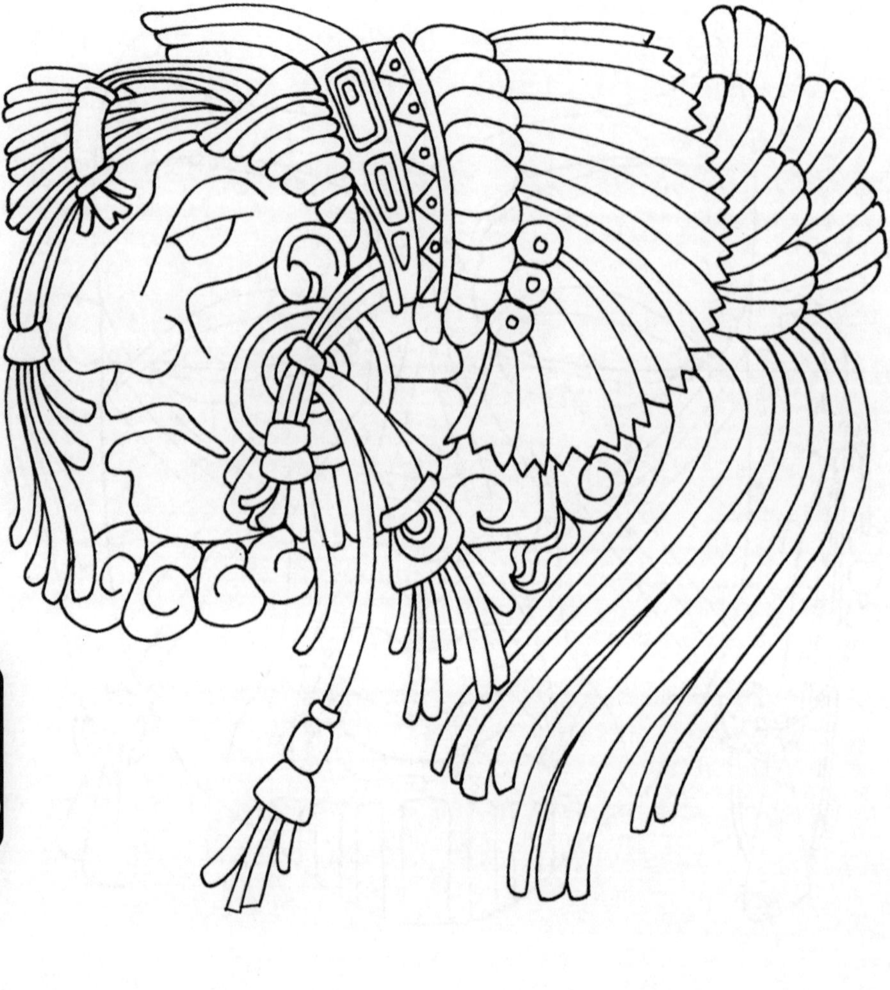

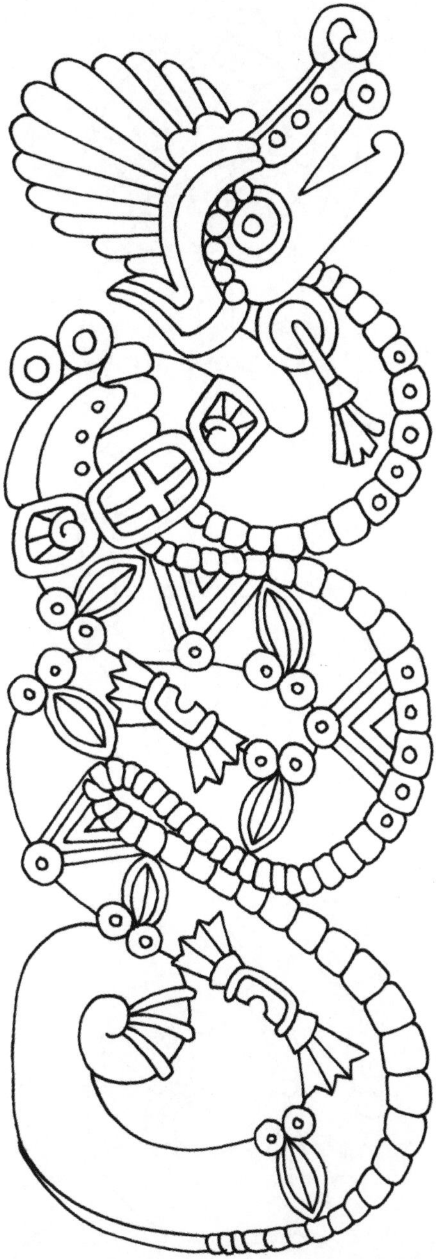

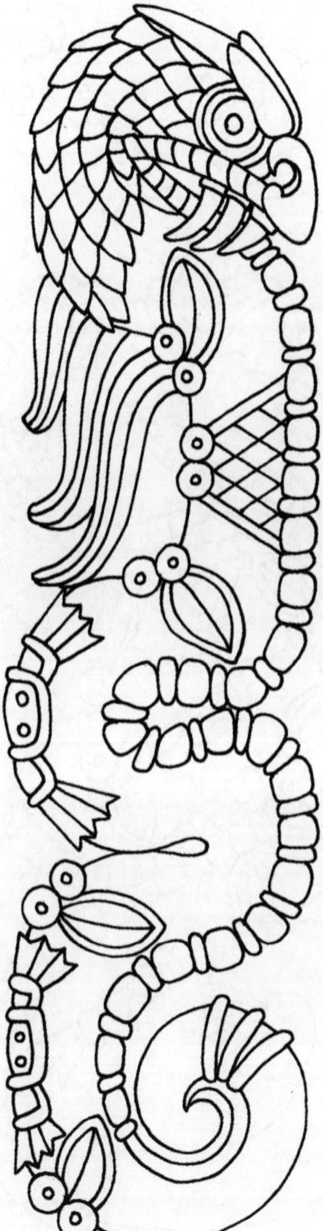

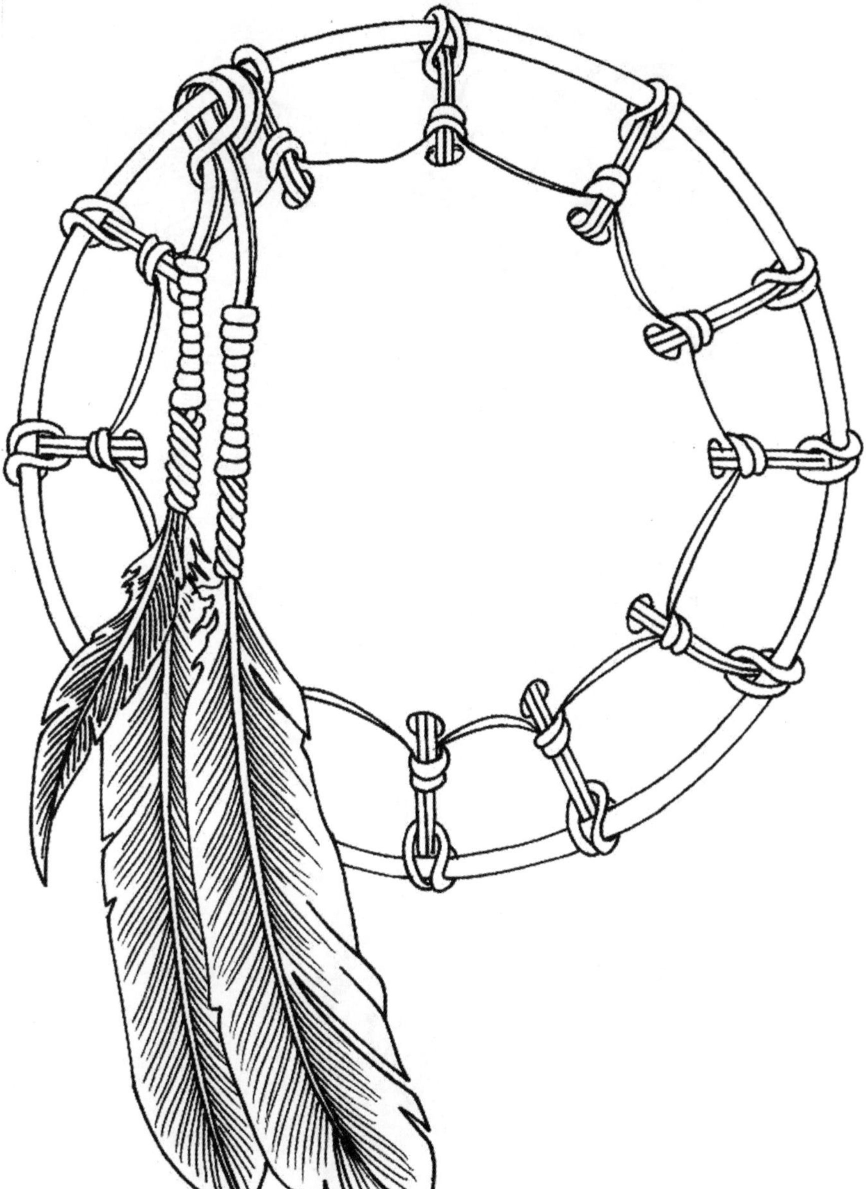

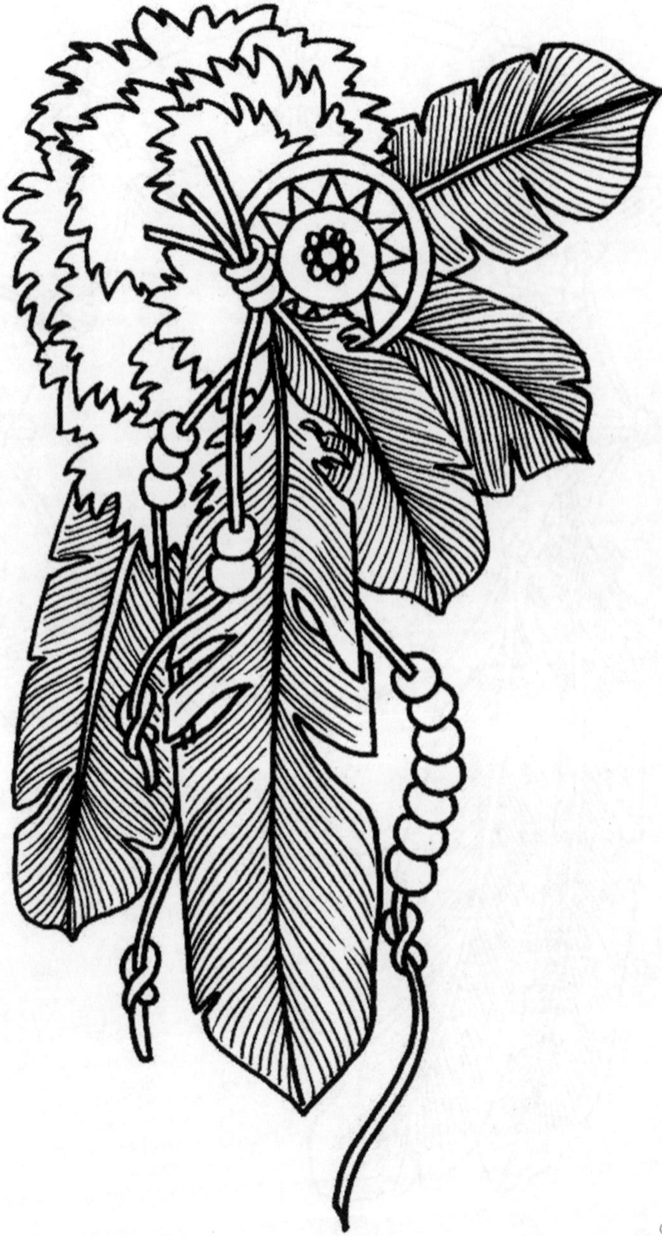

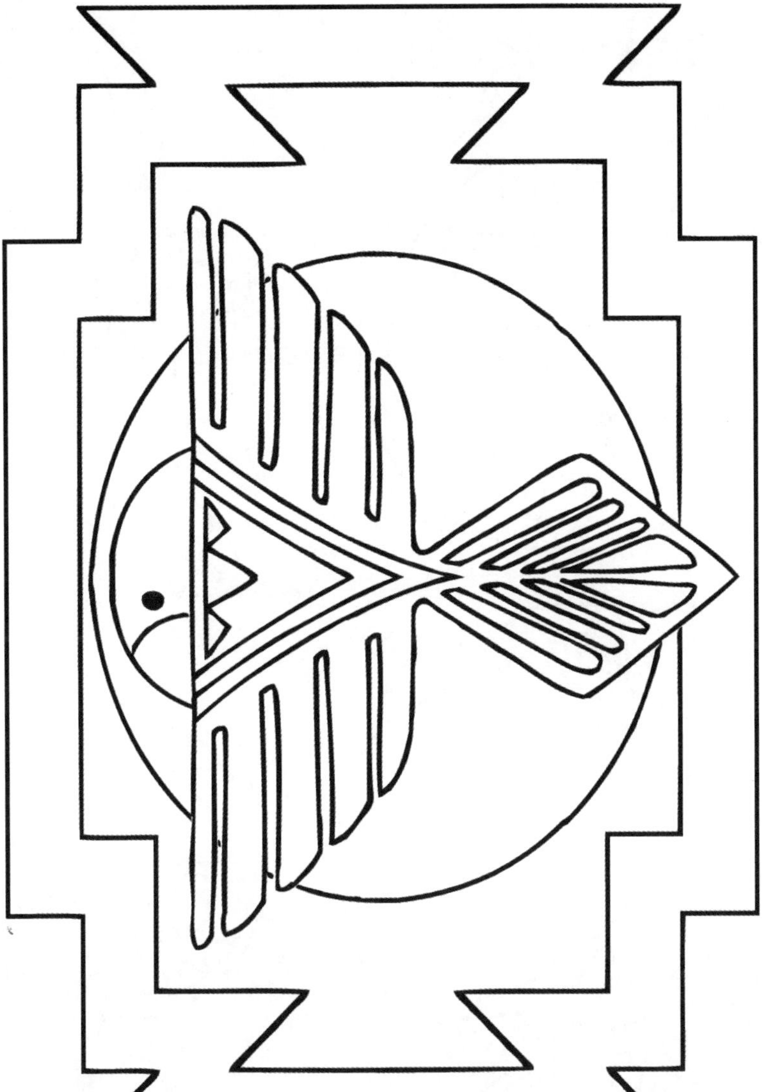

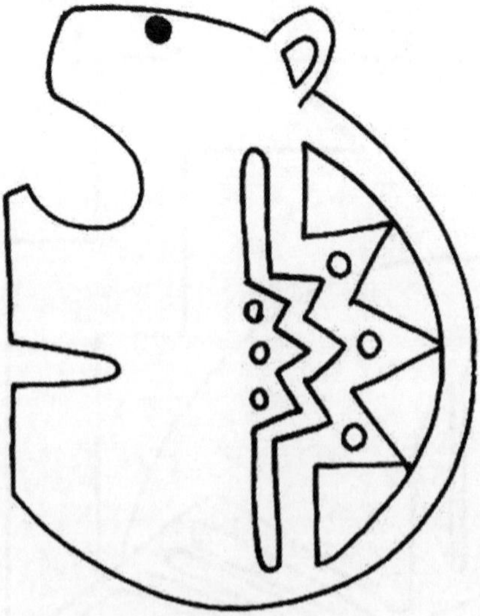

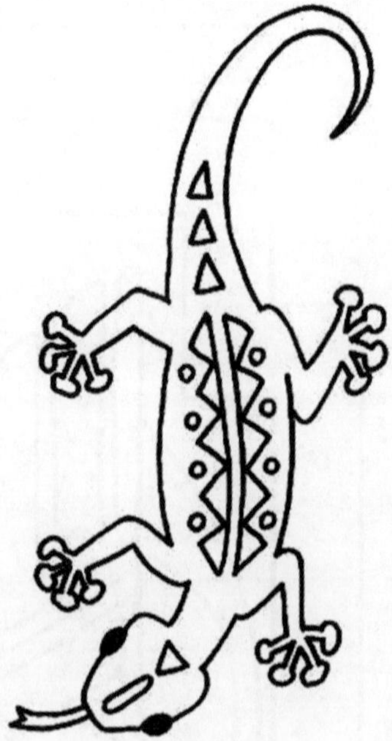

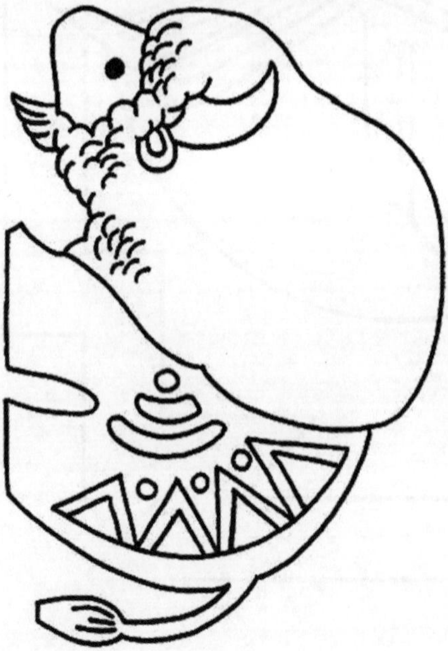

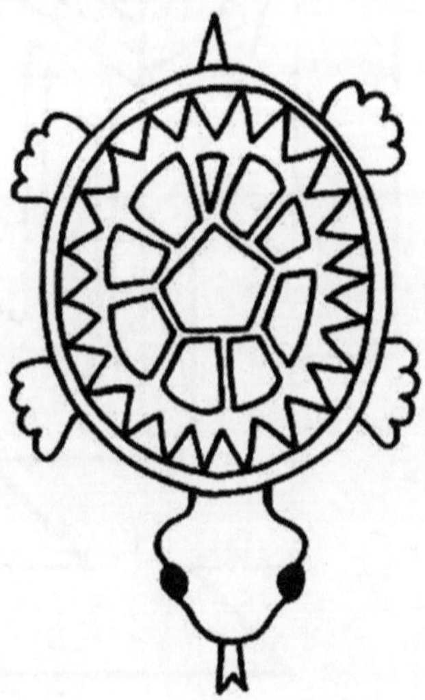

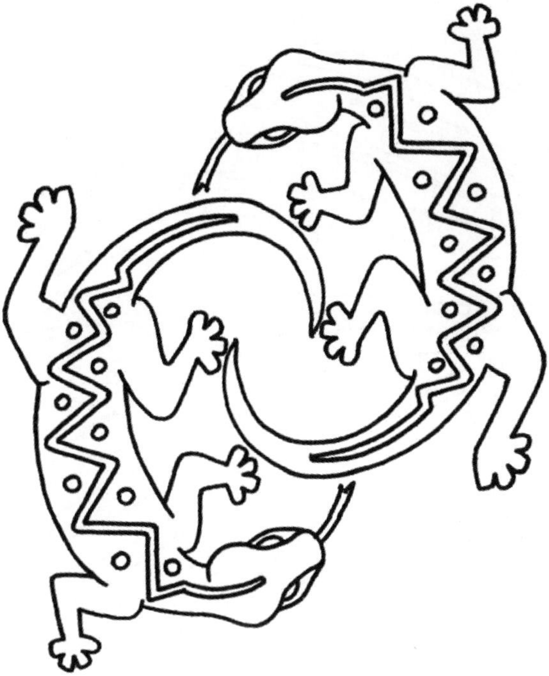

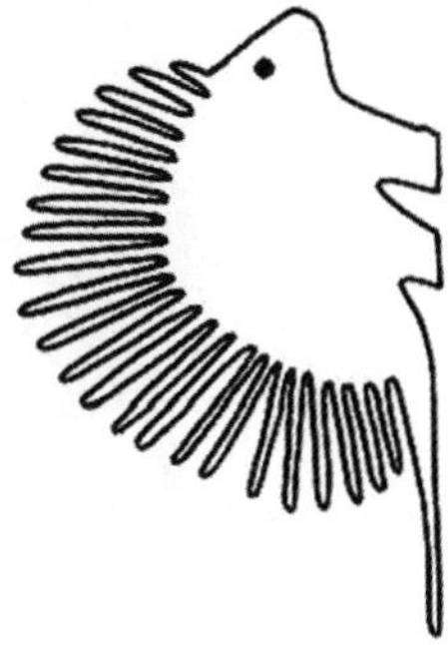

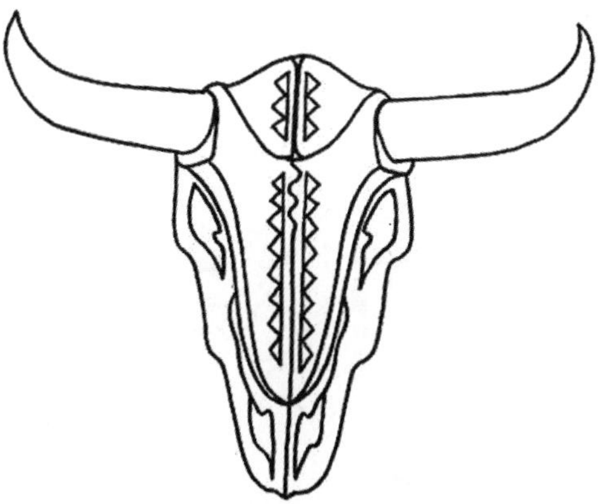

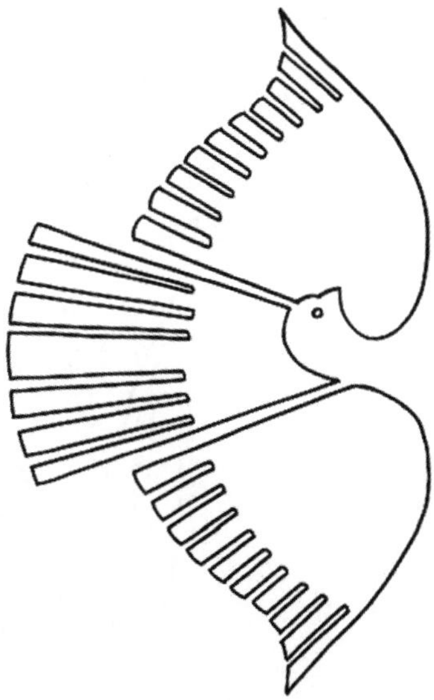

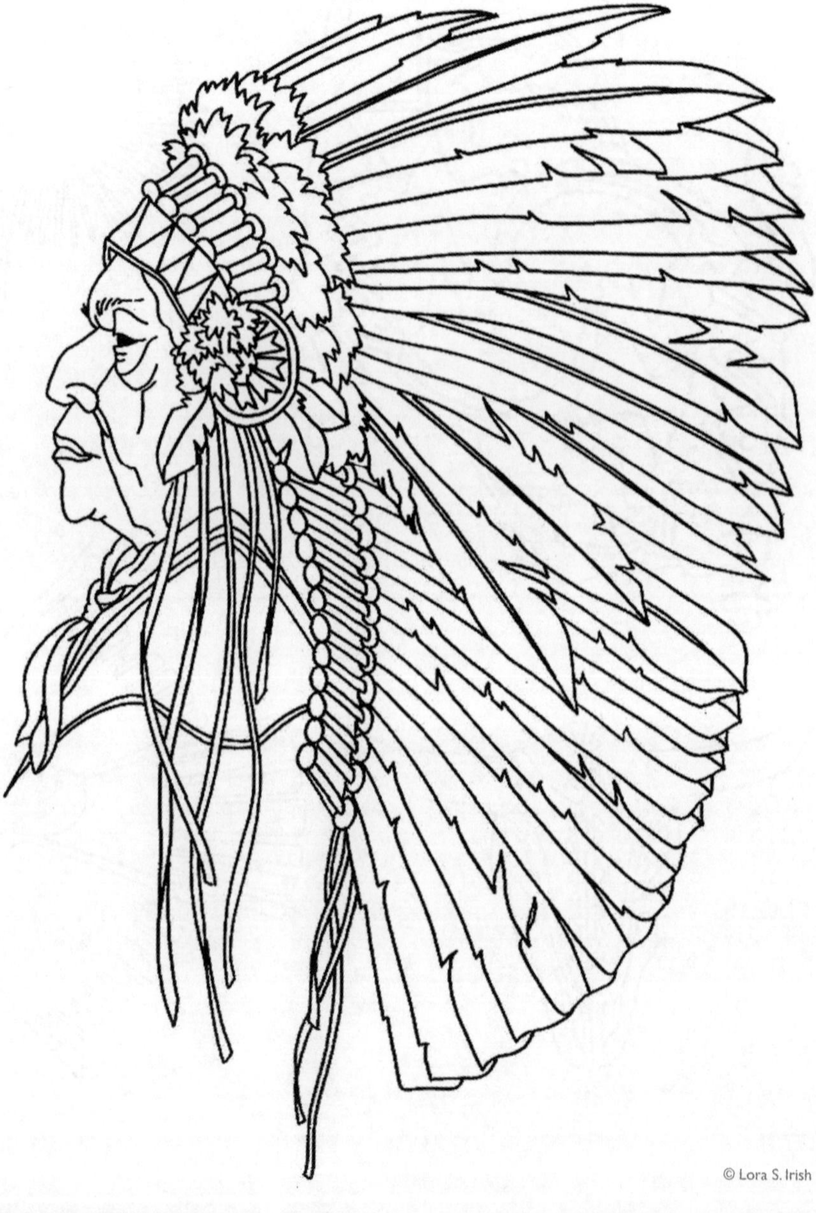

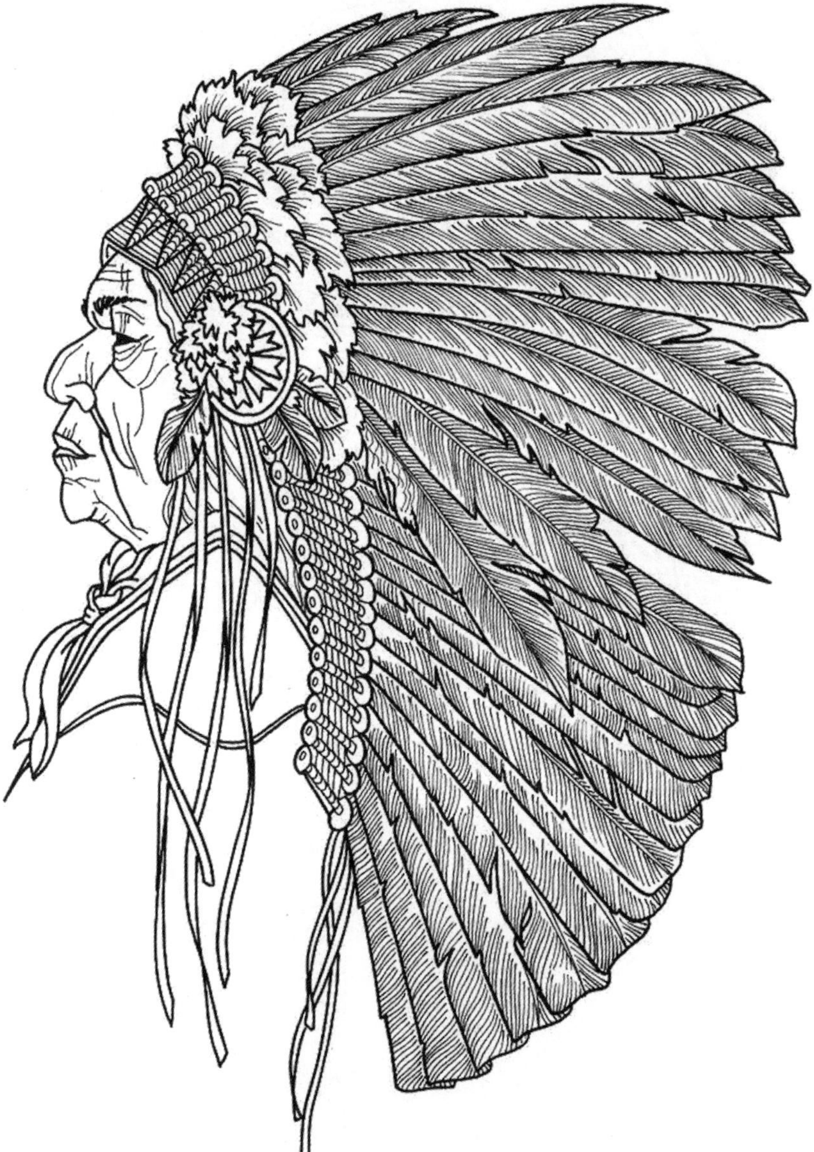

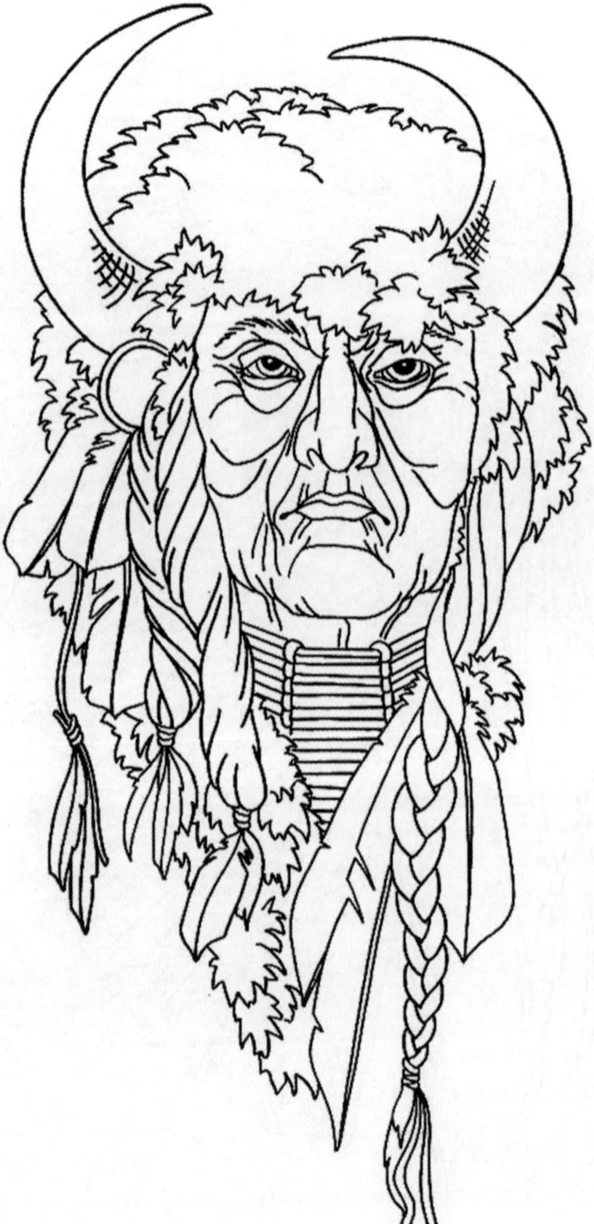

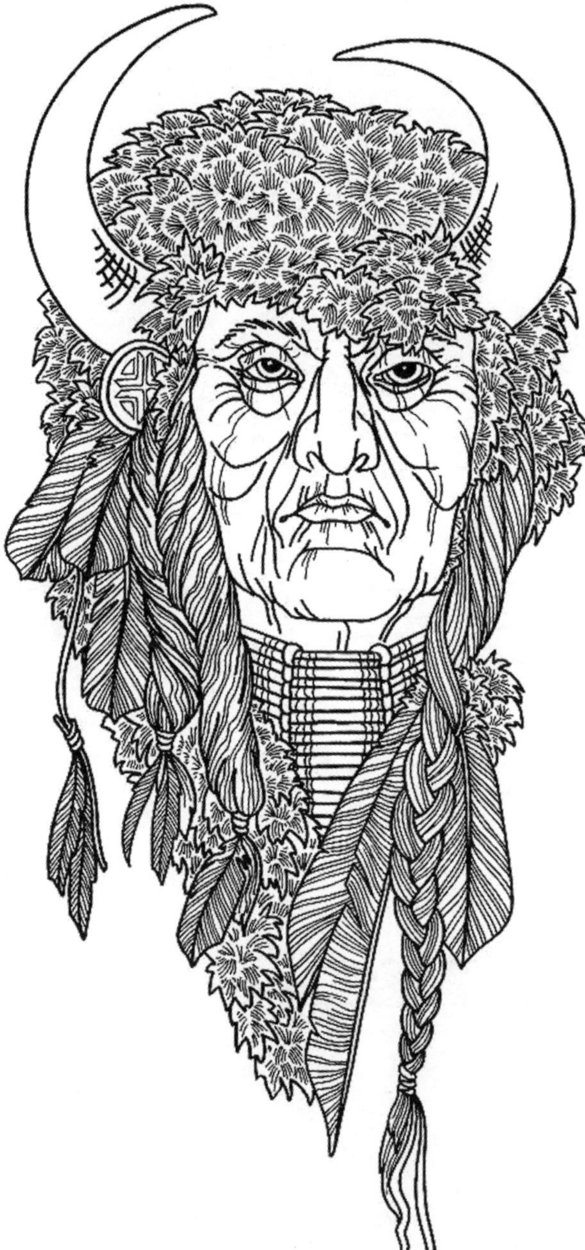

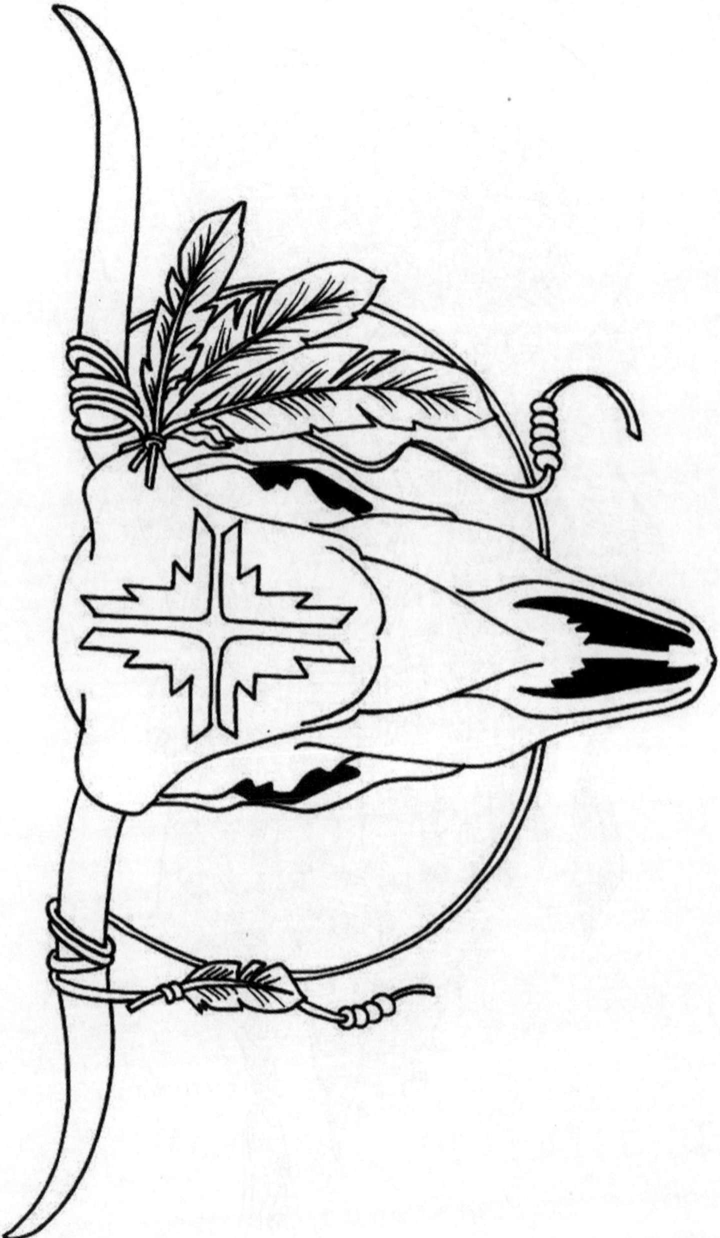

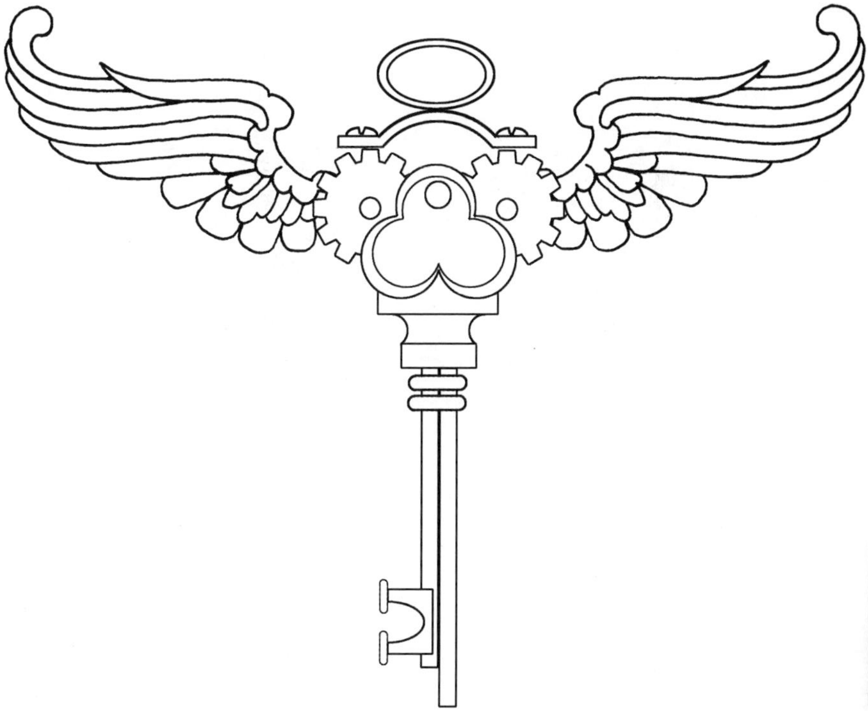

Symbols

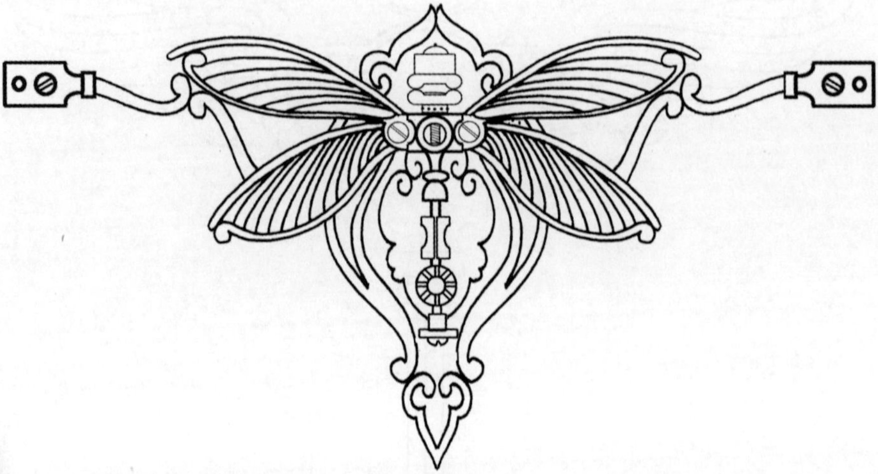

© Lora S. Irish

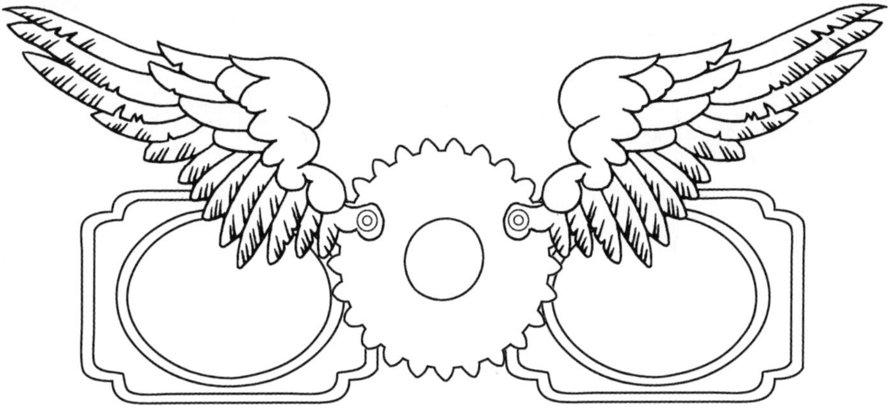

Symbols

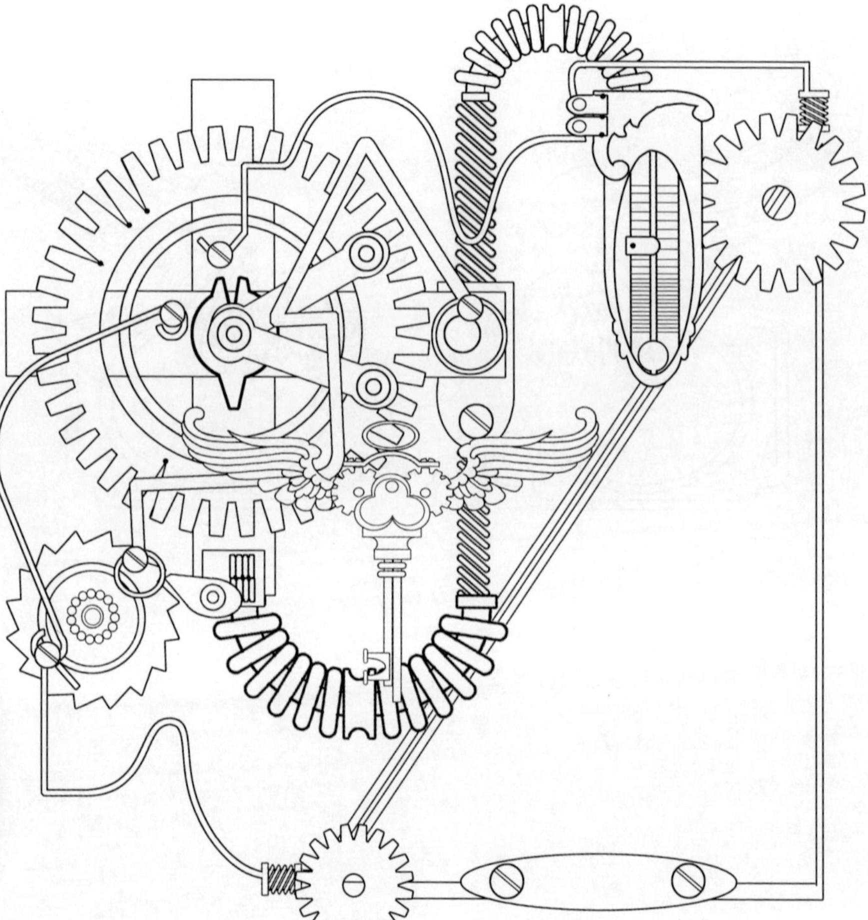

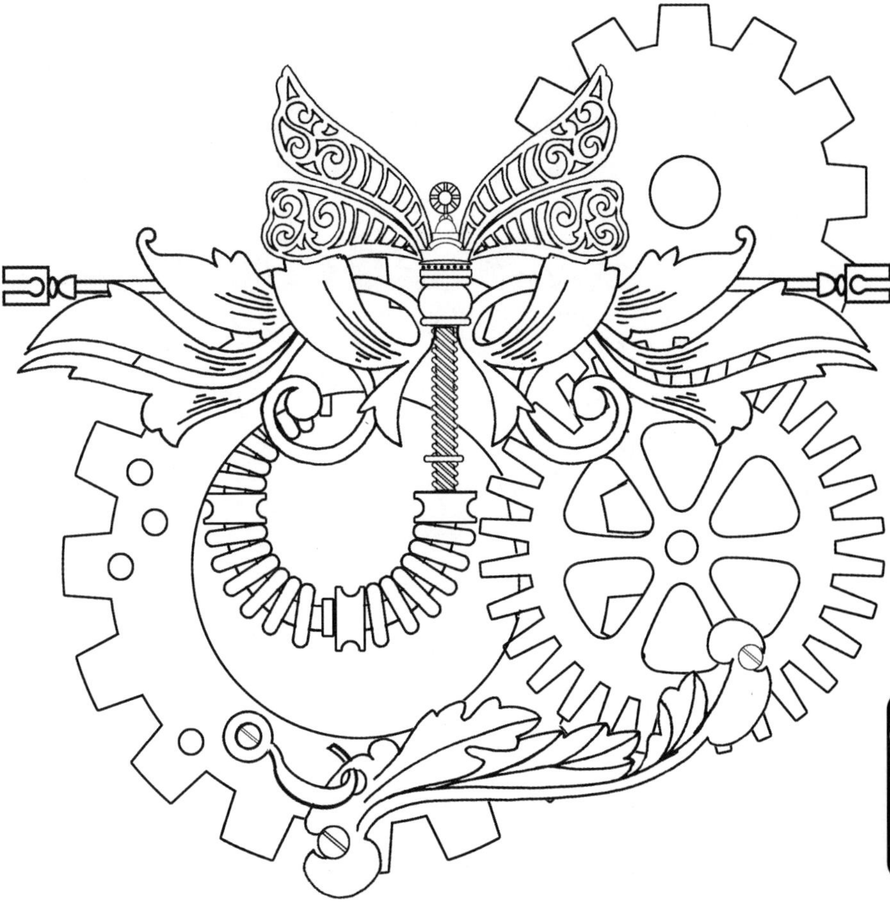

Symbols

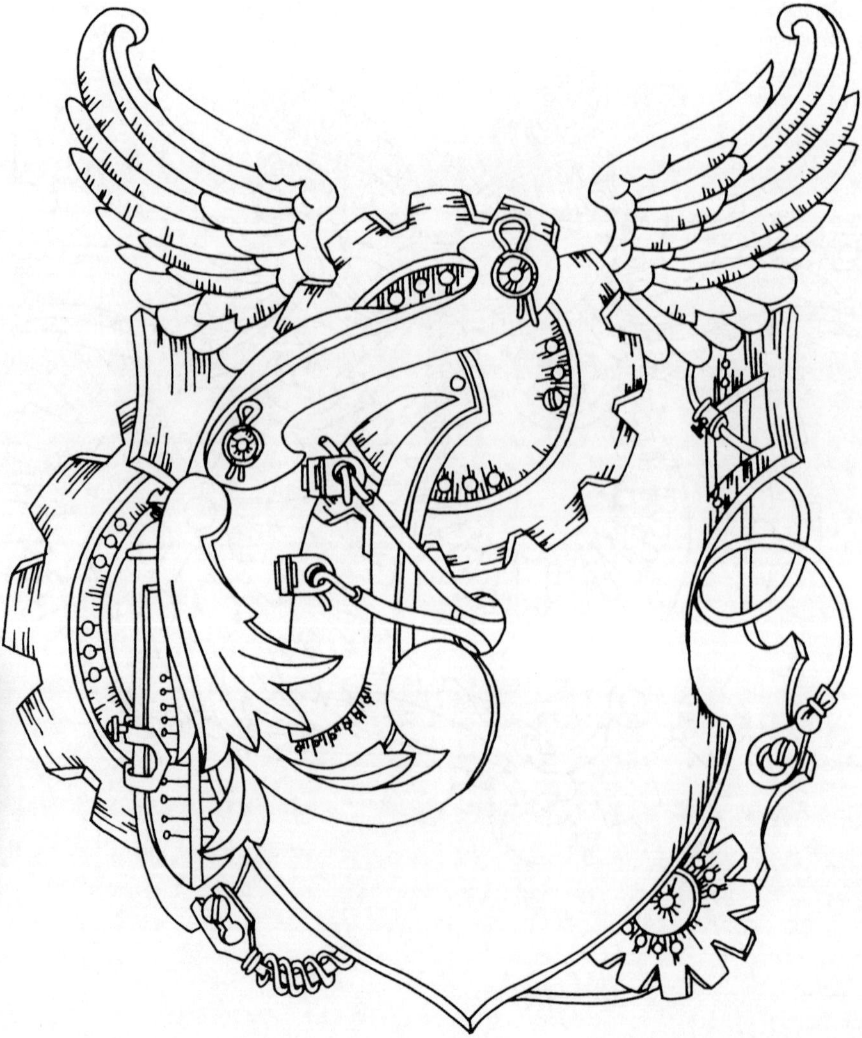

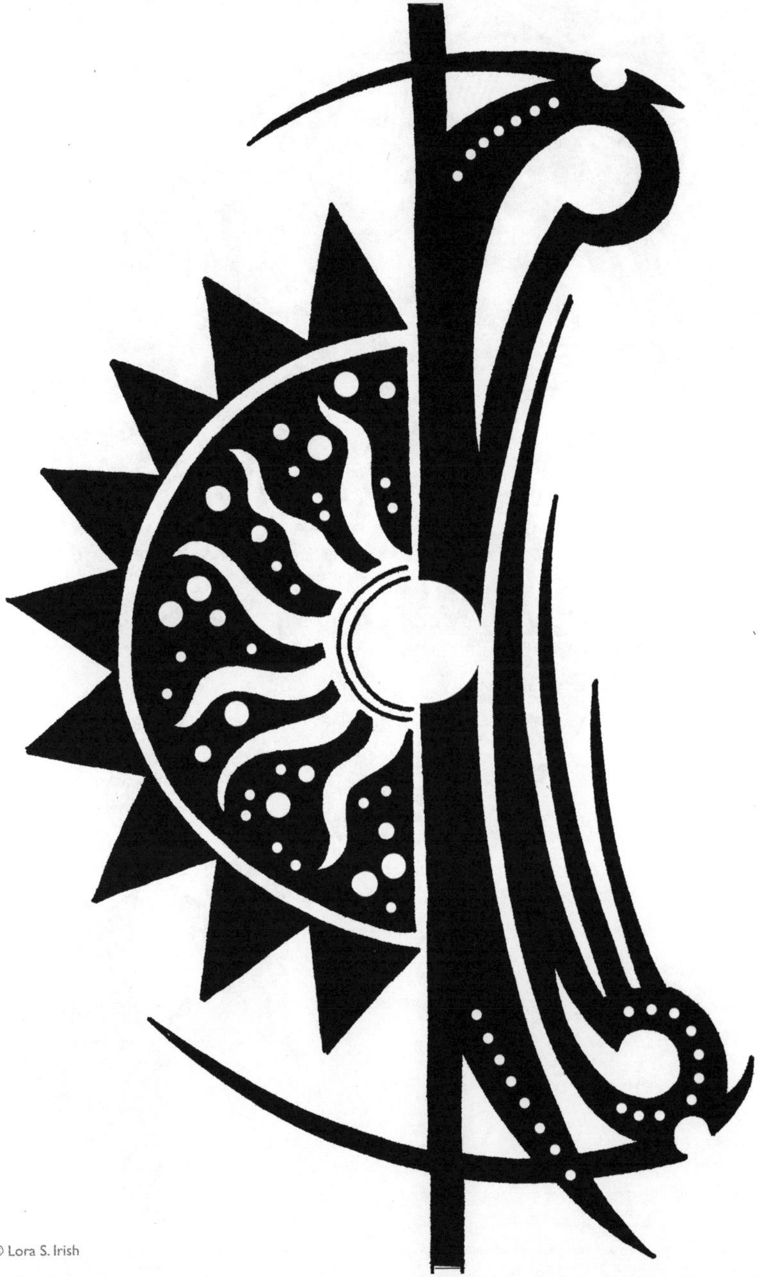

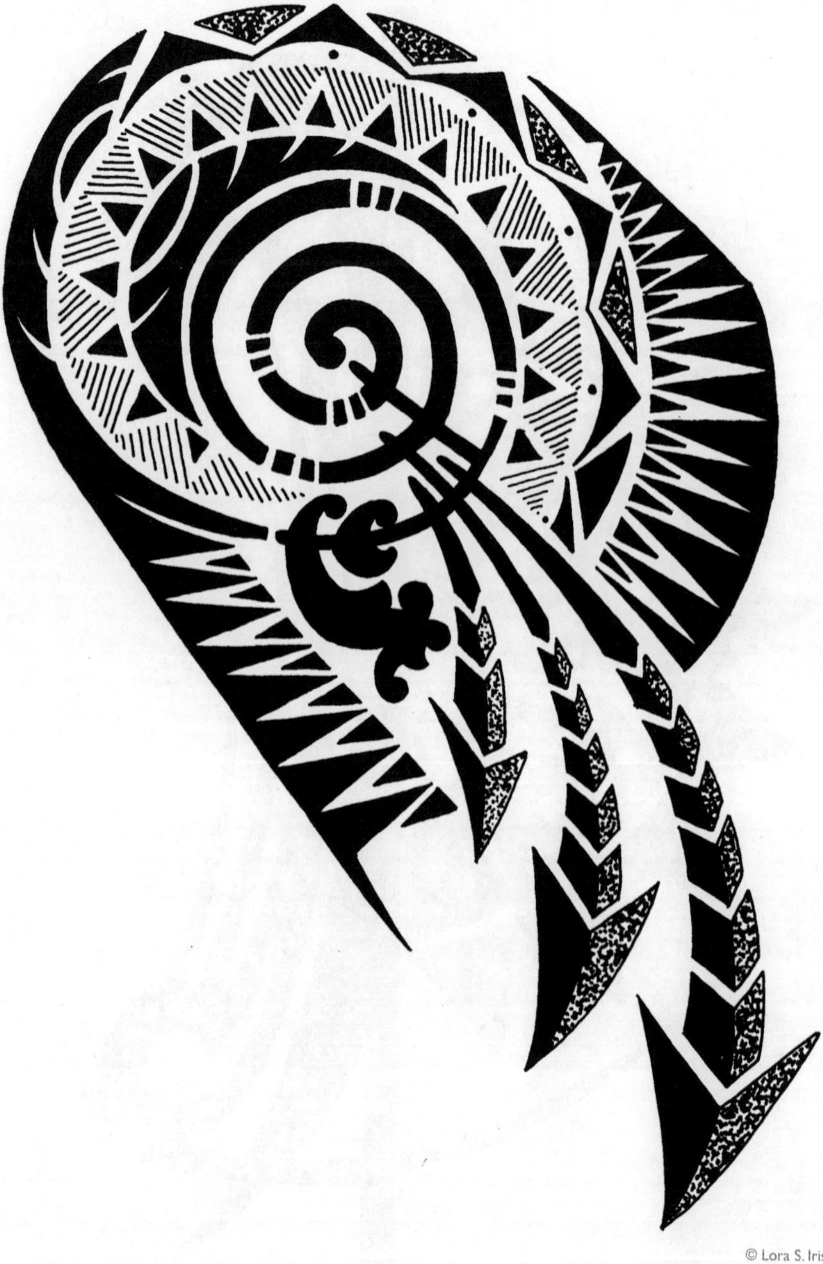

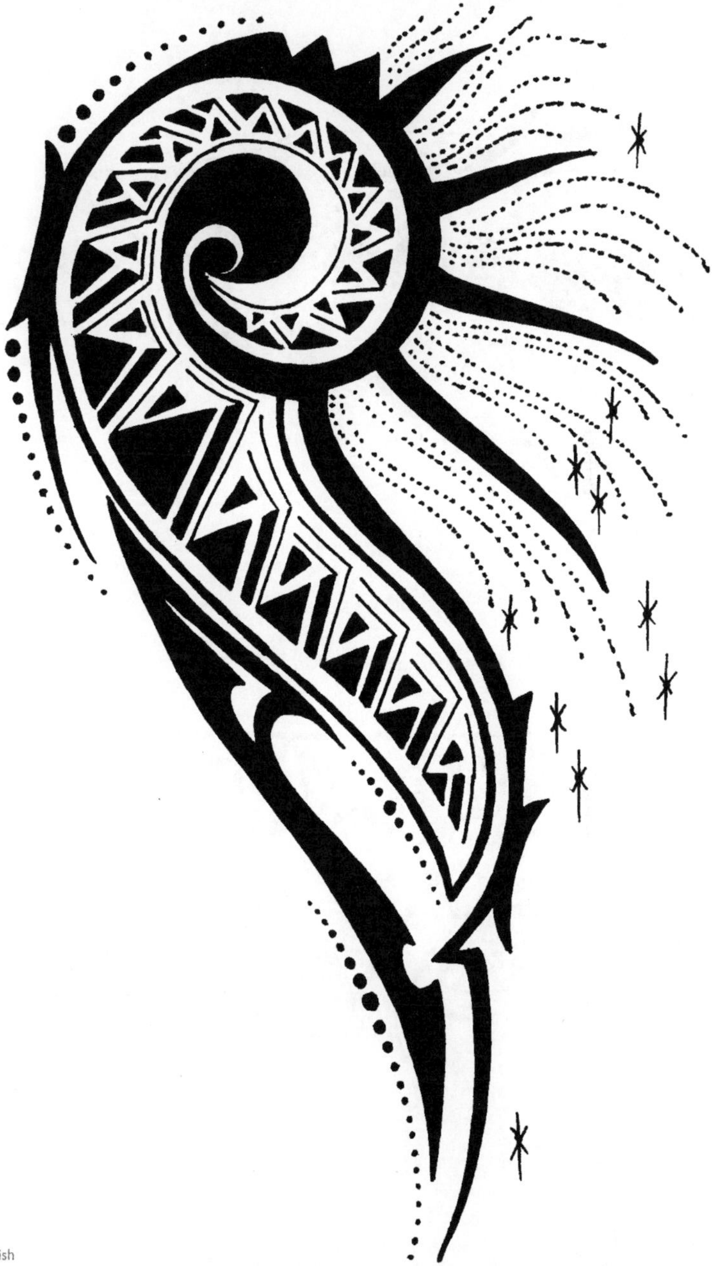

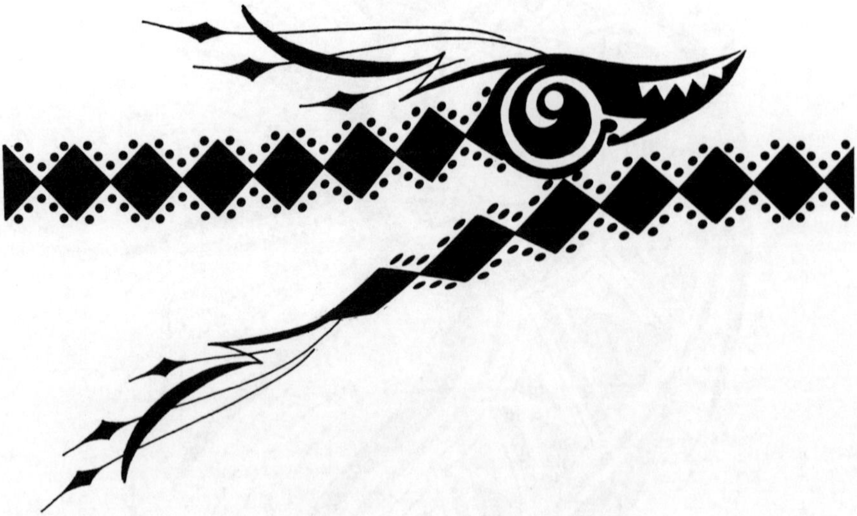

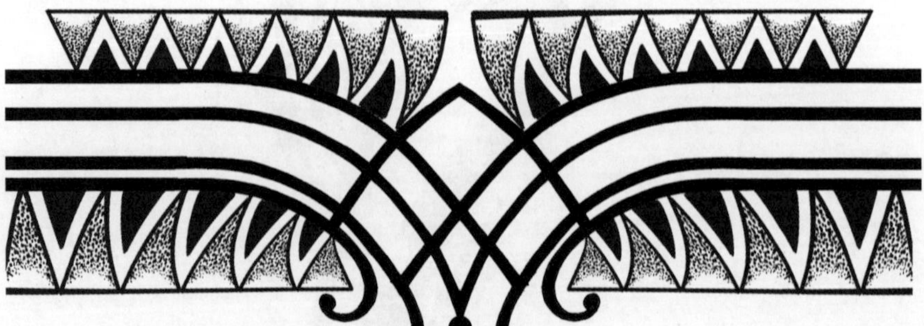

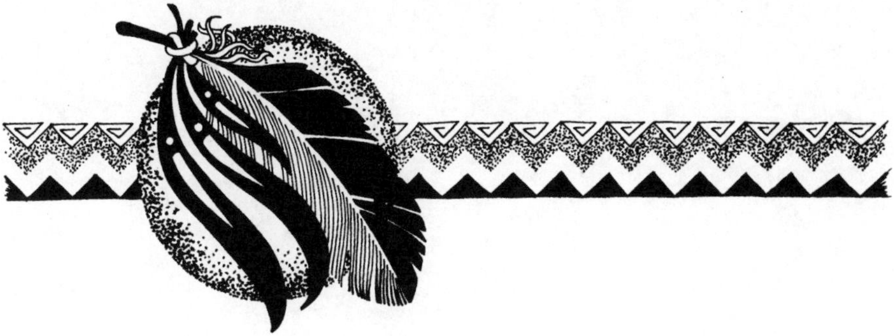

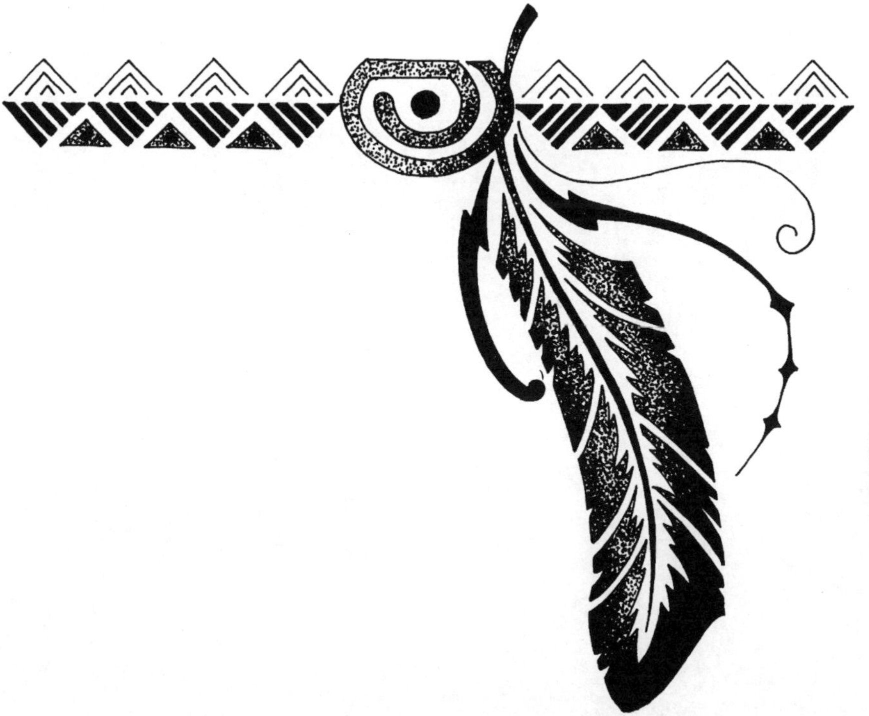

Symbols

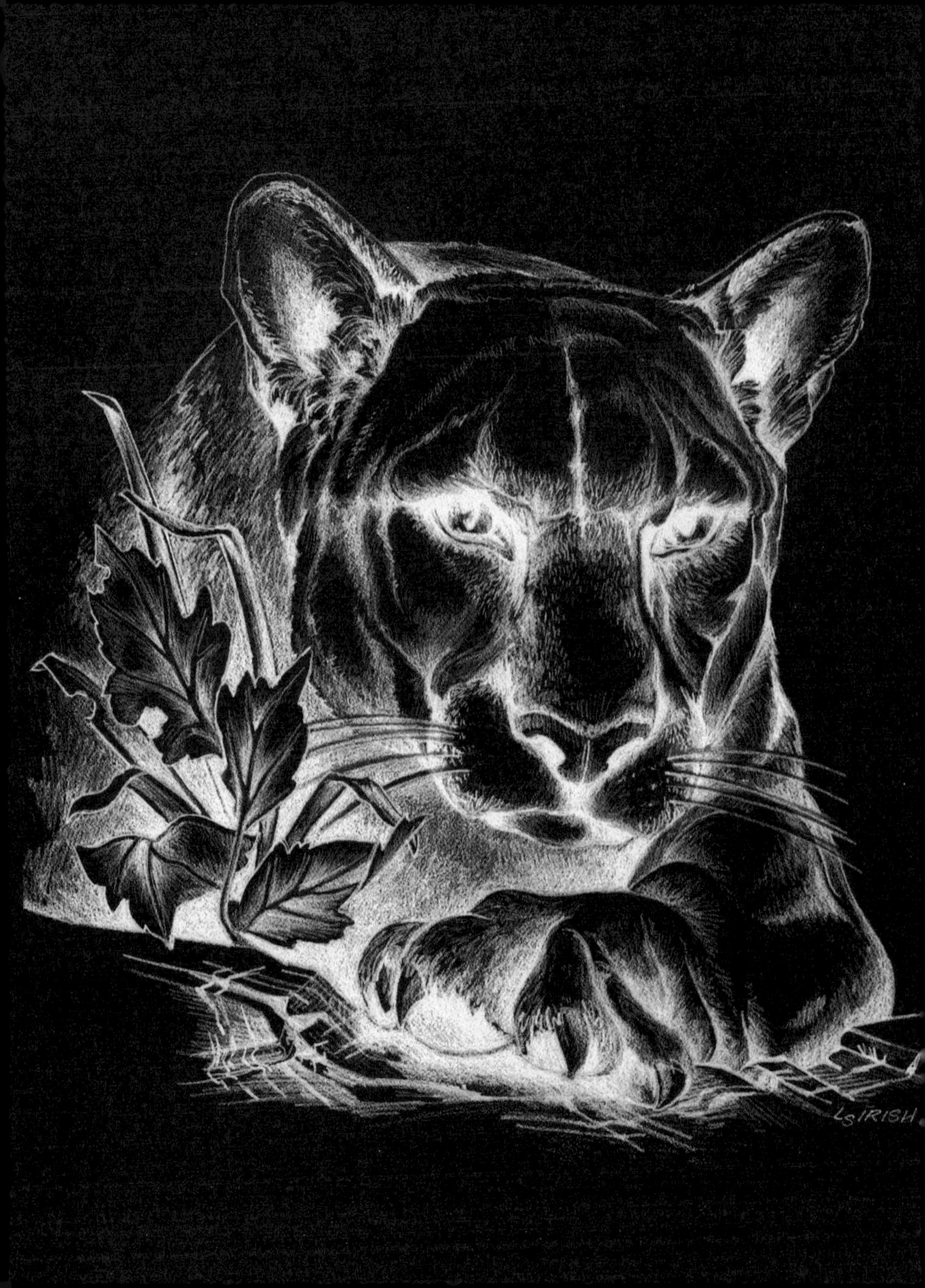
LS IRISH

Wildlife

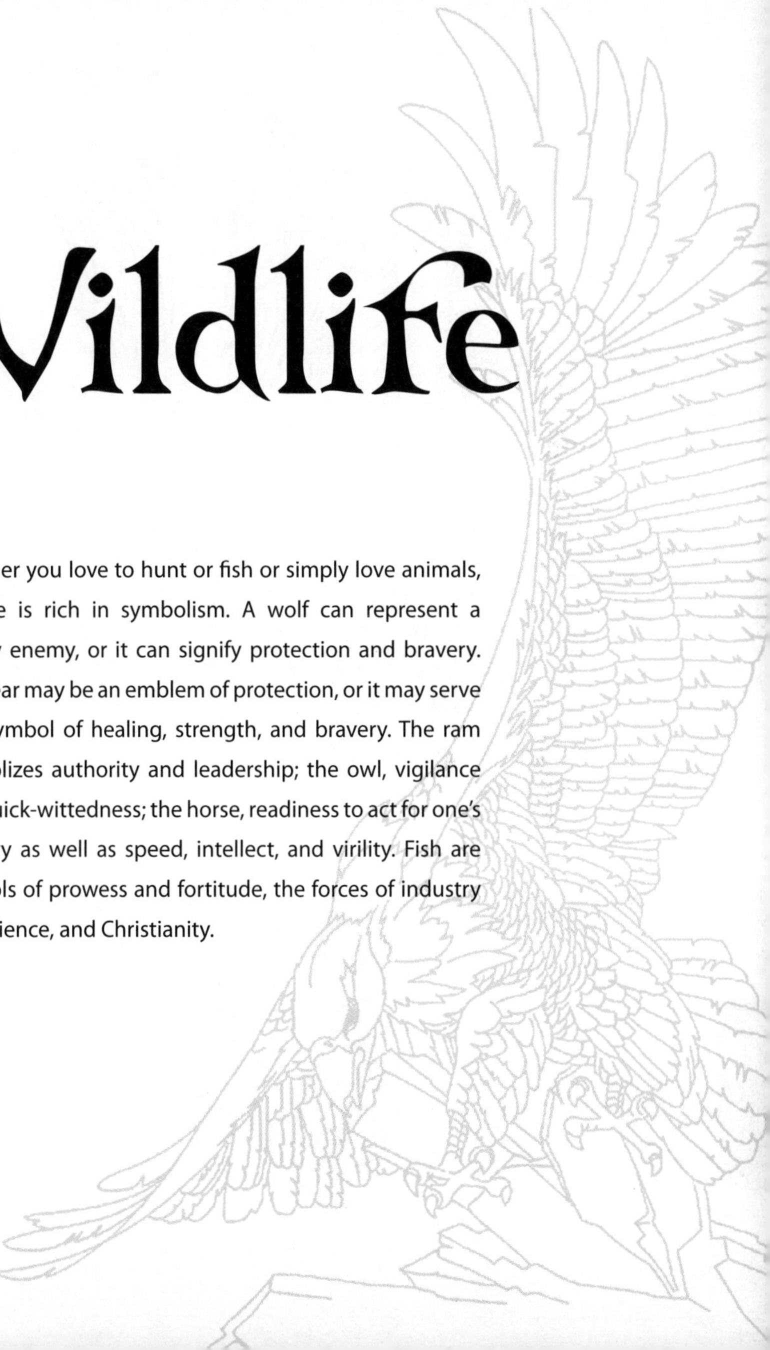

Whether you love to hunt or fish or simply love animals, wildlife is rich in symbolism. A wolf can represent a deadly enemy, or it can signify protection and bravery. The bear may be an emblem of protection, or it may serve as a symbol of healing, strength, and bravery. The ram symbolizes authority and leadership; the owl, vigilance and quick-wittedness; the horse, readiness to act for one's country as well as speed, intellect, and virility. Fish are symbols of prowess and fortitude, the forces of industry and science, and Christianity.

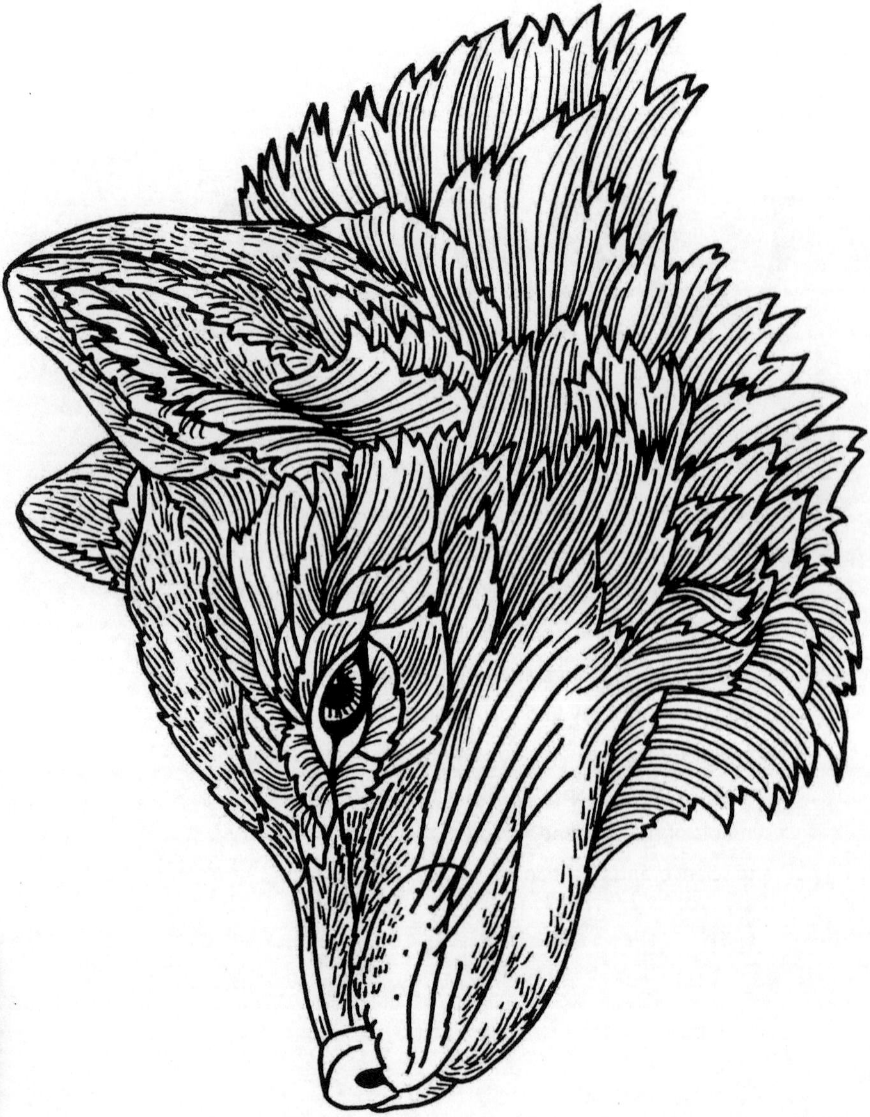

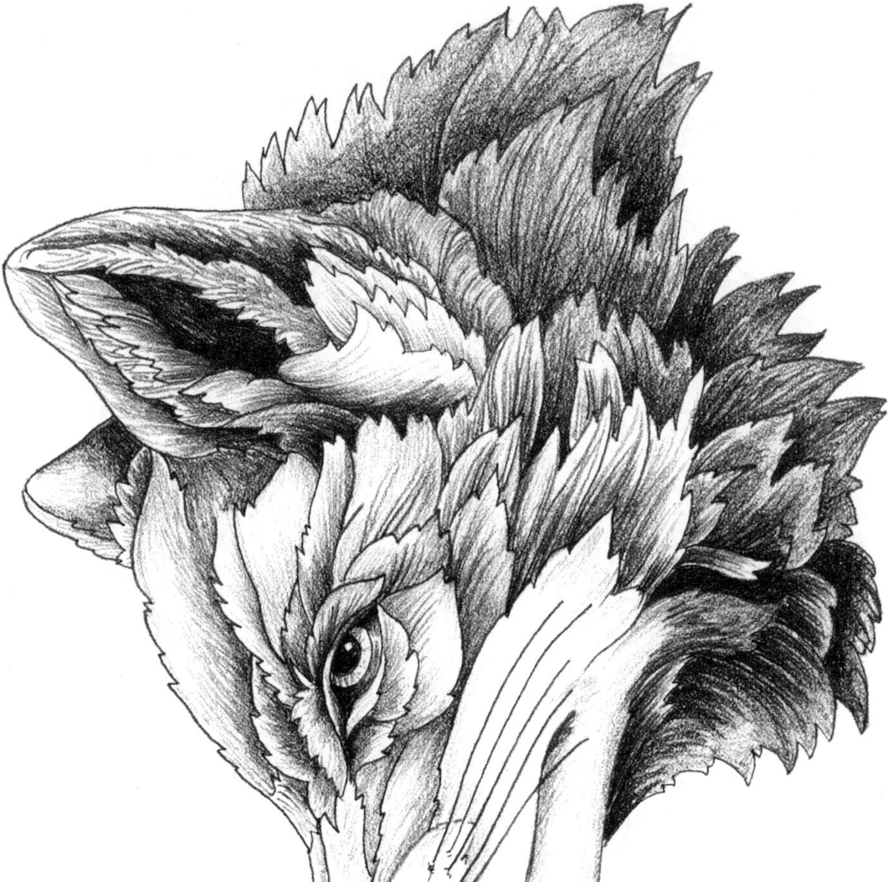

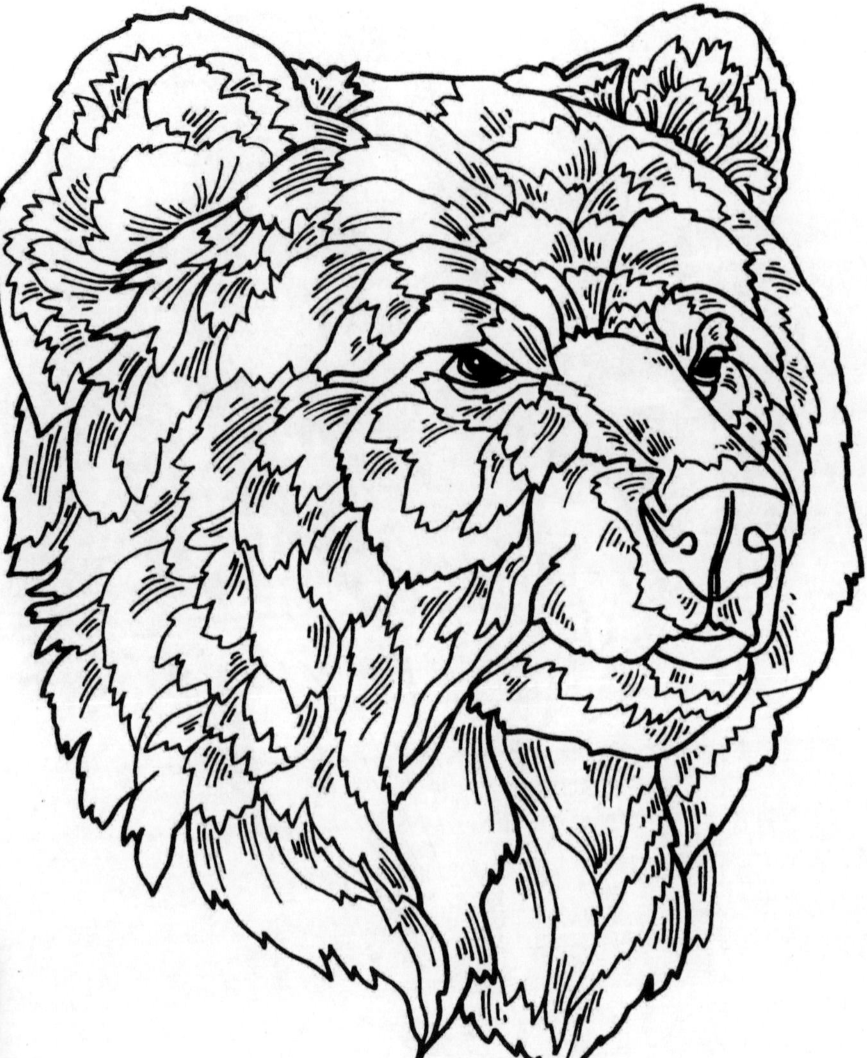

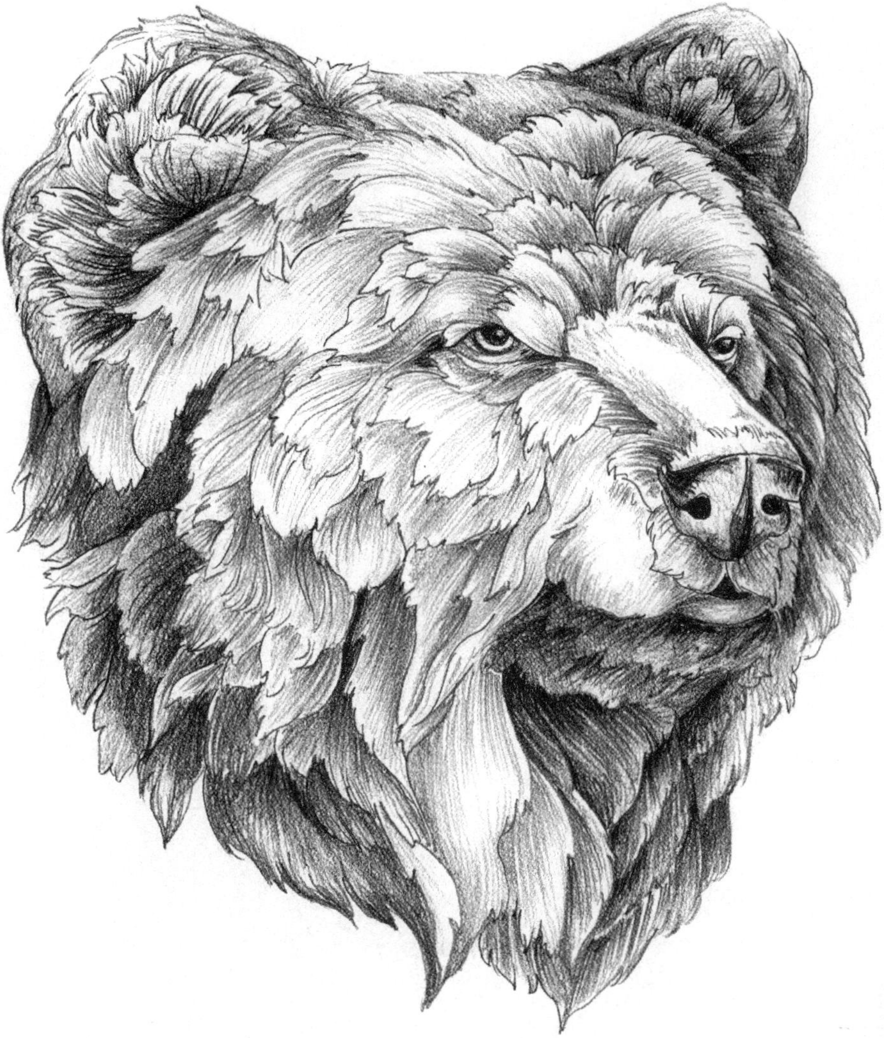

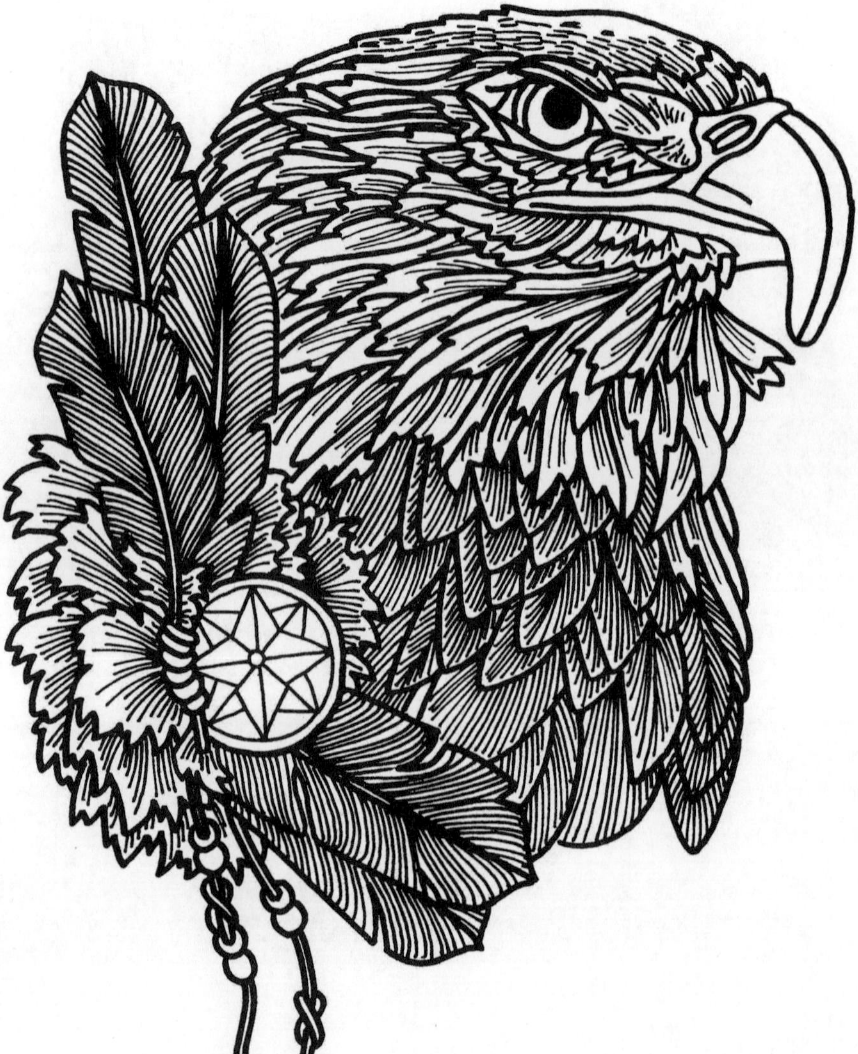

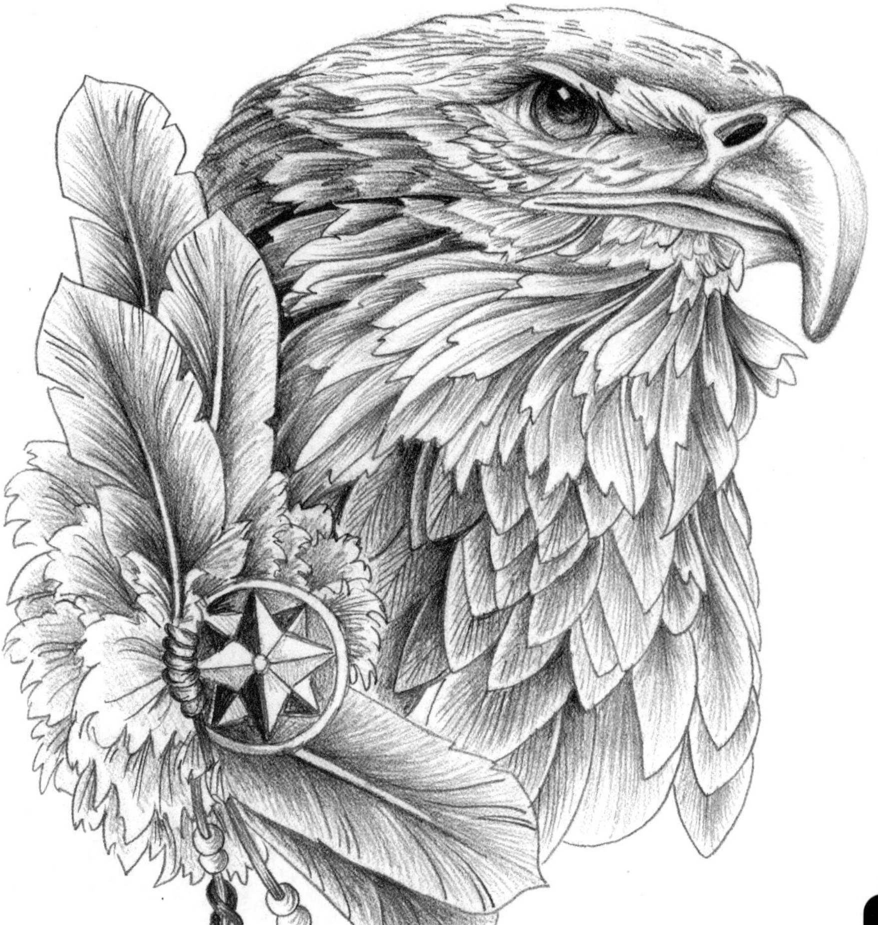

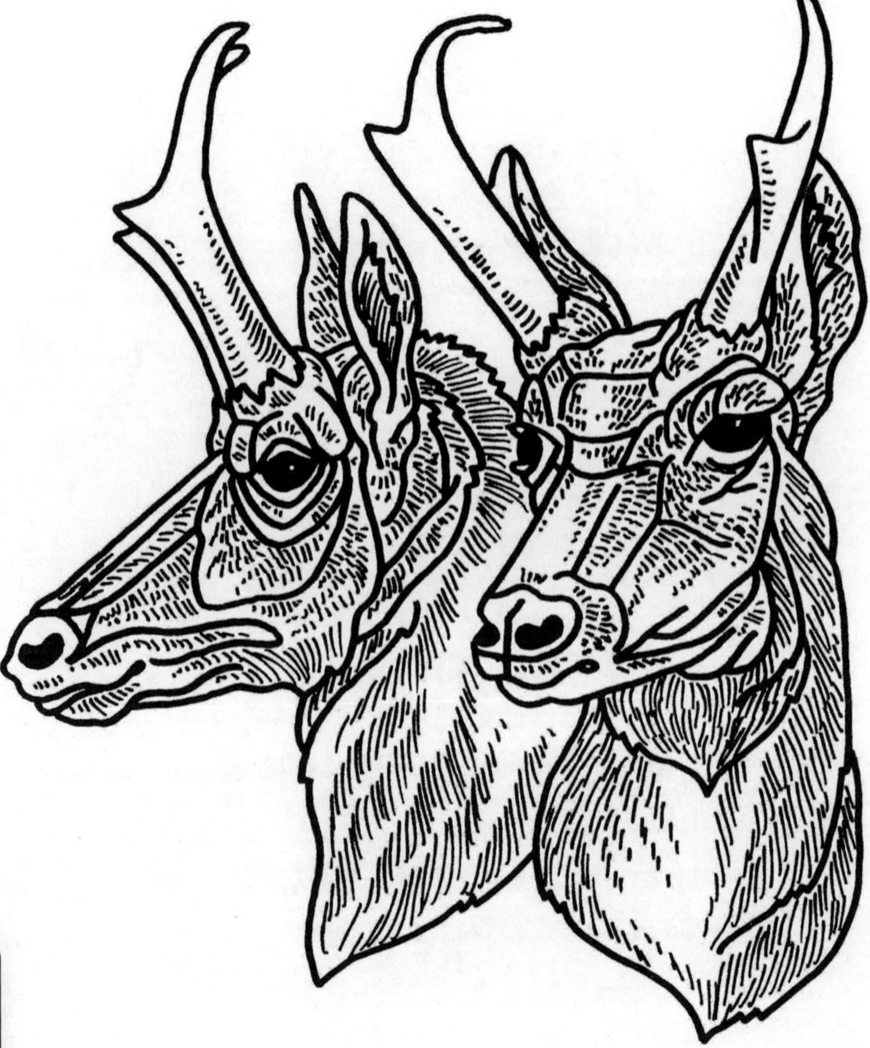

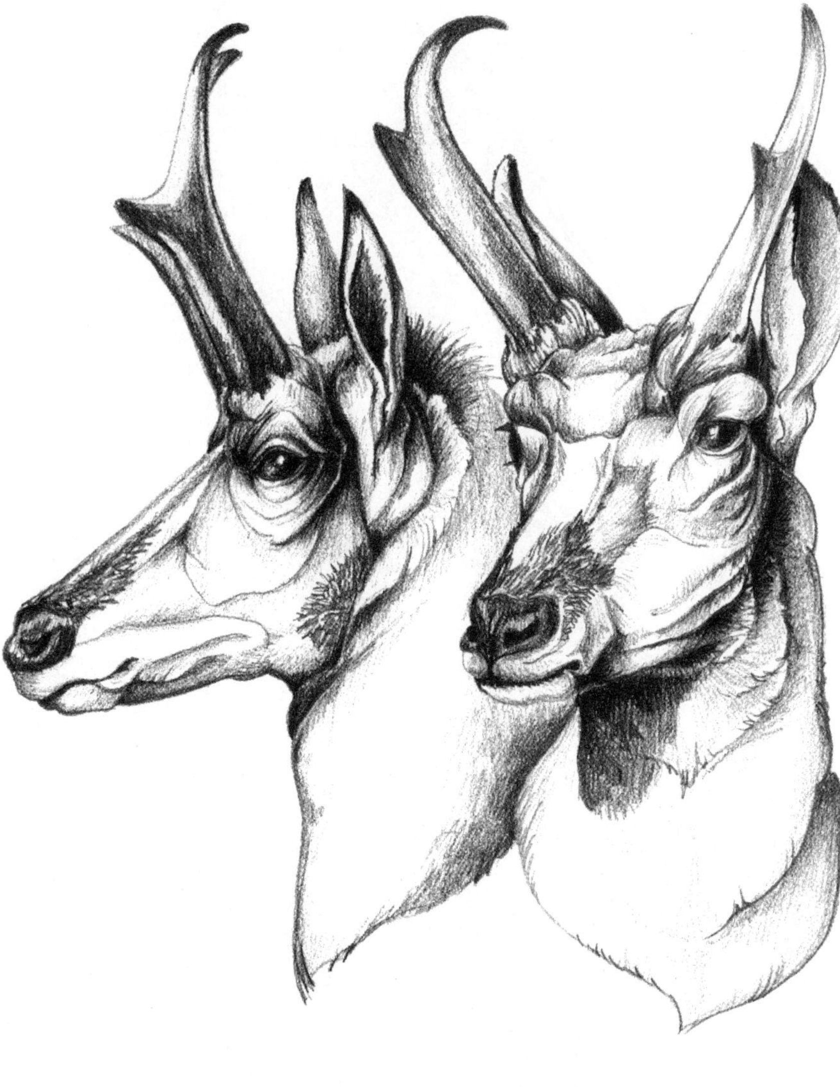

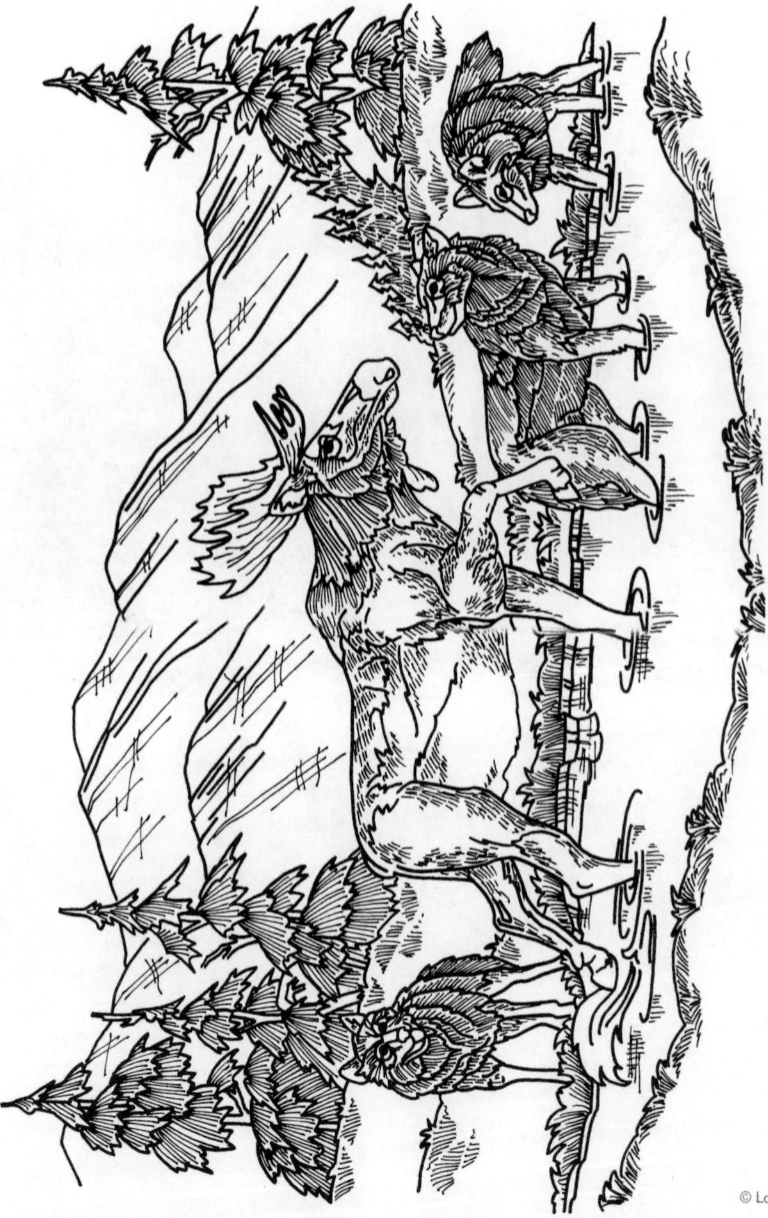

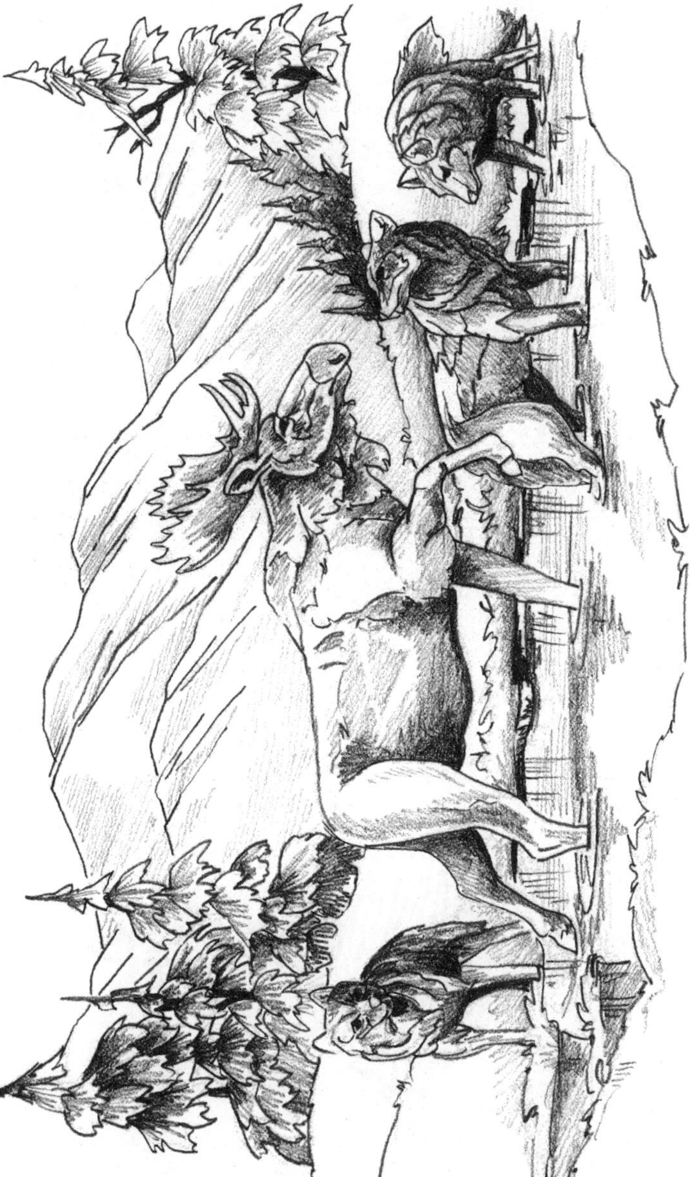

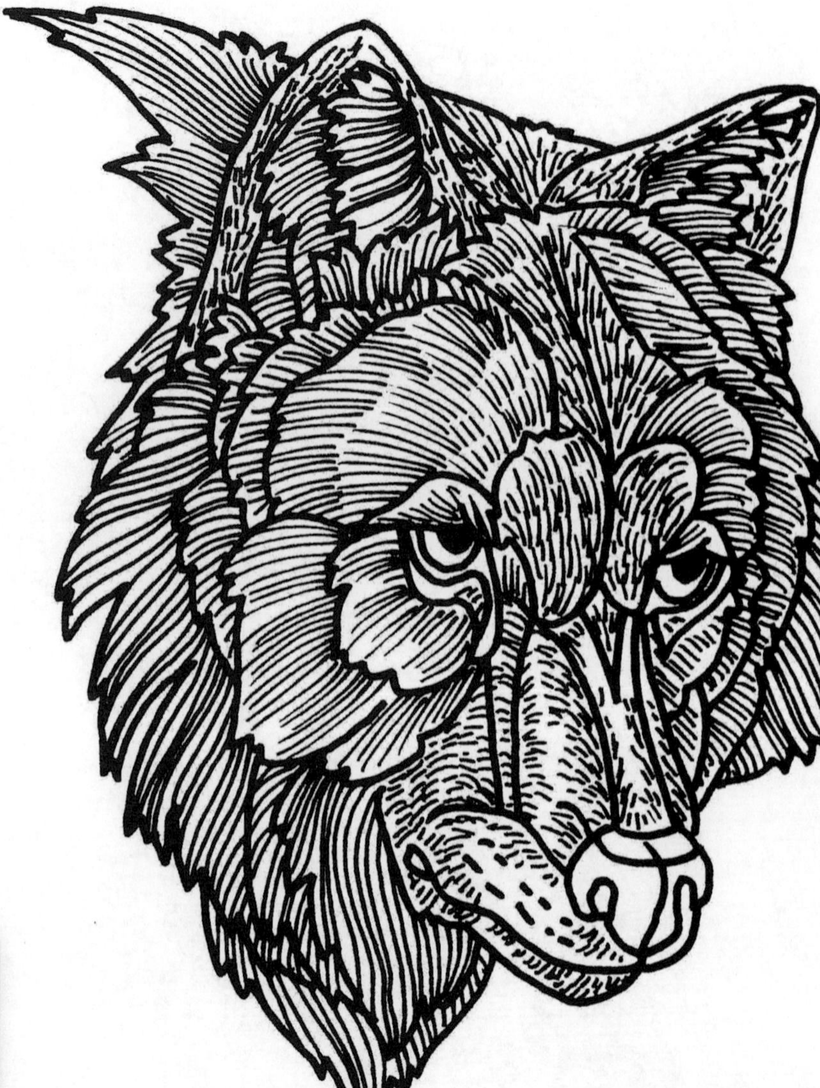

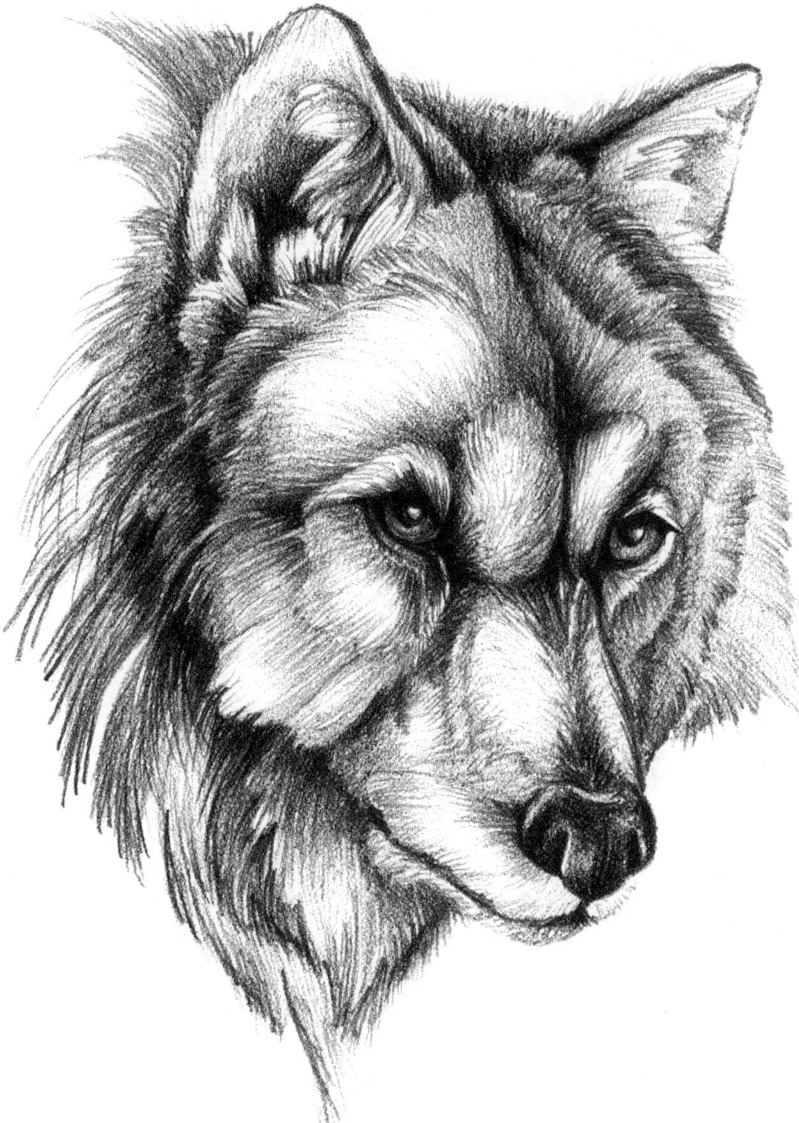

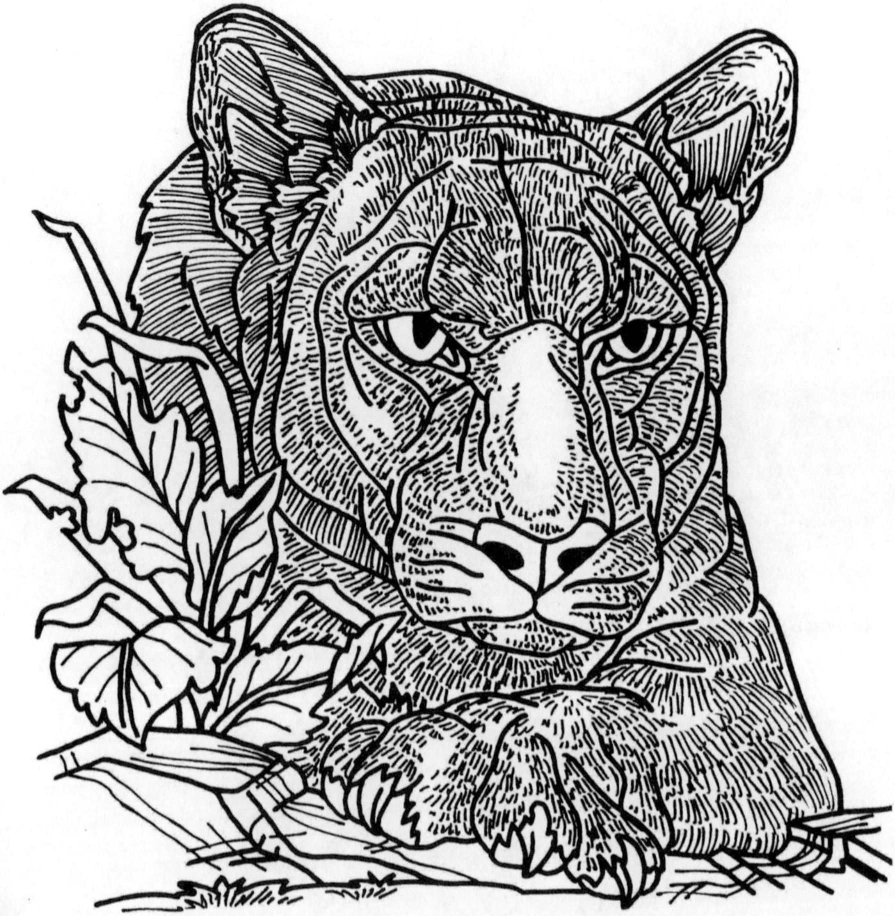

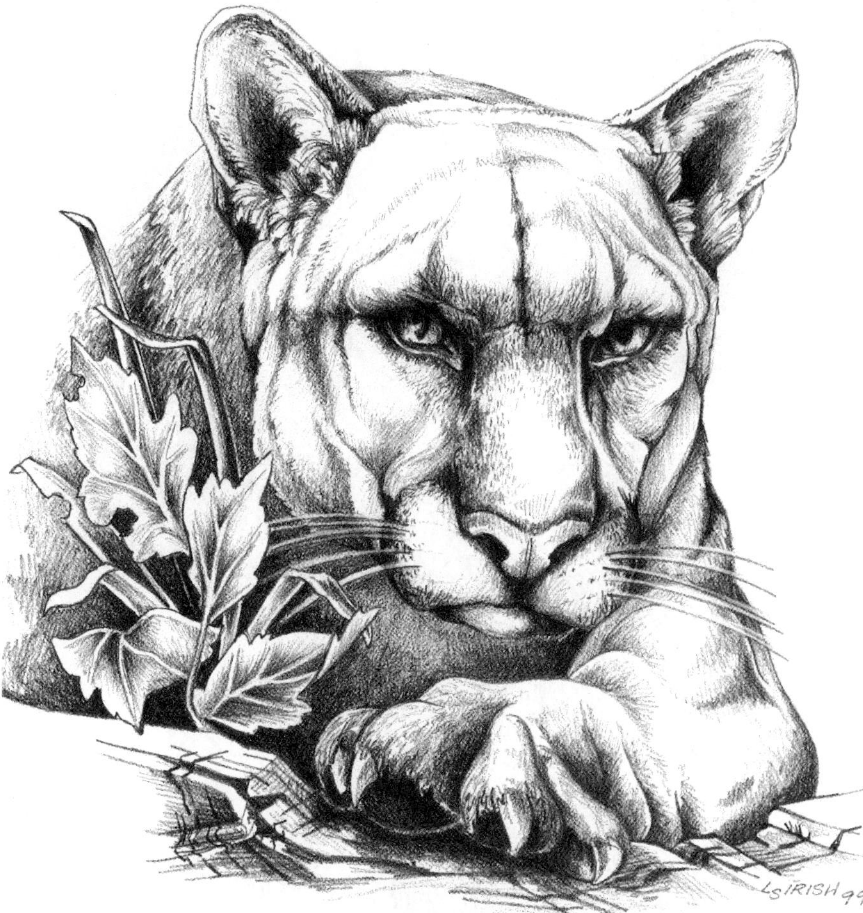
LS IRISH 99

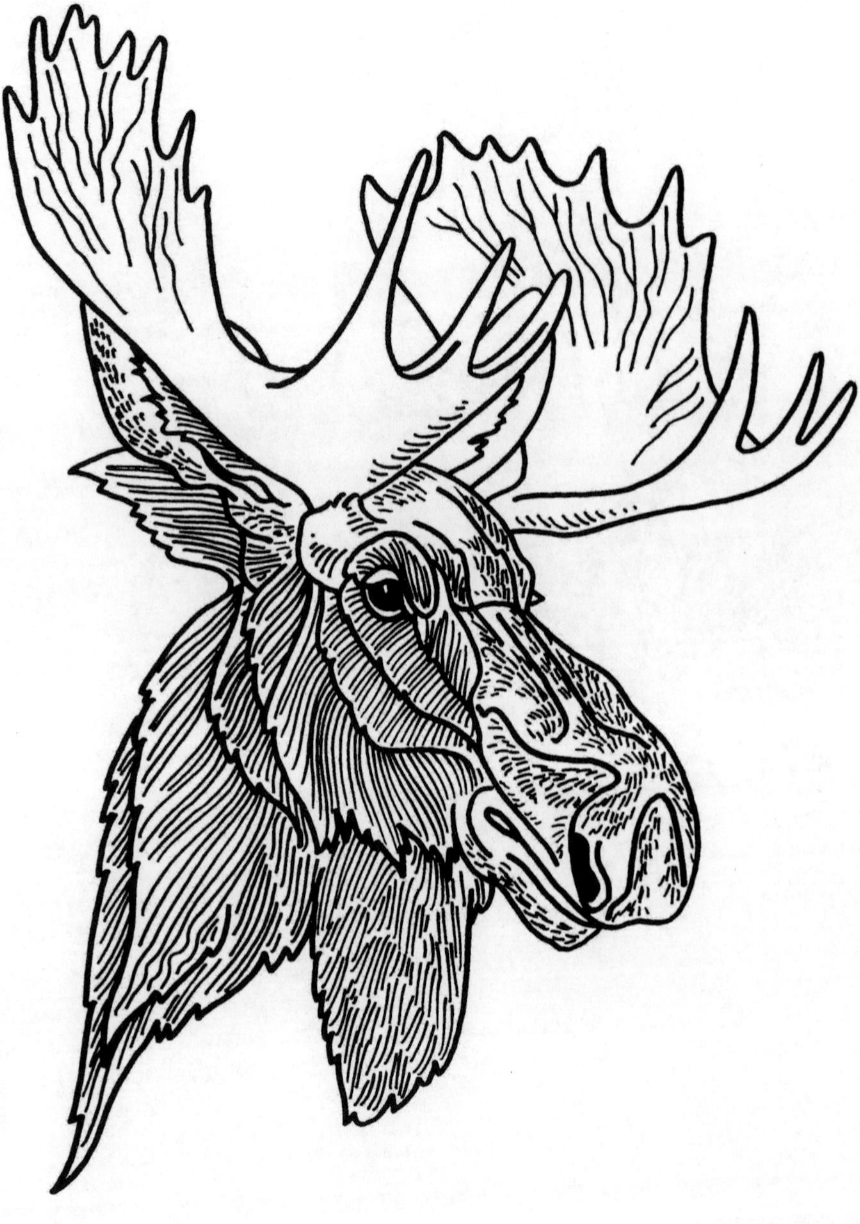

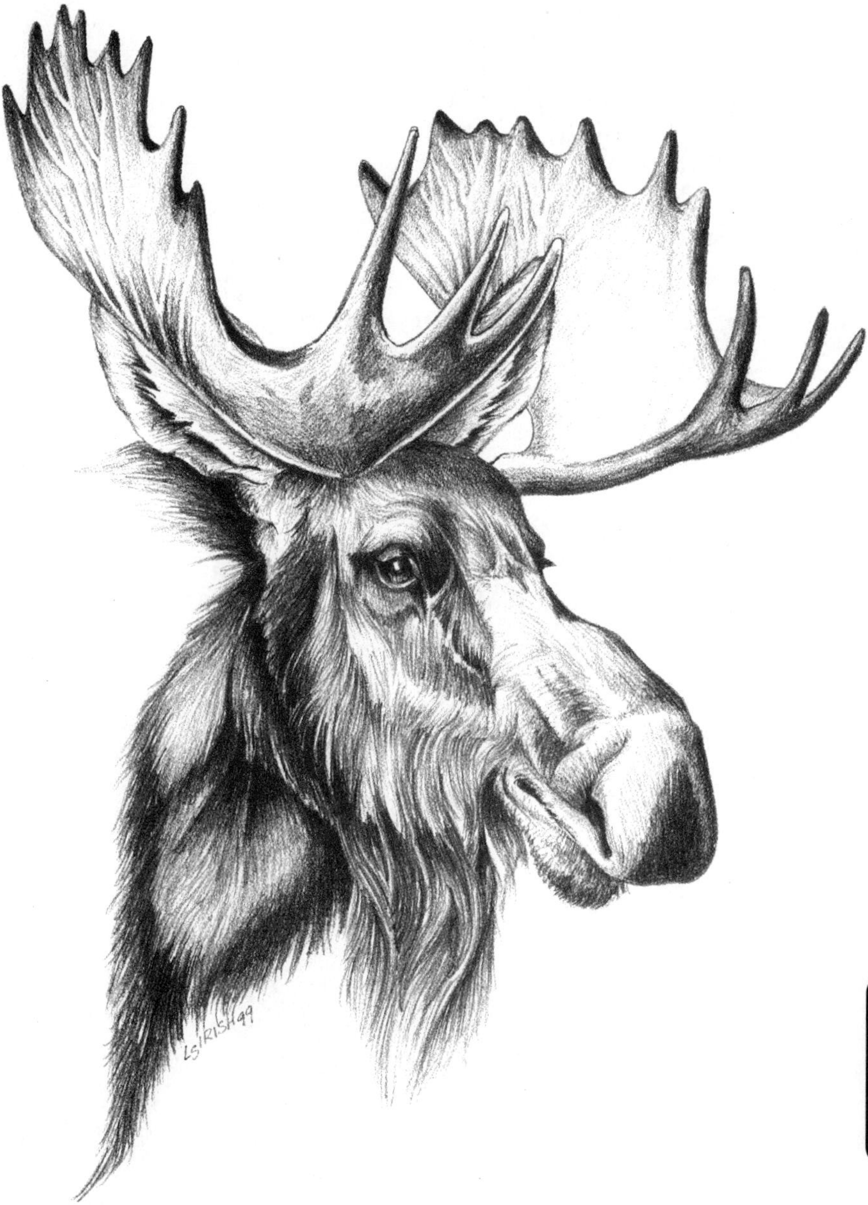
LSIRISH99

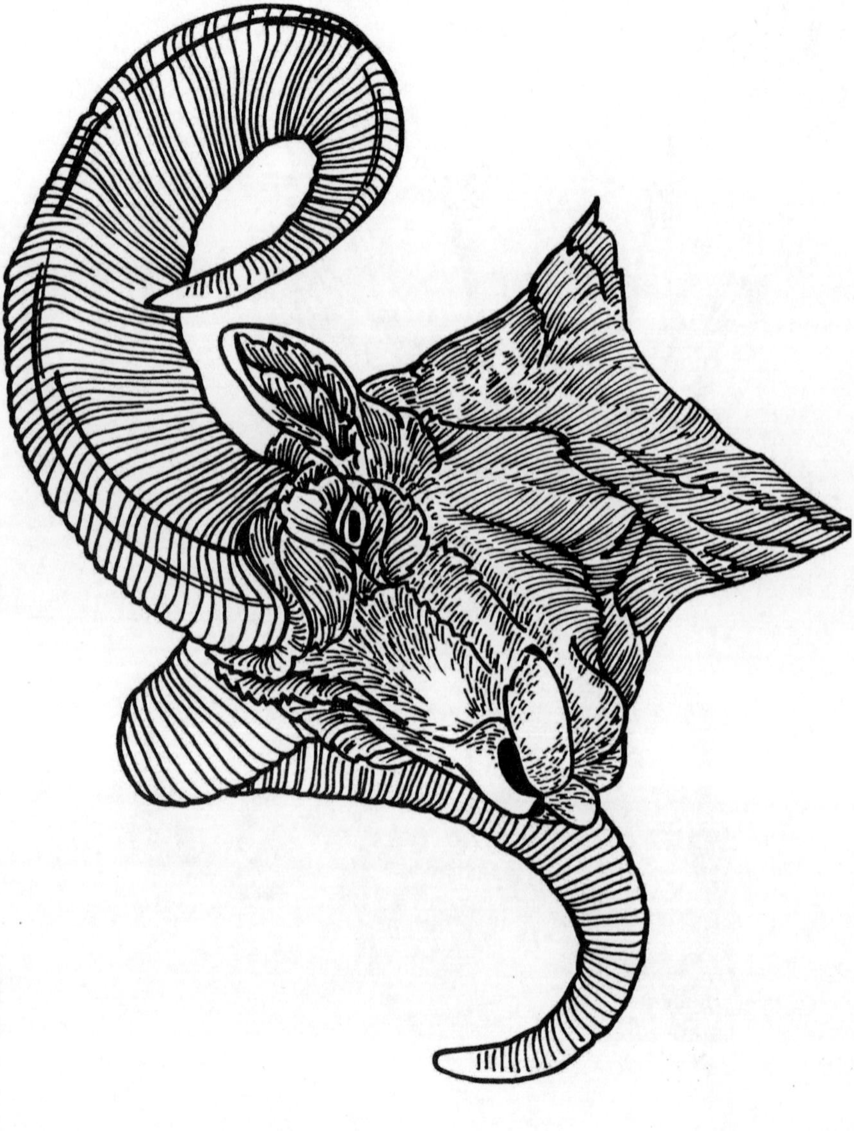

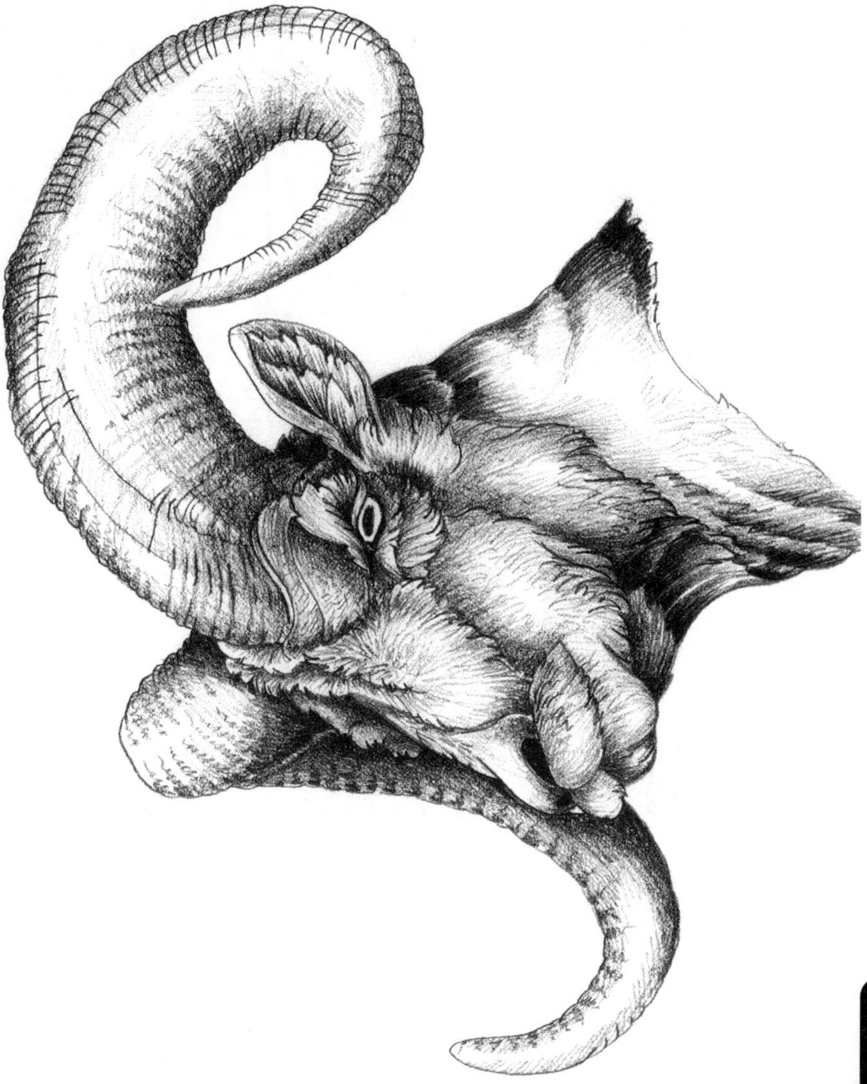

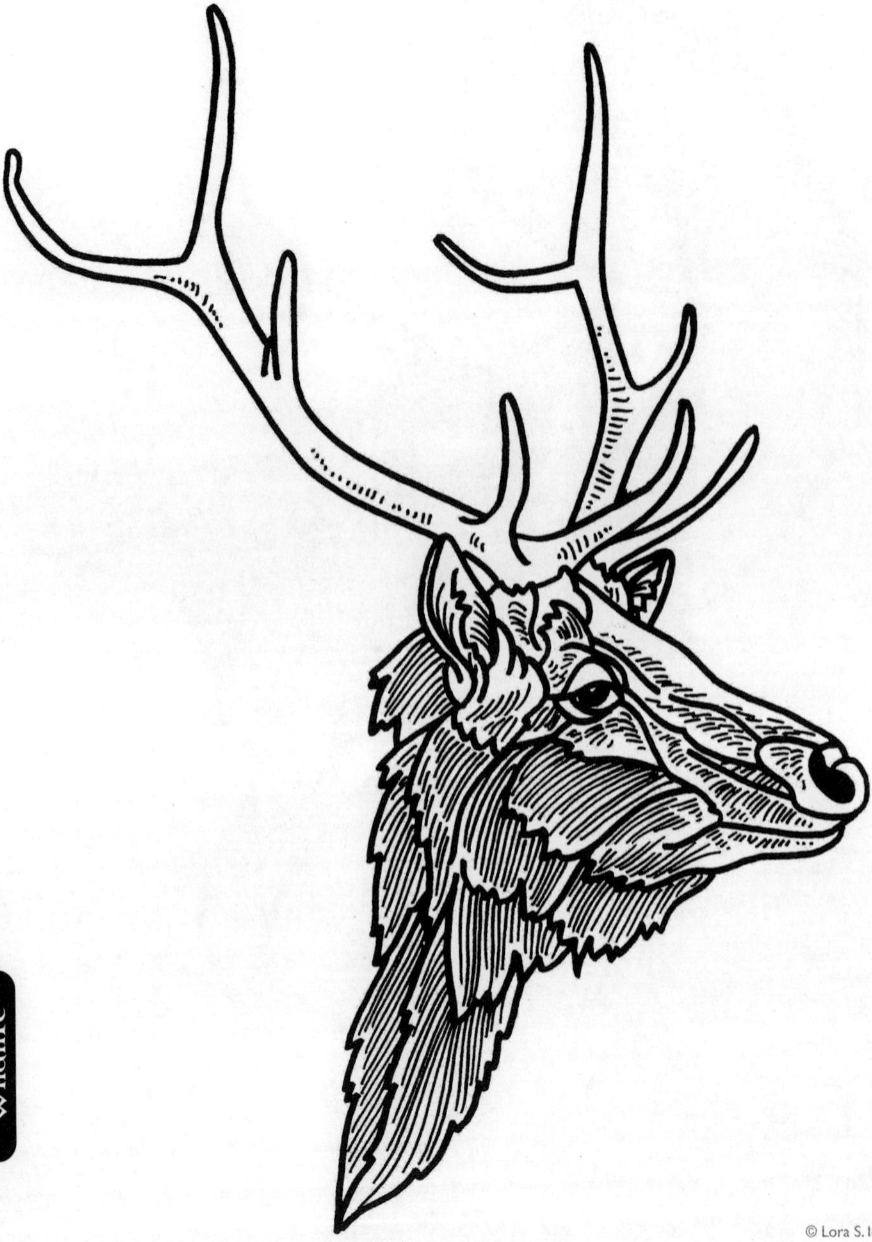

© Lora S. Irish

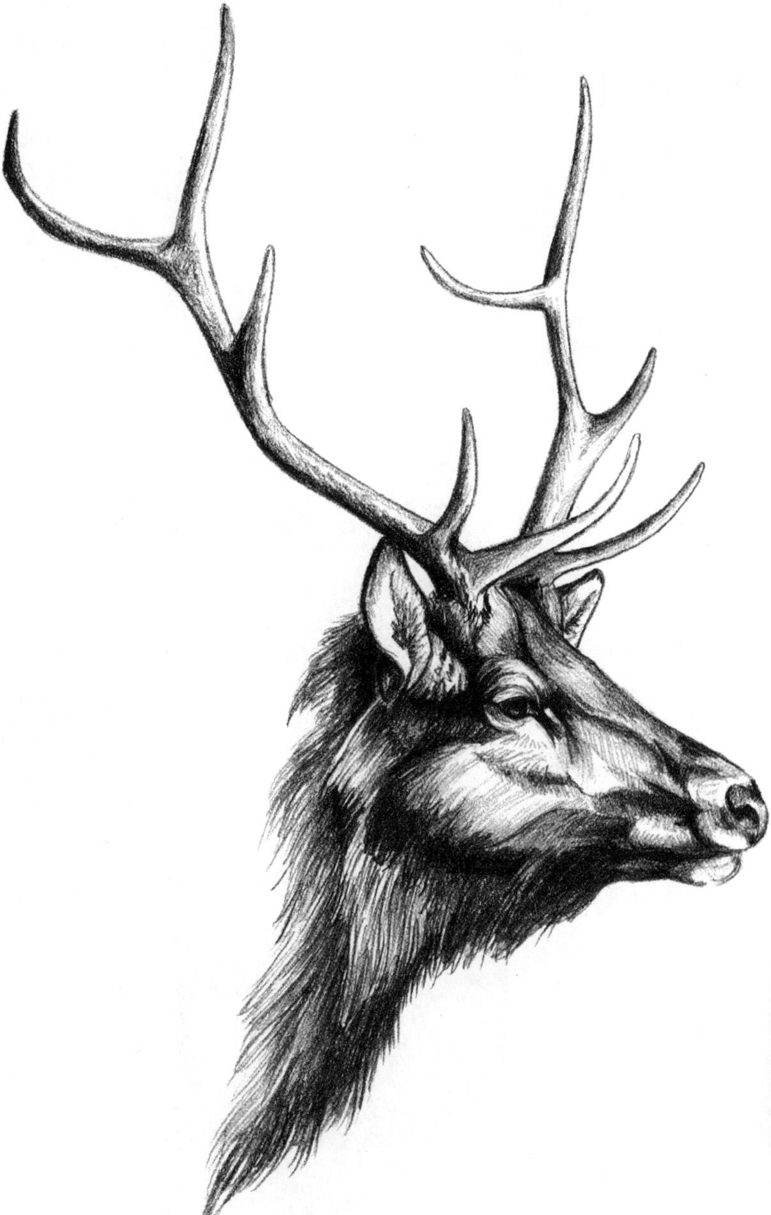

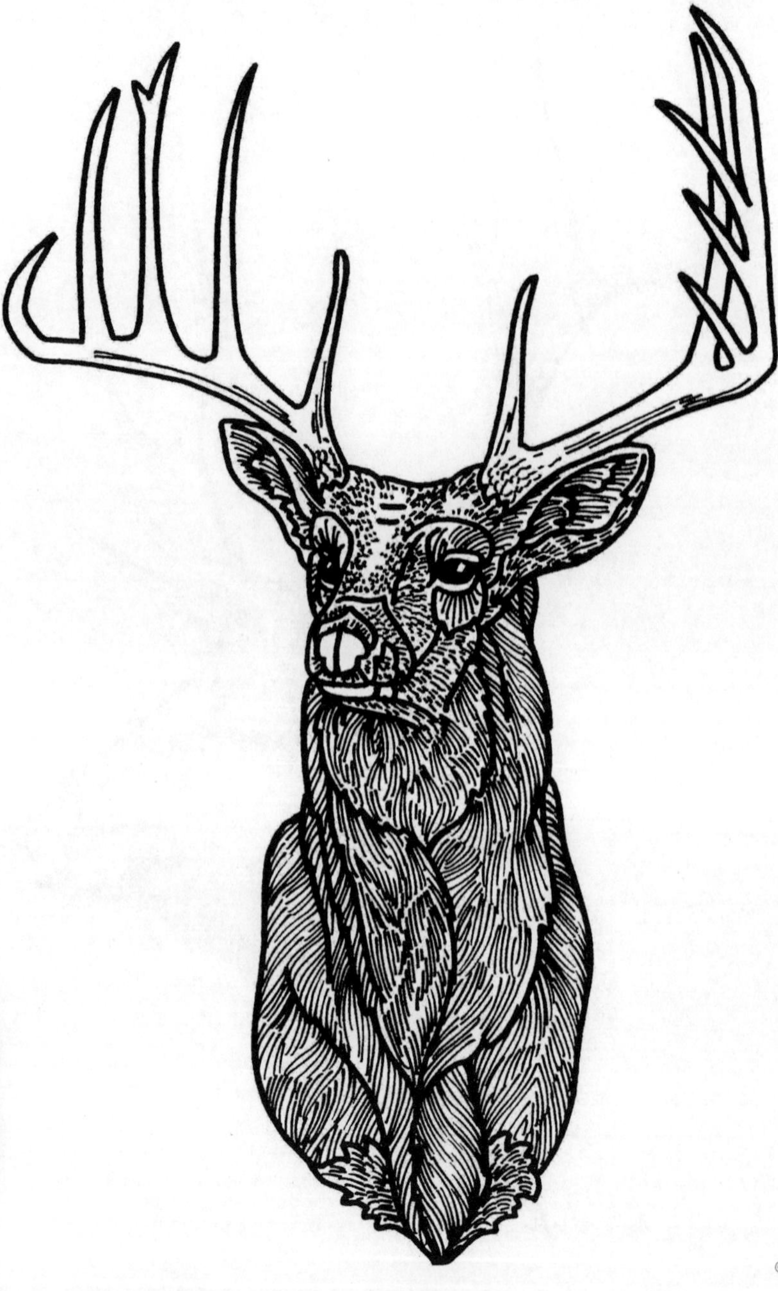

© Lora S. Irish

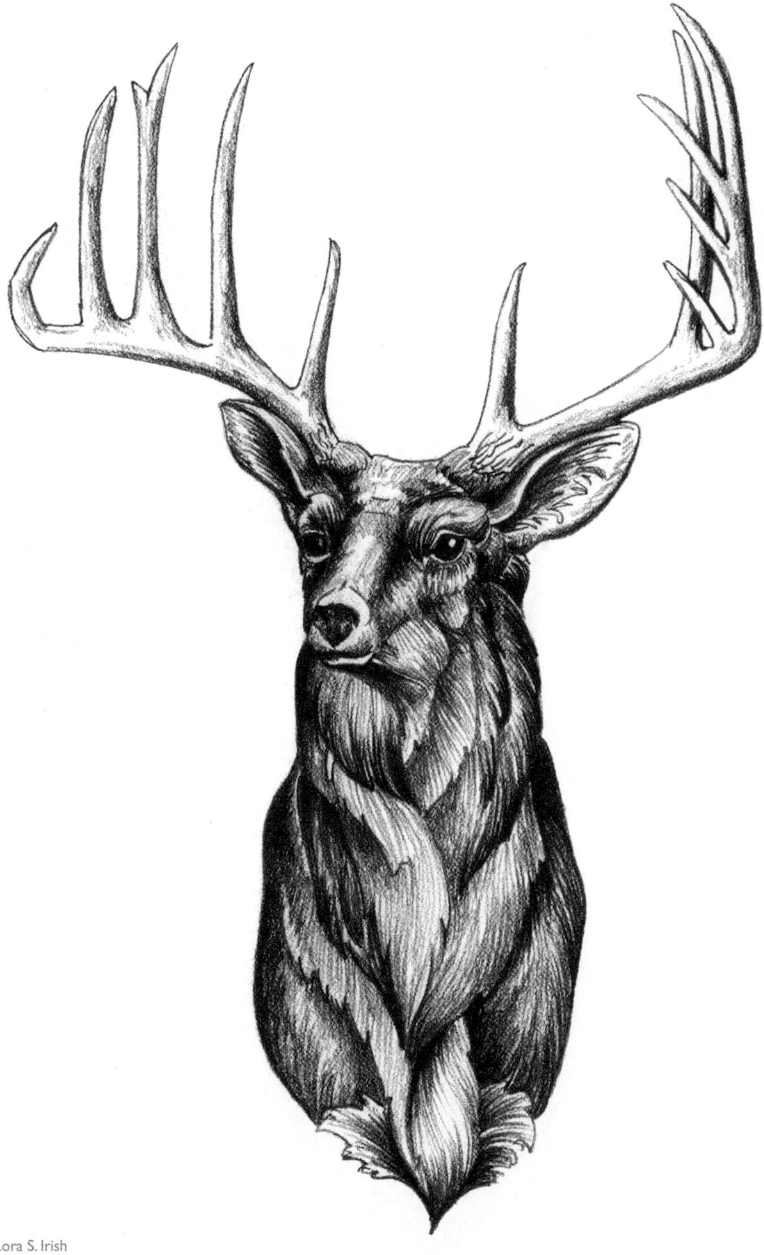

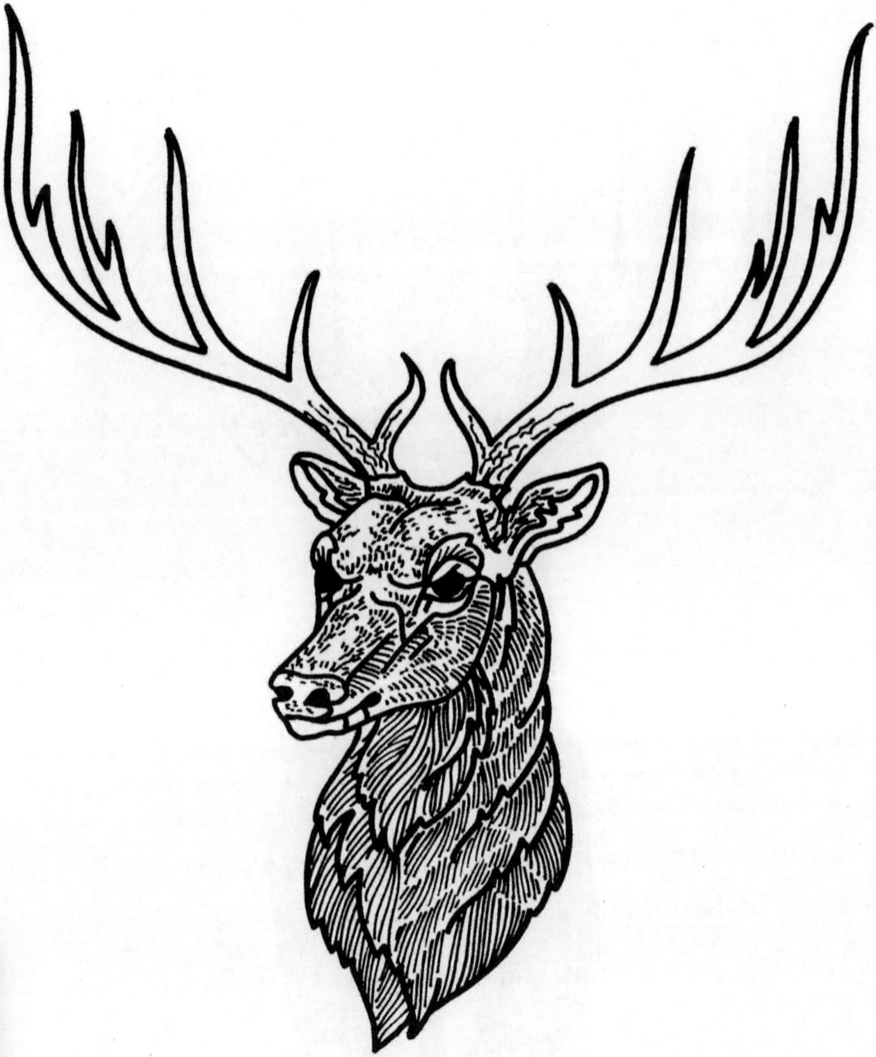

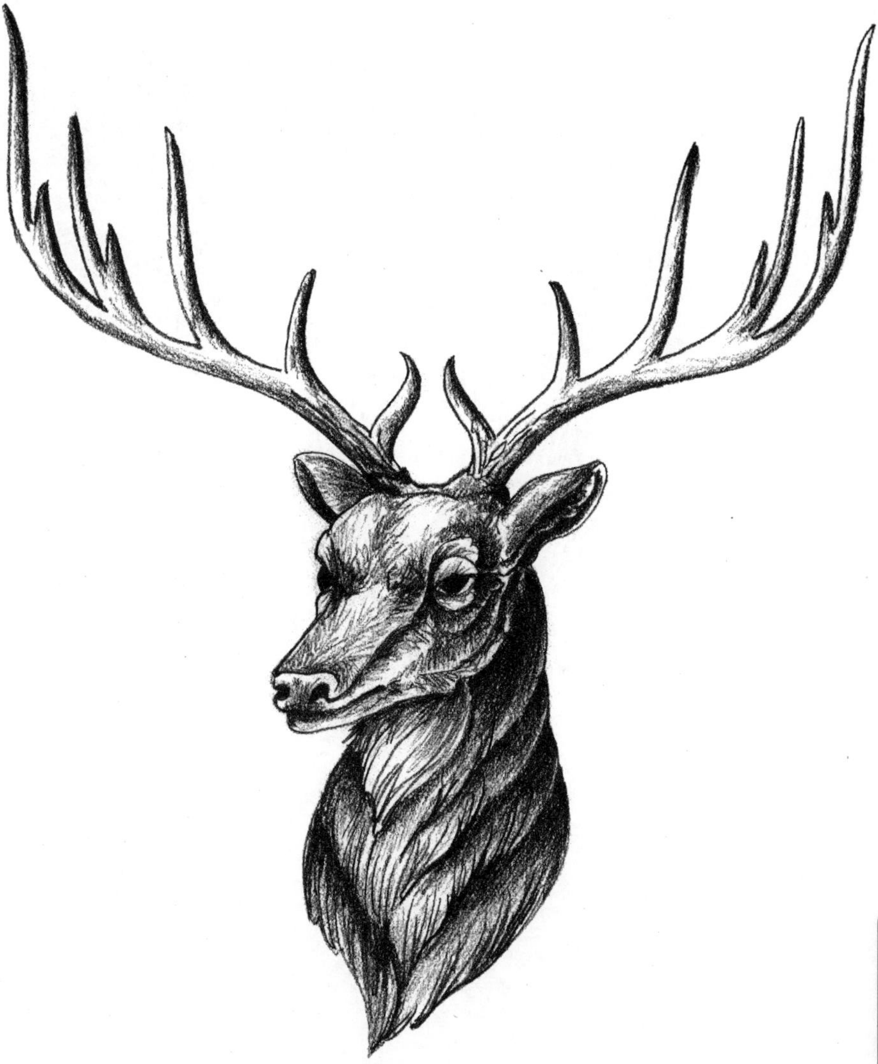

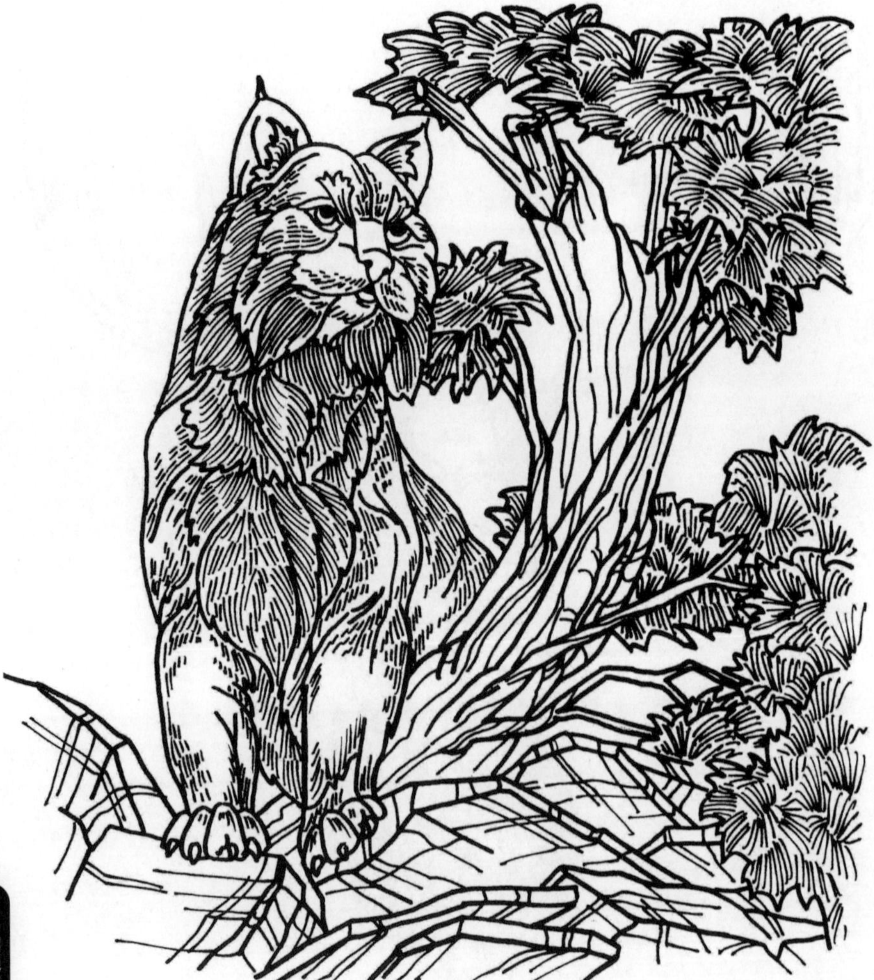

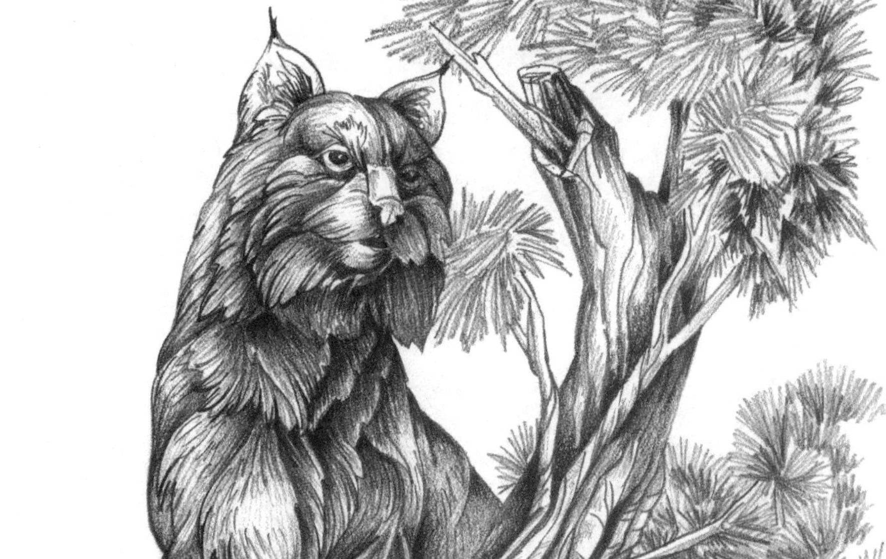

Wildlife

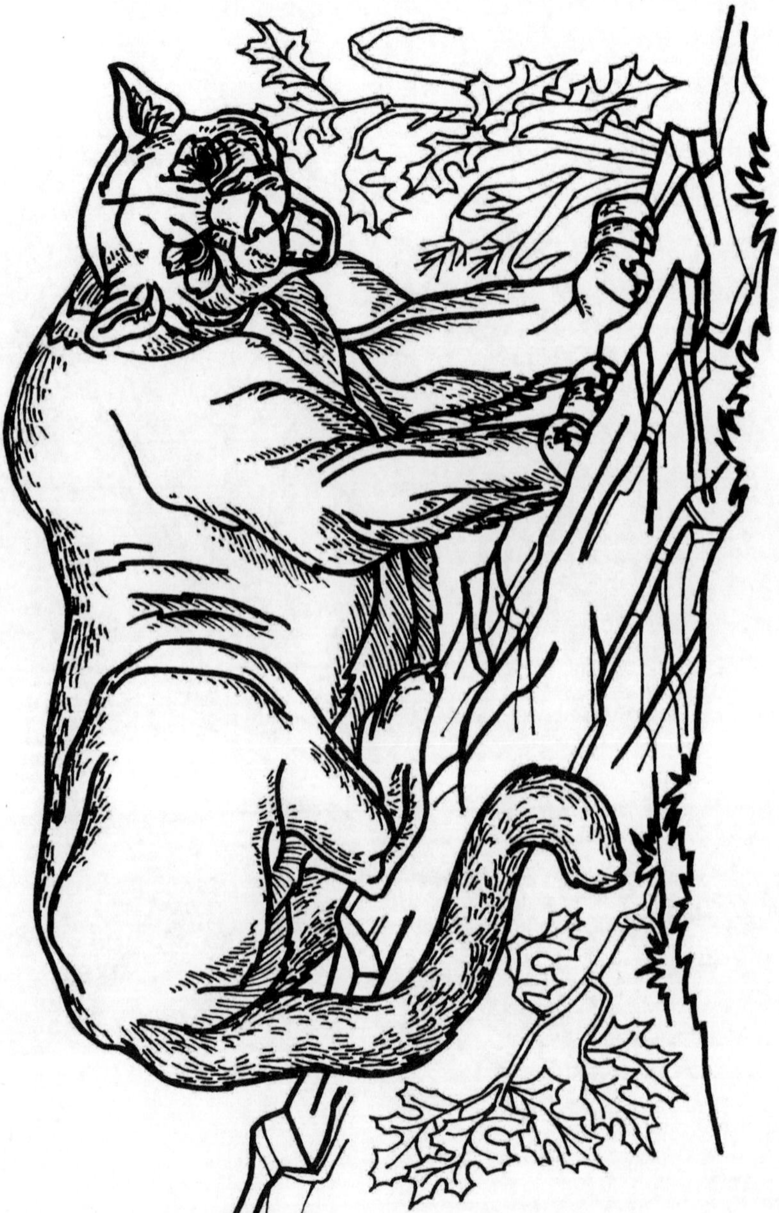

© Lora S. Irish

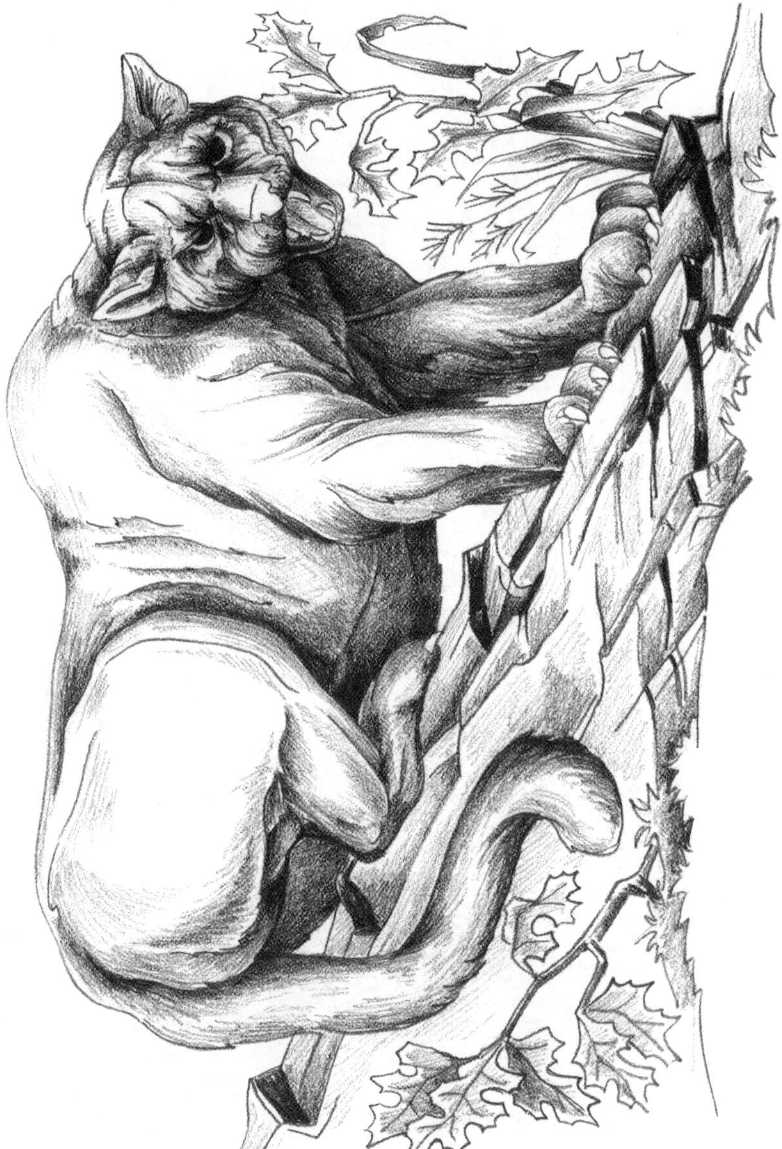

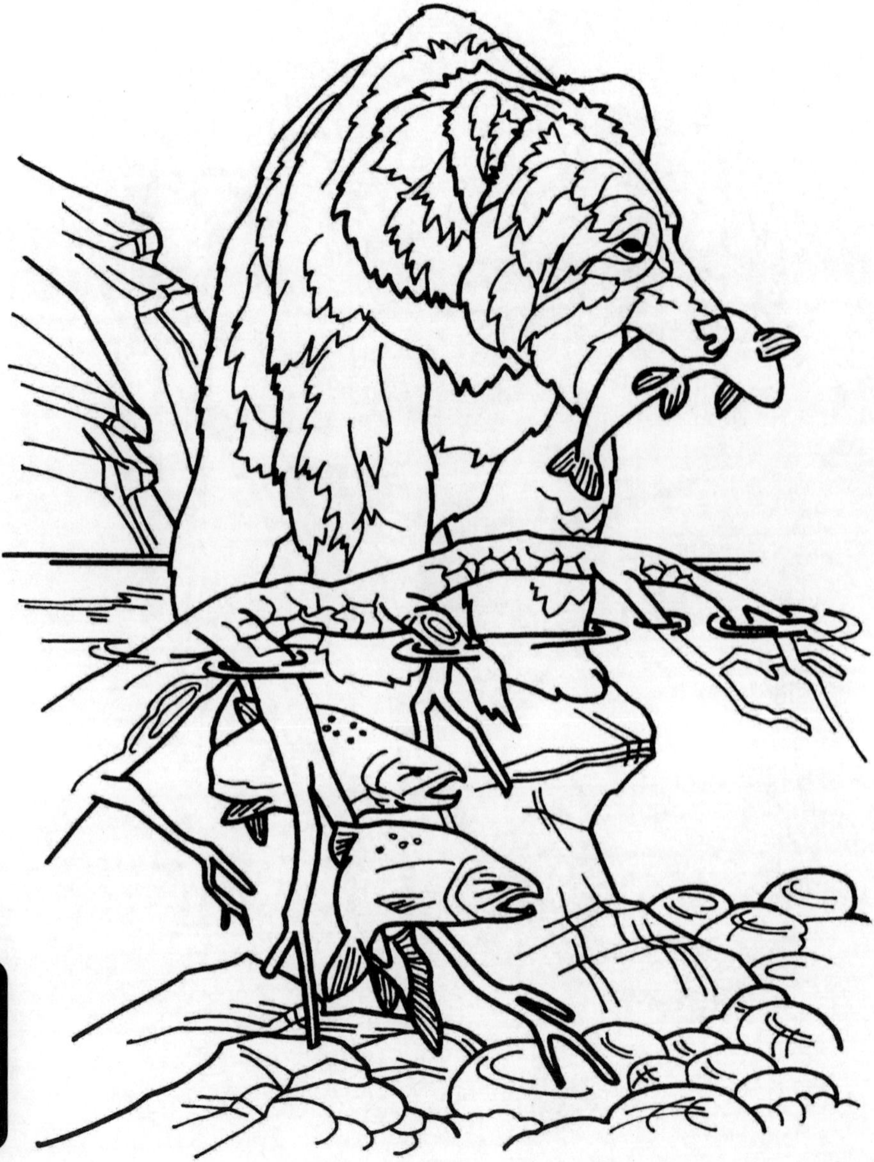

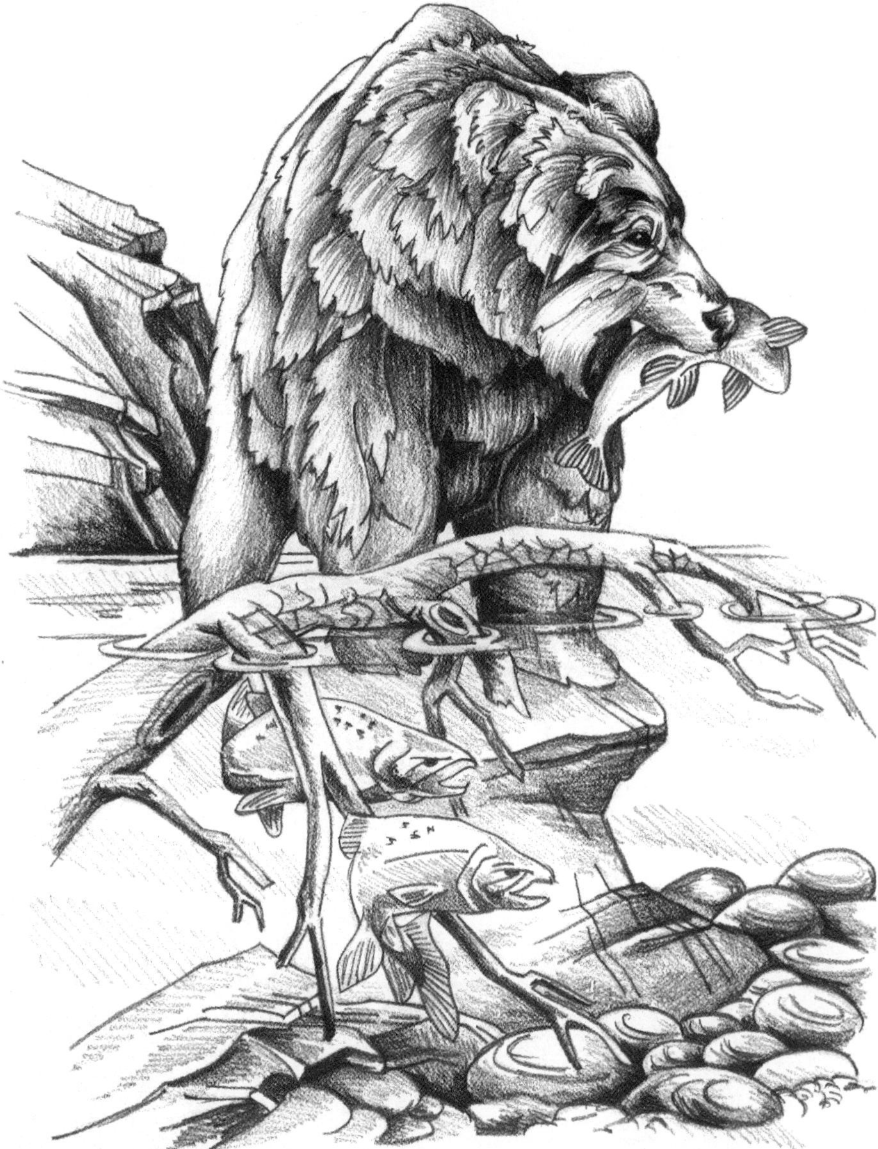

Wildlife

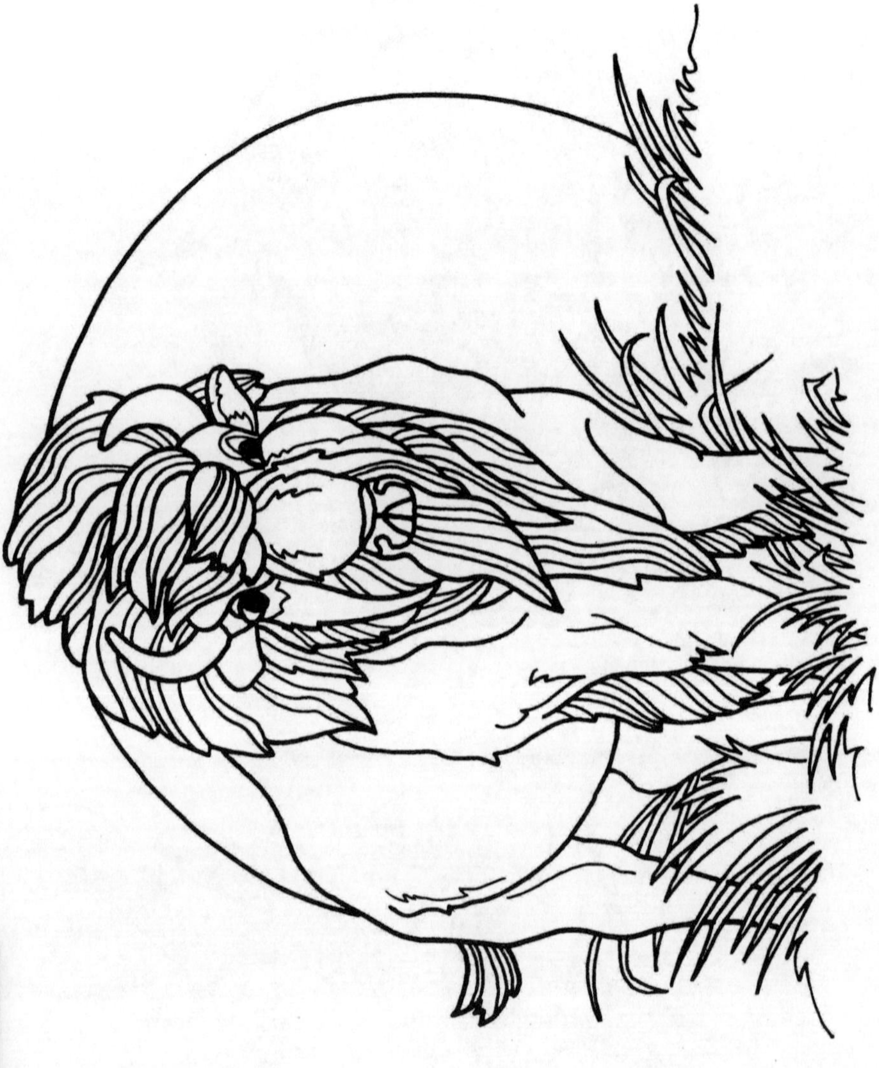

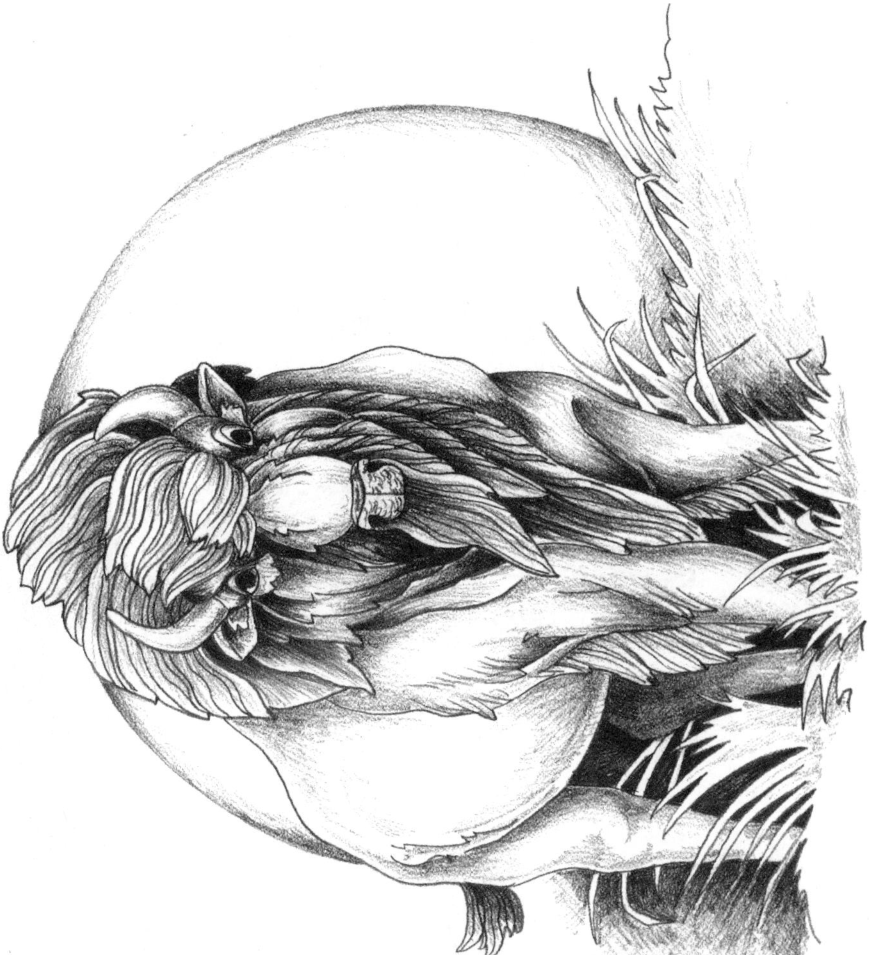

Wildlife

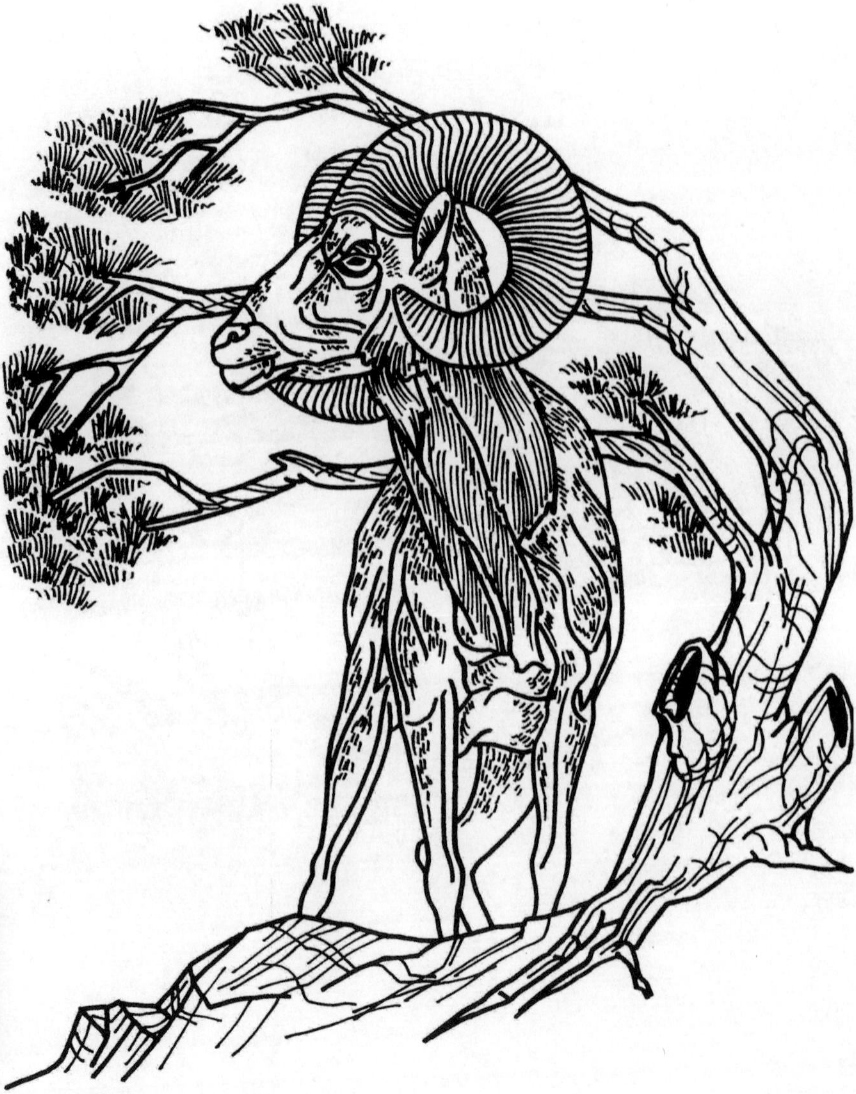

© Lora S. Irish

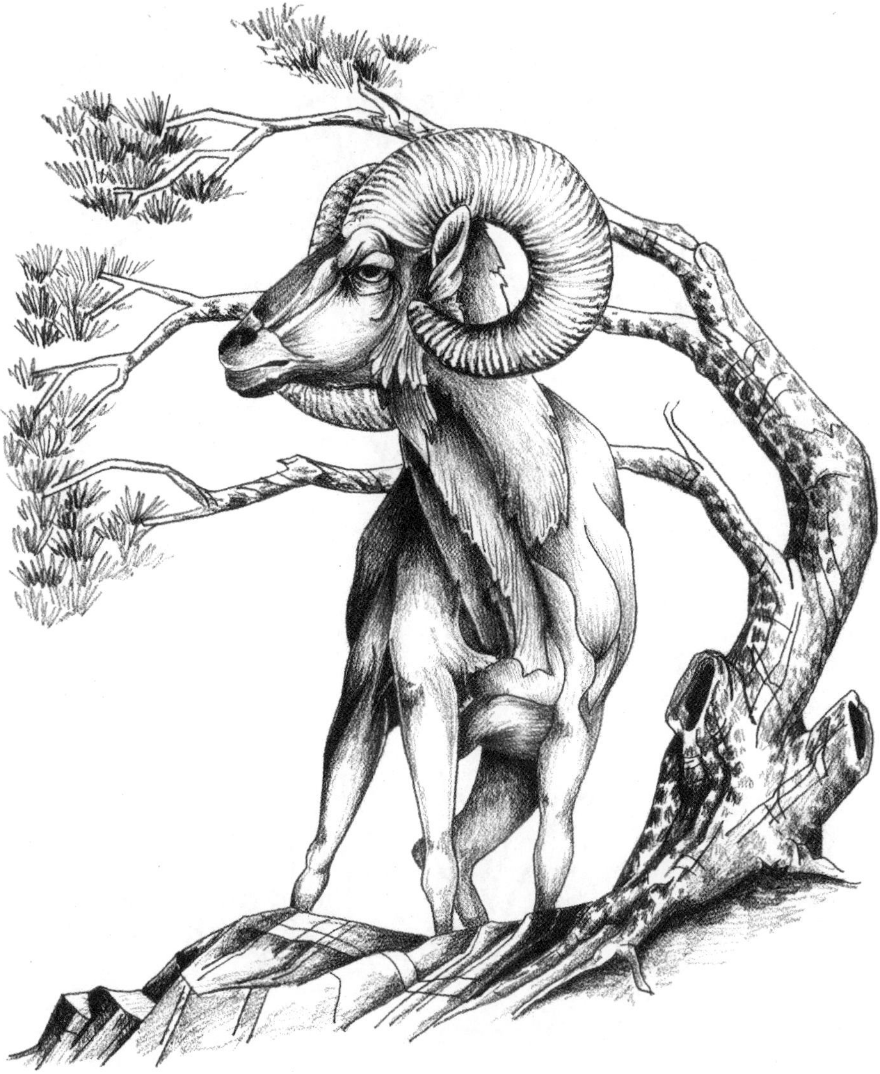

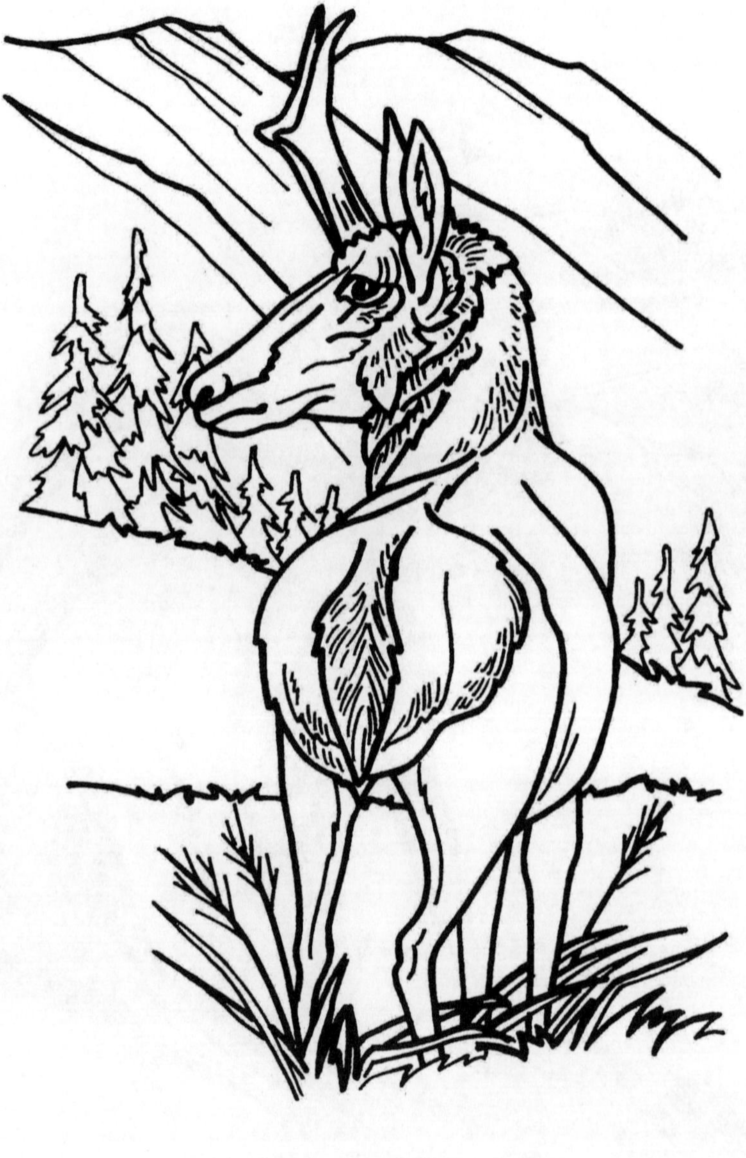

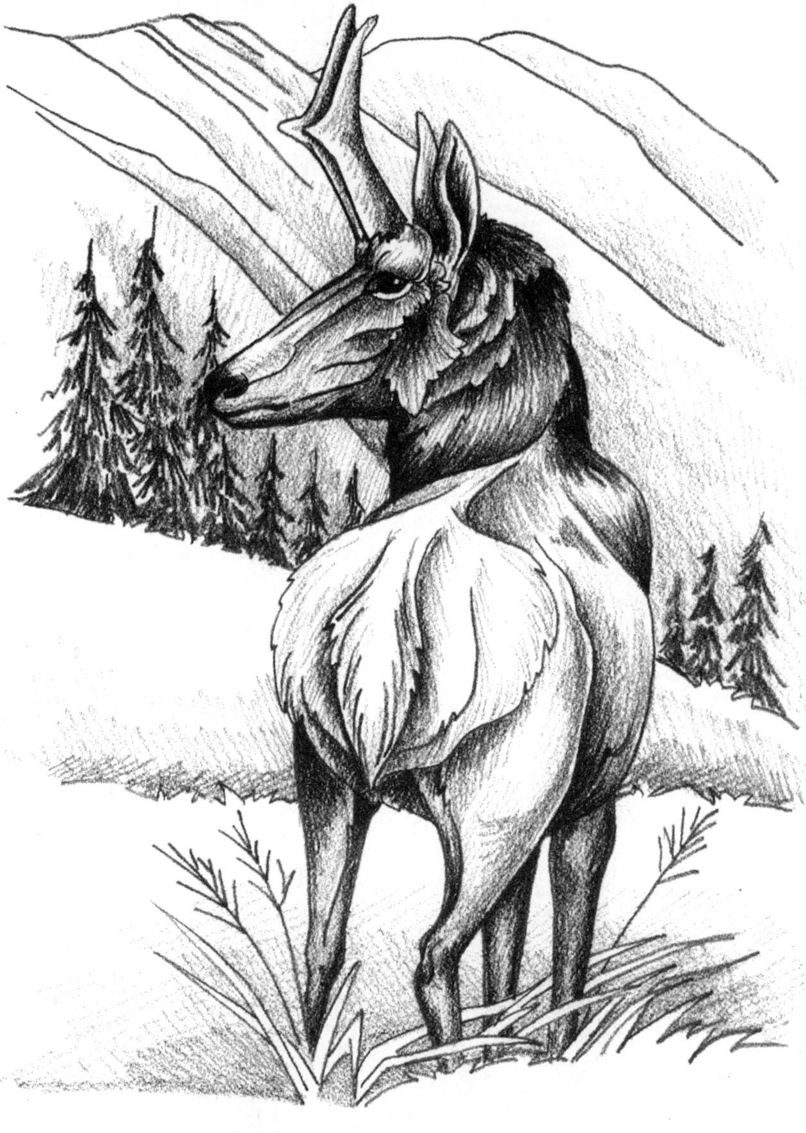

© Lora S. Irish

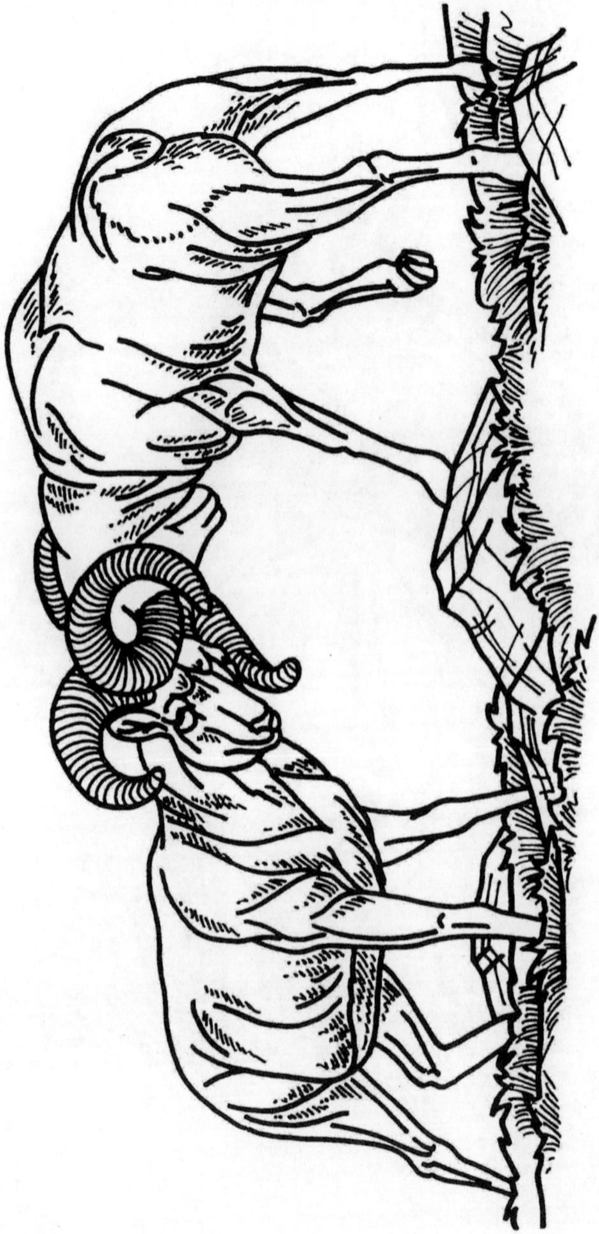

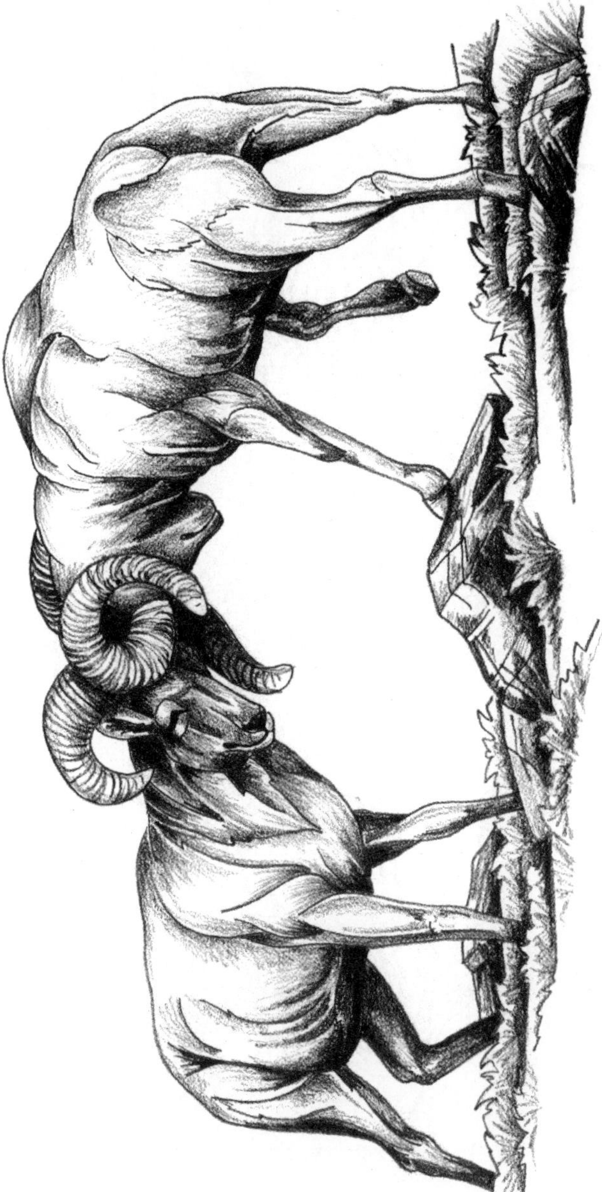

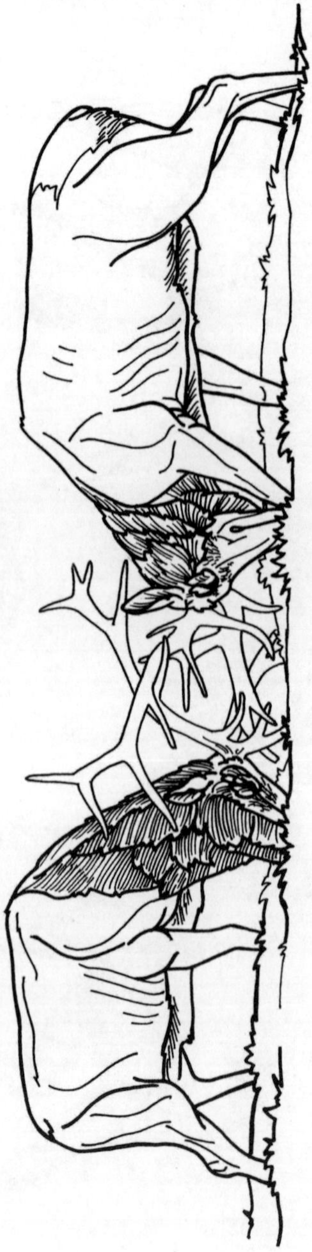

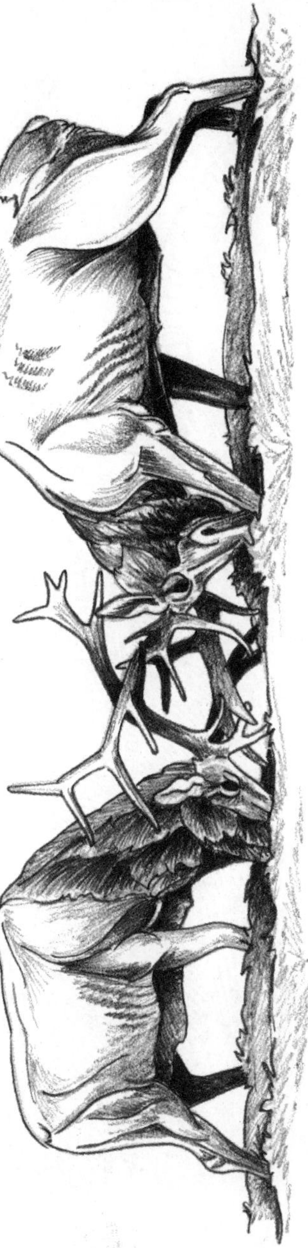

© Lora S. Irish

Wildlife

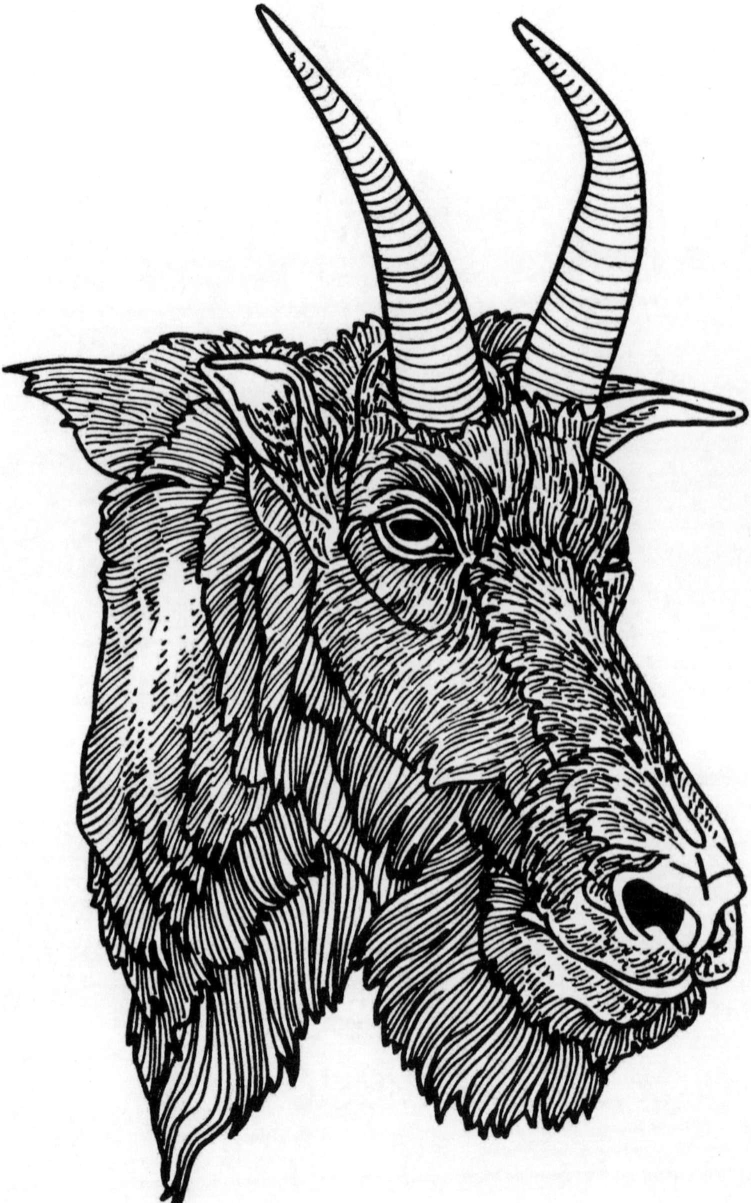

© Lora S. Irish

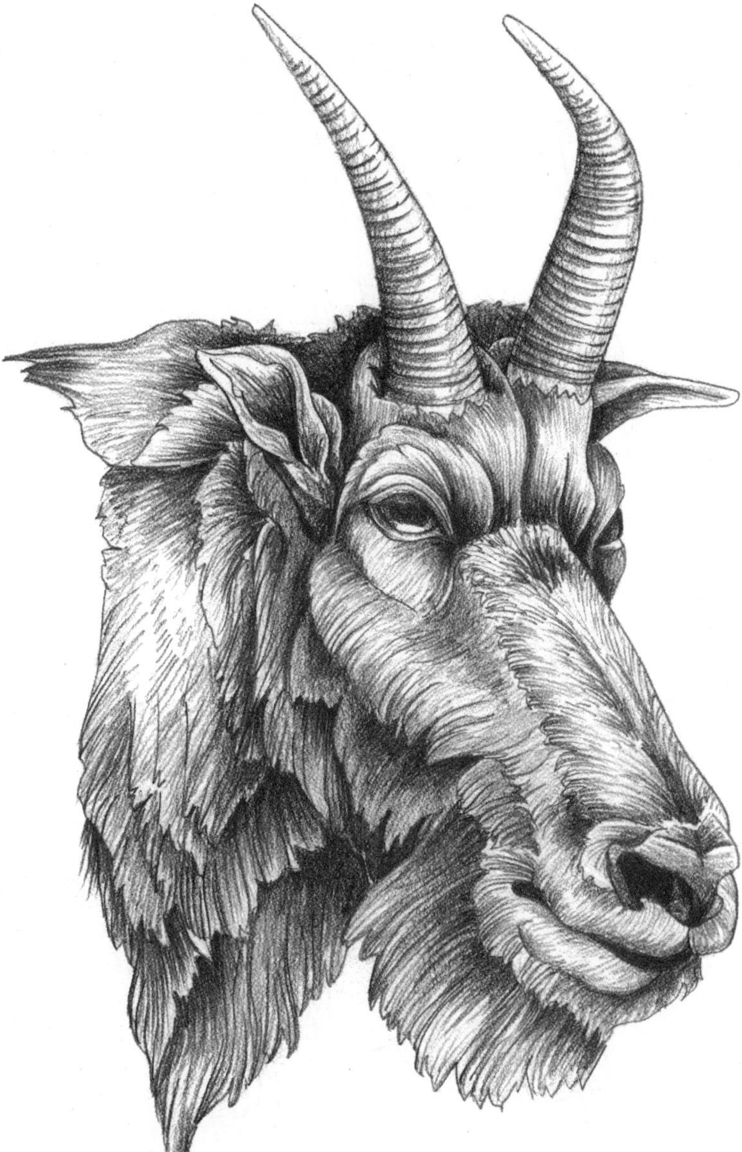

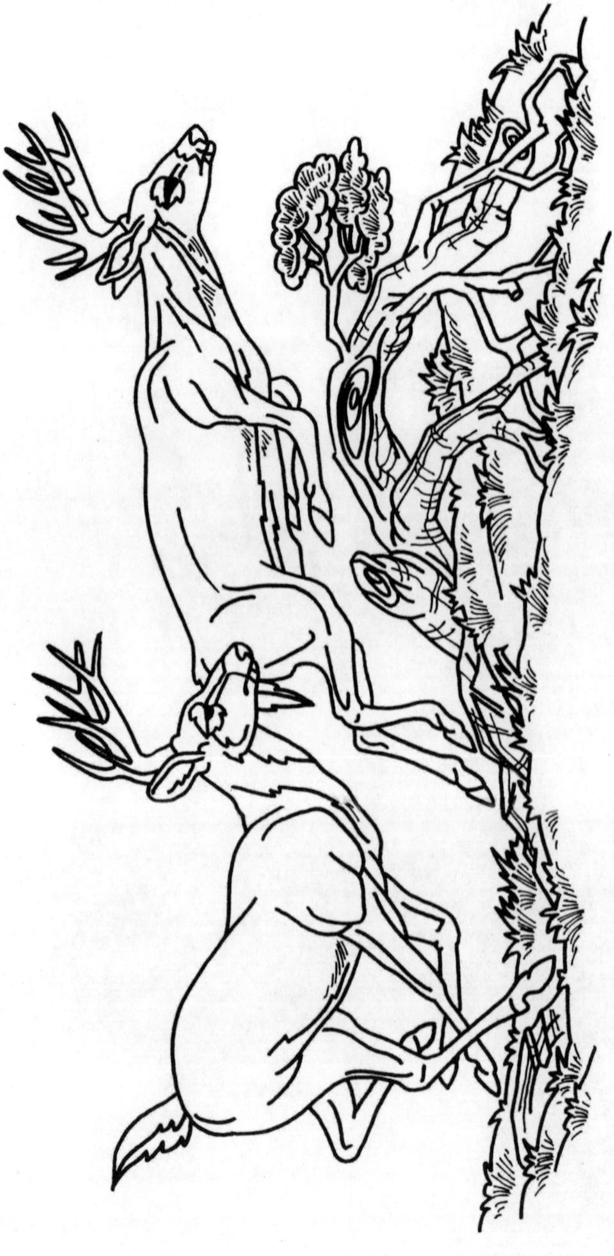

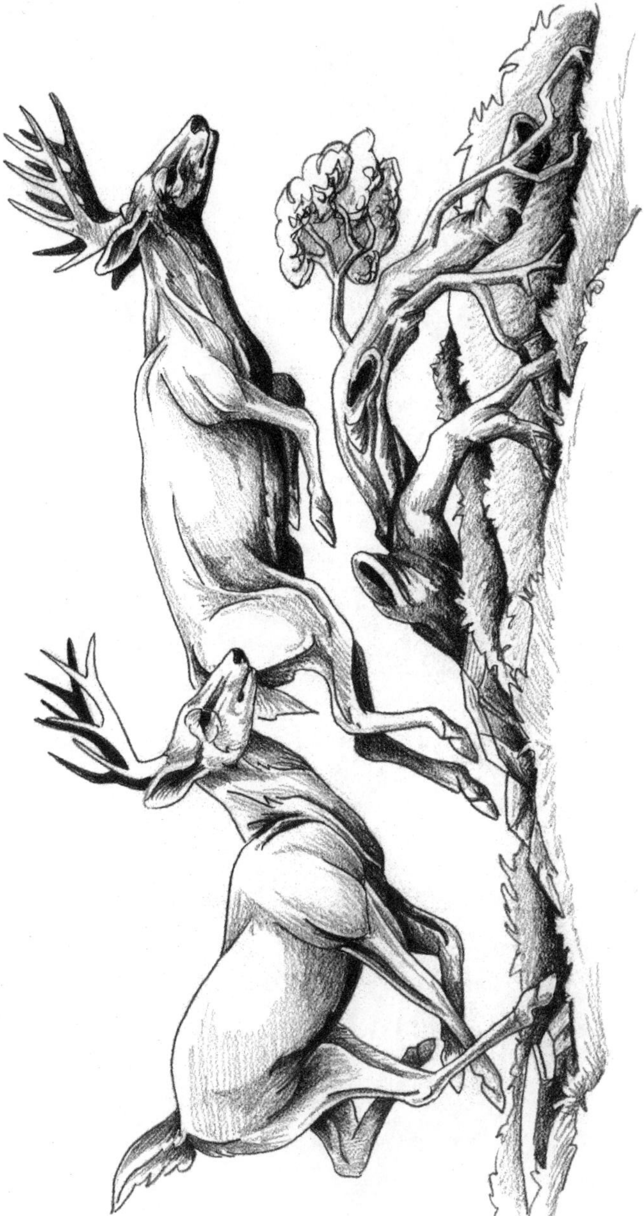

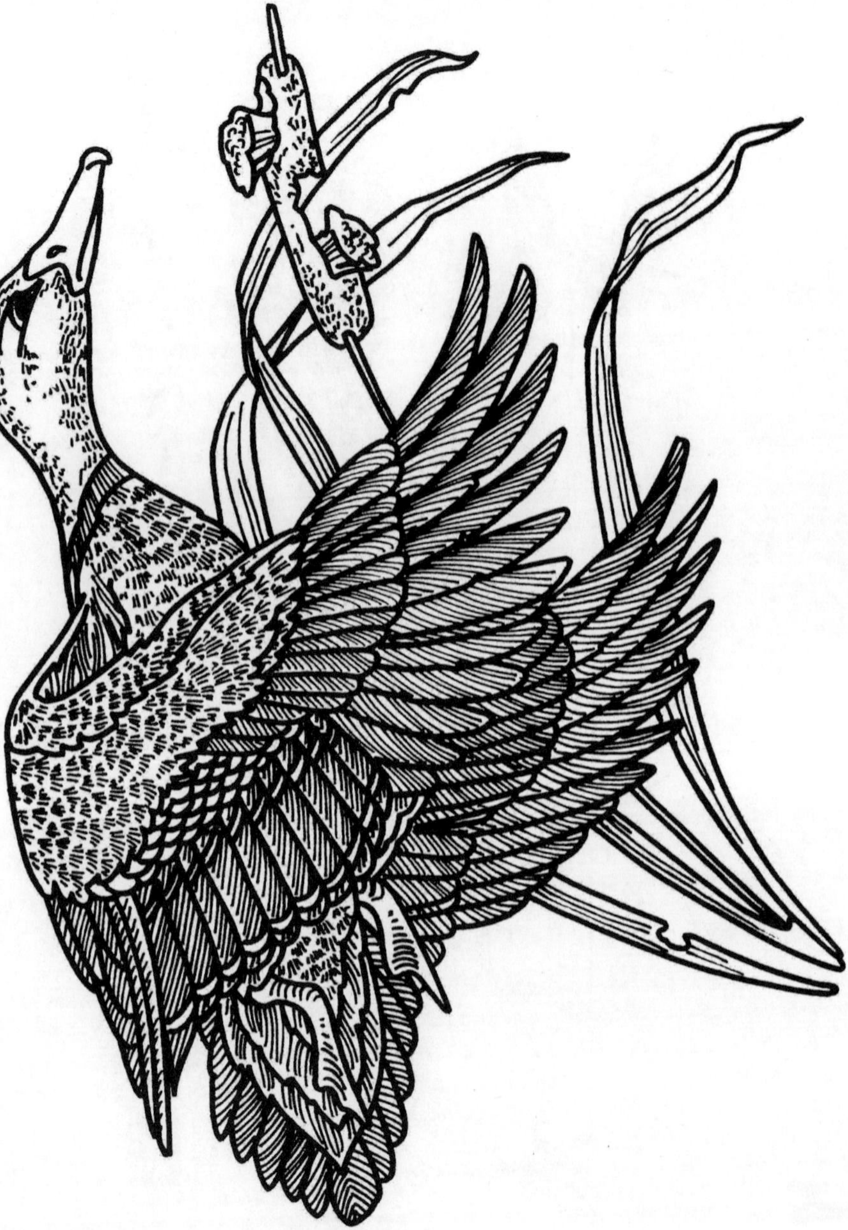

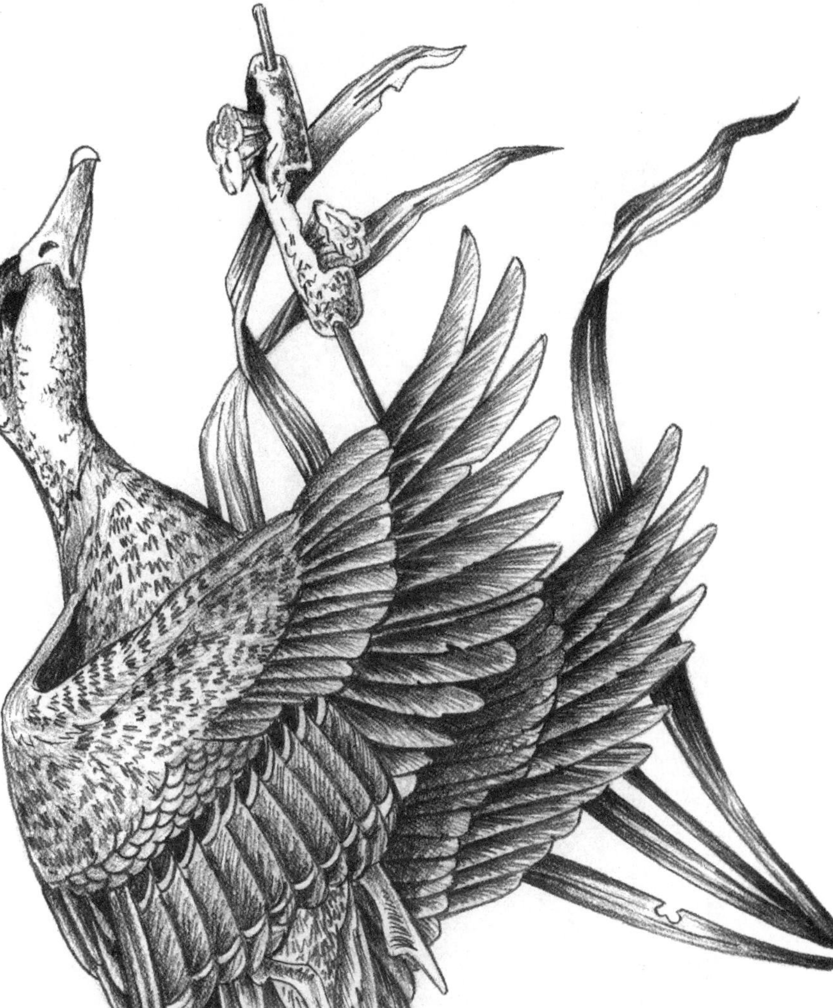

Wildlife

© Lora S. Irish

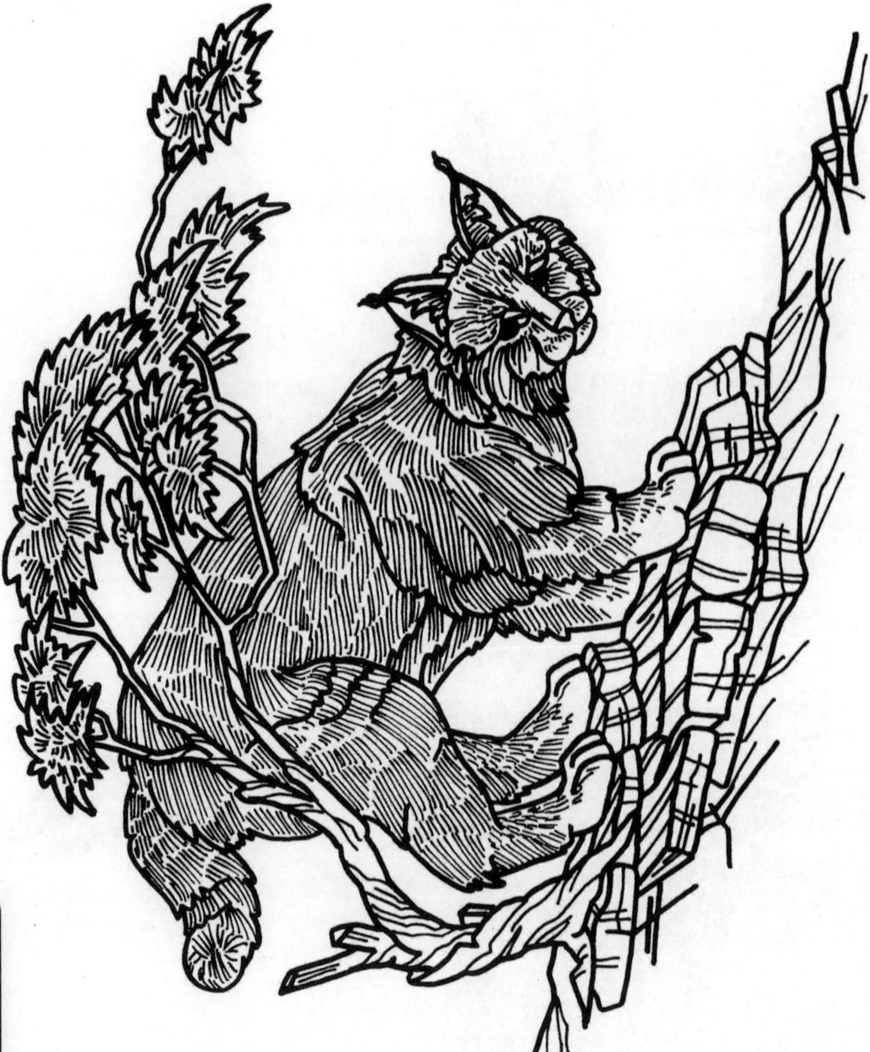

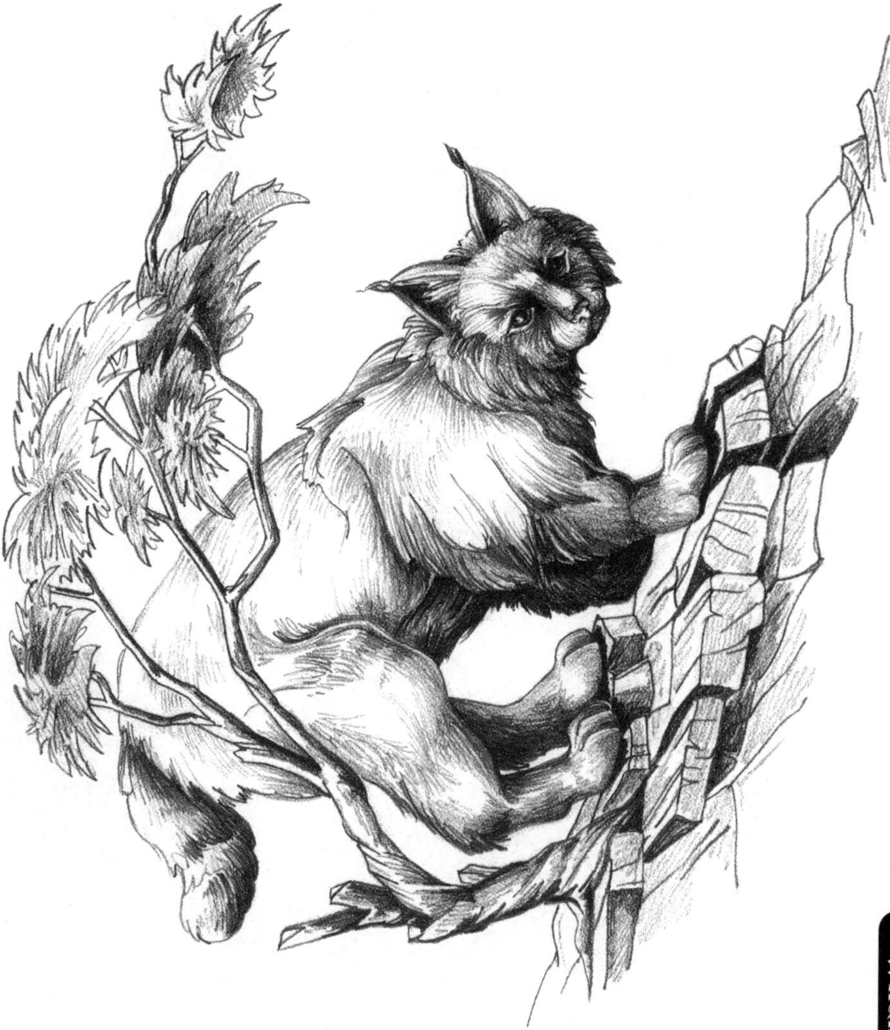

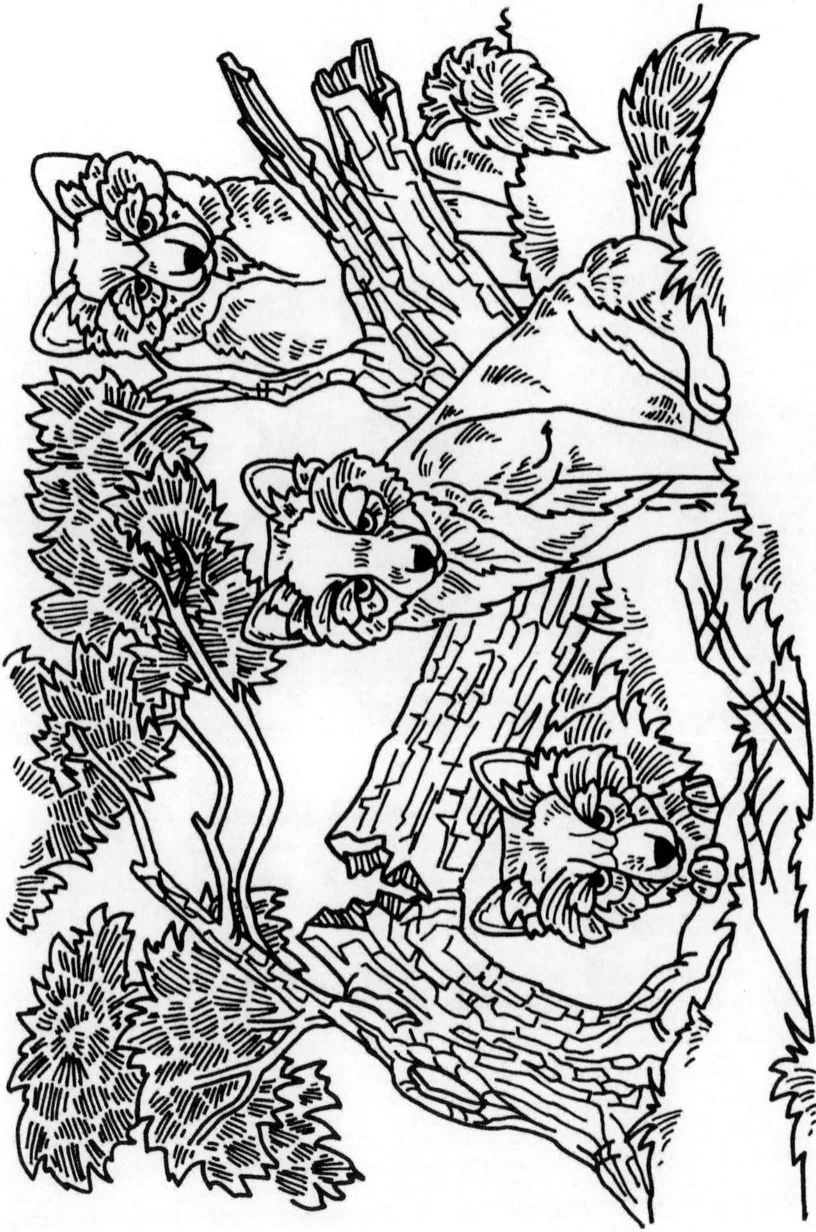

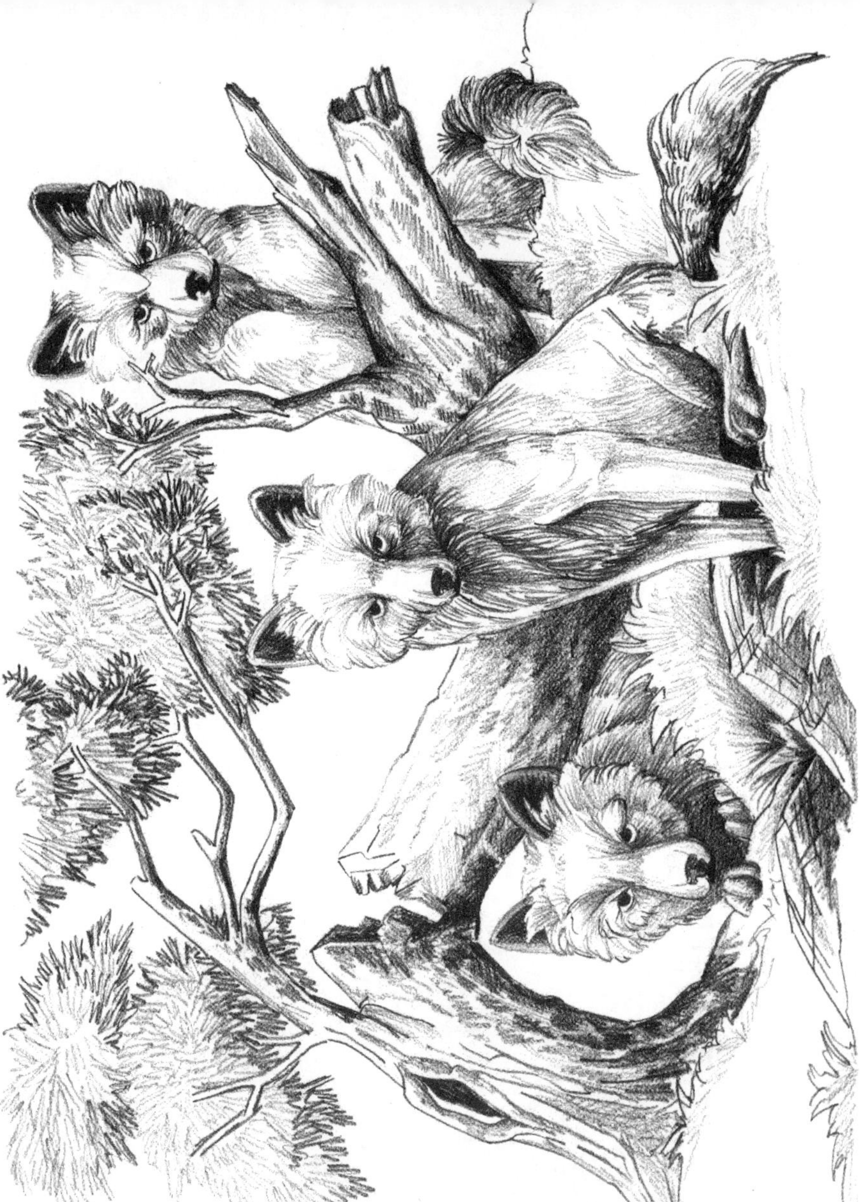

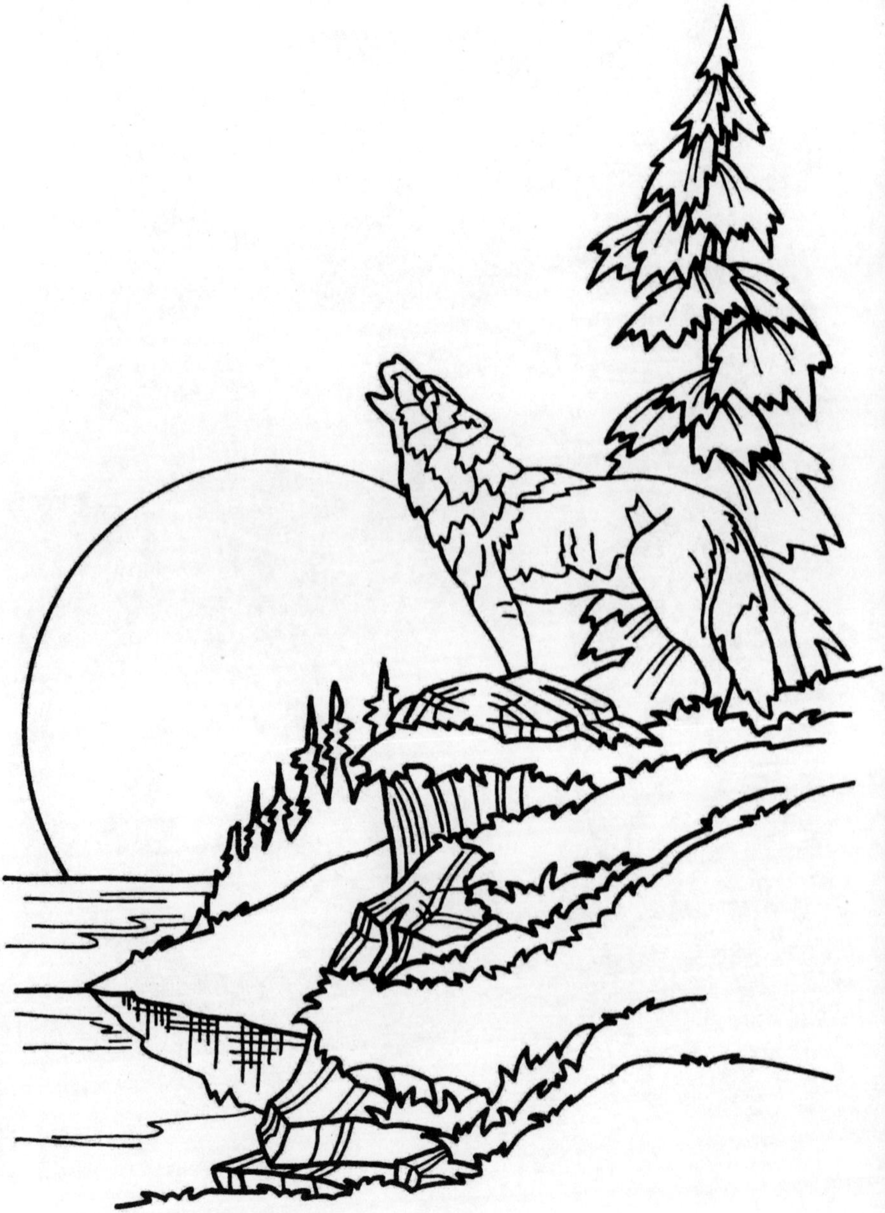

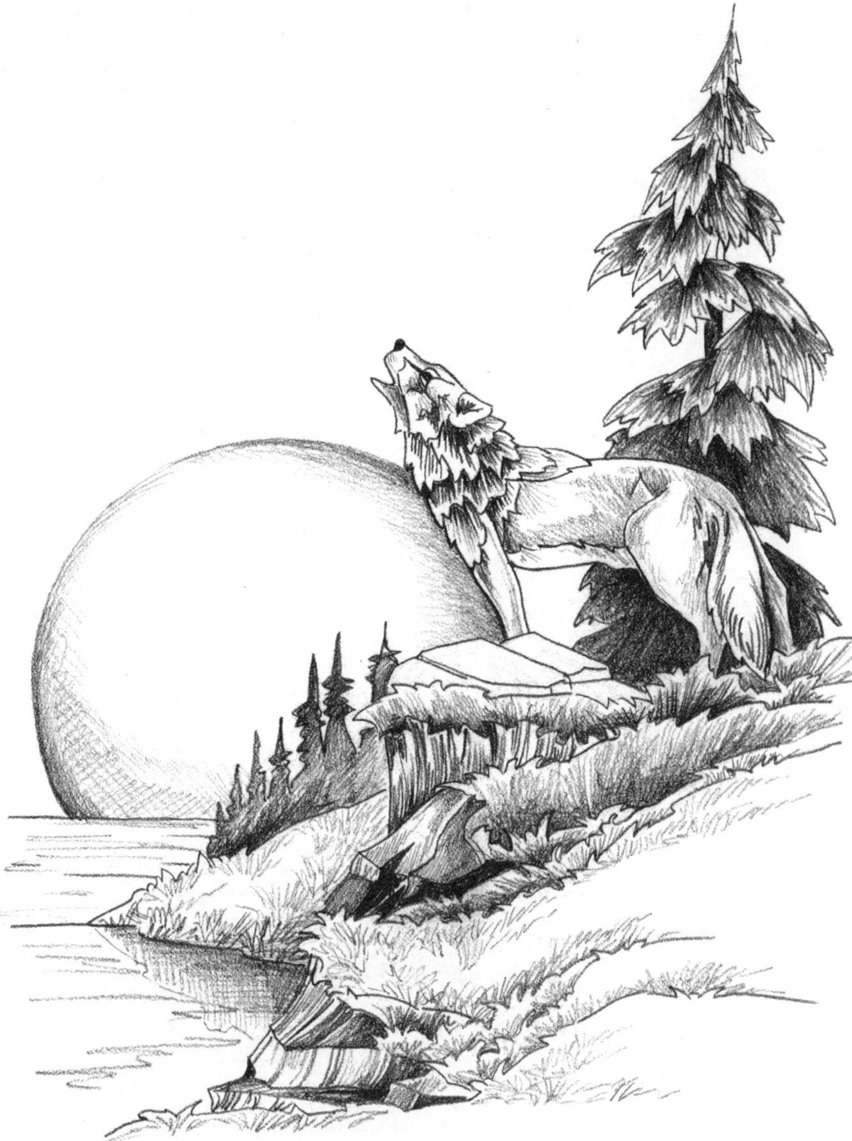

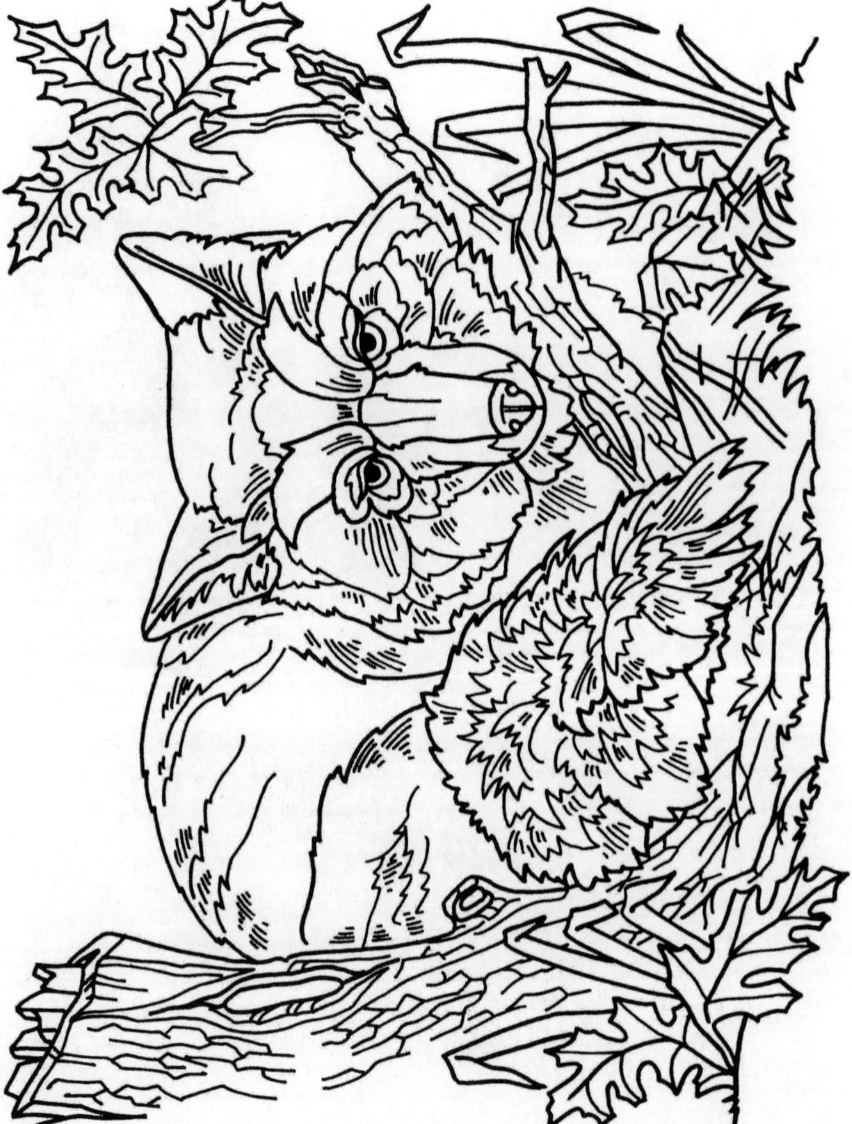

© Lora S. Irish

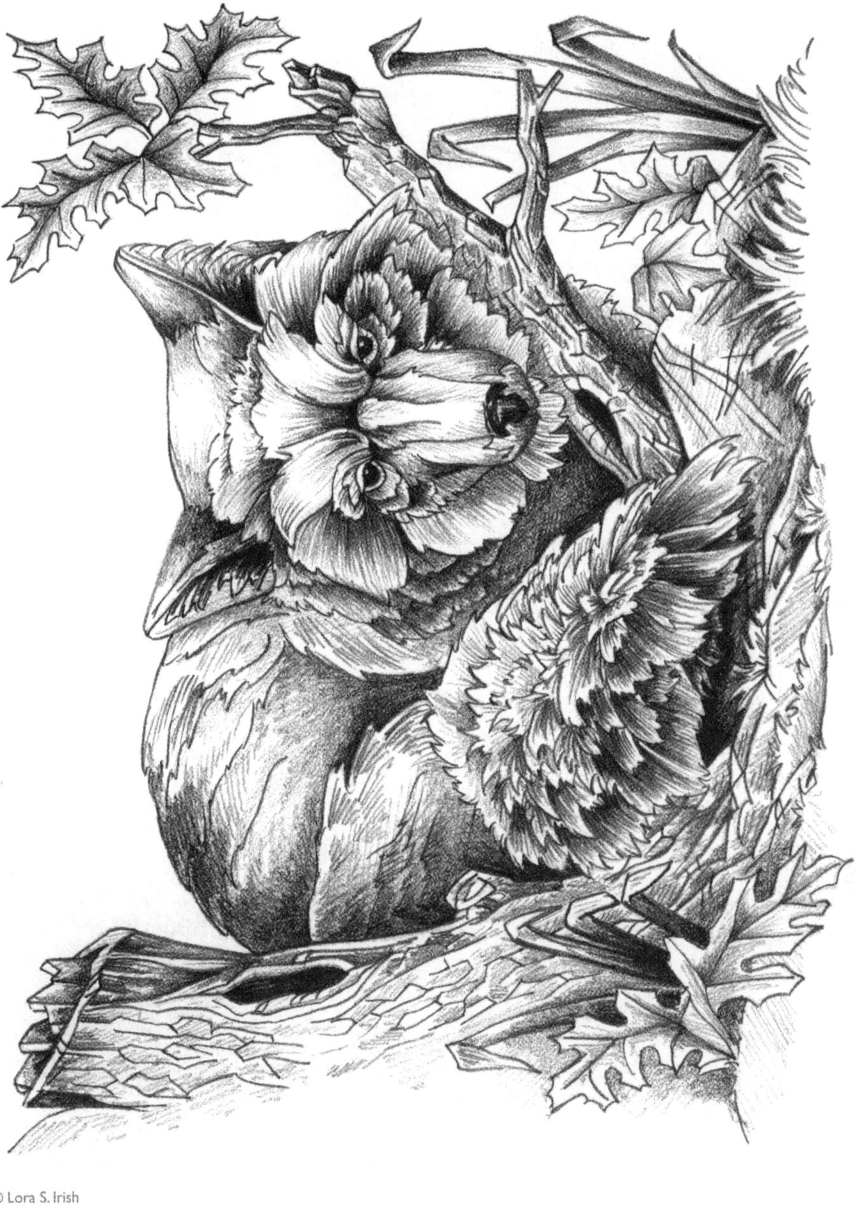

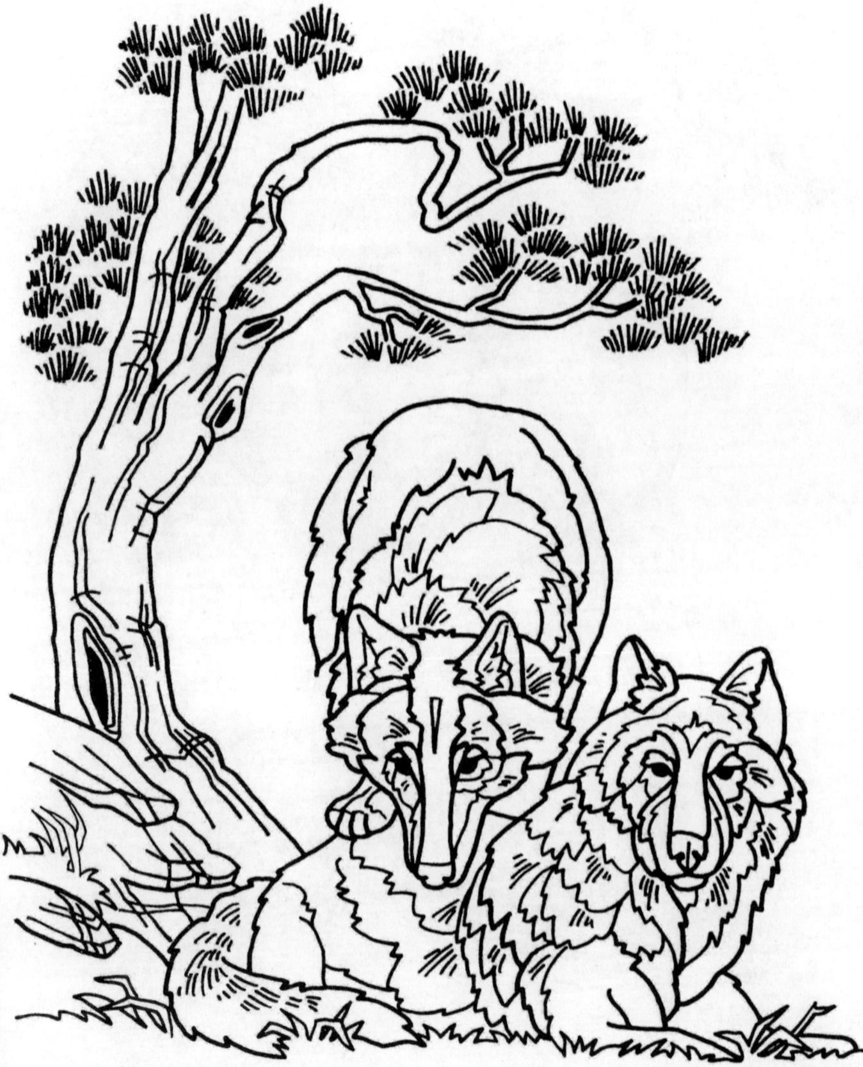

© Lora S. Irish

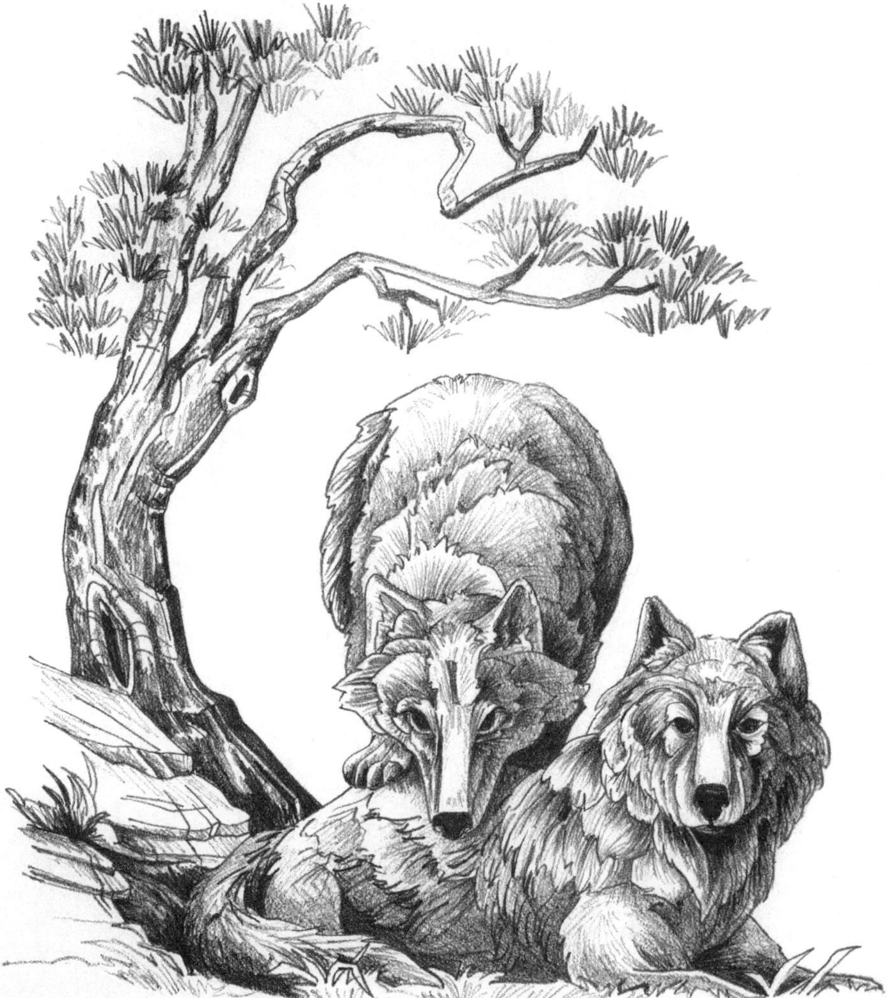

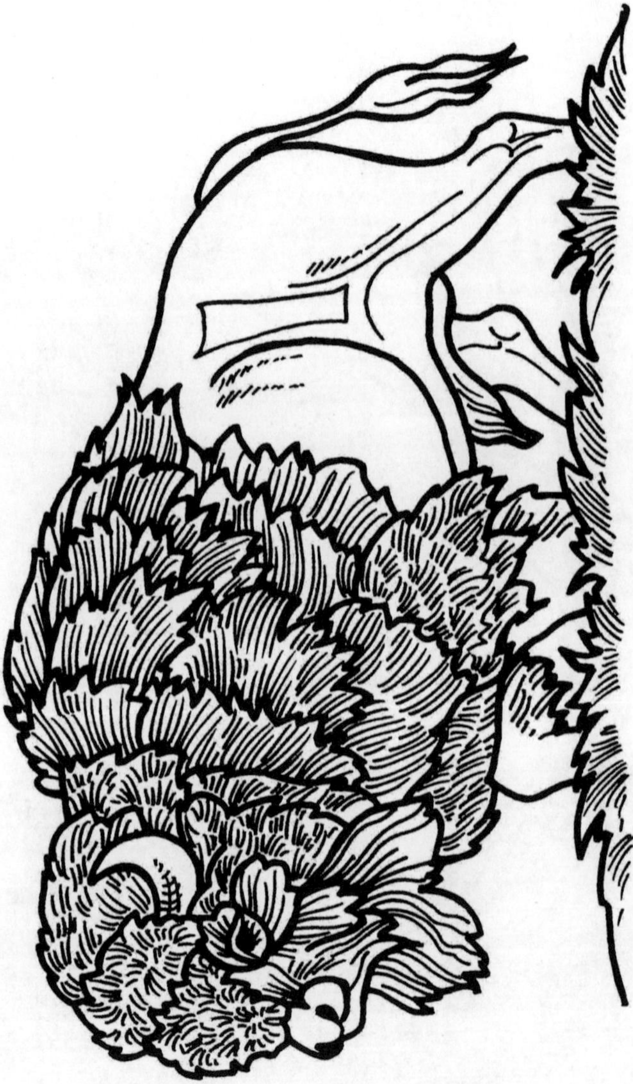

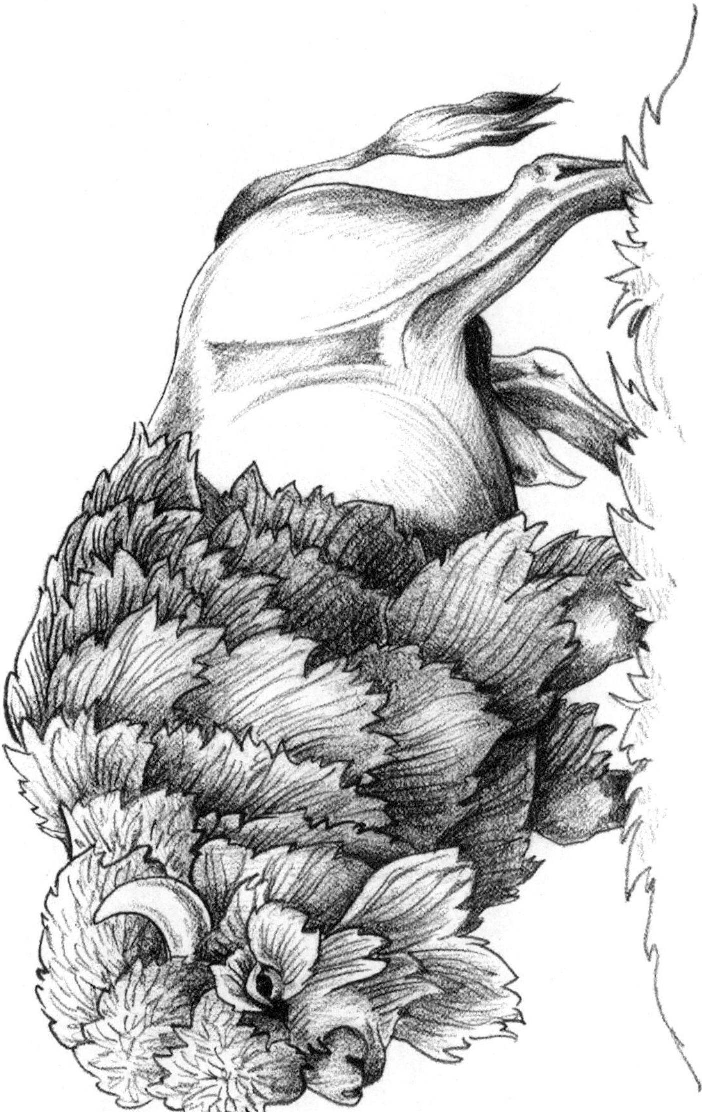

Wildlife

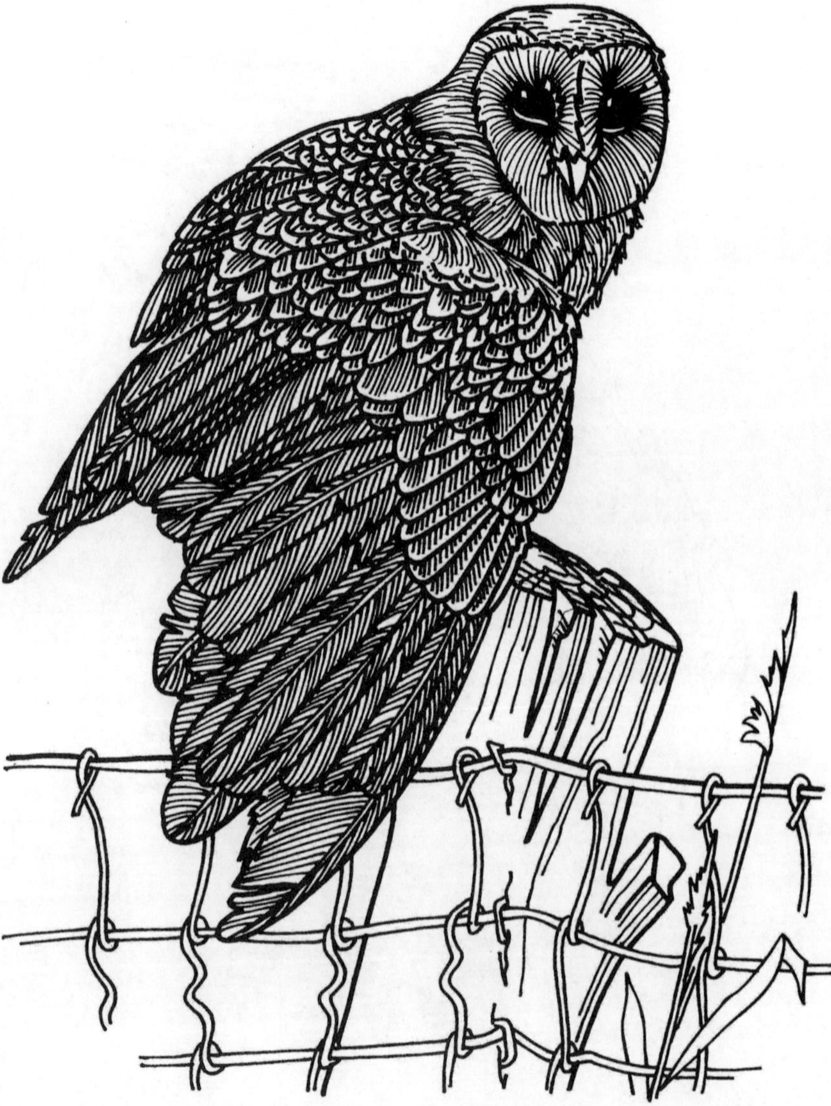

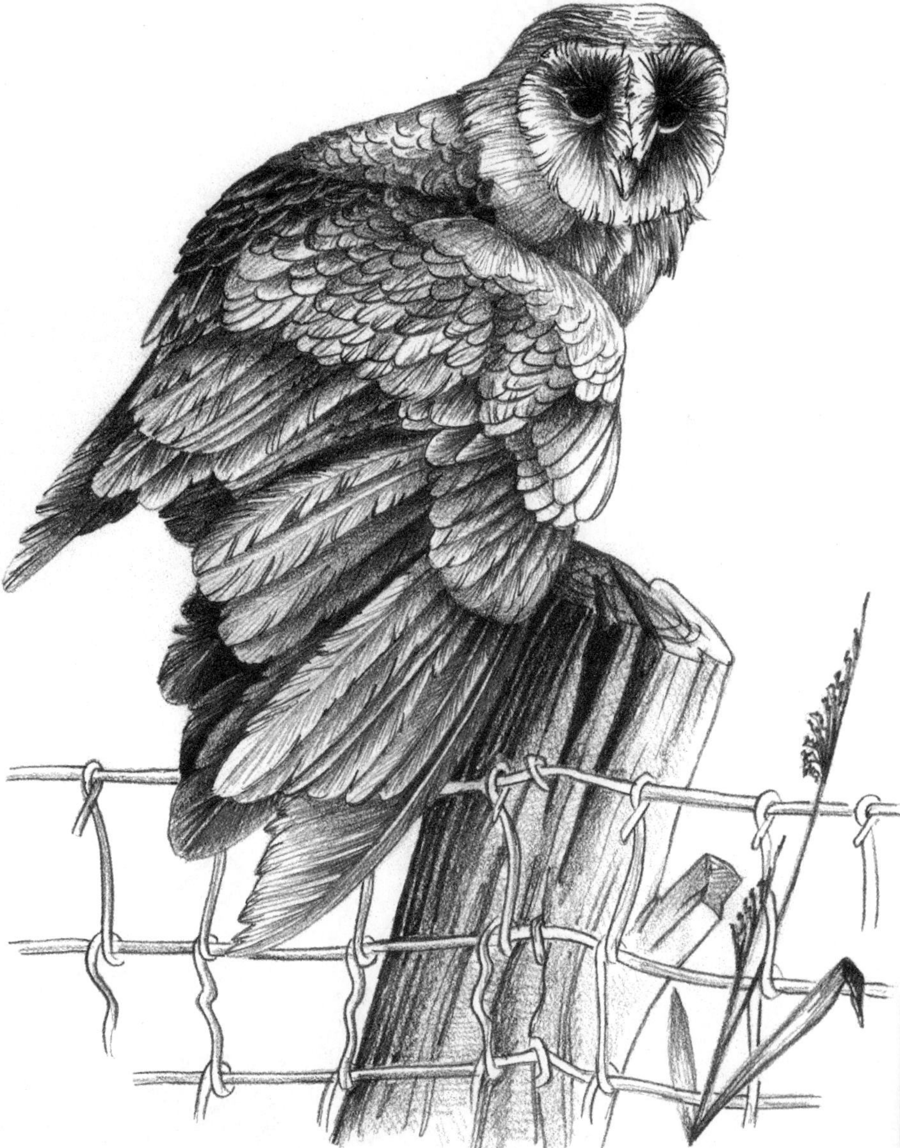

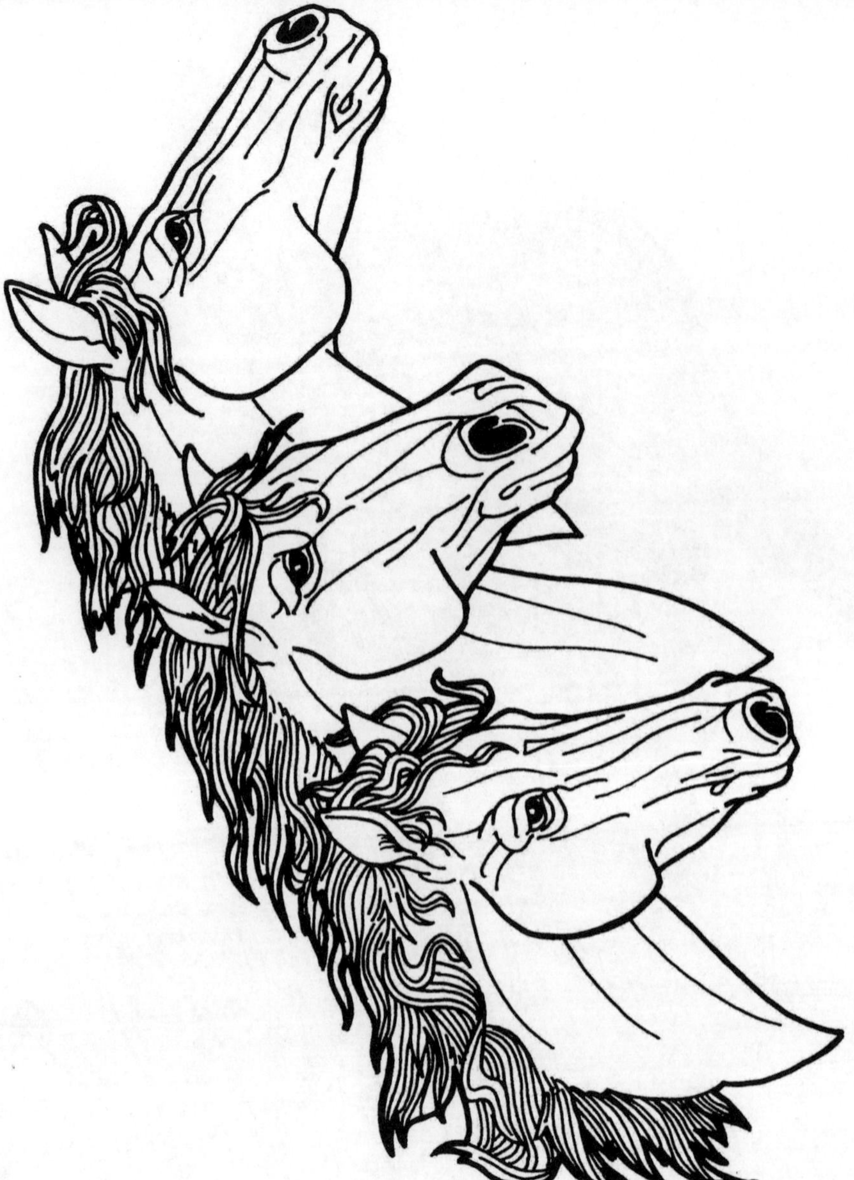

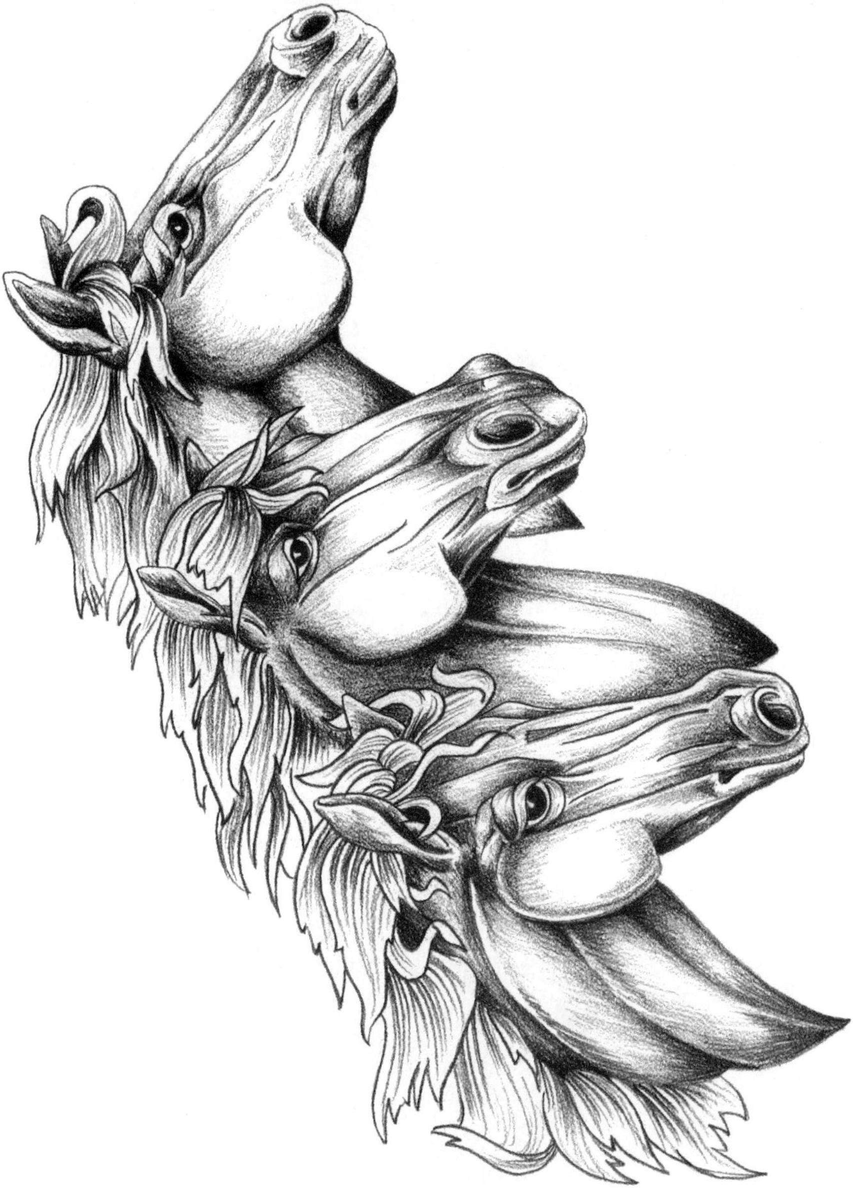

Wildlife

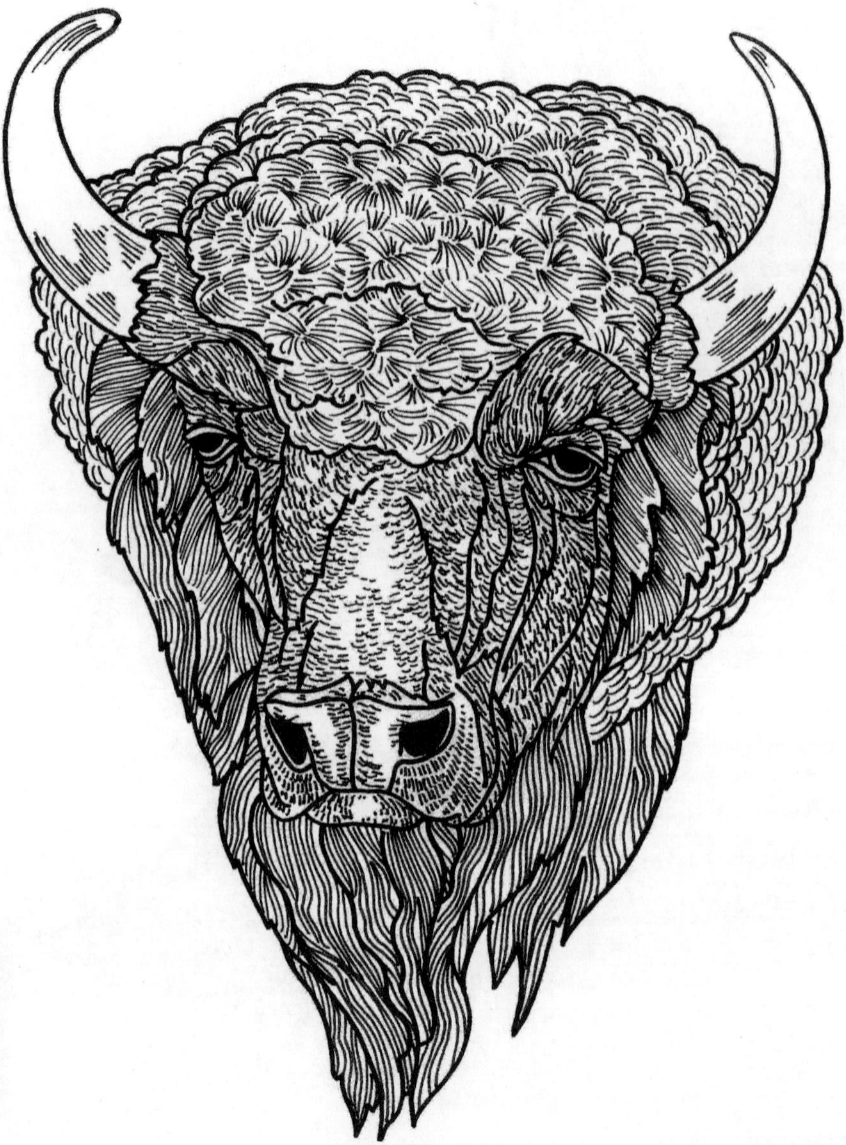

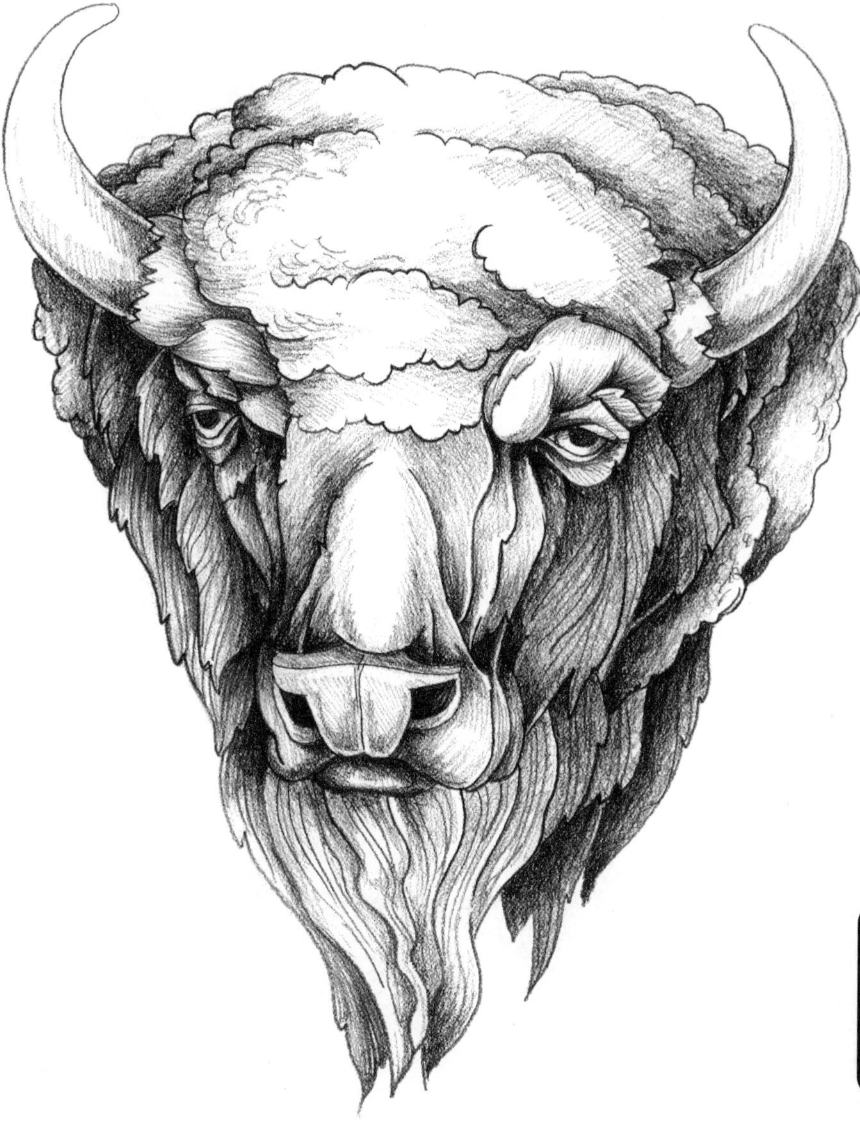

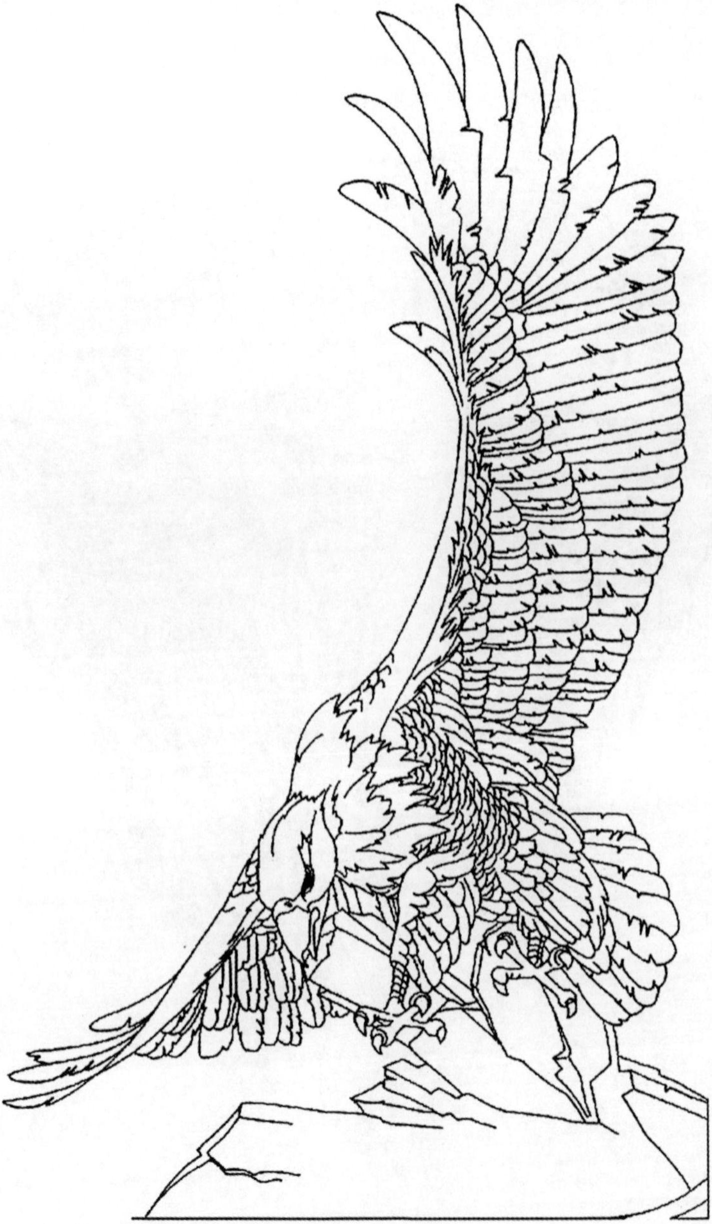

© Lora S. Irish

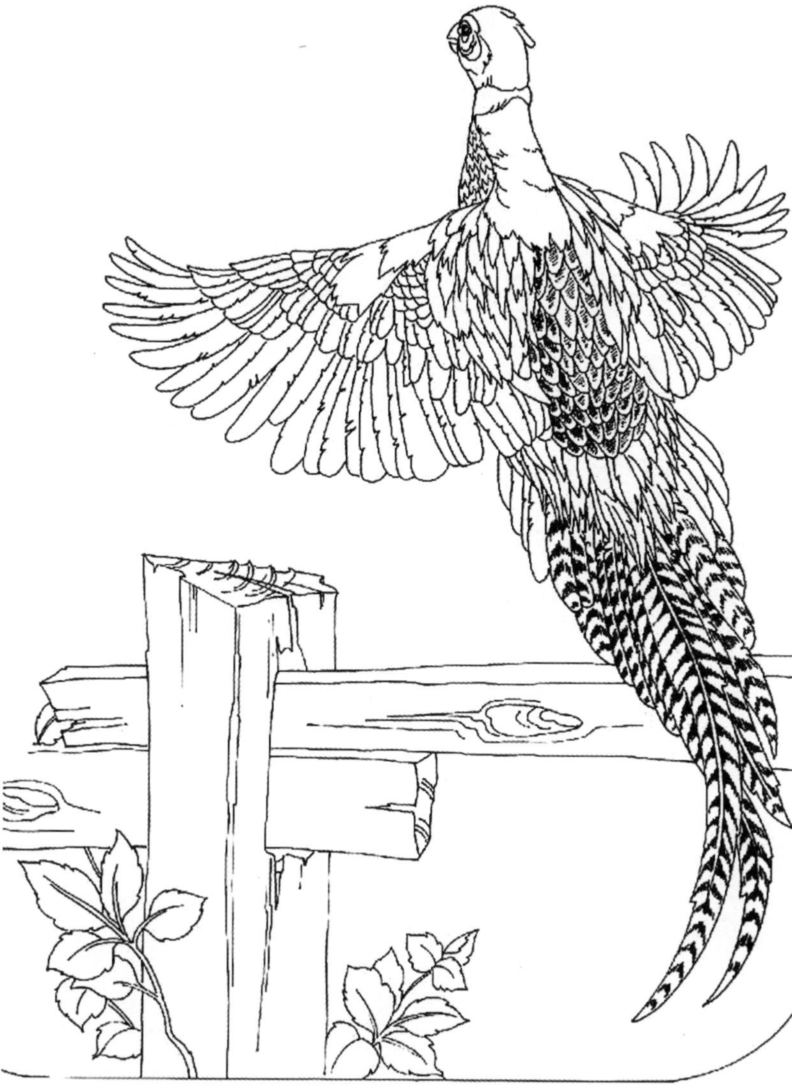

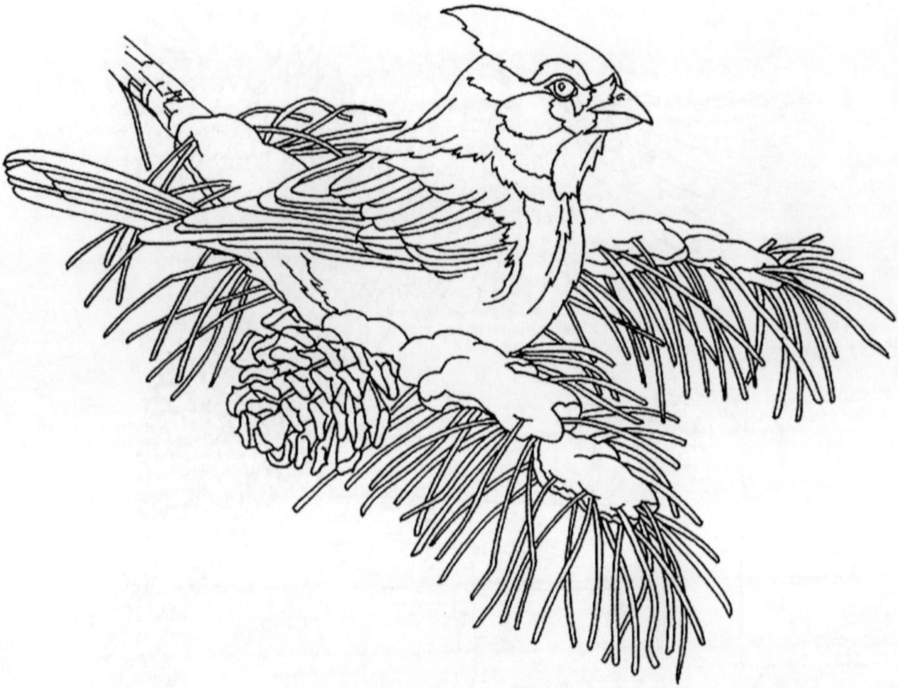

Wildlife

© Lora S. Irish

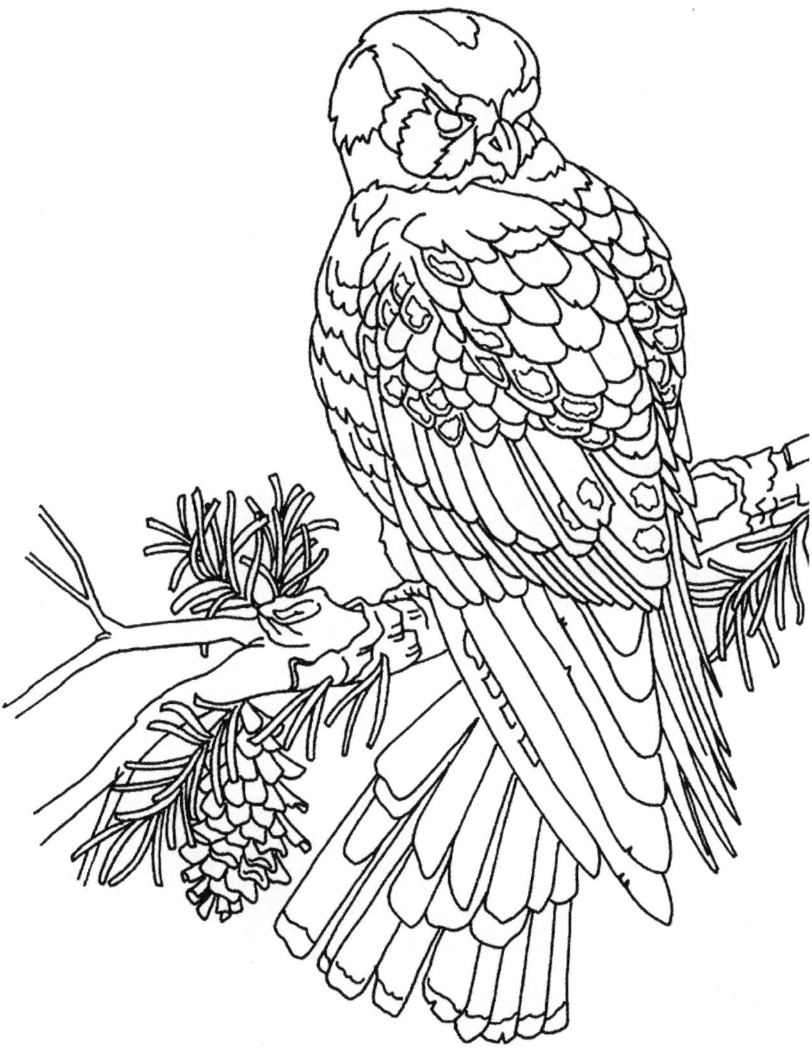

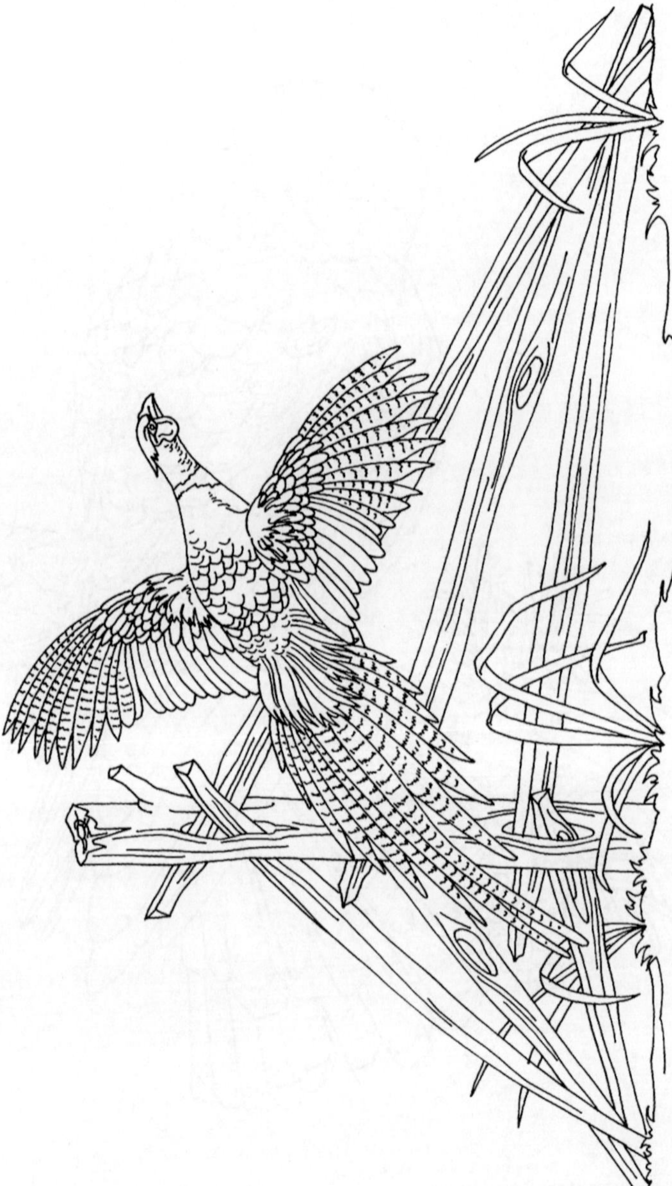

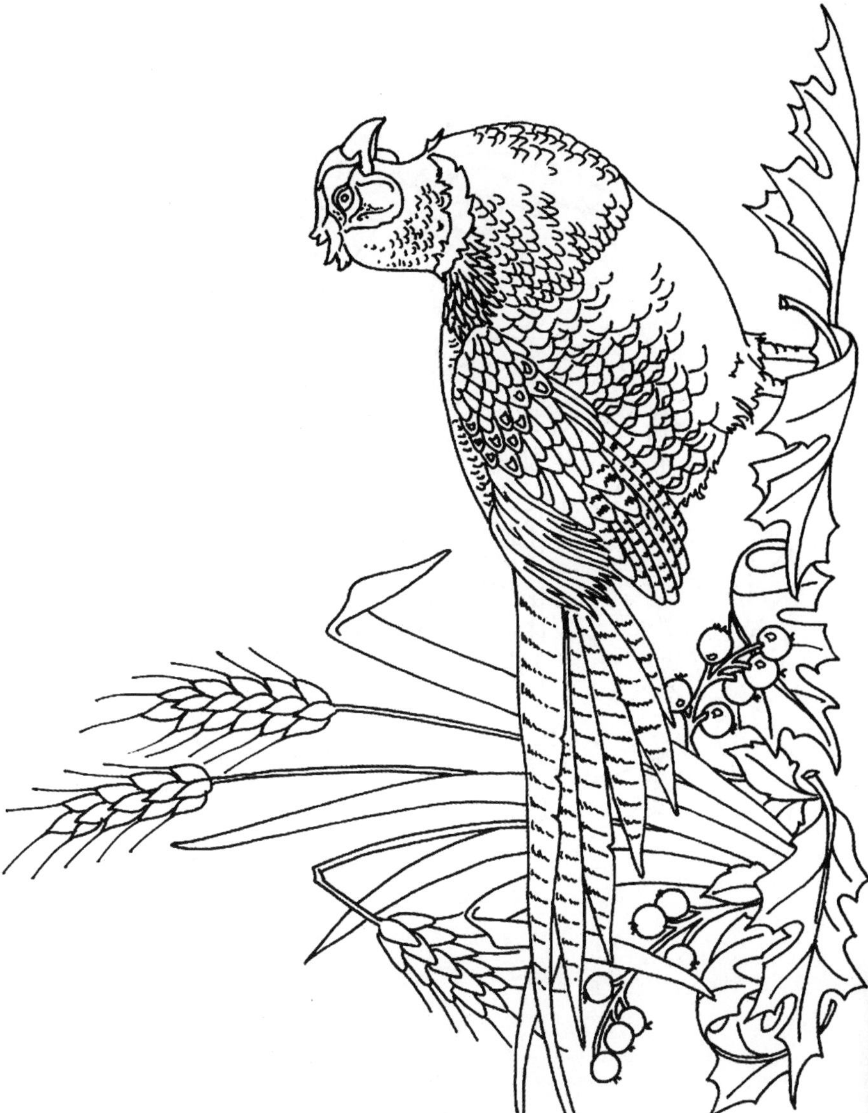

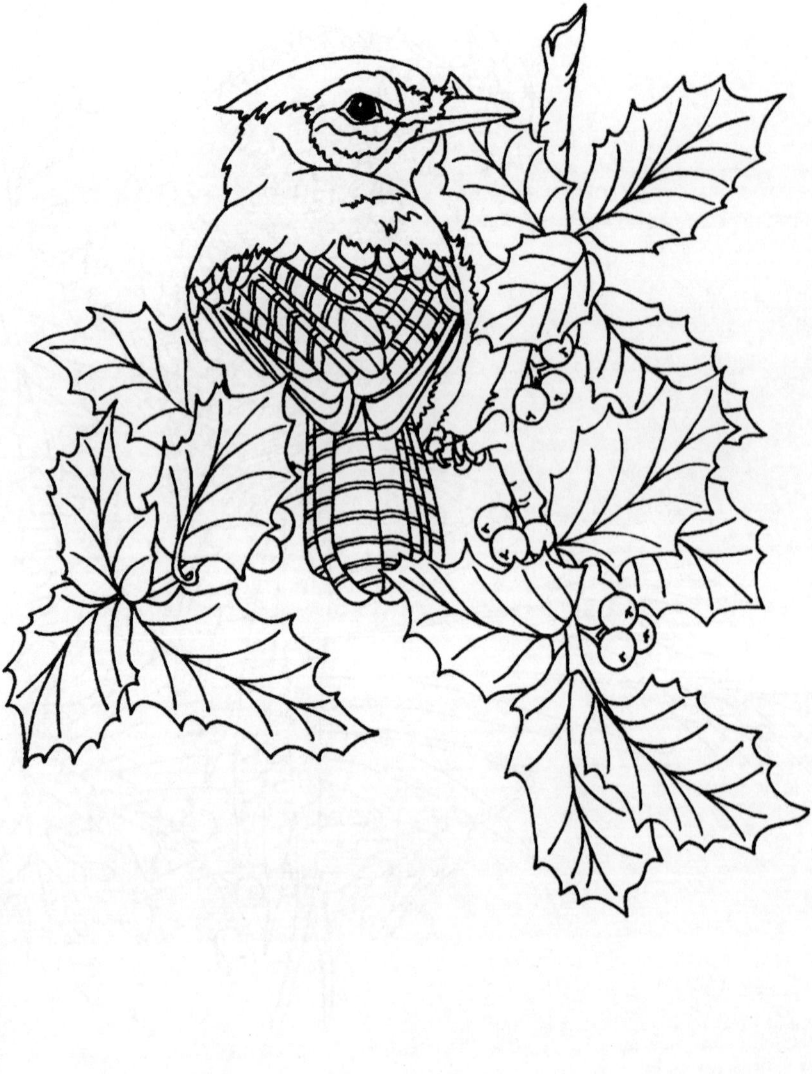

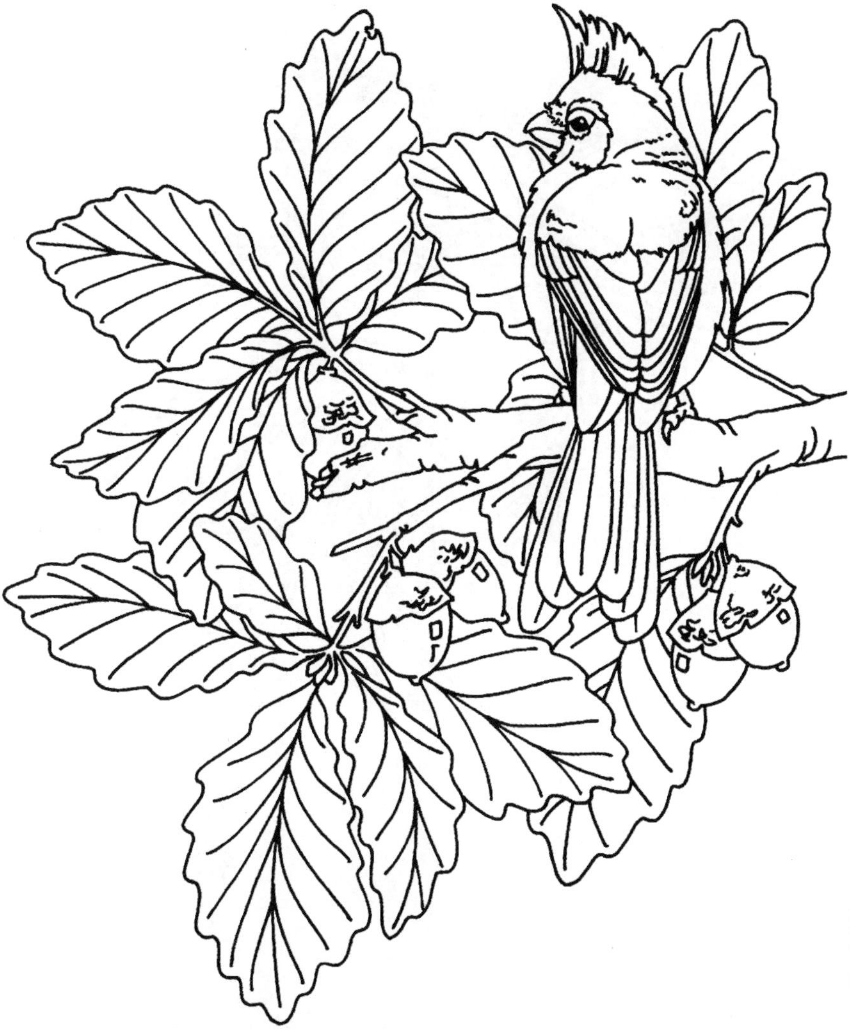

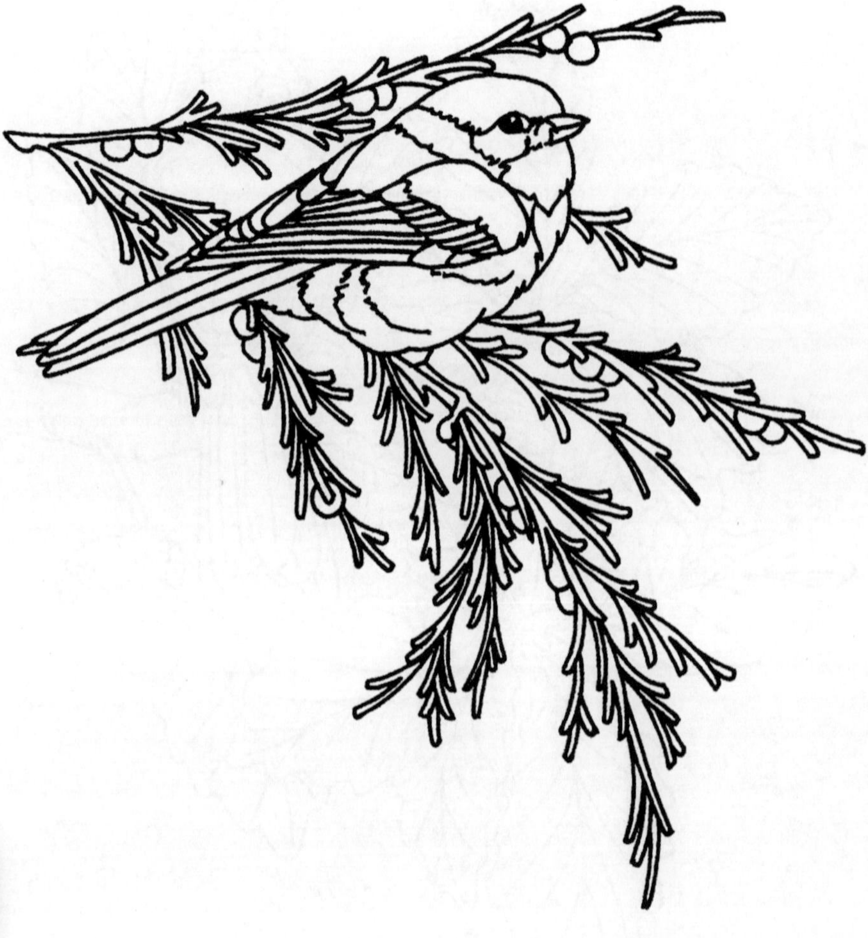

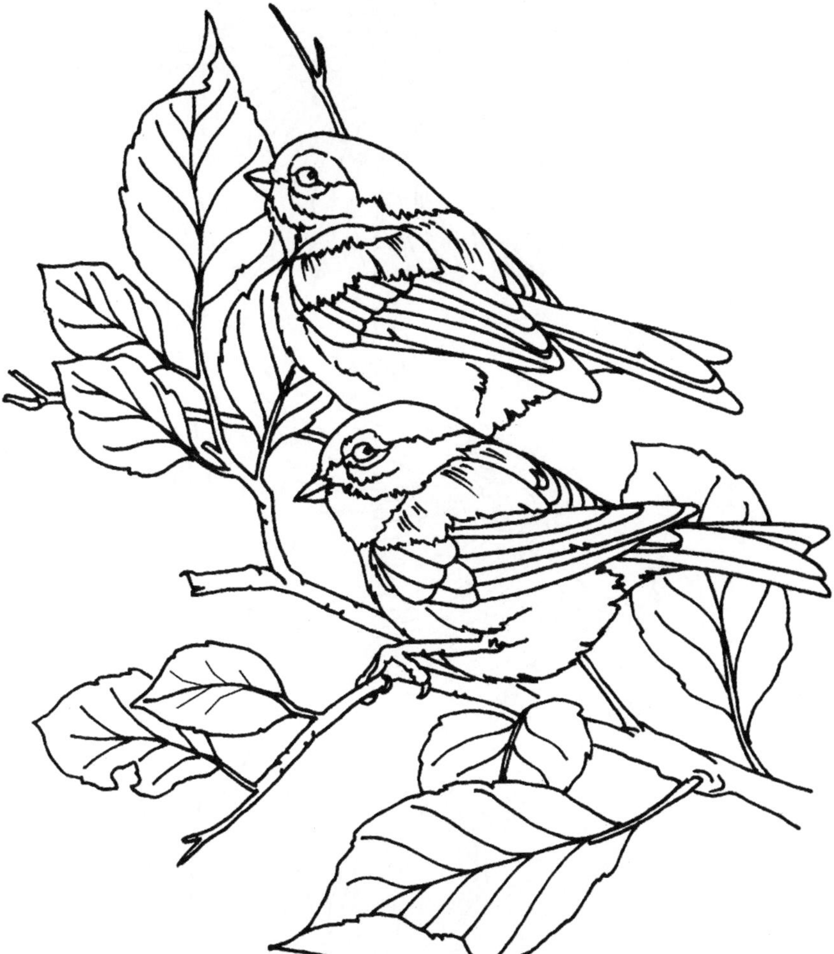

Wildlife

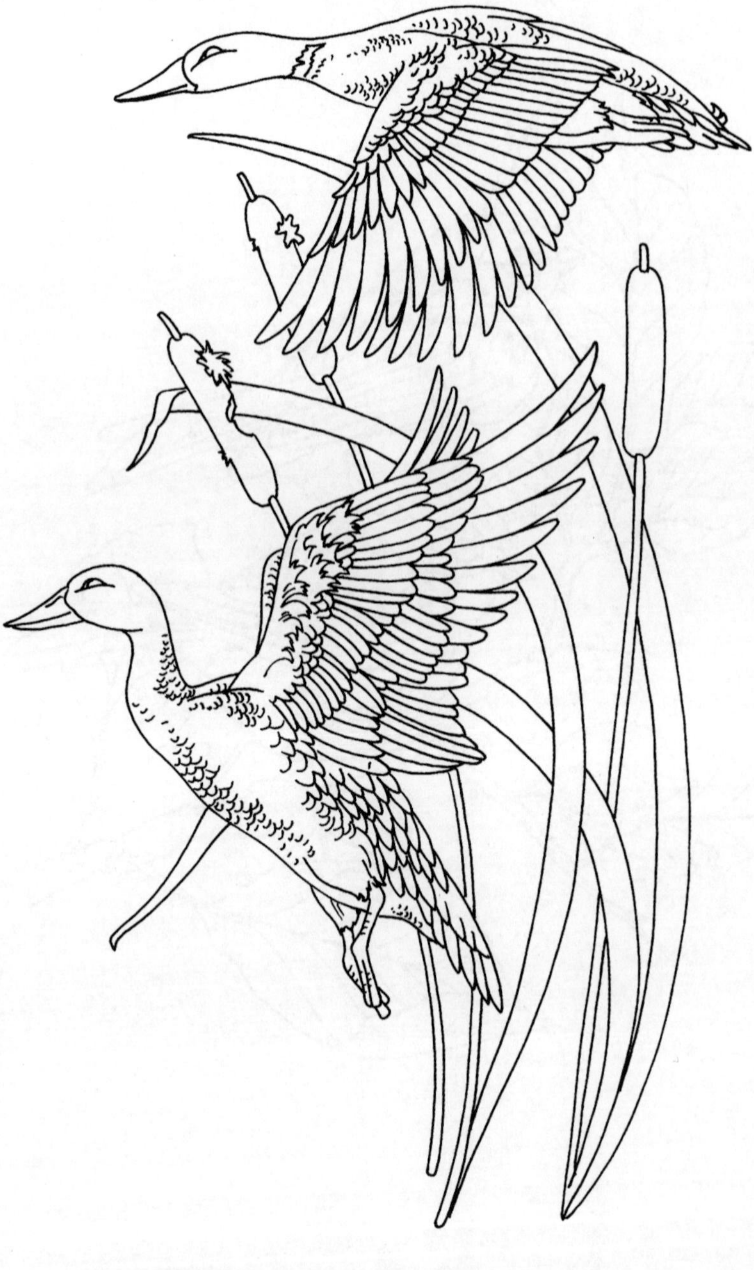

Wildlife

© Lora S. Irish

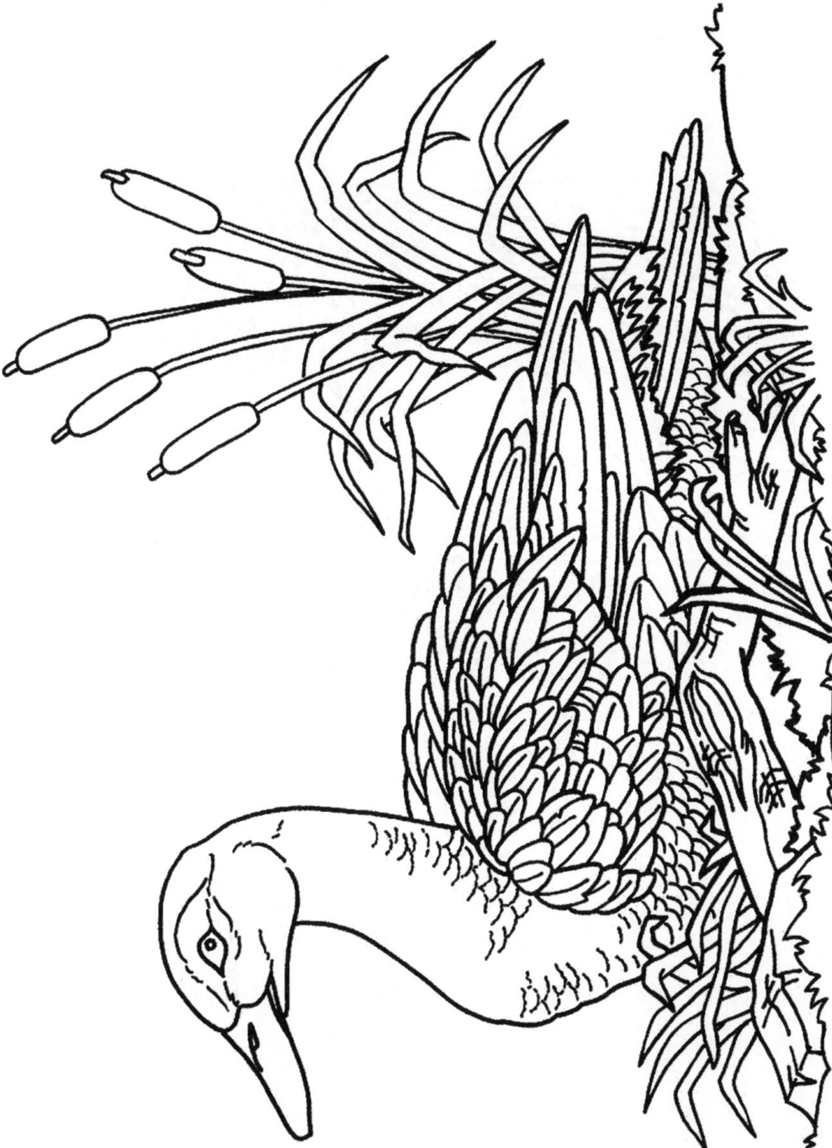

Wildlife

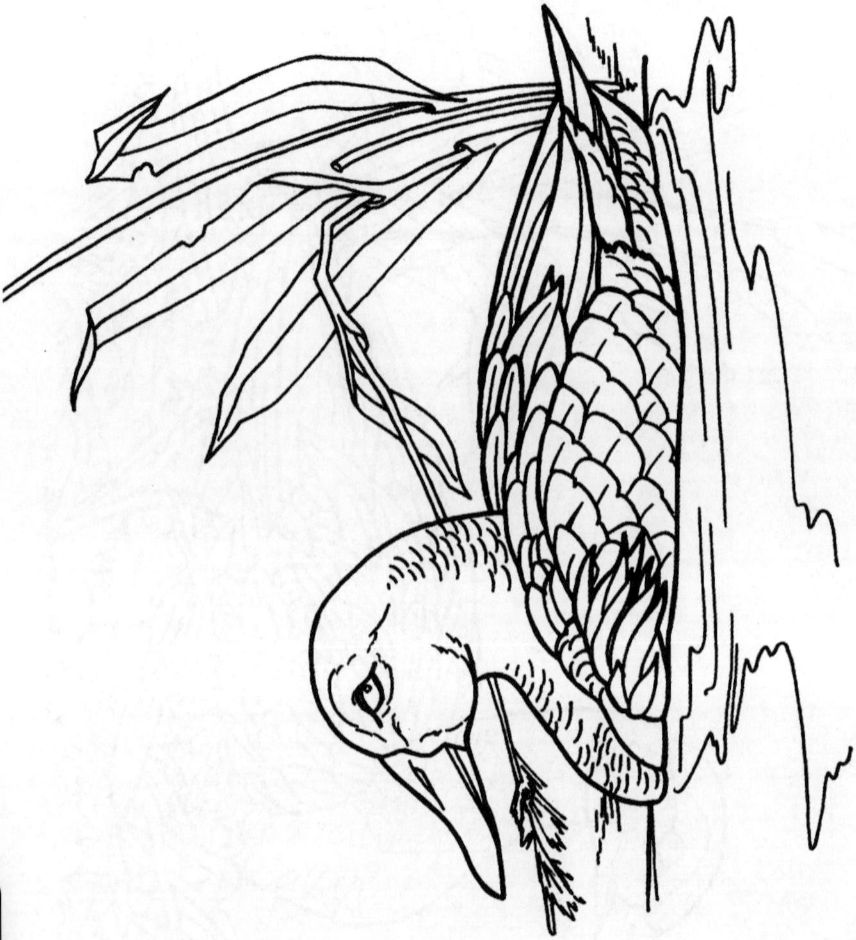

Wildlife

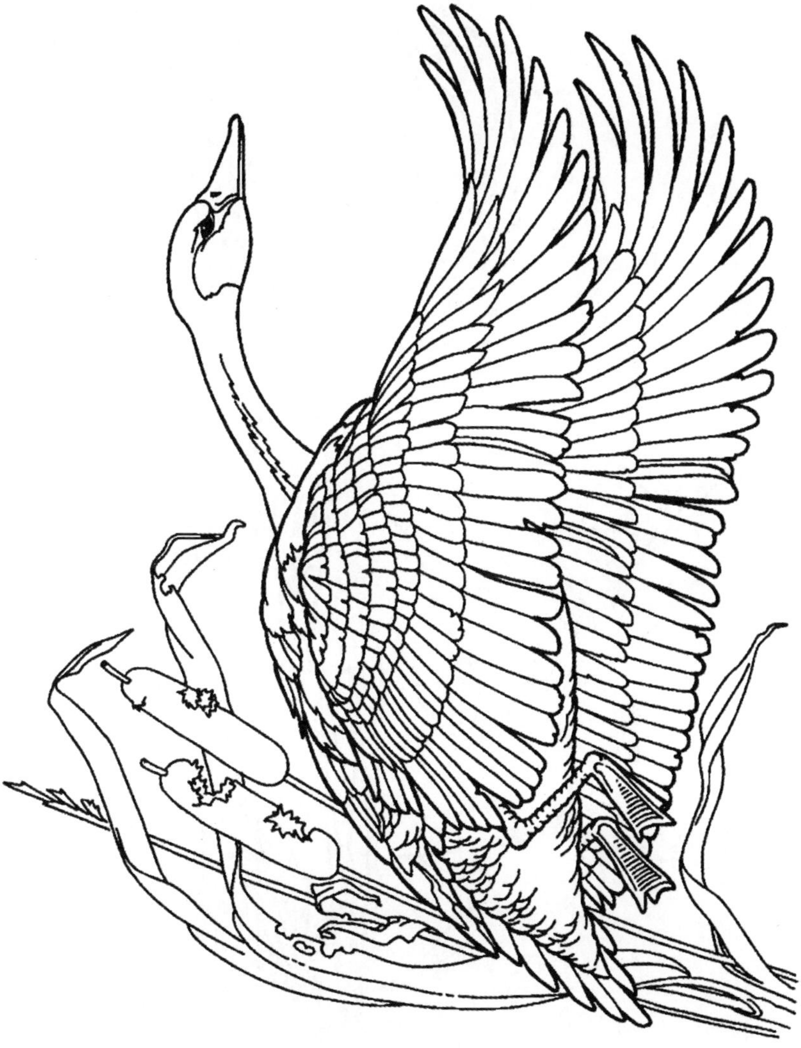

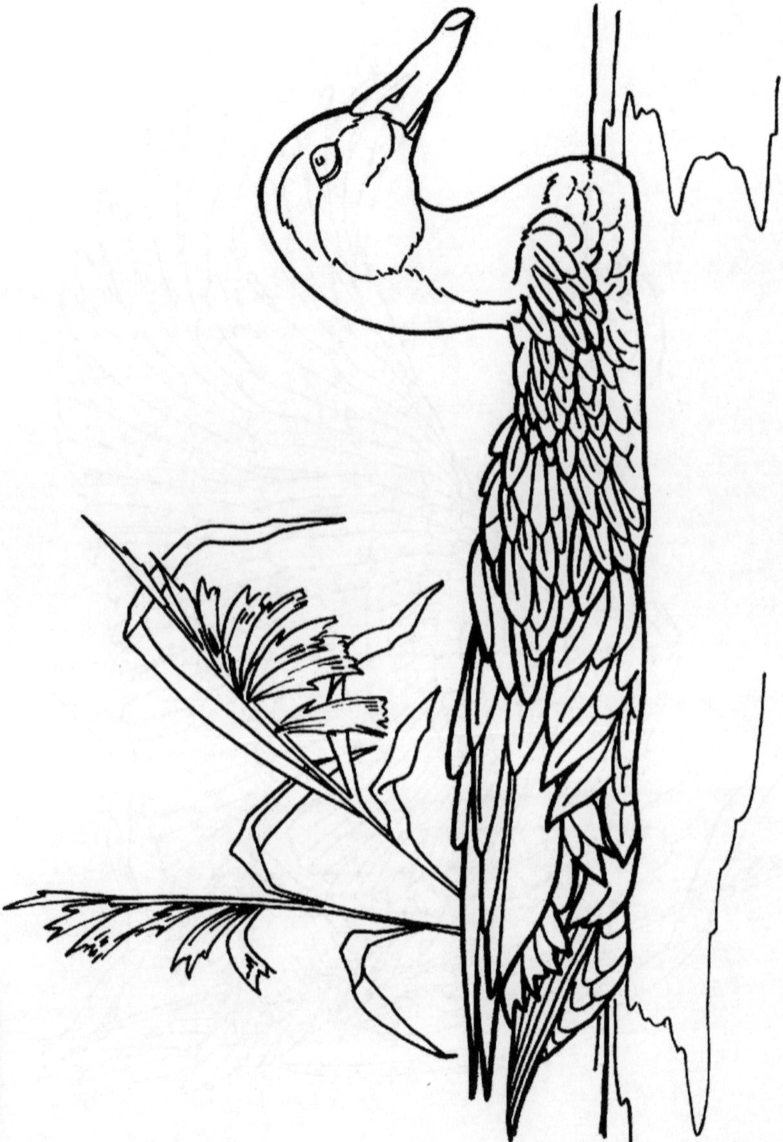

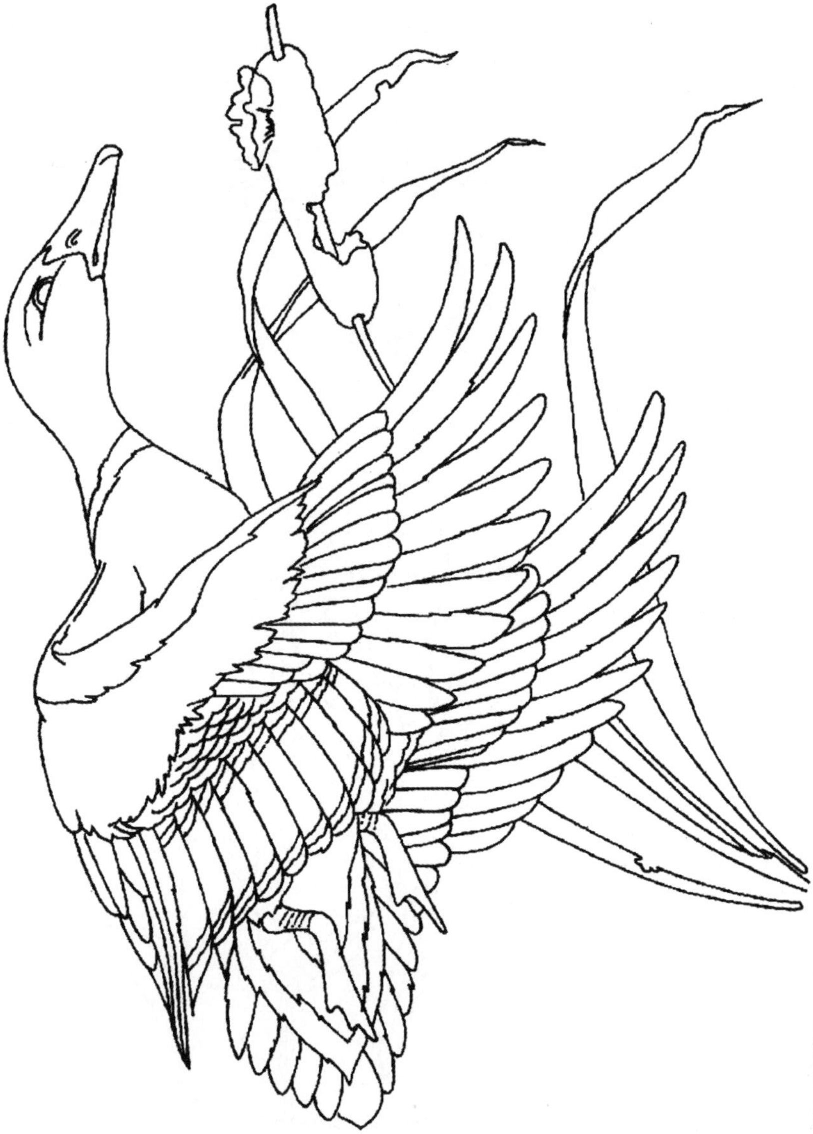

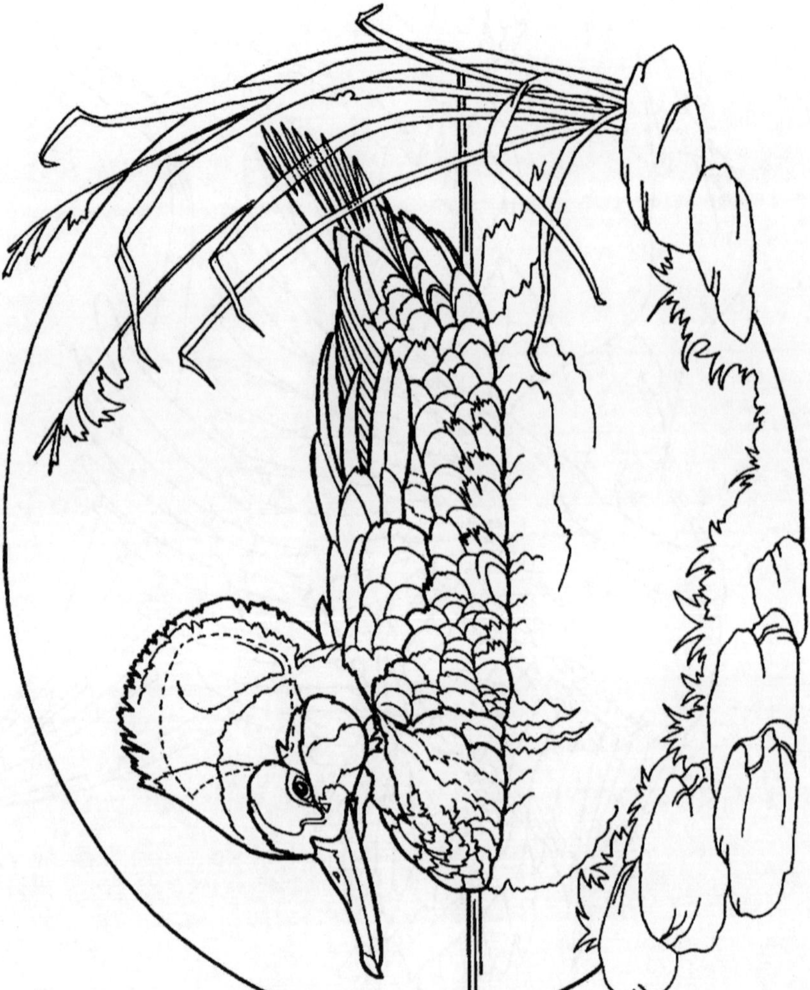

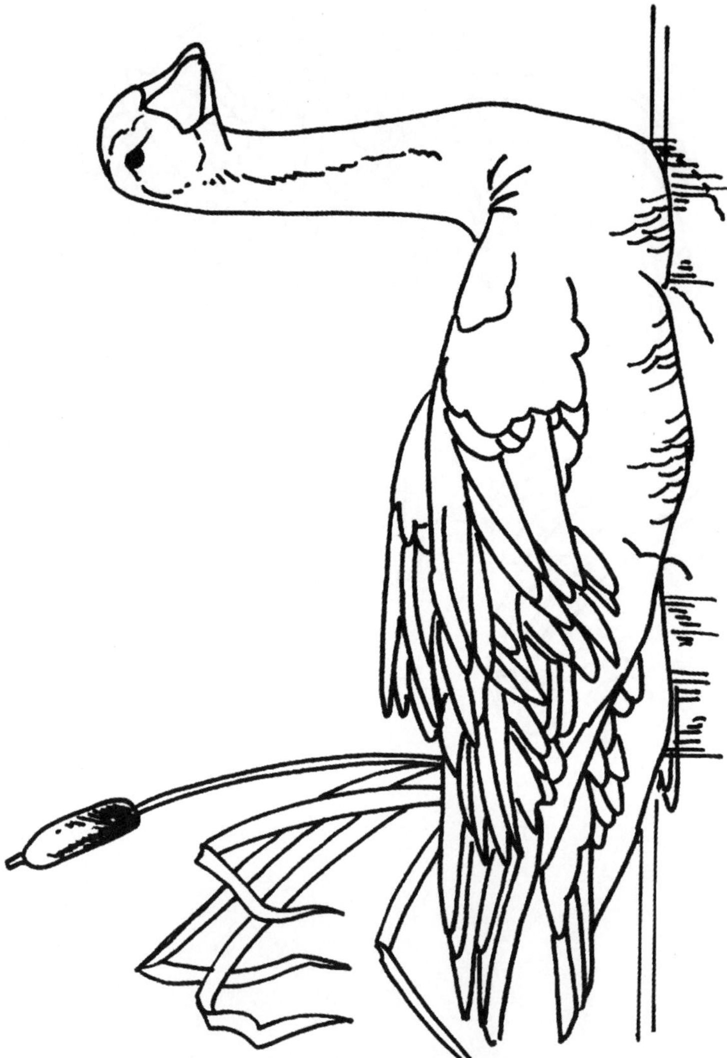

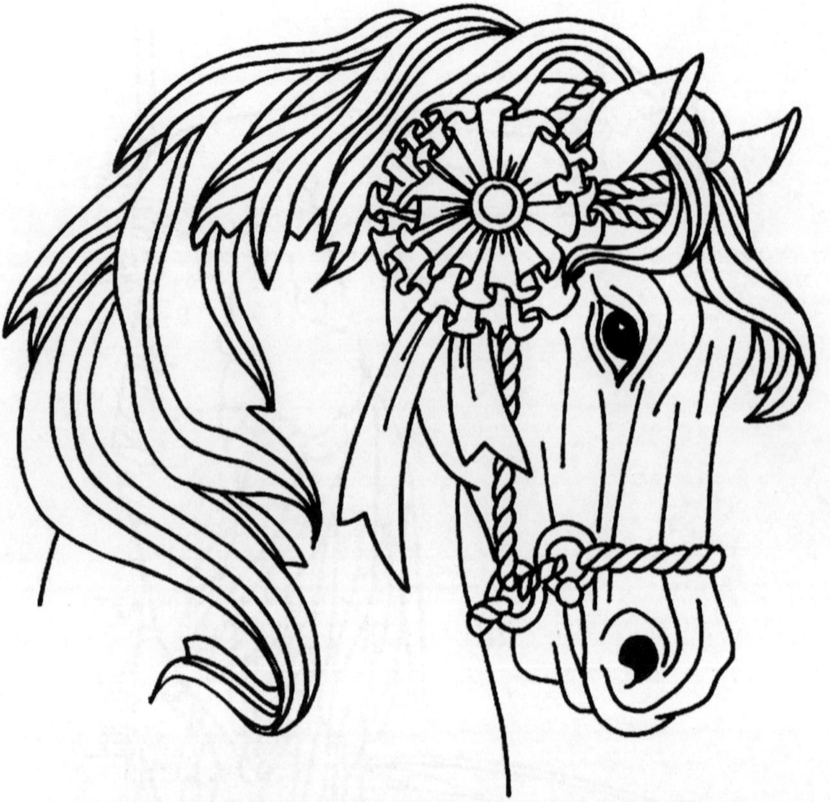

© Lora S. Irish

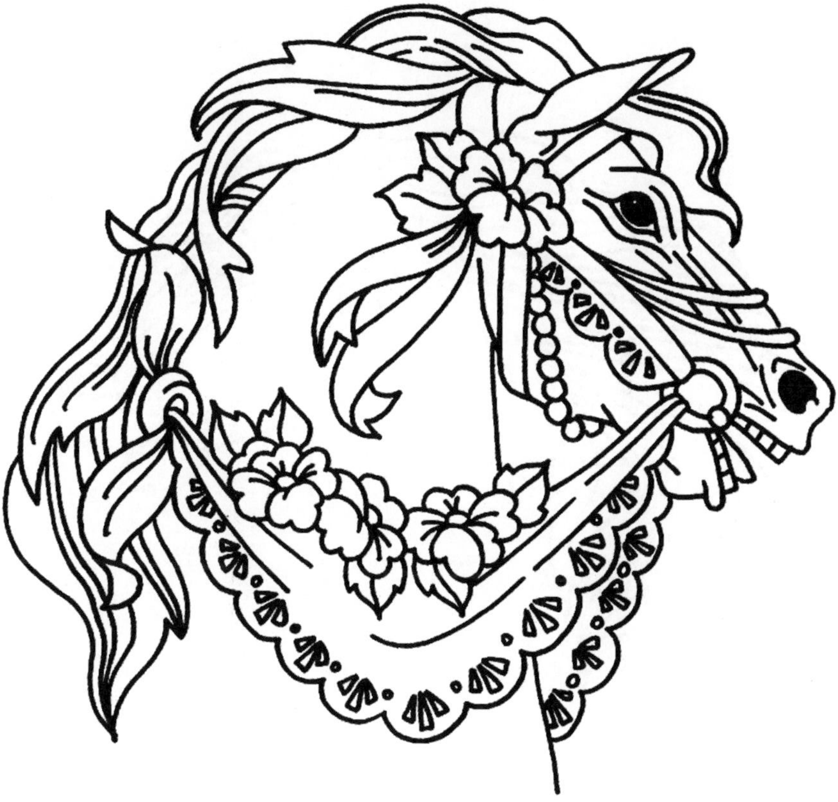

Wildlife

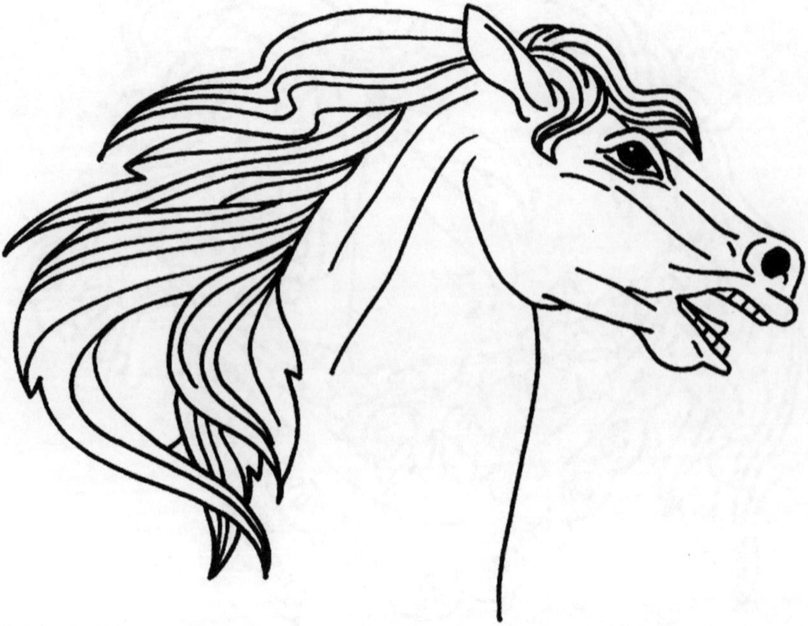

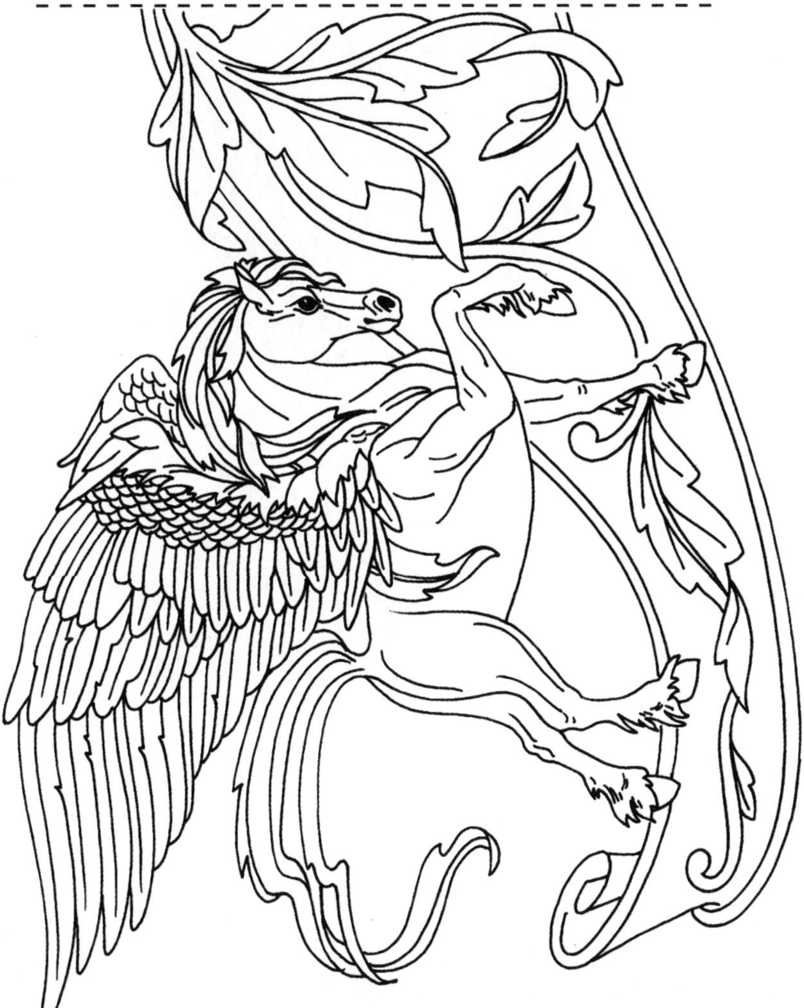

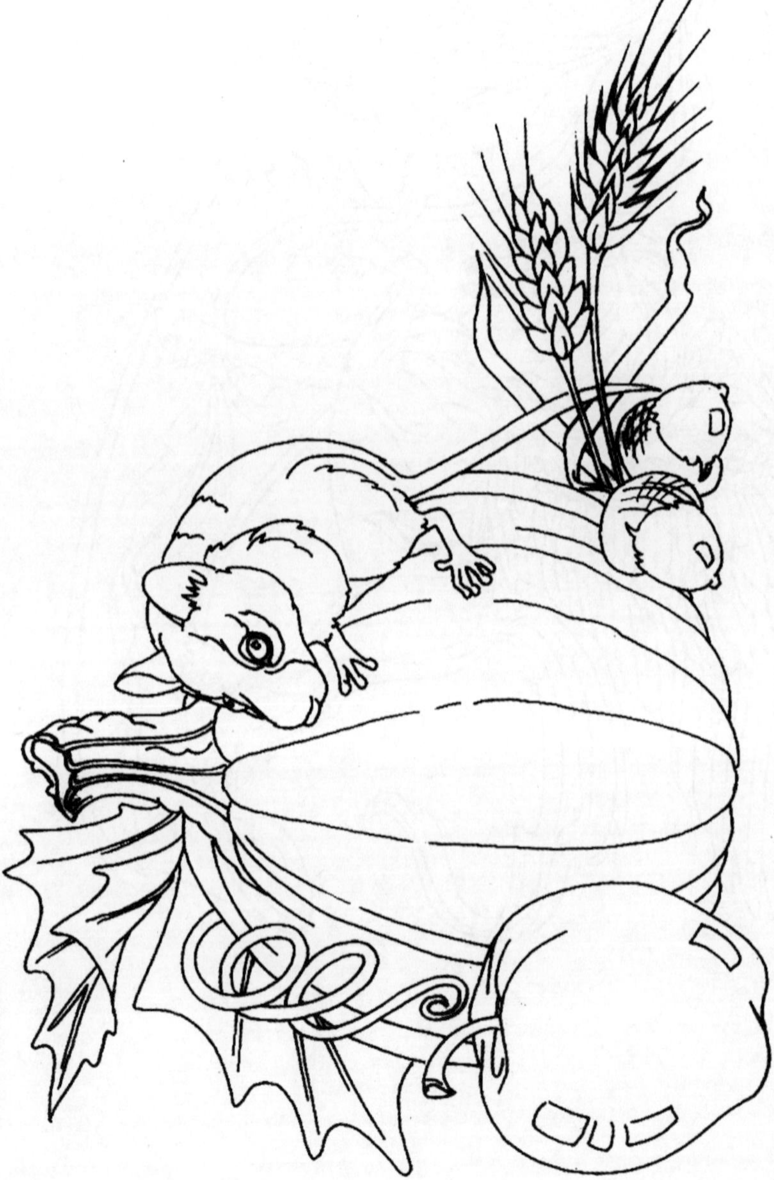

© Lora S. Irish

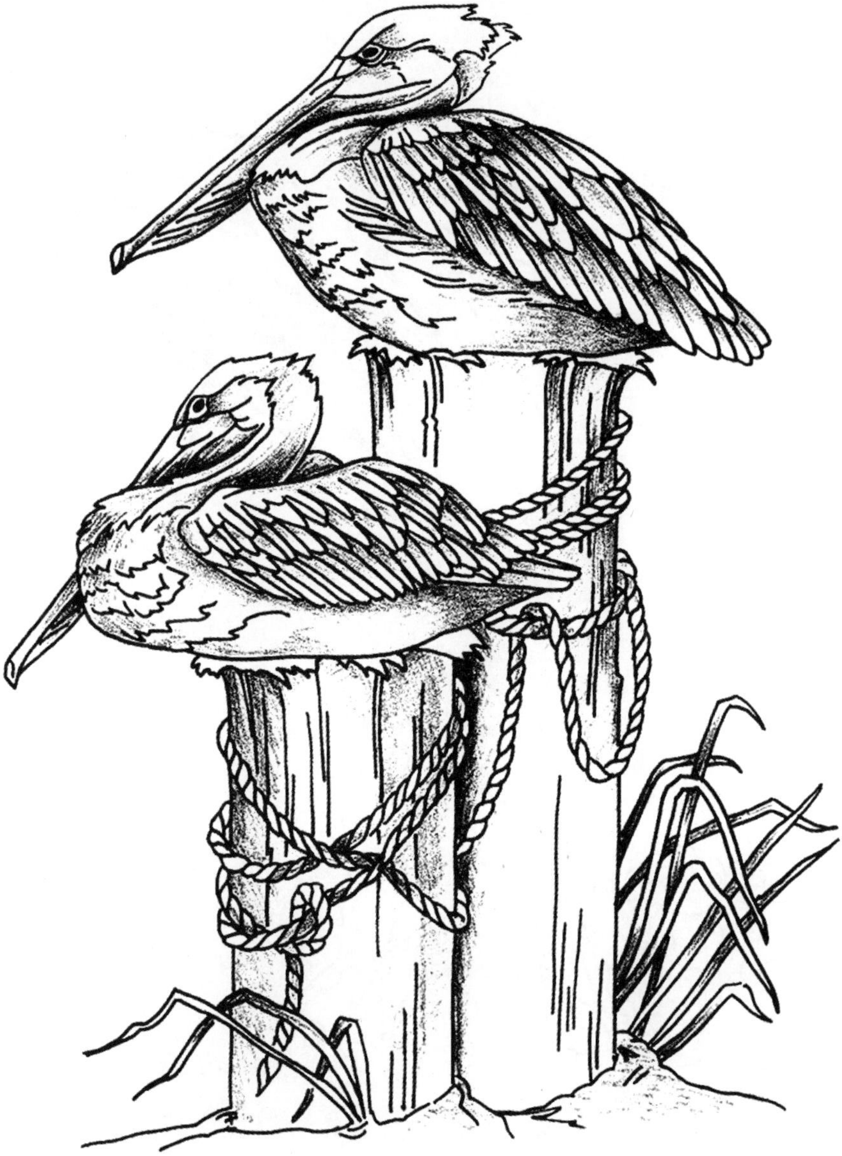

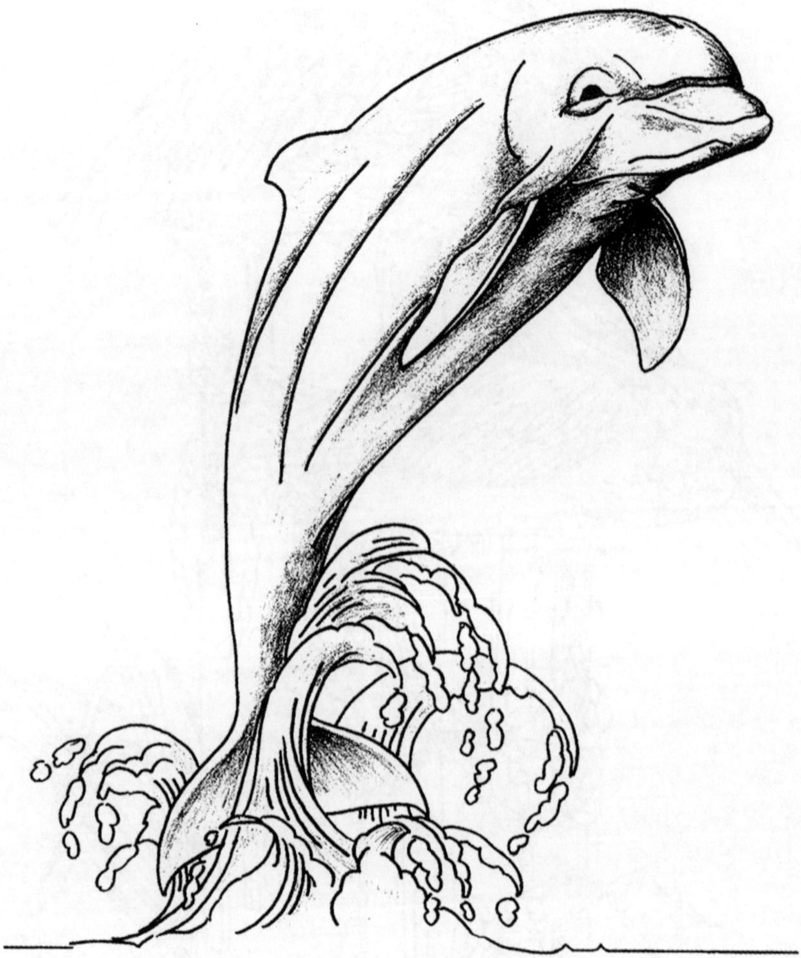

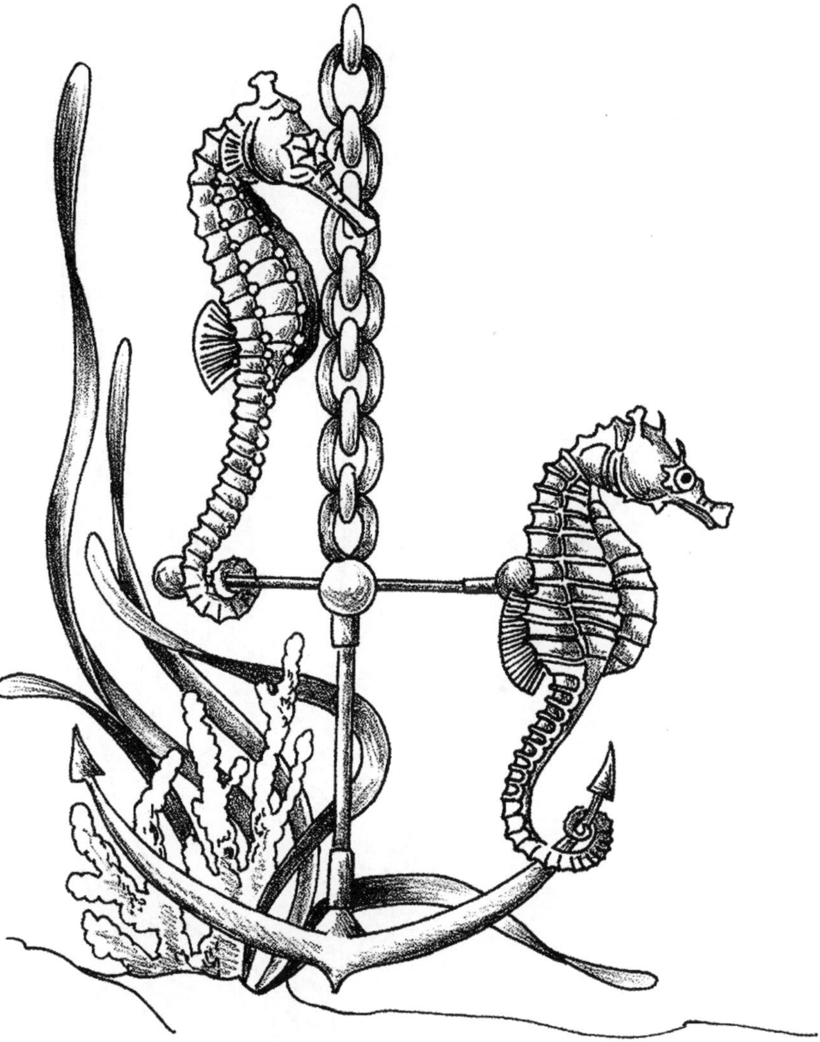

Wildlife

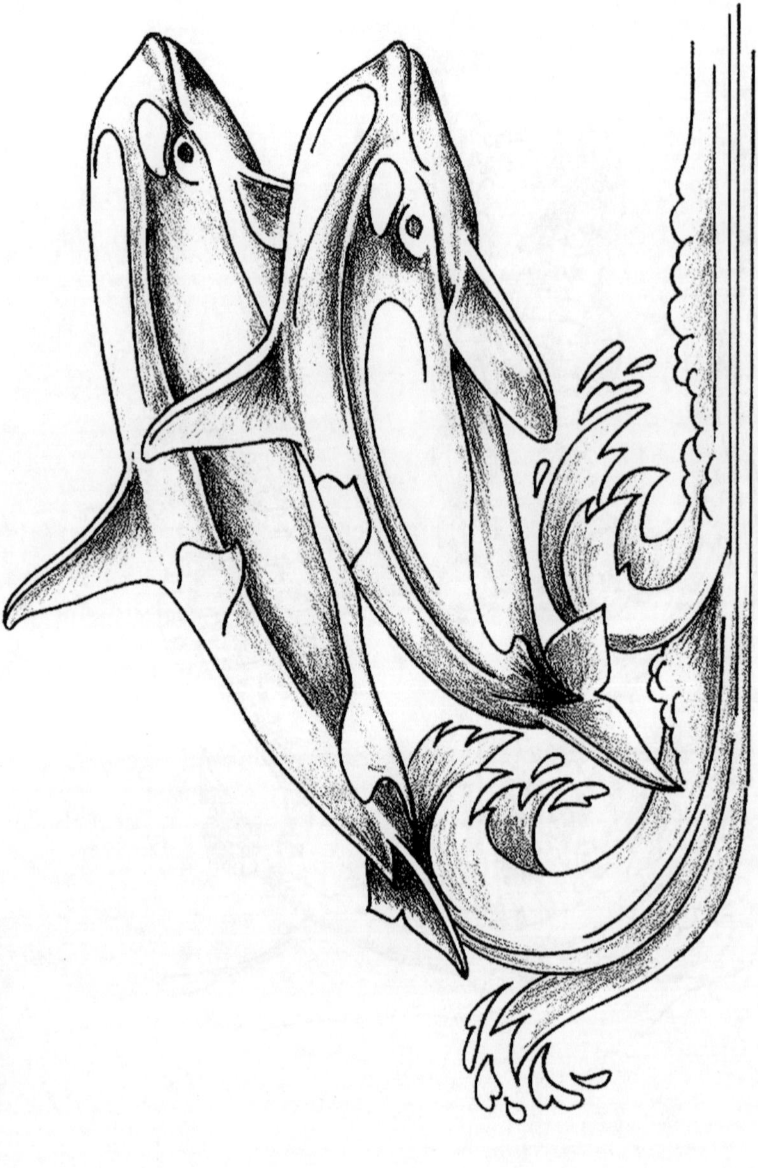

© Lora S. Irish

Wildlife

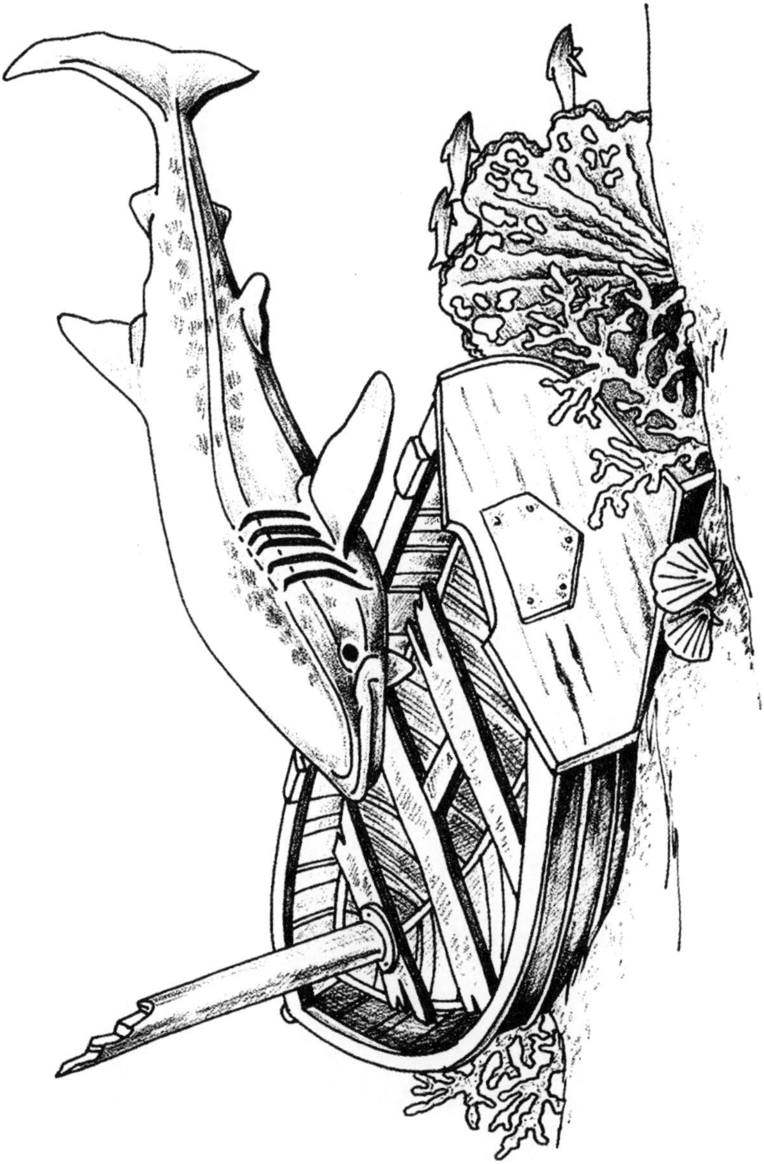

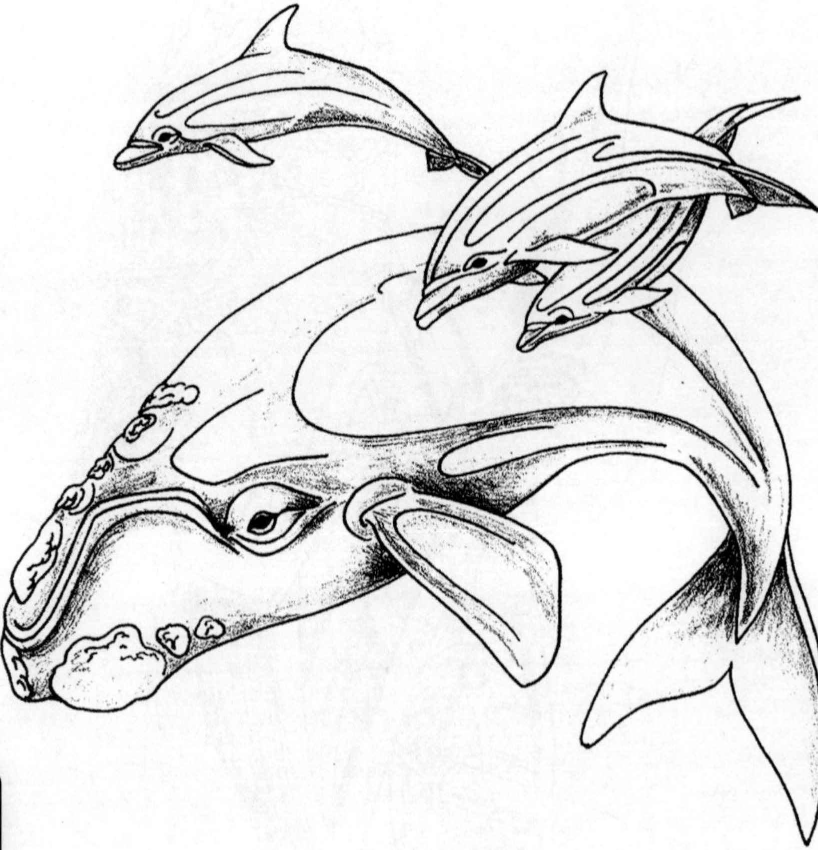

© Lora S. Irish

Wildlife

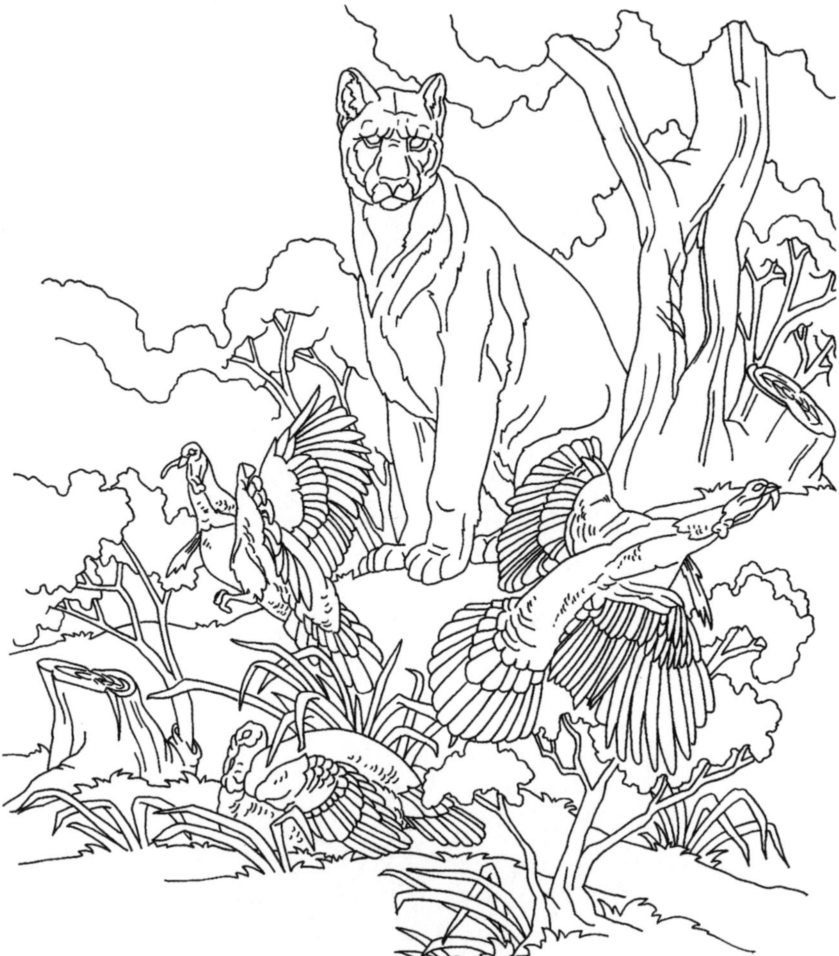

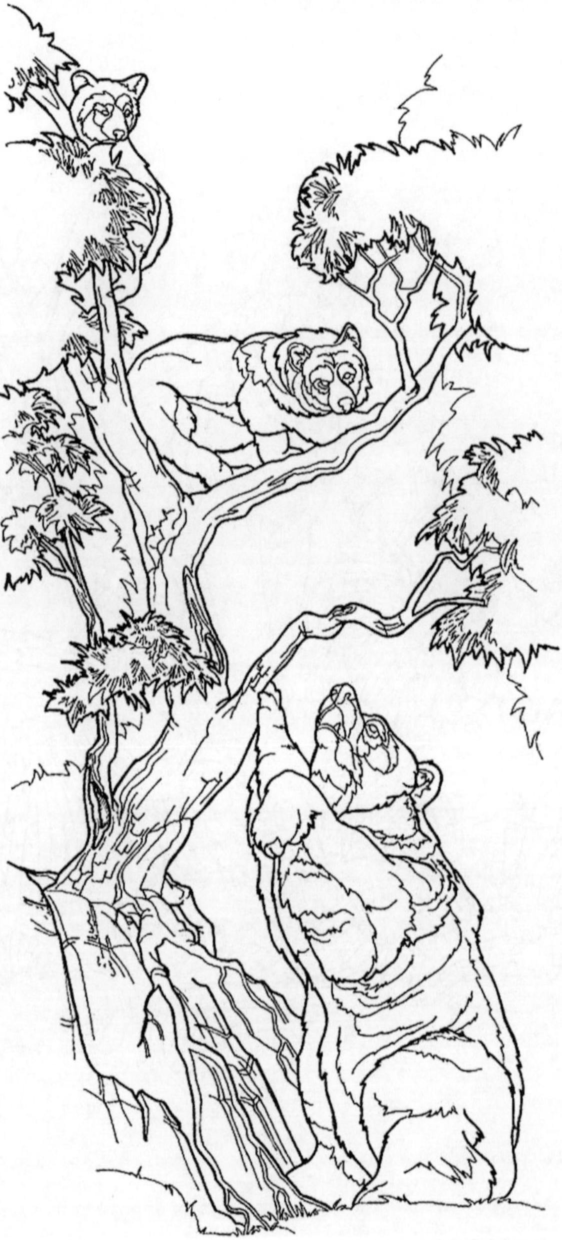

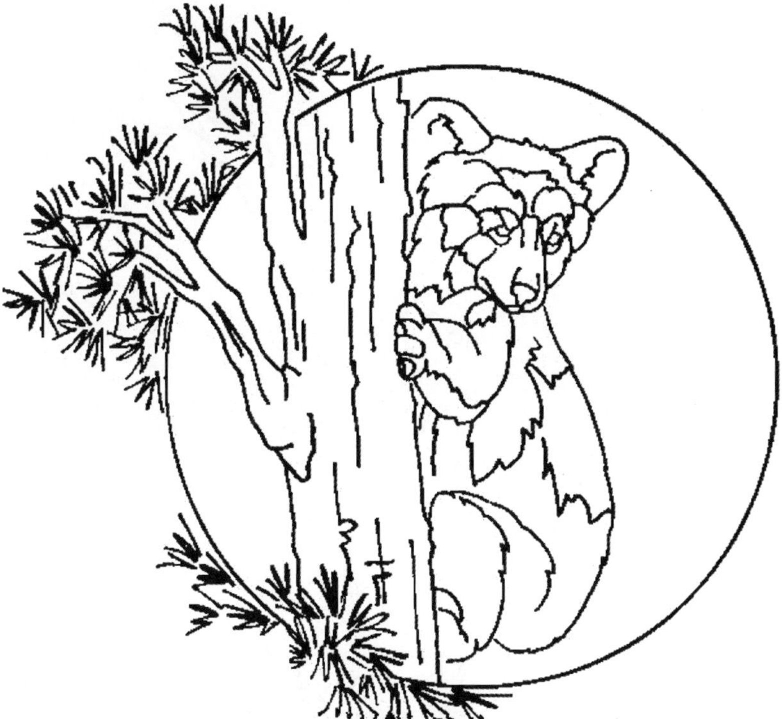

Wildlife

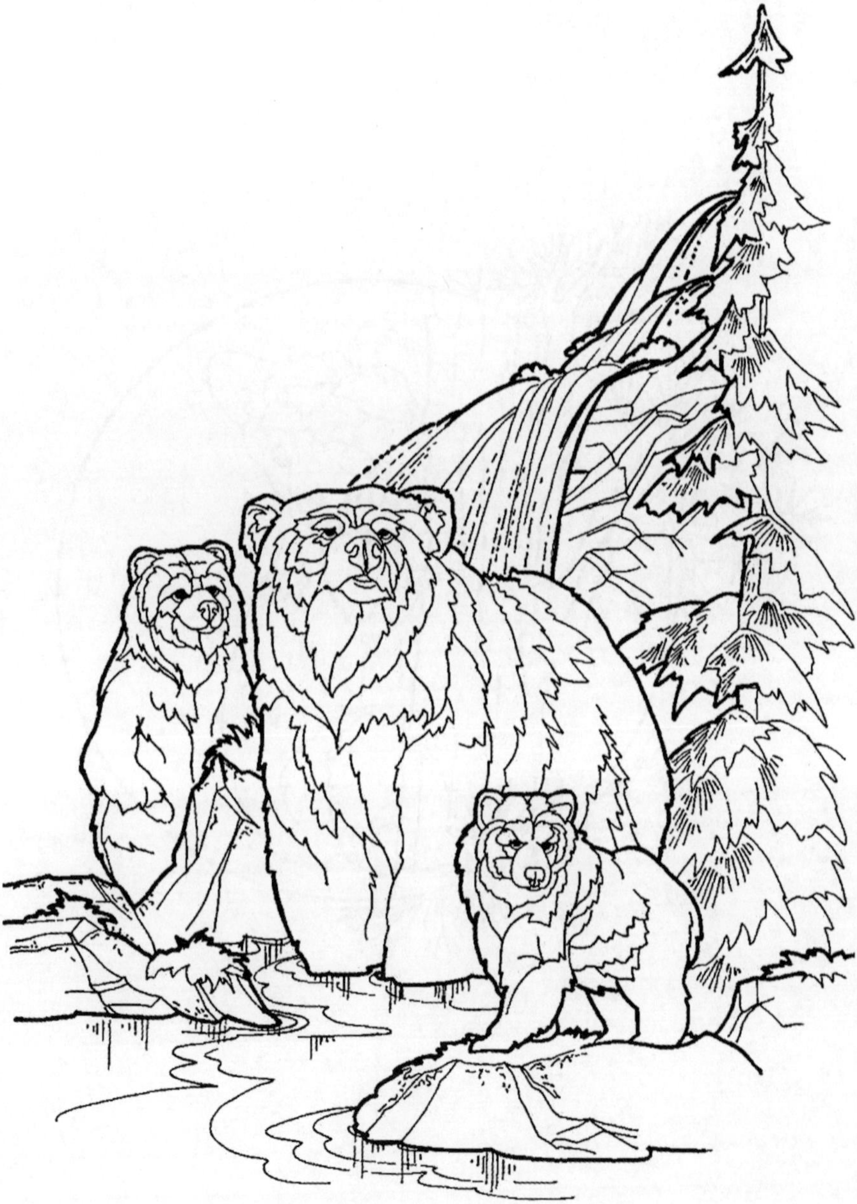

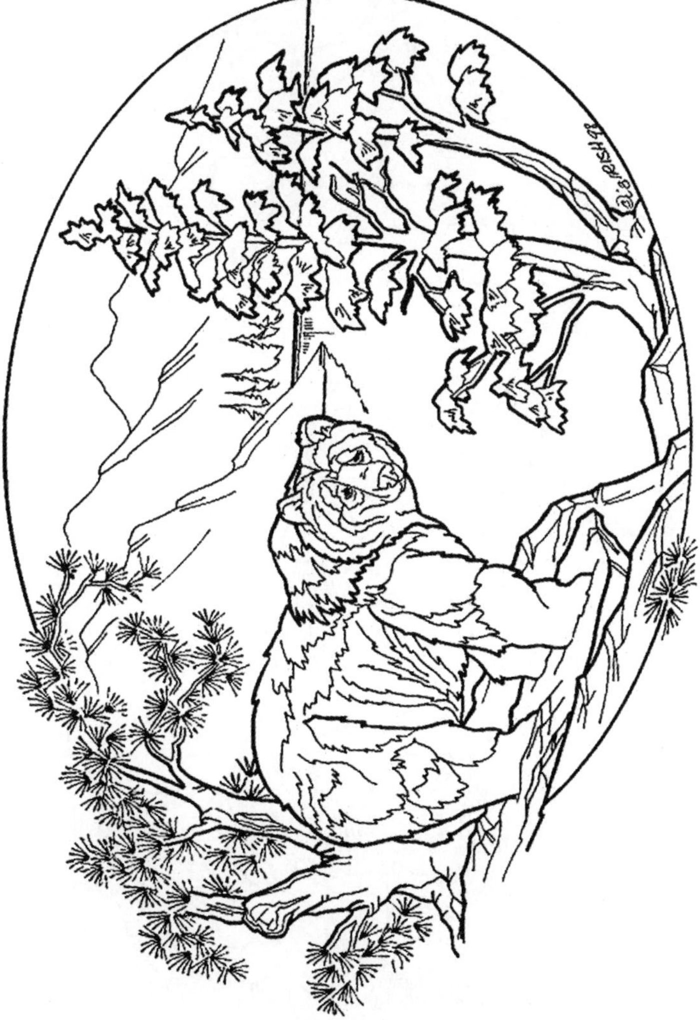

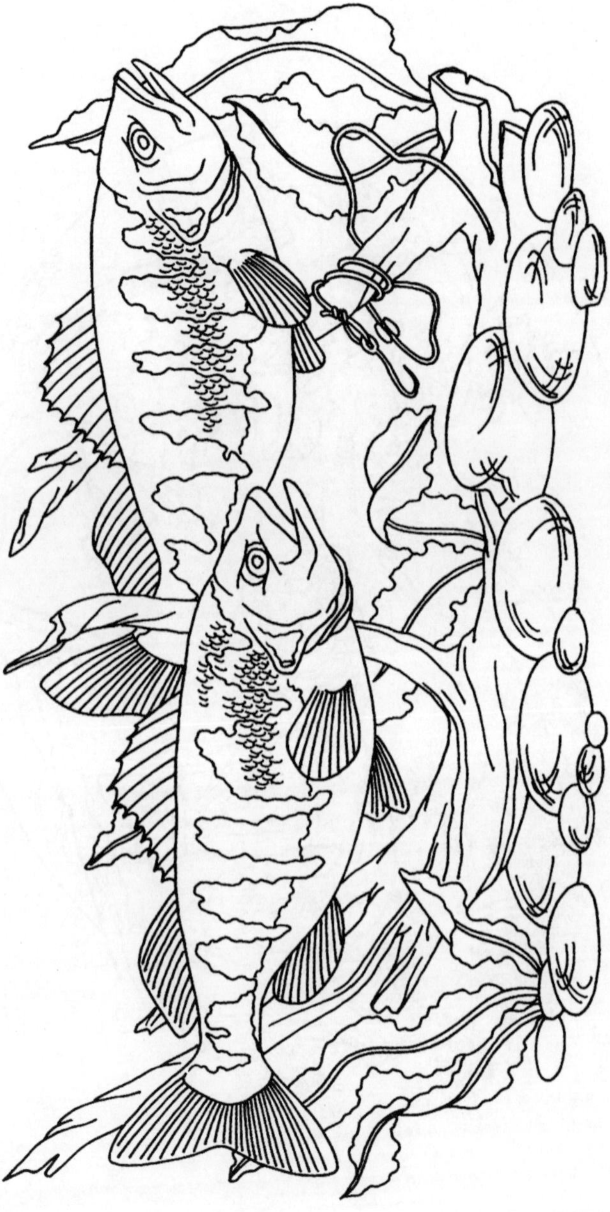

© Lora S. Irish

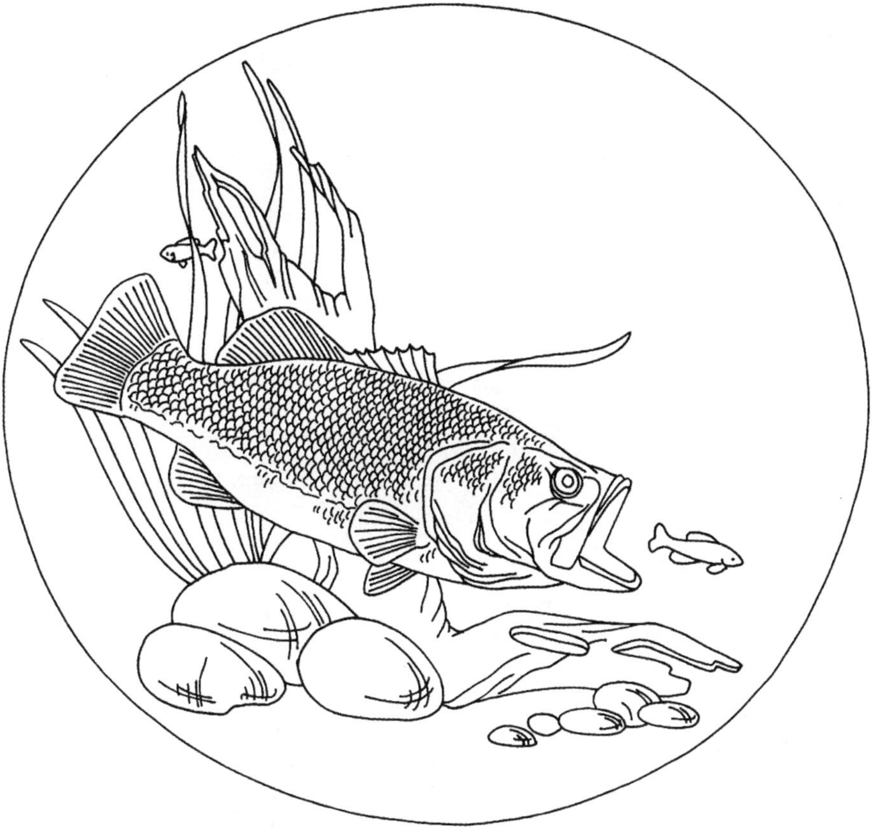

Wildlife

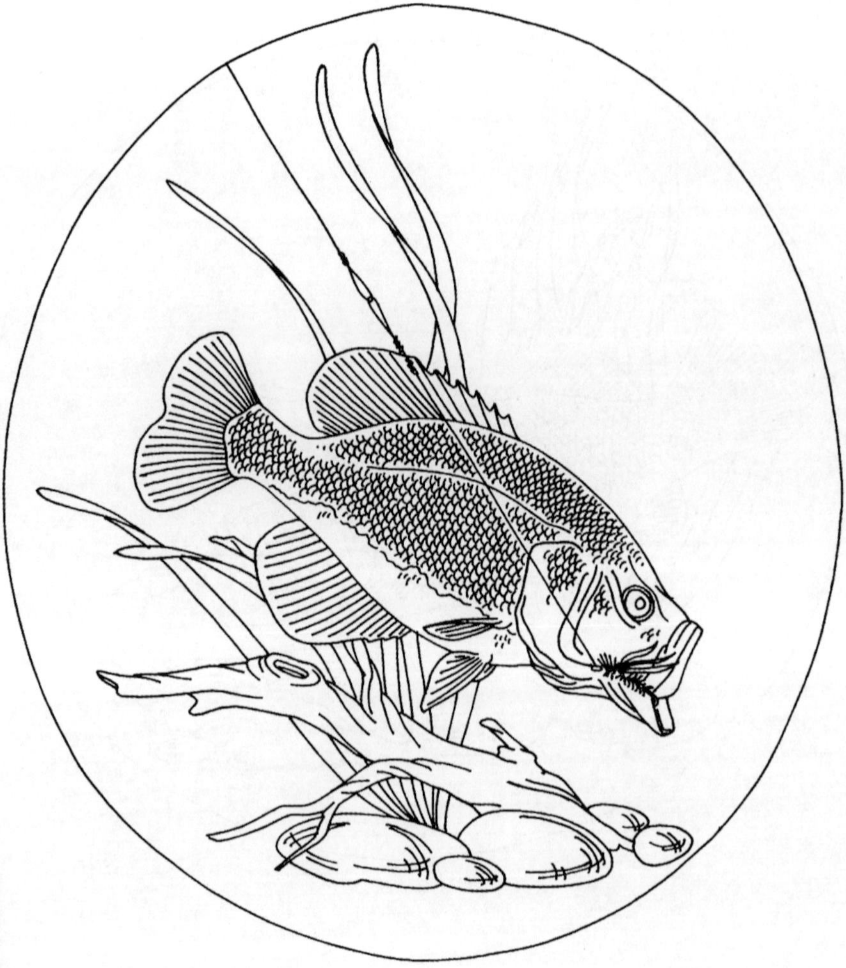

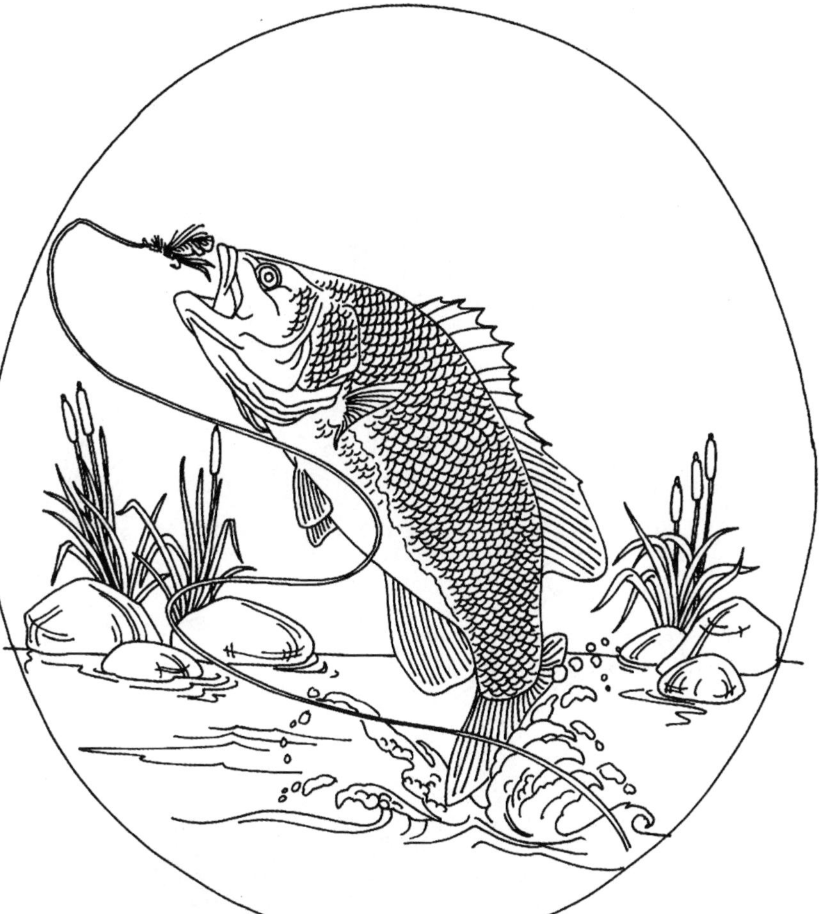

Wildlife

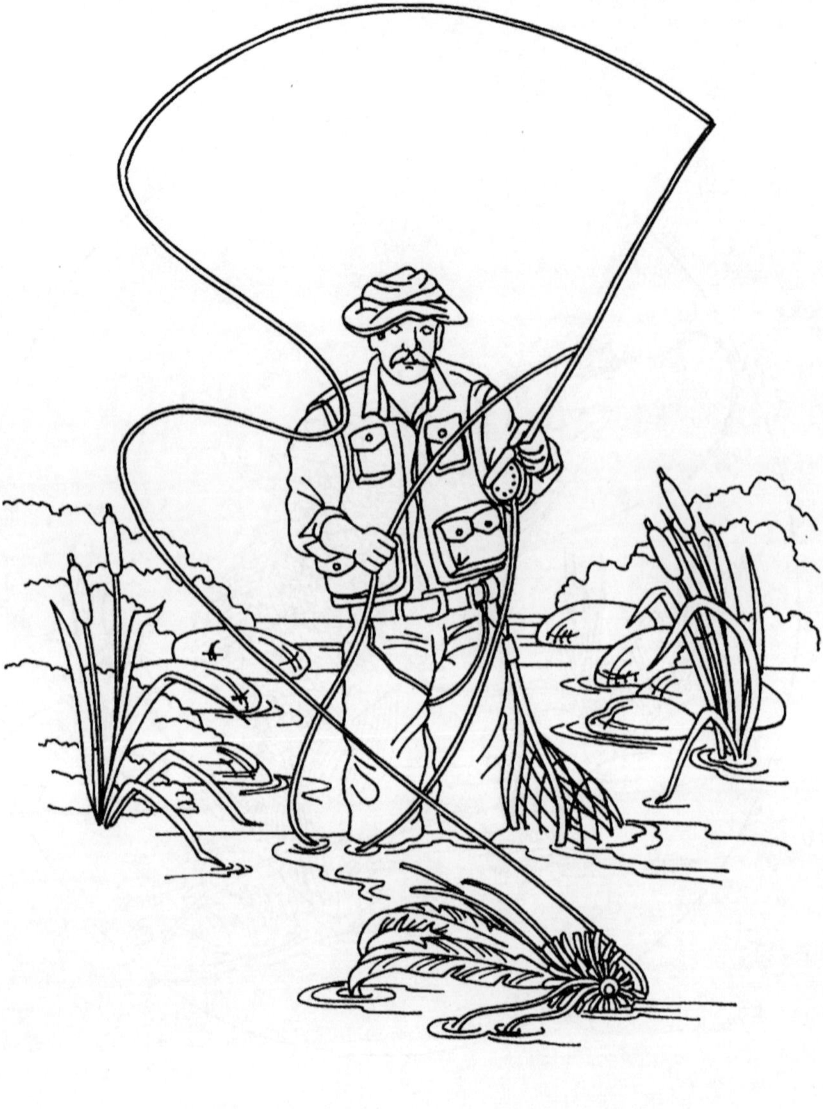

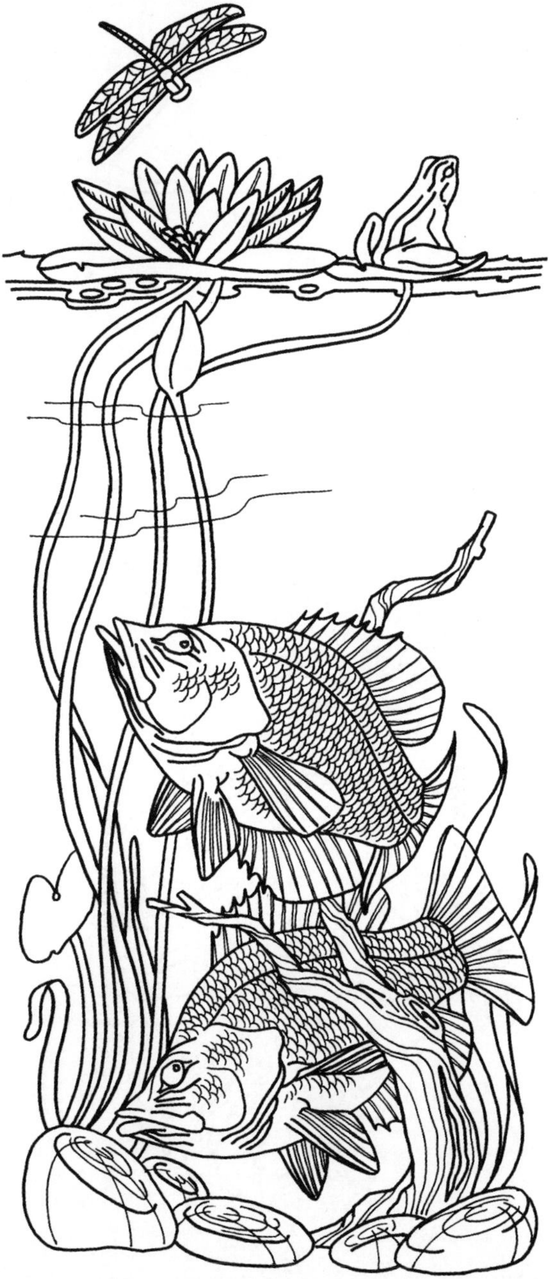

© Lora S. Irish

Wildlife

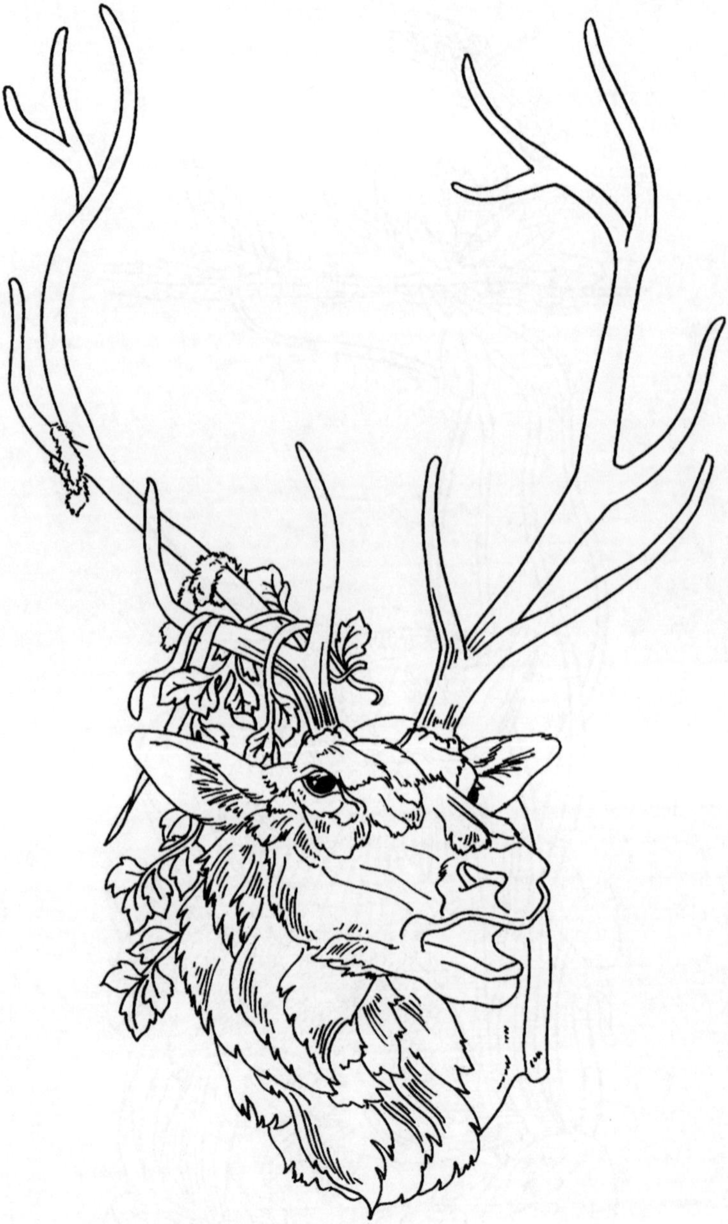

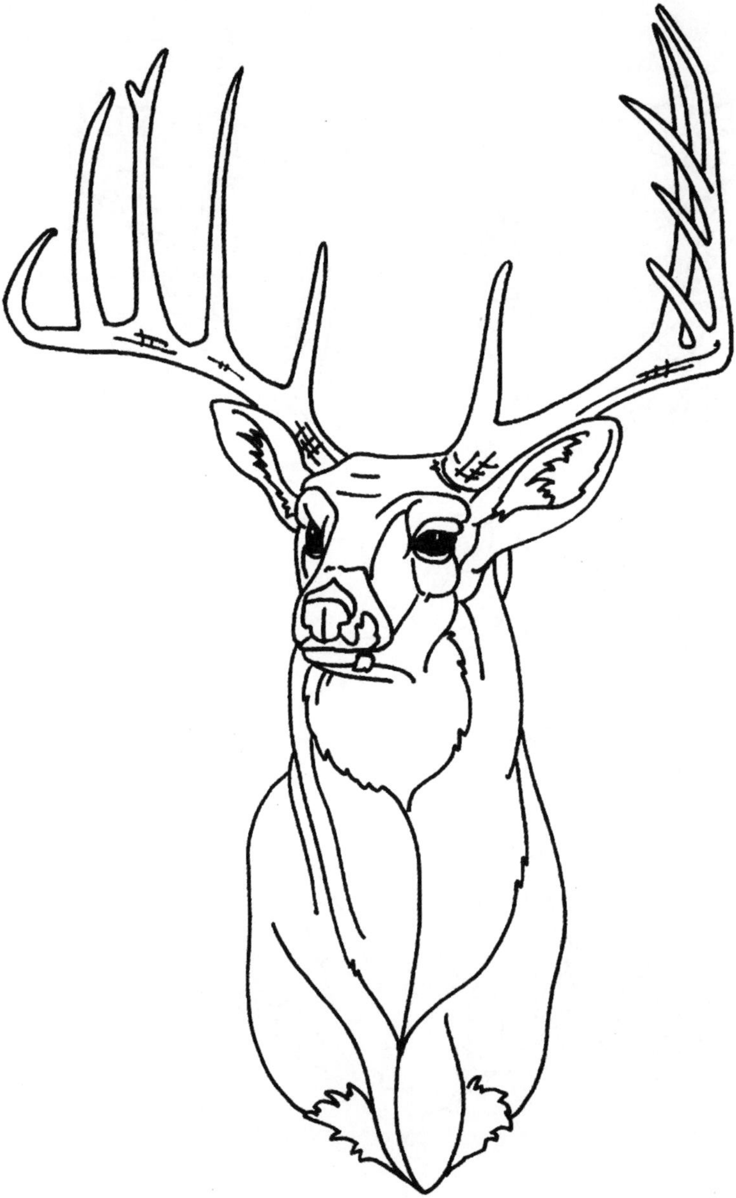

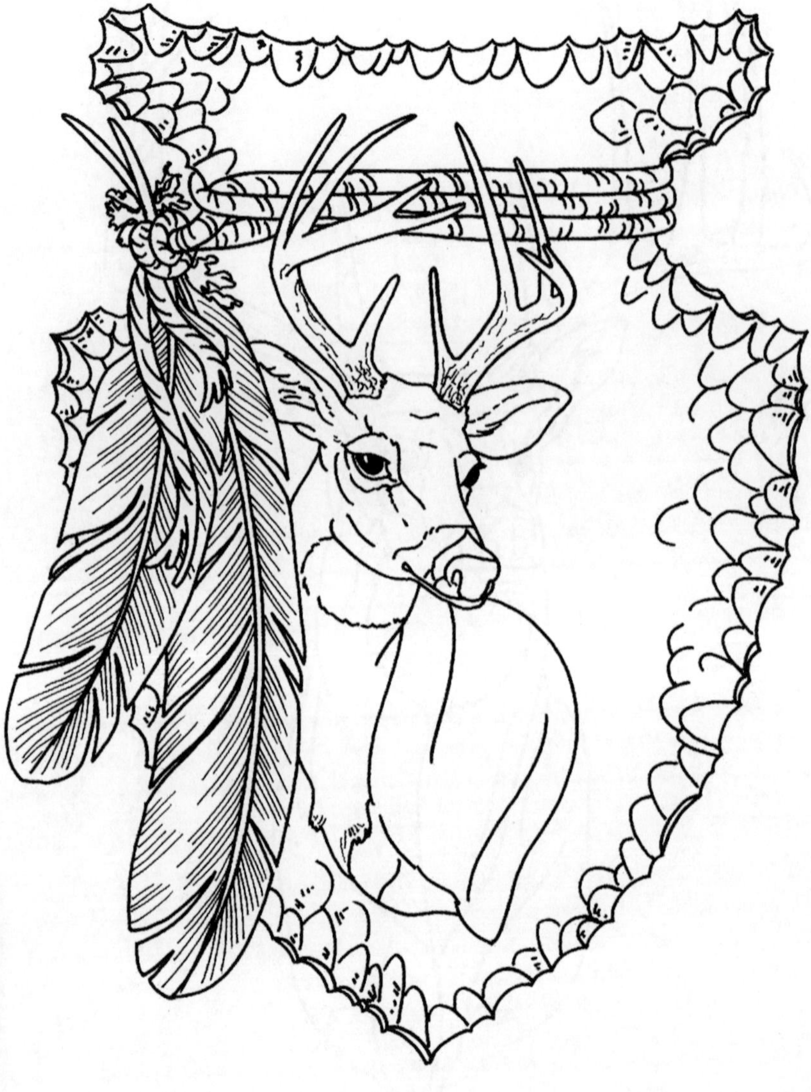

© Lora S. Irish

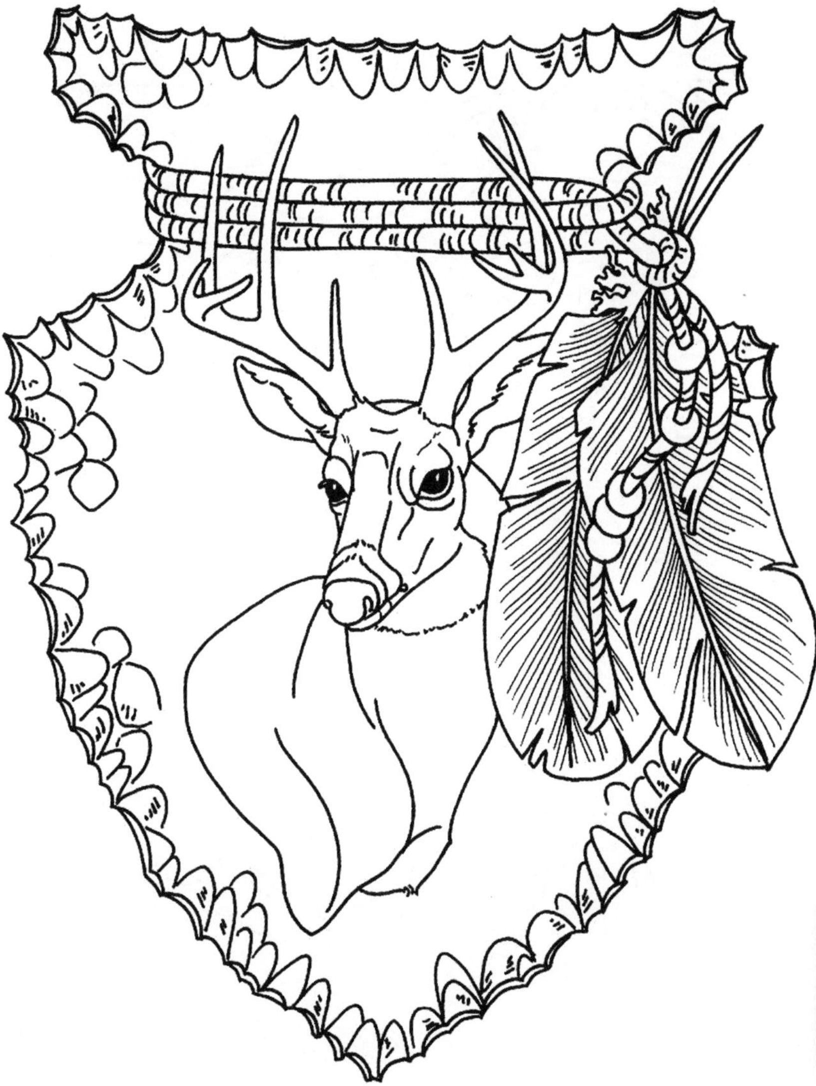

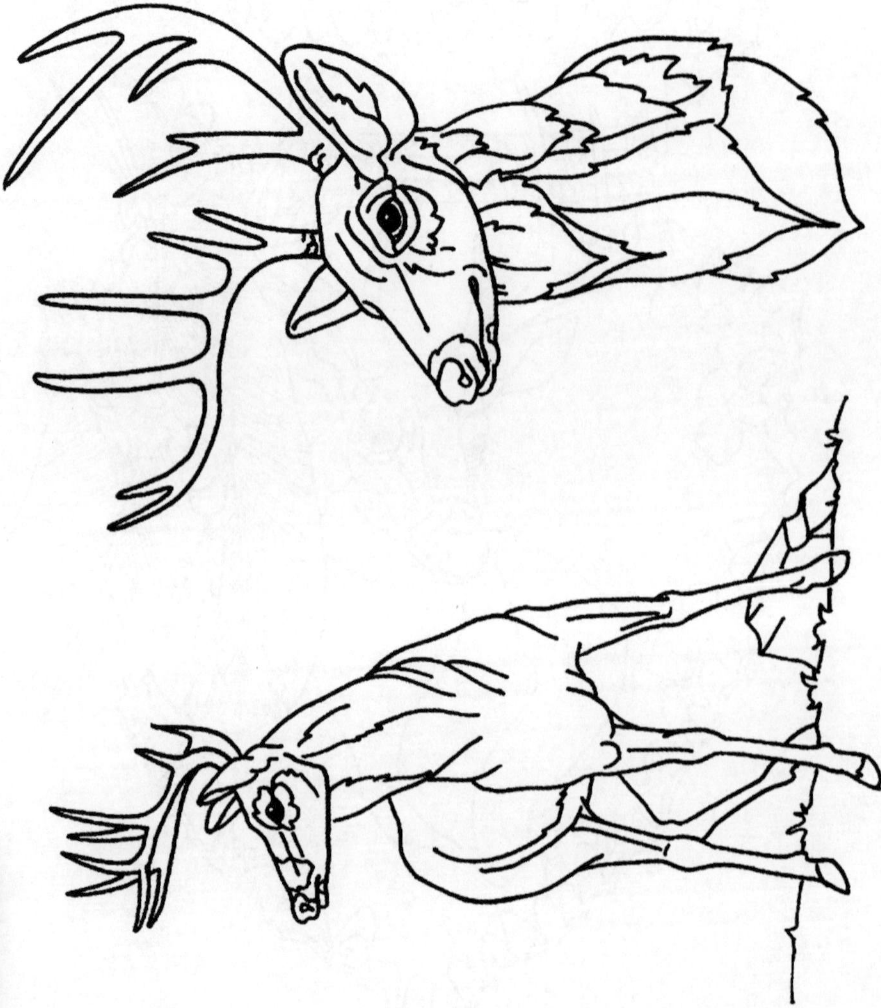

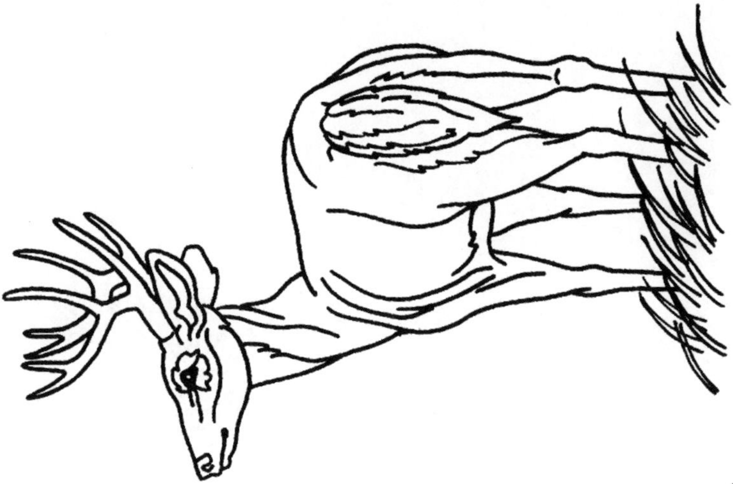

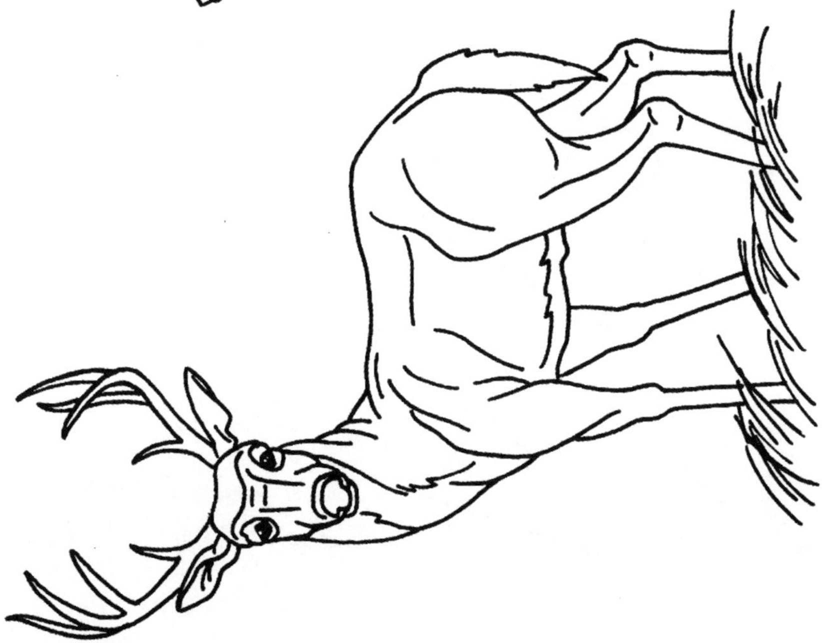

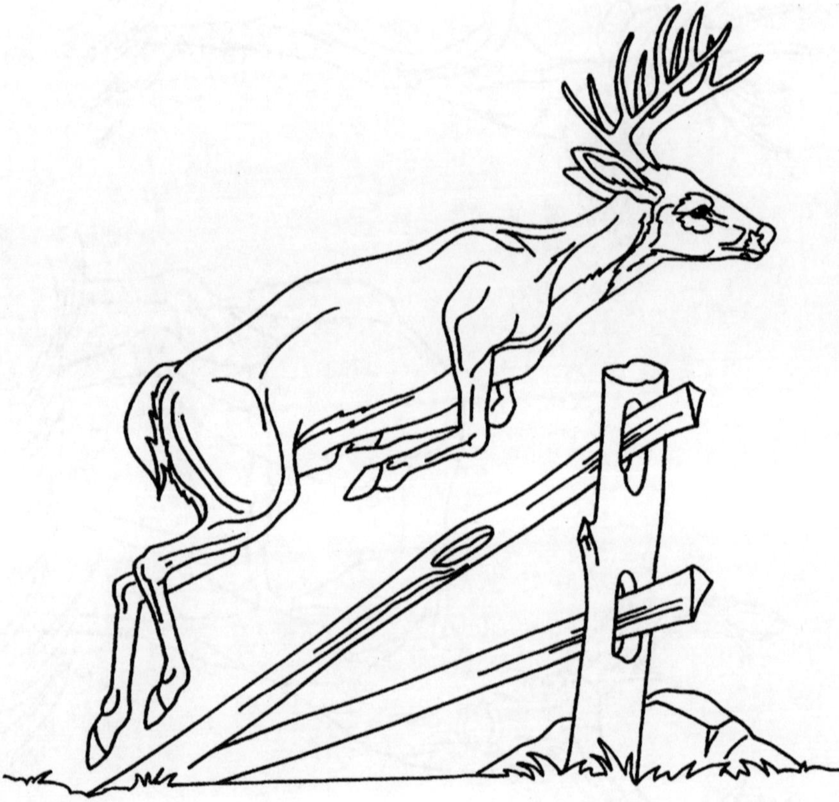

© Lora S. Irish

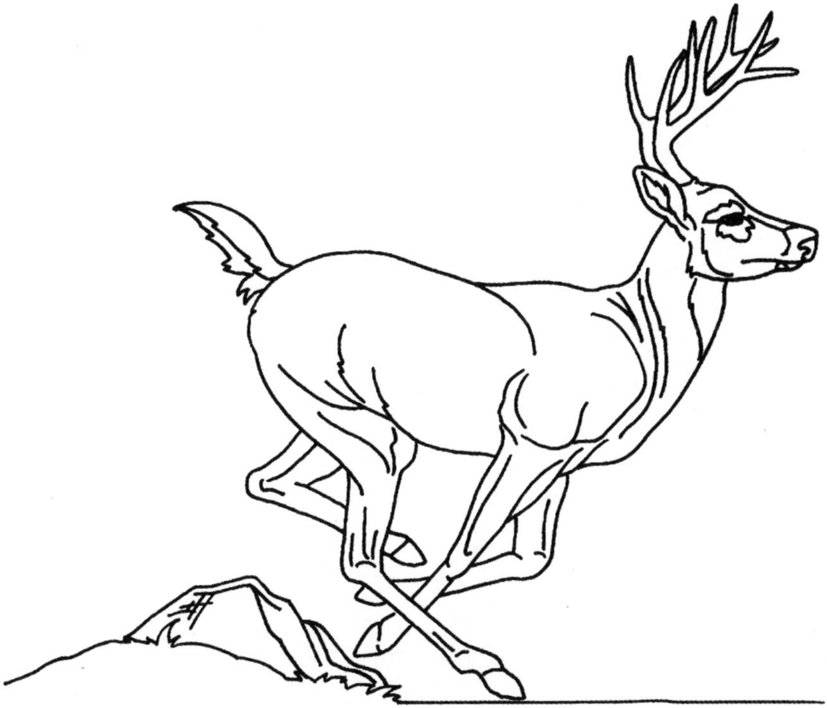

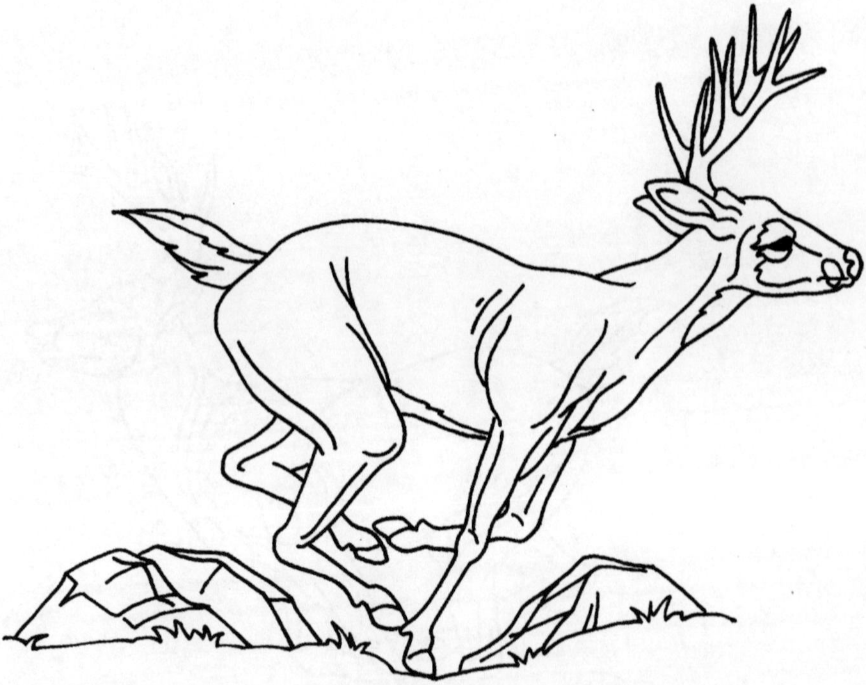

© Lora S. Irish

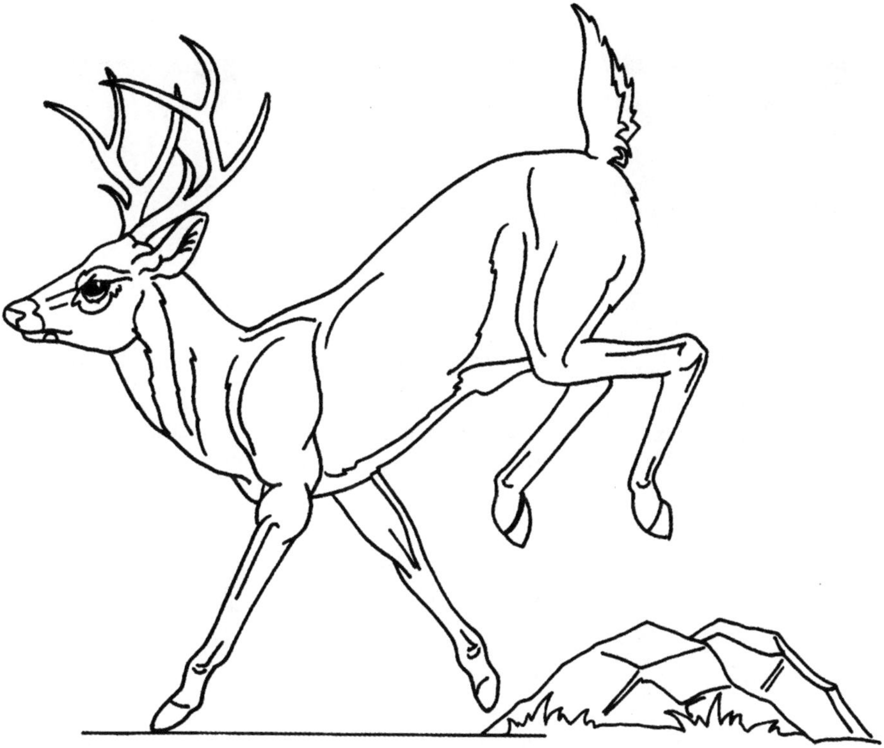

Wildlife